D1104428

The Lore
of the
Playground

The Lore of the Playground

One hundred years of
children's games, rhymes
and traditions

STEVE ROUD

BOOKS

Published by Random House Books 2010

2 4 6 8 10 9 7 5 3 1

First published in Great Britain in 2010 by
Random House Books
Random House, 20 Vauxhall Bridge Road,
London sw1v 2sa

www.rbooks.co.uk

Addresses for companies within The Random House Group Limited can be found at:
www.randomhouse.co.uk/offices.htm

The Random House Group Limited Reg. No. 954009

A CIP catalogue record for this book
is available from the British Library

ISBN 9781905211517

The Random House Group Limited supports The Forest Stewardship
Council (FSC), the leading international forest certification organisation. All our
titles that are printed on Greenpeace approved FSC certified paper carry the FSC
logo. Our paper procurement policy can be found at www.rbooks.co.uk/environment

Typeset by Palimpsest Book Production Limited,
Falkirk, Stirlingshire
Printed and bound in Great Britain
by Clays Ltd, St Ives plc

Illustrations are reproduced by kind permission of: xvi (tl), 139 (cr) Bert
Hardy/Getty Images; xvi (cr), 1 (c), 338 (cl) Henry Grant/Mary Evans Picture
Library; 1 (t), 56 (tr), 338 (tl) Haywood Magee/Getty Images; 56 (br) Lisa
Payne/Alamy; 56 (t) Imagestate/www.photolibrary.com; 138 (tr) Underwood &
Underwood/Corbis; 138 (b), 449 (t) NMeM Daily Herald Archive/Science &
Society; 139 (t) Tony Boxall/Mary Evans Picture Library; 139 (cl) ANSA/Corbis;
249 (t), 410 (cl) Mary Evans Picture Library/Alamy; 248 (tr), 410 (br) Sally and
Richard Greenhill/Alamy; 248 (cl) Hulton Archive/Getty Images; 339 (bl) Janine
Wiedel/Photofusion; 410 (cr) Bubbles Photo Library; 411 (t) Shirley Baker/Mary
Evans Picture Library; 448 (cl) Roger Mayne/Mary Evans Picture Library.

For Jacqueline and Stephanie . . .
the next generation

Contents

Part 4: Singing and Clapping

Part 5: Rules and Regulations

Part 6: Just for Fun

Part 7: Superstition and Tradition

Acknowledgements

My first thanks must go to the children who have contributed so much excellent material to this project. My 'special correspondents' Rebecca Wilcockson of East Finchley, and Natasha Bishop Wiltshire of Sheffield, supplied information and willingly answered questions throughout the project. Special thanks also to all the children who agreed to be interviewed, especially: Megan, Molly and Annie from Godalming; Ella, Helena and Luckshie from East Finchley; Harry, George, Harry and Justin from Maresfield; Kate and Joanna from Weybridge; Maddie, Dahlia and Rhea from Ealing; Cherry and Ella from Camden; Gus and Susie from Haddenham; Sam and Caitlin from Rochester; Maddie, Rebecca, Emily and Sophie from Lechlade; Adam, Irma, Bethany and Adele from Gateshead; and the school councils of Ravenstone School, Balham; St Mary's, Ardleigh; Robert Arkenstall, Haddenham; Okehampton Primary; Park Lodge Primary, Belfast; Estcots School, East Grinstead; and all the others who contributed material via the website and other channels. I could not have done the book without you all.

On the adult side, several colleagues in the field have generously given material from their own collections and knowledge, including especially Cathy Gould, Steve Gardham, Gareth Whittaker, Peter Millington, Ronne Randall and Julia Bishop; and thanks also to Mavis Curtis for contributing the chapter on the multicultural playground. Others who have helped signally in various other ways include: June Factor, Paul Marsh, staff at Random House, Susan Tilley, Caroline Oates, Robin Wiltshire, Fionnuala Carson-Williams and Maurice Leyden. Thanks also to all the people who contributed material via the website and all my previous childlore projects. Some of you may not even remember contributing years ago, but folklorists have long memories and capacious filing systems.

And thanks also to librarians and archivists all over the place, but especially those at the Vaughan Williams Memorial Library, the School of Scottish Studies, the Ulster Folk and Transport Museum and the London Library.

Thanks also to Caroline Pretty for doing her usual thorough job of copy-editing, and to Kate Faulkner for the index.

But a really special vote of thanks to Iona and Peter Opie for their excellent research, fine scholarship, wonderful books, humanity and generosity over the years. I only hope that my efforts come somewhere close to carrying on the work you started so well.

Introduction

> Children are forgetting how to play. To realise this one has only to . . . watch the pupils . . . in recreation time with their disappointed efforts at amusements, their unrelated racings and shoutings, their perfunctory attempts at leap-frog and kindred sports . . . but the village pastimes, the rhyming and rompings which were organised for children, and continued to maturity, are fast becoming obsolete. This is doubtless an inevitable result of modern developments, of the centralisation of town life and the waning prosperity of country districts.

This lament – from a 1903 article in *Leisure Hour* – is a familiar one, and has been repeated constantly down the years by journalists, parents and even teachers. All that has changed in subsequent decades is the bogeyman responsible for the perceived decline in children's play. In the 1900s it was city life. By the 1920s and 1930s commentators were pointing the finger at cinema's baleful influence. Television was the main culprit in the 1950s and 1960s, then video games in the 1980s and 1990s. Today it is sophisticated computer games. We all remember our childhood games with affection, and we are all convinced that the next generation is apathetic and uninterested.

The idea is so ingrained, and so widespread, that it is pointless trying to argue against it, but it is an interesting exercise to seek to explain it. The fact is that adult observers, often viewing the playground through the rose-tinted spectacles of their own childhood, tend to assume that if children are not playing precisely as they did when they were young, then nothing much can be going on. So, for example, they see children running around in a rather aimless way, and fail to recognise that they are actually playing a game of tig or war. They notice a solitary child by the gate and do not appreciate that he or she may have been put there by the witches or is a robber in jail. They glance at an apparently bored huddle of girls in the corner not doing much, and do not realise that they are playing 'Truth, Dare or Promise' or trying to work out, by complicated procedures, who loves who. And they register that some boys are kicking a rolled-up pair of gloves against the wall without understanding that they have a complicated scoring system or are practising special man-oeuvres for their own contentment while someone goes to find a ball.

Children's play has, of course, changed over the past century. Even the location of children's play has been modified as increased traffic and concerns about safety have brought about the virtual demise of games played in the street. At the same time, childhood itself has altered. A hundred years ago, many twelve-year-olds were out at work, and within living memory, fourteen was the normal school-leaving age. We believe today that children are 'growing up' faster, but they do not have to become adults as early as was the case for many from previous generations, and the teenage years now bridge the gap. Such changes dramatically influence our perception of childhood, and make the more pessimistic assume that it has lost the 'magic' or 'innocence' of previous eras.

What I have set out to do in *The Lore of the Playground* is to disprove the pessimists who think children no longer play, and show how games and rhymes have been endlessly modified and reinvented, or some-times abandoned and replaced, over the past century. To keep the subject within the bounds of one volume, I have not set out to cover every-thing: the emphasis here is on games, rhymes and traditions that are freely and widely shared, not board games or commercial crazes. Nor have I included organised sports such as football, netball, cricket, rounders and other bat-and-ball games. I have also decided, with some regret, not to look at imaginative play and 'pretend' games, even though they are a very important part of playground life, or the vast array of children's jokes and stories. These all form a vital part of a child's everyday life, but each is a book in itself. In addition, I have elected to exclude the more offensive – usually misogynistic – rhymes that are often part of the playground scene, though there are still plenty of rude and scatological ones here.

One notable thing is that the age range for the games, rhymes and other lore included in this book has narrowed considerably in the last fifty years. For their seminal work *The Lore and Language of Schoolchildren* (1959) Peter and Iona Opie routinely collected material from secondary schools, and they found plenty of fourteen-year-olds still playing tig and other chasing games in the playground. But nowadays, for the vast majority, such lore stops dead at the age of eleven, as children approach their move to secondary school. Girls who, at the age of nine, were apparently spending every waking moment doing clapping rhymes with their best friend, have trouble remembering the words two years later. They have already moved on.

This has serious ramifications for children's lore, especially their games. Not only is the 'game period' of the child's life severely truncated, so that they have less time to develop an extensive repertoire, but the games which require more developed intellectual or physical prowess have a tendency to wither away.

Nevertheless, the stock of games and rhymes remains a rich one. Some have clearly been passed down from one generation of children to the next; others arrived perhaps last year or only a few months ago. Some may have been imported directly from the Scouts, Guides, Cubs, Brownies, Woodcraft Folk and other youth organisations, or been taught in gym or sports lessons, or by other teachers. Others have come from parents, playground supervisors, summer-school leaders, *Tweenies* or *Wiggles* DVDs, comics or YouTube. The rude material might have been whispered by one child to another or have come from such books as Michael Rosen's *Rude Rhymes* (1992, 1994).

Word of mouth certainly remains a powerful influence. A game or rhyme may come from any source, but it usually enters the playground via one or two children, who then teach it to others. Childlore researchers are always being told, 'X taught us this one', 'Y learnt this from her cousin' or, quite frequently, 'Z made this one up'. The chances are, however, that the instigator is rarely the inventor. When I was talking to a group of children in Balham in 2010, for example, I was told about a game called 'The Tree Game', which they claimed they had made up, but once the rules were explained to me I realised that they were simply playing the latest version of 'Puss in the Corner', a game that has been around since the late seventeenth century.

In routine daily play it is usually acceptable for any member of a playing group to suggest changes or introduce new items, but it is also noticeable that there are often one or two individuals who are regularly cited as the source of new ideas and material. It is not clear whether these children simply have a particular interest in this kind of material, but they certainly receive a degree of prestige within their group for being the source of new rhymes or game variants.

In some cases, family influences are at work. Older siblings, who were usually at the same school, may help to keep a particular tradition going within the same 'community', co-opting a sometimes unwilling younger brother or sister to take part in, say, a clapping game that then gets transmitted to that younger child's peer group. Cousins may well be at a different school or live in a different area, and they may be instrumental in ensuring that a particular game or tradition gets passed from one part of the country to another. Parents, ever watchful of opportunities to extend their child's imagination and dexterity, will also introduce rhymes from their own childhood, attempt to teach skills and so on. It is surprising how many girls say that their first lessons in skipping came from their grandmother.

Children's lore is a huge field. It has a history going back to the dawn of time, but it also exists in the here and now, and is constantly changing. Every current child is a living repository, and everyone who has been a child has material or information to offer – even if they do not always realise it.

To get to grips with this vast sea of material, most workers in the field concentrate on one place or a few places for in-depth study, and then rely on comparison with other case studies to draw wider conclusions. The remarkable Iona and Peter Opie excepted, it is relatively rare for writers to attempt the broader geographical or temporal view taken in this book (but see Ewan McVicar's *Doh Ray Me* (2007) for an excellent Scotland-wide survey).

The challenge is how to get authentic material from a sufficiently wide sample in sufficient quantity to be representative and meaningful, both for past and present. To do this requires a range of methods.

The accepted 'gold standard' for childlore research is to visit a working playground and tape-record and video what is going on. This is the only way to get really under the skin of children's play, and if possible this should be done on a regular basis, in the same place, to chart the changes and cover all weathers, game seasons, crazes and so on. Anyone interested in this aspect of research should definitely read Iona Opie's *The People in the Playground* (1993), which comprises extracts from her fieldwork diary for 1979/80.

But without a team of researchers and a long-term project, this method is a very time-consuming and inefficient way of collecting material. Moreover, while it allows observation, it is not good for conversation. Informal interviews with children themselves, in small or large groups, yield much better results in some respects, and give the children the opportunity to explain why they do things as well as how. Interviews like these, in schools and in the children's homes, with girls and boys of different ages, have provided the backbone of the 'current' material in this book.

I have also had the benefit of being able to consult material from other researchers' work, for which I am extremely grateful. Their names are listed in the Acknowledgements. They have provided valuable insights from places I have not been able to visit personally, as well as different perspectives to balance my own views and habits. For the last two years there has also been a questionnaire on the *Lore of the Playground* website provided by the publisher (which is still open for business if anyone wants to contribute more material: www.loreoftheplayground.co.uk). This approach brought in some responses from children, but more importantly it stimulated the memories of a large number of adults, of different ages and from many different places, who contributed some fascinating information.

One obvious change in many playgrounds in recent decades is the presence of significant numbers of children whose families have recently migrated to Britain. How this has changed or contributed to the games being played is an important question, but one which needs specialist knowledge and research. So I have asked a friend and colleague, Mavis Curtis, whose expertise lies in this area, to contribute a chapter on the subject (see pp. 393–409).

For the older material, I also had access to a wealth of previous publications, which are listed in the Bibliography, along with unpublished collections in public repositories, and the results of my own collecting efforts, from adults and children over the past forty years.

All this adds up to a significant body of material. Nevertheless, I cannot claim that it is exhaustive, and all I can hope is that it is representative. If readers of this book recognise aspects of their own childhood reflected here, and learn something of how it continues, I will be content.

Schoolchildren at play, 1949

Chain Tig, 2010

Puss in the Corner, 1877

Playground scene, 1965

Prisoner's Base, 1909

Tig, 1950

PART ONE

Running Around

School playground, 1971

Horses, 1906

Duck Duck Goose, 2010

CHAPTER ONE

From Ancient to Modern

One of the striking things about children's play activities is the kaleido-scopic mix of tradition and innovation present in their everyday games. Many of the most mundane of activities can be shown to have a long history; others that have all the hallmarks of a long-standing game turn out to be no older than living memory. Games are combined or cross-fertilise with each other, a new feature added or another one dropped to suit the environment or the whim of the moment, and yet the same items can often be found at the same time in playgrounds from Cornwall to the Orkneys.

It is well established that when children say they have invented a game, rhyme or ritual, they often mean that they have changed a small detail and made it their own, and when they say that so-and-so invented it they usually mean that that person introduced it to the group. And when they really do 'invent' something, it often turns out to be very similar to some-thing 'invented' in similar circumstances by countless children before them. Many innovations fail to outlive the moment in which they were born, but others strike a chord or fulfil a need, and can make a lasting impres-sion. It is this constant interplay between past and present that makes childlore such a fascinating, rewarding and sometimes frustrating field.

An excellent example of the way children perpetually adapt games to suit the particular environment of their playground is the recurrence of games called 'Corners', or something similar:

'Four Corners': a playground game useful in the wet. In the playground was a rectangular covered area called the 'shed'. You had five players (mostly but not necessarily boys). One child stood with a hand on the pillar of each corner, and the fifth child stood in the middle. Pairs of 'corners' would swap places by running, daring the child in the middle to get there first and steal the corner. The person left over after a swap became the person in the middle. This game could last the whole playtime, especially in the rain.

NOTTINGHAM, 1950S

'Corner wall': There can be up to two people in each corner. The one in the middle shouts 1 2 3 or 4, which are the numbers of the corners. The people who are in the corner of that number have to run round (any way) the corners and back to their corner; if they succeed in getting back, everyone else has to run round the same way through each corner and back to their place. But they can get tigged between the corners and if you find you have been caught then you have to join the tigger in the middle.   *YORKSHIRE, 1975*

Similar games are still regularly reported from other schools that possess appropriately square features. When I was talking to the School Council at Ravenstone School, Balham, in January 2010, one girl mentioned a game she and her friends had invented that made use of trees standing in one section of the playground:

There are four trees in a square, there's one person in the middle and they have to spin round. And then when they get dizzy, you have to try and swap with the person opposite you without letting the person in the middle get to your tree first.

They call it 'The Tree Game'. Another member of the group, of a different age, said that his friends played a similar game, which they had also invented. In their 'Tree Game' the person in the middle does not spin round but calls out someone's name, who then has to swap with one of the others. A third member of the group, again of a different age, explained the game that she and her friends had made up:

Instead of calling out the person's name you put your two thumbs up to someone and if they go like that back to you, then you swap trees – but sometimes they're faking it and the catcher gets your tree.

They too called it 'The Tree Game'.
  Little did my young informants know, but they are continuing a very long tradition. 'Puss in the Corner' was a hugely popular game and is often

mentioned in literature, right back to at least the late seventeenth century. The only real difference between it and the Ravenstone games is that in earlier times the players in the corners taunted the middle person with cries of 'Puss, Puss, come here' or 'Puss, Puss, come and get some milk' and so on. The game was also popular at indoor parties, when the corners were usually represented by chairs. In Scotland it was often called 'Moosie in the Corner', and other, more recent, names for such games were 'Poles' and 'Catch-corners'. Similar games are found in many European countries.

A different type of continuity is evident in the traditional cry, still to be heard on a daily basis, whenever a child has possession of a hillock, tree stump or any other prominence:

> I'm the king of the castle
> You're the dirty rascal.

It is always said defiantly, even when no one is interested in trying to dethrone the self-proclaimed sovereign, but there is always the risk that some 'dirty rascal' will indeed attempt to unceremoniously oust the king.

The phrase has a long history, and there was once an actual game that went with it, although its rules were often flouted and used as an excuse for an uninhibited fight. George Forrest's book *The Playground* (1858) describes how the proper game was played in Victorian times:

'King of the Castle': The mound in the field made me think of it; and it is a capital game for cold weather. One of you is called 'king' and stands on top of the mound. The rest try to pull or push him off . . . It is not allowable to seize the clothes at all. The 'King' may be pushed, but not pulled, except by his hands or legs. If any player grasps his clothes, that player is obliged to retire from the list of assailants until the King is dethroned, and bears the name of 'Dummy'. The player who dethrones the King takes his place, and then the Dummy is allowed to rejoin the rest of the players.

The game was known all over Britain. In Glamorganshire around 1905 it was called 'Chwarae Cadw'r Castell, neu'r Twmpyn', and a Scottish version recorded in 1868 was called 'Willy Wassle':

A boys' play consisting of one or more established on a hillock, and the rest rushing up to pull him or them down. This was called playing 'Willie Wassle', and the cries both of defenders and assailants justified the name:

A Miscellany of Games

Games can be classified or organised in many different ways, but there are always a few that do not fit into the usual categories or that have features that are based on an 'unusual' pattern. The following is a selection of these 'different' games:

'Granny's Fridge': Someone's the granny, and there's these other people, and they're kids, and there's this fridge behind them and the granny says, in like a granny voice, don't touch my cake because I'm going to get more chocolate for it, and she goes out and she throws the key behind her back, for the fridge, and then while she goes away the children get the key and open up the fridge and they take all the cake and then when the granny comes back she looks in the fridge and the cake's gone and then all the people have to run away, and the granny has to chase them.   *BELFAST, 2010*

'Red Lips': There's a mummy, and she has, everyone who wants to play, they're the children, and there's doughnuts left in this cupboard, it's locked, and usually people rip up leaves and turn them into a key, and then she goes off to the shops, and she throws it behind her, and the children get it, and they open the thing and get the doughnuts out, and when the mum comes back they have to find an excuse why their lips are red, like, I ate an apple, or I thought I was kissing my boyfriend and I kissed the red paint door.   *BELFAST, 2010*

'Granny in the Graveyard': You have to close your eyes and sit on the ground, and then people run around, and they have to keep their eyes closed, and they say, 'Granny in the graveyard, Granny in the graveyard, Granny in the graveyard is asleep, Granny in the graveyard', but when they say 'is awake' the grannies get up but they have to keep their eyes closed, but they have to touch them, and when they get touched they have to go to the graveyard, and they just die.   *BELFAST, 2010*

'Fly away Peter': We used to have a metal climbing frame in the yard – the sort of thing that would now be banned – two children would hang their legs over the bars and hold on with their hands – they would then lean backwards so that they were hanging just by their legs, saying the words, 'Fly away, Peter, fly away, Paul'. They'd then come back up and re-grasp the bars with their hands, and say, 'Come back, Peter, come back, Paul'. *SOUTH WALES, 1960S*

'Roadkill': On the sportsday lines on the field – you have to get across them without being pushed over, slaughtered or hit by a car. We're on our knees and hands, but someone's on their legs trying to push us over – they have to get you on your back. *ESSEX, 2009*

'Human Dominoes': In the meadow we play dominoes, human dominoes, and we all line up in a row, and someone up the front has to pull us all down. *WEST LONDON, 2009*

This one is perhaps an echo of an older game from Cornwall, recorded in the *Folk-Lore Journal* of 1887:

'Solomon Had a Great Dog': The players kneel in a line. The one at the head, in a very solemn tone, chanted, 'Solomon had a great dog'; the others answered in the same way, 'Just so' (this was always the refrain). Then the first speaker made two or three ridiculous speeches, ending with, 'And at last this great dog died, and fell down', giving at the same time a violent lurch against his next neighbour, who, not expecting it, fell against his, and so on, to the end of the line.

Willie Willie Wassle
'Am in ma castle
An a' the dougs in yurn toon
Winna ding me doon.

A version from Edinburgh, described in James Ritchie's *Singing Street* (1964), was usually played on a street manhole cover, and was called, oddly enough, 'Burn the Bible'. An illustration entitled 'L'Assaut du chateau' in Jacques Stella's *Les Jeux et plaisirs de l'enfance* (1657) shows that the game was played in the mid seventeenth century, and one of the little tableaux in Brueghel's *Children's Games* (1560) is probably the same game.

A similar game, called 'Battle for the Banner', is described by Forrest. In this, there were two teams, and the one in possession of the 'castle' planted their flag there and defended it against the assailants. The same rules of combat applied:

> If a defender is pulled fairly off the mound, he is a prisoner of war and may not return to the defence; and if an attacker is thrown down, he is called a 'dead man', and may not return to the attack.

Not all games are competitive, and there are numerous activities that children enjoy which are so simple adults do not really notice them, but which nevertheless have their own rules and conventions, passed on from generation to generation. In memories of childhood written in the second half of the twentieth century, the game of 'Horses', for example, is frequently mentioned as one of the innocent games of childhood, and it was widely popular. Up to the Second World War, both country and town children would, of course, have been familiar with horses undertaking various tasks. For Rose Gamble in Chelsea in the 1920s they pulled buses:

> I was in the junior school and responsible for taking Joey to and from school . . . The only way to stop Joey dawdling was to 'bus-up'. All the little kids did it. We crossed our arms behind our backs and held each other's hands, pretending we were bus horses. We trotted most of the way home.

Children in country schools, on the other hand, may sometimes have pretended to own their horse and not to have been one. In its simplest form, one child grabbed the other's coat-tails or belt, but in winter scarves could be particularly useful as reins. Some even possessed specially produced equipment:

An enterprising parent, perhaps with problems of torn or pulled out-of-shape skirts and jerseys, had knitted many pairs of reins for the children's playtime. Kept in a large cardboard box, they came in all colours and had two holes for arms across the breast piece. We selected our colours and harnessed up teams of horses to parade and prance around the playground.

SOMERSET, 1950S

Two children pretending to be a horse and driver can still be seen in playgrounds up and down the country, although 'Horses' can easily change into 'Trains', or even 'Snakes', if more children join the line. Either way, the enjoyment of careering around in a line is the same.

In Rose Gamble's description, the children linked arms behind them. This is reminiscent of another game that was popular in the 1890s, called by Alice Gomme 'Alligoshee':

The children form pairs, one pair following the other, with their arms linked behind. While the first four lines are repeated by all, they skip forward and then skip back again. At the end of the last line they turn themselves about without loosing hands.

She recorded five different versions, from various parts of the country, and in each the children sang a verse as they skipped. The texts do not make much literal sense. This is from Gloucestershire:

Barbara, Barbara, dressed in black
Silver buttons all up your back
Allee-go-shee, allee-go-shee
Turn the bridle over me.

Here again there is a link from past to present – in this case an as yet unexplained connection between the Alligoshee verses and the more recent clapping rhyme *Miss Mary Mack*, who also had silver buttons 'down her back' (see p. 311).

Not all games and rhymes, though, can demonstrate such continuity. As the active age range for traditional games gradually shrank during the second half of the twentieth century, some became casualties, particularly complex, strategy-based chasing games. The typical children's chasing game nowadays is tig, which has its own history: its continuing vitality is reflected in the numerous versions that children all over the country report as still current in their playground. But it has never reached the heights of sophistication

or complication of several of the games routinely played by past generations and occasionally encountered today in youth organisations like the
Scouts and Guides, or perhaps in organised school activities.

'Prisoner's Base' was easily the best known of all chasing games in
Britain from the Middle Ages until the later nineteenth century, and was
played by adults as well as by children, under a variety of names, including
'Prison Bars', 'Chevy Chase', 'Chivy' or simply 'Base'. As already indicated,
the game is quite complex, and requires a higher degree of organisation
than any of the current playground repertoire. The nearest modern
equivalent is perhaps 'Relieve-o' (see p. 86).

The first reference to the game is from 1332, and it was so well known
in Elizabethan times that writers could refer to it in passing and know
that their readers would understand. Book 5, Canto 8, line 5 of Edmund
Spenser's *Faerie Queene* (1596), for example, focuses on the key feature of
the game – that each pursuer is also pursued by somebody else:

> As they had been at bace
> They being chased that did others chace . . .

William Shakespeare includes it as 'Country base' in Act 5, Scene 3 of
Cymbeline (1610). Public games between local teams were organised and
advertised, like cricket matches. So, for example, Roger Lowe of Ashton-
in-Makerfield, Lancashire, recorded in his diary for Saturday, 18 July 1663:

> Upon Latchford Heath there was a great company of persons with 2 drums
> amongst the young men were playing at prison barrs where I stayed awhile
> to see them but concluded it was but vanitie.

A full description of the game was published in *Boy's Own Paper* in
1887, written by someone who had played it in his own schooldays in mid
Victorian times.

> The game I liked best was 'Chevy', or as it is sometimes called, 'Prisoners'
> Base', in which, at the beginning at least, the antagonists were fairly matched.
> The two best runners in the school, or two who were as equal as possible,
> would first of all choose sides, so that the school was divided into two parties
> of equal strength. Then at one end of the playground was a line drawn along
> its whole length, about eight feet from the wall or fence. From the centre
> of this line to the wall another line was drawn, and in this way we got our
> bases. At the opposite end of the ground a line was drawn across each corner,

and the triangles so formed were the prisons. Our prison was opposite to the enemy's base, while the enemy's prison was opposite to our base. By this arrangement the would-be rescuers of the prisoners had to run diagonally across the ground. In some schools the bases are drawn so as to stand out from the end of the ground, and leave an open space on three of their sides, and the prisons are about three-quarters of the way down, so that the rescuers can approach on three of their sides. At one school I was at the prisons were two large elms in the corners of the ground, which the prisoners had to touch at the time they were released. All being ready, one of the youngsters from the side that had first choice, was sent out by his captain into the centre of the playground to cry 'Chevy!' One of the other side, say ours, then set off in pursuit and tried to touch him before he got back to his base. One of the other side then started after our man to touch him before he touched the chevy. One of ours then started off after him, and so on until nearly all the sides were out, each in pursuit of a particular foe, and each endeavouring at the same time to escape from his particular pursuer. Should he touch his enemy before his following enemy touched him, his pursuer had to make the best of his way back, for the break in the chain rendered things awkward for the pursued who had no one to pursue. When a player was touched, he had to go to prison and wait till he was released by one of his own side running out from the base and touching his hand.

A special watch was kept on these rescuers by their opponents, who endeavoured to cut them off and make them prisoners. The first prisoner would keep his foot in the prison, the second would hold his hand and reach out, the third held his hand, and so on, so that the distance between the prisoners and their friends was diminished with each capture. When a prisoner was released, he, like his rescuer, ran back to his base, and became, in his turn, a rescuer of prisoners, or a prison guard to cut off attempted rescuers. The prisoners were brought back in the order of their capture. And the game ended, when it did end, either by the side being all put in prison or by their accidentally leaving their base without an occupant, when the other side would run in and 'crown' it.

A busy, bustling game is Chevy when played loyally. The name of the pursued was shouted by the pursuer as he left the base, so that all the minor dodgery of pretending to do one thing in order to do another was prevented. Until the pursuers were released, no fresh 'chevy' could be started, so that matters were much simplified as the game progressed. The plan we found paid best for releasing prisoners was to start three or four rescuers together, and let those who got away best go on, while the others returned to their base. In this way the opposite side were kept in a state of hesitation until the very last moment.

Starting and Finishing Games

Despite the huge upheavals in society and education, in many respects the dynamics of the playground have not changed much in 100 years. Who plays with whom, how you join in, how you choose your game, and so on, have always been governed by local rules that, on the whole, children understand and abide by.

Most children nowadays play with their own immediate 'friendship group', but these groups overlap, and everyone knows who they can call on to make up the numbers necessary for particular games, and who they can join in with if their own friends are not available.

One of the strongest of unofficial rules is 'game ownership'. Sometimes it is obvious who the game belongs to, because they own the ball, or the skipping rope, but if not there is a strict etiquette to be followed. As Rose Gamble remembered Chelsea in the 1920s:

> The formula for joining a game was to approach anyone who was already playing and say, 'Gisser game.' The orthodox reply would be, 'T'ain't my game.' 'Who's game is it? you had to ask. 'Alfie's.' This meant that Alfie had suggested, or as we said, 'got up' the game, and had dipped up for sides with one of the other kids. So you had to approach Alfie, and await Alfie's convenience. 'Gisser game, Alfie.' If he wanted you on his side, he said so, otherwise you were lumped together with all the other kids he hadn't chosen.

Almost exactly the same situation is described in *Growing Up in the Playground* (1981), Andy Sluckin's book of his research in Oxford schools in 1980, and children in the twenty-first century say very similar things. Apart from when they are deliberately flouting the rules to be aggressive or destructive, the only time a child will simply join in without following this formality is if they are confident that they are sufficiently 'in' with the core group for it not to be thought necessary. Or they can try bribery or threats.

Choosing what to play can sometimes be a challenge. I vividly remember in the 1950s whole lines of boys with their arms across each other's shoulders stomping round the playground chanting, 'What shall we play? What shall we play?', which I thought was a waste of good playing time. They often spent the whole playtime chanting, whereas my group had always agreed beforehand what we were going to do. Others did the same long before my time:

> Long before playtime in morning school, one would have arranged by signs and whispers, or notes across the classroom, what one was going to play . . . so the boy of your set nearest the door, and therefore likely to be the first one out, was deputed to rush into the playground and 'bag' the best corner . . . which meant stamping about on it and shouting and waving one's cap fiercely in the face of any bigger boys who were late comers and shouting, 'I bags this for Jenkins's set' – always naming the biggest boy in your crowd. The code was inexorable. *SOUTH-EAST LONDON, C.1915*

Outside the playground, things were often a bit different. In your own street, where membership of the group was mainly defined simply by residence, many children did not need to worry about whether or not they were included. In Valerie Avery's street off the Old Kent Road in London, in the 1940s:

> There was no need for my friends to knock for me to come out to play after tea; Ronny, who was the leader of our gang because he had the loudest voice and the biggest brother, ready to bash up anyone who made trouble, would bellow out, 'Allee in ooz-a-playin!' You could hear his cry ten streets away. Then I would dash downstairs with bread and jam in one hand, coat in the other.

In the playground a game can just peter out, or the bell might announce the end of break. But in the street the ending is often less clear-cut. The traditional call was surprisingly similar, all across the country. Valerie Avery again:

> Allee 'ome, we ain't a-playin'! Allee 'ome! This cry was taken up by everyone until the whole area was one echo gradually dying in the night air.

And for Cathy Gould in 1970s Coventry:

> All-ee, All-ee in
> All-ee, All-ee in!

Another relatively complex game that has now disappeared is 'Barley-break' or 'Last Couple in Hell'. Again, it is mentioned so frequently in the writings of poets and playwrights from the mid sixteenth century onwards, including those of Shakespeare, Robert Herrick, Ben Jonson, Thomas Dekker, Sir Philip Sidney, Philip Massinger and John Fletcher, that it must have vied with 'Prisoner's Base' as the archetypal chasing game of the time, but it is usually referred to as a pastime for young adults rather than children. Although it is often mentioned, it is not usually described, so a degree of imaginative reconstruction has to be undertaken.

It was a game for three couples, one male and one female in each couple. One couple stands in the middle section, called 'Hell', while the other two stand at the far ends of the playing area. The couples at the ends must try to change partners with each other, by running across 'Hell', while the middle couple try to intercept and catch them. The couple in the middle must stay linked by holding hands, but the others may separate temporarily if need be.

In *An Etymological Dictionary of the Scottish Language* (1808) John Jamieson claims that the game was called 'Barley-break' because it was traditionally played around the barley stacks in the farmyard, but the game he describes under this heading is not the same as the one described above, and is simply a basic chasing game with a cumulative 'it' person.

In the context of popular games that have fallen from favour, another should be mentioned, since it was once so widely known that it gave the English language the saying 'I'm on Tom Tiddler's ground'. The game's main feature is that it reverses the notion of a safe place for the players by providing a place where they are in danger if they enter it. A line, or circle, is drawn to denote the area belonging to the one who is 'it', who is Tom Tiddler. The players are safe while they are outside this area, but when they invade they announce, 'Here we are on Tom Tiddler's ground, picking up gold and silver', or something similar.

Sometimes Tom Tiddler catches someone, and the game starts again immediately with this person becoming Tom, while in other versions he must catch them all, and place them in his prison. Occasionally the game is extended by allowing uncaught players to release their colleagues from the prison, and again in some versions the children take things more literally and place sticks and stones or other items in the area, to represent the 'gold and silver'.

Children called the game, and the character who was protecting his land, by many names, including 'The Friar', 'Boney', 'Old Daddy Bunchy', 'Pussey', 'Tom Tinker', and, in later years, 'The Dragon'. But in the adult world the game's name became standardised to 'Tom Tiddler's Ground', quite possibly because Dickens called one of his famous *Christmas Stories* by that title, and referred to the game in two of his novels.

The phrase 'to be on Tom Tiddler's ground' was widely used, and had two meanings. In some contexts it signified a place or situation where money could be got very easily, but in others it was a no man's land of dubious safety. It lasted in general parlance until Edwardian times, and could still be heard occasionally between the wars.

One final, formerly widespread game, 'French and English', is also worth noting. Like 'Barley-break' and others it required a higher degree of team-work and strategy than most chasing games. A line would be drawn, to separate two territories, and the two teams gathered in their own area. Each team placed a number of personal items – hats, coats, handkerchiefs and so on – in a pile some way behind their side of the dividing line. In some versions, only one item, usually a handkerchief, was designated as the team's flag. Players crossed the line, at will, and tried to capture one of the enemy's treasures, without being caught on the way. If caught they were put into a prison area, from which they could be freed by their colleagues. They could only be caught on the way to the enemy's pile; once they had picked up one of the treasures, they had free passage back to their own territory. Players had to be careful not to stand too close to the border, because a standard tactic was to seize an enemy across the line and drag him across. The game ended when one team had captured all the enemy's items, or all its players.

Generically called 'French and English', the game had many other names, depending largely on time and place. In the north it was more commonly called 'Scots and English', but in the twentieth century 'Germans and English', and in many places by names that referred to the items captured – 'Stealy-clothes', 'Seizing Sticks', 'Tak Bannets' and so on. It was certainly already well known in the late eighteenth century, and lasted well into the post-Second World War period, but it is likely that, if it survives at all today, it is encountered only as one of the games arranged by youth organisations.

CHAPTER TWO

Tig

It is a pretty safe bet that children everywhere chase each other and that they have some structure to their chasing that makes it a 'game' rather than just 'running about'. Structure means rules, and the fundamental rule, which again we can assume is universal, is that the role of 'chaser' – called the 'it role' by commentators but the 'itter', 'he', 'the man', 'the tigger' and so on by children – can be passed from one to another. How far back this notion goes, though, is not known.

One of the earliest descriptions of tig in Britain is to be found in Francis Willughby's *Book of Games*, a manuscript compiled in the 1660s, and it is interesting to note that there was an awareness even then that this was the fundamental chasing game:

> One boy touches another and cries, Tick. Hee that is touched runs after the other that touched him, to tick him againe, and then runs from him as soone as hee has touched him. Hee that is ticked, & cannot tick againe, is beaten. This is one of the first & most simple of the running sports, from which Prison Barres etc. seeme to be derived.

For something so simple, it is extraordinarily difficult to describe clearly what goes on in children's chasing games. The games are necessarily rule-bound, but there are so many variables, and the play is too fluid for strict classification. In general, children like to stick to the rules of a particular game, but they will change these at a moment's notice to suit differences in the environment or just for fun. Changes might stick and become part of the game, or even constitute a new game, or they might simply be temporary expedients.

Indeed, chasing games are one of the most inventive parts of play-ground life. The fact that many of these same inventions appear in different schools is one of the great mysteries of folklore.

The terminology involved in the basic chasing game is fascinating and confusing in equal measure. Children manage perfectly well when conversing among themselves, but when they talk about their games with grown-ups and outsiders, inherent confusions surface, and children have been known to get quite exasperated when adults cannot grasp what to them is very simple.

Here I am going to use 'tig' as the generic name for the basic game, and for the act of 'touching' someone during the game, but preserve the original terminology in any quotations from children and books. And I reserve the right to ignore my own rules when it seems appro-priate.

To get some theoretical handle on the vast sea of tig variants, it is possible to postulate a 'pure' form of tig in which only the fundamental rules apply. This theoretical game is completely free-form and has no restrictions on the number of players, their movements or the field of play (beyond being 'in the playground', etc.). There is one 'it' at a time, the role is passed on by simple touch, and there are no homes, safe places or timing restrictions.

This type of basic tig certainly exists, and takes place in hundreds of playgrounds every day. Its beauty is that it needs no planning, it can be started instantly, can last two minutes to an hour, and can be done virtu-ally anywhere. But to make the game more playable, more challenging or more fun, the players tinker with these basic features, either one at a time or all together, to invent their new variations.

An important rule, which often goes unnoticed by outsiders, is the question of timing. One of the easiest things to do in the basic game is to tig the one who has just tigged you, so there is often a rule of 'no returns', or a time limit to allow them to escape – you cannot re-tig someone within five seconds, for example. In addition, whenever there are homes or other safe areas there is the potential problem of the player who simply stays put, or who keeps putting off running across and so on. So again there are usually locally agreed timing rules.

Another basic variable is to redefine the field of play and therefore to change the very shape of the game. Sometimes this is merely to restrict the size – within this part of the playground, or only in the sheds, for example – but more often the change is more fundamental and governs where the players run. A common sub-category is to have the players run across an open space, from wall to wall or across the street, with the 'it' people in the middle.

Another variable is the 'it' role, which can be played by one person at a time, or cumulatively, as in 'Family Tig', or in teams from the start. More than one 'it' has the distinct advantage of evening out discrepancies in speed and ability, as the younger or slower players can gang up on the faster ones. A further refinement of the cumulative format is to alter the way the 'it' people move; 'chain tig' is a good example, where the chasers must hold hands.

The next feature to consider is the way that people are tigged. The simple touch is often not enough; the tigger might have to touch them on a certain place, or in a certain way – three taps on the head, or on the bottom as in 'Bum Tig' – or they might have to hold them for a required length of time, or while they repeat a certain phrase; or they might have to get them on the floor, as in 'Take-down Tig'.

If those who have been tigged do not immediately become 'it', they might be out of the game; or temporarily immobilised, as in 'Stuck in the Mud'; or they might have to hold the part of the body where they were tigged, as in 'French or Hospital Tig'; or they might be taken to a prison. The presence of a 'prison' area involves rules about how long they stay there, whether or not they can be freed by other players, and how and when this can be done.

Then there is temporary immunity, which might be a fixed home or den where players are safe, or a 'movable' immunity, such as when 'touching wood', or when their feet are 'off ground'.

A further refinement is when the 'it' people actually control the movements of the other players, by calling them across or otherwise dictating who runs where. This is one of the fundamental features used to define a game, and takes us out of the basic tig format. But there is also the presence or absence of less-obtrusive spoken elements. Sometimes the 'it' people have to give a warning before the chase starts, or they must say something when they tig someone, or it does not count. Other players may have to say particular words when reaching the home, such as 'Forty forty in!', or when freeing others 'Forty forty free!', and so on.

And lastly there is the ever popular category of 'character games', which is where imaginative play and chasing games meet. These can be old favourites like 'Cowboys and Indians', 'Cops and Robbers', 'Witches and Fairies', or be based on the latest television series or blockbuster film, or both. The characters sometimes affect the game: 'Cops and Robbers' nearly always has a prison; whereas chasing aliens might involve shooting them with a laser-gun rather than touching them, but they might be able to protect themselves with a force-field. I was recently told about a game called 'Jurassic Park': if the person chasing you is a Tyrannosaurus rex, all you need to do is stand completely still, because, as everyone knows, a T. rex's eyes can only detect movement.

THE MANY GAMES OF TIG

Some flavour of the sheer variety of games can be seen in the following list, which was included in a project on games put together by pupils of Mary Erskine School, Edinburgh, in 1990, now lodged in Edinburgh Central Library:

Aeroplane tig – When tug you stand with arms out like an aeroplane and can only be freed by another player running under your arm.

Animal tig – Everyone is a kind of animal and predators have to catch their natural prey.

Ball tig – 'It' has to throw the ball at people.

Budge – There are several bases where you are safe, but no one is allowed to stay on a base for long. If someone else gets to that base they say 'Budge' and you have to move on. You must not return to a base you have just left.

Chain tig – Everyone who is tug has to join the 'It', holding hands.

Fishes in the net – Similar to Bulldogs.

High tig – Players can't be tug while they are off the ground.

Hospital tig – If you are tug on the arm you can't use that arm, as if you were injured. If three parts of your body have been tug, you join the tigger.

Marco Polo – Plain tig but played in the swimming pool.

Shadow tig – Any piece of shade is a den.

Tackle tig – 'It' has to get people onto the ground.

Toilet tig – Stand with arms out, and can only be freed by another player pulling your arm, like a toilet flush.

Tunnel tig – Stand with legs apart and can only be freed by another player crawling between your legs.

Witch's fingers – Everyone holds one of the witch's outspread fingers. The witch tells a story and when s/he says a certain agreed word or phrase the others scatter.

Witches in the gluepot – A form of tig. When the witch catches you she puts you in the gluepot. You start sinking. The only way you can be rescued is by another team-mate taking you out. If you are not rescued you become a goblin helping the witch.

Many of these, and various other versions, merit a little closer scrutiny.

Family Tig

The simplest form of cumulative 'it' is when each one tigged has to become another 'it' person, but they are all free agents and are not constrained to act together or in any special way. Nowadays this seems to be mostly called 'Family Tig' or 'Team Tig', but in the past it was variously 'Help Chase', 'All Man He' or, in my South London playground in the 1950s, 'One-chase-all-chase'.

Stuck in the Mud

'Stuck in the Mud' has been a firm playground favourite for over fifty years, and is probably still the most widely known of the simple variations of tig. As with basic tig, 'Stuck in the Mud' is free-form and needs no boundaries or structure, and (usually) involves one chaser pursuing all the others, attempting to touch them. The essential difference is that when touched the players remain rooted to the spot, legs apart and (usually) arms outstretched ('like a scarecrow'). They remain stuck in this way until freed by one of their uncaught colleagues, and in most versions they vociferously demand, or plead for, release. The way I remember it, the only way to release someone who is stuck is to crawl between their legs, but there are many other ways in modern play-grounds: tap their nose five times, pat them on the head or shoulder, or simply go under their arms, for example – and these options are particularly applicable to girls if the ground is muddy or wet and they do not want to crawl on the floor. Not only this, but, as one ten-year-old boy from Sussex commented, 'If we play with the girls they don't let us go under them', although his nine-year-old friend added, 'Who would want to?'

Theoretically speaking, the game is limited. It lacks a way for the 'it' role to change easily among the players, as the traditional method was to wait until everyone was stuck at the same time before the game started again with a new chaser. With more than a handful of participants, the chaser has little hope of guarding all those stuck and chasing the others. But present-day children have a range of variants of the game to choose from, which all conform to the basic pattern but go some way to alleviate this fundamental problem.

In 'Melting Candles', or just 'Candles', those who are stuck have to count loudly and slowly, down from ten, as they gradually melt down to the ground; some people call this 'Sticky Toffee'. In 'Banana Splits' those caught have to stand with hands together above their heads, which they slowly bring down on each side, symbolising the peeling of a banana, and in 'Quicksand' they again sink to the ground. In all these, if they are not released by other players before they reach zero, they are out of the game, or join the tigger.

Even more fanciful is 'Octopus', in which the chaser constantly waves his or her arms around like an octopus, and those caught become 'seaweed', who also wave their arms around (but must not move their feet). Some people observe the rule that anyone touched by the seaweed also becomes stuck. In 'Toilet Tig', when you get tigged you are frozen to the spot and another player can only free you if you bend your knees so that they can sit on your lap and pretend to pull a toilet chain, or they just have to pull your arm down to simulate flushing. Then there is 'Sacrifice', in which anyone who altruistically frees a fellow player immediately becomes stuck themselves.

Finally, some children play the game nowadays with a 'tigger' as usual, but rather than all players being allowed to free people, just one designated person is allocated this role. In conversation these two roles go by various names, such as the 'stucker' and the 'unstucker', or the 'itter' and the 'un-itter'. Sometimes the unstucker is immune from being tigged, but at others they are just as vulnerable as the rest.

Even without these variations, the game goes by many different names, including 'Statue Tig', 'Freeze Chase', 'Tunnel Tig' and 'Underground Tig', but most children still usually recognise 'Stuck in the Mud' as the generic term.

Feet-off-Ground

After 'Stuck in the Mud', 'Feet-off-ground' is probably the commonest variant of tig. In this game the players being chased can gain temporary immunity by being off the ground:

'Touch off Ground': You might be hanging off a fence or dangling from a windowsill, or wrapped around a lamppost. It might not even be somewhere you'd be able to stay off the ground for long, just long enough for the chaser to go after someone else maybe.   WALES, 1970S

You're 'It'

The 'it' role is one of the brilliant inventions of childhood play, and there is nothing quite like it in the adult world. Not everybody calls it 'it', of course. In some places you are 'on' or 'on it', or, in Glasgow:

> Nobody fancied being 'het', whatever the game. But if there was one thing worse than being het it was to be called 'It' instead. 'It' was if you were cissy or English (which was much the same thing) or from Edinburgh, which was worse than either.

But the 'it' has a deeper function than simply designating who is to do the chasing, and is a fundamental factor in determining the success of a particular game. One basic problem, for example, is that in an ordinary chasing game the ones who are best at the game will never get caught, and the ones who are worst will always be 'it'.

Commentators have identified major differences within the role, depending on the game in play, and have noted a *high-power it* at one extreme, where the person has a great deal of control over the actions of the other players, and over who they chase, and a *low-power it*, where the it has no control and must simply rely on skill. Weaker players find the low-power 'it' role extremely frustrating and soon get bored, because the rules as well as their own lack of skill seem stacked against them, but the high-power role goes a long way to even out the skill differences.

The 'cumulative it', found in some chasing games, is a brilliant way of levelling the playing field in a group with mixed abilities, because the weaker players can gradually combine against the stronger ones. Another way in which the power differential is addressed in a chasing game is the question of whether the *last* person caught becomes the new 'it', rather than the *first*. Where it is the *first*, the next game is sure to start slowly and likely to become tedious, as one of the weakest players is bound to be 'it' each time. But where one of the most skilful is chosen, the game is likely to start much more dynamically.

There are also ad hoc strategies and practices that help the game along and prevent stagnation. Where there are palpable differences in the ages of players, new rules are often invented to help the younger ones. They might get three chances, or the older ones might accept a handicap. In chasing games, the stronger players do not simply disappear to the other end of the playground, but often stay close to the 'it'. Admittedly, this is usually taunting behaviour accompanied by mild verbal abuse, but the bolder it gets, the more likely that a mistake is made and the 'it' gets them. Finally, if the game is in danger of getting too tedious, a strong player may well sacrifice him- or herself to get things moving. There is no shame in this; indeed, it is a validation of the player's superior status in the world of the game.

There also needs occasionally to be some evening out in the other direction, by restricting the 'it's' movements or powers, to prevent misuse. In a game where players are safe while touching a particular feature, for example, there is often a rule that restricts the amount of time they can stay there in safety, but this is usually balanced by a rule that prevents the 'it', from standing too close.

Although the ethos of the game requires the players to try to avoid being 'it', it is a mistake to assume that the 'it' role is always an undesirable one. Stronger players are often happy to accept the role, because they know it will only be temporary, and they can enhance their status by being able to choose their victim, and in many games, such as 'Grandmother's Footsteps' the 'it' is actually the leader and dictates the actions of the other players.

Older children are often well aware of what makes a 'good' chasing game, and are able to express it when asked. This is not true of all children, of course, but it is quite surprising how they can often analyse and talk theoretically about their games. And they also approach their games dynamically, in that they are willing to try out new rules to suit the circumstances of the day, the environment and the people involved. In a stable play community – for example a year group that has been together throughout their time in the school – most members are well aware of the abilities and weaknesses of their companions.

The name of the game varies, but is usually a compound based on the local name for tig, for example 'Off-ground Touch', 'Off-ground He', 'Tig-on-high' and 'Dobby-off-ground'. There are local rules for what consti- tutes proper 'off-groundness'. Leslie Paul, writing about his childhood in South-east London about 1915, mentions the 'sitting down' method;

> 'Feet-off-ground' – which meant that you could not be 'had' once you got your feet off the ground either by climbing or sitting down with your feet in the air.

But in my London playground in the 1950s I remember thinking it a pretty poor show when people just sat on the floor and raised their legs in the air. That was too easy, and was banned in our version of the game. The game is also easily adaptable to particular playground features, and might become 'Bench Tig' if there are enough benches around, or can be played exclusively on the climbing frames, and so on.

As with all 'immunity' games, there are usually timing and proximity rules, in that players cannot stay on a particular safe spot indefinitely (thirty seconds is sometimes quoted) and the chaser must not simply stand next to someone waiting for them to move. Sometimes there are other refinements to the rules, as in Birmingham in the 1970s:

> During 'Off-ground Tig' you had to shout 'Arley barley feet off ground' and have your fingers crossed to be safe.

But the commonest variant, which many children regard as constituting a different game, so that it warrants a different name, is the rule that only one person can be on any particular safe spot at any given time:

> 'Egarty Budge' – This is a game like off ground tig, only two people are not allowed on the same thing and if one person moves onto an object and someone else is already on, the first one on has got to move onto some- thing else.   *YORKSHIRE, 1982*

The newcomer usually has to say something to shift the sitting tenant, and such words are usually admirably direct: 'budge', 'buzz off', 'shoo', 'hoppit' or 'scram', for example.

Other chasing games have similar features, such as the following recorded in Yorkshire in 1975:

'Bob 3 Times and Run For Your Life' – The game is played when one person
is chosen to be it and the others run away. After the person who is it has
counted to ten he then runs after the others. When he runs after them the
others can bob down and then the 'tigger' has to go after someone else. But
the people who are running can only bob down three times and then they
have to run for their lives.

This variant was widely known and went by a number of names, such as
'Touch Ground Tig', 'Low Tig', 'Bob Tig' and 'Squat'.

'Feet-off-ground' does not seem to be mentioned specifically before the
Edwardian era, although the basic idea is so simple and obvious that it
has probably been around a long time. The earliest concrete reference
appears to be in a list of London playground games published in *Notes &
Queries* in 1910.

French He/Hospital Tig

In 'French He' or 'French Tig' you have to hold the place on the body
where you were tigged. Presumably by coincidence, most of the earlier
descriptions of 'French Tig' come from London. Norman Douglas included
it in his *London Street Games* (1916), and Leslie Paul in his memories of
South-east London about 1915, while Valerie Avery describes playing it in
the Old Kent Road area in the 1940s:

> This was followed by 'French touch', where you could be 'ad three times
> before you became 'He', but you had to run round holding the place where
> you had been touched until you were released by somebody free. With every-
> body running round like crippled monkeys.

But it was also known elsewhere, and John Nicholson included it as 'Lame
Tig' in his book on East Yorkshire folklore, published in 1890. Other names
included 'Chinese Touch' and, according to the Opies, in Germany the
same game is called 'English Touch'.

In other variations you can only be tigged on a certain spot, but you
do not necessarily have to hold it:

> 'Bum it' is where you have to it someone on their bum – and there's also
> 'Shoulder it' when you have to it someone on their shoulder – and 'Head
> it' when you have to get them by the head.   WEST LONDON, 2009

And in 'Hospital Tig', as explained in the list of Edinburgh games, above, you cannot use the part that is tigged, and when three parts of your body have been thus 'paralysed' you have to join the tiggers. Both 'Hospital Tig' and 'French He' are still played.

Chain Tig

One of the most effective variants of the basic chasing games, which is still known in many playgrounds, is 'Chain Tig', where each player who is tigged joins the other 'it' people, but they hold hands while pursuing those who are still free. There are two main versions nowadays. In the commonest version the chasers form an ever-growing line, while in the second they can split into twos. The latter is, of course, a much faster-moving game, but the former is often more fun because only the people at the end of the chain are allowed to tig someone, and the whole chain has to be intact for the tigging to count. Once the chain grows past a certain point, it gets unwieldy, and intrepid runners can simply break through the middle and avoid being surrounded and caught by those on the ends. Leslie Paul remembered past glories in South-east London, about 1915:

> Nothing in after life has quite taken the courage it then took to face alone this thundering line, and run at it, and hurl oneself at it, and break it with one's body or fists before the hands of the extremities could wheel round and touch me. For months this swift and exciting game would oust all others in our affections.

Although the game is still known, it does not seem to be so enthusiastically played as in the past, and children from many schools today deny any knowledge of it. In my own playground in South London in the 1950s it was a great favourite, and was one of the games always played by boys and girls together. Nevertheless, modern versions still emerge:

> 'Spiral' – Every time someone was caught they linked hands to the last person caught, till a large chain of small children had linked hands, then the first person (it) shouted, 'Spiral,' and you would start spinning around the axis of the it till you hit such speed that children flew everywhere – the winners were the ones left standing.   ESSEX, 1980s

> 'The Blob' is a game when two people are it. They can't let go of each other's hand; when they tag someone they join the blob.
>   GLOUCESTERSHIRE, 2008

An interesting contemporary variant is described by Rebecca (nine years old) from Lechlade and her stepsister Maddie (ten years old) from Salisbury, in which the chaser cannot 'tag' people when they are linked together, holding little fingers.

'Chain Tig' has a long pedigree, and many nineteenth-century versions had much more complex rules than the modern ones. A small but significant detail owes itself to the literal nature of the child's mind. In many early versions the initial chaser had to run with their hands clasped in front of them – forming a chain of one.

There was also commonly a temporary reversal of roles within the game. Each time the 'it' people caught someone they all had to return to their base before they could chase anyone else, and until they did so they were open to physical attack with caps and knotted scarves from those still free. Vestiges of this kind of play survived well into modern times, and may still do so in some places. The Opies, for example, quoted in 1969 a twelve-year-old Forfar schoolgirl describing the local game of 'Bully Horn':

> If they let go hands we shout out loud 'Chainy broken – get them.' We run and hit them again before they reach the pavement.

In other cases, while the 'it' people were temporarily powerless they could be tigged by any still-free players and forced to give them a piggyback back to the base.

The other interesting feature of earlier versions is that they very often included words with which the chasers had to warn the others of their approach:

> Stag-a-rag-a-roaring
>   Very frosty morning
> What I cannot catch tonight
>   I'll catch tomorrow morning.
>
> *SHROPSHIRE, 1880S*

> Widdy widdy way
>   The morrow's the market day
> Slyarter, slyarter
>   Comin' away, comin' away.
>
> *NORTHUMBERLAND, C.1890*

One of the regularly occurring names for the earlier versions of 'Chain Tig' was 'Stag', and there are other occasional references to horned beasts. The games also went under an impressive variety of colourful names, including 'Widdy' (London); 'Widdy-waddy-way' (Northumberland/Cornwall); 'Stag-a-laggle' (Dorset); 'Stag-warning' (Staffordshire); 'Witto-witto-wee' (Isle of Man); 'Cock-warning' (Buckinghamshire); 'Hiry Hag' or 'Haggary Hag' (Yorkshire); 'Bloomer' (Somerset); 'Long Ticker' or 'The Press Gang' (Huntingdonshire); and 'Snakes' (Southwark). One early description, in Jamieson's *Etymological Dictionary of the Scottish Language* (Supplement, 1825), called it 'Hornie'.

Line Tig

Another very common variant of tig that takes advantage of features in the environment is 'Line Tig':

> Well, it's called 'Line Tig', and you've got to walk on the yellow lines, all round, and the person who is on it's got to try and tig you; it's like tig but on the yellow lines – the netball courts. And if you get tigged you're on it and you've got to chase someone else . . . if you're on a corner you're only allowed to go one way – you're not allowed to go backwards.　　　HAMPSHIRE, 1979

As indicated here, there are sometimes rules about which way round the players can move. The semicircles at each end of the netball court are crucial to most versions of the game. These are the only places you can overtake a slower player, and in some cases they are regarded as sanctuaries where the chasers cannot venture.

The game is still regularly played, but its inherent restrictions mean that it is often regarded as only really suitable for younger children.

Kiss Chase

One of the commonest variants of the basic chasing game is 'Kiss Chase', where the boys chase the girls, or vice versa, and when a chaser catches someone they have to kiss them. There are many variations within this basic framework. Sometimes each catcher chases only one victim, and when caught they are both out of the game until it is restarted, but more usually the chaser moves straight on to another player. In some versions the one who is caught has a choice of what will happen to them – they can be kissed or cuddled or tortured, for example.

One woman remembering her childhood in Yorkshire in the 1980s commented that 'Kiss Chase' was:

> . . . generally instigated by the girls and avoided by the boys. It was usually only popular amongst girls who were confident that one of the boys would want to catch them.

Talking to groups of girls, I have found that they are usually quite happy with the game and agree that it is sometimes they who initiate it; but there is often a minority who are clearly uncomfortable with the whole thing and prefer not to play, or who invent new roles for themselves, such as 'helping' friends who are caught. Boys, too, often show ambivalence about the game. Some see no point in it, others enjoy the chasing but not the kissing, while some are aware that they should want to kiss the girls, but do not quite understand why.

To a certain extent, of course, it depends on the age of the children involved. In interviews with modern ten- or-eleven-year-olds, I have found they usually state that they 'used to play' the game, and are touchingly condescending about their younger selves. 'They don't really know what they're doing,' said one such 'older child' at Ardleigh School, in Essex. But it is clear that the older children do sometimes play the game, even if only for old time's sake. In the past, when chasing games were regularly played by a wider age range, the game certainly had more serious intent, and was one of several games, including 'Kiss-in-the-ring', in which physical contact between the sexes was the whole point (see p. 43).

Although virtually every child recognises the phrase 'Kiss Chase', they often have a local name for the game, such as 'Kissy Catchy', 'Catchy Kissy', 'Kissy Girls' (when the girls are doing the chasing) and, where other elements are introduced, 'Kiss, Cuddle or Torture', or 'Kiss, Kick or Torture', which are fairly self-explanatory.

Shadow Tig

'Shadow Tig' is sometimes mentioned by schoolchildren who claim to have made it up, but it has been around at least since Norman Douglas published his *London Street Games* in 1916. In the usual version the 'it' person tigs others by stepping on their shadow, but there is another way of playing, as recorded in the list compiled by the Mary Erskine pupils in Edinburgh, given above, in which any patch of shadow is considered a safe home.

The Terminology of Tig

In their researches in the 1950s and 1960s, Iona and Peter Opie discovered that many different names were used for the basic chasing game, and also for the roles and actions involved. But these differences were markedly regional, and the Opies provided a series of distribution maps in their *Children's Games in Street and Playground* (1969), which quickly became the touchstone for childlore research. Research since their time confirms what they found, with some modification and the proviso that the picture on the ground was messier than a map can show.

What the Opies found, in summary, was that 'tig' easily trumped other names, being the dominant word from the Wash to the northern tip of Scotland and, strangely, in Cornwall in the far west; 'tick' was found in North Wales and the English Midlands; 'touch' was the word in South Wales and the western counties of Devon, Somerset and Dorset; 'tag' had a relatively small territory, comprising Hereford and Worcester, Monmouthshire and Gloucestershire; 'he' was predominant in London, Essex, Suffolk and the South-east.

There were, however, many anomalies: Birmingham children said 'tig' even though they were surrounded by 'tick' speakers; Nottingham children said 'dobby'; and 'tip' was found in various places, as were 'catch' and 'touch'. The latter word was the one most used in books of games, and was therefore something of an 'official' term.

The Opies argued that 'it' was 'common in the west country, and relatively uncommon elsewhere, except in Cambridgeshire and Huntingdonshire'. Recent fieldwork with people who were children at the time suggests, though, that it was a leading alternative name for many children, especially those in the 'he' area. The Opies may also have underestimated the incidence of 'tag' as an active name.

No one has undertaken a national survey since the Opies' time, but recent research suggests that while the geographical pattern they described is still broadly in place, it is gradually breaking down. 'It' now seems to be moving from being an alternative to actually replacing 'He' across the South-east, and may well be infiltrating the rest of the country. It is also possible that 'tag' is becoming the generic word, thanks, perhaps, to American influence. (The Opies thought that 'tag' might have been the general name across the whole of southern England at one time; if so, modern US culture is – as in other areas of children's lore – restoring an older usage.)

It seems almost certain that children did not invent these words. 'Tick' is related to Dutch *tikken* and Norwegian *tikke*, both of which mean 'to pat or touch lightly', and is recorded in English *c.*1440. 'Tig' appears in this general sense in 1721, and although the *Oxford English Dictionary* does not say categorically that 'tig' derives directly from 'tick', it admits the probability. 'Tick' as the children's game is recorded in the poet Michael Drayton's works in 1622, and in the manuscript description of games compiled by Francis Willughby in the 1660s, while a poem by Robert Anderson, dated 1802, names the game as 'tig'.

The earliest known usage of 'tag' for the game is found in the *Gentleman's Magazine* of 1738. This predates 'tig' but still leaves 'tick' as by far the oldest word. 'He' does not seem to have been used before the late nineteenth century, but it was used as the name of the chaser in a counting-out rhyme published in *Gammer Gurton's Garland* of 1810, which ends with 'You or I must be he'.

The word for the 'it' person is even more difficult to pin down than the game itself, because children are not always consistent, and in conversation will often use a word they think the interviewer will understand rather than the one that comes naturally to them. Thus they will refer to the 'catcher' or the 'chaser' to an outsider and then use a different word when talking to each other. There is also a subtle difference between the name of the person and the 'state of being it', which causes confusion.

As the Opies showed, the 'it' person is likely to be the 'man', or 'mannie', in Scotland, northern England and parts of the Midlands, 'it' or 'het' in many other parts of England and Scotland, 'he' in London and the South-east, and 'king' in the Orkneys. Sometimes the suffix '–er' is added, as in the 'tigger' and 'tagger', the 'stucker' and 'unstucker' (in 'Stuck in the Mud') and – not listed by Opies but quite common now – the 'itter'. The person can be 'on' in the Midlands and North of England, but 'on it' in Wales and western England. When it comes to describing the *act* of touching a player, those who call their game 'tig' or 'tag' can talk of a 'tigger' or 'tagger', who 'tigs' or 'tags' their victim. However, Londoners who play 'he' cannot really 'he' someone, so they 'have' them instead, and this can sound quite confusing in conversation: 'He has to have them, and when he has had them he has to . . .' Say that out loud, dropping a few aitches, and you will see the problem for the folklore collector. It is no surprise that children in the South-east occasionally call the game 'had' or 'hads'.

Lurgi/Fleas

The basic tig game takes on a different aura when the 'it' is identified with a disease, fleas or something else unpleasant. This can happen in the playground, for example recently at Ardleigh school in Essex, where the game 'Virus' is the same as tig but the children say 'virus' when they touch someone. But it also takes place in the classroom, or other confined spaces like the school bus, where there is no chance of running away, and it can easily acquire a rather cruel overtone.

Some nineteenth-century sources imply that tig suggests the notion of infection being passed on, but do not offer any clear description of this. The idea was, however, certainly widespread in the twentieth century, when 'Plague' and 'Fever' were alternative names for the game. Children quickly picked up (as did many of the adult population) on the term 'the dreaded lurgi', which was a catchphrase on *The Goons*, a radio programme of 1954. For some time afterwards this was the standard playground word for any transmittable disease, and it is interesting to note that over fifty years later it can still be heard:

> 'Lurgies' – same as 'it' but you have to say 'Lurgy' when you 'it' someone – but you can cross your fingers to protect yourself – or [say] 'injection of life'. A friend in one class says, 'Injection, injection, injection infection' or 'Injection, injection, injection, no infection'.   BALHAM, 2010

Cops and Robbers

In some chasing games, players must be caught rather than simply 'tigged', and instead of a 'home' or safe place, there is a prison. The commonest name for this is 'Cops and Robbers', which needs two teams:

> There's one group of cops and there's one group of robbers, and what happens is the robbers get a five-second headstart and they have to run off, and the cops have to go and catch them and put them back to jail, which is, say, one wall; but the other robbers can free any robbers who are against the wall.   WEST LONDON, 2009

In some versions the robbers who are caught have to stay in the prison until the end of the game, but often there is an agreed method by which they can be released by a team-mate, or there are ways in which prisoners can 'escape'.

Poison and Witch's Fingers

The game 'Poison' starts with the 'it' person holding out one hand or two (depending on the number playing), with fingers outspread. Each of the players holds a finger. 'It' then says, 'I went to the shop and bought a bottle of—' and the players must run and be chased if they say the word 'poison' but must stay put if they say anything else. Anyone who moves at the wrong word becomes 'it'. In some places the key word formerly used was 'Jumbo' or 'Bingo' or something else. The game survives in the form 'Witch's Fingers', included in the Edinburgh list given above, where the players hold the witch's fingers while she tells a story until a certain word is spoken and they all scatter. In North London it is one of several games called 'Sticky Toffee':

> 'Sticky Toffee': You have to hold people's fingers, and you say, 'I'm going to the market, I'm going to buy . . .' and when you say, 'Sticky toffee,' you have to run away. The person who said, 'sticky toffee' has to go and catch you.
>
> EAST FINCHLEY, 2008

Cross Tig

One chasing game that seems to have disappeared these days is 'Cross Tig':

> 'Cross Touch': In this game Touch chases one player until another runs across his path, between him and the boy pursued, upon which Touch must immediately run after the one who crossed until some other crossing between them must in his turn be followed; in this way the game continues until one is touched, who takes the office of Touch, and gives chase to the others.
>
> GAMES AND SPORTS FOR YOUNG BOYS, 1859

This seems hard on the chaser because with a little organisation on the part of the players he or she will be constantly facing fresh runners. One refinement not mentioned here is that the chaser must declare who he or she is chasing. 'Cross Tig' was already being played in the first decade of the nineteenth century, at Sedgley Park School for example, and was popular enough to be mentioned in many of the standard works on games throughout the century.

Last Touch

Children who have been playing tig in the playground can often be seen trying to get the last touch in while they line up to go back into school, as if it matters, even in jest, who will stay 'it' for the rest of the day. This impulse was formerly very well known, and in many minds constituted a distinct form of the game, played on the way home from school:

> 'Last-Bat-Poison': a game at tig, played as school children arrive at the parting of their ways in going home. The object is to give a 'bat' without being touched again, and the player on touching and running off calls out 'Last-bat-poison'.
>
> NORTHUMBERLAND, C.1890

In a Yorkshire collection of the same period, the writer advised, 'But be it remembered, this last tig had to be given on the skin, not on the jacket, or the boy would call out, "I wasn't born with my clothes on."'

Tiggy Touch Wood or Iron

The idea of temporary immunity from being tigged is not a new one, and in some games it becomes the main distinguishing feature. Throughout the nineteenth century and into the earlier twentieth, one such game was 'Tiggy Tiggy Touch Wood' or 'Ticky Ticky Touch Wood', in which the players who were touching wood were exempt from capture. Judging by the published descriptions, the emphasis of the game was slightly different from usual tig. Rather than the players running around and occasionally claiming immunity, the norm here seems to have been to run from one safe point to another:

> 'Tiggy-Touchwood': One player who is called Tiggy stands out and each of the others takes hold of or touches a piece of wood, such as a door, or rail, etc. One then leaves his 'wood' and runs across the playground, and if while doing so Tiggy can touch him he must stand out or take Tiggy's place.
>
> SHEFFIELD, 1880S

The game was extremely widely known, and so was the phrase 'Tiggy Touchwood'.

Given that the game was concerned with 'protection', and was well known to adults as well as children, it is almost certainly the origin of our modern superstitious practice of saying, 'Touch wood'. The claim that the latter goes back to when we believed in tree spirits is complete nonsense.

The earliest reference to the game is in Robert Anderson's poem *The*

Author on Himself, published in his *Ballads in the Cumberland Dialect* (1805). Remembering the joys of childhood, he writes:

> Or scamper, like wild-things, at hunting the hare
> Tig-touch-wood, four corners, or twenty gams mair.

Anderson was born in 1770, so if the poem is genuinely autobiographical it takes the game back into the eighteenth century. After the 1820s it is mentioned quite frequently in published works.

Ball Tig

'Ball Tig' is one of those games that is still sometimes mentioned by children describing their playground activities, but is clearly nowhere near as popular as it used to be. When the Opies commented on it back in the 1960s, when it was most commonly known as 'Kingy', it was clearly a nationwide obsession:

> This fast-moving game has all the qualifications for being considered the national game of British schoolboys . . . it is immensely popular (almost every boy in England, Scotland and Wales plays it) and no native of Britain appears to have troubled to record it.

The reason for its decline is not clear. Perhaps the problem is that nowadays school staff discourage games that involve throwing things at people. Or perhaps it is simply that the game was always the province of older children and now that children stop playing such games at an earlier age than they used to it has been left behind. It is certainly still played in organisations like the Woodcraft Folk and the Scouts.

The game varies little from place to place. The person who is 'it' holds a ball and tries to tig the other players by throwing it and hitting them with it. Sometimes there are agreed places where a player can be hit – for example, between knee and shoulder – but more often there is no restriction. The 'it' is cumulative, so each one tigged joins the growing team of 'it' people. The rule is often played that the first 'it' can run with the ball, or at least can move about while bouncing it, but once there are two or more 'it' people it is invariably the case that they cannot move while holding the ball and so must pass it between themselves to get nearer to their quarry. The only way the free players can defend themselves is to hit the ball away with their fists, but if an 'it' person catches the ball directly from a player's fist (i.e. before it has bounced), that player is tigged. An extension of the fist rule is that players can pick up the ball between their two fists and throw it away from them.

Another feature that formerly distinguished this game from other versions of tig was that players often had particular methods of starting the game. The commonest form was for boys to stand in a circle with their feet apart while the leader bounced or rolled the ball into the centre; whoever's legs it rolled through was 'it'. Alternatively, the players could line up against a wall, or sit on the kerb, but again, whoever's legs the ball rolled through was chosen.

CHAPTER THREE

British Bulldog and Other Chasing Games

When I recently started collecting games again, after a lapse of a few years, I was surprised to be told by many schoolchildren that they played 'Bulldog' a lot. 'British Bulldog' was, in my experience fifty years ago, a very robust game, played by males, mainly in relatively controlled situations of secondary-school gyms, Scout meetings and even army training camps. It was routinely banned in playgrounds, although I was aware that previous generations had played it in the schoolyard as a matter of course. The essence of the game is that players have to run back and forth across an allotted space, while a growing number of catchers try to stop them. To catch a player, the catchers must lift him bodily so that both feet are off the ground, and hold him up long enough to chant 'British Bulldog 1 2 3', or, in other versions, the player must be held down on the ground for a similar length of time. Played in this way, the game is one of rough macho excitement, with much dodging, ducking and diving, and it is a point of honour not to give in gracefully, but wriggle, writhe and resist in every way available, short of outright fisticuffs.

In my conversations with contemporary children it soon became clear, however, that nowadays children regularly use 'Bulldog' as a generic term for any game where players have to run across the playground. As a ten-year-old girl from West London (2009) said:

> 'Bulldog' – I love that game. There's one person who is it and we all have to parade across and if he catches us then we're a bulldog. One side to another. Sometimes there's 'Colour Bulldog' where you say if you're wearing

this colour then you run across – the people with that colour get across safely, and the person can't it them, but then when the person says 'bulldog' the other people have to run and the itter can get them.

My style of 'Bulldog' is still played, but under more specific names:

> A more violent version of this was 'Bring-down British Bulldog' . . . you had to knock to the floor as many people as you could (more like rugby tackling!) at each run past.   *NOTTINGHAMSHIRE, 1980s*

> We play Bulldog – but not 'Take-down Bulldog' which the boys play.
>   *WEYBRIDGE, 2009*

Also variable is the question of how the runners know when to go across, how they are caught or tackled, and the terminology involved. The way I remember it, each player chose his moment to run, but many versions have built-in rules that regulate the flow. Sometimes the bulldog names players, but when he or she calls 'Bulldog!' everyone runs at once. Sometimes as the single runner gets through, or is caught, the others all run. The essence of some versions is that the players select runners without the bulldog knowing, at least at first, who they are going to be:

> In 'Subject Bulldog', the catcher chooses a subject, like cars, pop groups or TV programmes. Then the players decide between them which one of that subject they want to be. Like, if the catcher chooses 'sports', one person might be football, one tennis and another rugby. When they have decided, the catcher says a sport. If that sport is the one you chose to be, you must run. This way, the catcher cannot choose who he wants to run, as he does not know which sport you have chosen.   *YORKSHIRE, 1990s*

The method of catching varies considerably, although most modern children play a version in which the runner has merely to be touched. The former style, where the players are lifted bodily from the floor, seems to be much rarer, and modern versions focus more on getting people on the ground. But there have been many degrees between these extremes, and the bulldog sometimes simply has to touch the runners' heads or backs, and say something – usually, nowadays, 'Bulldog'.

A significant majority of the children who spoke to me about 'Bulldog' volunteered the fact that it was banned, although some said that only the 'take-down' versions were forbidden. What is clear from many accounts is that it is not simply the tackling that teachers object to, but the 'headlong dash' of groups of children across the busy playground. But the more robust versions survive – sometimes they are allowed on the school field, sometimes they are played in the playground surreptitiously, although it is unlikely the 'authorities' really do not notice. A lad from Coventry told Cathy Gould in 2007 that the game was banned from his junior school so they renamed it 'Fast and Furious' to confuse the teachers.

The name 'British Bulldog', and the rougher elements of lifting or throwing down, seem to have become the norm during the twentieth century. Earlier references appear under many different titles, and concentrate more on unspecified 'detaining' or patting the heads of players. Alice Gomme, for example, included several versions of the game in her 1890s compilation. One, from Nairn, was called 'Cock', and the boy in the middle had to 'crown' players by placing a hand on their heads. In another Scottish version, called 'Rexa-boxa-king', the King called out those words to signal the general rush of players. In 'Click', reported from Marlborough in Wiltshire, the one in the middle had to hold a player long enough to say, 'One, two, three, I catch thee; help me catch another,' which sounds awfully polite, whereas in a Warwickshire version described in Joseph Wright's *English Dialect Dictionary* (II, 479) he had to declaim the less straightforward, 'Fox a' dowdy, catch a candle.'

The basic game appears in many books of games of the period. *Cassell's Book of Sports and Pastimes* (1907) calls the game 'King Senio': the King in the middle has to tap the others on the head and say, 'I crown thee king', while in Savill's *Organised Playground Rhymes* (1908), it is 'King Caesar' who says these same words. Indeed, it is noticeable that in these Victorian and Edwardian versions the person in the middle is regularly referred to as a 'King', and Gomme gives details of another Scottish version, called 'Rax' or 'Raxie-boxie', where the catcher was called 'King' or 'Queen' depending on whether it was boys or girls playing. The Opies provide details of several other descriptions, dating back to 1805, and also related games under the heading 'Wall to Wall'.

The basic format of running across a playground or, in earlier versions, across a street, is the defining feature of a range of games that are related in one way or another to 'Bulldog'. 'Red Rover', for example, is a game that for a while was extremely popular, although much less common these days. As played in Coventry in the 1990s, and recorded by Cathy Gould:

Two teams of players line up facing each other. They hold hands to form two chains. One team calls:

> Red Rover, Red Rover
> Send — over (naming someone from the opposite team)

The person named breaks rank and runs across with, hopefully, enough force to break through a link in the other team. If you manage to break through you return to your own team. If not, you join the opposition.

Again, the game has often been banned on the grounds of potential physical harm. As Catherine McKiernan recalled of her schooldays in Leeds in the 1980s:

> Bulldog and Red Rover were both banned in the playground, although Red Rover was unofficially allowed if only the older classes were in the playground . . . It was more talked about than played.

Strangely enough, given its potential for rough play, the game was formerly particularly popular with girls in Scotland.

The history of the game is not entirely clear. It is evidently played all over the English-speaking world, often under the Red Rover name, and very similar games are known on the Continent, but Iona and Peter Opie in *Children's Games in Street and Playground* (1969) could not find any version in Britain before the 1920s. This dating is confirmed by what Avis Butterfield remembered playing in York around 1920, and collected by Steve Gardham:

> 'Cookoo': Two teams face each other and each member of the team links arms with each other, then one team chooses a member of the opposite team to break a link in that team's chain. So that person runs across and jumps onto the arms of the two people in one of the links. If he breaks it those two people in the link join the other team, but if he fails he must join that team.

None of the earlier games suggested by the Opies, such as the Scottish 'Jockie Rover', printed in Alice Gomme's *Traditional Games* (1894), seem quite right as Red Rover's ancestors, and there is some confusion between this game and the other hand-holding game 'Chain He' or 'Chain Tig', and its own ancestors 'Warning' and 'Widdy' (see p. 26). On present evidence, it seems possible that Red Rover may have been introduced to Britain, probably from America or Australia, just prior to 1920.

Another game in which the players had to cross a space without getting caught by the child in the middle was a great favourite with my circle of friends in Streatham, South London, in the 1950s. We called it 'Cock-aroosha' or 'Hop the Barger', although 'Barge the Hopper' would have been more appropriate.

> Everybody on one side of the playground except one catcher in the middle. Every individual has to make it across the playground without being caught, but all players have to hop all the time, with their arms folded across their chests. The only way for the catcher to stop people is by barging them, and forcing them to put their other foot down. Anyone thus caught joins the one in the middle, so the odds against getting across safely gradually shorten, as the players hop back and forth.   *SOUTH LONDON, 1950S*

Childlore collector Cathy Gould noted exactly the same game from her father, who called it 'Hopping Jinny' and who played it in the street in Coventry in the 1920s.

The game was known all over the country, and went by a variety of names, many of which included the 'hopping' element ('Hopping Caesar', 'Hop and Dodge', 'Hoppy Bowfie') or the 'Cock' ('Cockarusty', 'Cockie Duntie', 'Cock Heaving') or both, as in 'Hopping Cockerels' in North-amptonshire. It is interesting to note that the names of games involving hopping often refer to 'cocks'. There were some minor local variations, but the only major difference was that in some places the middle person called the players individually to hop across, rather than all going at will.

There are many other 'run across' games in which the distinguishing feature is simply the different names given to the catchers and the runners. It is common nowadays for those in the middle to be called 'sharks', while the others are known as 'fish'. An extension of this idea, played in Belfast, combines the game with a feature more usually found in 'Stuck in the Mud' (p. 20):

> 'Octopus': There's one person 'it' – it's a bit like 'Bulldogs', and the people have to run forward and back and whoever gets tipped is the seaweed. Whoever's the seaweed they have to [stand still] and they have to catch other people, and they turn into seaweed.   *BELFAST, 2010*

Several of the games already mentioned include the motif of the players being called across individually, or being distinguished by colour or subject, but in some the dialogue between catcher and potential victim takes on a much larger role. 'Sheep, Sheep, Come Home' is one of these:

One [game] which springs to mind is 'Sheep, sheep, come home'. A caller
would stand at one end of the playground; in the middle would stand the
Wolf, with all the Sheep at the other end of the playground. The caller would
say, 'Sheep, sheep, come home', and the sheep would reply, 'We're afraid.'
Next, caller said, 'What of?' Whereupon the sheep replied, 'The Wolf.' The
caller then responded with, 'The Wolf has gone to Devonshire and won't be
back for many a year, so sheep, sheep, come home' (which was a blatant lie,
of course!). So the poor ignorant sheep would try to run home to the caller
and, inevitably, on the journey, whoever the Wolf caught would be 'out'. The
caller would then switch to the other end of the playground, to call again.
So it went on until the one sheep remaining would be decided the winner.

HEREFORDSHIRE, C.1940S

This game was immensely popular in the mid twentieth century, and
contributors to the *Within Living Memory* series, compiled by Women's
Institutes up and down the country in the 1990s, often mention playing
the game as one of their favourite childhood memories. In addition to
being a playground and street favourite, it was one of the games that
younger children learned in the home. It had been equally popular in the
previous century:

While I was still a very little child this same game made a fine squealing
indoor romp called 'Sheep, sheep, come home'. One player called these words
to the other players the other side of the 'den'. The sheep answered, 'Fraid.'
'What are you afraid of?' was the next call, and at the answer 'Wolf', the
assurance came, 'Wolf's gone to Devonshire! Won't be back for seven year.'
So then the sheep ran across the den and out came the wolf.

FARNHAM, SURREY, 1860S

Several writers on children's games comment on the palpable excitement that builds in games like 'What's the Time, Mr Wolf?' and the squeals
of mixed joy and fright as the wolf suddenly turns, and the chase begins.
There is perhaps less tension in 'Sheep, Sheep', but the dialogue functions
in a similar way.

The game has many other names, including the stark 'Wolf', under
which title five different versions are given in Alice Gomme's *Traditional
Games* (1898).

CHAPTER FOUR

All in a Circle

One of the natural ways of organising people for group activities is to get everyone into a circle, and it is no surprise that many children's games take this basic shape. But what happens next in the game varies considerably. Many of the older and more formal singing games take a circular form, with the children holding hands or dancing (see Chapter 16), but in each of the games considered in this chapter the players interact in different ways with each other while preserving the circular shape.

One important group of interrelated circular games, which all share key features, includes some of the most widespread games of the past 200 years or so. The best known of these games is nowadays called 'Drop Handkerchief', 'I Sent a Letter to My Love' or 'A-tisket A-tasket', but before the Second World War 'Kiss-in-the-ring' was the version commonly played. The newest recruit to the stable, 'Duck Duck Goose', is known to so many present-day children that if its popularity continues it will, in its turn, become the best known, if not the most played, in adult circles.

In all these games the participants stand or sit in a circle; one (Player 1) goes round the outside and chooses another (Player 2), at random. These two then chase or race each other back to Player 2's place in the circle. What happens in between, however, is what gives each game its particular flavour. It is not always easy to separate them, or to disentangle their respective histories.

As played by Lynda Rose in Birmingham in the 1960s, the game was as follows:

In this game we sat in a circle and one of us was chosen to be a 'postman'.

The postman walked around the circle and we all sang:

> I sent a letter to my love
> And on the way I dropped it
> Somebody must have picked it up
> And put it in their pocket
> Thief! Thief!
> Drop it! Drop it!

On the words 'drop it', the postman dropped the 'letter' (a beanbag or a screwed-up ball of paper). The postman was then chased by the person who'd had the letter dropped behind them. The postman usually made it safely back to the empty spot.

Most modern versions follow this pattern, although after the fourth line it is more usual for the one going round to repeat something along the lines of 'It isn't you', until he or she suddenly says, 'It's you!' Over the years, various items have been used – a handkerchief, glove, scarf, and so on – and a common feature is that the players in the circle must not look behind them until Player 1 has passed them. In some versions Player 2 runs the same way round as Player 1, but in others they run in opposite directions.

Another notable difference between previous eras and today is that in the past, rather than having to take over immediately as Player 1, Player 2 was sometimes forced to go into the middle of the circle and suck their thumb while there. They were relieved by the next person to fail. In a few cases, everyone who failed went into the middle and as the game progressed there were fewer and fewer in the circle and a growing number in the middle.

What distinguishes 'Kiss-in-the-ring' from the other 'Drop Handkerchief' games is, as its name suggests, the motif of kissing. If Player 2 fails to catch Player 1, or fails to get back round before them, Player 1 is entitled to claim a kiss – usually undertaken in the centre of the circle in full view of the company. Obviously, there is wide scope between a chaste kiss on the cheek and the flirtatious struggle for a more adventurous kiss, and in many cases Player 2 will actually want to fail, so the chase or race takes on a degree of pretence.

This interaction between Players 1 and 2 is a crucial variant in determining the nature of the game being played. In some it is a simple 'race', where both parties have to try to get back to the vacant spot first, while in others it is a 'chase', because Player 2 must try to catch Player 1 before that player gets back to that spot. These may sound very similar, but the 'chase' option provides scope for more complicated routes, in and out and through the circle, and in many versions Player 2 must follow exactly the route taken by Player 1 or be penalised.

This leads us to 'Cat and Mouse', the final major game in this group. In this form of the game, there are no preliminaries or singing, but merely the chase in and out of the circle. The players in the circle often hold hands and then raise them up to make arches for the others to run under.

As well as being played in the playground and street, all these games were once immensely popular at children's parties, family get-togethers at Christmas and other festivals, and Brownie and Guide meetings. It is also clear from many nineteenth-century sources that 'Kiss-in-the-ring' was particularly popular with young adults, and writers such as Charles Dickens (for example in *Sketches by Boz*, 1836) and a contributor to William Hone's *Every-Day Book* (1825) regularly mention large enthusiastic games at open-air fêtes and fairs. Even at the end of the century the *Westminster Gazette* (10 August 1899) could report:

> A peculiar custom on Hampstead Heath for the week following Bank Holiday is the playing of Kiss-in-the-ring on a large scale on a special part of the West Heath.

While the third part of Flora Thompson's *Lark Rise to Candleford*, published in 1943 as *Candleford Green*, describes the scene at local church socials of the period:

> After 'Postman's Knock' and 'Musical Chairs' and 'Here we go round the Mulberry Bush', a large ring was formed for 'Dropping the Handkerchief', and the fun of the evening began. 'I wrote a letter to my love and on the way I dropped it. One of you has picked it up and put it in your pocket,' chanted the odd man or girl out as they circled the ring, handkerchief in hand, until they came to the back of the person they wished to choose and placed the handkerchief on his or her shoulder. The chase which followed took so long round and round the ring and always eventually out of one of the several doors, that two separate handkerchiefs kept two couples going in the Church Social version of the game. There was supposed to be no kissing, as it was a Church function, but when the pursuer caught the pursued somewhere beyond the door with a smudged roller towel upon it, who could say what happened. Perhaps the youth sketched a stage kiss. Perhaps not.

The essential difference between the Hampstead Heath and Candleford Green escapades is not simply that one was outdoors on a bank holiday and the other indoors at a church function, but that the degree of social control varied. All the young people at Flora Thompson's gathering would have been from the local community, and would have known perfectly well that their behaviour was being monitored, and that any transgressions would be followed by social repercussions. Indeed, the 'roughest' elements of local society were probably not invited and would have shunned such an affair anyway. But in a public gathering, on a summer's day, in holiday mood, among strangers, the behaviour of the young people could be far more uninhibited.

It is tempting to conclude that the adult game of 'Kiss-in-the-ring' was gradually cleaned up and transformed into one suitable for children, but the available evidence does not support this hypothesis. The earliest clear reference to any of these games, which is to be found in the *Little Penny Pocket Book* (1767), contains no hint of kissing. The picture included there shows eight figures (four men, four women), seven of whom are holding hands in a circle, while one is on the outside, and a letter lays on the floor. The picture is captioned 'I sent a letter to my love', and the accompanying verse reads:

> The lads and lasses here are seen,
>   All gaily tripping o'er the green;
> But one among them, to her cost,
>   The treasure of her heart has lost.

Despite the pastoral implications of the verse, the picture clearly shows them indoors.

The name 'Kiss-in-the-ring' is first found in Strutts's *Sports and Pastimes of the People of England* (1801), where his entry for 'Cat after mouse' ends with:

> When this game is played by an equal number of boys and girls, a boy must touch a girl, and a girl a boy, and when either of them be caught they go into the middle of the ring and salute each other; hence is derived the name of Kiss in the Ring.

J. S. Udal's detailed description of Dorset games in the *Folk-Lore Journal* of 1889 gives two versions of the game, called, respectively, 'Kiss-in-the-Ring' and 'Drop the Handkerchief'. Of the former, he comments, with due emphasis, 'if a capture is effected (*as is nearly always the case*), the chaser is entitled to lead the first player back into the centre of the ring and claim a kiss'. Of the latter, he writes:

> In this last it will be noticed there is no kissing, and I am assured by several persons who are interested in Dorset children's games that the indiscriminate kissing (that is, whether the girl pursued runs little or far, or, when overtaken, whether she objects or not), with which this game is ordinarily associated, as played now in both Dorset and in other counties, was not indigenous to our county, but is merely a pernicious after-growth or outcome of later days, which had its origin in the various excursion and holiday fêtes, which the facilities of railway travelling had instituted, by bringing large crowds from the neighbouring towns into the country. I am told that thirty years ago such a thing was unknown in the country districts of Dorset, when the game then usually indulged in was known merely as 'Drop the handkerchief'.

As with the Hampstead Heath get-together, the picture here is of relatively rough and indecent 'open-air' public gatherings, eliciting more than a hint of disapproval from social 'superiors'.

The modern game of 'Duck Duck Goose' closely follows the basic 'Drop Handkerchief' format, but in a simplified form. All the players, except Player 1, are seated in a circle. Player 1 walks or trots round the outside tapping each head and saying 'duck' for each one. But at any moment Player 1 can say 'goose', and the person thus designated has to chase Player 1 round the circle back to the space they have just vacated. If Player 1 gets back without being caught, Player 2 becomes the new Player 1; but if Player 2 manages to catch Player 1, the latter continues as Player 1 and starts again.

This game is now widely known in infant schools across the country, and is often the first 'playground game' that newcomers to school learn. It is often taught by teachers and playground assistants, and is played in PE lessons. Many children, though, claim that they first learnt it from other children, so it occupies a 'semi-official' place in children's lore. It is noticeable that there seems to be very little variation between versions from different schools.

'Duck Duck Goose' seems to have been introduced to British schools as recently as the very early 1990s, but it has a much longer history in North America and Australia, stretching back at least to a Toronto version collected by Edith Fowke in 1960. Again there is a mixture of adult–child and child–child transmission, but it seems likely that the former came first. Childlore researcher Simon Bronner, for example, has found several versions in American books aimed at PE teachers that pre-date the ones collected in the field, including *Physical Education Activities for High School Girls* by Louise Patterson van Sickle (1928).

In the plethora of lesser-known variations on the theme, Iona and Peter Opie identify two worth mentioning. One, which eschews the handkerchief motif and which they call 'Bump-on-the-back', is also described in Alice Gomme's *Traditional Games* (1894), under the title 'French Jackie'. The other is the aptly titled 'Whackem', in which the participants stand in a circle with their eyes closed and hands behind their backs. Player 1 places a short piece of rope into the hands of Player 2, who immediately starts to belabour his or her right-hand neighbour. This person then has to run round the circle back to place to avoid the blows.

There are also many circle games that do not involve the players chasing each other. 'Down in the Jungle', for example, brings in a clapping movement. Players stand or sit in a circle, with their hands out beside them. Each person's left hand is on top of their neighbour's right, and their right hand is under their other neighbour's left. One person starts by bringing their left hand over and slapping the left hand of their neighbour (No. 2). No. 2 then slaps the hand of No. 3, and so on, round and round the circle, while a rhyme is sung or chanted. Whoever gets slapped on the last word is out, but if they are quick enough they can pull their hand away just as their neighbour tries to strike, and if they succeed their neighbour is out instead.

Games with the same format and similar rules are known in many countries, sometimes with nonsense rhymes attached and sometimes with straightforward recitations such as a sequence of numbers or the alphabet. These simple sequences are known in Britain too, but more often children chant a rhyme which begins, 'Down by the river of hankie pankie' or 'Down in the jungle'. In the following version the slapping takes added urgency because of what is being passed on:

> Down in the jungle where nobody goes
> There's a great big gorilla picking his nose
> And he picks it and he flicks it, see where it goes
> Who's gonna get that
>   Who's gonna get that
>   Who's gonna get that
>   Slimy Snot.

WEST LONDON, 2009

In the interests of equality, it should be pointed out that the verse is not always about a gorilla. At Park Lodge School in Belfast, in February 2010, it was a hippo.

Another ring game, 'Chinese Puzzle', has been a great favourite for decades, and the Opies in their *Children's Games in Street and Playground* (1969) use it as an example of a game with many different names – 'Chinese Muddle', 'Chinese Puddle', 'Jigsaw Puzzle', 'Chinese Knots', 'French Knots', 'Chain Man', 'Tangle Man', 'Policeman' and 'Cup and Saucers'. It is no surprise to find that it is still popular in the playground, and equally that it now has a completely different name:

> 'Doctor, Doctor, we're in a twist!': Someone is chosen to be 'on' (Player 1); the other children form a circle holding hands. Player 1 goes off to somewhere and covers their eyes so they can't see the next step; without letting go of each other's hands, the group tie themselves into a terrible knot, going under arms, twisting, etc. They then shout, 'Doctor, doctor, we're in a twist!' and Player 1 returns to untangle them all and return them to the original circle. COVENTRY, 2004

> 'Doctor Doctor': You're in a group, say you're in a circle, and you have to tangle yourselves up so much without letting go hands, and say Mollie would be Doctor, she would direct us all and try and get us back into a circle. GODALMING, 2008

Many singing games have one person placed in the centre of a ring, their role being either to choose a lover or act out a story. But in the past there were also several games in which an 'it' person was placed there, their movements strictly confined, while the other players moved more freely around the outside. Examples with a long documented history are found all over Europe. In many cases the middle person is named after an animal, and whereas in some the players torment, tease or belabour him or her, in others it is the creature's job to break out.

'Baste the Bear' was played in Britain till at least the 1920s. Here it is described in *Games and Sports for Young Boys* (1859):

> The players should toss up for the first bear, who kneels on the ground within a circle marked out for the purpose; each bear may select his own master, whose office it is to hold him by a rope, and use his utmost efforts to touch one of the other players, as they try to thrash the bear with their handkerchiefs knotted and twisted very tightly. If the bear's master can touch

one of the assailants without dragging the bear out of the ring, or letting go the rope, the boy touched becomes the bear, selects his keeper as before mentioned, and the sport is continued.

As the Opies have pointed out, an illustration of a very similar game appears in a book of French games published in 1695 under the name *La Poire* ('The Pear'), and this may link it to a popular English game of the Elizabethan period called 'Selling the Pears'.

While the bear is constrained by a rope, the key player in 'Frog in the Middle' must simply stay sitting down with his legs under him. The other children form a ring, and they:

> ... pull or buffet the centre child or Frog, who tries to catch one of them without rising from the floor. The child who is caught takes the place of the centre child ... They sometimes sing or say:
>
> > Hey! Hey! Hi! Frog in the middle and there shall lie;
> > He can't get out and he shan't get out – hey! Hey! Hi!

In an American version from 1831, the people on the outside taunt the frog with 'Frog in the middle and can't catch me', but the person in the centre suddenly jumps to catch one unawares.

'Bull in the Barn (or Park)' was far more aggressive. Here the children hold hands in a ring around the bull, and there is usually a dialogue before the action. In the version printed in Charlotte Burne's *Shropshire Folk-Lore* (1883), one of the outside ring is designated the king:

> BULL: Where is the key of the barn-door?
> CHORUS: Go to the next-door neighbour.
> KING: She left the key in the church-door.
> BULL: Steel or iron?

The bull then forces his way out of the ring, and whoever catches him becomes the new bull. In a version from Hampshire, printed by Alice Gomme in 1894, the bull addresses each player in turn with the question 'Where's the key of the park?' and each one replies, 'Ask the next-door neighbour', until the last, who says, 'Get out the way you came in', which is the signal for the bull to break out.

In a very similar game from Cornwall, published in the *Folk-Lore Journal* of 1887, the circle taunts the 'Pig in the middle and can't get out', who declares, 'I've lost my key but I will get out', and tries to do so. Another version, from Scotland, also printed by Alice Gomme, is called 'The Tod i' the Faul', or 'The Fox in the Fold'. Here, too, the animal must break through the linked hands of the circle and is then chased by everyone else.

A number of illustrations and descriptions seem to demonstrate the wide popularity of this game format – in France, Germany and modern Greece, for example – but the earliest reference must be from the second-century Greek writer Julius Pollux, whose *Onomasticon* (9. 113) includes a description of a game called 'Chytrinda'. In this, one boy (called the *chytra*, or 'pot') sits in the middle while the others pluck, pinch and strike him as they circle round. If he succeeds in catching one, they become the new pot. But while such games may have survived until the twentieth century in Britain, there is little evidence that they are played here any more.

Boys and Girls

The question of whether boys and girls play together or separately, and whether this has changed over time, is not an easy one to answer, because factors other than gender play a part, and the picture changes with the age of the children and their situation. Broadly speaking, in mixed schools nowadays the younger children play almost entirely in single-sex groups. As they get older there is more mixing between the sexes, but for specific purposes only, such as for games like tig, which require larger numbers, or 'Kiss Chase', which obviously needs both sexes. By the time they reach the last year of their primary school, however, boys and girls are happier to spend much of their playtime together. This pattern was confirmed by most of the children interviewed for this book, but there were exceptions. Occasionally a boy would adamantly claim that he and his friends *never* play with girls, and sometimes a girl would say the same.

> At my little boy's school (rural Sussex) if you want to play something like 'goose', you go round saying, 'Who wants to play goose? No girls!' The girls do the same ('No boys!').
> SUSSEX, 2008

There are also exceptions in the opposite direction. There are always individual girls who like playing football, for example, but it is ostensibly the game, rather than the company of boys, which is the attraction. But when individual boys like to play with the girls, they often feel that a reason needs to be given. Speaking of a particular boy who often joins in their pretending games, one group of girls said '— often plays with us, but he wants to be an actor', and at another school, '— often plays with us, but he's Italian', as if that explains it all.

But even when boys and girls play separately, there is often interaction between them. It is commonplace for the boys to rush in and 'spoil' the girls' activity, and in conversation the boys often regard this as a legitimate 'game'. The girls usually get very cross and exasperated at this wrecking behaviour, but again in conversation sometimes refer to it as if it were part of the game. Sometimes, also, it happens the other way round – the girls will invade the boys' space and try to kiss them or upset them in some way.

One factor that sometimes alters this pattern is the size of the school. In smaller schools there appears to be far more mixing of the sexes, simply because there are fewer playmates to choose from and certain games need more than a handful of participants. The size of school is even more relevant to the mixing, or otherwise, of age groups. All things being equal, children in the playground tend to stick to their own year group, but again, in smaller schools the force of circumstance brings different ages together – to get enough people for a decent game of football, for example, the boys of years 5 and 6 have to combine.

Looking at the history of children's play, it should be remembered that in most pre-war schools the sexes were quite rigidly segregated. If the school was big enough, there were two playgrounds: one for the infants and junior girls, and one for the junior boys. Inside the school the boys and girls were also kept apart as much as possible. The large red-brick three-storey schools built in Edwardian times as board schools, which still dominate the skylines of many London boroughs and other towns, were models of segregation. The infants occupied the ground floor, the junior girls the second and the junior boys the third. Mixed playing was only possible at home, in the park and in the street. This all changed after the Second World War, with the move towards co-educational classes and playgrounds.

At any given time, in a given school, there will be a consensus on which games are played by boys, which by girls and which by both, but in interviews with modern children there is little sense of people being barred from certain games because of their sex – it was more a question of choice. Boys, however, are often contemptuous of girls simply because they cannot play football.

In the past the division between boys' and girls' games was certainly more rigid, and girls were actively discouraged by parents, school, church, and so on from taking part in any 'unfeminine' activities. But the historical picture is far from clear-cut, and there was change over time. Skipping, for example, was a regular pastime for both boys and girls throughout the nineteenth century, but in general boys had lost interest in the game by the time the twentieth century dawned. For other games, such as fivestones, there was no real consensus, and we have equally adamant statements, from similar periods, claiming it as a girls' game and a boys' game (see p. 157).

Other games were played by both sexes, but with in-built differences. Boys and girls played with hoops, but the boys' ones were larger and made of metal, while the girls' were made of wood (see p. 148). They all played with tops, but the designs were very different, as were the ways they played with them (see p. 152). We can perhaps find a clue to explain some of the apparent confusion between play and gender if we look at the comment made by Don Haworth in his book of reminiscences of childhood in Lancashire in the 1930s. Writing of tops, he relates how the girls played with them all year round, while the boys played only in the season. Boys had to be very careful to avoid the 'double contempt of playing a game which was out of season and, being out of season, a girl's game'. There were clearly fine gradations in notions of masculinity and femininity, which elude us in retrospect.

On the question of boys and girls playing together, voices from the past paint a picture of more rigid separation; nevertheless, they say remarkably similar things to modern children, and when speaking of the other sex they demonstrate, in equal measure, amused tolerance, grudging admiration, outright condemnation and everything in between:

> Normally girls did not join in our play. They played their games and we played ours. We shared the street without quarrelling. The paving stones they chalked for hopscotch, the railings to which they fastened their skipping ropes, and the lamp-post on which we chalked our wickets were established by custom . . . Deliberate spoiling of somebody's game was rare and clamorously condemned. Accidental collisions were frequent. The right of rebuke belonged to girls alone. They caricatured the exasperation of women mill workers telling off the tackler. 'You are a pain, lad. Why don't you look where you're going?' . . . [after describing tops] Girls did most things better. They were good with the biffbat, sharply repelling the ball that scutched back at them on a length of elastic. They could fling yoyos in all directions. A few could even play diabolo . . . Girls persisted in the proper purpose. In this and in other street games they developed the skill to make their pleasures last. They did their own things better and one girl at Todmorden Road School did ours better too.   *LANCASHIRE, EARLY 1930S*

The playground of the Junior School was covered with asphalt and perhaps it was a bit unappealing, but it was large. This meant the boys could play

fast games with a leather football, with laces in it, blown up hard, or they
could play even rougher games with each other, shouting and chasing and
striking sparks from the nails of their boots as they ran. So if the boys were
absorbed in playing with each other, the girls too could play together and
we usually went to the little playground on the left of the school porch.
This was a warm sheltered spot beneath the infants' classroom windows
and beside the garden plots . . . In this little playground we were safe from
the sight and sound of the horrible boys.   *DORSET, 1930S*

Although most of us had sisters, except at home, or if there was no other
boy, we never played with girls. They were always useless at football and
couldn't play cricket for toffee. They had no idea how to throw a ball properly, and were hopeless at flicking cigarette cards. Our games of tops, they
said, were far too rough and they could only manage wooden hoops. In
general, girls were no use at all. We could never see the point of jumping
up and down to let a rope pass under you, particularly when accompanied
by silly rhymes.   *SUSSEX, 1920S*

It may be noted here that, except for a few games played by the very young,
a sharp line was drawn between those [games] played by boys and those by
girls, a boy being called a cissy and a girl a stag if crossing the line.

LANCASHIRE, C.1914

The marked and invariable contempt exhibited by the boys to the softer sex
seems quite unjustifiable, as in a large number of games the girls are formi-
dable rivals, if not actually better players.   *LONDON, 1891*

It is not easy to find evidence of earlier practice in this sphere, but
one mid Victorian writer offers a brief historical perspective. Writing in
Notes & Queries in 1868, 'Bushey Heath' contrasted the games played in
the Scottish border counties around 1820 with those of his present day:

In nothing is the change of manners more remarkable in country places
than in the alteration of the early intercourse between the sexes. There is
now a separate course, and a propriety laid down, and somewhat prudishly
insisted upon, which the partakers in the simple and innocent pastimes of
other days can hardly understand. But what they thought or knew no evil
of, is now looked upon as indecorous, if not vicious.

Blindman's Buff, 1900s

Hopscotch, 1950

Hot Cockles, 1822

Broken Bottles, 2010

Handslapping, 2010

What's the Time, Mr Wolf? *c.*2000

Hopscotch, 1950

PART TWO

Games of Skill

Leapfrog, 1906

Piggyback fight, 1900s

Hopscotch, 2010

CHAPTER FIVE

Athletic Feats

HOPSCOTCH AND OTHER GRID GAMES

Hopscotch has been a great favourite with children for well over 300 years, and is still regularly seen in playgrounds, although its hold may be weakening. Many of the different versions played in the past, with their wide variety of layouts, have disappeared and left the field clear for a relatively standardised form, which is found all over the country. Where hopscotch grids are provided on the school playground these days, they tend to be the same pattern.

The earliest grids were all straightforward ladder-shaped affairs, with anything from seven to ten identical oblong beds, and the first development seems to have been the addition of a semicircular place at the far end. This is shown clearly in the illustration included in the *Little Penny Pocket Book* (1767), where the beds are numbered 1 to 9 but a final one is marked 'PT' (probably short for 'pots'). Later adaptations involved much more complex patterns, with the oblongs divided to double the number of beds, diagonals drawn across rectangles, and so on.

Many other patterns have been reported, usually based on variations of the rectangular format, but a markedly different shape has the squares drawn in a spiral, like a snail shell or curled snake. This format was already in use by the 1890s, and when seen in seaside settings or in places famous for fossils, such as Portland in Dorset, it has often prompted commentators to believe that the local children had been influenced in their play by their environment. The only problem with this theory is that the shape is found everywhere, and the earliest examples are from city locations.

The 'aeroplane' pattern, which now seems to be the standard form, at least in England, was introduced just before the turn of the twentieth century, and Iona Opie in her playground researches suggests that the pattern came in as paving stones were introduced to our streets. The main feature of the new grid was the alternating single and double squares, which brought with it the characteristic hop, two-feet, hop, two-feet movement that practised players seem to achieve so effortlessly but is not so easy as it looks. It was described by Claire and Emma Taylor (aged ten and seven) of Andover, Hampshire, in 1979 as follows:

> On the first one it's hop, hopscotch, hop, hopscotch, hop, hopscotch, hop, then you turn around and come hop, hopscotch, hop, hopscotch, hop, hopscotch, hop, until you come to the beginning.

Before this pattern became widespread, the more usual method of locomotion was hopping all the way. The second characteristic feature of this new design was the weakening, and eventual removal, of kicking a stone before you as you progressed; in the new design it is more usually picked up on the way back.

Scotland has long had the reputation for being the place to see the game at its best, and the plethora of shapes and game rules there is amply demonstrated by the chapter in James Ritchie's book of games, *Golden City* (1965), where he gives twenty different diagrams and even more descriptions from the streets and playgrounds of Edinburgh alone.

The shape of the grid determines the rules to a certain extent, but other factors are largely independent of the layout. Throwing the stone and hopping are constants, but there are also many variables. In some games, for example, after a successful navigation of the grid, players can 'reserve' a square by throwing the stone into it and chalking their initials therein. Other players must not set foot in such squares owned by others. As already mentioned, in most games nowadays the stone is picked up, usually on the way back after the player has successfully travelled to the top of the grid, but in the past the normal method was to kick the stone. Picking it up introduced many other possibilities, based on different ways of carrying it – on the back of the hand, on the foot, head or even eyelid.

> You drew squares in a traditional pattern on the paving stones. One, then two together, then one again, etc., with 'home' at the end. You had to throw your stone to the first square, then hop up the squares without putting your foot on the square with the stone on it. Then you'd have to throw your stone on to the second square and do it again. On the double squares (two

and three, for example) you could put both feet down, unless your stone was on that square of course. Once you'd got through all the squares once (no easy feat, for it was hard to throw your stone on to the higher-number squares from behind square number one) you were allowed to choose a square to call your own. Other players were not then allowed to tread on that square as they hopped through the squares. Once a number of squares were taken by other players, it became quite difficult to hop through, because mostly you had nowhere to put a second foot down. We also played ball hopscotch, where you bounced a ball as you went through the grid. The ball hopscotch grid was a little different. *LONDON, 1950S*

There was also much variation in the materials used for the throwing part of the game. It is quite possible to use any stone picked up by the roadside, but many players swore by certain things, such as pieces of broken tile or crockery. And a surprising number of twentieth-century descriptions and photographs reveal that shoe polish tins (the old-fashioned round flat ones) were particularly favoured.

Hopscotch is often claimed to be much older than the evidence will support. It has been given a spurious ancient history, based mainly on a misreading of some floor markings in ancient Rome and the apparent religious symbolism of Continental versions. J. W. Crombie's 'History of the Game of Hop-Scotch', published in the *Journal of the Royal Anthropological Institution* in 1886, is an early example of the style of erudite and informed argument based on the shakiest of propositions that characterised his generation, but has proved surprisingly tenacious.

Much of his argument is based on the twin assumptions that any religious symbolism in a game must reflect its original form and is necessarily evidence of a very long history. But a game with religious symbolism can be invented at any time, and religious symbolism can similarly be introduced at any stage in its history. The presence of beds named 'heaven' 'paradise', 'hell' and 'purgatory' is most likely to be merely one more example of the persistent propensity for religious officials to intervene in all aspects of everyday life and imbue them with religious meaning whenever possible.

In fact, the earliest evidence for any form of hopscotch is as late as the second half of the seventeenth century, although it was clearly already well established by that time. One of Jacques Stella's strange illustrations shows his usual naked cherubs playing 'La Marelle a Cloch-pié', in his *Les Jeux et plaisirs de l'enfance* of 1657. In England, Francis Willughby's manuscript collection of games, compiled in the 1660s (and published in 2003), contains

Hopscotch Grids

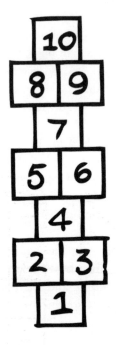

The 'standard' modern aeroplane grid.

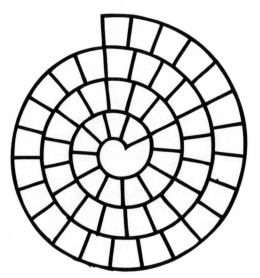

The widely known spiral or snail shape.

Throw your stone into one of the boxes, hop to the middle without touching the box with the stone in it, on the way back pick up the stone, hop to the end, and if you get there and back without stepping on a line or falling over, chalk your name in the box your stone landed on. That box is now yours, and the others have to hop over it for the rest of the game.

GATESHEAD, 1960S

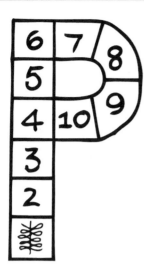

Children in the 1960s made their grids in the shape of letters.

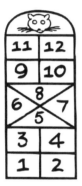

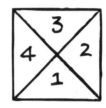

Four of the ten shapes published by Alice Gomme in 1894.

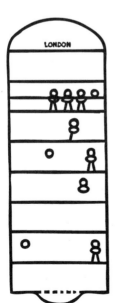

One of the standard patterns for the game 'London'.

a detailed description of how the game of 'Scotch Hopper' was played at the time. This section is written in a child's hand, not Willughby's, and includes a diagram showing seven oblong beds lettered A to F, with the furthest one marked as 'M'. 'They play with a piece of tile or a little flat piece of lead, upon a boarded floor, or any area divided into oblong figures like boards', the manuscript reads. The play is essentially the same as those of later descriptions: throw the tile into B, hop all the way to the top and back, kicking the tile before you as you reach it on the way back. Throw it into C and do the same, and so on. There are also detailed rules covering such things as hopping on lines and putting two feet down. The item thrown clearly had a special name, as the manuscript states, 'The piece of tile or lead is called —', but unfortunately the space is left blank.

For many people, hopscotch and skipping are the most obvious examples of playground games that boys rarely play, if at all. But both have a complicated gender history. Early illustrations and descriptions show hopscotch being played exclusively by boys, although this is not conclusive proof of contemporary practice, given the male bias of most publications of the time. Nevertheless there was a definite shift during the nineteenth century towards the game being played primarily by girls, and Iona Opie estimates that this process started around the 1820s. By the turn of the twentieth century it was taken for granted by many that hopscotch was purely for girls. Recalling his childhood games in London, around 1910, C. H. Rolph commented:

> Hopscotch, for example, I merely watched, never understanding the rules –
> and always wondering why it was played only by girls . . . After I had left
> school I found that it was very occasionally played by boys, but this seems
> to have been but a brief revival.

Edwin Pugh's 'Some London Street Amusements' of 1905 tells a similar story:

> [Girls' games] are shrouded in a mystery impenetrable to the mere mascu-
> line intelligence, even among juveniles. No boy ever really arrives at the true
> inwardness of Hopscotch, for instance. It is as baffling as feminine human
> nature itself, whether it be of the variety that depends on a series of circles
> or numbers, or on a drawing known as 'Spider's Web' which rather resem-
> bles a periwinkle-shell in outline and has initials written on it in set spaces.
> The tiny maids, hopping on one leg, kick at a piece of china or a flat stone;
> and if they fail in their incomprehensible endeavours they seem to go on

just the same, and if they succeed they are as pleased as a cat in the fender, though it seems to make no difference either way.

This situation has continued to the present day, and although there have always been some boys willing to join in, hopscotch, like skipping, has been female territory for a long time now.

The game's recent decline stems partly from the fact that formerly it was as much a street as a playground game, and street playing for most of the population is now very much a thing of the past. Another reason is that few schools allow pupils to go around chalking on the playground surface. Given what sometimes happened in the past, this is perhaps not surprising. A photograph of children busily drawing on the pavement in *All In! All In!* (1984), Eilís Brady's book of Dublin street games, is knowingly captioned, 'Once there is chalk to be had, no surface escapes'. And the concern for clean playgrounds is nothing new. In the early 1960s, Edinburgh girls were already telling James Ritchie, 'In ma last school ye got the belt for drawin' peever beds in the playground. Fae the heidmaster tae!', and, 'At Abbeyhill ye could play peevers in the playground, but the jannie [janitor] was aye moanin'.'

When I talked to children in English schools in 2008–9, it became quite clear that if hopscotch patterns were provided on the playground surface, some girls still played the game, but if they were not, nobody did. Younger children often play on them, and they know that they have to hop from square to square. However, they do not always know any other rules – a sign that the game's hold is weakening. If the rules are not passed on, the game will die, whether the grids are there or not. That said, it is apparent that in some schools the tradition is still strong enough, and the children know most of the rules and play the game when the fancy takes them.

Children often assume that the name 'hopscotch' means it is a Scottish game, but it is well attested that the 'scotches' are the lines scored on the ground to make the pattern. Before 'hopscotch' became the general name, the game was more likely to be called 'Scotch-hoppers', but it has gone by a bewildering array of local names in its time, including 'Peevers', 'Pallie', 'Beds and Tables' (Scotland and elsewhere); 'Hoppy Beds' (Cumbria, 1930s); 'Hippy-beds', 'Hitchey-dabber' (Northumberland, c.1890); 'Hopscore' (Yorkshire, 1820s); 'Hap the Beds' (Galloway, c.1824); 'Heck-a-beds' (Wexford, c.1811); 'Pillatte-hache' (Guernsey, 1975); and 'Pickie' (Co. Kerry, 1890s).

There were also many other variations on the hopscotch principle, including one that involved bouncing a ball, described here as played in Durham about 1900:

> 'Bays' was almost invariably a girls' game. The 'bay' was drawn on the pavement in chalk, with either four or eight rectangular divisions, with a semi-circle at the top called 'pot'. Generally a small group of six girls played, one playing while the others watched carefully, for there was a ritual attached to this game and if it was broken, the player was 'out'.
>
> The player began by saying 'Welcome Onesy!' and then stotted or bounced the ball in each division without standing on a line. The ball was then rolled or 'booled' into bay two. The player ran after it, picked it up while still in that bay, and stotted it through the other bays. So the game continued, rolling the ball into each bay and catching it before it rolled out, and 'stotting' it round. In the eight-bay game, the bays were in double column, and in bays five, six, seven and eight, the player had to run through bays one, two, three and four before catching the ball. The final rolling was to 'pot', and this, involving a run through all the eight bays, was most difficult.
>
> Before the ball was rolled each time the player had to say 'Welcome Onesy or Twosy', and so on. If she omitted this she was out. Nor must she stand on a line when running round or stotting, nor must she miss a bay.
>
> The next round was 'hard labour'. This consisted of hopping on one foot, through all the bays, stotting the ball as she went. Then followed 'blindies', the most difficult of all. Holding the ball in the right hand, with the eyes shut, and face upturned, the player had to walk through the bays to 'pot', without touching a line, then back to one again.

Hopscotch is not the only game to utilise a grid pattern chalked on the floor. In Frances Low's article on London street games in the *Strand Magazine* for 1891, for example, she gives a detailed explanation of a game called 'London':

> 'London', so far as I can gather, is a completely modern game, and is more in vogue in the north and west of London than in the east. The accompanying illustration shows the figure that is drawn in chalk on the pavement, the two side loops being for the player's marks. Should there be three or four players, the figure is made longer with an additional number of lines, and there are extra side loops; the game is, however, usually played by two persons. The bit of china is put on the bottom line and 'nicked' or 'spooned' along with the finger. If it rolls on, say, 2, the player draws a mark in the side loop nearest 2 from opposite corners. The other player has then a turn,

each player going in alternately. The second time the player's china goes on the same number a line across the opposite corners is drawn; the third time this occurs a line is drawn across the middle of the square horizontally, and the fourth time perpendicularly. Here the real pleasure of the player begins. Her object is now to get the china again into 2, the number by which she has obtained her marks. If she does this she exclaims aloud triumphantly, 'Now I've got a soldier's head!' She then draws a little round close up to her square, but on the other side of the line. She then has another turn, and, if the china again goes into 2, she cries, 'Now I've got the soldier's belly!' and adds a large circle on to the one she calls the head. If it goes into 4 or 5, and she has not previously nicked the china into these numbers, she simply makes a stroke, as before. The sixth time that the china goes into 2 the player gets the soldier's legs, and she has now got her soldier. The one who obtains most soldiers is the winner. If the china goes over any of the boundaries, or on the lines, the player is out and has lost the game. The chief attraction of this game appears to be in the naming aloud of one portion of the soldier's anatomy; the little girls seem to have some sort of idea that the language is not quite polite, and I observed they looked at me half doubtfully, as if in expectation of finding a shocked expression on my face, which might result in jeopardising the promised pennies. Nothing of the sort, however, being visible, they proceeded with great gusto to describe another soldier, much to my amusement.

'London' cannot be said to be particularly common, but it is mentioned sporadically in the games literature of the twentieth century, and something of the game survived into the post-war period. A photograph in the North-West Film Archive in Manchester, for example, probably taken in that area in the 1950s, shows two boys bent over a grid that looks like an overgrown shove-ha'penny grid, chalked on the pavement. But it has the word 'LONDON' clearly marked in the semicircle at the top.

And another game of the same name was collected by Cathy Gould from someone who was at school in Halifax, Yorkshire, in the 1960s and 1970s. The word 'LONDON' is chalked on the ground in large letters, one above the other. The player stands below the 'L':

To play a pebble is thrown onto the first letter, and then the player jumps onto that letter, turns and jumps back. Then a pebble is thrown onto the second letter and so on. If you fail to hit the correct letter with your pebble or fail to reach the correct letter in one jump, you have to start again.

FROM HANDSTANDS TO PIGGYBACKS

Hopscotch and 'London' are well-developed games with long documented histories behind them, but many children's activities seem so obvious and casual that adults do not even consider them proper games. Children have always had a way of making even the simplest of movements into a social event, and often add rules and rhymes to increase the enjoyment. Standing on your head or spinning around to make yourself dizzy are perfect examples of this kind of game, while simply trying to stand on one leg might develop into a hopping game, and jumping on each other's backs might turn into a piggyback race or a game of leapfrog.

Handstands and headstands are not often mentioned in recent books on games, but they regularly feature in earlier illustrations of childhood, such as Pieter Bruegel's famous painting *Children's Games* (1560) and in one of the illustrations in Jacques Stella's *Les Jeux et plaisirs de l'enfance* (1657), entitled 'La Culebute', which shows five upside-down cherubs.

In Victorian times in Britain, as now, handstands were popular with children. In Dorothy Tennant's article on London ragamuffins, published in the *English Illustrated Magazine* in May 1885, her 'best subject' (she was an artist) was named Canon Southey, and he explained that such acrobatics were not only undertaken for mere fun:

> He was very desirous of being painted in some momentary or impossible attitude – doing the wheel, or standing on his head, an accomplishment he was very proud of. 'I can beat boat chaps at walking on my 'ead, only it don't pay like the cat-wheel. Gents chuck down coppers from the buses for the wheel, but they don't care for this 'ead-walking'; and Canon, with his feet in the air, head downwards, proceeded to walk about on his hands with unsteady steps.

The article includes two engravings of Canon doing a handstand and 'the wheel'.

Handstands remained in vogue, even without the incentive of adults throwing money, but many of the post-war references describe it as a craze that came and went. In a piece on her children's crazes in *The Times* (16 April 1956), an anonymous mother wrote:

> Next came handstands and mothers grew accustomed to finding their daughters at any time and in any place cavorting and gyrating at all angles. To an accompaniment of tears, rages, and despair small girls everywhere struggled

in private with the difficulties of projecting themselves into an upside-down position.

Several people I have spoken to have confirmed the 'craze' status of handstands – for example in Edinburgh in the 1970s, and Cambridgeshire in the 1980s – but other sources indicate that there was more to it than just turning upside down, showing how children will turn a simple activity into a more complex game.

In Andover, Hampshire, in 1982, for example, the girls had a rhyme that they chanted, in an urgent tone, before launching themselves on to their hands:

> Rain, snow, thunder, lightning
> My mother caught me fighting
>> She said go to bed
>> I said no
>> She said go!

And in Robert Arkenstall School, in Haddenham, Cambridgeshire (December 2009), the game was more involved:

You all do handstands and whoever does it the longest goes into the middle and says:

> I am the greatest
> Oh no, you're not
> Not for the longest [or 'Knock on the longest']
> Under over, Pepsi Cola
> One, two, three.

Then they all do a handstand and the person in the middle sees which one does it the longest, and then they go in the middle.

This game sounds very similar to what veteran childlore researcher Brian Sutton-Smith found in New Zealand schools, and he claimed it as an example of one of the major characteristics of girls' play:

At several Dunedin schools in 1949, I found girls playing at the game of standing on their hands. The leader told the girls when to go up on their hands. She then judged which was the winner, or, rather, the winner was the player who stayed up the longest and the leader announced the verdict.

The winner then became the new leader. It is noticeable that girls' games of skipping and their informal activities often fall into this leader type of organisation, with one player taking a commanding role over all the others.

In Coventry in 2008, the girls described performing the following routine, patting each part mentioned and doing the appropriate action:

> Head, head
> Hip, hip
> Bum, bum
> Wiggle, wiggle
> Jump, jump
> Turn around, touch the ground
> I can do a handstand.

Or alternatively:

> Salt and pepper
> Scooby dooby doo
> The boys go ——[*blowing kisses*]
> The girls go wooo! [*go into handstand*]

Children don't just enjoy turning themselves upside down; they are also fascinated by the dizziness brought on by twirling or spinning, and will incorporate it into a game at a moment's notice. For Catherine Burke, it is a fond memory of growing up in Waterford in the 1990s:

> We would play 'Dizzy' or 'Umbrellas' where you would basically spin around and around until there was only one person standing.

But some players are not so keen. Fred Bason, remembering Southwark around 1917, wrote:

> Twisting (or Twisters) was a game I never did like. Two children joined hands and twisted round and round. I always got dizzy. Mostly girls played this game, but when a girl and a boy played Twisters they were usually fond of each other and, having whirled round and round, they got dizzy and had a good reason to sit down, hold hands and do some kissing.

Spinning round is also a feature of many other games.

In more than one school (I cannot recall how many), when asked about hand and arm games the children have enthusiastically told me of a game which had no name, and which they could only make me understand by demonstrating it. Child 1 stands with hands clasped, held stiffly about shoulder height but slightly forward, away from the body. Child 2 adopts the same posture but takes a few running steps towards Child 1, hooks her arms over, and at the same time Child 1 turns her body sharply and the centrifugal force lifts Child 2 off the ground and swings her round.

I took little notice, thinking it too trifling to document, until I read the following around from June 1979 in Iona Opie's *People in the Playground*:

They are still enjoying the nameless, casual lifting game I have noticed over the past ten years and have thought of as too unimportant to be worth describing. Today it had a name, which must raise its status. It's called 'Run, pick up, and throw'.

I must remember to take more notice of the children's own judgement on their games.

And then there is the traditional style of carrying or swinging a child, by two people crossing arms and holding hands or wrists. This can still be seen occasionally in the playground, especially when older girls are playing with the little ones. It is unlikely, though, that anyone remembers the rhyme that, in Victorian times, invariably accompanied the game:

London Bridge is broken
And what shall I do for a token
Give me a pin to stick in my thumb
And carry my lady to London.

The rhyme varies a fair amount from version to version, but the 'Carry my lady' line is relatively constant, and that is the only part that makes literal sense. The game is also depicted in Bruegel's *Children's Games* painting of 1560.

Carrying someone on your back or shoulders is presumably a universal human trait, and illustrations from the late Middle Ages in Britain and Europe, and from classical Rome, confirm that the activity has been regularly practised for centuries. It is only a short step from carrying to fighting, and piggyback fights also have a long history.

Talking to modern children about their games, I find that piggyback races are still mentioned frequently, but piggyback fights much less so.

They are just the sort of thing to incur the disapproval of playground staff, and when children refer to them at all they tend to say, 'We only play that when we're on the field', where the potential for injury is obviously lessened. When children do play the game, they say they have no rules, but when pressed they reveal that they play in a similar way to their predecessors: the 'horses' can only barge each other, their riders can push or pull each other, but hitting is not allowed.

Most of the earlier written sources make it clear that the pretence of the game was of people riding horses. The riders were called 'knights', the fights referred to as 'jousting', and the riders sometimes held sticks. But in a description from the Scots border country in 1868 the model seems to be a monkey on a horse:

> The 'monkey battle' could compete with the most outrageous in these contingent particulars. A small boy on the shoulders of a stout fellow tugged for victory against another monkey so mounted; and the antagonism was equal to a battle of centaurs. Sometimes there was a dismount, and sometimes a 'horse' fall, and sometimes all were down together. But at any rate there was always plenty of equipments (clothes) torn off the backs of the gallant combatants.

One of the regular names for shoulder-mounted fights, which by definition are more unstable than piggybacks, is 'Flying Angels'.

Apart from the simple piggyback, there were various other configurations of boys carrying each other, which were usually given other animal names like 'Elephants' and 'Rhinos'. The one called 'Camels' (or sometimes 'Donkeys') is worth mentioning, because exactly the same format is illustrated in Bruegel's *Children's Games* painting of 1560: one boy stands upright, another bends down behind him, holding on to the first boy's waist or hands, and the rider climbs on to the second boy's back. This was called 'Chariot-fighting' in Cambridge in the 1960s.

The term 'piggyback' perhaps needs some explanation, as pigs are never impersonated in the game. In fact, there was a lively discussion in the pages of *Notes & Queries* and other periodicals in the 1890s on just this topic, with many people insisting that the proper name was 'pick-a-back':

> In my younger days in Derbyshire this was always 'pick-a-back'. 'Give's a pick-a-back' = 'pick me up on your back', and this was a very common amusement amongst boys, when they broke out of school with whoops and

yells on half-holiday occasion, or at other times when spirits ran too high for repression.

Another correspondent, on the other hand, wrote, 'It was always "pig-a-back" when I was a child in North London in the forties.'

For a time it looked as if the difference was merely of dialect, with people in the northern counties saying 'pick' and the southerners saying 'pig', but a glance at the *Oxford English Dictionary* shows that 'Pickback' or 'Pick-a-back' was being used at least as early as 1565, while the first reference to 'Pig Back' is from 1783.

To return to the horse theme, one particular game was called by various names, such as 'Bucking Bronco', 'Shaking Horse' or just 'Donkey':

> There was another game in which the captor was rewarded with a ride back to the catch, and it was called *Chware Ceffyl yn Pori* (the grazing-horse game) . . . The game was played in a field in which any number of children could join; one, called *Yr Hen Geffyl* (the old horse) had preceded the others into the field, where he pretended to be quietly grazing. The children first of all moved along the hedge, gradually edging towards the 'old horse', until they got near enough to spring on his back, which it was his main aim to prevent. If a child succeeded he was given a ride as far as the hedge.
>
> WALES, C.1904

LEAPFROG

Leapfrog is another of those games that was immensely popular in nineteenth-century Britain and the first half of the twentieth century but has since lost favour and is much more rarely seen in playgrounds today, although everybody still knows how to do it. What has survived is a mere shadow of the wide variety of games based on the basic leapfrog pattern. Back in 1916 Norman Douglas gave the names of over fifty leapfrog games in his book *London Street Games*, although he was maddeningly vague about how much variation was needed between games actually to warrant a new name:

> You could write a whole book about sports of this kind, each with its separate rules and separate name – fancy names they are, some of them – and each with its 'showman' or 'duty-man' or 'namer' who decides what things are to be done.

In its basic form, leapfrog can be done with two players, but it is clearly more fun with more, and can be an everlasting game if those bending stand in a line, the last one jumps over them all in turn and then bends down at the front, while the new last one starts working his way up the line, and so on. The great advantage of this style is that everyone gets a turn at jumping and bending down, and it was very popular with children who wanted to play on the way to somewhere, such as to and from school.

Most of the more complicated versions hinge on changing the way people jump, or the use of particular props, particularly caps and handkerchiefs. In the widely known 'Foot-and-a-half' a leader dictates to the others a certain style of jump, and the number and type of steps taken to reach the 'back'. In the equally popular 'Spanish Fly' a cap is placed on the back of the bending player and the jumper must pick the cap up with his teeth and either carry it with him, throw it forward or, most difficult of all, toss it backwards over his shoulder. In another version, as each players leaps over, he leaves his cap on top of the others, so that the pile gets higher and more difficult to jump without knocking over. In most leapfrog games, anyone who fails in any way is punished by being the one who bends down.

Vaulting over people's backs would seem to be a fairly obvious thing to do, and therefore likely to go back beyond documented history. But leapfrog is not one of the games found illustrated in classical sources, and it only really comes into its own in early modern times. It is frequently portrayed in European illustrations such as Pieter Bruegel's *Children's Games* of 1560, and Jacques Stella's *Les Jeux et plaisirs de l'enfance* (1657), where it is called 'La Poste'. In Britain, the name 'leapfrog' was already well known enough at the turn of the seventeenth century for writers to mention it in passing. Shakespeare does so in Act 5, Scene 2 of *Henry V* (1599) – 'If I could win a lady at leap-frog, or by vaulting into my saddle' – as does Samuel Rowlands in *The Letting of Humours Blood* (1600), but no earlier reference has yet come to light. It is fully described under the title 'Hop-Frog' in Francis Willughby's *Book of Games*, compiled in the 1660s.

From Shakespeare onwards, the game is frequently mentioned in various literary genres, and is one of those whose popularity is demonstrated by the figurative use of its name in general parlance. In literature, leapfrog is often synonymous with boyhood and youthful exuberance, as in Charles Dickens's description of a clear crisp frosty day in *Pickwick Papers* (1836–7):

It was the sort of afternoon that might induce a couple of elderly gentlemen, in a lonely field, to take off their great-coats and play at leap-frog in pure lightness of heart and gaiety; and we firmly believe that had Mr Tupman at that moment proffered 'a back', Mr Pickwick would have accepted his offer with the utmost avidity.

To 'make a back' was a generally accepted synonym for 'bend down'.

Ever eager to draw adult morals from children's behaviour, many writers drew analogies from the game. In John Newbery's *Little Pretty Pocket-Book* of 1744, for example, under a charming woodcut showing the game in progress, the reader is offered a verse and moral:

> This stoops down his head,
>   Whilst that springs up high;
> But then you will find,
>   You stoop by and by.

> *Moral*: Just so 'tis at Court;
>   To-day you're in place;
> To-morrow, perhaps,
>   You're quite in disgrace.

The 'frog' part of the name presumably refers to the leaping action involved, with the arms providing the impetus, but the game had many other names, and some more robust versions conjured up other animal-images. In Galloway in the 1820s it was called 'Loup the Bullocks':

A very rustic sort of amusement. Young men go out in a green meadow, and there, on 'all fours', plant themselves in a row about two yards distant from each other. Then he who is stationed farthest back in the 'bullock rank' starts up, and leaps over the other bullocks before him, by laying his hands on each of their backs; and when he gets over the last one, leans down himself as before, whilst all the others, in rotation, follow his example; then he starts and leaps again. But what makes this fun of a bullock or brutish description, is the severe tumbles the leapers often meet with; for that bullock is considered the most famous of the 'herd' that can heave up the 'rump' highest and smartest, when the leaper is going over, and can launch him on his nose, to the effusion of his blood on the meadow.

'Loup' or 'lowp' means 'to leap' in Scotland, Ireland and many parts of northern England. As with many of the older games, there was also a rich tradition of local words used in the process of playing: 'fudging', for example, meant the devious practice of suddenly dropping lower as someone springs on your back, and various phrases were called out to warn the 'backs' that a jumper was coming, for example 'Tuck in yer tuppenny', or 'Tuck in your napper' in London; 'Leap-toss-coming-in' (Cornwall, 1929); and 'Tip on the bot, Spanish fly' (Isle of Man, c. 1876). These make sense in the context of the game, but another Cornish version recorded in the *Folk-Lore Journal* (1887) defies all attempts at explanation:

> The first as he jumps says 'Accroshay', the second 'Ashotay', the third 'Assheflay', and the last, 'Lament, lament, Leleeman's (or Leleena's) war'.

Many older illustrations of the game depict boys standing almost upright, bent only from the shoulders instead of from the waist. These may seem unlikely, but Jim Bullock's recollections of life in a Yorkshire mining village before the First World War, published as *Bowers Row* (1976), indicates that they are perfectly accurate:

> Leap Frog was another favourite amongst the boys and girls, though the girls' frocks were a great hindrance. We got so good at it that we could jump over each other when only the head was bent. We used to run and put our hands on the next boy's shoulders and leap straight over him.

The basic leapfrog idea exists – or existed – in other games as well. Here, for example, is Norman Douglas describing a game he calls 'Swimming in Blue Water', in 1916:

> One boy stoops down in bending attitude, and another boy lays on his back crossways, and does the action of swimming; if the boy who is swimming falls off, he has to be down.

Far more popular though, particularly in the 1920s and 1930s, was a game called 'Hi Jimmy Knacker'. In 2009 John Earl, from South-east London, recalled it as follows:

> 'Hi Jimmy Knacker' was, for me, easily the best of all the playground games and the one that I remember with most pleasure. This was played by bigger

boys in secondary, not junior school. In my case that meant 1939–43. Any number could play, but you needed at least five a side. Seven was probably ideal. One side provided a long horse (my term – I don't remember it having a name), with one boy standing, back to wall, with hands linked at groin level to form a cup. Next boy made a back with his head in the cupped hands, holding on to the first boy's waist. Next boy tucked his head into the second boy's backside, holding his legs – and so on, down the line. The boys on the other side then ran and leapt, one at a time, on to the horse. The art of the thing was to take as long a run as space allowed, landing as heavily as possible, and as far forward on the horse as you could. Ideally you landed on the back of another rider, since this placed maximum strain on the back of some poor lad below. When all riders were in place, they sang out

> Hi Jimmy Knacker, one, two, three
> Hi Jimmy Knacker, one, two, three
> All o-ver!

and dismounted – well, fell off – with unmerciful clumsiness. If the other side had managed to survive the whole ideal, they were 'strong horses', if they collapsed they were 'weak donkeys'. But the result was really of no consequence. The important thing was to change sides quickly and keep going, turn and turn about, until the playtime whistle blew. It looked (and still sounds) like a rather rough game, but it was always played with good humour and I can never remember anyone getting hurt.

Harold Walker, remembering Walthamstow about 1916, agreed:

The melee of arms and legs accompanied with hysterical laughter, and frantic shouts from the riders who would delight in derisively shouting, 'Weak horses!', was the highlight of the game as the usual expected debacle followed. There were no winners! It was just boisterous fun. The collapsing was always on purpose and contributed to the game. Even in later years when picnics were held during courting days it was played with considerable success. I leave the scene of the collapse to your imagination . . . No one was ever injured to my knowledge.

There were many variations in the game. In most versions, for example, the leapers had to remain where they landed, but sometimes they were allowed to creep forward to make room for others on their team. Similarly, in some games the 'horse' remained still, while in others it was allowed to jiggle and buck in an effort to dislodge the riders. Often the jumpers had to shout a traditional warning – 'Warnie!', for example – before running up.

There were also possible elements of strategy: in the placing of the stronger and weaker boys in the 'down' team, for example, and the nice judgement of deciding in which order the jumpers would proceed.

> There was usually found in every team one with a body of lead and joints of wood. He was out last; but he usually made up for the stiffness of his limbs in the power of his grip, and thus hanging on grimly, with his feet tucked up only two or three inches from the ground, he seldom let his side down. A method resorted to sometimes was to send the clumsiest on first and to ask him to lean forward and then put our hands on him as we jumped, treating him, in effect, as a member of the opposite team.
>
> *CARMARTHENSHIRE, C.1906*

Typically the riders had to remain mounted (or at least not touching the ground at all) for a set period, which tested both the endurance of the horse and the tenacity of those on top. Sometimes this was for a certain number of seconds, or even minutes, but it usually lasted while a rhyme (which often furnished the local name for the game) was shouted, as in John Earl's example above, or as in East Anglia about 1890:

> Challey wag, challey wag, one, two, three
> Challey wag, challey wag, one, two, three
> Challey wag, challey wag, one, two, three
> And off go we.

And in Nottinghamshire about the same time:

> One, two, three
> One, two, three
> Bum Bum, Barrell
> And off we go.

In its most complex form, the rigmarole chanted by the riders was the same as in another game, usually called 'Buck Buck' (see p. 105):

> The game was played in Northants in my boyhood, about 1890 ... The captain of the mounting side jumped on last, and while all were 'mounted', he held up a number of fingers and said, 'Buck, buck, how many fingers

hev I up?' 'Fower.' 'Fower thou says, and two I hev; buck buck lie down.' The jumping side then had a turn. If the guess was correct, the speech was, 'Fower tha says, and fower I hev, buck buck stand up.' The 'down' side then had a turn at mounting.

Many writers and informants agree with John Earl and Harold Walker that the game sounds rougher than it really was, but others tell a very different story. C. H. Rolph in his memories of London before the First World War commented that the game 'produced some nasty injuries and (I remember) cost one boy all his front teeth', and, according to Sid Knight, a game of 'Sally-on-the-mopstick' in Worcestershire about 1910:

> . . . was no namby-pamby game for cissies; at times it could be dangerous and result in a broken bone . . . I was at the receiving end once when Candy Neal swung up one of his hobnailed boots and gave me a terrific bender on the nose, leaving a scar with the imprint of his two fat hobnails that persisted for many years. On top of this I had a lovely nosebleed.

Mari de Garis writes that in Guernsey a game of 'Saute Moutaön' 'always ended in a fight'.

It even impeded the national war effort:

> Whilst I was serving overseas on active service in the first world war, I can recall that the officers and men of 'K' Battery, R.H.A., enjoyed playing this game when out at 'rest' (sic!) behind the fighting line in 1917. It was played very vigorously and during one session the commanding officer – Major Palmer – sustained a rather serious injury to his knee which placed him hors-de-combat.
> LETTER TO THE TIMES, 1951

It is only on the rarest of occasions that we hear of girls playing the game, but some certainly did:

> When I was a schoolgirl in Cornwall 30 years ago, we played a game known as *Pomperino* – in the same way as *Hi Bobberee* and *Munt-a-Cuddy* were played in London and on Tyneside. The girls played as well as the boys, but not together.
> LETTER TO THE TIMES, 1951

The game, then, was hugely popular, and it lasted in some areas well into the 1970s. However, it appears to have rapidly faded from the scene in the last decades of the twentieth century.

A bewildering variety of names have been recorded for this game, and even the Opies, with their nationwide reach, could not detect any regional pattern. 'Hi Cockalorum' and 'Hi Jimmie Knacker' are probably nearest to general names, at least in England, but the following is a small selection of other titles: 'Warnie', 'High Bobbery', 'Jimmy Nacko', 'Jimmy Wagtail', 'Hi-diddy-Jacko' (London); 'Mobstick' (Bedfordshire); 'Bunge Barrel' (Hampshire); 'Crambo', 'Jump Diddy Wacko' (Cheshire); 'Saute Moutaön' ('Leap the Sheep') (Guernsey); 'Mountie Kitty', 'Jump', 'Ump-tiddy-ardy', 'Jumpety-whack', 'Bung the Bucket' (Northamptonshire); 'Munt-a-cuddy' (Co. Durham); 'Pomperino' (Cornwall); 'Agony-oss' (= 'Hang on Your Horse'?) (Midlands); 'Challey-wag' (East Anglia); 'Bum Bum Barrell' (Nottinghamshire); 'Jack Mop', 'Johnny Mop', 'Bull Stag', 'Little Jack Aguwary' (Leicestershire); 'Dick', 'Prick', 'Polony', 'Long-back' (Yorkshire); 'Ride-a-kench' (Lancashire); 'One, Two, Three and the Hopstick', 'Sally-on-the-mopstick' (Worcestershire); 'Ocky Ocky All On' (Coventry); 'Whare Jumpers' ('Playing Jumpers'), 'Strong Horses and Weak Donkeys' (Carmarthenshire); 'Bomberino' (South Wales); 'Cuddie's Loup', 'Cuddie's Weight' (Edinburgh); 'Winchy My Donkey' (Isle of Man); 'Jump Little Nag-tail' (*Games and Sports for Young Boys* (1859)).

CHAPTER SIX

Hiding and Creeping

HIDE-AND-SEEK

Several different games have been called 'hide-and-seek' over the years, including ones in which an item is hidden and others where a small child is temporarily covered and revealed, to the accompaniment of 'Boo!' But here I am restricting the name to the games in which people hide and others try to find them. There can be few children in Britain who arrive at school age not already knowing this game of hide-and-seek. In its basic form it is one of the first active games that small children learn, and it remains a firm favourite with preschool children everywhere. It is hardly surprising, therefore, that hide-and-seek, like tig, forms the basis of a number of games of varying style and complexity, by which it is adapted to different abilities, environments and circumstances. But the 'hiding' element of the game makes it more dependent on environment than most chasing games.

One of the limitations of the basic game is that it is quite static: the hiders have to stay put until they are found (although this is perfectly suitable for indoor play). So often the first detail to change is the introduction of an element of movement for the hiders, the usual method being to create a base to which players can run or sneak back. Rules are then needed to regulate how and when this can happen. Occasionally, however, the static hiding remains an integral feature – as, for example, with 'Sardines'.

The next alteration is to regulate the seeker's actions while the others hide. In the simplest forms the seeker simply stands with eyes shut or covered, counting out loud, but there are various other ways of occupying his or her time. In one extremely widespread variant, one of the players kicks or throws an item, such as a tin can, which the seeker must retrieve and place back on the 'base' before the seeking starts. Alternatively he or she must run to an agreed spot and back. Not only do these actions effectively divert the seeker's attention, but they also introduce an interesting randomising element, as the time available to the hiders will not be the same on each occasion.

Other modifications focus on a difference between merely *seeing* a hider, or having to *touch* or physically *catch* him or her. To a certain extent this is determined by the environment in which the games takes place, the amount of space available, and the availability of good hiding places. Many descriptions of the game also mention the fun of playing the game in the street or in the countryside as it begins to get dark.

If played in the street or countryside, with plenty of places to really hide and no easily discernible boundaries, it is virtually impossible for one person to find everybody without the game dragging on too long. Versions have therefore developed in which there are two teams, one hiding and the other seeking, or in other circumstances it was traditional to have two seekers – one to go looking and the other to guard the base.

One further marked feature of hide-and-seek games is the frequent occurrence of spoken, or rather shouted, elements – special words and phrases that must be said at certain points in the game or when particular circumstances arise. One regular rule in earlier versions, for example, is that the hiders have to make noises periodically, either at will or as the result of a request or command from the seeker. Other phrases are shouted by the seeker on starting his or her hunt, or by the hiders as they reach home, and there is often a 'finishing' call, to alert those still hiding that the game is over.

Adults tend to see all this as one game that has a lot of variants. Children, however, generally regard each variant as a game in its own right. It is certainly the case that different versions foreground different aspects, and it is the interplay between the 'hiding and finding' and the 'chasing and releasing' elements that count most in defining the nature of the game. Perhaps the most satisfying are the ones that involve both in equal measure. In recent times the decline of street-playing has resulted in a narrowing of the choices on offer. This is not to say that there has been a complete sea-change of style, or to claim that some of the older forms are not still to be found, but the overall tendency of a shift from 'hiding' to 'racing' can certainly be discerned.

Judging by people's memories, it seems that hiding games involving a tin can or its equivalent were extremely popular throughout the nineteenth century and into the twentieth. They went by a huge number of names, including 'Tin Can Tommy', 'Tin Can Turkey', 'Tin Can Squash', 'Tin Can Copper', 'Tin Can Lurky', 'Mount the Tin', 'Kick Can Policeman', and 'Kick the Can'. The following is an example from Nottinghamshire around 1910:

> Draw a large ring on the road; put an old tin inside it. One of us would throw the tin as far as he could, then one would have to fetch it back and put it in the ring; while he was doing this the others would run off and hide themselves, he would then have to try and find them; when he found one he would say 'Lurky' and call him by his name, then run back to the ring and touch the tin with his foot; if the one he had found got to the tin first, he would shout and all the others would come out, and the same proced-ure would be gone over again. If the one who was found failed to get to the tin first he was out, and the hunt would go on for the others; if they were all found without any of them getting to the tin before the one who was seeking them, then the one who was found first had to do the seeking and he who had done the seeking went to hide with the rest. But there was always the risk when you had found anyone, of someone popping up from somewhere and getting to the tin before you got back, and in that case you had to do the seeking again.

Quite often the can was kicked away at the beginning, rather than thrown, and sometimes the seeker had to keep his or her foot on the tin, which meant that the game was one of 'seeing' rather than 'chasing'. Harold Walker, remembering his childhood in Walthamstow, East London, about 1916, described his version of 'Tin Can Copper':

> Another exciting and diversionary pastime especially when played at dusk, and always played in the street. Again the object required was an old tin can . . . A boy was delegated as 'a copper'. The can was thrown as far as possible by the best thrower, who with the rest ran off to hide in the oppos-ite direction. Meanwhile, the 'Copper' retrieved the can and returned to base. Placing his foot on the tin he called out the names of those he could see hiding. He had to state name of hider and the exact description of the hiding place. For example, 'Jack Jones in Mrs Stotter's garden, One, Two, Three', while stamping his foot on the can at each number mentioned. This disclosure meant that the one discovered had to give himself up . . . It was incumbent on any hider to creep up unobserved by the 'Copper', and indulge

in a tremendous push in the back, to dislodge him from the stance of having
to keep one foot on the can on which he had to stamp. If this attack was
successful the can would be taken and thrown allowing the captives to escape
and continue in the like fashion. This game also had an indeterminate ending
and created a great deal of noise and laughter. The alternative was that if
all were caught the last man became 'Copper'.

In games where the hiders had to be physically caught, there was a wide
range of possibilities. Sometimes they were simply touched, as in games
of tig, or patted on the back three times, and so on. In team games they
were often physically restrained by the seekers, and could struggle free.
Another occasional feature was that the victim had to give his or her victor
a piggyback ride:

> 'Spy-Ann': A game of hide and seek, with this difference, that when those
> are found who are hid, the finder cries 'Spyann'; and if the one discovered
> can catch the discoverer, he has a ride upon his back to the dools.
>
> GALLOWAY, C.1824

And on the Isle of Man in the 1920s:

> 'But-Thorrin' or 'Butt-Thurran' [lit. 'Stack-butt']: A game of hide and seek
> around stacks. 'One was putting his head against the stack and the rest
> getting away among the other stacks, and then the one that was lying was
> coming out and trying to tip someone and make him lie in his stead, and
> if he chased one to a certain distance from his own stack, whoever would
> catch him then he had to ride them back to his stand again. We used to
> spend moonlight evenings in the winter at that game.'

The words and phrases used in many hide-and-seek type games were
also interestingly variable:

> If the finder failed to find all the players he would shout, 'Ooper oller,
> opperay, if you don't oller I don't play.' Whereupon the hidden person would
> make a small noise to give a clue.   BUCKINGHAMSHIRE, 1950S

'Cuckoo' was often the word that the hiders were supposed to utter,
and close variants are found up and down the country. In a glossary of
the Northumberland dialect compiled by Richard Heslop and published
in 1892, the word 'coo' is glossed as 'to hide oneself, as in "When yor hidden,

mind ye cry *coo*'''. In Anne Baker's dictionary of Northamptonshire words, published in 1854, 'cuckoo' is defined in the following terms:

> A child's cry at the game of hide and seek to announce that she has concealed herself; and, Hoop or Hoopit: When a child is playing at the game of hide and seek, and has concealed herself, she calls out 'hoop! hoop!, to signify to her playmates that they may begin to search for her.

'Hoopie' was also what the game was called on the Isle of Wight in the 1830s, while on Guernsey it was sometimes 'Couk', and in Lancashire, around 1914, it was 'Whip':

> Among the variations of 'Hide and Seek', the most common was 'Whip' (why so-called is obscure) . . . when spotting one he would shout 'You're whipped' and race back to the den . . . Curiously, all over South Lancashire, it was the custom, when deciding to abandon the game, for all those in the den to shout aloud 'Tiddley-up-tup-tup, tiddley-up-tup-tup' until all the players returned.

Among the other bewildering number of names for hide-and-seek in the nineteenth and early twentieth centuries were 'Bicky' (Somerset); 'Ho Spy', 'Hospy' and 'Hy Spy' (Scotland); 'Hey Spy' (Co. Antrim / Co. Down); 'Spy' (Cork); 'I Spy' (Hampshire/Cheshire); 'I Spy I' (Berkshire); 'Felt and Laite' (Sheffield); 'Felto' (Whitby); 'Hed-O' (Holderness); 'Hide and Fox' (Kent); 'Hidy Buck' (Dorset); and 'Lam-pie-sote-it' (North Yorkshire).

As already indicated, there were versions where the hiding took more prominence than the seeking, as in a Yorkshire mining village about 1903:

> 'Hide and seek kick out the can' . . . Of course this was a great game, because boys and girls played it together, and there were so many wonderful places to hide. In the closets you could fasten the door from the inside and remain in seclusion with your little girlfriend; in the pigsties you could hide in the straw heaps. Sometimes the game was played in the woods, sometimes in coal houses; but boy and girl always ran away together. The game was very keenly played, because 'it' always knew that some boy or girl was hidden somewhere with his or her sweetheart.

In modern times, straight hide-and-seek is still played frequently, especially in the infants' playground, but sooner or later most children graduate to more challenging versions, and the commonest nowadays is usually called 'Block' or 'Forty Forty', in which the emphasis is more on racing back to the base than on the hiding.

> There's 'Forty Forty Touch' and 'Forty Forty See'. 'Forty Forty See' is like hide-and-seek, where you don't go and find them but you stay nearer your base. (If you stay too close it's called 'cat-guarding'.) If you see someone you say, 'Mollie by the stage – forty forty out', and you have to touch the base. And people hiding have to get back to the base before the person who's seen them.
>
> In 'Forty Forty Touch' there's more fun. It's like hide-and-seek at the beginning, but you have to try and run in. The person who's on is trying to it you – it doesn't matter if you see them, you don't have to hide. If they hang around too close to the base, it's 'No fools around the pole' or 'Forty forty scat!'　　　　　　　　　　　　　　　　　　　GODALMING, 2008

The local name for the game is usually reflected in the words that both the seekers have to call out when they see someone and the hiders have to shout when reaching the base. In Wales a common name for the same game is 'Mob':

> The person who was it would count to 100 leaning against a 'mobbing post' – ideally a pole that could be approached from several directions (e.g. a telegraph pole), but it could be a specific part of a wall. This person would then hunt for the others, who were hiding. When 'it' spotted someone she or he would run back to the mobbing post, and if she or he got there first would slap the post with their hand and shout, 'Mob Mob —[name of the person found] one – two – three'. The first person mobbed would then become 'it' in the next round. However, at any point during the game, any hider might sneak back to the mobbing post and mob the person who was 'it', or if spotted by 'it' could race him or her back to the mobbing post with the aim of mobbing 'it'. If 'it' got mobbed by one of the hiders, the hider would shout, 'Mob Mob — [name of 'it'] one – two – three, followed by 'Save all' if 'it' had mobbed any people up to that point. In this way the hider would save those people who had been mobbed from becoming 'it' in the next round. 'It' would have to mob more people after the save to secure a replacement for the next round, or he or she would be 'it' again. When 'it' mobbed the last hider of the round he or she would shout 'All out' after the mob call, to finish the game.　　　　　　WALES, 1970S

Other names and phrases are variants of 'Block In', 'Ackey 1 2 3' and 'Rally 1 2 3'. 'Relieve-o' (sometimes 'Release-o') was a particularly widespread form of the game through most of the twentieth century in Scotland, Wales and much of England.

It is interesting to see that the modern games have to a certain extent kept up the tradition of calling out interesting phrases. As a nine-year-old boy from Coventry told Cathy Gould in 2007:

> Before the game starts the person who is 'on' can shout, 'No fools around me in all directions' – this stops someone just standing right next to the rally post and when you open your eyes they just touch the post and shout, 'Rally 1 2 3.' Also 'No stampedes', which disallows everyone breaking cover at once and charging to the rally post.

The Opies in their *Children's Games in Street and Playground* (1969) give other versions of the phrase shouted by the seeker at the start of the game, including 'No backs, no sides, no front' (Scarborough) and 'No behind the cat's tail' (Caerleon).

One of the regular tactics adopted by those already caught is to reach out to anyone trying to save them:

> There's an itter and they count to forty, and everybody else runs and hides, and then when that person finds you, you have to run to the homey [usually a tree] and say, 'Forty forty home' when you get there; and you can, like, one person can hold on to the tree and you can all hold hands, and make a chain to get to the person – a homey line – and as long as you're touching the person, and you're on the chain, you can come off homey.
>
> *WEST LONDON, 2009*

Other, less colourful, modern names for the game include 'Manhunt' and 'Cops and Robbers', and at one private school in Cambridgeshire in the 1960s it was called 'Wavie' because those who had been caught and confined could be released if they could see a still-hidden player waving at them.

As I have already mentioned, many seeking games are best played when it is getting dark, and some have features that only work well in those conditions:

> 'Dickie Dickie Shine-a-Light' was played after dark with torches. My father asked for, and was given, a torch especially for this game. Players split into two teams. One team goes and hides. The other team then shouts, 'Dickie Dickie shine a light!' On this command the hidden team all flash their

torches for a brief moment. This gives the searchers a brief chance to memorise where to start looking and then they go off and try to find everyone using their own torches to help seek them out.   *COVENTRY, 1920S*

'Show a Light' games are documented back to the seventeenth century.

In country areas many 'Hares and Hounds'-type games were formerly played in a similar way, but ranging over a much wider area:

> 'Hare and Hounds': This was a kind of hide-and-seek, played in the streets at night when it was dark. The hares started off from the den, and when about a hundred yards away, one of them cried 'Ahernt!', the hounds immediately giving chase. The hares sought cover in doorways, blind alleys, dark passages, or anywhere they could hide. When a hound caught a hare he immediately yelled, 'Ahernt, you're caught.' All the players then returned to den, the game proceeding as before, the former hounds in turn becoming the hares. When one hare was caught they were deemed to be all caught, the cry 'Ahernt, you're caught!' being an intimation to the other hares that they were discovered.   *ISLE OF MAN, C.1876*

'Hare and Hounds', which was a widely known game, also went by such names as 'Fox and Hounds' and 'Hunt the Hare', and was played from at least the early seventeenth to the mid twentieth century. It can be organised in teams, but more usually has one or two hares and as many hounds as like to join in. The rules are simple, and were clearly contrived to mirror a real hunt, with the hounds giving the hares some time to get away, and then following as fast as they can. The chase can lead anywhere, and in the countryside often goes on for miles, but if the hounds lose sight of their quarry they have a set of words to call out:

> Sound your holler
> Or my little dog shan't foller.
>
> *WARWICKSHIRE, 1890S*

> Uppa uppa holye
> If you don't speak
> My dogs shan't folly.
>
> *CORNWALL, C.1860S*

The hares must answer, to give a clue to their whereabouts. If the hares are caught, they are often handled roughly.

A game recorded in Alice Gomme's *Traditional Games* (1894), also under the title 'Hare and Hounds', was contributed by her husband, and was presumably from his own boyhood in the 1860s. In this game, which would nowadays be called a 'paperchase', the hare carries a bag full of strips of paper and must leave a trail for the hounds to follow, but he still tries to get away from them and to reach an agreed finishing place before they catch him.

One other game with a hiding aspect to it that was particularly ideal for the countryside was called 'Bogey'. Here, though, it was the 'it' person who did the hiding:

> The best time of all, though, was when the hay was cut on the village green. Then the children played 'Bogey won't be out tonight'. One child would lie down and be covered with the cut hay. The other children then danced round singing 'Moonlight, starlight, Bogey won't be out tonight', until they saw Bogey throwing off the hay. This would send them shrieking in all directions, while Bogey chased them until one of them was caught. That one had to be the Bogey, and the game started all over again.
>
> *SURREY, 1930S*

There was presumably enough grass around in East London at the time of the First World War to play this game, as Norman Douglas describes the same procedure in his *London Street Games* (1916) under the name 'Green Man Rise-o'.

But it could also be played in city street or country lane, and was a great favourite on the way home from school. Flora Thompson recalled it in her classic *Lark Rise to Candleford*, remembering life on the Oxfordshire–Northamptonshire border in the 1880s:

> [Laura] never really enjoyed the game the hamlet children played going home from school, when one of them went on before to hide and the others followed slowly, hand in hand, singing:
>
> > I hope we shan't meet any gipsies tonight!
> > I hope we shan't meet any gipsies tonight!
>
> And when the hiding-place was reached and the supposed gipsy sprung out and grabbed the nearest, she always shrieked, although she knew it was only a game.

GRANDMOTHER'S FOOTSTEPS AND OTHERS

Another way of organising a game is to have the 'it' person on one side, usually facing a wall, with the other players creeping up behind him or her. The commonest of these is 'Grandmother's Footsteps', which seems to be known to almost all children in the country, and everyone seems to have played it at some point in their lives.

The basic game is simple: one child, the grandmother, stands with their back to the others, who are some distance away. They all have to creep up on the grandmother, who can turn round at any moment, and if she sees anyone moving they are sent back to the start line. Whoever succeeds in getting close enough to touch the grandmother wins, or becomes the new grandmother. Alternatively, as the children at Okehampton Primary School described it in 2010:

> We play it like there's a granny, and people, and they turn around and look, and then they turn back and you have to run, and if they see you moving as they turn round you have to go to the back again, and it's the first person to go, 'Hello, Grandma'.

Nowadays most children recognise the name 'Grandmother's Footsteps', but a number of different names for it existed in the past. Cathy Gould, for example, states that it was called 'Mother's Headache' in Coventry in the 1970s. The Opies, writing in 1969, called it 'Peep Behind the Curtain' and demonstrated that this was the prevalent name in South and South-east England, while 'London' predominated in western England and the southern half of Wales, and 'Sly Fox' in the northern half of Wales and in the English Midlands and North. Other names included 'Peeping Tom', 'Creeping Jenny', 'Piggy Behind the Curtain' and in Scotland 'Black Peter', 'White Horse' and 'Statues'. They also commented that the game's name in the first recorded examples, around the turn of the twentieth century, was 'Steps', and that 'the name "Grandmother's footsteps" seems to be known mostly in private schools'.

More modern widespread names include 'Chocolate Fudge', 'Hot Chocolate' and 'Ice Cream'. These often reflect the words that have to be called out when someone reaches the 'granny' person, but they also some-times indicate a slightly different set of rules – sufficiently different from the classic version of 'Grandmother's Footsteps' to prompt children to regard these food and drink titles as constituting a separate game.

Collector Gareth Whitaker observed a version of 'Hot Chocolate' being played by six or seven ten-year-old girls in Denholme, Yorkshire, in 2002, and his notebook reads:

> 'On' facing wall, others 5 metres away in a line creeping forward. 'On' spins round trying to catch someone moving; if she does this they must go back to the beginning. Game soon develops into fun game of striking poses as 'on' spins round – aim of reaching the wall forgotten (huge fun – all laughing and enjoying themselves).

This reminds us how quickly one game can change into another, and the dangers of being too dogmatic about the 'rules' of particular games.

One of the regular variations in the way the game is played includes the rule that the grandmother cannot turn round completely at will, but is constrained by having to recite a phrase or numbers:

> 'London': In this someone faced the wall and spelled out L-O-N-D-O-N loudly. While they were doing this the others who were standing some way away had to advance towards the caller. At the end of the word the caller turned round quickly and anyone still moving had to go back to the start. You could vary the speed of the call – very quickly or a mixture of slow and quick to try to catch them out. The winner was whoever managed to reach and touch the caller. GLASGOW, 1940S

These days, the 'grandmother' may also sometimes have to chase all the other players as soon as someone reaches her. And sometimes things get even more complicated:

> 'Chocolate Fudge': 'He' has to stand with back to the other players, he shouts 'go' and the others have to silently creep up. He turns round suddenly, and anyone seen moving has to go to the front and stand beside the 'He', holding hands. When the last one gets there, they shout 'Chocolate Fudge' and all have to run back to the starting line without being tug by 'He'. If someone is tug they become 'He', but if not, part two of the game starts. Everyone holds one of He's outspread fingers and gets ready to run. 'He' starts telling a story, and as soon as 'He' says 'Chocolate Fudge' they must run to avoid being tug. If anyone starts to run too soon, they have to go down on one knee. EDINBURGH, 1990

A very similar game, reported by eleven-year-old girls in Godalming, Surrey, in 2008, is called 'Pink Potion':

It starts off like 'Grandmother's Footsteps', when you try to get up to the grandma without them looking and if they see you moving you've got to go up to there, and the last person to get on – everyone else holds hands and they weave in and out telling a story. And they might say, 'Once upon a time there was a rat who used pink shampoo', but if you say 'pink potion' everyone has to run back and the person telling the story has to catch you.

Very similar 'creeping-up' games are known in Austria, Germany, Italy and elsewhere on the Continent.

'What's the Time, Mr Wolf?' is organised on the same principles as 'Grandmother's Footsteps' and is just as well known. From the responses to the *Lore of the Playground* online questionnaire, and interviews up and down the country, it seems that everyone nowadays knows and plays it in more or less the same way:

Everyone will stand at one end apart from somebody chosen to be a wolf. The wolf will face the other way. The rest will ask, 'What's the time, Mr Wolf?' The wolf will say —o'clock. Whatever o'clock he or she says, the rest will take that many steps forward. This will continue until the wolf thinks everyone is near enough. They will ask him or her what the time is and the wolf will spin round to face them and say, 'Dinner time!' Then everyone will run and the wolf will try to catch them. If he or she catches someone they will be the wolf, but if not he or she will be the wolf again.

INVERNESS, 2008

When played in the modern playground, the wolf usually stands facing a wall, but when the game was formerly played in the street he often walked along, with the others trailing behind and asking the questions. Variant names, such as 'What's the Time, Mr Fox?' and 'Mr Bear', have also been recorded. In all versions, though, the main excitement of the game is the rising tension at each question, as the children know that the chase is coming soon, and the squealing that usually accompanies the pursuit when it finally arrives.

The Opies in *Children's Games in Street and Playground* (1969) record examples of the game back to the 1890s, and draw parallels with older games, in Britain and abroad, in which a potentially dangerous animal is taunted with questions before a chase or capture takes place.

The idea that the players and the 'fox' enter into a dialogue is also a key feature of a range of games that are characterised by people asking permission before they can move. The favourite of these permissions games has long been 'May I?' or 'Mother, May I?', in which the players take it in turns to ask the 'mother' if they can move towards her, and she dictates what type of steps, and how many, can be taken:

'Please, Your Majesty can I come and see you in your beautiful castle?' – and she'll say, 'Yes, you can. Take, say, five steps.' Before you go you have to remember to say, 'May I?', and if you don't say it and you start just walking forward you have to go back to the start. GODALMING, 2008

In nearly all versions the players must utter the prescribed words before moving, but the real essence of the game is the range of steps that are allowed:

In this game there were three types of steps, called pigeon steps, which was heel to toe; normal step, or giant step, in which you took the biggest step you could without your other foot leaving the ground or you falling over. If you fell over or jumped you had to go back to the beginning. 'Mother' would call out someone's name and say, '—, move five pigeon steps', at which point — would then say, 'Please mother, may I?', Mother would say, 'Yes, you may' or 'No, you may not'. If — had moved without asking then she'd have to go back to the beginning. LONDON, 1980s

Other versions have a much wider repertoire of movements. In Coventry in the 1960s, for example, there was 'giant steps', 'lamp posts' (lying on the floor and then moving along that length) and 'spitting kettles' (spitting and moving along to where it landed); and in the 1990s, 'baby steps', 'banana splits' (taking really big steps) and 'round the world' (one rotation while moving forward). In Glasgow in 1998 there was 'lamp post' (lying down and standing on place where the head reaches), 'round the world' (running round in a circle till 'on' tells you when to stop), 'fairy step' (placing feet heel to toe), 'giant step' (taking as large steps possible) and 'banana split' (trying to do the splits and moving to the furthest place). James Ritchie's *Singing Street* (1964) even records the command 'take a minister's walk', which means close your eyes and move forward, pretending to hold a Bible in your hands. Iona and Peter Opie include forty-one different steps for this game in their *Children's Games of Street and Playground* (1969), many with delightfully inventive names.

A modern name for one regular variant of the 'May I?' principle is 'Red

Letter'. Previously it was more commonly called 'Names', 'Alphabet' or simply 'Letters'. Here it is as played in Edinburgh in the 1970s:

> There would be an 'it' on the side of the playground and the other players on the other. 'It' would say, 'The red letter is (for example) R.' 'It' would then shout a letter from the alphabet, and you used your full name and took a small step if it was in your name, or a big step if it was a capital letter in your name. If she shouted out, 'The red letter' and you moved, you would have to go back to the start. The aim of the game was to reach 'it' first.

A more recent description from Edinburgh shows the steps being more closely regulated:

> Red Square is played on squares. A letter of the alphabet is chosen as the red letter. The leader calls out letters. If these are in your name you move forward one square. If the letter is a capital in your name you move forward two squares. When the leader calls the red letter, nobody should move, but if they do they have to go back to the start. First to the finishing lines wins, and becomes the new leader.   EDINBURGH, 1990

The basic game is essentially the same wherever it is played, but sometimes a chase is added:

> The first person who gets there tags the person who is on and then the person who is on has to chase everyone else and you try and run back to the beginning.   GODALMING, 2008

A very similar game is 'Colours', in which the 'it' person simply calls out a colour, and anyone wearing that colour is allowed to move. The essential difference between this and 'Mother, May I?' is that there is no dialogue, or choice of steps. Previous generations had similar games that focused on other features of the players, such as 'Aunts and Uncles', or 'Relations', where the 'it' person called out a name and anyone who had a relative with that name was allowed to move.

In some 'permissions' games, the traditional across-the-playground chasing is combined with elements of control by the 'it' person. The usual pattern is for the 'it' person to allow certain people, defined by a stated criterion, to cross unmolested, while the others must rush across and take their chances of being caught. A regular feature is a relatively developed rhyme or dialogue, which is spoken each time:

Jack, Jack, may we cross the water
　To see the king's daughter
To push her in the water
　To see if she can swim?
What colour is she?

Crocodile, crocodile, may we cross the water
　To see your fairy daughter
Dressed in water?
　What colour do we choose?
I will want you to wear pink
　If you have pink you may cross
If you don't you better wait
　Cos I'll catch you if you dare try.

PLAYERS: Please Mr Crocodile, can I cross the water
　To see your ugly daughter
　Before she goes to bed? [or sometimes 'In a rubber ring']
CROCODILE: Only if you've got blond hair. [or 'You're wearing red', etc.]

The rhymes vary considerably from place to place, but a regular feature is a river, or at least a stretch of water, which the players must cross.

The Opies list numerous names for this sort of game in their *Children's Games of Street and Playground* (1969), including 'Farmer Farmer', which was once the most regularly found title. They make the interesting comment that 'this is probably the most popular game in the streets of Britain today'. It can hardly claim that crown nowadays, but it is still regularly seen, in one form or another, in playgrounds all across the country. The earliest references to the game date from around the turn of the twentieth century.

CHAPTER SEVEN

Questions and Answers

The creeping and permissions games described in the previous chapter all feature stylised dialogue between the 'it' person and the other players, but there are other games in which the verbal element takes a more prominent place – sometimes as a prelude to other action, sometimes as the main purpose of the game.

In their *Children's Games in Street and Playground* (1969), Iona and Peter Opie set out quite an involved sub-category of 'racing games': 'Games in which only two competitors run against each other at a time, one of them generally being instrumental in the selection of the other'. The current game this most effectively describes is 'Polo', which seems to be popular in playgrounds as far apart as Cambridgeshire, Coventry, Lechlade, Belfast, Glasgow and Edinburgh. 'Polo', though, does not quite follow the same form as any of the games described by the Opies, and it may therefore be of relatively recent vintage.

Here is 'Polo' as described by Megan, Mollie and Annie (aged eleven), from Godalming, Surrey, in 2008:

> Basically, someone's on and they say, 'I choose (Mollie)' and she'll come up as a messenger and I'll tell her a question and she goes back – it might be 'What's your favourite colour?' One will say 'blue' and another 'green', and she'll say to me, 'One blue, one green'; and I'll call out either 'blue' or 'green', and if I called out 'blue', Annie would have to run. You have to have two walls and the person who's on starts on one wall and everyone else starts on the other, and you just run to the other wall, and you say 'P', and then 'O', 'L', 'O', and then 'Polo'. It can be any question – what's your favourite

animal, or your favourite TV show. If there were two blues, it would be 'blue 1' and 'blue 2'.

The only difference for Maddie, Rhea and Dahlia (all ten years old), of West London, in 2009, was that the person doing the choosing was called 'the queen'. Adults from Kent and Yorkshire reported playing essentially the same game in the 1970s and 1980s.

The second part of the game, the racing against each other, is found in other games, such as 'Peter Pan Said to Paul', recorded in James Ritchie's *Singing Street* (1964). Here, one girl is 'it' and faces a line of players, who hold out their hands. She goes along, slapping each hand in turn, saying:

> Peter Pan said to Paul
> Which do you like the best of all
> Kerb or hearthstone wall?

Whoever the rhyme ends on has to make the choice. If she chooses 'kerb' she must run first to the kerb and back, and then to the wall and back, while the 'it' person does the opposite. The 'it' person can delay the rhyme on the last line by saying, 'Kerb or hearthstone, stone, stone . . .' and it is only when she says 'Wall!' that the race begins.

'Television' games follow a similar course, but here the race is between the players rather than between the 'it' person and one player:

'Television game': You get a paper, television paper, and you find a programme you watch, and then you say the beginning letter of the programme, and the person's got to try and get it, and when they get it they have to run up, run back down, and run up and shout it out, and if they've got it wrong they have to go back down again, if they don't get it. HAMPSHIRE, 1979

'TV game': First of all you find two posts, walls, or whatever is convenient, that you can run between. A wall to line up against is best so that you are all starting level with each other. One person is chosen, usually by a dip (I will call them the caller here, but they don't have a special name at school) and they have to think of a TV programme. The caller then tells the others the channel, time and day of the programme. If anyone thinks they have guessed it, they run to the other post and back, with everyone else making sure they *touch* it and don't cheat. When they get back home they shout out their guess. If they are right they become the caller. As soon as someone starts running the caller stops giving clues, to stop people running just to get ahead, i.e. before they know the answer. If no one can guess with the information given, the caller thinks of more clues, giving the initials and/or describing what happens. The guesser can ask the caller to repeat their clues and sometimes you can ask questions. If you get back and say the wrong programme, you must run again before you have another guess. An important development to the game, which makes it more interesting, and stops you running out of TV programmes, is that other categories have been formed. We now also have adverts, pop, cinema and video, football teams and theatre.   *SOUTH LONDON, 1987*

These descriptions in turn match a game called 'Film Stars', which was described by the Opies in *Children's Games in Street and Playground* as being very popular in the 1960s. Not surprisingly, the game could also be played with pop star and pop group names:

'Pop Groups': The game takes place on a square pitch. 'It' is the person who calls out group names. 'It' calls out the initials of a pop group. If the group guess wrong, the 'It' takes one pace towards them. If it is guessed, the players and the 'It' run from one end and back; the first person back is it.
                                                      YORKSHIRE, 1975

Ultimately, the pedigree of such games stretches back even further. 'Trades' or 'Two Poor Tradesmen' or 'Jolly Workmen' (to mention only three of the names variously used) was very popular from at least the 1820s until the 1960s. Like its successors, it involved guessing and chasing, but it also included the element of miming. For D. Parry-Jones, writing of Wales in Edwardian times, it was called 'Three (or Seven) Jolly Welshmen':

Whatever the name, the game proceeds in the same manner: one acts the part of the employer, who is visited by these jolly Welshmen looking for some work; upon being asked what sort of work they can do, they reply, 'Oh, ev'ry sort.' 'Then show me one.' They then go through the action of doing some work previously decided upon – very much like the present television game of 'What's My Line', which, I am sure, was suggested by it. The employer tries to guess their trade, and if he guess aright, the jolly Welshmen scatter in all directions, while he tries to catch one of them. If he succeeds, the one caught remains with him to help catch the others the next time, for the game goes on till they are all caught. In the county of Glamorgan, village boys often played it in the evening under the light of the street lamps – and the one who imitated his trade badly was chucked out and another took his place.

A description in *There is an Isle* (1998), Criostoir O'Flynn's account of his boyhood in Limerick in the 1930s, shows that the game was known in Ireland, and young Londoners were doing the same sort of thing about the time of the First World War:

> Please We've Come to Learn a Trade (also called Guessing Words or Dumb Motions) – another game for boys and girls. There are two parties, one on each side of the street. One of them has to think of a trade, such as picking hops, for instance; then they take the first letters, P and H, and go over to the others and say, 'We have come to work a trade.' When the others ask, 'What's your trade?', they must answer 'P. H.', and pretend to be picking hops with their hands. If the others guess what trade they mean, they must shout it out and chase them across the street.

Late nineteenth-century descriptions show a similar pattern. Earlier versions, though, display some marked differences: the tradesmen often name their chosen trade, but mime a particular tool associated with it; and instead of a general chase, the tradesmen or the person who guesses wrongly are belaboured with knotted handkerchiefs or caps. The earliest known version in Britain appears in a little book entitled *School Boys' Diversions* published around 1820, but the Opies (in *Children's Games in Street and Playground*) mention Continental versions that date back to the sixteenth century.

Alongside the 'Polo' and 'Film Star'-type games, there have been many in which the verbal element is accompanied by physical action, but without any chasing or running. 'Honeypots' is perhaps the classic example from the late Victorian and Edwardian playground. A number of children stoop down in a row, clasping their hands under their legs, representing the pots of honey. Two act as owner and purchaser. The purchaser asks, 'Have you any honey pots for sale?' and is informed, 'Yes, plenty; will you walk round and taste them?' The purchaser then goes along the row, pretending to taste each one, finding fault, until one is chosen. The purchaser and owner then test the pot by lifting it up by the arms and swinging it backwards and forwards. If the child can keep his or her hands clasped it is a good pot, but if not, it is a bad one and set aside. In many versions of the game a rhyme is sung or chanted at the start or while the swinging is taking place:

Buy my fine honey today
Which shall I buy?
Taste 'em and try.

LONDON, 1890s

Take her and bake her
   And into pies make her
And bring her back
   When she is done.

LONDON, 1890s

Honey pots, honey pots, all in a row
Twenty-five shillings wherever you go
Who'll buy my honey pots?

DUBLIN, 1890s

The same game was called 'Hinnie-Pigs' in Galloway in the 1820s, and was played by boys; the illustration in *A Nosegay for the Trouble of Culling* (1813) shows the involvement of both boys and girls.

Judging by the number of affectionate references in books and articles of the period, 'Honeypots' was a particularly popular game throughout the nineteenth century. Even the little eight-year-old watercress-seller from Clerkenwell, interviewed by the journalist and social investigator Henry Mayhew in 1851, who had little time to play and who had never even heard of a park, mentioned it:

Sometimes we has a game of honey-pots with the girls in the court, but not often. Me and Carry H— carries the little 'uns. We plays, too, at 'kiss-in-the-ring'. I knows a good many games, but I don't play at 'em, 'cos going out with the creases tires me.

The game lasted into the twentieth century, though Norman Douglas, writing in 1916, called it 'a little old-fashioned'.

'Honeypots' may have gone the way of all flesh, but 'Concentration' in today's playground fulfils the same role of combining words with some physical actions. The game may possibly have originated in the classroom or at Girl Guide meetings but it has now very definitely acquired a life of its own in the playground:

Concentration [*clap clap clap*]
Sixty-four [*clap clap clap*]

No repeats [*clap clap clap*]
Or hesitation [*clap clap clap*]
I'll go first [*clap clap clap*]
I'll go second [*clap clap clap*]
Starting with [*clap clap clap*]
Anything [*clap clap clap*]
Bananas [*clap clap clap*]
Apples [*clap clap clap*], etc.

EAST FINCHLEY, 2008

The game can be played in pairs or with a group who arrange themselves in a circle, the losers staying around to try to distract those still remaining. The clap-clap-clap rhythm is common, but is not the only one available to children. A version noted in Edinburgh in 1990, for example, has a much more difficult routine:

Concentration [*slap thighs, clap, click fingers*]
Start with [*slap thighs, clap, click fingers*]
Determination [*slap thighs, clap, click fingers*]
If so [*slap thighs, clap, click fingers*]
Let's go [*slap thighs, clap, click fingers*]
[Leader says word] [*slap thighs, clap, click fingers*]
[Next says associated word, etc.] [*slap thighs, clap, click fingers*]

Even more popular in the current playground is 'Truth or Dare', one of those games that adults often find pointless, or even regard as unacceptable, but children never seem to tire of. As played by older children in the unsupervised street or park, as it was in the past, there was a real danger of participants 'daring' each other to destructive or antisocial behaviour, from knocking on doors to setting fire to derelict buildings, or swallowing noxious substances. As played nowadays in the junior-school playground, though, it is pretty harmless: the dares are generally kept under some sort of control, and they are rarely that audacious. What is noticeable is the proliferation of categories from which the victim must choose. A contributor to the *Lore of the Playground* questionnaire, remembering her childhood in Berkshire about 1970, wrote:

A major game was 'Dare, double dare, truth, love, kiss or promise', where a group of us would select one of the challenges. The others in the group made up the challenge. So, 'dare' meant the others chose a daring action for

Bad Behaviour

One of the less desirable aspects of the unsupervised street-play of yester-year was that many children got involved in mischief which went beyond naughty and became dangerous, antisocial or even illegal. Adults often have a double standard in this respect. We roundly condemn vandalism and lack of respect in today's children, and fret about the peer-pressure involved in games of 'Truth or dare' or 'Follow my leader', while some-what shamefacedly smiling over some of the antics we got up to back when we ourselves had the chance to misbehave.

There is no end to the mischievous invention of children when left to their own devices, and the more forbidden the better, but one example must stand for the countless acts of vandalism down the years. Playing beside the railway was bad enough, but one writer confessed to further misbehaviour:

> There was always an element of adventure as we were never certain when the next train would arrive. The railway signal stood high on the embank-ment and each day a man would walk up the line from Horrabridge station to place an oil lamp to illuminate the signal. My two elder brothers were crack shots with an air rifle and would regularly break the glass in the lamp – eventually the stationmaster gave up replacing it. *DEVON, 1920S*

But certain types of 'bad behaviour' seem to be traditional in the sense that they persisted from generation to generation, and children regarded them as legitimate 'games', which had rules and conventions of their own, while in areas which have traditions of an annual 'Mischief Night' (see chapter 26), some children still believe that they have the right to misbe-have on that day at least.

Much of the standard antisocial behaviour of the past focussed on annoying householders in some way, by tying door handles together or smearing knockers with grease or treacle, and so on. But by far the most common of all such games was undoubtedly that of knocking on doors or ringing doorbells, and running away. This is generally called 'Knock Down Ginger', but is known by a very wide variety of local names, including 'Knocking Ginger out of bed', 'Knock door run', 'Nicky nocky nino', 'Bing bang scoosh', and the less obvious 'Squashed tomato', 'Rabbit chase', 'Robber's knock', and 'Rosy apple'. There are many reports of added refinements, which either escalate the vandalism involved or increase the danger of being caught:

> The local lads enjoyed the game 'Knock and Nash' around the village of Dalston. Very annoying, I'm sure, but relatively harmless. They would fill a water barrel and lean it against a door, then knock on the door. The door would open and in went the water. CUMBERLAND, 1930S

The heyday of door-knocking games ended with the general demise of street play, although they still take place on occasion, and have clearly been a problem for a long time. The Town Police Clauses Act (1847), for example, specifically names 'wilfully and wantonly disturbing any inhabitant by pulling or ringing any door bell or knocking at any door' as criminal behaviour.

Other tricks took planning and careful execution, and relied on skills passed on through the generations. An extremely widespread procedure was the 'window-tapper', which was described in characteristically fine detail by C. H. Rolph in his memories of his Edwardian childhood in London:

> With chewing-gum or cobbler's wax we secured one end of an 18-inch length of black cotton to the centre of one of the glass panels in the upper half of the widow. At the other end, about nine inches below the window-frame centre and two inches from the glass of the lower window, hung a half-inch metal nut or a pebble with a hole in it; and just above the nut or pebble would be fixed four stiff-paper wings to catch the wind. A decent breeze would have the thing tapping irregularly at the widow, and as a rule the occupier would come out a surprising number of times before he decided to investigate and then found our evilly-inspired apparatus.

Other versions of the window-tapper were less elaborate and were operated by a long piece of cotton pulled by a child hidden in the garden, although this ran the risk of the perpetrator being caught if the householder 'cottoned on' quickly and gave chase. Parents who worry that delinquent behaviour necessarily results in a life of crime should be reassured to learn that Rolph later became a Chief Inspector of the City of London Police.

the person to do, 'double dare' (which no one ever seemed to select!) was extra daring; 'truth' meant they could ask any question and the person had to answer truthfully; 'love' meant that the group asked the person if they loved a particular person (interestingly we often asked the person, 'Do you love God?' to which the answer was always yes); 'kiss' meant that the group told the person to kiss someone (usually on the hand!); and finally 'promise' meant that they had to promise to do something. This game was played by us when we got a bit older – from maybe ten to twelve and nearly always with a mixed group of boys and girls.

As with 'Kiss Chase' (p. 28) it is clear that while many children relish the game, others find it goes well beyond their comfort zone. A group of boys aged eight to ten in East Sussex in 2008 had an ambivalent opinion of the game:

It's got to be something embarrassing. The dares can be as worse as shoving a worm down your trousers, hitting yourself, or kissing a girl . . . 'Black dare' you definitely have to do it. 'Donkey dare' if you don't do it they have to pound you fifty times. 'Truth, Dare, Double Dare, Kiss, Command or Cuddle' – that's boring, I hate that game. Normally it's the girls what play it.

It is likely that 'Truth or Dare' is a direct descendant of various games played by both adults and children in the past, under titles such as 'Questions and Commands' and 'King I Am', as described in *Round about the Coal Fire*, a little book of 'Christmas Entertainments' of 1740:

When the commander may oblige his subject to answer any lawful question, and make the same obey him instantly, under the penalty of being smutted, or paying such forfeit as may be laid on the aggressor; but the forfeits being generally fixed at some price, as a shilling, half a crown, etc., so every one knowing what to do if they should be too stubborn to submit, make themselves easy at discretion.

Obviously, the potential for such games depends on the nature of the gathering, and of the company, but a hint of the scope allowed in past centuries is provided by an example quoted by the Opies from *Gratiae Ludentes* (1638) – a sample question posed to a gentlewoman: '*Question*: Suppose you and I were in a room together, you being naked, pray which part would you first cover? *Answer*: Your eyes, sir.'

BEHIND YOUR BACK

Many question-and-answer games inevitably involve doing things on or behind the player's back and asking them to guess what is happening. Quite a few can be found in the modern playground, but it is perhaps worth looking first at a couple, 'Buck Buck' and 'Hot Cockles', that appear to have disappeared from the scene, because both demonstrate just how far back certain types of play can be shown to stretch.

Here is 'Buck Buck' as described in East Yorkshire in the 1880s:

> Another boys' game is played by three boys. One stands upright against a wall, another bends down with his head against the stomach of the first, while the third leaps on to the back thus formed, and holding up so many fingers, speaks to the one on whose back he is,
>
> > Buck, buck
> > Hoo mony fingers div I hod up?
>
> 'Buck' answers as many as he thinks, say four. If this were wrong it would be said
>
> > Fower thoe says
> > An' three there is
> > So buck, buck, etc.
>
> until the correct number is guessed.

The boy standing against the wall was not always necessary; the one bending down could always, if needed, lean over a chair or a table, or hang on to a gate or some other suitable object.

This game was certainly well known all over Britain and Ireland throughout the nineteenth century, and only started to die out in the first decades of the twentieth. The basic format was remarkably similar from place to place, although some versions were rougher than others, involving thumps and slaps on the stooping boy's back:

> If the one stooping down guessed correctly the two changed places; if incorrectly, all the others beat upon his back with their clenched fists, crying out, 'Row, row, rad-i-o; row, row, rad-i-o', for several minutes.
>
> *WILTSHIRE, 1880S*

And in a Scottish version printed by Alice Gomme:

> If the guess was wrong, the Rider gave the Buck as many blows or kicks
> with the heel as the difference between the correct number and the number
> guessed.

In some versions the words recited are specifically 'how many *horns*'
rather than 'how many *fingers*', which is significant in the light of the
frequent recurrence of the word 'buck' in the game. The name varied from
place to place, including, in Wales and Cornwall, 'Buck Shee Buck'; in
Suffolk, 'Huck-a-buck, Huck-a-buck'; in Ireland, 'Hurley Burley'; and in
Glasgow, 'Bairdy Bairdy, Buckety-buck'. In Huddersfield, about 1880, the
rhyme was:

> Inkum, jinkum, Jeremy buck
>   Yamdy horns do au cock up?
> Two tha ses, and three there is
>   Au'll lea'n thee to la'ke at Inkum.

In an extensive survey of 'Buck Buck' published in the Irish folklore
journal *Béaloideas* in 1942, Paul Brewster demonstrated the truly international nature of the game, and his study was supplemented by further
material in the Opies' *Children's Games in Street and Playground* (1969).
Their findings revealed that the word-stem *bok* or *buc* occurs in versions
of the games recorded in German, Swedish, Dutch, Swiss, Danish,
Norwegian and other languages.

Just how old the game ultimately might be is hinted at in the following
passage from *The Satyricon* of Petronius Arbiter, written about AD 65:

> Trimalchio, not to seem moved by the loss, kissed the boy and bade him
> get on his back. Without delay the boy climbed on horseback on him, and
> slapped him on the shoulders with his hand, laughing and calling out 'Bucca,
> bucca, quot sunt hic?'

Neither Brewster nor the Opies go so far as to claim the actual survival
of the game in Britain since Roman times, but the astonishing similarity
not only of the game's actions but also the words 'buck' and 'bucca' certainly
argue for a direct link of some form or other. Perhaps the game was
imported, presumably from the Continent, at some point in its history,
or possibly even newly planted here by someone translating directly from

the ancient literature. The earliest reference to it in this country is in the late seventeenth century, and it is not fully described until its appearance in *Nancy Cock's Pretty Song Book* (*c.*1781, but the Opies believe first printed *c.*1744). But it certainly existed in other parts of Europe well before this, and is clearly illustrated in Pieter Bruegel's *Children's Games* (1560).

'Buck Buck' occasionally gets confused with the game 'Hi Jimmie Knacker' (see p. 74), because both involve one player on another's back. In practice they were in fact occasionally combined. A localised version, played in a very similar way, was 'Husky-bum, Finger or Thumb', which the Opies found was widely known in the North and Midlands of England, but not, apparently, elsewhere. Here, the choice declared by the rider was on the lines of 'Finger, thumb or rusty bum?', the latter being a fist, or 'Stick, roger or dodger', which was the thumb pointing up, sideways, or down. Again, there were sometimes several boys bending down in a line as in 'Hi Jimmie Knacker'.

Continuing the theme of guessing what is going on behind a player's back, 'Hot Cockles' was another very widespread game, commoner in the home or at Christmas parties than in the street, and therefore more civilised than 'Buck Buck', although still with some scope for a little violence.

The standard form was for one player to be blindfolded and to lay his or her head in another's lap. This was already the style when someone wrote a description in Francis Willughby's *Book of Games* manuscript in the 1660s:

> Handie Back or Hockcockles is when one stoopes downe and lays his head in anothers lap, that hoodwinks him, and his hand spread upon his breech, which one of the rest strikes with the palme of his hand as hard as hee can. If hee can tel who struck him, hee is free & hee that struck must ly downe. But if hee mistake & name a wrong person, hee must ly downe againe, & so till hee guesses right.

A fourteenth-century illustration published by Joseph Strutt in his *Sports and Pastimes of England* (1801) shows the game in progress. It is first mentioned by name in Britain in 1549, and appears regularly in literary sources for the next 300 years or so. The scope for flirtation inherent in these party games is neatly portrayed in John Gay's *The Shepherd's Week* (1714):

> As at Hot-cockles once I laid me down
> And felt the weighty hand of many a clown

> Buxoma gave a gentle tap, and I
> Quick rose, and read soft mischief in her eye.

As with 'Buck Buck', there are close parallels in the ancient world, and it seems that the idea of guessing who touched a player's back has been around for a very long time. The Opies identify an ancient Greek game called 'Kollabismos' and a picture on the wall of a tomb at Beni Hassen, c.2000 BC, which shows 'a player on his knees while two others, unseen by him, thump or pretend to thump his back with their fists'. They go on to suggest that the passage in the Bible, where the guards blindfold Christ, smite him with the palms of their hands and say, 'Prophesy unto us, thou Christ, who is he that smote thee?' may even be a reference to this game (Matthew 26:67–8; Mark 14:65; Luke 22:64).

Today there are still various games around in which one player has to guess what activity is going on behind his or her back or even what is being traced on the back with a finger. In the 1960s, for example, the Opies described a game called 'Stroke the Baby', in which one child strokes another's back and challenges him or her to identify the hand or finger used.

> Strokey back, strokey back
>   Which hand will you tak'
> Be you right or be you wrong
>   Which hand stroked you?

Snakes and (particularly these days) spiders also crop up. Jim Duerdin, for example, who grew up on Tyneside in the 1960s, explained that the procedure described by the Opies was added to a counting-out rhyme, the idea being to determine how the count (which would give the others a chance to get away) would proceed. First of all the rhyme would be recited to select which child should do the counting; then that child would turn round and another child would trace a snake on their back, poke them and say:

> I draw a snake upon your back
> Which finger progged it?

The counter then had to guess which finger had been used for the 'progging' or poking. Sometimes the choice was one hand, sometimes two. If he or she was right with their first guess the count would go up in fifteens; if the second guess was correct, tens; if the correct answer came with the third guess, fifteens, and so on. The whole thing would then be repeated to determine how many the count should go up to – with each guess counting as 100.

Iona and Peter Opie's 1969 survey devotes several pages to this procedure, as they found it so widespread in the 1950s and 1960s as a prelude to hide-and-seek games. Some of their examples were more complex, but were still concerned with setting the conditions of the game to follow. So, for example, the child whose back was drawn on had to guess who did the poking, but before being told whether the answer was correct had to set a task (e.g. 'run round that car five times'). If he or she was right, the person who poked must undertake the task and then be 'it', but if the answer was incorrect, he or she had to do the task while the others ran off to hide. This uncertainty dictates a nice judgement on how arduous the task should be.

Nowadays a modern version of the snake-on-back procedure more often involves a spider and is part of a hybrid game. It starts with clapping, then goes into 'Rock, Paper, Scissors', then the creature on the back, and finally the winner ritually beats the loser's forearm as a punishment. Versions of this game seem widely known, and in recent enquiries (2009), similar examples came in quick succession from North and South London, Essex, Devon and Cambridgeshire. Here it is as recorded recently in South London:

> Tick tack toe
> Give me a high give me a low
> Give me a three in a row
> Polly got shot by a UFO

Then you do 'Rock, Paper, Scissors'. Then you do the thing where whoever wins, the other person turns round and you go:

> Little spider up your back
> Which two fingers did that

And they have to guess which fingers did that. And then if they get it wrong you go:

> Ha ha, you lose
> You got the biggest bruise

And you hit their arm like this.   *BALHAM, SOUTH LONDON, 2009*

A couple of variants come from the children at Robert Arkenstall School, Haddenham, Cambridgeshire. Instead of a spider on the back, they say:

> Little finger on your head
> Which finger wet the bed

And if the person guesses correctly:

> You win, that's fair
> Now I get to pull your hair

The 'spider on the back' can also be a game in its own right. Ella from North London demonstrated the following on her friend Cherry's back in December 2009, reciting in an urgently dramatic voice:

> Spiders crawling up your back [*fingers crawling upwards*]
> Getting ready to attack
> Bite! Bite! [*pinch hard on both shoulders*]
> Blood trickling down your back [*fingers crawling downward*]
> Bite! Bite!
> Blood trickling down your back
> Spiders crawling up your back
> Getting ready to attack
> Bite! Bite!
> Blood trickling down your back
> Tight squeeze [*squeeze back of neck*]
> Cool breeze [*blow on neck*]
> Now you've got the shiveries.

This was a particularly fine performance, but similar procedures are known, often in shorter versions, from Devon to the Orkneys, and often starting with drawing lines and dots on the person's back:

> Dot dot line line
> Spiders crawling up your spine
> Cold breeze
> Tight squeeze
> Now you've got the shiveries.

ORKNEY, 2004

Line line
Dot to dot
Curly wurly
Electric shock [*tickle waist*].

DEVON, 2010

Surprisingly, the game has been around for at least twenty-five years. Compare this piece from the *Australian Children's Folklore Newsletter* of November 1984:

10 nails in your back
Blood running down your back [*fingers on upper back*]
Spiders running up your arm
Spiders running down your arm [*fingers creeping on forearm*]
Feel a little breeze [*blow*]
Feel a little squeeze [*pinch*]
Now feel the chill [*spoken very mysteriously*]

5 upper primary girls lying on towels at a pool, Ashburton, Melbourne, January 1984. Girls sat on each other's backs to chant this, whilst doing actions on the back of the girl lying down. Intonation very important for dramatic qualities. Game became a mass of rolling, giggling bodies as excitement rose to a pitch.

In the USA, versions without the blood and the scary voices are very common in preschools and nurseries, very often starting with the well-known phrase 'Criss cross apple sauce'.

CHAPTER EIGHT

Party and Parlour Games

Games historians often distinguish between different types of game by the context in which they are usually found, such as party or parlour games, as opposed to playground ones. But children can always be relied upon to cut across carefully constructed adult categories, and will adopt any activity for playground use that takes their fancy. So it happens that a game like 'Blindman's Buff', a long-time staple of the party-game repertoire, also makes a regular appearance in the playground, even though it works best in a relatively confined space. It is one of those games that always seem to be on the decline but everyone still knows, and it pops up again when it is least expected.

The game is simple: one person is blindfolded and he or she then has to catch one of the other players, who usually dance around the 'blindman', tempting and teasing and pushing each other into his or her reach. Usually the person caught immediately becomes the new blindman, but in some versions they must first be identified. Identification is more difficult than it sounds if the players have taken the precaution to swap clothes, hairbands, and so on.

It seems that everyone has always known the game. It is mentioned by generations of writers, including William Shakespeare, Oliver Goldsmith, John Gay, William Blake and Charles Dickens, from the 1560s onwards and more times than any other similar game. Samuel Pepys refers to it in his diary entry for 26 December 1664:

> Then to my office to enter my day's work; and so home to bed, where my people and wife innocently at cards, very merry. And I to bed, leaving them to their sport and blindman's buff.

He recorded the next day that the merrymakers did not go to bed till four in the morning. Note that the date of Pepys's entry is Boxing Day – the game has long been a particular favourite at Christmas parties.

Earlier names for the game were 'Blind Hob' and 'Hood-man Blind', and the latter reminds us that the original way of 'blinding' someone was to turn their hood back to front. A fourteenth-century illustration in the Bodleian manuscript copy of the *Romance of Alexander* shows this clearly, and also shows another element of the game that has now been lost: the use of knotted hoods or scarves by the other players to 'buffet' the poor blindman. This resulted in a potentially much rougher game but, paradoxically, improved it. To flick someone with your hood you need to get in closer, which gives the blindman more of a chance to catch you, or to grab your hood.

It also perhaps explains the name of the Roman game from which 'Blindman's Buff' probably descended, 'The Brazen Fly': one can imagine the players buzzing around and 'stinging' like bothersome insects. It is interesting to note that the game is still amenable to variation. When three ten-year-old girls in West London were describing their games in 2009, they mentioned 'Marco Polo' and said that it is like 'Blindman's Buff' but that when the person gets confused they call out 'Marco' and the others have to answer, 'Polo'.

A very different escapee from the parlour and youth group meeting is 'Wink Murder', which is extremely popular with current junior schoolchildren. Indeed, it has been mentioned by nearly every group of children interviewed in the past three years. The players sit in a circle; one is chosen to be the detective, and goes out of the room, or is temporarily isolated from the group. Another is chosen to be the murderer. The detective comes back and stands in the middle of the circle. The murderer kills people by winking at them. They have to die, although not necessarily immediately; in some versions their death must be audible, but in others silent. The detective must work out who the murderer is, and accuse him or her of the crime.

The name changes a little, from group to group: 'Wink Murderer', 'Blink Murder', and so on. In Gateshead it is called, rather abruptly, 'Drop Dead'.

The same format has been adopted for other games where one player must identify another as a result of actions carried out. So, for example, the same children in Gateshead described their game of 'Dance Inspector':

All stand in a circle, except one who is the 'Dance Inspector' who stands apart while the others secretly choose one of their number to be the leader. The leader starts dance movements, which all the others must follow. The inspector returns and stands in the circle, and has to guess who the leader is.   GATESHEAD, 2010

Another very popular nursery and birthday party game for younger children is 'Musical Statues', in which the players have to stand perfectly still the moment the music stops. 'Statues' is also a popular game in the playground, and its basic principle has been introduced into several other games. Some modern clapping rhymes (p. 296), for example, end with the word 'freeze', and 'Stuck in the Mud' (p. 20) is also sometimes called 'Statues'. 'Grandmother's Footsteps' (p. 90) is also clearly related:

> 'Statues' was another group game. The crowd would go to one side of the street and after being counted out the last one would go to the other side of the street. He or she would face the wall for a second or two, then turn round and everyone would stand stock still, like statues, in all kinds of attitudes. They would be trying to reach the other side of the road without him seeing them move. If someone was seen to move that one would go to the other side of the street and the rest would go back and start again. Both boys and girls played this game.   DEVON, 1920S

If the turning-round element is not present, there has to be some mechanism to let everyone know when to stop moving, and sometimes this is simply supplied by a leader who randomly shouts, 'Freeze!' But there is another popular variant, usually called something like 'Flinging Statues' or 'Flying Statues', in which a leader spins each player round in turn and suddenly lets go. They must then hold the position into which they are 'flung'. Once all the players have been thus dealt with, the leader chooses the best one.

In another variant, particularly popular in the past, each player is given a choice – 'Bread, honey or wedding cake?', 'Egg, bacon or chips?', and so on. Although the words vary considerably, they all mean 'fast, slow or medium' or 'hard, soft or medium'. This game was well known in the early twentieth century, as indicated by descriptions like the following, from Norman Douglas's *London Street Games* (1916), but it does not seem to have been recorded before that time:

> There are 'Ugly statues' and 'Pretty statues'. When you play this game you have to line yourselves up against a wall or a house; then the judge comes along and pulls one of you forwards and in that moment you have to make

a posture and a face, sometimes pretty but mostly ugly, and pretend to be a statue. It spoils everything if you laugh over this game.

An old feature of many parlour and party games dating from Victorian and Edwardian times is that the players must remain serious, despite the ridiculous words or antics of those whose task it is to make them laugh or smile. Some of these games have lived on at parties, and in youth organisation meetings, but they can also be found on occasion in the playground. The children of Okehampton Primary School, in Devon, for example, told me of 'Sausages' or 'Granny's Knickers':

> You have someone sat in the middle, and everybody round the edge, and you have to ask them a question. All the person is allowed to do is answer, 'Sausages', or in 'Granny's Knickers' it would be 'Granny's knickers', and if they laugh or smile they're out, and they'd swap, and the idea is to try and make the person in the middle laugh. I remember we used to do really rude ones we used to get ashamed to do – really funny stuff.

They also have 'Gobbledegook', played between two people, 'and we have to speak in our own language without laughing or smiling'.

There are several games like this in the party-game repertoire. Cecily Rutley's *Games for Children* (1928), for example, has a whole chapter on them. Probably the best known nowadays is 'Poor Pussy', in which one player must miaow and behave like a cat, and the others take it in turns to stroke the cat and say, without laughing or smiling, 'Poor Pussy' three times. By far the best known in Victorian times, on the other hand, was 'Buff', which dates from the 1830s at the latest. One child approaches the others, holding a stick, and involves each of the players in turn in the following dialogue:

(1) [*Thumping the floor with a stick*] Knock, knock!
(2) Who's there?
(1) Buff
(2) What says Buff?
(1) Buff says Buff to all his men
 And I say Buff to you again
(2) Methinks Buff smiles
(1) Buff neither laughs nor smiles
 But looks in your face
 With a comical grace
 And delivers the staff to you again.

Anyone who fails to remain serious is then compelled to pay a forfeit.

One whole area of parlour games – those involving fires – has, not surprisingly, disappeared altogether, but it is worth mentioning briefly because it nicely demonstrates how, while many games develop over time, perhaps turning into new ones, some inevitably vanish completely as society, domestic arrangements – and attitudes to personal safety – change.

In earlier times it was not unusual for people to gaze into a fire and tell stories of the castles and dragons' lairs they could see in the flames. And there were many other innocent pleasures, too:

> When sitting round the fire, on a winter evening, it used to amuse us to throw pieces of paper therein, and then watch the bright sparks race across the ashes. We used to call them 'Folks leaving church', and the names of local characters were given to them as the peculiarity of motion suggested.
>
> *EAST YORKSHIRE, 1880S*

But there was also a range of games, involving burning sticks, that would make a modern parent's hair turn white. John Jamieson's *Etymological Dictionary of the Scottish Language* (1808) defines a 'Dingledousie', for example, as 'a stick ignited at one end; foolishly given as a plaything to a child'.

The most commonly reported fireside game involved all the players in turn holding a burning stick. The basic game, often called 'Robin's Alive' or 'Jack's Alive', was also played as a parlour game, as described in S. O. Addy's *Glossary of Words Used in the Neighbourhood of Sheffield* (1888):

> Jack's Alive: A number of people sit in a row, or on chairs round a parlour. A lighted wooden spill or taper is handed to the first, who says:
>
> > Jack's alive, and likely to live
> > If he dies in your hand you've a forfeit to give.
>
> The one in whose hand the light expires has to pay a forfeit. As the spill is getting burnt out, the lines are said very quickly as everybody is anxious not to have to pay the forfeit.

It was also played by children. In Galloway in about 1824 it was 'Robin' who needed to be kept alive:

> Robbin-a-Ree: A game of the ingle-nuik . . . in passing the brunt-stick round the ring, the following rhyme is said:

Robin-a-Ree, ye'll no dee wi' me
Tho' I birl ye roun' a three-times and three
O Robbin-a-ree, O Robin-a-ree
O dinna let Robin-a-Reerie dee.

In other versions the players actually fought with the burning sticks, as here in the Isle of Man game called 'Doagan', or 'Firebrand':

In this game each player has a stick the point of which has been reddened in the fire. Each combatant whirls his stick about to keep it burning while at the same time he endeavours to knock the burning head off the stick of his opponent. [saying in Manx] Here's the *Doagan* for you. What did the firebrand say? By the cross, by the mark, by the little straight stick, and a bend in the other little [one] over yonder, if you will put the head off the firebrand I'll put your head off for it.

Another name for the game in Scotland was 'The Priest's Cat'.

A seemingly more innocent rhyme reported in Charlotte Burne's *Shropshire Folk-Lore* (1883) probably refers to the traditional forfeits associated with this game:

Children wave a burning stick in the air, saying:

A girdle o' gold, a saddle o' silk
A horse for me as white as milk.

Forfeits, incidentally, are recorded in one of the earliest descriptions of the game, which appears in Francis Willughby's *Book of Games*, a manuscript compiled in the 1660s:

Robin Alive: One of the boys holds a stick in his hand that is a little fired at one end and swinging it about in the air says, 'Robin Alive and alives like to be, if it dies in your hand your back shall be saddled and bridled and sent to the King's Hall with a huf, puf and all.' Or sometimes he says, 'Your back shall be saddled and a pack put upon it.' Then he gives it to his next fellow who repeating the same words gives it to a third &c., till it hath gone through them all and about again till the fire go out. He in whose hand the fire doth go out in must be saddled, that is must stoop down and lay his head in one of his fellow's laps, who hoodwinks him as in Hockcockles [see p. 107]. Another holds any thing as cushions, chairs, tongs &c., asking him,

'What hold I over you?' If he guess right, he is free and another fire stick must be carried about as before, but if he guess false and cannot tell what is held over him it must be laid upon his back, and something else must be held over him till he do guess right. When they lay things upon his back they used to say, 'Lie there till more comes', or 'Lie there tongs'.

The 'saddling' routine lasted well into the nineteenth century, probably because the game became associated with Christmas festivities. A remarkably similar description to Willughby's appeared in Eliza Leslie's *American Girl's Book* of 1831.

It is hard to imagine many parents now allowing their children to wave lighted sticks around. That said, 'Jack's Alive' did manage to survive well into the twentieth century. The following account shows that it was alive and well in the repertoire of Scout troops in the late 1920s:

Players in a circle, leader in centre has a cork which he holds in the middle of a candle till it is smouldering; the leader then passes the cork to one of the players who blows on it and passes it on saying 'Jack's alive'. The player in whose hand the cork stops smouldering is suitably decorated by the leader drawing with burnt cork on his face.

CHAPTER NINE

Hand Games

Many apparently inconsequential children's games involve the manipulation of hands or arms – for example the 'Hand Pile Game' (my title). As played by two people it involves one person laying their hand palm-down on the table; the second player then places one hand on top; the first player places their other hand on top; the second player does likewise. Now that a pile of four hands has been made, the first player removes their hand from the bottom and places it on top of the pile, the second one follows suit, and this continues as each bottom hand is removed and put on top. The game gradually speeds up and usually ends in a mad scramble of slapping hands. When played with more than two players it can be even more hectic.

It is such a common and unremarkable game that most people would hardly give it a second thought. Yet it turns out to be at least 200 years old – and by late Victorian times it was, according to Alice Gomme, 'a well-known game for small children in London' – and to have acquired some interesting names. On the Isle of Man it was called 'Bassag' or 'Badhag', from the Manx *bass*, the palm. In Forfar it was 'Neivies'. In Galloway in 1824 it was known as 'Dish-a-Loof', which John MacTaggart explains was quite a rough game:

A singular rustic amusement. One lays his hand down on a table; another clashes his upon it; a third his on that, and so on. When all the players have done this, the one who has his hand on the board pulls it out, and lays it on the one uppermost: they all follow again in rotation, and so a continual clashing or dashing is kept up; hence the name 'dish'. Those who win the game are those who stand out the longest, viz. those who are best at enduring pain. Tender hands could not stand it a moment; one dash of a rustic loof would make the blood spurt from the top of every finger.

A more developed version, entitled 'Bread and Cheese', is printed in *American Girl's Book* (1831) by Eliza Leslie. Two girls place their hands in the pile as usual, starting with the right hand, but then a dialogue takes place. The one on the bottom says, 'What have you there?'; the other replies, 'Bread and cheese.' 'Eat it up,' says the first; the second one removes her left hand and puts it to her mouth, pretending to eat. They repeat the sequence the other way round. They do it a third time, so that only the first player's right hand remains, but closed, rather than flat. The second player then starts the following dialogue:

> What have you there?
>   A chest.
> What is in it?
>   Bread and cheese.
> Where is my share?
>   The cat has got it.
> Where is the cat?
>   In the woods.
> Where are the woods?
>   Fire has burned them.
> Where is the fire?
>   Water has quenched it.
> Where is the water?
>   The ox has drunk it.
> Where is the ox?
>   The butcher has killed him.
> Where is the butcher?
> Behind the door cracking nuts; and whoever speaks the first word shall have three twitches by the ear, and three squeezes by the hand.

They then compete to see who can remain silent the longest, and whoever speaks first has their ear tweaked and their hand squeezed.

When I was talking about the 'Hand Pile Game' with children in the Robert Arkenstall School Council in Haddenham, Cambridgeshire, in December 2009, one girl demonstrated a version in which fists are used instead of flat hands. She accompanied this with the well-known rhyme *One Potato, Two Potato*, which was formerly a very popular counting-out rhyme (see p. 348). Whoever's fist is on the top when the rhyme reaches the last word, 'more', she explained, wins the game. Children from other schools have since confirmed that the fists version is widely known, and that the *One Potato* rhyme survives much more in the context of this game these days than in the counting-out repertoire. The use of fists in the pile was recorded in Victorian times by G. F. Northall in his *English Folk-Rhymes* (1892). He also printed the rhyme that accompanied the actions:

> Here's one hammer on the block
> My men, my men
> There's one hammer etc., My man John
> Dibble the can, blow, bellows, blow
> Fire away, lads, for an hour or so.

Another hand game that seems so instinctive as to be scarcely worthy of note is hiding one or more items in a closed hand, and asking someone to guess which hand is holding the object or how many objects are involved. Again, this is a game that turns out to have a venerable history, and it is also a game that was once rather more elaborate, involving rhymes and rules which today we have largely forgotten.

The best known was 'Handy Dandy', which existed in numerous versions, such as these three contributed to *Notes & Queries* in 1883:

> Handy dandy
> Sugary candy
> High, Jack, or low?
>
> SOUTH-EAST CORNWALL

> Handy Andy
> Picardy pandy
> Which hand will you have?
>
> NORTH LINCOLNSHIRE

> Handy spandy, Jack-a-dandy
> Loved plum-cake and sugar candy.
>
> SUSSEX

The phrase 'Handy dandy' was proverbial for centuries for an either/or choice, or for the sleight of hand involved in switching a concealed item from one hand to another. The fourteenth-century poem *Piers Plowman* includes it, as does Ben Jonson's play *Bartholomew Fair* (1614), among many other literary works. Perhaps the best-known example comes in Shakespeare's *King Lear* (Act 4, Scene 6):

> See how yon justice rails upon yon simple thief. Hark, in thine ear; change places; and handy-dandy, which is the justice, which is the thief?

In the North of England, Scotland and Ireland, where 'neif' or 'neive' means a fist, there was a very different rhyme with a similar purpose:

> Nievie, nievie nack
> Whether hand wilta tak?
> Under or aboon
> For a singul hauf-croon?
>
> NORTH YORKSHIRE, 1883

> Nievie nievie nick-nack
> Whilk hand will ye tak'?
> Tak' the richt or tak' the wrang
> I'll beguile ye if I can.
>
> FIFE, C.1900

'Nievie Nievie Nack' may well be as old as 'Handy Dandy', as it is mentioned in one of Alexander Montgomerie's poems of around 1585.

There seems almost no end to variations to the simple hand game. In Ireland in the late nineteenth century, for example:

> It was a favourite amusement for children to collect pins at Christmas time, to use as stakes, the game being played by spinning a tee-totum, or by guessing. This is a rhyme that was used in guessing. One of the players took a pin and placing his hands behind his back concealed the pin in one of them, then holding out his hands in front, the other player points with his finger to the other's hands as each word is repeated:

> Pippety, poppety play me a pin
> Open the door and let me in
> Let me lose or let me win
> This is the hand the pin lies in.

If the hand that he pointed to when saying the last word of the rhyme held the pin, the rhymer won it – if not he paid a pin as forfeit. Where this game was too slow for sporting characters, there was a quicker way of winning or losing pins. One player concealed a number of pins in his hand and said:

> Peep at the bush
> I'll break your smush, was the reply
> How many times?

If the number given was correct, the guesser won, if not an equal number was forfeited.

In Galloway in the 1820s the game was called 'Headim and Corsim', and the purpose was to guess which way the pins lay in the hand. As John MacTaggart, the compiler of the *Gallovidian Encyclopedia* (1824), commented of this game:

This is the king of all the games at the *preens* [pins], and let it not be thought that it is a bairn's play; by no means; it is played by lads and lasses as big as ever they will be and by those whom age has again made young; the game is simple and harmless, and not uninteresting.

Another example, from East Yorkshire, in the 1880s:

A quieter indoor game with marbles is called 'Eggs in a bush'. A boy takes a number of marbles and shakes them in his hands, asking, 'How many eggs in a bush?' The one who guesses must pay the difference between the number he says and the actual number, afterwards taking his turn at shaking and asking; but, if he guess correctly, all are his. A similar game is 'Odds and evens', a few being held in one hand, which is kept closed. If odds be guessed, and there are evens, the guesser gives one; but if odds be guessed, and there be odds, then they become the property of the guesser.

D. Parry-Jones's *Welsh Children's Games and Pastimes* (1964) reports similar hand games in Wales. The following rhymes were used when guessing how many items were held:

> Bwch mewn llwyn ['A buck in the bush']
> Dorrws I drwyn ['Broke his nose']
> Sawl gwaith? ['How many times?']
>
> Dyma'r hawl ['This is the question']
> Twrch Penllwyn ['The buck of Penllwyn']

Tor dy drwyn ['Break your nose']
Sawl gwaith? ['How many times?']

Another rhyme, used for the pin game, goes:

Pi – pa – po – pin
Yn hwn ma'r pin ['In this is the pin']

Lastly, in a game played in Forfar called 'Straik the Buttonie', which is in some ways akin to 'Queenie, Queenie, Who's Got the Ball?', the following rhyme is recited:

Hey the button, ho the button
Guess you fa [= who] has the button.

The players stand in line with their hands together as if praying, and one of them conceals a button in his or her hands. The seeker must guess who is holding the button, and may stroke their hands in the process.

Hands can also be used to do battle, and several traditional methods are in circulation. 'Thumb Wars', for example, seems to be found in every part of the country. Two opponents both crook all four fingers of one hand and link them, with thumbs raised. The idea is to trap your opponent's thumb and hold it down for a prescribed time – usually four seconds. One widely known routine is to get into position, then declaim, 'One, two, three, four, I declare a thumb war', and then start the wrestling. Once one is trapped, some say, 'Four, three, two, one, I am the strongest one', while others say 'Five, six, seven, eight, try to keep your thumb straight'.

Thumb-wrestling hit the big time in media terms in 2006, with the launch in the USA of the *Thumb Wrestling Federation* television cartoon series, with associated spin-off games and other merchandising. But it is difficult to assess how old the game is. It was certainly known by teenagers in Britain in 1992, and was mentioned in *Time Magazine* on 16 July 1973 as if it were already an old game.

In the past, children (mostly boys) could be seen testing their pain thresholds with a game called 'Knuckles', 'Knucklies' or something similar:

Two boys stand facing each other, with their right fists together, knuckle to knuckle. Player 1 quickly raises his hand and brings his knuckles down hard on his opponent's hand. Player 2, however, can withdraw his hand as soon as Player 1 makes his move, but he must not retract *before* Player 1 moves, and Player 1 can feint several times before delivering the blow. Whether he is successful or not, the turn now passes to Player 2, and they continue, alternating, until one or other has had enough.

In this version, as played in the 1950s, at least you had a chance of escaping some of the blows, but in *Children's Games in Street and Playground* (1969) the Opies describe a game in which the players simply take it in turns to 'knuckle' each other, with the one on the receiving end not being allowed to move at all. The game thus becomes one of endurance rather than of skill or dexterity.

'Knuckles' has been around for over 100 years at least. C. H. Rolph, writing about his childhood in London, about 1910, observes:

> [This game] transferred the endurance test from the conker to the bare knuckles, each boy taking turns to hit the other's closed fist with his own. I never saw any boy endure this for long, but I've heard that in sterner times the little idiots would bash all the skin of their knuckles rather than give in.

And Florence McDowell confirms its existence in Antrim, about 1905:

> You and your friend could each make a fist and try to knock the knuckles off one another. This game was, credibly, called Hardiknuckles.

In the research for this present book, all children were asked if they knew the game, and the vast majority did not. Significantly, the ones who did recognise the description said they had learnt it from their dad, so it seems that the game is now largely a thing of the past.

But another way of inflicting pain on each other's hands is very much alive, and usually goes by the name 'Slaps':

> One particular two-person game involved putting your hands together as though in prayer and holding them tip to tip with the other child's hands. You had to try to slap the other's hands; they had to anticipate and move their hands away in time. If they flinched when you weren't actually about to try and hit them, then you could slap their wrist – the first child to have a reddened wrist lost. *CAMBRIDGESHIRE, 1960S*

The rules are very similar everywhere, although the punishment for premature removal varies a little:

If the slappee manages to get clear before being slapped he then becomes
the slapper. One complication is bluffing. If the slappee twitches and makes
the slappee pull his hands away unnecessarily three times, the slapper is
entitled to hold the slappee's hand still while he slaps it once really hard.

COVENTRY, 1960S/1970S

The collector of the Coventry example, Cathy Gould, admits to having
invented the terms 'slapper' and 'slappee' to explain what was going on.
    Also from Cathy's collection of Coventry lore is 'Peanuts':

Two players hold their hands up, grasp each other's hands with interlocked
fingers. The aim of the game is to either twist your opponent's hands down
or push their fingers back until they surrender by calling out, 'Peanuts!' It
is seen as a game of strength and there are no turns, both players 'going for
it' at the same time.

Again, this game is widely known and still commonly played. Children in
Gateshead recently confirmed that 'peanuts' was the surrender word in
their version of the game, but in many other places the victim has to cry
'Mercy mercy' before he or she is released.
    Another hand contest described by members of the Robert Arkenstall
School Council, in Haddenham, Cambridgeshire, in 2009, appears to have
no name. Two opponents clasp their own hands, with fingers interlinked,
but thumbs up and index fingers extended and pointing forwards. They
take it in turn, using their extended fingers, to bash their opponent's fingers
and attempt to break them apart. If one succeeds, the victim must then
extend middle fingers instead of index fingers, and so on, down to the
little fingers. Exactly the same game was collected by Gareth Whitaker in
Denholme Primary School, Yorkshire, in 2002, again with no name.
    Not so much a contest, nor a real test of endurance, is a set of procedures
particularly popular with girls nowadays, in which a story is told and
someone's forearm marked:

Along come the crabs
   Pinch pinch pinch
Along come the elephants
   Boom boom boom
Along come the snakes
   Sssssss
Along come the horses

> *Gallop gallop gallop*
> Along come the tigers
> *Scratch scratch scratch*
> And they all make the red carpet for the Queen.
>
> NORTH LONDON, 2009

This bears some clear resemblance to the finger and hand games that children play on others' backs (see p. 105).

Hands and arms have also inspired a genre of visual jokes. One simple but effective performance which is quite widely known is 'Bob' or 'Freddy'. The first version is from Kate and Joanna (aged eleven and twelve), of Weybridge, Surrey, talking in 2009:

> Write 'THIS' on the back of your fingers, between the knuckles, one letter per finger. Draw the figure of a person on the palm of one hand. Draw a red scribble or smudge on the palm of the other hand.

> This is [*show knuckles*]
> Bob [*show palm horizontally*]
> Bob says hi [*show palm vertically*]
> Clap for Bob [*clap hands*]
> Bob's dead! [*show other palm*]

The above was said slowly and deliberately, in a slightly declamatory style, although this may simply have been for the interviewer's benefit. But for the more complex second version below, the collector Cathy Gould noted, 'When this was demonstrated to me, it was done really quickly allowing for good rhythm and rhyme.'

As above, in this version the children write 'THIS' on the knuckles of one hand, and draw a spider on one palm, and a mess on the other. They then say the following:

> This [*show 'THIS'*]
> is [*cover the TH to show 'IS'*]
> Freddy [*show spider*]
> Say Hi! [*cover the T & S to show 'HI'*]
> Freddy jump! [*raise hand showing spider*]
> Freddy fly! [*sweep hand across, above the head*]
> Freddy splat! [*bring hand down and slap other palm*]
> Freddy die! [*show other palm to audience, showing the messy smudge*]

And one more, from Rochester, in Kent:

Write 'THIS' on fingers. Show all fingers when saying 'This'; bend down the TH fingers to show 'is'; bend down the T and S for 'hi':

> This is Buggy
> Buggy says hi
> Buggy jump
> Buggy fly
> Buggy splat
> Buggy die
> Bye bye Buggy.

Rough Play

It is noticeable that children, especially boys, indulge in a great deal of physical horseplay in their everyday dealings with each other, and that between friends and equals it is a normal part of play, although the same behaviour in other contexts constitutes bullying and victim-isation. All schools are aware of bullying as a potential problem, and take active steps to prevent it, and in the modern playground there is markedly less physical roughness and fighting than there was a few generations ago.

But 'rough' play is still of great interest to anyone studying playground lore, because many of these activities are just as 'traditional' as any skip-ping rhyme, being passed on from child to child, and from generation to generation, by informal methods. Tradition is not always benign or pretty.

Probably the most commonly reported form of minor physical attack in the twentieth century was the 'Chinese burn', to accomplish which you hold a person's wrist with your two hands, then turn your hands sharply in opposite directions. This seems to have been extremely well known in the post-war years all over the country, and was definitely around as early as the 1930s. Many informants comment that it was mainly done by boys, but it was also known to most girls, even if actually done more rarely, or gently, by them.

It is interesting to note that everyone interviewed or contacted on the subject called the procedure a 'Chinese burn', or occasionally 'Chinese torture', except for one person who reported that in Sheffield in the 1950s it was known as an 'Indian burn' (the name by which it is generally known in the USA). The procedure certainly survives among modern children, but judging by the fact that many nowadays do not know of it, it would be safe to say that it is far less widespread than before and, possibly, gradually dying out.

A 'chicken burn' is different, as recorded by Cathy Gould, from Coventry in the early 1970s:

> The wet sleeve of a jumper rubbed vigorously against someone else's skin on the back of the wrist until red raw or even bleeding. If you pull away or ask for it to stop, you are 'chicken'.

'Chicken scratching' was similar – scratch someone with your nails or a ruler (or let them scratch you) until that part of the body is red raw and the victim gives up.

There is a wide range of other ad hoc attack procedures which can be carried out at any time, often without premeditation. 'Dead legs' have been widely known for at least fifty years, involve a sharp blow to the outside of a person's thigh (usually administered by the knee), which hurts a great deal and incapacitates the leg for a while. A similar effect, called a 'dead arm', can be achieved with a sharp rap of the knuckles on the upper arm muscle. Other procedures involve making someone trip over when walking by coming up behind them and as they raise one foot in the air tapping it sideways with your own foot so that it catches behind their other one; making a stationary person crumple by pushing sharply, with your foot or knee, behind their knee; and, if two people are standing talking, crouching down behind one of them so that the other, seeing you there, can easily push them over you. A practice reported from a boys' school in Ipswich in the late 1970s was called 'nipple cripple': the perpetrator grabbed the victim's nipple between his knuckles and twisted sharply. Girls seem to favour bending fingers back, sometimes as a punishment or simple attack, but at other times to test someone's truthfulness or fortitude.

An example of the longevity of tradition is provided by the following two reports, almost 100 years apart:

> In Warwickshire and Staffordshire they torture an unfortunate victim by throwing him on the ground, and falling atop of him, yelling out 'Bags to the mill'. This summons calls up other lads, and they add their weight.

> 'Pile On', when you pushed someone over and lay on top of them, and yelled 'Pile On!' to everyone else – which they did.   GRIMSBY, 1980S

Reports from Victorian and Edwardian times tend to reveal much more complex, structured procedures, which are perhaps more worthy to be designated 'games' than most modern ones. The following, certainly too visible to be tolerated these days, was recorded by Richard Church in his autobiography, as it took place in South London, about 1905:

> A game popular with the bigger and heavier boys, who formed themselves by joining hands into a living lasso, which hurled itself across the concrete playground and wrapped itself round the small, shrinking fauna of the lower standards, throwing them to the ground and dragging them to a corner, where they were released with velocity against the wall, to whimper there, and ruefully staunch the blood flowing from grazed knees, elbows, or noses, and to wonder what would be said at home about their own garments.

This is not very different from a violent game played by boys in Hull in the 1950s:

> Another playground favourite in the 1950s was crossing hands 'bell-oss' fashion and marching up and down the playground chanting, 'Anybody in the road gets a good kick', repeated for as long as the game lasts, by kicking anybody who doesn't get out of the way smartish. Bell-osses was just as violent. Three boys cross hands to form a linked line of three and charge about the playground knocking into people.

Indiscriminate violence like this was quite commonplace in playgrounds in the past, as in the following example from Cricklewood, North-west London, in the late 1970s:

> A perennial favourite was to line up with arms around each other's shoulders, usually starting with around three or four boys with more joining us, and march around the playground kicking anyone in our way. The chant was:
>
> > We won the war, in nineteen-sixty-four,
> > Guess what we done, we kicked them up the bum.
>
> The kick being administered on the beat directly after 'bum'.

The *We Won the War* rhyme was certainly widespread at the time, but only sometimes involved the kicking motif. A further two examples from the past reveal similar motifs in different guises. The first is from northern England in the 1860s:

> When a 'Cobbing match' was called, all the boys rushed forward and seized the unfortunate of the match by the hair, repeating these lines:
>
>> All manner of men, under threescore and ten
>> Who don't come to this cobbing match
>> Shall be cobbed over and over again
>> By the high, by the low, by the wings of the crow
>> Salt-fish, regnum, buck or a doe?

> I spare you the details of the tortures named salt-fish and regnum; buck was a rap on the skull with the closed hand – doe a tug at the hair, dragging out many a lock. Those who bore no part in cobbing the victim were liable to be cobbed themselves; so were those who were so unlucky as not to be able to touch the hair of the victim or who while repeating the verse neglected the proscribed rites, i.e. the standing on one leg, closing one eye, elevating the left thumb, and concealing the teeth.

The second from East Yorkshire in the 1880s:

> Should a boy be detected in cheating, or in committing an offence against the boys' unwritten law, the discoverer would cry 'Ringlins! Up!' when all within hearing would rush up, and seizing the unfortunate culprit by the hair, lug (tug, pull) right merrily, until the leader cried, 'off'. During the time of the punishment, each one must hum, and he who did not pull hard enough, or who did too much by not ceasing when the signal was given, was treated to the same; and so the fun ran on, until all had been 'ringled', or the players had grown tired.

Indeed, hair and ears seem to have been particularly popular targets. A common twentieth-century procedure, which went by various local names (e.g. 'scrubs', 'nuggies'), was to grab a boy in a headlock, with his head trapped under your arm, and with your free hand to run your knuckles roughly over the top of his head. A 'crow's nest' involved a spider-like hand on somebody else's scalp. Another procedure, from Hull in the 1950s, could only be done in the right season:

> A particularly nasty trick which was called 'Chinese torture' involved taking a stem of grass I know the species now to be called 'Timothy'. You strip the

flowerhead, which resembles a thick fluffy tail, and the stripped end of the grass is then inserted into the victim's hair and the stem spun as if winding spaghetti. The result is that the hair becomes entangled in the fine barbs left on the grass stem. The stem is then pulled until either grass or hair gives way. Nasty stuff.

As for ears, they seem to be crying out for assault:

> I was evacuated to Wales with my secondary school in 1939 and we had a time in the early forties when ear clipping, either as a losers forfeit or for no reason at all, became popular. The clip was usually administered from behind the victim, with an open hand, swung in a short, sharp horizontal movement, so that the tips of the stiffened fingers made slicing contact with the top of the ear. The lawfully recognised clip touched only the rim of flesh, never the head and never any lower part of the ear. Once the technique was perfected (simply a matter of regular practice) you could end up with a classroom full of boys nursing red and painful, but generally harmless, swellings.

In Mansfield, Nottinghamshire, in the 1950s, ear flicking from behind was called 'tabbing', and in modern Coventry a 'cauliflower ear' is when you creep up behind someone, grab their ear and pull and twist it. In the same city, boys indulge in 'wet willies', which involves wetting your finger, sticking it in someone's ear and twisting it around.

A key time for licensed attacks by all and sundry on an individual is their birthday. For much of the twentieth century it was customary to give people 'the bumps' on this day, in schools, youth organisations and many other places. For many people, 'the bumps' is so common as to need no further comment, but as the custom is rapidly going out of fashion, and future generations may well not know what it was, it is as well to attempt a description.

The perpetrators lay the victim flat, hold his or her wrists and ankles, and raise and lower their arms in unison so that the victim's body flies up and down. One lift is given for each year of age, and 'one for luck'. If done carefully and properly, the lifters do not let go when the victim's body is high in the air, nor do they allow it to hit the floor on its descent. But done badly, it is very painful and dangerous to the person's back. In more recent times someone was often detailed to kneel down and support the victim's back as it approached the floor.

Another old custom, very similar to 'the bumps' but not restricted to birthdays, was tossing in a blanket, which involved placing somebody on a blanket and literally throwing him or her in the air by people holding each corner. Again, it could be done relatively gently or very roughly, and it was one of the favourite tricks that older public schoolboys played on the younger ones. A letter from Augustus Hare, a pupil at Harrow, on 21 January 1847, for example, related the following incident:

> A boy met me at the door, ushered me in, and told me to make my salaam to the Emperor of Morocco, who was sitting cross-legged in the middle of a large counterpane, surrounded by twenty or more boys as his serving-men. I was directed to sit down by the Emperor, and in the same way. He made me sing and then jumped off the counterpane, as he said, to get me some cake. Instantly all the boys seized the counterpane and tossed away. Up to the ceiling I went, and down again, but they had no mercy, and it was up and down, head over heels, topsy turvy, till someone called out 'satis' – and I was let out, very sick and giddy at first, but soon all right again.

And even 'the bumps' had antecedents. Edward Moor, who was at school in the 1770s, included a definition of the word 'bump' in his *Suffolk Words and Phrases* (1823):

> The punishment of a school-boy for telling tales or for any act of treachery, coming immediately under the summary jurisdiction of his peers, is 'bumping'; and this is performed by prostrating the coatless culprit on his back, in the immediate vicinity of a large block of wood, or of a wall. A strong boy seizes the right ankle and wrist, another the left, and lift him off the ground; and after a preparatory vibration or two to give a due momentum, he comes in violent contact with the block, *a posteriori*. This is repeated six or eight more times, according to the enormity of the offence, or the just resentment of the executioners.

This is exactly the same as one of the treatments often meted out to youngsters on the annual 'beating' of the parish boundaries. Boys were 'bumped' on boundary stones as a way of ensuring that they remembered where they were. Newcomers and strangers were also treated in the same way, for fun.

Returning to birthdays, a more recent tradition comprises birthday 'beats' or 'digs'. Childlore collector Cathy Gould described the situation in Coventry in 2004. There had previously been a relatively harmless birthday ritual whereby you got thumped on the arm as many times as the years celebrated, i.e. fourteen on your fourteenth birthday, but this had escalated:

> If you are spotted on your birthday and someone shouts 'Birthday beats!' anyone around feels allowed to join in and basically beat you up. Boys are consistently pushed to the ground, kicked and punched. Boys try to keep their birthdays secret and if it gets out are sometimes removed from lessons to protect them.

The boy who told her this was hiding from attack at the time, and was really annoyed that a girl he knew who shared his birthday and who was walking round with an 'I am fourteen' balloon was only receiving cards, presents and good wishes. Cathy discovered, however, that girls did get 'birthday digs' on their arms, but in a much more controlled way. Another treatment favoured by girls was to pull the hair of the person with the birthday, one pull for each year.

The theme of thumping on the arm also features in another game reported by Cathy Gould, called 'Sixes and Saves', played by schoolchildren of Coventry and Solihull in the 1970s. This was usually part of a consenting game, however, and so, although unpleasant, did not involve really hard thumps.

To get 'sixes' or 'sixes on yer' was to be thumped six times, usually on the upper arm. Sixes were given for various reasons, for example saying, 'What', or 'Marrow', or passing wind. 'Marrow was a joke,' Cathy Gould was told, 'as no one was likely to say it in conversation so you had to be tricked in some way to say it, or would say it on purpose to provoke a chase or as a dare.'

Saying 'Saves' quickly after the offending act (and before anyone has time to call 'Sixes!') saves you from being hit. Two girls remembered having whole conversations using phrases like 'What, saves, are you doing tonight?' 'I don't know. What, saves, do you fancy doing?' and so on. At one school it became the habit to say 'Saves' in an over-acted, satisfied manner after farting. After 'Sixes' had been called you had certain comeback chances. Calling 'Bouncebacks!' or 'Returns!', quickly, allowed you to return any sixes given. 'Sixes, no bouncebacks!' or 'Sixes, no returns!' used as the original call stopped these retaliations.

Even packs of cards could be involved in games of physical violence:

> A very popular game at the secondary school in Beverley where I worked in the 1980s and 1990s was played with a pack of cards. It involved dealing

out the pack to all present and then swapping cards and discarding sets and pairs and whoever ended up with the Queen of Hearts (I think it was), had to endure the dealer holding the whole pack in his tight fist hitting the loser hard so many times on the back of the hand, just above the knuckles, with the edge of the pack. The result was quite painful and temporarily stopped the blood flow to the veins and made them swell. Obviously it was a daredevil game, and was eventually banned when discovered.

There are also various word games that end in some form of pain. Adults find them silly and say, 'But surely they would only work once.' Children, however, never seem to tire of them. For example, one child will say to another:

> Adam and Eve and Pinch-me
> Went down to the river to bathe
> Adam and Eve got drowned
> Who do you think was saved?

The other child quickly discovers that the answer also seems to be an instruction.

The Opies include a number of different versions in their *Lore and Language of Schoolchildren* (1959) that are either clever extensions on the same pattern, or weak attempts to disguise the rhyme. Thus the protagonists become 'Pinch-me, Punch-me and Treadonmytoes', 'James and John and Little Nippon', or 'The cock, the hen, and the pullet'. The basic rhyme was already in circulation in the 1850s, and there are similar versions in several European traditions.

One of many similar tricks is to say to someone, 'Punch and Judy had a race. Judy came last. Who won?' And when they answer 'Punch', you punch them.

The catalogue of physical attacks, games and tricks is apparently endless. Here is another example:

'Smell my cheese': when a child would hold out his hand, with his other fist on the wrist, and invite another child to 'smell my cheese' – when the child put his nose to it, he would get punched on the nose.

Flicking someone's tie up was also common and irritating trick, which could be done casually or as part of a 'joke':

'What does the Queen Mary do when she comes into dock? Ties up and drops anchor', and you flick their tie up and stamp on their foot.

Presumably this is going out of fashion now that fewer school uniforms include ties. In any case, who now knows what the *Queen Mary* is?

Short-rope skipping, 2010

Long-rope skipping, 1939

Tops, 1906

Buck and Gobs, 1880s

Long-rope skipping, 1946

Conkers, 1970s

PART THREE

Games with Things

Marbles, 1948

Two-balls, 1948

Marbles, 2010

Marbles, 1906

CHAPTER TEN

From Ancient to Modern

The facility with which children can make games and home-made toys out of just about anything that comes their way is legendary. Back in the 1950s, for example, a great favourite in my playground was 'Lolly Sticks'. It was played by two contestants, each armed with an old-fashioned wooden lolly stick (there was one brand – a Mivvi? – which had a compressed cardboard stick and was therefore useless in a games context). Player 2 held his stick at each end, about 20 to 30cm in front of him. Player 1 held his stick between his thumb and the middle knuckle of his crooked middle finger, with his index finger extended along its edge. He then took a whack at the middle of player 2's stick, trying to break it. If he was unsuccessful, the roles were reversed, and they alternated until one of the sticks was broken in two. The winning stick took on a number, as in conkers. We were quite happy to pick up discarded lolly sticks in the street or out of bins.

A decade earlier, Sunderland children were using lolly sticks to play a game that is now produced commercially. A generous supply of lolly sticks would be dropped from a height of approximately two feet, landing in an unruly heap. Each player then had to dislodge a lolly stick without moving others. If by accident he or she disturbed another stick, then the next player would take over and the game would continue until all sticks were removed.

Games with lolly sticks belong to a clearly identifiable era and are probably even now a thing of the past, but games with other found objects such as string and stones still form part of children's activities and often have quite a lengthy history to them. The well-known cooperative string game 'Cat's Cradle', for example, retains its popularity, though it tends to be one of those crazes that comes and goes and is often learnt from books. It has been around for something like 300 years, the earliest reference being in Abraham Tucker's *The Light of Nature Pursued* (1768), where the author describes it very much as it is today:

> An ingenious play they call cat's cradle, one ties the two ends of a pack-thread together, and then winds it about his fingers, another with both hands takes it off perhaps in the shape of a gridiron, the first takes it from him again in another form, and so on alternately changing the packthread into a multitude of figures whose names I forget, it being so many years since I played at it myself.

Tucker was born in 1705, so if he is referring to his own childhood, it must take the game back to the early eighteenth century. Similar games are known almost all over the world, and it is usually assumed that our version was imported from Asia. It has been suggested that the name 'Cat's Cradle' is a corruption of 'Cratch Cradle', 'cratch' being an old word for a manger – but this seems unlikely: after all, many small things in colloquial English are designated 'Cat's . . .'.

A hundred or so years later, Alice Gomme in her *Traditional Games* (1894) included eight figures, from her own direct knowledge: 1. Cradle; 2. Soldier's bed; 3. Candles; 4. The cradle inverted, or manger; 5. Soldier's bed again, or diamonds; 6. Diamonds, or cat's eyes; 7. Fish in dish; 8. Cradle as at first. Moor's *Suffolk Words and Phrases* (1823), for its part, included: 1. Cat's cradle; 2. Barn-doors; 3. Bowling green; 4. Hour-glass; 5. Pound; 6. Net; 7. Diamonds; 8. Fish pond; 9. Fiddle.

Skimming stones across a flat stretch of water is an even older pastime, though whether this really dates back to the Stone Age, as some claim, is no more than guesswork. It seems such an instinctive activity that we rarely give it a second thought, but the following nineteenth-century account shows that it once had its own terminology:

> 'Ducks and Drakes': A boyish pastime, played by casting stones on to the surface of a still piece of water, slantingly, that they may dip and emerge several times. If once, it is a 'duck', if twice, 'a duck an a drake', if thrice, 'a duck an a drake an a fie'penny cake', four times is 'a duck an a drake an a fie'penny cake an a penny to pay the baker'. If more than four, 'a duck', 'a duck an a drake', etc., are added. These distinctions are iterated quickly to correspond in time, as nearly as may be, with the dips of the stone. A flat-tish stone is evidently the best for this sport. From this pastime, which

however dull in description, is animating and not to be despised – has probably arisen the application of the term to a spendthrift – of whose
approaching ruin we should thus speak – 'Ah! he 'av made fine ducks and
drakes of a's money, that 'a have.' As much as to say he has cast his means
upon the water; or to the winds.   SUFFOLK, 1820S

In Wales about 1905 the game was called '*Torri Cwt y Gath*' ('Cutting the
Cat's Tail') or '*Ceiliog a Giar*' ('Cock and Hen'). The sequence the children recited went, '*Dic, dac, do, deryn ar y to*' ('dick, dack, doh, a bird on
the roof').

Today the colourful terminology has gone. Instead, every now and then
an article appears in the press about scientific studies on what makes a
throw successful. The diagrams and mathematical formulae reveal what
most of us know already: that it is the angle at which the stone hits the
water that determines how efficient the skim will be. Researchers at
the University of Marseille (reported in the *Guardian*, 1 January 2004), for
example, discovered that:

> an angle of about 20 degrees between the stone and the water's surface is
> optimal with respect to the throwing conditions and yields the maximum
> possible number of bounces.

Sadly, they do not reveal how to programme one's arm to achieve the
correct angle. In the USA, where the accepted terms seem to be 'stone-
skipping' or 'gerplunking', there are websites devoted to the game, and, of
course, world championships. At the time of writing, the official world
record is held by Russ Byars, from Franklin, Pennsylvania, who in July
2007 achieved fifty-one 'skips' with one throw.

Until the Second World War another very popular game with stones
was called 'Duckstone'. This involved throwing, racing and tagging, and
was clearly widely played, mostly by boys, all over the country back to at
least the turn of the nineteenth century. An account from Wales gives a
description of the basic game, as played in the early twentieth century:

> *Ali Bwl Dab, Bwl Rag* or *Y Bwl a'r Dab*, to give a few of the names by which
> this game went . . . All that was needed was a big stone with a fairly flat top,
> placed so as to stand rigidly, with plenty of room behind it. About eight or
> ten yards away, a line was drawn as a catch, at which the throwers took their
> stand. Any number of lads could join in and each one provided himself
> with a stone – the *bwl* – about the size of a handball, a round one if possible,

and if one was near a river-bed or sea-shore, one could obtain them in abundance. The first thing to do was to choose one to 'go in', who then put his own stone on the *dab*, standing as near it as he dared in order to snatch at every opportunity that came his way once the game started. The others now took their stand on the catch and threw their stones (*bwls*) at his *bwl* on the *dab*, each in his turn; if they failed to dislodge it, each ran to take his stand by his *bwl*, now well beyond the *dab*. If, however, one succeeded in doing so, the boy by the *dab* had to retrieve it as quickly as he could and replace it on the *dab*. While he was doing this, the boys standing by their stones picked them up and ran back to the catch as fast as they could, endeavouring to avoid, as they did so, being touched by the lad who was the guardian of the *dab*, for, having replaced his stone, he was free to engage in that further task – he could not try and catch anyone unless his stone was on the *dab*. The one he did manage to touch, automatically went in, put his stone on the *dab* and the game started all over again. It was rather a dangerous game unless marksmanship was of a fairly high order. Many readers will recognise the game as a variation of *Duckstone* or *Duck on a Rock*.

Elsewhere in Britain the game was essentially the same, although the terminology was different, and urban environments also required some alterations. When played in the street, for example, the duck was commonly set up on a brick standing on its end. In another variation the players who had missed, and were standing by their stones, could shuffle them with their feet towards the safety line, as long as they did not touch the stones with their hands. But the essential core rules, which held in almost every version of the game, were that the 'duckman' could not chase the others until his stone was replaced, and the others could not run to safety without their own stones in their hands.

Many of those recalling the game remember it as quite dangerous, because of the stones flying about. It is also interesting to note that as early as 1891 there was an additional concern that children became so engrossed in the game they were at risk from traffic:

In 'Duck', which is the name given to the stone which acts as a target, a hole is scooped in the road, in front of which a stone is placed. The game consists in knocking the duck into a hole from a little distance; but, if the player is unsuccessful, he may have another turn, provided he can pick up his own stone and reach the pavement without being touched by his opponent. During the operation the boy or girl says: 'Gully, gully, all round the hole,

One duck on.' This game, which is principally played in the road, is, however, fraught with some danger to the limbs of the players, who are too intent upon grasping their stones and eluding their pursuers to regard passing vehicles with much attention.   *LONDON, 1891*

Duckstone was by far the commonest name around most of Britain, but it also had other local names, including: 'Huddle-duck' (Wiltshire); 'Knock-down-run-back' (Isle of Man); and 'Ducks Off' (Dorset). It continued to be very popular into the immediate post-war years, but then began to fade away, and it was probably concerns over stone-throwing that contributed most to its decline, together with the fact that it was clearly best suited to older children, who were already beginning to give up playing such games. It was gradually replaced by similar games in which things were still knocked over as a prelude to a chase, but using a ball as the missile. These games went under various names, but 'Cannons' was the most widespread.

One other game whose inherent risks may well have contributed to its demise was 'Splits'. This involved any suitable sharp object that lay to hand, and was very popular in the late 1950s and 1960s. It could not be played in the playground because it required soft ground, but it could be played on the field – when the teachers were not looking. Two players would stand facing each other and would take it in turns to throw a knife, a tent peg, a pair of dividers from a geometry set or some other sharp object into the ground a few inches (no more than twelve) to the side of their opponent's feet – either to their left or their right. The opponent then had to move his nearest foot to the place where the knife was sticking, before picking it up and having his go. The players' feet therefore got further and further apart, until one of them could not stretch any further, or they fell over trying to reach the knife. At any time one player could throw the knife between his opponent's feet and then his opponent would have to turn round and face the other way. The game was certainly played by junior schoolchildren, but more seriously by adolescents. It was mainly a boys' game, but girls sometimes played it themselves, or joined in with the boys. This was particularly popular with boys in the 1960s, when miniskirts were in fashion, which is perhaps the reason why I remember it so well.

There were plenty of tales of people getting a knife through their foot, or losing a toe. These added to the thrill of the game, but I never actually witnessed any accidents. The Opies included the game under the title 'Split the Kipper' in their *Children's Games in Street and Playground* (1969). They revealed that it was still popular at the end of the 1960s and, perhaps surprisingly, that my generation was probably among the first to play the game.

Other children played to slightly different rules, but the principle was always the same. In some places it was called 'Knifie', and this was also the name of a much older game, which was particularly well known in Scotland:

> As for 'Knifey', I'm pretty certain this was never as traditional or as old as bools and conkers. I know we played it for several years, but I've a feeling it came from *The Wizard* or *The Rover* or another of the other avidly read boys' papers of the day. Knifey was played with a sheath or penknife. You stuck the tip in the ground then flicked it with your open hand. The knife had to do a complete turn and stick in the ground again. Then you did two turns and three and more.   FIFE, 1940S

The immediate source for that writer's knowledge may have been a boys' comic, but the game had been around for about 400 years before that. In the version described by James Ritchie in his *Golden City* (1965), the player had to flick the knife – in turn – off the back of the hand, back of any finger, the point of a raised toe, a raised knee, the edge of a hip, the end of an elbow, chin and eyebrow (with head tilted back), and in each case it had to stick into the ground.

Items specially manufactured for the playground are as subject to the vagaries of fashion as 'found' objects. Perhaps the classic example is 'Battledore and Shuttlecock'. Now virtually forgotten (although badminton is its direct descendant), it was once a hugely popular game that brought with it a host of other traditions.

Writing about her childhood in Derbyshire in the 1880s, Alison Uttley remembered the pleasures of the game:

> Battledore and shuttlecock came into season at pancake-time. It was an exciting day to drive down to our village to buy oranges and also to get half a dozen shuttlecocks and two wooden battledores. Shuttlecocks were lovely things with red and blue feathers, which I thought came from exotic birds, or our white feathers from hens, and the cork end was bound with gold tinsel. All the girls took their shuttlecocks to school, for it was a feminine game. The air was filled with the flock of these bright birds flying up and down, and the sound of tap-tapping of the battledores echoed through the playground. It was an indoor game too, and I had a special house battle-dore, made of double parchment like a shallow drum, with red morocco

handle and edges, trimmed with gold braid, which I used in the parlour. Hardly had the shuttlecock season begun than it was over. The winds were too strong, the feathered cocks were carried up to the roofs where they lay in the launders, and the game was done.

The game was played by adults as well as children, and was so prevalent in the nineteenth century that Shrove Tuesday was in many places known as Shuttlecock Day.

One interesting feature of the game is that in children's hands it developed a divinatory aspect, on similar lines to many other activities that have a counting element (see p. 462). Trying to keep the shuttlecock in the air as long as possible, children would chant:

> Shuttlecock, shuttlecock, tell me true
> How many years have I to go through?
> One, two, three . . .

At Wakefield, Yorkshire, in the 1870s, they had a whole series of sequences to determine their marriage prospects:

> This year, next year, long time, never
> Monday, Tuesday . . .
> Tinker, tailor . . .
> Silk, satin, cotton, rags
> Conch, carriage, wheelbarrow, donkey-cart.

Shuttlecock had a long and prestigious history. The earliest evidence is pictorial, a fourteenth-century illustration of the game, redrawn and published by Joseph Strutt in his *Sports and Pastimes* (1801), while the first recorded mention of the word is found in John Skelton's *Why Not to Court* (1522): 'I trow all wyll be nought, Nat worth a shyttel cocke.' Other references from the sixteenth and seventeenth centuries show that the game was already linked with Shrovetide, and that shuttlecock was already being used figuratively for something tossed lightly back and forth. The game was particularly popular at the highest levels of society. John Manningham, Attorney of the Middle Temple in London, for example, recorded in his diary for February 1602/3 that 'The play at shuttlecocke is become soe much in request at Court that the making shuttelcocks is almost growne to a trade in London.'

The game seems to have gradually lost its popularity as the twentieth century progressed, and finally left our playgrounds sometime after the Second World War. Plastic shuttlecocks sometimes find their way into the school equipment cupboard – a rather faded reminder of the game's former glory.

HOOPS

Shuttlecocks are not the only objects to have largely disappeared from view. When Women's Institute members and their husbands were asked to write about their childhoods in the 1920s and 1930s for the *Within Living Memory* series of books, the toys they mentioned particularly frequently were hoops and tops. Neither means anything to contemporary children. Until relatively recently, though, both enjoyed astonishing popularity.

Each autumn, hoops came in: the game involved a lot of running, and this was a great way of keeping warm. They came in various sizes, but there was definitely a feeling of 'bigger is best'. Status could be acquired by possessing a large hoop, and everyone desperately tried to avoid being seen with one 'too small' for them.

It was also one of those areas of play that had a sharp distinction between boys and girls. Boys had iron hoops and girls wooden ones, and the demarcation was apparently quite strictly enforced. Some girls professed to dislike boys' hoops, and complained about the awful noise they made on cobblestones; others envied them for the very same reason (many older adults recalling their childhoods remember the *sound* of the hoop with particular pleasure). The way hoops were controlled also differed according to gender. Girls always had a stout wooden stick, but boys could opt for a metal hook or ring, mounted on the stick, which greatly altered the way the hoop could be handled, and certainly increased the noise factor by several degrees.

Hoops could be bought at the local shop, but in rural areas they were often made by the local blacksmith or cooper, and these craftsmen also stepped in when hoops broke or got bent out of shape. Children's author Alison Uttley, growing up in Derbyshire in the 1880s, usually bought hers:

> One day, without any warning, a boy would come to school trundling an iron hoop, and the sound of the iron handle hissing as it rubbed against the hoop was sweet to our ears. It was an autumn game, it kept us warm with running, and the winds could not spoil it. My last year's hoop was lifted from the high wooden peg on the whitewashed wall of the barn where

it hung among the scythes, flails, and old harness. It was cobwebbed, and I scrubbed it at the horse-trough. It was slightly oblate, it would do for home, but I couldn't appear at school with a crooked hoop. So down to the village I drove with my father the next Saturday morning, to visit the wonderful shop which sold everything from Browning's poems and Scott's novels to penny dolls and lucky-bags, from newspapers to valentines and masks. There, hanging from the ceiling, were white wooden hoops for girls and iron hoops for boys. The wooden hoops were of many sizes, and I chose one nearly as tall as myself, with a smooth short stick to beat it.

D. Parry-Jones, growing up in Carmarthenshire about twenty years later, similarly remembered the annual trip to the local forge:

Hoops were one of the few things we did not make ourselves but, all the same, we saw them made. When their season arrived, we would receive father's permission to call on Sam, the blacksmith, to ask him to make us one. We had not only the thrill of ordering a hoop, but the pleasure of watching it in the making. Our eyes followed Sam as he selected one of the long slender iron rods from a stock that he had got in in readiness. Having measured it and cut off the right length, he began hammering it on one of the angles of the anvil, and as he did so we could see the curve gradually growing until, in the end, the two ends met in a circle. They were then put in the fire until they were red-hot and finally hammered together in one round piece, and lo! our hoop was made. But there was one thing yet to come, and that was to put it in a tub of cold water, where it sizzled and threw up a cloud of steam. It was left there while he fashioned the hook or bowly. Then, taking the hoop out of the tub, giving it here and there a few taps on the anvil, he threw it into motion towards the door – in this manner did we always receive our hoops. Off we went after it and out through the door, happy as boys have always been from the days of Ancient Greece, following a hoop.

In his autobiography, *A Small Child in the Sixties* (1927), set in Farnham, Surrey, George Sturt commented how lucky he was to be the son of a wheelwright and to be allowed to ask his father's workers to make him a hoop.

Much of the pleasure of playing with a hoop was simply gained by running alongside, keeping it going and guiding it with skilful application of the stick or skimmer. This could be done alone or in groups. The journey to and from school was a particularly good time for long-distance hoop-running. But in other versions of the basic game hoops featured in more imaginative ways – in races and obstacle courses, for example, or bowling a smaller hoop through another while it was moving. And there were 'fights', where two or more hoops were bowled at each other in an attempt to knock the others over. You could even make sparks fly from your iron hoop on suitably stony ground. Girls also often used their hoops for skipping.

Several memoir-writers comment that girls were often more skilful than the boys at hoop control, primarily because they had more patience and practised more. Wilfrid Tapp commented that in his time in Thornton, Yorkshire, in the 1890s, 'Girls kept their hoops until they were into their teens, but it was considered "cissy" for a boy to bowl a hoop after he was seven or eight.'

Above all, a hoop was a living companion. George Sturt wrote:

A good hoop-stick of course was useful for guiding the hoop too; could be used as a brake; and was in short the only tool with which a self-respecting boy could be seen 'trolling' a hoop. I despised the boys who 'scaled' their hoops, with iron hooks. The milksops! And what freedom could an unhappy hoop enjoy (and hoops were live things) held in with a hook in its driver's hand? A hoop in front of a hoop-stick would bound and run – run away from you, down a hill if you were not a good driver. And there was a way of tossing it forwards so that it seemed to scamper back behind you – oh it was fine to be a boy with a hoop!

And Alison Uttley:

A hoop was the best of toys, except a cricket-bat, for it was a friend and a companion. It ran very fast, it leapt down fields and I leapt too. It was filled with vitality and imaginative power. It was a personage, with a character and a life of its own, and I could share that life. I never felt lonely when I had my hoop with me, to accompany me running through lanes and down pastures, in wind and rain, in sunshine and by the light of the evening star.

TOPS

Adults writing in the second half of the twentieth century of their pre-war childhood days tend to recall tops with as much affection as hoops, and there is an extensive literature about them that stretches back even further in time. Here is Alison Uttley on the subject:

A well-spun top emitted a hum like a contented bee, lovely to hear. The tops 'went to sleep', spinning so quickly they seemed to be motionless, and they could be lifted by a good spinner, even taken up in a spoon to spin there. When they rolled over and fell on their sides they were said to be dead. To walk down the village road in top time was as difficult as to walk on ice. Tops flew under one's feet, whips curled around ankles, and little boys looked baleful when somebody touched a long-spinning top and made it die. Drivers kept a watchful eye, for the tops dashed out like wild things under the horses' hooves and boys ran after them. *DERBYSHIRE, 1880S*

There is a noticeable difference in tone between women's and men's memories of tops. Like Alison Uttley, women often focus on what might be called the 'gentle art' of top-spinning; they record colouring the tops with chalks or pieces of paper to make pretty patterns, and the pleasures of watching tops spinning. Men, on the other hand, remember the competitive games, and the danger to life and limb involved. Indeed, so many of them mention windows being broken that one begins to suspect such tales are largely apocryphal, although such accidents definitely did take place on occasion, and some styles of top were indeed called 'window-breakers'.

As with all games that both sexes played, the boys were desperate to avoid being accused of behaving in a girlish way. It was not just making sure that you had the right sort of top; you also had to make sure you played the game in the 'right' way. Don Haworth, describing his Lancashire childhood in the early 1930s, recalls:

For boys tops was a craze of limited duration which needed to be strictly observed to avoid the double contempt of playing a game which was out of season and, being out of season, a girl's game. Having limited practice, we never rivalled the skill of girls who could drive a top the length of the street pavement and back. We tried to cut a dash by buying 'window-breakers' tops which were not conical in section but T-shaped.

And George Sturt, writing ruefully in later life of his inability to really master the game:

But then, the little peg-tops called French tops (I had one, painted green) would always spin all right, thrown 'underhand'; but I was ashamed to be so 'girlish'. None the less, the proper 'manly' throw from the shoulder downwards (and that was the only way to damage somebody else's top) could never be achieved. *FARNHAM, SURREY, 1860S*

A later account gives some idea of the physical difference between boys'
and girls' tops:

> Boys always had peg tops, which had a tendency to fly through the air if
> not struck properly. Most of us had whips made of a piece of wood and
> string, but a lucky few, which did not include me, had leather whips, often
> made of bootlaces from a working man's boots. Girls' tops were different
> from the peg tops we had. Ours were about an inch and a half high up to
> a spread out top, giving them the impression of a tall mushroom. They
> came in many colours, although dark green or brown seemed to predom-
> inate. Those used by the girls were far bigger round and almost the same
> thickness all the way up. They were far more stable than the peg tops with
> their tendency to fly through the air if hit incorrectly.   SUSSEX, 1920S

There go the windows again.

There were numerous games involving tops, but most were variations
on a few basic patterns. One was to draw a circle, in which marbles, fivestones, buttons or other small items were placed, the idea being to push
these items out of the circle with your top. Another was to create a similar
circle, set a top spinning in it, and then throw in other tops to knock the
first one, or each other, out. Yet another game involved two teams whipping their tops towards opposite goals. And then there were one-to-one
duels:

> Another way in which tops were played was what we called 'Top Fights' and
> was usually only played by older and bigger boys. In principle, this was
> simple. Two boys started spinning their tops and then took it in turns to
> try and knock the other top out with theirs. Soon turns became forgotten
> in a frenzy of whipping tops in the direction of your opponent and then
> arguments as to who knocked who over, particularly if they both fell down.
>   SUSSEX, 1920S

One of the most important skills to learn was to catch or pick up a
spinning top on the palm of your hand or other implement, so that it
could be placed or thrown elsewhere as part of the game:

> 'Chip'ems' – This was played with a piece of cord, a long-pegged top and
> a crown cap from a beer-bottle. The best tops were made from creamy-
> coloured boxwood, hard as stone and called 'boxers'. We threw the top
> spinning into the air and caught it on the palm of our hand, and while it

was still spinning chipped it down on to the metal cap, whizzing it along the ground. We played in partners, each chipping the bottle top in opposite directions.   LONDON, 1920S

There were different styles of tops, including many home-made varieties, and therefore different ways of getting them started and keeping them going, as described in C. H. Rolph's highly detailed memories of Edwardian London:

The spinning tops were of two kinds, the 'throwdown' and the 'whipper'. A throwdown was usually a pear-shaped wooden ball with a long metal peg at the small end, the wooden body being grooved to take the folds of string. You bound it up tightly with the cord, held it between forefinger and thumb with the left-over string bunched tightly in the remainder of your fingers; and as you threw it down from shoulder height you jerked the string to give the top an extra twist as its peg struck the ground. Until you were really expert its peg didn't strike the ground at all, and your twisting energy merely sent your top rolling ignominiously and swiftly away on its side, looking ridiculous. As for the whipping top, its control was always a bit of a mystery to me. Nevertheless, it was so much easier than that of a throwdown as to be almost sissy for people over five, though you could condone it in girls of any age and even in mothers and aunts. For one thing, you started it spinning with your two hands, which anybody could do; or, more rarely, and expertly, you bound it up with the string of your whip, balanced it on its peg, steadied it with the forefinger of the non-whipping hand, and then smartly pulled the string away, making it revolve fiercely. The best whipping top was mushroom-shaped, because here the string, being wound round the stalk, had more coils to unfold and spin the top more strongly. Once it was spinning you lashed it along the ground. There was absolutely no skill in this. At each blow the string coiled itself round the top, which tightened the coils by its own motion, and then as you pulled the whip away you gave fresh impetus to the spinning.

One of the main styles of top was called a 'peg-top', the peg being a metal (preferably brass) tack or screw inserted into the lower tip to protect the wood and to give a hard smooth surface on which to spin. When a top was broken 'in combat', the victor claimed the 'peg' of the vanquished top as his prize, and kept it as a trophy. During the season some skilled operators acquired a substantial number.

Like most other children's games that go back a long way, the world of tops is replete with arcane terminology. The types of top, the games and the moves within the games often had local names, which were everyday terms for the participants, but incomprehensible to outsiders. The general word for a top in Scotland, for example, was 'peever'. On Guernsey they were *les piroues*. In Buckinghamshire the tall thin tops were 'carrots' and the short fat ones 'cabbages', and in Suffolk the latter were 'tulbys'. One regular game went by the name of 'Gulley Ulley', while the ring game illustrated in the *Little Penny Pocket Book* (1767) was called 'Peg-farthing'. When a top was happily spinning it seemed to be motionless, and so was said to be 'asleep' – hence the expression 'to sleep like a top'. When it slowed and fell over, it was 'dead'.

There is no doubt that top spinning is older than recorded history. Illustrations of people whipping tops are found in many classical Roman and Greek sources, and actual tops from ancient Egypt, *c.*1250 BC, have survived. In Britain, illustrations of top playing go back to at least the fourteenth century, while one of the earliest descriptions appears in Francis Willughby's manuscript *Book of Games*, compiled in the 1660s. Here, as elsewhere in his book, the writer is clearly interested in the science of top spinning, and includes three rough shield-shaped drawings, with the following commentary:

> Top: The top is a cone or rather a conoide of this figure [gives diagram]. The top or apex . . . is inverted and set perpendicularly upon the ground, & giving the basis or broad end . . . a twirle with their fingers it gets a verticity & makes it run upon the ground. They carry a stick in their hands with a piece of cord or whiteleather tied to the end of it, & with this they follow the top & whip it to keepe it up as long as they can. At [the top] is a brasse naile driven in, to keepe the top from wearing. They must play upon smooth boards, as ice &c. Gigs are little tops made of the tips of hornes.

The literature on tops is highly informative and quite extensive. Alice Gomme includes detailed descriptions of several top games played in Victorian Britain in her *Traditional Games* (1894 and 1898), under the following headings: 'Gully', 'Hoatie', 'Hoges', 'Peg in the Ring', 'Peg-Top', 'Tops', and (in the appendix) 'Chippings'. Iona and Peter Opie present their usual masterly account in *Children's Games with Things* (1997), and D. W. Gould's *The Top: Universal Toy, Enduring Pastime* (1973) includes a worldwide survey of tops and their history. Yet for all the fascination they evoked and for all their erstwhile popularity, tops were already in decline in Britain by the 1950s. By the late 1960s they had disappeared from the playground altogether.

FIVESTONES AND JACKS

Extravagant claims for the age of children's games are easy to make, rarely easy to sustain. But there is abundant evidence that the game of fivestones, or something very similar, was played in Classical Greece and Rome, and probably ancient Egypt as well. The game has undergone major changes over the years, and has been called many things, including 'Astragals', 'Knucklebones' and 'Hucklebones', and a plethora of local names, but the similarities outweigh the differences and we can honestly say that the same game has been played over more than 2,000 years of human history.

In its earliest incarnations, the game was played with natural animal bones or stones. These were later replaced by substitutes, manufactured from a variety of materials, including ivory, bone, ebony, stone, clay or metal. Broadly speaking, the man-made substitutes gradually stylised the natural shapes, and pebbles picked up on the beach evolved into square cubes, while angular bones became metal 'jacks'.

Even without the variety of local names, there is a major problem with terminology. Writers on the subject often use deliberately archaic names, such as 'Astragals' (the Latin name for a bone in the ankle), while ordinary people were calling them 'Dibs' or 'Snobs'. There were also two major branches in the game's development, between the one with just the five playing pieces and the other with an added ball (or marble). Given the complexities of the game's history and terminology, it is as well to start with the period of living memory, and then move back to earlier styles, names and ultimate origins.

When I was a boy in South London in the 1950s there were two distinct games available – fivestones and jacks – the former played by boys and the latter by girls, I thought, but this was apparently not definitively true. Fivestones was played with five small cubes about half-an-inch square, made of clay or chalk, each one a different pastel colour. They were ribbed on four sides, and smooth on top and bottom. Wooden ones were also available, which had stronger colours, but they were too light to be of use in the proper game, and were mainly used as freight on the back of our Dinky lorries.

A set of jacks, however, consisted of five (some girls played with ten) three-dimensional star-shapes consisting of six spikes, each with a bulbous end, and a rubber ball. Although the basic games were very similar, consisting mainly of throwing up, catching and carrying out set procedures on the ground, the rhythm was very different indeed. Jacks players let the ball bounce before catching it, while the fivestone(s) had to be caught on the first fall. I just could not condition myself to the rhythm of jacks – then or now.

My basic game of fivestones consisted of three main parts: (A) Throwing them up, catching them on the back of the hand, then throwing up those caught, and catching them in the palm of the hand; (B) Throwing up one stone (or more) and picking up others before catching it; (C) Throwing up one stone (or more) and doing a variety of set procedures before catching it. There seems to be no generic name for these procedures, so I may as well use the word 'figures', adopted from the dance world. These figures are many and various, and of widely different degrees of difficulty, and they are largely responsible for making the game look incredibly complicated. Each figure is distinct, but they can be put together in any order at will, or as decreed by local custom. No two groups of children, even within the same school, were ever likely to agree totally on their order. A contributor to the *Boy's Own Paper* of 2 July 1881 (see p. 151), called 'Toodles', contributed a list of twenty-nine figures, but this was highly unusual, and most players in my experience only had a repertoire of between six and twelve.

It is worth noting that when you made a mistake and were temporarily 'out', you did not go back to the beginning but on your next turn continued with the figure on which you left off. 'I'm on threesies,' or 'I'm on Nelson's Column,' you would say.

The following sequence gives some idea as to how complex the game could be:

Part A: (1) Hold all five stones in the palm of your hand. (2) Throw them up in the air (not too high or fast), turn your hand over, open your fingers (not very wide) and try to catch all the stones on the back of your hand. If you do not catch any you are out. The stones that do not stay on your hand must be left on the floor. (3) Throw those on your hand up again, and catch them in your hand. If you drop any at this stage you are out. Put aside all the stones you have caught, except one, which you keep in your hand.

Part B: (4) You now have to pick up the stones left on the floor from the first movement, one by one ('onesies'). Throw up the stone that is in your hand, pick up one stone, catch the descending stone. Put the one stone aside. Repeat with each of the stones on the floor. If you drop the thrown-up stone at any time you are out.

(5) Repeat right from the beginning, but this time at point (4) you must pick up two stones at a time ('twosies'). Repeat again for 'threesies', and again for 'foursies'. If there are not enough stones on the floor (e.g. only three when you are on foursies) you must pick up all that are there.

If you are playing the 'sweepsies' rule, you must pick up the right number of stones in one sweep of the hand. If you are playing the 'nudgies' (I am not sure that is the right word) rule, you can gather them together by throwing up the stone, nudge a stone towards another, catch the stone, and so on, as long as you do not drop the thrown-up stone, and when you do pick them up you must make sure you grab the right number all at once.

Some of the figures I remember for Part C are:

Fivesies: Your opponent places the five stones on the back of your hand, in any configuration he or she chooses, and you must throw them up and catch them all in one go – which is quite difficult if they are spaced out.

Name for this movement forgotten: Keep the stones in your hand. So, for example, when picking up one stone at a time, keep it in your hand rather than laying it aside. This makes it progressively more difficult to catch the next stone thrown up.

Nelson's column: Make a tower of four stones. Throw up the fifth one, remove the top stone and catch the thrown stone. Repeat with each of the stones in the tower, without knocking it over.

Bridges: Make an arch with the thumb and forefinger of your left hand. Throw up a stone and nudge another stone towards the arch, Then catch the thrown-up stone. Continue with each stone until it is through the arch.

Crabs: After catching the stones on the back of your hand, pick up any missed stones between your fingers and keep them there while throwing the stones off the back of your hand and catching them.

The terminology of fivestones is second only to that of marbles for local colour and variety. In a brief survey of late nineteenth- and twentieth-century sources, the following names for the game occur, but this list is far from exhaustive and, as will be seen, some areas have more than one word:

Alleygobs: London.
Bobber and Kibs: Cheshire, Lancashire.
Buck and Gobs: London.
Checks/Checkers: Lancashire, Yorkshire, Lincolnshire.

'Knuckle Bones' in 1881

From Capt. A. S. Harrison: I beg to enclose a full description of the game of Knuckle Bones. The game is played with five bones; the stages are:

1. *Beginnings*: The five bones are gathered in the palm of the hand and thrown up, any number being caught on the back of the hand; they are then tossed up again, and caught in the palm. One is selected, thrown into the air, and one at a time the remainder picked up, while the one thrown is in the air. This must be caught and again thrown for the next bone. The bone thrown up is called the 'dab', and must be caught clear, without touching any part of the person but the right hand under all circumstances of the game.

2. *Ones*: The five bones are thrown onto the table, the dab selected is thrown up, and the remainder are taken up, one by one, without touching any other bone.

3. *Twos*: The same again, but two taken up for each throw of the dab.

4. *Threes*: Three picked up, and then one.

5. *Fours*: Four picked up.

In twos, threes, and fours, it is permitted by consent of the adversary to push the selected bones together while the dab is in the air. The touching of any other than the selected bones, or the failure to pick up the proper number, forfeits the turn.

6. *Short spans*: Two bones are placed on the table, each side of the left hand, one pair close to the thumb, the other pair at the tip of the little finger. Each pair must be taken up separately, without any pushing together.

7. *Long spans*: A bone is placed at the extremities of the thumb and little finger, stretched out to the widest. Another pair is put in the same way about six inches farther on the table. These pairs must be taken up without any touching together; any bone misplaced may be put back again *three* times; failure on the third trial forfeits the turn.

8. *Creek mouse*: The five bones are tossed from the palm, and any number caught on the back of the hand; all but one are shaken off; the remainder are then gathered into the palm, without disturbing the one on the back, which is then tossed and caught in the palm, with the others.

9. *Second creek mouse*: The five bones are tossed from the palm, as before, and one is retained on the back. The remainder are taken one between each finger

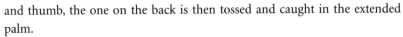

and thumb, the one on the back is then tossed and caught in the extended palm.

10. *Bridges*: The hand is laid on the back on the table, the bones held between the fingers are then dropped in a row on the table. An arch is formed with the first finger and thumb of the left hand at about six inches from the left-hand bone of the four. They are then one by one pushed through this bridge; when all are through the left hand is removed, and the four are taken up at one sweep. No touching together is allowed.

11. *Cracks*: The bones are thrown on the table, and the four are picked up one by one; the dab in falling and being caught to make a *distinct crack* on the one picked up.

12. *No cracks*: Same as before, but the dab must be caught without touching the other bone. The slightest sound forfeits the turn.

13. *Exchanges*: The four bones are laid at the corners of a square, a full span on each side. The first bone is picked up from the lower right-hand corner, and at the next throw is exchanged for the one above. This is exchanged for the one at the top left-hand corner, this for the lower left, and that is placed at the point of starting. The bones are then taken up in diagonal pairs.

14. *Everlastings*: The whole of the bones are tossed from the palm, and any number caught on the back. These are tossed from the back and caught in the palm; and any that have fallen in the first toss have to be picked up while the whole of the others are in the air, so that at one moment there may be four dabs and one to pick up. This task, as the name implies, approaches the everlasting.

The game is an excellent one for exercising and developing that perfect sympathy between the eye and the hand which is certain to be of great service in after life.

BOY'S OWN PAPER, *28 MAY 1881*

Contributed by 'Toodles' a few weeks later:

Order of Knucklebones: Practice, ones, twos, threes, fours, creepmouse, chuck-ups, dux 1, dux 2, dux 3, dux 4, clicks, non-clicks, postman's knock, double postman's knock, fingers, inches, spances, short arms, long arms, and triangles; squares, daggers, swords; pockets 1, pockets 2, pockets 3, pockets 4, everlastings.

BOY'S OWN PAPER, *2 JULY 1881*

Chucks/Chuckies: Northumberland, Scotland in general.

Clinks: Cumbria, Northamptonshire.

Dabs/Dabbers: Hertfordshire, Buckinghamshire, London.

Dandies: Wales.

Dibs: Dorset, Northamptonshire (the Opies say this is the most prevalent name in the South of England).

Dids: Warwickshire.

Dobber and Jacks: Lancashire, Derbyshire.

Fivestones: Worcestershire, London, Dorset, Cambridgeshire, Norfolk.

Jackstones: Northamptonshire.

Jinkstones/Jinks: Cambridgeshire, Norfolk, Hertfordshire.

Snobs: Leicestershire, Rutland, Suffolk, Nottinghamshire, Warwickshire.

Historically speaking, 'Checkstones' seems to be the oldest, being mentioned in several sources from the 1580s onwards.

The evidence on the question of whether it was a boys' or girls' game is, to say the least, unusually contradictory. Many writers state categorically that it was played by boys, while others are equally certain it was purely a girls' game, and these statements include both items written from memory and from contemporary accounts, and are from some of our most trusted sources. 'I never saw girls at it,' writes C. H. Rolph in *London Particulars* (1980); 'Dibs was a girls' game,' noted Flora Thompson in *Lark Rise* (1939); 'It was not considered a game for girls,' writes L. C. Tredinnick in *Old Cornwall* (1931–6); 'A girl (never a boy) knelt on the kerbstone,' says Robert Roberts in *Ragged Schooling* (1976), and so on. And to confuse matters more, D. Parry-Jones in *Welsh Children's Games and Pastimes* (1964) comments, 'Though it was really a girls' game, we boys were equally fond of it.'

Unfortunately, the contradictory claims do not divide neatly on geographical or even temporal lines, but in numerical terms the references to girls outweigh those to boys, probably about three to two. Perhaps the answer lies in the similar gender confusion outlined in the discussion of tops (see p. 153): that boys played the game enthusiastically in the season only, while girls played it all year.

As mentioned earlier, the game is ancient, but this statement needs some qualification. The game is certainly documented in ancient Greek and Roman times, and in Britain from the 1580s onwards, but the automatic assumptions that (a) its existence in Britain must therefore stretch back to classical times, and (b) the game has had an unbroken existence here ever since, cannot be tested, and therefore cannot be proved. On the other hand, it is only fair to say that in the considered opinion of Iona and Peter Opie (*Children's Games with Things*, 1997), 'There is probably no country in the world where fivestones is not played.'

One result of the accredited antiquity of the game is that scholars have taken more notice than they usually do of children's activities, and many studies trace its development and describe its features, although not always in helpful detail. In particular, few sources give details of the figures used and how they were played. The following sources are worth noting because they do include this level of detailed information: *Boy's Own Paper* (28 May 1881 and 2 July 1881); Alice Gomme's *Traditional Games* (1894), which includes descriptions under several headings, the one under 'Fivestones' being particularly detailed; the journal *Folk-Lore* 12 (1901), which contains three detailed descriptions, from Derbyshire, Essex and Buckinghamshire; *Old Cornwall* 2:7 (1931–6), which describes the game as played in Cornwall; James T. Ritchie's *Golden City* (1965), which describes the game as played in Edinburgh; and Iona and Peter Opie's *Children's Games with Things* (1997) which gives a general survey.

As with tops, though, enthusiastic adults and a whole body of literature about fivestones have not guaranteed its survival. Many children today are given cloth bags containing a rubber ball and a set of fivestones – usually by nostalgic parents – but few seem to play with them on a regular basis, and even fewer understand the intricacies of the game.

CHAPTER ELEVEN

Skipping

A lison Uttley (1884–1976), best known now for her children's books about characters such as Little Grey Rabbit, was also an excellent chronicler of Victorian country childhood, second only to Flora Thompson and her *Lark Rise to Candleford* (1945). Uttley's *Country Things* (1946) includes a long piece on skipping in her childhood in Derbyshire, from which the following extracts are taken, which gives important information about the state of play at a crucial point in the game's development:

Skipping was a favourite among all the games we played. Every little girl had her own skipping-rope. The poorest children had shabby bits of rope with frayed ends, others had brand new ropes white as snow, with pale-blue or scarlet handles, and small bells jingling there. The handles were picked out in gold and tapered in an elegant way. However, there was no class distinction, and we shared our ropes happily. We carried them wherever we went in the skipping season.

We skipped our way to school along the rough grassy lanes, through the wood and along the sloping field paths. It was a quick way of getting anywhere, it gave wings to our feet. We skipped in the playground with one big rope which the pupil teachers turned, and forty little and big girls in a long procession danced their way through the game 'Keep the pot a-boiling'. First they all ran through the skipping rope without touching it. Then they skipped one, two, and progressively higher numbers, falling out when a mistake was made or when the pot was not kept boiling, so that the rope was never empty.

The best skipping game was Questions and Answers, when the rope became the Oracle of Delphi. First we went through the letters of the alphabet to find the name of the sweetheart. Next –

He loves me, he don't
He'll have me, he won't
He would if he could but he can't.

We went through the list of wedding garments

Silk, satin, muslin, rags

Then followed the journey to the church

Coach, carriage, wheelbarrow, muck-cart

Next the date of marriage

This year, next year, sometime, never.

Then the number of children we should have, and we longed for a great many, but the rope went fast and our children were limited. It ended with 'Salt, mustard, vinegar, pepper!' and with the cry of 'pepper!' the rope was turned so rapidly it whipped the ground and tripped our feet.

There are two basic forms of skipping, which are both described by Uttley: 'short rope' and 'long rope'. Short rope is when a single skipper turns the rope over themself, and long rope is when two people hold the ends of a rope and turn it for others to jump over.

In short rope, apart from speed and endurance, the main features a skipper can introduce are fancy footwork and different ways of swinging the rope:

Young skippers practise a lot by themselves, for they must be able to skip backwards as well as forwards, and in 'crossie' the hands have to be crossed over. To allow the whirling rope to pass, the skipper must have both feet lifted in the air, and afterwards while some may let both feet together touch the ground, a number of players prefer the style of hitting the ground again with either foot alternately. *EDINBURGH, 1960S*

Skipping on one foot is often called 'hopsie'; skipping on each foot alternately is 'climbing the stairs'; and another version of 'crossie' is to cross and uncross the feet rather than the rope.

With a modification to the steps it is possible to move along while skipping, and one aspect of the game that was extremely common in past times but is now rarely seen is the practice of girls skipping on their way to the shops or all the way to and from school. In the fascinating film of Edinburgh street play *The Singing Street* (1951), several sequences show girls travelling down the pavement, often in pairs, side by side, sharing one rope and stepping in perfect unison. The basic action for going somewhere is a running step, but this can be varied with fancier footwork, such as the occasional 'hop hop hop' when the rhyme dictates it, and swinging the rope from side to side and jumping in turns.

Oddly enough, it seems that hoop skipping sometimes preserves the travelling mode:

> We used plastic hoops to do skipping with at times. With the hoops, it was often a 'moving' skipping game, where you would work your way across the playground by skipping with it.   SUSSEX, 1980S

There is also scope for two, or even three, to share the rope, even in the static version:

> In pairs you stand in front of each other and then one person swings the rope normally but the other person will have to jump as well.
>
>   GODÁLMING, 2008

But, both for the spectator and the participant, short-rope skipping is rarely as interesting as what can be achieved with the long rope. By dividing the labour between rope-turners and skippers, and thereby freeing the hands and body of the latter, long rope has far greater possibilities, and a wider variety of movements have become attached to it. Most importantly, there can be any number of skippers, they can undertake a range of movements, and they are free to come and go.

Turning the rope requires a certain amount of strength and skill but is rarely a coveted position, and strategies and rules have been developed to regulate who takes on the role. The simplest method is for a skipper who is 'out' to take the place of an ender and stay there until someone else is out, although sometimes, where there is a rapid turnover, players have several chances. There is usually a tradition of 'first' and 'second' enders, in that the 'first' ender is the one who will become a skipper when the next person is out. When this happens, the second ender becomes the first ender, and so it goes on.

At the beginning of the game, selection is often decided by a normal counting-out procedure (see p. 341), or being the last to say, 'Bagsy no ender' or its equivalent, or simply being the last two to turn up. But some methods are specific to the genre, such as the following, which has echoes of the old fairground gambling game 'Fast and Loose':

One of the girls takes the rope and bending her left arm she coils the rope round her elbow and the palm of her hand, concealing the two ends well. Each child takes a loop and whoever gets the loop nearest the ends are 'on it'.

DUBLIN, 1980s

When the rope-turners and skippers are equal to the task, it is possible, and very effective, for the enders to walk slowly round in a circle, while the skipper gradually turns with them.

Many long-rope games are simply variations on the theme of girls entering, skipping and leaving in a set sequence, and each replacement is often signalled in a rhyme, such as 'When I go out, — comes in'. The idea of continual rotation is also enshrined in the terminology of the game, in phrases such as 'Keep the kettle boiling' or 'Don't leave the rope empty':

> Keep the kettle boiling
> Miss the beat you're out.

SOUTH LONDON, 1960s

Or, as each skipper enters, she pushes out the previous one:

> Down in the meadow
> Where the girls go *push*.

WILTSHIRE, 1978

And in Follow-the-leader games each girl has to replicate in her turn the timing and movements of the first skipper.

One standard pattern for perpetual motion was often called 'Over the Moon', in which the skippers lined up on one side and jumped over the rope one by one, and then back again from the other side:

'Over and Under the moon' was one we played. Two girls held the ends of a long rope and turned it laboriously in a great arc, while the rest of us lined up on one side. As the rope swung towards us we ran through it, one at a time – that was 'under the moon' and easy. From the other side, 'over the moon' was much more difficult. With the rope still turning you had to jump over it just as it touched the ground, and run away quickly or you got tangled in the rope. *WARWICKSHIRE, 1930s*

This was often done in a figure of eight, in which the line of girls went round each of the enders in turn. But they did not always simply run through:

Over the sun and under the moon: Running into the turning rope from either
side and jumping increasing numbers; e.g. run in on the rope with it coming
towards you (under the moon), jump once; run in on the rope with it going
away from you (over the stars), jump once. Then again, jump twice, etc.

MANCHESTER, 1970S

Another obvious advantage of long-rope skipping is that the skippers'
actions are not constrained by the need to hold the rope, so they can turn
around, touch the ground, do fancy steps or even cartwheels, and can interact
freely with each other. One regular basic sequence for two skippers is:

> Back to back
> Face to face
> Shake your partner's hand
> And change your place.

WEST LONDON, 2009/GODALMING, 2008

Two skippers changing places is sometimes the main feature of the game,
a procedure often called 'criss cross' or 'up and down the ladder'; they both
count how many times they can change places before being out. Moving
up and down the rope was already being performed in the 1890s, as shown
by the game described by Alice Gomme in which the skipper has a dialogue
with each ender in turn, beginning with, 'Father give me the key' (see
p. 169).

Many games also include hand or body movements, as dictated by the
rhyme or story being enacted (see *Teddy Bear* on p. 175, for example), and
these can be done by a solo skipper or by several in unison. Some of the
best-known simple skipping rhymes indicate the speed of the rope: *Salt,
Mustard, Vinegar, Pepper*, for example, where 'salt' is slow and 'pepper'
very fast; again, this was already in circulation in Alice Gomme's time in
the 1890s. But other rhymes indicate the height of the rope as well as its
speed:

'High, low, swing, dolly, pepper, hop, choice,' sung again and again until you
made a mistake. The word that was being sung when you made the mistake
dictated what style you had to skip in when you got your next go. 'High'
meant the people turning the rope would hold it up high so it never touched
the ground; 'low' would mean that it was low so you had to crouch as you
skipped; 'swing' would mean they would swing it back and forth rather
than in a full circle; 'dolly' would require you to skip with your thumb in

your mouth while turning round; 'pepper' meant fast (no time for little preparatory jumps between your rope jumps); 'hop' meant you had to hop; and 'choice' meant you could choose one of the options. *WALES, 1970S*

In Hampshire in 1983, 'high' and 'low' were used in the same way, but for 'dolly' you had to crouch down and suck your thumb, and 'pepper' involved skipping while turning round on the spot, holding your nose and saying, 'Atishoo, atishoo, atishoo.'

F. C. Husenbeth, who attended Sedgley Park School near Wolverhampton, around 1805, recorded that in his day the speeds were called 'cabbage', 'faster', 'bacon' and finally 'double ones'.

Another common stylistic flourish is nowadays called 'bumps', and is probably what Husenbeth meant by 'double ones'. In normal skipping, as the player jumps, the rope passes under her feet just once, but with 'bumps' or 'doubles' it passes twice. James Ritchie gives an example of a simple pattern in which the bumps occur at the end of each line:

> Ali Baba and the forty *thieves*
> Went to school with dirty *knees*
> The teacher said, 'Stand at *ease*'
> Ali Baba and the forty *thieves*.
>
> *EDINBURGH, 1960S*

Another description from Scotland, around 1918:

> What we called French skipping. We sang a rhythmic variation on the numbers one to seven in French – rendered by us 'ong, dee, twa, katara, sang, see, seh' – and at the end of each line of the tune we jumped high so that the skipping rope passed twice under our feet. I played this in Glasgow at the end of the First World War, so I assume that it must have been brought by Belgian refugee children.

The word 'bumps' seems to be the most widely used for the technique, and has been around since Edwardian times, but there were others, and Ritchie notes that in Dundee the name was 'fireys'. In Redcar in the 1990s the technique was called a 'double whammy', a phrase much in the news as it had been used in the Conservative Party's election campaign of 1992.

In one distinctive class of skipping game, the rope is swayed back and forth for a while, and then swung over into a normal skipping routine.

Skipping Rhymes in 1898

This is the full set of rhymes printed by Alice Gomme in her *Traditional Games* (1898), which represents one of the earliest published collections and may well be the nearest we can get to 'first generation' skipping rhymes in Britain. The last example was collected by the Revd Moxon in 1907.

Ipsey Pipsey tell me true
Who shall I be married to?
A B C etc.
SUSSEX

Half pound tuppenny rice
Half pound of treacle
Penny 'orth of spice
To make it nice
Pop goes the weasel.
KENT

When I was young and able
I sat upon the table
The table broke
And gave me a poke
When I was young and able.
DEPTFORD

Up and down the ladder wall
Ha'penny loaf to feed us all
A bit for you and a bit for me
And a bit for Punch and Judy.
PADDINGTON GREEN

Every morning at eight o'clock
You all may hear the postman's knock
1 2 3 4, there goes—
(Girl runs out another runs in)
MARYLEBONE

(As they run thus, each calls in turn, 'Red, yellow, blue, white.' Where they tripped, the colour stopped on marks that of your wedding gown.) *DEPTFORD*

(Each of the two girls turning the rope takes a colour, and as the line of children run through, they guess by shouting, 'Red?', 'Green?' When wrong, nothing happens; they take the place of the turner, however, if they hit upon her colour. Another way is to call 'Sweet stuff shop' or 'green grocers' and guess various candies and fruits until they choose right.)

DEPTFORD

(When several girls start running in to skip, they say,)
All in, a bottle of gin
(As they leave at a dash, they cry,)
All out, a bottle of stout
(While 'in' jumping, the turners time the skippers' movements by a sing song:)
Up and down the city wall
Ha'penny loaf to feed us all
I buy milk, you buy flour
You shall have *pepper* in half an hour.
(At 'pepper' they turn swiftly.)
DEPTFORD

Up and down the ladder wall
Penny loaf to feed us all
A bit for you and a bit for me
And a bit for all the familee.

Up and down the city wall
In and out 'The Eagle'
That's the way the money goes
Pop goes the weasel.
LONDON

Dancing Dolly had no sense
For to fiddle for eighteenpence
All the tunes that she could play
Were 'Sally get out of the donkey's way'.
DEPTFORD

My mother said
That the rope must go
Over my head.
DEPTFORD

Andy Pandy
Sugary candy
French almond
Rock.
DEPTFORD

B L E S S I N G
Roses red, roses white
Roses in my garden
I would not part
With my sweetheart
For tuppence hapenny farthing
A B C etc.
DEPTFORD

Knife and fork
Lay the cloth
Don't forget the salt
Mustard, vinegar
Pepper!
DEPTFORD

(They sometimes make a girl skip
back and forth the long way of
the rope, using this dialogue:)
(GIRL SKIPPING:) Father give me
the key.
(FATHER:) Go to your mother.
(GIRL jumping in opposite direc-
tion:) Mother give me the key.
(MOTHER:) Go to your father.
Lady, lady drop your handkerchief
Lady, lady pick it up
(suiting the action to the words, still
skipping)
Rhyme to time the jumps:
Cups and saucers
Plates and dishes
My old man wears
Calico breeches.
LONDON, 1907

All the boys in our town
lead a happy life
Excepting Freddy —, he wants a wife
A wife he shall have and a-courting
he shall go
Along with Florrie —, because he
loves her so
He huddles her and cuddles her
And sets her on his knee
Says 'Darling do you love me?'
I love you and you love me
Next Sunday morning
the wedding shall be
Up comes the doctor
Up comes the nurse
Up comes the devil in a dirty
white shirt
Down goes the doctor
Up comes the cat
Up comes the devil in a dirty
straw hat
Salt, mustard, vinegar, pepper.
LONDON, 1907

An extremely widespread pattern is for the routine to start with the phrase 'Bluebells, cockleshells', or something very similar, but then to diverge into a range of lines usually taken from other rhymes:

> Bluebells, cockleshells, eesy icy over
> How many boys did you kiss last night
> One, two, three, four . . .
>
> *SHEFFIELD, 2008*

> Bluebells, cockleshells
>   Eevy ivy over
> Mother's in the kitchen
>   Doing a bit of stitchin'
> How many stitches did she do?
>   Ten, twenty, thirty . . .
>
> *WILTSHIRE, 1978*

> Bluebells, cockleshells,
>   Eevory, ivory, over
> Mummy rocks the baby
>   Daddy gets the meat
> How many hours will the baby sleep?
>   One, two, three . . .
>
> *HALIFAX, 1970s*

> Bluebells, cockleshells
>   On the sea shore
> Now the waves are coming over
>   Jump for the shore!

On lines 1 and 2 the rope is just swayed at ground level; line 3 it does a complete turn; line 4 the player has to get out of the loop.

COVENTRY, 1983

Other widely known verses with a similar pattern include one about 'Eever Weaver', or, as recorded in London around 1916:

> Eaper Weaper, chimbley-sweeper
>   Had a wife but couldn't keep her
> Had anovver, didn't love her
>   Up the chimbley he did shove her.

The rope is swayed to and fro for the whole verse, and then turns for
'How many miles did he shove her?'. In other places it is:

> Swish swosh, barley wash
>> Turn the bucket right over
> Swish swosh, barley wash
>> Turn the bucket right under.

SOUTHERN ENGLAND, C.1916

A BRIEF HISTORY OF SKIPPING

There is some disagreement as to whether boys or girls were the first to take
up skipping. A common view is that skipping was exclusively a boys' game
originally, and was then taken over by girls in the later nineteenth century,
at which point boys began to drop it. This notion is probably based on careless readings of nineteenth-century sources that were exclusively concerned,
as so often in those days, with the male sex. But it has also been circulated
by some influential modern writers, such as Roger Abrahams in his *Jump-
Rope Rhymes: A Dictionary* (1980), where it constitutes the first sentence of
the book's introduction, and it is still regularly repeated. There is abundant
evidence, however, of girls (and boys) skipping, both in written and in
unambiguous pictorial sources, back to the eighteenth century.

Iona Opie, in *Children's Games with Things* (1997), tries diplomatically
to square the circle by stressing the difference between solo skipping and
long-rope skipping and suggesting that while the former was regarded as
suitable for girls, the latter was more of a boys' game. But even here there
is contradictory evidence, and it is safest to accept that both sexes skipped
quite happily, until boys began to give it up as the twentieth century
approached.

Nowadays boys are often encouraged to skip by school staff, ostensibly
because it helps to keep them fit and is a form of exercise adopted by professional sportsmen, but also because the adults are trying to break down gender
divisions in games. Many boys take quite readily to the activity (albeit in short
bursts) but they are rarely interested in the rhymes or actions which are an
essential part of the girls' games, and their skipping is almost entirely concerned
with how many skips they can achieve, or how fast they can do it.

There is perhaps a danger that the idea that skipping is 'good for you', and
the purposive and competitive view that sometimes prevails, will replace
rather than augment the tradition of rhymes and games. That said, the notion

that skipping is a healthy activity is not new. Many nineteenth-century sources stress its healthful nature, for both sexes, and it must be said that girls have long included endurance as part of their skipping traditions:

> Well, whoever went into the rope and could skip without making a mistake, that was if your foot hit the rope then you were out . . . anything up to 100 skips, whoever could go to 100, we didn't often get to 100 . . . the more you played it the more proficient you got at it, and if you got to 50 or 60 you were doing well, but the winner was usually whoever got to 100, and it depended whether you were tall or long-legged, you could do better than somebody else. [The people turning did the counting; did they make it more difficult?] Oh yes, yes, by turning it faster they did, yes, but . . . it was a rhythm . . . if you got into the rhythm you could go on and on and on, but if you made a mistake or didn't concentrate and your foot hit the rope and that was it, you were out.   BELFAST, 1920S

Nowadays there are sponsored skips and skipping competitions, again sometimes organised partly to raise the profile of a 'girls' activity. It would be a pity, though, if skipping became solely a keep-fit exercise or a competitive sport.

Skipping is not one of those games that can be shown to go back to classical times, and indeed it is only if we include skipping with hoops that we can say it is even as old as the late sixteenth century. Iona Opie, in *Children's Games with Things* (1997), shows that jumping through hoops can be seen in *Les Trente-six figures* (1587), and again in Jacques Stella's *Les Jeux et plaisirs de l'enfance* of 1657, while the earliest reference to skipping with a rope is in Jacob Cats' *Silenus Alcibiadis* (1618). The second edition of this book, published in the same year, also includes a picture of the game. The earliest known mention of skipping in Britain dates only from 1737.

It is interesting to note that many of the early sources in Britain refer to the game as 'jumping rope'. This is a common American usage today, and demonstrates how the USA quite often preserves an earlier form that has been superseded in Britain. The word 'skip', in this context, seems to appear just before the turn of the nineteenth century.

Given that the game may well be no older than the early eighteenth century, it is not surprising that the first detailed descriptions only appear in around 1800. F. C. Husenbeth's account of life at Sedgley Park School near Wolverhampton, around 1805, which is quoted many times in these pages, demonstrates that the game was certainly well entrenched there in his time:

Skipping with a rope was a favourite game, played usually in the playroom, but very often in the 'Bounds' [the school playground] also in dry weather. 'Long-rope' was when two boys held and turned a long rope, and a boy had to step in, and skip, and step out of this rope, without touching it or disturbing its turns. He called to the turners, to signify at what pace they were to turn. There was also 'bells', where, instead of turning the rope, they swung it backwards and forwards on the ground, and a boy kept stepping over it and back again in measured time.

Even more surprising than the relatively recent date for the introduction of skipping is the fact that the accompanying songs and rhymes, which are nowadays so much part of the skipping experience, seem to be little more than 100 years old. There is no mention of them in the nineteenth-century sources until well into the 1880s, although the evidence is not quite as clear as we would like. The first person to mention a rhyme seems to be W. H. Babcock, who collected a great deal of children's lore in Washington, DC in that decade, but he found only the one, which he published in *Lippincott's Magazine* in 1886:

> By the holy and religerally law
> I marry this Indian to this squaw
> By the point of my jack-knife
> I pronounce you man and wife.

A writer in the *Girl's Own Paper* (12 March 1892), who knew enough to describe skipping in New York in detail, specifically states:

> Curiously enough, there are no 'skipping-rope songs', though the nature of the game would seem conducive to some sort of rhythmical accompaniment. The following is the only verse I have heard sung by American girls while they are skipping: Skip, skip, skip to the barber's shop.

So, the first mentions, positive and negative, come from America, and it is not clear if the same situation prevailed on this side of the Atlantic. Alison Uttley's testimony, which I quoted earlier, shows that by the early 1890s English girls were at least using skipping for divination, even if she does not quite say that rhymes were chanted. But by the time Alice Gomme published the second volume of her seminal *Traditional Games* in 1898, she had received a group of rhymes from one of her contributors, mostly collected in Deptford, London. Only eight years later, the Revd Moxon of St Anne's, Soho, published more than twenty rhymes in his parish magazine, and claimed to have many more in his collection. Norman Douglas included about fifty in his *London Street Games* (1916), although as usual his studiedly demotic style never really makes it clear which were used for skipping and which for other purposes. So, if rhymes were only used from, say, 1890 onwards, the repertoire certainly became extensive in a very short time.

Rhymes are not confined to one genre alone, and can be used for clapping, skipping, two balls and so on, as the whim takes the child, as long as the rhythm and any actions prescribed in the text work well enough together. But one striking characteristic of skipping rhymes, which is shown by reference to the early collections, is their longevity and relative stability. Many of them lasted in recognisable form into the late twentieth century, and the same themes occur time and again.

One of the dominant themes is the divination of love and marriage prospects, and this was already the case in the 1890s, as noted by Alice Gomme:

> The second class of games consists of those cases where the skipping is accompanied by rhymes, and is used for the purpose of foretelling the future destiny of the skipper.

Rhymes doing precisely this can still be heard in many a modern playground. In skipping, in particular, any rhyme can end in 'How many ... ?', 'What colour ... ?' and so on, to give a degree of divinatory meaning, but it is usually the ones concerned with boyfriends that take this notion to any length.

SKIPPING RHYMES

My experience recently has been that when you ask girls for skipping rhymes, *Teddy Bear* and *Bumper Car* are usually the first two which spring to their minds. The main feature of *Bumper Car* is that the word 'corner' is elongated so that the skipper has time to leave the rope, run round one of the enders and rejoin the rope:

> I'm a little bumper car
> Number 38
> I went round the cooorner
> And slammed on the brake.

LONDON, 2009

While she is chanting the last word the skipper stops the rope with her foot.

Sometimes the rhyme is extended to give the skipper more time in the rope:

> Bumper car, bumper car
>   Number 48
> Went round the coooorner
>   Brakes didn't work
> So it's slide down the hill
>   How many miles did she do?
> Ten, twenty, thirty . . .
>
> *HAMPSHIRE, 1980*

> Bumper car, bumper car
>   Number 48
> Went round the coooorner
>   And slammed on the brakes.
> But the brakes didn't work
>   So I took another coooorner
> Stopped at the traffic lights
>   And slammed on the brakes.
>
> *HAMPSHIRE, C.1983*

Then you count down every time you go round, so instead of 68 you go 67, and then it will be bumper car 66. Sometimes you don't do 'slam on the brakes' each time, but 'He mustn't be late', and sometimes 'How many laps did he do?'   *GODALMING, 2008*

Teddy Bear is the commonest of the 'action' rhymes, in which the skipper is expected to mime the things mentioned in the text:

> Teddy bear, teddy bear, turn around
>   Teddy bear, teddy bear, touch the ground
> Teddy bear, teddy bear, show your shoes
>   Teddy bear, teddy bear, that will do
> Teddy bear, teddy bear, say your prayers
>   Teddy bear, teddy bear, turn out the light
> Teddy bear, teddy bear, say goodnight.
>
> *LONDON, 2009*

Teddy bear, teddy bear, turn around
　　Teddy bear, teddy bear, touch the ground
Teddy bear, teddy bear, show your shoes
　　Teddy bear, teddy bear, jump right through.

BELFAST, 2010

The actions for 'turn around', 'touch the ground' and 'say your prayers' are obvious; 'show your shoe' usually involves hopping and lifting one foot, 'turn out the light' requires pretending to operate a pull-cord, and on 'say goodnight' or 'jump right through', the skipper stops or leaves the rope.

Exactly the same rhyme is also found with *Ballerina, Lady, Lady, Spanish Lady* or another character doing the same things, and as part of other rhymes. Essentially the same rhyme appears as *Lady-Lady* in the article that Revd Moxon wrote in 1907.

Alongside *Bumper Car* and *Teddy Bear*, several other rhymes are regularly found today, including *All in Together, Girls* and *I Like Coffee*:

All in together, girls
　　Never mind the weather, girls
When I say your birthday
　　Please jump in
January, February, March . . .

SHEFFIELD, 2008

When everybody is jumping the rope, you repeat the rhyme but change the penultimate line to 'Please jump out'. An alternative way of getting everyone out is as follows:

All in together, girls
　　This cold and frosty weather, girls
Put your hats and jackets on
　　Tell your mum you won't be long
When I count twenty the rope must be empty
　　Five, ten, fifteen, twenty.

OMAGH, CO. TYRONE, 1930S/1940S

The first two lines of the rhyme go back to at least the 1890s, but in these earlier versions the skippers entered and left simultaneously rather than one by one. This was also particularly popular in 'public' skipping situations.

Rose Gamble, for example, in her book *Chelsea Child* (1979), recalled evenings in the 1920s when several skipping ropes would be tied together, stretched across the street, and the whole community took part:

> When it was time to pack up, and some of us were called up for bed, we begged for another five minutes, until someone shouted, 'All in together.' This was the recognised finale and everyone joined in, even some of the watching mums in their pinafores. We crowded, packed in the rope, clutching hands until the turners shouted, 'Ready?' After many false starts we leaped unevenly over the rope as it turned and chanted:
>
>> All in together
>> This fine weather
>> I-spy Peter
>> 'Angin' out the winder
>> Shoot, bang, fire!
>
> On the word 'fire' everybody ran out of the rope, shouting goodnights, and leaving the owners of the ropes struggling to undo the scuffed-up knots.

Again, this rhyme appears in the Revd Moxon's article of 1907.

I like coffee is another regular favourite today, which allows for a simple rotation of skippers:

> I like coffee, I like tea
> I like — in with me.
>
> I like coffee, I like tea
> I like — out with me.
>
> *GODALMING, 2008*

The named person either joins or leaves as the words dictate. The second verse varies more than the first, and is often 'I don't like coffee . . .' or 'I hate coffee . . .', and sometimes the skipper's exit is delayed while some other action takes place:

> I like coffee, I like tea
> I like — to jump with me
> One, two, three, change places
> Four, five, six, change places, etc.
>
> *EDINBURGH, 1970S*

Another simple action rhyme is:

> Cowboy Joe from Mexico
> Hands up
> Stick 'em up
> Drop your guns
> And pick 'em up.

> *SOUTH LONDON, 1960S*

And then there is Cinderella, who always wears the same colour:

> Cinderella, dressed in yellow, will you marry me?
> No
> Cinderella, dressed in yellow, will you marry me?
> Yes
> Turn around, touch the ground
> And jump over me.

> *EAST LONDON, 1978*

> Cinderella, dressed in yella
> How many princes did she marry?
> One, two, three . . .

> *NORFOLK, 1990S*

> Cinderella, dressed in yella
> Went upstairs to kiss her fella
> By mistake she kissed a snake
> How many doctors does it take?
> One, two, three . . .

> *WEYBRIDGE, 2009*

One of the most popular divinatory rhymes is *Rosy Apple*; the 'aliens' in this version is presumably a recent addition:

> Rosy apple, lemon tart
> Tell me the name of your sweetheart
> A, B, C . . .
> —, —, will you marry me?
> Yes, no, yes . . .
> Where we getting married?

Church, pigsty, mansion . . .
How many children will you have?
One, two, three . . .
Angels, devils, aliens . . .

BELFAST, 2010

The first four lines of *Not Last Night* crop up in various places, as the following example shows:

Not last night but the night before
Twenty-four robbers came knocking at my door
As I went out they came in
And hit me on the head with a rolling pin
And this is what they said to me
 Ballerina, ballerina, turn right round
 Ballerina, ballerina, touch the ground
 Ballerina, ballerina, do the kicks
 Ballerina, ballerina, do the splits.

HAMPSHIRE, 1982

I'm a Little Girl Guide is also very popular, and exists in numerous versions, long and short. The 'blue' verse is the commonest and presumably the original, as that is the colour of the Guides' uniform, but it was probably inevitable that the other verses were added.

I'm a little girl guide dressed in blue
 These are the actions I must do
Bow to the king, curtsey to the queen
 And show my knickers to the football team.

WILTSHIRE, 1978

I'm a little Brownie dressed in brown
 See my knickers fa'ing down
Pull them up, pull them down
 I'm a little Brownie dressed in brown.

I'm a Girl Guide dressed in blue
 See all the actions I can do
Salute to the king
 Bow to the queen

Turn my back on the sailor boys
    One, two, three and out.

EDINBURGH, C.1950S

I'm a little girl-guide dressed in blue
    These are the actions I must do
Salute to the captain, bow to the queen
    And twist right round like a fairy queen.

I'm a little girl-guide dressed in red
    This is the time I go to bed
One o'clock, two o'clock . . . [*bumps*]

I'm a little girl-guide dressed in yellow
    These are the times I've kissed my fellow
One, two, three . . . [*bumps*]

I'm a little girl-guide dressed in black
    These are the times I've had the sack
One, two, three . . . [*bumps*]

SOUTH LONDON, 1970

Jelly on a Plate has also been a favourite for many decades. It is often restricted to the first verse, but again is infinitely extendable:

Jelly on a plate
Jelly on a plate
Wibbly, wobbly, wibbly, wobbly [*skipper wriggles*]
Jelly on a plate.

Sausage on the pan
Sausage on the pan
Turn it over, turn it over [*skipper turns round*]
Sausage on the pan.

Money on the floor
Money on the floor
Pick it up, pick it up [*skipper touches ground*]
Money on the floor.

IRELAND, 1980S

Jelly on a plate, jelly on a plate
    Wiggle-waggle, wiggle-waggle
Jelly on a plate.

Put some custard on the top
  Wiggle-waggle, wiggle-waggle
Put some custard on the top.

FORFAR, C.1950

Being a relative newcomer to the stable of children's games, it was natural for skipping to acquire some rhymes from older forms of entertainment. *On a Mountain Stands a Lady* is an example of a rhyme that was formerly found in a ring game concerned with courtship; it received a healthy new lease of life when adapted for skipping. In the first version it is a calling-in rhyme, but in other versions it takes on the standard 'how many kisses' style:

On the corner stands a lady
  Who she is I do not know
All she wants is gold and silver
  All she wants is a nice young man
So call in my very best friend
  Very best friend, very best friend
So call in my very best friend
  While I go out to play.

HAMPSHIRE, 1950S

On a mountain stands a lady
  Who she is I do not know
All she wants is gold and silver
  All she wants is a nice young man
So go to your —, dear
  And make it Mrs —
How many kisses did he give you?
  One, two, three . . .
Will you marry him, yes or no?
  Yes, no, yes, . . .
How many babies will you have?
  One, two, three . . .
Do you love him, yes or no?
  Yes, no, yes, . . .

SOUTH LONDON, 1974

On a mountain stands a lady
  Who she is I do not know
All she wants is gold and silver
  All she wants is a nice young man

> All right —, I'm telling your mother
> For kissing — round the corner
> How many kisses did you give him?
> Two, four, six, eight . . . [*speeding up*]
>
> HAMPSHIRE, 1975

Another widespread skipping rhyme previously used as a singing game is *The Wind* (see also p. 287):

> The wind, the wind, the wind blows high
> Blows — through the sky
> She is handsome, she is pretty
> She is the girl of the golden city
> She goes courting one, two, three
> May I tell you who 'twill be
> — says he loves her
> All the boys are fighting for her
> Takes her in the garden
> Sits her on his knee
> Says —, will you marry me?
> And we'll all have sausage and mash for tea.
>
> LANCASHIRE, 1950S

Hundreds of different rhymes have been recorded over the years, and in many cases numerous versions of each rhyme have been documented. Taken as a whole there is a bewildering range of subject matter, and although some of it is mundane and closely tied to the physical needs of the activity, there are also many flashes of humour, surrealism and sheer poetry.

OTHER GAMES WITH SKIPPING ROPES

There are a number of other ways to play with a rope apart from skipping with it, and some of these games are widely known. One is to swing the rope round in a circle:

> Sometimes we got two skipping ropes and we tied the ends together, just one end, so it would make it very long . . . and there's someone in the middle, and they would crouch down and swing it around and the other people

have to jump over it . . . you have to do it low . . . and if you get hit you
have to go in the middle.   *ESSEX, 2009*

Variations on this theme have been recorded all over the country. It is
often called 'Witches and Fairies' because those two words were chanted
over and over again, and if the rope hit you on 'witches' you were out,
or had to take the middle position, while if struck on 'fairies' you suffered
no penalty. It was also traditional to raise the height of the rope gradually, forcing players to jump higher and higher, or to start at head height,
with the players ducking under it, and to get progressively lower. But the
latter often ended in an accident and led to the game being banned in
some playgrounds. James Ritchie records in *Golden City* (1965) that the
game was called 'Round Rope Heights' or 'Roundie Heights' in Edinburgh.

Less well-organised but probably quite effective is the following:

One of my favourite games to play is called 'Bogie on a string'. We made it
up. One person is it. A green skipping rope is attached to an elasticky skipping rope. The person who is it throws the bogie whilst holding the elastic
at somebody. If it hits them they are it. If not then the thrower is still it.

INVERNESS, 2008

Another rope game involves players holding each end of the rope and
waggling it on or near the ground, while the others jump over it:

We also played colours. Two people would hold each end of a rope which
was resting on the floor; they would each think of a colour; and start to
shake the rope, from side to side. The others would then jump the rope and
call out a colour; if you guessed right then you took that end of the rope.

MIDDLESEX, 1950S

Colour Wand: A skipping rope is wiggled on the ground (a girl at each end
shaking it). The two girls have secretly decided between them on a colour.
Other girls then take turns to jump over the rope calling out random colours
as they jump. The winner is the girl who shouts out the secret colour. The
trick was to choose the most obscure colour you could think of e.g. maroon,
silver etc. to make it difficult.   *COVENTRY, 2004*

Interestingly, these are very similar to a game recorded by Alice Gomme
back in 1898. In this, the rope was simply wiggled for players to jump over,
without the added colours element, and was often called 'Snakes' or 'Wavies'.

A Miscellany of Skipping Rhymes 1940–70

Teddy on the railway picking
up stones
Along came an engine and broke
Teddy's bones
Oh said Teddy, that's not fair
Oh said the engine you shouldn't
have been there.
DUNDEE, 1940S

[The last line of this one is often: 'Oh
said the engine I don't care']

Ipsy gypsy Caroline
Washed her hair in turpentine
Turpentine to make it shine
Ipsy gypsy Caroline.
WILTSHIRE, 1940S

My pink pinafore
My pink sash
Fell in the water
Splash splash splash!
[*3 high jumps*]
HUNTINGDONSHIRE, 1947

Little Fatty Doctor
How's your wife?
Very well thank you
That's all right
But she can't eat a bit o' fish
Or a bit o' liquorice
I N spells in
O V E R spells over
And O U T spells out.
YORKSHIRE, 1950S

House for sale apply within
The people upstairs are drinking gin
Drinking gin is a very bad thing
As I go out Mrs — comes in.
WALES, 1950

Schwah schwah
Woppity woppity
Alla-walla bing bong
Ting-tong toosi
Oozey woozy woozy
On fah fey.
HAMPSHIRE, 1960S

All the girls in our town
Lead a happy life
Except for —
She wants to be a wife
A wife she shall be
Along with —
Because she loves him so
She kisses him
She cuddles him
She sits upon his knee
And says, 'Oh my darling
Won't you marry me?'
Yes, no, yes . . .
SOUTH LONDON, 1960S

Mr Speed is a very good man
He learns his children all he can
A-reading, a-writing, arithmetic
And never forgets to use his stick
For when he does
He makes them dance

Out of England into France
Out of France and into Spain
Over the hills and back again
On this hill there is a school
In this school there is a fool
On this stool there sat a fool
And her name is —.
LANCASHIRE, 1950S

Mrs D
Mrs I
Mrs F F I
Mrs C
Mrs U
Mrs L T Y.
SOUTH LONDON, 1950S

Mrs M
Mrs I
Mrs S S I
Mrs S S I
Mrs double P I.
HAMPSHIRE, C.1960

Down to Mississippi
If you miss the beat you're out
Up to Mississippi
If you miss the beat you're out
Turn to Mississippi
If you miss the beat you're out
Clap to Mississippi
If you miss the beat you're out . . .
SOUTH LONDON, 1960S

Ice cream
Penny a lump
The more you eat
The more you bump
Ice cream
Tuppence a lump

The more you eat
The more you bump bump . . .
SOUTH LONDON, 1960S

Vote, vote, vote for –1–
Call in –2– at the door
For –2– is a lady
And she going to have a baby
[or 'She plays the ukulele']
So we won't vote for –1– any more.
SOUTH LONDON, 1960S

Policeman, Policeman
Don't take me
For I have a wife and a family
How many children have you got?
One, two, three . . . [*bumps*]
SOUTH LONDON, 1960S

Drip, drop, drops in the sea
Please turn the rope for me.
SOUTH LONDON, 1960S

London County Council
L C C
You don't know your A B C.
SOUTH LONDON, 1960S

Saucy Mary Ann
Saucy Mary Ann
Walking down the street
With a nice young man
High-heeled shoes
Feathers in her hat
I'll tell mum
You saucy little cat.
SOUTH LONDON, C.1960S

Another fairly obvious thing to do with a rope is simply to jump over it, as in a high jump, called 'Jumps' in Dublin, and 'Higher and Higher' elsewhere, or duck under it. Another inventive use was recorded by Norman Douglas in his *London Street Games* (1916):

> In 'Polly Tell Me the Time' they wind a skipping-rope round a girl's waist a certain number of times, and then unwind her.

PUBLIC SKIPPING CUSTOMS

I have already touched on the notion of whole communities coming out to skip: Rose Gamble's description of people in her street joining in on summer evenings (see p. 177) is an instance of this. In some places, however, public skipping has become a tradition. At Scarborough in Yorkshire, for example, every Shrove Tuesday afternoon the foreshore is closed to traffic, an official bell is rung, and hundreds of people of all kinds and ages appear with long ropes, to indulge in their annual orgy of skipping.

Scarborough is the only place with an apparently unbroken tradition of annual skipping over several generations. In the past, though, the custom was far from unique. Similar public skipping was commonplace all over the country in the late nineteenth and early twentieth centuries, and usually took place on Good Friday or Whitsun. The best documented of these activities were at Cambridge, Brighton and elsewhere along the Sussex coast, where they survived until the Second World War. A contributor to *Notes & Queries* in 1937 also attested to its popularity in Devon:

> As a child in the eighties and nineties of last century, at Teignmouth, Devon, I well remember the skipping which used to take place annually on that day on the Den, which our nursery window used to overlook. A number of groups used to be formed on the extensive grass-plot, each consisting of about ten or twenty men and girls, and skipping would go on with great energy for most of the day. In each group a long rope was used, and swung hard and fast by two men, while two or more of the others skipped together. I do not remember this form of skipping taking place on any other day of the year, nor children taking part . . . I know of several other towns in Devon where similar skipping matches used to take place regularly on Good Fridays.

Various claims of ancient origins have been made for this custom over the years, each following the fashion of the time for such explanations. Those most often quoted are that the jumping was designed to encourage the spring crops to grow tall, or that the game is connected to the story of Judas Iscariot. This latter theory gets trotted out in many Easter custom legends, its validity seemingly confirmed by the fact that he hanged himself with a rope. Needless to say, these explanations are completely spurious. As we have no evidence of public skipping earlier than the mid nineteenth century, or rope skipping at all before the mid eighteenth, ancient or ritual origins seem astonishingly unlikely.

As a final note on skipping, though, it is interesting to find that skipping can be illegal. According to *The Times* for 8 April 1874:

> At Worship Street, Henry Neale, a brass finisher, and James Mortimer, a labourer, were charged before Mr Hunnay with playing a game of skipping-rope in Victoria Park, contrary to the 7th rule of Mr Ayrton's Royal Parks and Gardens Regulations Act. On Easter Monday the prisoners were turning a long rope for young men and girls to skip with in the park.

An estimated 20,000 people thronged the park on that day, and a number of men charged revellers a halfpenny or penny to skip in their ropes. But the regulations stated that no person should 'play a game' or 'sell a commodity' in the park, and the professional rope-turners therefore contravened both clauses, and had also refused to desist. The court fined them half a crown each. The park constable added that he did not interfere with children skipping, only with men who made a business of it.

ELASTICS

To play 'Elastics' or 'French Skipping', you need a continuous piece of elastic, tied in a loop. Two children stand facing each other, about a metre apart, with their feet about 30cm apart, and with the elastic looped round their ankles to make an oblong shape.

The players take it in turns to jump inside, outside and on the elastic in a set sequence, and with different steps. Once a player has successfully negotiated the sequence, the elastic is moved up to calf level, and then to knee level and so on. These heights are referred to either by numbers, or as 'anklies', 'kneesies' and so on. The width of the oblong can also be varied, to produce a narrower or wider field of play. Variations include 'hopsies' (on one foot); 'doubles' (two players at the same time); 'one eye' (with only one eye open); and 'blind' (both eyes closed). A slightly different slant is given to the game if three players put one foot inside the elastic to make a triangular shape, but the movements are very similar to the ordinary version.

Within the game there can be a number of rules that govern the play, and a very important one regulates how the feet land on each jump, because, except in special circumstances, the feet must land at the same time. One foot after the other was called 'foxtrots' by Wendy (aged eight), Joanna (nine), and Sonai (ten) in Croydon, Surrey in 1985, 'scissors' by Joanne Dyer, a ten-year-old who contributed an excellent description of the game to the *Australian Children's Folklore Newsletter* in 1981, and 'clip clops' by Cathy Gould in her childhood in 1970s Coventry.

In many reports from the 1960s and 1970s, girls describe making their first set of elastics by tying together a great quantity of rubber bands, presumably before persuading their mothers to buy a length of elastic or finding sufficient in their sewing boxes, and some used two skipping ropes tied together. Nowadays, the school equipment cupboard may well include elastic loops, ready made.

'Elastics' is extremely popular with girls of seven to nine, but usually in relatively short bursts – something to be done intensely for a short while, and then left behind. At the world-weary age of eleven, Megan, Mollie and Annie of Godalming, Surrey, struggled to remember their past crazes of three years before, and explained:

> We did it in year 3. The thing with French skipping, there wasn't a variety of things you could do with it, because you could just jump in and out really, and it was a bit more cramped so not many people could do it.
>
> GODALMING, C.2005

And it is this rather limited scope that tends to restrict its staying power. Nevertheless, the game has distinct advantages. It can be done in small groups, indoors and out, with little preparation, and can be broken off at any moment. You do not even need three people to carry it out, as in the playground a drainpipe or other piece of equipment can substitute for one of the 'standers', and in the house, a couple of chairs will allow the solo child to practise her skills perfectly well.

In 1989 Andy Arleo, a collector of French children's lore, sought to test the game's international reach, and found it actively played in twenty countries across Europe, North America and Asia, and after further research, Iona Opie concluded in *Children's Games with Things* (1997) that 'it would safe to say it had become worldwide'.

The game has had several names in Britain. 'Chinese Skipping' and

'American Ropes' were early titles, but for some time the commonest names have been 'French Skipping' and 'Elastics' – although the latter is usually rendered as 'Lastics', 'Laggies' or something similar – and is occasionally called 'Cat's Cradle' in reference to the hand string game. It has often been noted that many of the names hint at foreign origins, and for once this seems to be quite an accurate assessment of the game's history.

The game hit British playgrounds in about 1960, and James Ritchie's collection of Scottish childlore, *Golden City* (1965), was probably the first to have recorded its existence, under the title 'American Ropes'. It is fairly certain that it did indeed come directly from America, brought in by children of American armed forces personnel stationed here. In the USA the game is usually called 'Chinese Jump-rope', and again it is most likely that American children learnt it originally from Asian immigrants, although it is not clear whether it originated in China or Japan.

It certainly reached epidemic levels in England in the early 1980s, when my daughter Kathy was eight and at school in Andover, Hampshire. I wrote at the time:

> The craze came back with a vengeance in about February 1984 and remained the main pastime for Kathy and her best friend Natalie until we moved away. Indeed, for Kathy and Natalie, 'craze' is perhaps not a strong enough word as they seemed to be at it nearly all the time, and Kathy never went anywhere without her 'lastics in her pocket, just in case.

Several well-known rhymes accompany the actions, but they are short, limited in variation, and are chanted rather than sung. The commonest is *England, Ireland, Scotland, Wales*, in which the first line is fixed, but the second line varies somewhat. *Banana Split* is probably the second most frequently found:

England, Ireland, Scotland, Wales
Inside, outside, inside, on.

HAMPSHIRE, 1984

England, Ireland, Scotland,Wales
Inside, outside, on the rails.

NORTH LONDON, 2009

England, Ireland, Scotland, Wales
All tied up in monkeys' tails.

INVERNESS, 2008

England, Ireland, Scotland, Wales
Inside, outside, puppy dogs' tails.

GODALMING, 2008

Banana, banana, banana splits
Inside, outside, inside, on.

SOUTH LONDON, 1985

Jingle jangle, centre spangle
Jingle jangle, on.

EAST LONDON, 1978

Jack be nimble, Jack be quick
Jack jump over the candle stick.

SOUTH LONDON, 1985

Romans, Saxons, Normans, Danes
Inside, outside, inside, on.

YORKSHIRE, 1982

CHAPTER TWELVE

Ball Games

BALL BOUNCING AND TWO-BALLS

For at least 100 years, girls all over Britain regularly indulged in an orgy of ball-bouncing games, which could be played at any time but were particularly popular in the spring and early summer. The simplest version, although not nearly as easy as it looks, is played with a single ball, bouncing it on the ground. The player pats the ball up and down, usually to the rhythm of an accompanying rhyme, swinging her leg over the bouncing ball and sometimes doing other actions. The commonest rhyme starts 'One, two, three, a-leary', although the last word varies considerably in spelling, and is often pronounced 'a-lairy' or 'o-leary':

> One, two, three a' leary
> My ball's down the dairy.
> Don't forget to give it to Mary
> Not to Charlie Chaplin.
>
> *NORTH LONDON, 1950S/1960S*

> One, two, three, O'Leary
> Four, five, six, O'Leary
> Seven, eight, nine, O'Leary
> Ten O'Leary stop.
>
> *HAMPSHIRE, 1960S*

The second line of the first example was often rendered as 'My ball's down the airy', and many girls who were at school during the Second

World War, and soon after, assumed that this must be a reference to an air-raid shelter. In fact the rhyme is much older and refers to 'the area' of town houses with basements. The 'area' was the space left to give light to the basement windows, and where the 'area-steps' led down to where the servants worked. It was usually marked at street level by the 'area railings'.

The verse was much parodied, and rude versions were also used for counting out (see p. 341):

> One two three alairy
> I saw Auntie Mary
> Sitting on the tingle lairy
> Eating chocolate biscuits.
>
> *LEEDS, 1920S*

A much more highly developed ball-bouncing tradition needed a wall as well as the ground. The commonest was two-balls, but some experts could handle three balls or even four. They were bounced against the wall and off the floor, with the player throwing, patting or catching them in a set sequence and in different ways – under the leg, overarm, underarm and so on – or doing other actions and movements. This could be done silently, by numbers, or accompanied by a rhyme, and could be played solo or by two or more in succession. Once the rhythm was established the girls displayed a remarkable fluidity of action and keen sense of timing, even when the action or rhyme dictated a break in or stretching of the rhythm.

In past times the game was immensely popular, and when in vogue any suitable wall in the playground or near the home would resound with the thump of bouncing balls as girls practised their routines. It was one game in which the urban child fared better than her country cousin:

> For certain games there was an accepted separation of the sexes. The girls played intricate ball games against the wall, onesy, sixy and sevensy, patting and bouncing, under your leg, round your back and twisters. We used two balls, juggling with one hand and repeating the learned routines with stiffsy, dumbsy, one-leg, jiggety-jig and clapsy. The even brick walls were just right for these games and the ball bounced true on the concrete ground. One old girl used to tell us off, sticking her head out of her window to shout at us because the rhythmic thump of the balls against her living-room wall knocked her budgie off his perch.   *LONDON, 1920S*

But this is one of the games that seem nowadays to have disappeared from most, if not all regions. No English child interviewed or who filled in a questionnaire for this book mentioned it, and most had never even heard of the game which their mothers and grandmothers undoubtedly practised with enthusiasm. Even in Scotland, where the Opies found the strongest ball-bouncing (or 'stotting') tradition in Britain, the game seems to be largely forgotten, and when I spoke to a school council in Belfast in 2010, hoping to learn of an active tradition, only one girl said she did some ball bouncing at home. The following descriptions are therefore set in the past tense, but, unlike many other games that have disappeared, two-balls persisted until well within living memory and could perhaps be reintroduced with a little effort. One headteacher pointed out to me, however, that modern school buildings, with their large low windows, simply do not offer suitable walls.

The most notable feature of many two-ball games was the programmatic nature of the procedures involved. Either the players did prescribed movements to numbers, often counting down from ten, or they performed a strict sequence of variant actions, which had names like 'plainsies', 'upsies' and 'downsies', were carried out a set number of times and were included in the accompanying rhyme. This programmatic nature led to many girls calling the game 'Exercises', or number-derived names, such as 'Sevensies':

Our playground was surrounded on three sides with high walls and these were put to good use . . . We used them for our 'exercises'. These were different ways in which one could throw a small rubber ball – forwards, backwards, twisted from behind, bounced and patted – the variations were endless.

YORKSHIRE, 1930S

We would start by just throwing the ball to the wall and catching it; after twenty times if you hadn't dropped it, you went on to a more difficult move such as clap hands or roll your hands, catch with right hand then left hand, under one leg then the other. All sorts of variations could be played and each had to be done ten times, starting from scratch every time you dropped the ball or made a mistake.

WARWICKSHIRE, 1940S

The named movements were many and various, but a good practitioner could manage at least ten in succession, and sometimes more. Caroline Brewser, for example, who went to school in the Vale of Glamorgan in the 1970s, described the different movements as follows:

We had *plainsies*, where you maintained a constant rhythm of throwing one ball then the other in quick succession against the wall. These throws would

be interspersed with many, many specialist moves in time with the words
of a song. These moves included:

Upsies (throw the ball up into the air)

Dashums (bounce the ball against the wall by first bouncing it on to the
floor, then catch it on rebound from the wall)

Dropsies (throw the ball against the wall, and let it drop on to the floor
before catching it)

Underleg (throw the ball against the wall under your right leg)

Otherleg (same but under left leg)

Buckets (as for dropsies, but form a loop with your arms through which
the ball would drop before hitting the floor)

Upsi-buckets (as for buckets, but throw the ball in the air first rather than
against the wall)

Under-dash (a dashum under the right leg)

Otherdash (a dashum under the left leg)

and one where you would use only one hand to throw the ball; and others
where you would turn round and catch the ball, either without it bouncing
first or after a bounce.

You would sing the rhyme again and again, and do a different specialist
move for each repeat of the verse until you made a mistake – so first time
through plainsies, then upsies, then dashums, etc. With good timing you
and a friend could keep throwing the balls with the same rhythm while
swapping from one of you doing the throwing to the other.

Two of the simpler rhymes remembered by Caroline were:

> Drink a pint of milk a day
> M. I. L. K. [with the specialist throws on the letters M I L K]

> Big Ben strikes ten
> T. E. N.

Chantel Cousins, at school in London in the 1980s, reported a range of
similarities and variants, and commented, 'There was a specific order to
most of the rhymes – they got harder to do':

Plainsies (just juggling against the wall)
Overs (overarm throw)

Unders (underarm throw)
Upsies (throw up in the air)
Downsies (juggle against the ground)
Dropsies (let the ball bounce before you catch it)
Digsies (throw to the ground so it bounces against the wall and back to you)
Underleg (throw under your leg)
Otherleg (throw under your other leg)
One-handsies (juggle with one hand)
Other-handsies (juggle with other hand – especially hard!)

A simple example of how these fitted into a rhyme is:

> Plainsies Mrs Brown, plainsies Mrs Brown
> Plainsies, plainsies, plainsies, plainsies
> Plainsies, Mrs Brown.

And then repeat with the other actions.

If you managed to overcome these obstacles, there were other rules to keep you alert:

> Every time you miss you lose something – so, one hand, down on one knee, on two knees, then out. But you could redeem each one if you caught the ball.   ESSEX, 1970S

Caroline Oates, born in 1955 in Gateshead, recalled an intricate version of what she and her friends called 'Two-baller':

> Juggling two balls against a wall (right hand, palm upwards, chucks one ball at wall while left hand, palm down a few inches above the right, catches other ball on rebound from wall and passes it straight down to right hand) while chanting 'Two-baller' rhymes:
>
> > Once there was a princess
> > Princess, princess
> > Once there was a princess
> > Many years ago, princess (just straight two-baller)
> >
> > The princess's name was Snowdrop
> > Snowdrop, Snowdrop
> > The princess's name was Snowdrop

Many years ago, Snowdrop (and on each 'drop', the ball would be allowed to bounce on the ground before catching it)

Her father's name was Jacob, etc. (and on each 'ob' of Jacob, which rhymes perfectly with 'up' (i.e. Jacup) one ball would be thrown in the air instead of at the wall and caught, keeping the same rhythm)

Her mother's name was Clover, etc. (and on each 'over', one ball would be thrown overarm at the wall instead of underarm)

A prince he came a-riding, etc. (trotting actions while trying to keep 'Two-baller' rhythm and not drop the balls)

The prince's name was . . . (I can't remember his name, but I think the action was chucking one ball to bounce on the ground before it hit the wall and returned to the catching hand)

He asked for her hand in marriage, etc. (hold up one hand while continuing two-baller with the other hand)

And since I never managed to get any further than that without dropping all the balls and being out, I don't know what came next.

It would seem logical to expect ball bouncing of this nature to be a twentieth-century invention, because it needs, after all, a good bouncy ball, a flat wall and a good smooth, hard floor to give the necessarily predictable effect. Games with hand-sized balls existed, however, in the mid eighteenth century, and were often connected with 'divination'. It is probable that these developed from a procedure in which the ball was mostly thrown up and caught, or where balls were 'juggled', to one where the bouncing was an integral part of the game. Balls made from materials such as cork with a leather or cloth covering made pretty good bouncers. By the later nineteenth century, balls of India rubber or gutta-percha were available to the better off, and by the 1920s good mass-produced rubber balls were within the reach of everyone, at which ball bouncing really took off. Our two-balls game certainly existed in Victorian times, and the indefatigable Alice Gomme included several versions in her *Traditional Games* (1898), under the name of 'Pots'. She gives no rhymes for two-balls, but her descriptions include recognisable sequences of throws and actions, with one or two surprises, including at one point an instruction to catch the ball 'dog snack' fashion, i.e. with knuckles upwards 'as a dog snacks'.

Gomme also gives a single-ball game, as played in her time in Fraserburgh and Galloway:

One girl takes a ball, strikes it on the ground, and keeps pushing it down with her hand. While she is doing this, the other players stand beside her, and keeping unison with the ball, repeat:

> Game, game, ba' ba'
> Twenty lasses in a raw
> Nae a lad amon them a'
> Bits game, game, ba' ba'.

If the girl keeps the ball dancing up and down – 'stottin' – during the time the words are being repeated, it counts one game gained. She goes on 'stottin' the ball, and the others go on repeating the words till she allows the ball to escape from her control.

One thing that has fascinated commentators for at least 100 years is the meaning or etymology of the word 'a-leary', 'a-lairy' or 'a-laira', which is so common in the rhymes used for games in which the ball is bounced under the raised leg. According to the *Oxford English Dictionary* the word 'aliry', describing crooked legs, appears in the fourteenth-century poem *Piers Plowman*, and it is tempting to see a link here. But this begs the question whether a word that for the next half a millennium went otherwise unrecorded could nevertheless have survived among children. As we have no indication that the game which involves an under-the-leg movement existed before the twentieth century, it also begs the question, What were the children using the word for in all that time? And if it was indeed in more general use, why is it not recorded anywhere?

THE RHYMES

In addition to the sequences of numbers and movements, a range of rhymes were also used for ball bouncing. Some were exclusive to the genre, while others were adapted from other genres such as skipping. *Want a Cigarette* could be used in solo bouncing, with the leg being thrown over the ball on 'sir', or in two-balls when the ball is allowed to bounce on the floor:

> Want a cigarette, sir?
> No, sir
> Why, sir?
> Because I got a cold, sir
> Where'd you get the cold, sir?

From the North Pole, sir
What're you doing there, sir?
Catching polar bears, sir
How many did you catch, sir?
One, sir, two, sir . . . [up to ten]
The rest caught me, sir.

HAMPSHIRE, 1975

A very similar version from Newcastle in the 1960s started with four lines, sung to the tune of *Here We Go Round the Mulberry Bush*:

Johnny get up and light the fire
Turn the gas a wee bit higher
Go and tell yer Aunt Maria
The baby's got the hiccups.

Nebuchadnezzar, who the *Oxford Companion to the Bible* insists should really be 'Nebuchadrezzar', may have been the King of Babylonia (605–562 BC), but to children he was simply one of those biblical names that trip off the tongue and seem to be made especially for them:

Nebuchadnezzar, King of the Jews
Bought his wife a pair of shoes
When the shoes began to wear
Nebuchadnezzar began to swear
When the swear began to stop
Nebuchadnezzar bought a shop
When the shop began to sell
Nebuchadnezzar bought a bell
When the bell began to ring
Nebuchadnezzar began to sing
Doh re mi fa sol la te doh.

KENT, 1940S

Nevertheless, his fame did not save him from the corrupting influence of oral tradition, and his name was often garbled beyond recognition, becoming, in one case, 'Archie Boo, King of the Jews'.

In long-rope skipping one of the most impressive sights is when girls follow each other in and out of the rope in a seemingly effortless sequence, without missing a beat or upsetting the smooth operation of the game. A similar small miracle happens with expert two-ballers, who can simply take over from each other without a hitch or stumble. This can be done at any time, but is sometimes the main feature of the game, and utilises a short rhyme that was once found all over the country, repeated as each player takes over:

> Matthew, Mark, Luke and John
> Next-door neighbour carry on.
>
> *HAMPSHIRE, 1960s*

The first line of this rhyme has a long history and was widely known in a very different sphere. Since at least the mid seventeenth century it has been the memorable beginning of a night-time prayer, sometimes referred to as *The White Paternoster*:

> Matthew, Mark, Luke and John
>   Bless the bed that I lie on
> Four corners to my bed
>   Four angels round my head
> One to watch and one to pray
>   And two to bear my soul away.

This was regarded almost as a magical charm by many people, to the constant worry of Protestant reformers down the ages.

The apparently obsessive counting instincts of two-ballers also led to the adoption of another rhyme, which exists in other spheres:

> When I was one I sucked my thumb
>   And all I got was a fruity drop
> When I was two I buckled my shoe
>   And all I got was a fruity drop
> When I was three I climbed a tree . . .
> When I was four I kicked a door . . .
> When I was five I sat on a hive . . .
> When I was six I picked up sticks . . .
> When I was seven I walked to Devon . . .
> When I was eight I climbed the gate . . .
> When I was nine I walked the line . . .
> When I was ten I found a hen . . .
>
> *HAMPSHIRE, 1975*

The English language is sadly deficient in usable rhymes for five, six and seven, but children do their best:

> When I was one I ate a scone
>   Ate a scone, ate a scone
> When I was one I ate a scone
>   Under my leg and over.
>
> Two – I buckled my shoe
> Three – I hurt my knee
> Four – I locked the door
> Five – I learnt to drive
> Six – I chopped down sticks
> Seven – I went to heaven
> Eight – I swung on the gate
> Nine – I reached the line
> Ten – It starts again.
> [tune: *I Saw Three Ships Come Sailing in*]
>
> LANCASHIRE, 1950S

All these various rhymes are based on the same principles, but the number of lines given over to the 'non-numeric' section, which acts as a chorus or refrain, varies considerably. In the first example given above it is simply 'All I got was a fruity drop', but in another widely known treatment of the theme, the chorus dominates the rhyme:

> When I was one I sucked my thumb
>   Over the Irish sea
> I jumped aboard a pirate ship
>   And the captain said to me
> 'We're going this way, that way
>   Forward and backwards
> Over the Irish sea
>   A bottle of rum to fill my tum
> And that's enough for me.'
>
> When I was two . . .
>
> SOUTH LONDON, 1950S

Obviously, you have to jump on 'jumped', move forward, back and side to side when instructed, and even salute when the captain is mentioned.

OTHER BALL GAMES

The following games can all, to a greater or lesser extent, be found in the modern playground. Some – 'Bad Eggs', for example – have been popular for a long time and we know quite a lot about their history. Others – such as 'Piggy in the Middle' – have been little commented on by previous generations, perhaps because they seemed too basic to be deemed worthy of note.

Stocking Ball

An article in *The Listener* (4 November 1954), which reported on a recent radio programme, hailed 'Stocking Ball' as a brand-new game:

'Have you ever heard of this?' asked Leo Beharrell in *The North-Countryman*:

> I spy Cinderella
> Cinderella up a tree
> I spy bumble bee
> Bumble bee in a basin
> I spy James Mason

If you have not you soon will! That is only a bit of it, and it is the incantation to a new street game that schoolgirls are playing. The girl stands with her back to the wall and bounces a tennis ball which is swinging in an old stocking. I said it is a new game – it could not be newer – because the stocking *must* be nylon. I am told nothing else will do. There she stands, like a little statue except for the one arm swinging: up – down – across – left – right – down – across, the speed increasing and the rhyme going on and on until the stocking suddenly develops a hole and the ball bounces away. Then she ties another knot in the stocking, puts the ball in again and carries on. A tennis ball in a nylon stocking is certainly 'modern' enough, but it is only a development of the older bouncing games . . .'

The game was not quite as new as the writer believed, but he was right to note that it inherited the rhymes and basic moves of existing ball games, including the rhyme *I Spy Cinderella* and the moves in the following, contributed to the *Lore of the Playground* questionnaire by Manchester-born Joanne Wallwork, remembering the 1970s:

A Miscellany of Two-balls Rhymes

I went into the garden
I found a little farthin'
I gave it to my mother
To buy a baby brother
The brother was a sailor
And sailed upon the sea
And all the fish that he could catch
Was one, two, three.
FORFAR, C.1950

Alice in Wonderland
Alice in Wonderland
Oh Alice, poor Alice
Alice in Wonderland
Olay!
SOUTH LONDON, 1978

Upsy Walls ice cream
Bouncy Walls ice cream
Dropsy Walls ice cream
Slamsy Walls ice cream.
LANCASHIRE, 1980S

Poor Mrs Fluffyball
Went to see a waterfall
She fell in and couldn't swim
Poor Mrs Fluffyball.
YORKSHIRE, 1980S

Mrs Minny had a pinny
Upside down
First she wore it
Then she tore it
Upside down.
SOUTH LONDON, 1960S

Gipsy Ipsy lived in a tent
Couldn't afford to pay the rent
When the rentman came next day
Gipsy Ipsy ran away.
SOUTH LONDON, 1950S

Over the garden wall
I let the baby fall
My mother came out
And gave me a clout
She gave me another
To match the other
Over the garden wall.
SOUTH LONDON, 1950S

Each peach pear plum
I spy Tom Thumb
Tom Thumb in the wood
I spy Robin Hood
Robin Hood in the cellar
I spy Cinderella
Cinderella in the stable
I spy Betty Grable
Betty Grable is a star
S T A R.
SOUTH LONDON, 1950S

Oliver, Oliver, Oliver Twist
Bet your dolly can't do this
Bend your knees
Stand at ease
Quick march
Over the arch
Oliver, Oliver, Oliver Twist.
SOUTH LONDON, 1960S

P K penny a packet
First you lick it
Then you smack it
Then you stick it to your jacket
P K penny a packet.
SOUTH LONDON, 1971

Brownie number one
She made me suck my thumb
She pulled my hair and made me swear
Brownie number one.
Brownie number two . . .
HAMPSHIRE, 1975

Peter Pan said to Paul
Clap your hands and drop the ball.
SOUTH LONDON, 1960S

Under, over, chocolate soldier
Over, under, drop.
HAMPSHIRE, 1960S

Plainsies, Clapsies
Rollies to Backsies
Right leg, left leg
And under we go
Up in the air
And down again
Twirl around
And back again.
CO. WICKLOW, 1977

1, 2, 3 and over
4, 5, 6 and over
6, 7, 8 and over
9 and over catch the ball
1, 2, 3 and under [put ball under the leg]
1, 2, 3 and dropsy [let the ball bounce]
[same again with one hand only]
WALES, 1950S

Eight girls' names I'm sure to know
So wish me luck and here I go
[recites eight girls' names]
Seven boys' names, etc.
Six towns, etc.
Five flowers, etc.
Four trees, etc.
Three cars, etc.
NEWCASTLE, 1960S

I went over and under
Over and under
Cross the Irish seas
A bottle of rum
To fill my tum
And that's the life for me.
HAMPSHIRE, 1950S

Plainsy, clapsy
Around the world and backsy
First your heel
And then your toe
Then your knee
And back you go.
SOUTH LONDON, 1950S

Ball in a stocking, played by standing with back to wall (no windows) – swing ball from side to side and under leg whilst singing strange song:

> Want a cigarette, sir
> No, sir, why, sir
> Cos I got a cold, sir
> Where d'ya get a cold, sir
> From the North Pole, sir
> What you doing there, sir
> Catching polar bears, sir
> How many did you catch, sir
> One, sir, two, sir, . . .

The ball could be attached to a piece of elastic, rather than a stocking – something not easy to improvise at home, but available commercially. A contributor to *Cumbria Within Living Memory* (1994) remembered things bought or won at the fair that came to Crosby at Whitsun and in October:

> The ball was what we coveted most – our Shirley Temple ball on a bit of elastic. We sang songs about Shirley and practised our skills against the wall. Up and down the ball would go on its long elastic, then it would be short-ened and we sang the rhymes as we sprang the ball over our hands, over our legs, over our heads if we dared, against the wall. Once the elastic gave way we used an old stocking. The bigger girls were better than me and they seemed to be 'in' for hours, but it was fun to watch them and await my turn with the rest.

Queenie, Queenie

'Queenie, Queenie' was widely popular for well over 100 years, and can still be found today:

> Queenie, Queenie, who's got the ball?
> See I haven't got it
> See I haven't got it
> Who's got the ball?

One person stood at the front with their back to the crowd. They threw the ball over their shoulder, when someone caught it and shouted 'ready'. They would turn round and point to one person they thought had it, that person would say, 'Who's got the ball?' twice and hold out each hand in turn saying, 'See I haven't got it' etc., and they'd try someone else. If the person who had the ball was found, they became the next thrower.

LONDON, 1950S

There were formerly numerous variations. A version played in Nottingham in the 1950s, for example, was played in a circle, and instead of 'Queenie', the call was:

> Alla balla boosha
> Who's got the ball?

And often the text was extended, as here from Andover in 1982:

> Queenie, Queenie, who's got the ball
> Is she fat or is she small
> Or is she like a cannon ball?

Here, Queenie could call on individual players and say, '— do the twist.' If she did not think that person had the ball she would say, 'Lettuce', but if she thought that person did, she would say, 'You're the dustbin.' In Southwark, around 1917, the game was called 'Queenie' if it was mostly girls playing, but 'Kingie' if it was mainly boys.

A more formal 'parlour game' version, entitled 'Lady Queen Anne', appears in Eliza Leslie's *American Girl's Book* (1831). One child leaves the room, or hides her face in the corner. One of the others takes the ball, and they all stand in a row with their hands hidden under their aprons. The seeker comes back and says to one of them:

> Lady Queen Anne, she sits in the sun
> As fair as a lily, as brown as a bun
> She sends you three letters and prays you'll read one
> > *Answer*: I cannot read one, unless I read all
> > Then pray, Miss —, deliver the ball.

This seems to be the earliest published reference to the game, and is similar to other nineteenth-century descriptions. In 1898 Alice Gomme printed fifteen versions along the same lines.

'Queenie' could be found in playground, street or parlour. A much rougher version, again played in the streets of Southwark about 1917, was called 'Dead Man's Cap':

It was only played by boys, and they had to have caps. It was played rather in the same way as 'Queenie', but the boys stood in line some three feet apart, behind each other. The 'Dead-man' threw his cap over his shoulder. One of the boys had to catch it – and hide it quickly. The 'Dead-man' had to guess or discover who had the cap. If he guessed right he had to return to the spot where he started from before the boy with the cap hit him with it. And a peaked cap could really hurt – especially if the other boys obstructed your run 'home'.

Another game that seems to have some affinities with 'Queenie' is 'Queen Sheba', which Jean Rodger included in *Lang Strang*, her little book of Forfar rhymes and games, published about 1950:

> The girls stand in a line with their hands clasped in front of them. Queen Shebah stands in front. One player stands back.
>
> > Queen Sheba-ah has lost her gold ring
> > Guess who has found it.
>
> Queen Shebah, holding the ring between her clasped hands, holds her hands over each of the others in turn. Into one person's hands she drops the ring. The one who was 'out' guesses who has found it. If she guesses wrongly, she is 'out' again. If correctly, she takes the place of the one who had it. That person becomes Queen Shebah, and the former Queen is 'out'.

Bad Eggs

'Bad Eggs' was formerly an immensely popular game in street and play-ground, and it is still played, although the complexity of its rules and the degree of organisation necessary mean that it is more often found now-adays in the repertoire of youth organisations like the Scouts and Guides than in the playground. From what I can recollect from my own experi-ence in the Woodcraft Folk in South London in the late 1950s, it works as follows. All players are given a number, from one upwards. As the game proceeds, each player tries to avoid getting a point against them, termed a 'bad egg'. Anyone who reaches a certain number of bad eggs, usually three or six, has to undergo a punishment. The game starts with one person (say No. 1) throwing the ball up in the air and calling a number (say No. 2). Everyone scatters, except for No. 2, who has to catch the ball. If they catch it before it bounces, No. 1 gets a bad egg and the game starts again with No. 2 throwing it up. If, however, No. 2 fails to catch it cleanly, as soon as it is in their hands they must shout, 'Stop!' All the players must then freeze. No. 2 must now try to hit one of the others players with the ball, after taking three steps towards them (say No. 3). If No. 2 hits No. 3 with the ball, No. 3 gets a bad egg; if No. 2 misses, No. 2 gets the bad egg. No. 3 is not allowed to move or flinch, and if they do they get the bad egg, unless they can catch the ball, in which case No. 2 gets the bad egg. The game starts again with whoever got the bad egg throwing the ball up. They do not have to wait for the far-flung players to get back to the centre, but can start immediately, which is the risk that those who run a long way out must take.

A more recent – and rather more human – description comes from eleven-year-old girls in Godalming, Surrey, in 2008. They called the game 'Spam':

> You throw the ball up – you're all numbered – and one person just throws the ball up and says (number 4) – say that's Mollie – she will have to try and catch the ball and we have to run away as far as possible – and when she's caught it she says, 'Spam', and she'll look who's closest and she can take three steps towards them and they can be as big as she likes, and she's got to try and throw it at them and they can't move their feet, but they can duck or they can lean – you have to get them out by hitting them. And if it hits you you're S, but if it misses you the person who throws it is on S. Then the next time it's P, then A, then M, then Spam.

The spelling out of a word was also a regular feature in the past: others included 'spuds' and 'donkey'. Another common detail was that the players were given names instead of numbers – days of the week, for example, or months if there were more than seven of you.

In some versions of the game the thrower does not throw directly at a chosen player, but can pass the ball to others. As long as the recipient does not drop the ball, they do not get the point against them, and it is only the one at the end of this chain of passes, who is actually 'hit' with the ball, who loses the point. In playgrounds, and other areas where there are places where the runners can get out of sight of the thrower, the rule is usually that they must always show at least one hand.

The main difference between recent and older versions of the game is that in the past, rather than throwing the ball up in each round, players would throw it into a series of holes, or the caps of the players all lined up at the foot of a wall. Whoever's cap or hole the ball landed in was the one chosen to throw the ball at the others. In these versions a stone was placed in the cap of the person who had lost the point, and this feature explains why the game's many names often include a reference to 'eggs'. Local names for the game are legion, including 'Egg-in-cap', 'Eggety Budge', 'Hat Ball', 'Hats and Holes', 'Monday', 'Tuesday', 'Kingy', 'Egg Flip', 'Flinchers' and, in Galloway in 1824, 'Burly Whush'.

As the main aim of the game is to avoid losing points, there is nearly always an agreed punishment for those unfortunates who reach a certain number of 'bad eggs'. Three traditional punishments are widely associated with the game, although their names vary considerably. 'Aunt Sally' is where the player bends over and all the other players line up to take it in turns to throw the ball at his or her posterior. In 'Under the mill' or 'Through the gauntlet' all the players stand in a line against a wall with their left arms raised, to make a tunnel. The victim runs through under the arms, and the players belabour him or her with their right hands. In earlier versions, another regular punishment was for the player to stand with their back to a wall, with one arm extended and the hand of that arm flat against the wall with fingers outspread. The others took turns to throw the ball, as hard as they liked, at the outspread hand.

The game is recognisable in the traditions of many countries, albeit with numerous local variations, and in *Children's Games with Things* (1997) the Opies refer to it as 'one of the major European games'. They demonstrate that it was already being played in Prague around 1580 and in Britain as early as the mid seventeenth century.

The game's probable immediate ancestor, 'Hat Ball', ultimately fell victim to a change in children's clothes fashions. As its name implies, 'Hat Ball' (or 'Ball and Bonnets', 'Ball in the Decker', 'Hats in Holes', 'Nine-holes', 'Egg-hat' and many other variations on the theme), requires players to have hats or caps – accessories that started to fade out some time after the Second World War.

A full description was published in *Somerset Notes & Queries* of 1896–7, referring to Somerset in about 1846:

> 'Caps': I can well remember this game was very popular fifty years ago in the playground at Crewkerne Grammar School when my father was Head Master, and I have often played it there . . . Half a dozen boys elected to play it and arrange their caps at the foot of a wall. A line was drawn about five yards distant from the row of caps and one player began by trying to pitch the ball into one of the caps, his own or someone else's. As a rule, unless he was a very good shot, he chose another cap than his own. As soon as the ball had lodged in one of the caps, the owner thereof had to run as quickly as he could

and picking it up hurl it at one of the other boys so as to strike him. We called it 'corking' him. If the shot told, the boy so hit had to cork another, and the boy who failed had to put a small stone in his cap, which was called an egg. Any boy who got three was said to be out and had to remove his cap from the row for the moment. As soon as the ball was safely in one boy's cap all the other players used to run away, and if they could run round a corner so as to hide all their bodies except a finger so much the better. But it was necessary to be careful in doing this, as it was lawful for another boy B to accept, if he could catch it, the ball from A and with it cork C who was close by him in fancied security. Or A, on seeing that it was impossible to cork anyone, might at once accept his egg, call play suddenly and pitch the ball into the cap of a boy who was too far off to run up and seize the ball, while the other boys were near at hand. Five or six boys might be corked in succession until a miss was made; and then the party so missing received an egg and proceeded to pitch the ball again into one of the caps. The game went on until all the players were out but one; and he won the game.

    Then all the other players had to pay the penalty of their want of success. Each of the losers in succession stood up facing the wall, and taking the ball in his left hand threw it between his legs as far as he could. The winner, taking his stand on the spot where the ball first touched the ground, used to cork his victim from that spot as hard as he could three times. When all had taken their punishment bravely the game was over.   SOMERSET, C.1846

This game was clearly popular in the nineteenth and early twentieth centuries. Another correspondent in the same volume remembered playing it in Dorset around 1850, under the title 'Egg-hat', and another full description of 'Pillar the Hat' was published in the *Dublin University Magazine* in 1862, as played in Co. Wexford fifty years before. In the *Boy's Own Book* of 1846, a very similar account is given under the heading 'Nine-Holes or Hat-Ball', and an Isle of Man version was described by A. W. Moore in his *Vocabulary of the Anglo-Manx Dialect* (1924).

    As indicated, the detail that the stones placed in the caps to keep score were called 'eggs' probably explains why the successor game is often called 'Bad Eggs'.

Donkey

One of the variations of games involving bouncing balls off walls is 'Donkey', an immensely widespread game in the late twentieth century, though less popular nowadays. It involves throwing a ball against the wall and the players jumping over it on the rebound, or at least letting it bounce between their legs. In one version the ball has to be caught on the rebound:

> A ball was thrown so that it bounced, then hit the wall, and was caught on the return. A player who failed to catch the ball got a 'D' and passed the ball to the next player. The next time she missed she got an 'O', and so on, until she had 'DONKEY' and lost the game. NOTTINGHAM, 1950S/1960S

Some children use different animals' names.

Kerbsy

A number of games are based on the simple fact that the angle provided between a horizontal and a vertical surface is a good place to bounce a ball. This particular game is still popular, and is usually called 'Kerby' or 'Kerbsy' when played against the kerb in the street or a step in the playground, or 'Ledger' when a window ledge or similar fixture provides the necessary surface:

> Kerby – Is a game for two players, and you have to have two kerbs. The rules are, you get a ball, it is a big ball, you stand on one kerb and throw the ball at the other kerb and if you hit it, it should come back to you.
>
> YORKSHIRE, 1980

In its commonest form the players simply keep a score of how many bounces or catches they have achieved, but sometimes there are cumulative restrictions on how the ball is thrown, as in two-balls (see p. 191).

Slam

A widely known game, which boys regard as both a game in its own right and good practice for their football skills, is usually called 'Slam' or 'Spot':

> 'Slam' is played against a wall. All contestants take it in turn to kick the ball against the wall. If you hit the wall, the ball rebounds and the next person takes his/her shot from where it lands. If you miss you lose a life. You have four lives, called S, L, A and M. When you lose a life you gain a letter. When you have spelt out SLAM you are out. If the ball hits you and it is not your turn, you also lose a life. You can gain an extra life by hitting

the wall twice in one go, if it hits, then rebounds, then rolls back and
hits the wall again.   *YORKSHIRE, 1990S*

The rules are almost always as described here.

Dodge Ball

'Dodge Ball' has been mentioned at nearly every school contacted for this
book, and is clearly a popular game, although it varies a little from place
to place. Probably the commonest form is that described by Cathy Gould,
as played in Coventry in the 1990s:

> Children line up and take turns to run along against a wall. The person who
> is 'on' tries to hit them below the knee with a ball (tennis ball size). If you
> are hit you are out, if not you can run behind the thrower and re-join the
> queue to have another go.

In other versions the children do not run across but simply stand in front
of the wall and have to dodge from side to side. Sometimes a person who
is hit immediately becomes the thrower, but in that case the tension of
gradual elimination is forfeited. The game also goes by the name of 'Wallie',
'Slam' and others.

But the name 'Dodge Ball' has also been applied to other forms of game,
such as the following:

> 'Dodge Ball': There are two teams, one on this side and one on this side,
> and there's like a line between, and they have this sponge ball, and they have
> to throw it at the other team, and if they hit somebody below the waist,
> then they're out, and then they have to sit down somewhere; but if some-
> body catches the ball on the team then they can come back in, but it can't
> bounce.   *WEST LONDON, 2009*

Champ

'Squares', 'Scrubby' or 'Champ' is a widespread ball game often taught by
teachers and games instructors but is also played spontaneously by children:

> '4 Square' – (1) You must paint or chalk four squares [i.e. one large square
> divided into four] and the squares must have A B C and D in all of them; (2)
> The person in square A hits the ball to any square he wants to; (3) The ball

can only bounce once in each square; (4) The ball must be hit with the palm or the heel of the hand; (5) If a person in A B or C gets out he is automatically placed into square D; (6) You can get out by two people passing the ball to each other's square, then one suddenly passes it to your square and if you miss it you are out.   YORKSHIRE, 1975

The game is still played enthusiastically in many playgrounds, wherever the squares are painted on the floor, and when in fashion there is often a queue of people waiting for their turn. It is nearly always called 'Champ' nowadays.

Head Catch

In a circle; a person in the middle throws the ball to others in turn and says 'head' or 'catch'. If they say 'catch' you have to head it, and if they say 'head' you have to catch it. If you do it wrong you are out.   GATESHEAD, 2010

Fists

You all stood in a circle (the bigger the better). It started with one of you with a tennis ball held between two clenched fists throwing it with one bounce to someone else in the circle. If they failed to catch it between their clenched fists they were out and the ball was returned to you for another throw. If it did not reach them first bounce you were out.   GLASGOW, 1940S

Broken Bottles

In 'Broken Bottles' all the players stand in a circle and throw the ball randomly to each other, until someone drops it. They are then out, or lose a life, or, in the more interesting version, are progressively handicapped each time they miss a catch. First time they 'lose' an arm, second time a leg, third time they have to go down on one knee and so on. But each time they catch the ball they reclaim one handicap.

The game has gone by various names – 'Broken Bottles', 'Wounded Soldiers', 'Donkey' (in which you gain a letter each time you miss, until you spell 'donkey' and are out), and even the evocative 'Sick, Ill, Dying, Dead'.

Piggy in The Middle

Norman Douglas includes a description of 'Catch' or 'Teaser' in his *London Street Games* (1916), which, judging by the spelling and grammar, was written for him by a child (unless Douglas was trying to imitate one for effect):

> Two boys stand at each side of the road and one in the middle, that's Hee. One of them tries to get the ball over middles head for the other to get but if middle gets it the throer goes Hee.

Most readers will recognise this as 'Piggy in the Middle', which is still regularly played in the playground, and a game name so familiar it has supplied an idiom to the general language. But the name was previously used for other games, such as 'Bull in the Ring', in which a person tried to get out of a circle, and a version of 'British Bulldog' (see p. 37). These are much better documented, and are more likely to have supplied the idiom.

Hot Potato

> There's a circle of people and you've got a sponge ball and you have to pass it around like it's really hot – hot potato, hot potato – and if that person drops it then they have to run around the circle before someone picks it up and throws it around, bounces it on their place, if they're not back in time.
>
> WEST LONDON, 2009

CHAPTER THIRTEEN

Marbles

In contrast to many areas of children's lore, where we have to piece together a history from a few scattered hints and references, the literature of marbles is extensive, at least in the nineteenth and twentieth centuries. This is partly because compilers of local dialect dictionaries realised that the terminology for the game in their region was colourful and seemingly archaic, so they invariably went into detail on the subject. But it is also a real measure of the popularity of the game. It is clear that many people who wrote about children's games, and those who published memoirs and accounts of their early days, remembered marbles with particular affection as a symbol of the happy pastimes of childhood. The game has continued to fascinate adult writers, but there is little doubt that the glory days of the game lie in the past.

The hold of the game on children's affections was already beginning to weaken when school staff took a firmer grip over playground activities. In many schools today marbles are discouraged, if not actually banned, on the grounds that no items should be brought to school that might be lost or fought over. And marbles, like many other games, including cigarette cards, cherry oggs and buttons, was in its heyday a form of gambling, and there are many tales of fortunes won and lost.

It is interesting that when you talk to modern children about games like marbles they are particularly intrigued by the gambling aspect of the game, and find the concept of losing your possessions in a game quite strange.

Overall, the range of marble games in circulation has diminished, and the finer points of rules, technique and arcane terminology are disappearing fast. The record, though, is extremely patchy. Many children look at you blankly when you ask if anyone plays marbles in the playground, although some say they play it at home. But in some schools, enthusiastic marble playing continues, or certainly did until recently. Marc Armitage's investigations into the design and use of school playgrounds, for example, summarised in *Play Today* (2001), drew on fieldwork in ninety locations in Yorkshire, Lincolnshire and Nottinghamshire during the 1990s. He found that about 65 per cent of the schools surveyed reported regular marble playing, and that the game was still seasonal, reappearing every spring with renewed vigour. As he comments:

> The playing of marbles becomes so popular here that the headteacher has introduced a method of drawing the season to a close – she opens her diary during an assembly and exclaims, 'I see from my diary that the marble season ends a week on Friday.' And sure enough, it does.

One noticeable feature of more recent marble games is the predominance of those utilising metal drain or manhole covers. Games like these have no doubt existed since drain covers were invented, but from the 1970s onwards they seem to have become the norm. In all but two of the schools where Marc Armitage found regular marble play, the game took place exclusively on such covers. As these metal covers vary considerably in size and the complexity of the patterns made by lettering, handles and so on, the games differ to suit the local situation. It is interesting to note that the children are well aware of which covers are the 'hardest' and which the 'easiest', and it is common practice for the latter to be left to the younger children.

The general name for the marbles themselves has varied considerably according to time and place: they have been 'marlies' in Ireland; 'bools' in Scotland; 'chonks' in the West Midlands; 'marables' in Yorkshire in the 1820s; 'bobbers' or 'merps' in Lancashire; 'doddies' in Buckinghamshire; 'jorries' in Northamptonshire; and 'taws' in various places. There have also been words for the different types of marble, the different games and the rules by which they were conducted.

Some measure of the rich variety of marble words is indicated by Elizabeth Mary Wright, whose husband compiled the mammoth *English Dialect Dictionary* (1898–1905), and who included the following synopsis in her *Rustic Speech and Folk-Lore* (1913):

> *Different types of marble*: balser, bobber, bullocker, dobber, dogle, dolledger, fifer, frenchie, kabber, ligganie, pot-donnock, etc. *Different games*: bungums, dab-at-the-hole, doorie, drop-eye, dykey, follow-tar, lag, langie-spangie, nanks, plonks and spans, rackups, ringhams, rumps, etc. *Exclamations and expressions*: A-Rant, no custance, dubs, fen keeps, gobs, heights, layers, lights up and no bird-eggs,

lodge, no first my redix, roonses, to fub, to fullock, to gull, to grumphey, to hagger, to murl, to plonk, to strake, to play freezers, to play kibbly, etc.

The methods of shooting or throwing are also variously named, as in the following sample culled from Anne Baker's excellent *Glossary of Northamptonshire Words and Phrases* (1854):

> *Dobbing*: when one boy strikes another boy's marble, without his marble first touching the ground, he is said to 'dob' on it; *Dribbling*: shooting slowly along the ground, in contradistinction to 'plumping'; *Fubbing*: an irregular and unfair mode of ejecting the taw, by advancing the whole hand instead of the thumb only; *Plumping*: a mode of shooting at marbles, by raising the hand, so that the marble does not touch the ground until it reaches the object of its aim; *Knuckle down*: when the marble is shot from the hand with the knuckle resting on the ground.

The words for the type of marble usually refer to its size, material, colour and value, or a combination of these.

The histories of the two commonest words, 'alley' and 'taw', are the most elusive, precisely because their meanings have changed over time. 'Alley' originally probably meant a marble made of alabaster, first used around 1720, but it soon lost its material connection and began to be used to refer to any ordinary marble. The derivation of 'taw', on the other hand, is less clear, and its history is much more complicated. The *Oxford English Dictionary* provides the first known use, from *The Tatler* in 1709, in the phrase 'he is hiding or hoarding his taws and marbles', but has no suggestion to offer on its etymology beyond the fact that it might be an abbreviation like 'alley'. Down the years, in everyday language, the word 'taw' was used either as a generic term for a marble, or to mean a particularly valued marble, usually the one used to shoot at the others.

This is made clear in George Forrest's *The Playground, or The Boy's Book of Games* (1858), which is written as a narrative concerning one Thomas, who arrives at a new boarding school and has to learn the local games from his new schoolfellows, who obligingly explain all the rules and give useful advice:

> Let me tell you, too, that you will lose a fortune in marbles if you have a bag of such good ones as those in your pocket. Why, they are all taws! You should get a bag of cheap marbles to put in the ring as 'shots', and keep the

others as your own taws. And take care to choose a taw of a curious or striking colour, because then there will be no disputes about its ownership.

In other sources the word 'taw' was used to mean the game, or, in many cases, the line from which the shooting was carried out.

Another way of looking at marbles has been according to their perceived value, and expert marble players in the past usually had an agreed scale of values, which took size, colour, decoration and rarity into account. This also engendered in-group terminology: a 'taw' was usually the most valued; those at the bottom of the scale would be dismissed as 'commoneys', a word already in circulation when Dickens included in *Pickwick Papers* (1837) the phrase 'whether he had won any alley tors or commoneys lately' (Ch. 34).

More modern names are, in general, more obvious:

Cullies for the multi-coloured ones, Smokies for the slightly cloudy ones, and Gobstoppers for the big ones. *WEST MIDLANDS, 1970S*

Queenies, Kingsies, cats eyes, petroleums, weenies, chinas.
KENT, 1970S/EARLY 1980S

Skettis were the best marbles to have. They looked like they had spaghetti in them. *ESSEX, 1970S*

Marbles that were opaque were called Allis and the big ones were called Dobbers. *BRISTOL, 1970S*

One of the beauties of the marble is that it can be used in so many ways, but certain games stood the test of time and were found all over Britain, although, as usual, they went by various names. Probably the best known of traditional marble games is 'Ring-taw' or 'Ringy':

In 'ring taw' a large circle is drawn on the ground, within which the players each place the same number of marbles. They then fix a place some ten or twelve feet distant from the circle, and bowl a large marble to it. The one who gets nearest goes first, and the others in order of nearness, but if the bowling marble enter the circle, it is dead and the bowler must take the last turn. The first player now shoots his marble at the full ring, and all those he drives out are his; and he can continue shooting until he fails to drive any out, or his own stays in, and then the next in order follows, and so on, until the ring be empty.   *EAST YORKSHIRE, 1880S*

The size of the ring depends on the number of players, and there are two main variations in layout. In one form there are two concentric circles, with the marbles inside the smaller one and players shooting from the perimeter of the larger. In the commoner version the marbles are simply placed in a ring and the players shoot from a line drawn outside the circle. The placing of the marbles in the ring also varies considerably. In some games they are placed randomly in the centre, in some they are carefully set into a pattern, and in some they are placed at intervals around the perimeter.

Another game that was once widespread was 'Long-taw' or 'Follows'. It proved particularly popular when the players were on their way somewhere:

> It was along the gutters, on the way to school, that several games of marbles would take place, one set following a few yards behind the other. This was what we called travelling – one bowled his marble along the gutter for a few feet and his opponent tried to hit it with his. If he succeeded he picked it up and the other fellow would have to bring a fresh marble out and start again. The crisis came when a drain appeared. Someone had to go ahead to stop the marbles going down! This game soon got children to school where they were promptly rebuked for having dirty hands. *KENT, 1930S*

The game could be played in a more static way, to a point and back again, and there was also a solo version, as graphically described by Gordon Mills, who grew up in Edinburgh in the 1930s:

> Now guttery, like many street games, is a game requiring great skill. The aim of the solo game is to knuckle a bool as far down the gutter as possible, without ending up on the roadway or vanishing into the lower depths of a silver [drain]. There were always hazards on the way. Hazards like soggy remains of sherbet dabs, spat out chewing gum, squashed cigarette packets, or the greasy sauce spattered leavings of last night's unfinished fish supper. And if you were very unlucky, petrified or – even worse – fresh mounds of horse dung. Hazards could not be removed before a game started.

A third regular pattern for marbles was 'Pyramids' or 'Castles', as played by C. H. Rolph in North London just before the First World War:

> [Of all the marble games] I remember only 'Pyramids', a game in which one

boy arranged all his marbles in a three-sided pyramid on the ground and drew a chalk circle round it. The rest of us then shot at it in turn with our own marbles, flicking each one by pinching it between the knuckle of the bent thumb and the curves of the forefinger. For each shot you paid one marble to the boy with the pyramid. But if you hit the pyramid (which very few people did) all the marbles which then rolled out of the chalk circle belonged to you; and the pyramid had to be rebuilt for the next contender.

The antiquity of this particular game is demonstrated by a passage in Francis Willughby's manuscript *Book of Games*, compiled in the 1660s:

Cob-castle: They lay three nuts or cherrie stones close together in a triangle, and another in the middle upon them. This they call a Cob-castle, and setting it a prettie distance off, they throw a nut at it. If hee that throws a nut, or boules a little bullet at it, can knock it downe, he wins the four nuts that made the Cob-castle. But if hee misses, the other that ownes the Cob-castle has as manie nuts as are thrown.

One of the obvious ways of playing marbles is to make holes at which they can be aimed, but there was a surprising variety of ways in which such holes could be used, depending on whether the marbles were rolled, thrown or dropped into them:

Another game was bung-in-the-hole, where you scooped out holes in the grass verge and bowled marbles or small pebbles into them. Each hole scored a pre-set number and each player had a fixed number of marbles. This was harder than it looked as the marbles bounced out again, it was quite a game of skill.   GLOUCESTERSHIRE, 1940S

Far more sophisticated, and requiring more skill, was 'Three Holes', as described in the *Papers of the Manchester Literary Club* (1936):

The object being to get your marble in three holes usually set at the points of a triangle and to prevent your opponents from so doing by knocking their marbles away as opportunity presents itself. The round of the holes is made three times.

J. P. Emslie offered a very similar description, in Alice Gomme's *Traditional Games* (1898), as he remembered playing the game in London in mid Victorian times.

A more rough-and-ready approach to marbles, which was more suited to the needs of the hard-core gambler, was also described by the *Manchester Literary Club* writer:

> [Another] favourite game is 'tipping'. One gambler challenges another one to tip him. Each stakes the same numbers of marbles and one tips the lot from the palm of his hand into a hole in the ground, preferably against a wall. If an even number comes out, the tipper wins. If not, the other boy takes them all. If all the marbles stay in or come out, no contest is declared and the tip is taken again. When one is skinned, he is given a set, that is, one out of each four marbles he has staked and lost, presumably to set him up again. He is at liberty to stake these or to retain them. It is a proud boast to be able to say, 'I was down to my set and then skinned him.'

A writer in the *Nottingham Journal* (22 April 1952) paints a similar picture of games played in holes, 'about the size of a matchbox', gouged out between the cobbles in the street. He comments on how large numbers could be won or lost in short order:

> But there was a certain ostentation about this, and only the wealthy could afford the lavishness of such gestures, though the truly lordly might even cast a precious 'blood ally' or two amongst the small change.

Playing on drain-hole covers has already mentioned as the preferred style nowadays. It seems to have been around since at least the 1950s:

> We used to find a drain grid and starting from the outside, it was a case of seeing who could get their marble to the middle hole of the drain first.
>
> NORTH LONDON, LATE 1950S/EARLY 1960S

But there were many other ways to play. Boys made marble-boards with cut-out arches through which players tried to bowl their marbles, and this game was often played indoors on a table-top. Marbles could be placed in a ring for people to try to knock out with their spinning tops. And W. F. Turner, writing in the *East Anglian Magazine* in 1954, remembered spending winter evenings in Suffolk, about 1910, making 'cock bird' shapes out of molten lead, using a hollowed-out brick as a mould. Other shapes could also be made, such as a swan, fox, dog, horse or tree, and in the same way as fairground workers set up their shies, when the marble season arrived the 'cock birds' could be set up in the playground for all comers to shoot at. If you knocked

down a bird, you won it, but the owner of the shy claimed all the unsuccessful marbles.

> A quieter indoor game with marbles was called 'Eggs in a bush'. A boy takes
> a number of marbles and shakes them in his hands, asking, 'How many eggs
> in a bush?' The one who guesses must pay the difference between the number
> he says and the actual number, afterwards taking his turn at shaking and
> asking; but, if he guess correctly, all are his. A similar game is 'Odds and
> evens', a few being held in one hand, which is kept closed. If odds be guessed,
> and there are evens, the guesser gives one; but if odds be guessed, and there
> be odds, then they become the property of the guesser.
>
> *EAST YORKSHIRE, 1880S*

Of the many arcane rules that govern marble play, the most often
mentioned is that the player must use the regulation hand position and
shoot the marble in the correct way:

> Of course, you never threw a bool at another one. You knuckled it by curling
> your forefinger round the bool and with your thumb behind, flicked it out.
> If your thumb was too deep behind the bool, you might be derided for
> having a 'pussy knuckle'. The top notchers merely put the tip of their thumb
> behind the missile and got more force that way.   *FIFE, 1930S*

Or, as Thomas's helpful friend in Forrest's *The Playground* (1858) explained:

> You have stuck your marble in the bend of your forefinger, and you cannot
> make it fly any distance without pushing your hand after it, which we don't
> allow. Look here, put the marble between the tip of your forefinger and
> thumb, and then you can make it go almost any distance . . . When you
> shoot you must put one of your knuckles on the ground and keep it there,
> or it is not counted a fair shot.

'Knuckle down' was already in the marble player's parlance in 1740, and
subsequently entered the general language as a phrase meaning 'to apply
oneself diligently to a task'.

Edwin Grey, remembering life in a Hertfordshire village in the 1870s,
wrote of 'luck breeders'. These were boys who had the reputation of being
'good luck', and marble players would hire them simply to stand close by
during a game, although they were usually paid by results.

In some places the standard punishment for an infringement of the rules was for the miscreant to place their knuckles on the ground for the other players to shoot their marbles at. As usual, the procedure had a special name: in Heslop's *Glossary of Northumberland Words* (1892), for example, the punishment was called 'Beaks', while in Moore's *Vocabulary of the Anglo-Manx Dialect* (1924) it was 'Canokes' or 'Grunks'. And, as W. R. Lee commented in his 'Pastimes of Youth' article in 1936, 'This is no small ordeal on a cold and frosty morning.'

Over the years there have been a fair number of references to girls playing marbles, but in far more it is described as strictly a boys' pastime, and it is clear that this was generally the case. With this in mind, though, it is worth highlighting a delicious memory recorded by Mollie Harris in her book *A Kind of Magic* (1969), which chronicles her childhood in Oxfordshire in the 1920s:

> Boys *and* girls played the game, but it was really considered more of a boy's game. The marbles were carried around in flannel bags secured tightly at the top with a thread of tape. Once, from somewhere, I'd got four marbles and a glass tally and one night after school I plagued the champion of the village to play. He was a big bully of a lad and sniggered as I challenged him. 'I shall take your few fust game, you see if I don't! Hark at yer challenging I, thur yent nobody in the school as can beat I.'

Under the watchful eyes of Bert's gang they played, and whereas Mollie had amazing luck, Bert could do nothing right and to everyone's amazement she cleaned him right out.

> Mad with temper he flung his super lucky tally at me, hitting me sharply in the face. 'There, take that!' he said, 'I'll win 'um all back tomorrow, you see if I dun't.' Then he and his gang moved off, shouting and swearing. I stuffed my winnings into Bert's flannel marble bag that he'd left lying on the ground and ran off home.

But her glory was short-lived:

> When I got to school next morning, Bert and his gang were bowling their iron hoops in the playground. 'En't you going tu try and win 'um back?' I asked, clutching my bag of marbles. 'No I blumen well en't,' he said, 'shove off. Marbles is a girl's game', and they tore away and charged round the playground like a herd of young bullocks. In fact nobody wanted to play. They were all too busy bowling their hoops.

Anyone interested in the early history of marbles would do well to start with the Opies' summary in their *Children's Games with Things* (1997). They write of small clay and glass balls from Egyptian and Cretan tombs, which archaeologists date to the Minoan period, 2000–1700 BC, but point out that these may have been used in board games or for some other purpose. In the classical period, children certainly played at rolling nuts, but it is only in medieval times that hard evidence for marble playing starts to appear, and only with the sixteenth and seventeenth centuries that marbles can be said to have become a commonplace game in Europe.

Collectors and dealers classify marbles by material, method of production, place of production, and then size, decoration and so on, and they have identified a bewildering variety of makes and styles over the years. But there does not seem to be a simple straightforward progression, with one type replacing another in a neat, orderly fashion. Balls found in archaeological sites, for example, which are presumed to be marbles, are usually of clay, but there are also glass ones – which may of course be beads. Clay marbles – generally regarded as cheap and inferior – were probably the first to be made and were still being made in the mid twentieth century. Glass ultimately supplanted them, but marbles have also been made of china, stone, metal, agate and alabaster.

It is very difficult to get a handle on what was available where at any given time, partly because people rarely describe what they take for granted, and partly because the situation varied so much from place to place. A very useful summary, published in *Games and Sports for Young Boys* (1859), gives the picture in the mid nineteenth century:

> There are many different kinds of marbles; those made of agate are prized above every other sort, and indeed their pre-eminence is fully justified by the exquisitely beautiful veining of some of them, and the rich and harmonious colouring of others. *Alleys* are made of white marble striped and clouded with red, and when this colour predominates, they are called *blood-alleys*. These marbles rank next in value to *agates*. *Taws* or *stoneys*, of brown marble, streaked with darker tones of the same colour form the third class; *French taws* of stained or coloured marble the next; the gaudy Dutch marbles of glazed clay, painted either yellow or green, and ornamented with stripes of a dark colour, constitute class the fifth, while the unpretending yellowish clay marbles, or *commoneys*, form the very lowest class, and are held in little repute by those who can procure the superior kinds.

There is no mention here of glass marbles, but a writer in *Notes & Queries* in 1899 commented that in his childhood in Belfast in the 1850s glass marbles 'were the newest inventions and not so much used'. Such marbles were mainly made in Germany but they took a long time to penetrate the market in Britain, and right up to the Second World War many players regarded glass marbles as something special – they were still called 'glessies', 'glarnies', 'glass alleys' or something similar. The situation was transformed by the influx of wonderfully colourful mass-produced marbles made in Asia, which almost overnight became the norm and set the style for what most people nowadays would regard as 'normal' marbles.

CHAPTER FOURTEEN

Conkers

Children love conkers, and as soon as they can toddle they enjoy finding them among the autumn leaves. It always seems a great shame that there is nothing much in practical terms you can do with them, although older people may remember a drive to collect them for cattle feed during the Second World War, and in the mid 2000s a belief started to circulate that keeping conkers in a room would keep spiders away.

There is little doubt that the word 'conker', denoting both the tree and the game, derives directly from predecessor games in which natural objects were pitted against each other, either by hitting or squeezing. These all featured the word 'conqueror', either as the name of the game or simply the designation for the winning contestant, and this shared name makes the early literature ambiguous. The modern conker game is probably little more than 160 years old, but it is difficult to date its exact beginning. The horse chestnut tree (*Aesculus hippocastanum*) is native to the Balkans, and was not introduced to Britain until the late sixteenth century. Although an attractive tree, prized for its ornamental features, its wood is of little economic value, and its spread across the countryside was relatively gradual over the following 300 years.

The most widely reported of the conqueror games that foreshadowed conkers involved snail shells. Here is the poet Robert Southey remembering his days at school at Corston, near Bristol, in 1782:

> One very odd amusement, which I never saw or heard elsewhere, was greatly in vogue at this school. It was performed with snail shells, by placing them against each other, point to point, and pressing till the one was broken in, or sometimes both. This was called conquering; and the shell which remained

unhurt, acquired esteem and value in proportion to the number over which it had triumphed, an accurate account being kept. A good conqueror was prodigiously prized and coveted, so much so indeed, that two of this description would seldom have been brought to contest the palm, if both possessors had not been goaded to it by reproaches and taunts. The victor had the number of its opponents added to its own; thus when one conqueror of fifty conquered another which had been as often victorious, it became conqueror of an hundred and one.

It is perhaps significant that he had not come across the game before. 'Conquerors' may have been the generic name, but nineteenth-century dialect dictionaries provide a range of local terms, such as 'Cocks and Hens' in Northumberland, and 'Coggers' in Northamptonshire, which could all have derived from the same root. The assumption that the snail-shell game is ancient, and has always been called 'Conquerors', has led many amateur etymologists to state that the word derives directly from the word 'conch', which entered the English language from Latin via French sometime before the late fourteenth century. At various times it was used to describe all sorts of shelled creatures, although more often shellfish than snails. The derivation is possible, but there is no firm evidence to support it.

The earliest clear reference to horse chestnut conkers is provided by one R. Tucker, who wrote to the *Athenaeum* in January 1899:

> I remember that about the year 1848, when I was a schoolboy at Newport, Isle of Wight, I often played conquerors with both horse-chestnuts and walnut shells. Further, we boys used to play the game with snail shells, by forcibly pressing the hard terminal tops against one another.

He was recalling a period fifty years earlier, and may possibly have got his dates a little wrong, but the game was definitely around in the following decade: Charles Higham wrote in the same journal that he played 'Conquerors' with horse chestnuts on a string at the grammar school in Loughborough in 1855–7; the game is mentioned in the 1856 edition of the *Boy's Own Book*; and George Sturt's memoir of his life in Farnham, Surrey, *A Small Boy in the Sixties* (1927), shows that by about the mid century mark all the elements of the later game were already in place:

> 'Conquerors' (shortened into 'Conkers') or 'Mounters' were horse-chestnuts, threaded on stout string. A gimlet bored a raw-smelling hole, and many

chestnuts – a rope or necklace of them – could be threaded on to one string like birds' eggs. But you wanted a good strong one for 'Conquerors'. Two played at that game; and indeed you took your 'Conquerors' to school with you, so as to be ready for a challenge. Each player in his turn held up his 'conqueror' – chestnut – threaded on a string and kept by a sufficient knot from swinging off, while his opponent swung his own 'Conqueror' against it – once only in each turn – as hard as he could, in the hope of breaking the other. The end of the game was when one of the chestnuts split.

Nevertheless, right into the 1880s and 1890s, many writers seemed unfamiliar with the horse chestnut game, and were still referring to 'Conquerors' as involving snails. It seems certain that although chestnut conkers were by then fully familiar to many people, the game had a long way to go before it achieved the widespread popularity that it was to enjoy in the twentieth century. So, for example, on 6 October 1898 a writer in the *Pall Mall Gazette* submitted a piece entitled 'Conkers', which described schoolboys playing the game, while another contributor to the same magazine, on 12 December 1898, could write of boys avidly collecting conkers and could comment, 'But beyond picking them up and putting them in their pockets and comparing notes as to how many they possess, I am not aware that they do anything with them.'

The basic rules are simple enough. One player holds his conker almost at arm's length, slightly above shoulder height, dangling on its string. Holding his own string, Player 2 swings his conker to hit player 1's, as hard as he can. They take it in turns, until one conker breaks and falls off its string, and thereby loses the game. There are, however, many possible variations. In most circumstances, for example, the players simply take it in turns, and a hit or a miss counts as a player's go, but some people allow three attempts per go, while others adopt the rule that a player's turn lasts for as many successful hits as he can manage, and only passes to his opponent when he actually misses. In early descriptions of the game, the conker on the receiving end was not held on its string, but placed on a hat or piece of turf and so on.

Conkers inherited from its predecessors the delightful notion that particular nuts not only attain their own score, but also acquire the successes already achieved by any vanquished opponent, and all numerals are graced with the suffix '-er'. Thus a conker which has beaten three others is a 'three-er', but if it beats a 'five-er', it becomes a 'nine-er' (3+5+1). The game has also enjoyed a rich terminology of its own, starting with a formulaic phrase to claim the first hit: 'Oblionker! My fust conker!' in Worcestershire

Seasonal Games

'Are the dates known at which children commence and conclude their games?' was the question asked by one J. K. in the antiquarian journal *Notes & Queries* in 1879. He continued:

> In the course of a tolerably extensive experience of the alleys and slums of London I have learned that tops, marbles, tip-cats (*ehue!*), battledore and shuttlecock, and other favourite games of both girls and boys come out and disappear at a given date. Whether there exists some *lex non scripta* [unwritten law] concerning these things, and what may be the cause of the observance of seasons, are matters on which I should be glad of information.

It is significant that nobody gave a definitive answer to his question.

'Game seasons' is one of those areas of childlore that is generally misunderstood and misremembered by adults, often because they are convinced that there was *one annual season* for games such as tops, hoops, marbles, skipping and so on, and that a season started and finished on particular days. Reality, though, was much messier:

> I can assure you that the dates of the opening of the seasons of hoops and tops were almost as arbitrary as those of cricket and football. Hoops were produced directly the last bonfire of November 5 had been extinguished, and continued to menace the pedestrian until February, when the first spring day was the signal for the opening of the top season. This for some unknown reason reached its zenith in boat race week; and though solitary enthusiasts were still to be found practising their art until the end of April, the pitches were mostly taken over by marbles players. These continued to occupy street corners until the hot weather made fields and hedgerows more attractive than pavements and roads.   HERTFORDSHIRE, 1920S

What most adults are, in fact, remembering or noticing is the palpable *coming in* time for games, when they take the general fancy. There is often a kind of 'shared consciousness', which dictates whether a fashion or craze takes the children's fancy and thus takes hold for a while.

> The date of their advent was a mystery, and once when I turned up at school with a skipping-rope before the correct skipping season, I was regarded as

if I had committed a crime. Much ashamed, I folded the rope, twisted it round the blue handles, and quietly put it out of sight.

DERBYSHIRE, 1880s

Some enthusiasts, of course, have always played particular games, such as marbles, all through the year, or at least when circumstances permitted or when other 'phases' were not dominant. The point about the 'season', though, is that everyone seems to be doing it, and there is an urgency and exhilaration involved – *all the rage* is the appropriate phrase here. Out of season there is no mass feeling of commitment. In the past it was noticed that gender had a part to play: some perceptive commentators noted that whereas the boys would play enthusiastically with, for example, fivestones and tops at particular times, girls played them all year round.

There can also be short-lived revivals at any time, brought about by a newcomer to the school, a dominant child within a group, or an outside influence such as a story in a book or comic or, nowadays, a television programme or film. One key aspect that determines whether a revival 'takes' or not is whether the game has been in fashion recently. As with 'crazes', there is a strong element of novelty, which wears off as the 'boredom' factor takes over.

Some games, such as conkers, are completely in the hands of nature and the seasons. But nature shapes the popularity of other games, too. It is difficult to manipulate fivestones or marbles with cold hands, or in gloves; shuttlecocks do not work well in windy weather and, as one ten-year-old girl said to me, 'You try being whacked round the legs with a sopping-wet skipping rope!' On the other hand, many games seem attractive in spring, while summer invites the playing of intricate static games.

Commercial outlets were well aware that certain games came in at particular times, and would stock up on hoops or marbles as appropriate; children were reminded of a particular game by seeing it in the local shop window. Writers were commenting on games seasons from at least the 1750s. However, it does seem to be the case that the hold of 'seasons' gradually weakened as the twentieth century progressed and that today, when children can get equipment from the school games cupboard whenever they like, they do not have to worry whether taking, say, a skipping rope to school is appropriate for the time of year. That said, phases and crazes still persist, and presumably they always will.

in 1878; 'Obli, Obli, O, My first go' in Herefordshire, 1878 ; 'Cobley Co, my first go' in Wales; and 'Hick, hack, first smack' and 'Fuggy smack' in Yorkshire in the mid 1940s.

Conkers with a flat side were formerly almost universally called 'cheeses', 'cheesers' or 'cheese-cutters'. When strings became entangled a player could claim an extra turn by shouting 'strings' before his opponent, and it was perfectly acceptable for a player to stamp on his opponent's conker if it ended up on the floor, unless the owner had already cried 'No Stampsies!' or its local equivalent.

As with all games worth their salt, conkers is not simply a matter of brute force but involves a degree of preparation and strategy that will separate the seasoned player from the mere novice:

> Conkers are not lightly to be led to victory. They should be veterans of a past autumn, hidden – and their hiding place not forgotten – through the year. They can be groomed for the tourney by being put in the oven or treated with alum or vinegar. The skill with which they are pierced and supported by well-knotted and not too thin string can make all the difference to their fortunes.   THE TIMES, 1952

How short should you make the string (by winding it round your hand) for the attack? A short string increases accuracy but at the expense of using the full force of a long sweeping swing. When on the receiving end, you need to decide whether to hold the string lightly enough to ensure that some of the force of the attack is absorbed in the conker being knocked out of your hand, or whether this runs the risk of your nut hitting the ground hard enough to crack it, especially if you are not quick enough with your cry of 'No Stampsies!' There are other subtle ways to exploit the physics of conkering:

> The rules of combat are simple enough. The bigger boy generally has the first whack, because he is the bigger boy. Carefully measuring the swing of his arm plus the length of the bootlace, he grasps the latter firmly with his right hand, and places the conker between the tip of the first and second fingers of the left hand. Both hands are raised over the right shoulder, just such a distance apart as to keep the bootlace fairly taut without checking the blow at the start. The smaller boy, meanwhile, allows his conker to hang motionless awaiting the blow. And in this the great art of the game consists. Palpably to move your chestnut out of the way as the other is descending is to 'fudge', and this is theoretically a most dishonest practice. But a very

slight 'give' at the moment of impact materially aids your champion to receive his whack without splitting. The blow delivered upon a retreating body loses half its force, and perhaps glances harmlessly aside. But you must catch the exact psychological moment for the 'give', and your opponent is watching for the psychological moment, too. Once, or even twice, he may feint; and if you are deceived his quick eye will detect the movement, and there will be a world of contempt in his accusation that you are 'fudging'. This, of course, you strenuously deny, and while the words are on your lips whiz! crack! comes his conker.   PALL MALL GAZETTE, *1898*

There is no doubt that, although conkers was popular throughout most of the twentieth century, it has lost much of its hold on the childish imagination in the last two or three decades. Every year there are letters in the newspapers commenting on the fact conkers are left lying on the ground in great quantity, whereas fifty years ago they would all have been avidly collected by local schoolboys. Some adults blame overzealous health-and-safety-minded teachers, and circulate stories of children being made to wear safety goggles before they are allowed to play. The game has certainly been discouraged in some schools, but judging from conversations I have had with children in recent years, it is clear that they have generally lost interest rather than been told not to indulge. Nevertheless, the game is not dead yet, and many children still play it every year.

CHAPTER FIFTEEN

The Collecting Instinct

I t goes without saying that children have a highly developed collecting instinct, and that this is nothing new. They get a great deal of pleasure from things that come in 'sets' or can be accumulated. Publishers and manufacturers have known this for many years and have sought to satisfy the need. Most of us can remember the pleasure we got from collecting things when young, whether our passion was lead soldiers, Dinky cars or My Little Pony.

Certain items, such as cigarette cards and marbles, are obvious candidates for collecting, but children in the past also gathered everyday items such as pins, buttons, cherry stones and pieces of broken china, either for their own interest or for use in particular games, and these items often became the unofficial currency of childhood. There was a locally agreed scale of values for marbles, for example, with large colourful ones being worth four or five 'commonies', and coloured pictures were always more sought after than black-and-white. Cigarette cards on certain subjects had more value than others, and even pieces of broken china ('boody') were worth more if they had some gold on them. In every community there seems always to have been particular children who were well known for their sharpness when it came to swapping and dealing, and many writers remembering their childhoods wonder whether these 'cigarette card barons' or 'marble entrepreneurs' later became successful bankers.

Nowadays a thriving industry caters for children's collecting instincts, but children still take pleasure in gathering other things, such as pebbles or shells from the beach, or conkers in the autumn, or pencils, rubbers and other items of day-to-day life. For many children in the twentieth century, though, it was cigarette cards that got the collecting bug going:

Cigarette cards were our passion, and the game most likely to delay us on the way home from school was 'Faggers' or 'Fag-cards'.

So wrote Leslie Paul of his London childhood around 1917, and he was not alone in his enthusiasm for the little picture cards that were given away, first in cigarette packets and later in other products. Cigarette companies started issuing cards in the 1880s, and within a decade children were avidly swapping, collecting and playing various games with them, and they continued to do so for nigh on 100 years. Cigarette manufacturers stopped including the cards during the Second World War, and some children continued to use the flattened cigarette packets instead. But manufacturers of other commodities aimed at children, such as 'sweet cigarettes', comics and bubble gum, soon stepped into the breach and began providing free cards, followed by the tea manufacturer Brooke Bond.

While they lasted, cigarette cards joined marbles as one of the key currencies in the child's economy. As Leslie Paul continued:

Almost everything within reach of a boy's pocket could be valued in cigarette cards. A boyish diary of mine had an entry, 'Swopped Wicksy 50 faggers for his nife'.

But getting the cards in the first place could be a task in itself. No self-respecting child would pass a discarded cigarette packet in the street without checking to see if the card was inside, and everyone tried to pin down their adult relatives and neighbours to ensure a steady supply. Some took more direct methods:

We got most of our fag-cards from the football crowds that passed the buildings on the way to the game at Stamford Bridge on Saturday afternoons. We hung about outside our gate, crying, 'Giss a fag-card mister.' Some men stopped and opened their fag packets and handed us a brand-new card. Others had to be pestered, and we ran alongside them begging, 'Go on, mister, giss one, ay mister?' Sometimes they took a swipe at us, and we ducked and dodged among the crowd, but persistence often paid off and we all got some.   LONDON, 1920S

Children tried hard to collect full sets, and later suppliers, such as Brooke Bond, produced albums in which the cards could be placed, pored over and cherished. Many of the cards were broadly educational, and while it was the pictures that most attracted the attention, the printed explanations

on the back were read with interest and helped inform the rising generation on a wide range of topics. Films stars, sports people and cars were
always the most sought after, but British regiments, wonders of the world,
foreign countries, kings and queens, major battles, characters in the works
of Dickens and Shakespeare, and every conceivable aspect of science and
nature, were also covered. Many adults have commented, only half-jokingly,
that their general knowledge of the world started with the information on
the back of the humble fag-card.

The only cigarette-card-related game I remember being involved in
during the 1950s had no special name, apart from 'Fag Cards'. A card entrepreneur would place four, or perhaps six, cards a few inches apart, leaning
them up against the wall at a relatively wide angle. All comers were invited
to flick their cards at these, and if you succeeded in knocking one down,
you won the cards that had missed and were still lying about. I cannot
remember, however, whether you paid the entrepreneur a card or two to
have a go, or whether he took a percentage of your winnings. He must
have had some way of making a profit, because that was the whole point
of the exercise, and there would have been a complex arrangement of capital
and shared risk to take some of the gamble out of the transaction.

I was never dextrous enough to be any good at flicking the cards, but I
had friends who were. And I had a good collection of cards, primarily because
I had two older brothers who had grown out of such things, so I inherited
the family collection – a good shoebox-full if I remember rightly. I would
lend cards to skilled friends, who would get to keep some of their winnings
and give the rest to me – if they won, of course. I always insisted on the
'swapsies' rule, because the player always wanted a new, stiff, undamaged
card to flick, but these were too valuable for me to risk. 'Swapsies' meant that
you could substitute inferior cards for the good ones you had lost.

This game was one of the two commonest forms of fag-card play, and
was often called a variation of 'Stick-em-ups', although Rose Gamble
recorded that in the 1920s it was called 'Lick-ems' because players always
licked the edge of the card before throwing it, as this was reputed to make
it fly more truly.

The other common game was to flick the cards and try to cover your
opponents' cards, which were lying on the floor. This was often done
against a wall, but could also be done by two players facing each other,
or three or more in a circle, pitching cards into the centre. Agreement had
to be reached beforehand on how much of a card had to be covered before
it counted, and as this was not a precise science, arguments often ensued.

Other ways of playing with the cards also existed. One, which was clearly based on other pitch-and-toss games, was to throw an agreed number against a wall and the winner was the one whose card was closest to the wall. Or you could draw a circle:

> In the playground, and sometimes in the street, we drew a 12-inch circle on the ground, about three inches away from the wall. You stood six feet away from that (in the street you simply stood on the kerbstone) and 'flicked' a card against the wall in the hope that it would drop into the circle. A card that did this earned its flicker five points. When all the cards had been flicked you took it in turns to 'tip' into the ring, with your thumb-nail, all those left lying outside it, one point for each. When you failed your opponent took over, and when all the cards were in the ring the game ended.
>
> *LONDON, 1920S*

'Cigarette cards' – still so called, even when they came in a packet of tea – remained a staple of playground life into the 1970s, but faded quite rapidly from the scene thereafter. Other cards took their place, but these were mainly ones which were produced for sale, rather than being given away with other products – although these still satisfy children's collecting and swapping habits. What has been lost, though, are the older throwing and flicking games, although children certainly play 'card games' with their collections.

The range of these cards seems endless, as the industry cleverly creates and satisfies the needs of the market at the same time. Any blockbuster film, such as *Star Wars*, can engender its own spin-off series, while factual cards on subjects like football teams and cars are perennial favourites. A brief glance at the card section of the local toy shop in May 2010 garnered the following: 'Pokémon', 'Match Attax', 'Yugioh', 'Andrenalyn XL', 'Stardust Overdrive', 'Card-Jitsu' and 'Crazy Bones', all of which are no doubt household names to children and their parents, but, I suspect, completely foreign to the rest of us.

A major part of the appeal of cigarette cards was the sheer joy of collecting the coloured pictures and swapping them with friends. For girls, though, while cigarette cards might well have their appeal, 'scraps' were often more popular.

> Exchanging 'scraps' was a favourite game. These were coloured pictures of flowers, fairies, cherubs, angels, clowns and nursery rhyme figures. One big one was worth two small ones and we usually sat with our friends on the doorstep to do the 'swapping'.
>
> *LANCASHIRE, 1930S*

Scraps were printed on large colourful sheets which were sold at the local shop, and the girls cut them up to make individual pictures, although these could be augmented with illustrations from various other sources such as magazines.

> You took the scraps you wanted to exchange with you to school in a book. Most of us used a children's book we still had, but thought babyish. You put each scrap between a page on its own. Those the owner was willing to exchange, she put up at the top of the page, so they stuck out of the closed book. The girl who wanted to have the scrap asked you what you would change it for from her collection. You could change a scrap for one scrap or for more, if yours was valuable. If everyone wanted angels you sold yours dearly. Scraps with glitter on were worth more than those without.   GLASGOW, 1950S

The collection and swapping of scraps also lasted well into the 1970s. Earlier generations had a game, too which some children turned to their material advantage. Scraps were placed between the pages of a book, and competitors invited to stick a pin, at random, between the pages. If they hit on the right page, they won the scrap. If they failed they had to either forfeit the pin or pay a scrap to the proprietor of the game. This game was well known in Victorian times and Alice Gomme describes it, under the name 'Dab', as generally popular in London in the 1860s. In Scotland it was called a 'Lottery Book', and there were unofficial rules regarding the number of scraps included. Girls with such books would call out, 'Dab, dab, dab at the picture-book, yin in every four leaves and four for the prize', but, according to Robert M'Nair in *Glasgow Past and Present* (1884), the pages holding the grand prize were cut a little smaller to make them harder to locate with the pin.

Another object that to today's child would seem worthless but to previous generations was highly collectable is the humble cherry stone. Not only did twentieth-century families gorge on cherries when they became available, but children pestered shops and market stalls for over-ripe fruit, and they were quite happy to pick them up in the street – something few parents would allow these days. Some children even spent some of their pocket money acquiring stones. In 1850 a fruit-seller told Henry Mayhew, who was gathering material for his magisterial *London Labour and the London Poor*, 'Boys buy, I think, more cherries than other fruit, because after they have eaten 'em they can play at cherry-stones.'

The stones, and their games, went by a variety of local names, including cherry-oggs, -bobs, -odds, -wags, -wobs, -gobs and -cobs, and in Scotland they were widely known simply as paips or papes. They were in such demand when in season that they temporarily eclipsed other things, even marbles, as a currency among children, and could be either 'gambled' in games of chance or skill, or used to pay for other treats or pastimes. In many games they were thrown or bowled, as this early definition from Jamieson's *Etymological Dictionary of the Scottish Language* (1808) makes clear:

> *Paip*: A cherry-stone picked clean, and used in a game of children. Three of these are placed together, and another above them. These are called a castle. The player takes aim with a cherry-stone, and when he overturns this castle, he claims the spoil.

This is very similar to a marble game called 'Pyramids' (p. 218). J. R. Rae, remembering his childhood in Hawick, about 1910, wrote a whole article for the *Scots Magazine* about the many games for which participants were charged a 'pape-a-go', including another throwing challenge:

> The simplest one was a grid chalked on the pavement with a number printed clearly in each box. Standing at a given mark, the pape was flicked with grim concentration towards the grid. If it landed in a box, the appropriate number of papes was paid out, but all too often it bounced outside the lines and was lost.

An illustration of such a grid can be seen in James Ritchie's second book of Edinburgh games, *Golden City* (1965), with the added detail that the stones were 'poodled' or squeezed between forefinger and thumb, rather than simply thrown.

Another way of gambling your cherry stones was recorded by the poet Richard Church (1893–1972) in his autobiography:

> I recall, too, the seasonal games, such as the mid-summer sport of 'cherry-oggs', when ingenious boys made castle facades of cardboard with doors through which their mates were invited to pitch dried cherry stones, so many being paid out if the stone passed through. I have no doubt that some of the more persistent of those promoters are now successfully running football pools.   *BATTERSEA, SOUTH LONDON, C.1901*

Albert Paul's reminiscences of life in Brighton just before the First World War include the following description of another game that may seem rather lame to us but was very popular in its time:

Us boys used to go round the streets in the town picking up cherry pips. We would get a big bag full, take them home, wash them well, then dry them in the kitchen range oven. Out we would go, meet the other boys who had done the same, then say 'Play you Cherry Lobs?' 'Yes!' 'Right. How many up?' Perhaps we would decide 10 up (any number of boys would play together). On a certain rainwater pipe (with a good shoe at the bottom) you would put 10 cherry pips in your hand, and thrust the hand hard up this shoe, which would send the cherry pips well up the rainwater pipe. Then, when they all rolled down again we would take notice where the pip had rolled away from the pipe farthest. If it was yours you would keep your eye on it. All the other boys would follow, each sending their 10 pips up the shoot (or pipe). Well, at the end the boy whose pip had rolled farthest would pick up all the pips. Should there have been 6 boys playing, the winner would collect 60 cherry pips. We called this game Cherry Lobbing.

One other game which involved throwing or rolling was 'Screws'. Again, this was popular enough to be remembered fondly – by Harold Walker, for example, in his evocation of life in Walthamstow, East London, around 1916:

A screw would be placed on its head, and invariably secured in place by a deposit of spit. Although a curious and unhygienic custom, it was never-theless religiously carried out. The 'oggs' or date stones would be pitched with the object of dislodging the spittle based screw. The person achieving this would collect all the surrounding stones.

Cherry stones were also used in more homely ways:

Cherry time was lovely because we all sat out on the step playing 'cherry hop, cherry hop'. The others had to guess how many cherries I'd got in my hand and then they'd take a turn.   *DEVON C.1910*

We used to sit for hours, rubbing a cherry-stone, till it got a hole in and make a necklace. A bit of spit, rub and rub, until it got so thin it got a hole in.   *KENSINGTON, LONDON, 1930S*

Minnie Dingwall, who wrote that last piece, also remembered charging a cherry stone a go to see her 'grotto' – a shoebox with a fairy scene inside, made of coloured paper and flowers (see below, p. 243). At the end of the day, the cherry-stone speculator could gloat over his or her takings, and, at least in Scotland, even this procedure was dictated by tradition. J. R. Rae writes:

Every night the papes were counted to assess the day's profit or loss, and this ritual had a vernacular all of its own. Four papes constituted a cad, so when counting it was yin, twae, three and a cad, a cad and yin, a cad and twae, a cad and three, twae cad and so on. It was generally understood that the word cad was a corruption of the French word *quatre* (four), and in the absence of any firm evidence to the contrary this explanation was happily accepted.   *HAWICK, C.1910*

Children's obsession with cherry stones goes back a long way. The game of 'Bob Cherry', in which players have to catch cherries floating in water or hanging from a string without using their hands, dates back certainly to the early eighteenth century (the rules are very much the same as for the much better-known 'Bob Apple'). 'Cherry-pit', the older name for the game involving throwing stones into small holes, is, according to the *Oxford English Dictionary*, first referred to as early as 1522. Shakespeare mentions it in *Twelfth Night* (Oct 3, Scene 4) – 'Tis not for gratuity to play at cherrie-pit with Satan' – and there are also references in Robert Herrick's *Hesperides* (1648), and John Ford's *Witch of Edmonton* (1658). Interestingly, 'cherry-pit' was for a long time proverbial for the innocence of childhood or for a simple, trivial pastime.

Buttons, too, were formerly very popular, with their own agreed values and terminology, and, like cherry stones, they could be played with:

'Buttons' or 'Pitchers' was also a very favourite game. The 'pitchers' were large metal buttons, cut from off gentlemen's servants' discarded livery, army buttons, and so on, those being heavy, were used (when the shanks were knocked off or flattened) to pitch at the 'mottie' or mark. These 'pitchers' were from six to ten times the value of ordinary buttons, of which there were several classes, viz: 'Brasses', 'Tinnies' and 'Bonies', etc. A boy with a pocket full of marbles and buttons was looked on as a boy of substance and wealth, and much sought after, but the 'button and marble' world was subject to great changes, for a boy might one week have quite a marble and button fortune, while the following week he might possibly be holding trousers and braces together with bits of wood or wire, the buttons having all disappeared from the pockets and also from the entire garment.

HERTFORDSHIRE, C.1870

The various games nearly all involved throwing or flicking. The buttons could be tossed against a wall, and the winner was the one whose pieces fell nearest the foot of the wall, as measured by the span of a hand; they could be pitched into holes, or perhaps into a chalked ring; or they could be placed in a ring with spinning tops, which would push them out, and so on.

> The girls played buttons . . . they would collect all kinds of buttons (any size). They would ask their mothers for old clothes to cut off all the buttons, and didn't you have to watch your sisters. They would cut off your buttons if your coat was hanging up (there was many a fight between brothers and sisters over this). A girl would mark a large square in chalk up near the wall of a house. They would always mark 'OXO' in the centre. The same procedure decided how many buttons each would play, say ten each. Each girl, one after the other, would place ten buttons on the kerbstone, in line with the chalked square. Then they would flick each button (with thumb and finger) forward until they all went into the square. After all the girls (say 6) had flicked their buttons onto the chalked square, the girl whose button was nearest, or on the 'X' of 'OXO', would gather up all the buttons, 60 in all. The girls called this game 'Up the Buttons'.
>
> BRIGHTON, SUSSEX, C.1910

There is a discrepancy in the historical record as to who played these games. Some writers stress that button games were played mainly by girls, while others are adamant that they were the province of the boys. The truth seems to be that both sexes played, perhaps at different times and in different places.

> Buttons: This game is almost entirely confined to the boys, possibly because the little girls are not able to supply the necessary playing instruments in the shape of trouser buttons and a big piece of lead, which is melted and flattened in the fire, and called a nicker. Brass trouser buttons are articles of immense value in the eyes of street boys; they are difficult to obtain, and in the majority of cases are cut off by the boys from their own garments . . . 'Buttons' consists of seven or eight buttons being thrown as near as possible a specific line on the pavement. The one who gets nearest goes in first. He stands on the kerb, takes his nicker, and aims it at a button agreed upon by the rest. If he hits it, he gets the button, and has another turn; if he misses, the next boy goes in, and the one who has got the most buttons is the winner. This game is called 'Nicking'. Another consists in putting all the buttons close together on a line and hitting one out of the line, without touching the others. This is called 'Hard Buttons', and its successful play necessitates a very neat and steady aim. Almost all the other games of

buttons, of which there are at least some seven or eight variations, are played on similar lines; and the fact that the winner may keep all the buttons he takes no doubt accounts in a measure for their great popularity.

LONDON, 1891

In another milieu, the humble button even featured in a pub and party game:

'Passing the button' was a game played both in the house, in the pub, at chapel socials, and in the open air. It is not as easy as it sounds. We used to sit in a ring, which varied in size according to the number of people playing. One would sit in the centre; one of the circle would show him the button and then the game started. The one in the middle had to guess who had the button. They hid it behind their backs and made lightning movements with body, head and arms, whether they had the button or not. Someone would act as if he had dropped it and everybody would look down pretending to hunt for it. It was quite bewildering. In the pubs they had experts at this, and their movements were really acrobatic. *YORKSHIRE, C.1912*

It is hardly possible to say where and how button games started, because the same games could be played with other objects – stones, marbles, counters, bottle tops and so on. But buttons were certainly popular, and widely reported, from the mid nineteenth century to the post-Second-World-War period. Alice Gomme's *Traditional Games* (1894) gives three button games, 'Banger', 'Buttons' and 'Crosses and twisses', and also provides a useful list of the relative values of different types of button at the time.

Alongside cherry stones, scraps and old buttons, broken china also had a part to play in a whole range of games, from around the 1820s until the pre-war period, and it also had a terminology all of its own. The way the pieces were used was pretty much universal, although the words varied from place to place. In the counties of Northumberland, Durham, Yorkshire, Cheshire and Northamptonshire, and probably elsewhere in the North of England, such bits of broken crockery were called 'boody', 'booly', 'bowdie' or something similar – one of their commonest uses was the making of 'boody-houses', usually just for fun but sometimes as part of a street calendar custom such as grottoing (see below) – while on the Isle of Man they were 'guys' and in Limerick in the 1920s they were 'chainies'. A. W. Moore gives the following examples of 'guys' used in local speech in his 1920s dictionary of the Anglo-Manx dialect:

Guy: a broken bit of earthenware or china. 'The children are playin down on the shore with guys. They're playin makin guy houses. She took an oul' drain-pipe and stuck guys all over it with putty, and you wouldna believe the nice it was; aw, fit for the Queen's parlour it was.'

The other widespread use of china was as a general currency, as recalled by Pete Elliott, of Co. Durham, from his childhood in the 1930s:

When we were kids we used to do what you call 'boody concerts' and your entrance fee was a piece of 'boody'; this was what you paid to get into the 'boody concert'. Boody was a precious commodity to children, and it was little pieces of pottery, any piece of a broken cup or anything like that, because cups were hard to come by. And all the kids sang a song. Whoever was running the boody show, whoever was going to end up as the boody bandit, the boody baron of the neighbourhood.

It is no surprise to learn from other sources that coloured or patterned boody was prized above plain white pieces, and, as previously noted, anything with gold on it was particularly precious.

Broken china – along with pins, cherry stones and marbles – also formed a useful currency for another regular feature of the playground and street from at least the mid nineteenth century to the inter-war years: the peep-show. Its form changed over time, but the essential principle was that the customer paid a fee to peep at something pretty, interesting or amazing. The earlier versions were two-dimensional, as Alice Gomme, who was born in London in 1853, described from her personal experience in her *Traditional Games* (1898):

I remember well being shown how to make a peep or poppet-show. It was made by arranging combinations of colours from flowers under a piece of glass, and then framing it with paper in such a way that a cover was left over the front, which could be raised when one paid a pin to peep. The following words were said, or rather sung, in a sing-song manner:

> A pin to see the poppet-show
> All manner of colours Oh!
> See the ladies all below.

Children probably copied the style of the rhyme from showmen they heard at local fairs and other gatherings, although they did not necessarily repeat the words accurately. A verse printed by S. O. Addy in his *Sheffield Glossary* (1888) ran:

> A pinnet a piece to look at a show
> All the fine ladies sat in a row
> Blackbirds with blue feet
> Walking up a new street
> One behind and one before
> And one beknocking at t' barber's door.

Later manifestations took on a further dimension, and were often housed in that essential feature of childhood in the past, the shoebox:

> Then there were grottoes. If you had an empty shoe box, you would take one end out and put in a bit of greaseproof paper, and then you'd make a scene in there, perhaps a fairy scene; a few rocks, a few flowers and a couple of fairies, all made out of paper and painted by hand. You'd take ages to make this grotto. You wouldn't know what you were going to see. 'It's a cherry-stone for a go. You've got to give me a cherry-stone and then I'll let you have a peep.' All on the pavement – you'd sit out all day with your grotto.   KENSINGTON, LONDON, 1930S

This writer's name for the activity links it with the late-summer grottoes built on the pavements of London and other towns (see p. 479), but the shoebox variety was more usually called a 'peep show', like its glass predecessor. Girls may have been satisfied with fairies and pretty flowers, but boys had other tastes, as documented by C. H. Rolph in his *London Particulars* (1980), which recalled life in the capital in Edwardian times:

> One of the respectable ways of getting marbles was the shoe-box peep show. One end of the box was cut out, leaving a half-inch margin to which you would stick a square of tracing paper, butter-muslin, or something similar that would let in the light. You cut two eye-holes at the other end. And then with cardboard cut-out figures filched from old scrap-books (or you could laboriously make your own), you mounted some silhouetted and harrowing scene like the Execution of Lady Jane Grey. Boys would pay 'a meggie a peep'.

Town and Country

It is astonishingly difficult to generalise about childhood, because the vast differences in personal situation and general environment, which are beyond children's control, have such a major effect on their everyday experiences. But when it comes to general environment, it is possible to argue that one of the major divisions in the past, and to a smaller extent in the present, was the difference between living in the town and living in the country.

Obviously, rural settings lend themselves to a wider range of 'natural' games – scrumping, tree climbing and so on – and country children have always readily availed themselves of all such opportunities. D. Parry-Jones, for example, writing of his childhood in Edwardian Carmarthenshire, lovingly describes how the children made their entertainment from the hedgerows – whistles, pop-guns, stilts, bows and arrows, catapults, and:

> . . . from the hazel hedge, too, we got material for a sling, a thing beloved of every boy, for with its aid he could hurl a stone four times as far as he could with his unaided arm . . . It was far from being a weapon of precision, and I do not remember ever trying to hit any particular object with it – what we aimed at was distance.

His memory is probably a little selective here, because other writers clearly remember that country boys threw stones at anything which moved – rabbits, birds, farm animals and each other. Female writers like Flora Thompson and Alison Utley, on the other hand, usually stressed the pleasures of collecting wild flowers and the opportunities for unsupervised socialising.

But there are other, less obvious, factors which result in a different play experience. It is often assumed, for example, that country playgrounds must be the best places to collect traditional lore, but although this may have been the case in the distant past it has not been true for a long time. All childlore researchers agree that larger schools have more 'lore' than small ones, simply because they have a bigger pool on which to draw, and a constant influx of new children bringing new material. Big urban schools thrive in this respect; small rural schools, on the other hand, suffer. That said, smaller schools have other characteristics, which may be regarded as beneficial to social play. It is noticeable, for example, that in smaller schools there is much more inter-generational play, and more mixing of the sexes, simply because you need the others to form a big enough group for some games.

Broadly speaking, country children tend to have further to go to school, and the opportunities for socialising and play on the way have always been greater than in urban areas, where schools were not far from the children's homes. In previous times this was even more marked:

> At the age of four I walked a mile to the village school with my six-year-old sister. We met other children and if we were early we put a stone on the gate post to say we had gone, and if a stone was already there we hurried to catch up with the others. When we got bicycles, to share them we would 'ride' and 'tie', which meant riding on ahead, dropping your bike for another child to ride and setting off to walk. The next person repeated the proce-dure so we got to school more quickly.   NORTH YORKSHIRE, 1930S

But all was not rural sweetness and light:

> Until my brother was old enough to start school I walked from Hallsannery Farm to the school on my own, and they were lonely narrow rough roads. I dreaded meeting a steam engine and threshing machine, it was usually on the way home from school after they had finished a day's threshing corn on a local farm. There were very few passing places, and I remember running to the nearest gateway to let them pass, they were such big noisy things, it was really frightening for a little child. Then my father used to keep a bull at Hallsannery and there always used to be somebody driving cows along the lane to the farm, it was horrible, they used to be so wild sometimes. Then there used to be the odd tramp with a perambulator or wheelbarrow

with their worldly things in, I used to be frightened of them. At Apps there was a slaughterhouse and you'd pass the gate where the poor old sheep were penned up and two men slaughtering away like mad, stunning them and cutting their throats, then they'd put them on a wheelbarrow and take them in to hang them up. 'Twas horrible the things I used to see on the way to school.   *DEVON, 1930S*

Urban children of the period may not have needed to worry about meeting animals and farm machinery, but they had other fears to contend with. The nearest school was often outside their 'home territory', and the journey involved traversing streets that belonged to others, with all the potential for conflict that entailed.

There was a long tradition of secondary children travelling to the nearest town by train, at least until the decimation of rural railway branch lines in the 1960s, but the commoner route now is by school-bus, and the steady closure or amalgamation of small rural primary schools in the post-war period has meant that increasing numbers of younger children also have this twice-daily experience. Many children find this very daunting at first, mainly because of the mixture of ages, but in most cases they soon settle into the natural pecking order which prevails. This aspect is a regular feature of children's comments quoted in Colin Ward's *The Child in the Country* (1988):

I was like everyone else, I started up at the front near the driver and edged my way further back every year . . . The quiet ones stay in the middle . . . It was both boys and girls at the back. You have to remember that some people were on that bus for eleven years, dropping off at the primary school for the first six of them and staying on for the high school for the rest of the time. They knew each other since they were infants.

Like the old walk to school, the journey is a great time for relatively unsupervised sessions of talking, swapping, arguing and playing static games. One by-product of all this, which many secondary schoolchildren have noted, is that while the bus schedule makes it difficult for children to stay behind for extra-curricular activities, it also discourages teachers from giving them detention.

The town/country divide is not the only one that once prevailed and still exists to a certain extent today. Those living on the coast similarly had and continue to have a different experience from those who dwell inland, the seashore offering plenty of opportunities for play, as this snippet from the Isle of Man makes clear:

Rock the cradle: a game played on soft yielding sand by the sea-side. The players rock from side to side and whoever sinks deeper wins the game.

ISLE OF MAN, 1920S

Ring a-ring a-roses, 1907

Clapping game, 1990s

'O then she was a lady . . .', 1943

Clapping game, 2010

Poor Mary is a-Weeping, 1880s

Ring a-ring a-roses, 1950s

PART FOUR

Singing and Clapping

Dancing in the street, 1900s

The Big Ship Sails, c.1913

CHAPTER SIXTEEN

Singing and Dancing

SINGING GAMES

If any children's game seems designed to delight an adult's eye and melt their hard heart, it is a singing game. There is something so right about children hand-in-hand in a circle, singing a pretty tune, with words only half understood but clearly archaic, occasionally breaking into another tempo, or doing a little dance, or bobbing down, taking it in turns to be the one in the middle innocently acting out matters of love and marriage, and life and death itself.

When worried commentators from the Victorian era to the inter-war years said that 'children do not play any more' it was often the decline of the organised singing games that they were lamenting. Certainly, compared to 100 years ago, very few can still be seen being played spontaneously by children in the playground, let alone the street or village green. The decline has been slower than the Victorian social reformers feared – when the major collectors of the post-war period, such as Damien Webb, James Ritchie and Iona and Peter Opie, went out into the field, they found many games still being played enthusiastically in streets and playgrounds all over the country. Nevertheless, even in the Opies' time the repertoire was dwindling, and the overall decline continued, and gathered pace, as the twentieth century drew to a close.

It is difficult not to see this decline in pessimistic and nostalgic terms. Many of us have a built-in cultural response to these matters, and we just *know* that the past was more innocent, better adjusted, kinder and more community-spirited than the present. Most of all, it was more rural – and somehow singing games seem part and parcel of a rural environment.

In Chapter 9 of *Lark Rise* (1939), entitled 'Country Playtime', the inimitable Flora Thompson provides us with what has become the classic description of the way singing games were played in rural areas of Britain in the 1880s:

> Then, beneath the long summer sunsets, the girls would gather on one of the green open spaces between the houses and bow and curtsey and sweep to and fro in their ankle-length frocks as they went through the game movements and sang the game rhymes as their mothers and grandmothers had done before them. Some of these were played by forming a ring, others by taking sides, and all had distinctive rhymes, which were chanted rather than sung.
>
> The boys of the hamlet did not join in them, for the amusement was too formal and restrained for their taste, and even some of the rougher girls would spoil a game, for the movements were stately and all was done by rule. Only at the end of some of the games, where the verse had deteriorated into doggerel, did the play break down into a romp. Most of the girls when playing revealed graces unsuspected in them at other times; their movements became dignified and their voices softer and sweeter than ordinarily, and when hauteur was demanded by the part, they became, as they would have said, 'regular duchesses'. It is probable that carriage and voice inflexion had been handed down with the words.

Thompson was well aware that the children were following a long tradition, surviving from what she regarded as 'an older, sweeter country civilization'. She also felt that her generation would be the last to play them in such rural simplicity, as they 'already had one foot in the national school'.

> No one inquired the meaning of the words of the game rhymes; many of the girls, indeed, barely mastered them, but went through the movements to the accompaniment of an indistinct babbling.

She then went on to give descriptions of a number of their singing games, including *Oranges and Lemons, London Bridge, Here we go Round the Mulberry Bush, Here Come Three Tinkers, Isabella, Thread the Tailor's Needle, Daddy, Honeypots, The Old Woman from Cumberland, Poor Mary is a-Weeping, Waly Waly Wallflower, Green Gravel, Sally Sally Waters, Queen Anne Queen Anne, Queen Caroline* and *The Sheepfold*.

Flora Thompson's observations were, as ever, perceptive, but even she could not escape the tinge of pessimism which by her time had become ingrained in the collective consciousness. Throughout the second half of the nineteenth century, there was a growing unease among the educated classes about the perceived decline of physical, spiritual and moral standards in the nation and in particular in the 'working classes'. The twin horrors of urbanisation and industrialisation, it was increasingly argued, were destroying all that was best in British culture. Many active social movements set out to remedy the situation. Some campaigned for better education, housing and working conditions; others attacked on the cultural front by promoting arts and crafts, along with the folk songs, dances and singing games of a supposed rural golden age.

Children, in particular, were singled out as being in need of moral and cultural reclamation. By the end of the century, people up and down the country were teaching children, and teaching their teachers, the singing game repertoire of the previous generation, or at least the part of it that met contemporary standards of respectability and innocence. The campaigners' objectives were laudable and their motives sincere, and we should be grateful that they documented many things that would otherwise have left no trace. That said, their romantic notions of a 'Merrie England' were historically unsound and their methods undoubtedly patronising, condescending and often misguided.

The parallels with the modern age are obvious. Although the feared reasons for decline today are different (the breakdown of community and the rise of computer games rather than urban and industrial life) the cry is the same, and the response very similar. When concerned teachers, parents and social reformers go into schools to 'teach children to play' it is often singing games that they focus on. And the net result, to be brutally frank, is the same as it was 100 years ago. The children love the games, but they do not play them for long after the instructors have moved on, and the games do not get passed on to the next generation. Singing games declined in the past because, for some reason or set of reasons, they no longer satisfied children's needs. That still seems to be the case, however much adults might wish things to be different.

What has happened therefore is that the classic singing games have continued to disappear from children's daily repertoire, while a select few are kept going by being regularly taught to nursery-school-age children by parents and teachers, and via television programmes and DVDs aimed at preschoolers. This means that these chosen few items – *Ring a-ring a-roses*, *London Bridge*, *The Farmer's in His Den* and so on – are still known to almost everybody in the land. However, they rarely appear in the playground beyond the staff-led games of the reception class.

This is very different to how it was 120 years ago, when girls would play these games right into their teens. As with so many other playground games, children nowadays feel themselves already too old for singing games at eleven.

That said, it should not be assumed that singing and dancing are leaving our playgrounds – far from it. Any observer can still see song-and-dance routines on a daily basis. What seems to have been happening is that the old singing games have gradually been replaced by clapping games, often involving an increasing emphasis on body actions, as if the urge to dance is breaking through.

It is also worth pointing out that many games that are not specifically 'singing games' nevertheless involve song or dance elements. Girls pick up very quickly on the latest pop music routines from television and Internet, and adapt them for performance in the playground. Very few last much longer than the time they are on the television, but new ones come along to replace them. When I was visiting playgrounds in the early 1980s it was Madonna and Bucks Fizz songs. A decade later the Spice Girls were making a huge impact – though even their songs have not lasted well. The details may change but the tradition of picking up on the latest trends in popular culture persists. Arguably, children today have access to a far larger pool of material than ever before.

There are dozens more of the older-style singing games than could be included in this book, but all I can do here is to look at a sample, focusing on those that are still around or survived within living memory. Anyone interested in pursuing the genre should first consult the work of Alice Gomme and the Opies (as listed below), and the games are also included in my *Folk Song Index*, which is available on the website of the Vaughan Williams Memorial Library of the English Folk Dance and Song Society (http://library.efdss.org/cgi-bin/home.cgi). This index includes nearly all the major books, recordings and manuscript collections of folk-song material in the English language and is designed to help the enquirer find other traditional versions of songs and games. The 'Roud number' given here in the notes to each singing game is the key to finding other versions within the *Folk Song Index*.

The literature on singing games is extensive. Many Victorian antiquarians and folklorists were interested in games as part of their general folklore collecting, and their publications include many examples from up and down the country. William Wells Newell's *Games and Songs of American Children* (1883; second edition, 1903) and Alice Gomme's seminal work *The Traditional Games of England, Scotland and Ireland* (1894 and 1898) really put the genre on the map and contain a huge amount of material from Victorian and preceding eras. Several of the enthusiastic folk-song collectors of the Edwardian period, such as Cecil Sharp, Frank Kidson, Anne Gilchrist and Alice Gillington, took particular notice of the genre, and in the first decades of the twentieth century numerous books of singing games were published, the best with material collected from children themselves, but many simply recycling what had been printed before.

Collections continued to appear between the wars, although more slowly, but a resurgence of interest in children's lore after the Second World War resulted in a great deal more fieldwork, and the publication of Iona and Peter Opie's masterly *The Singing Game* (1985). This was the first book since Gomme's *Traditional Games* to take a serious look at both the history and the contemporary situation of the genre. It is still the standard work, twenty-five years later.

Singing games come a close second to nursery rhymes in the indignities they have suffered at the hands of those who are determined to find hidden meanings and ancient histories. Starting from the assumption that all children's rhymes are (a) extremely old, and (b) have hidden meanings, origin-seekers simply seize upon a particular version (usually the modern standard one) and pick on a particular detail from which they extrapolate backwards to come up with a wholly spurious explanation. They, or someone else in the chain of transmission, then marshal other 'facts' to support the theory. This is the way all legends (i.e. spurious stories told as true) work.

The best-known example is the claim that *Ring a-ring a-roses* is about the plague. The original notion was probably suggested by the word 'posies', which brought to mind some vague idea that people held flowers to their faces in the past to guard against infection. Once this idea took hold, the totally inaccurate 'facts' that sneezing was the first sign of the plague and that the victims broke out in red sores (a ring of roses) were trotted out as supporting evidence. A similar but less widespread notion maintains that *In and Out the Dusty Bluebells* is about slave auctions. In Liverpool (where 'slave trade' legends abound), someone noticed that some local children sang '*dusky* bluebells', which was enough to suggest black slaves, and the tapping (auctioneer's hammer) and the 'I am your master' line clinch it.

Sometimes the thought processes involved are a little more convoluted. For example, one legend that has arisen quite recently holds that the novelty dance/game *The Hokey Cokey* was originally a cruel Protestant parody of a Roman Catholic mass. It is therefore deemed offensive in a modern tolerant society, and some people really have sought to get it banned from church socials. In fact, what has almost certainly happened here is that someone has ingeniously guessed that the phrase 'hocus pocus' is a parody of the *Hoc est corpus* of the Eucharist (which is almost certainly not the case), assumed that 'Hokey Cokey' must be related to 'hocus pocus' and therefore decided that a perfectly innocent song is up to no good.

The early folklorists, struggling to claim a scientific credibility for their new discipline, came up with several fundamental theories. The most important of these was the doctrine of cultural survivals, which argued that all societies pass through identifiable stages of development from savage to civilised (i.e. the Christian West). This meant that any cultural item found in a society deemed more 'primitive' than ours could be used as direct evidence about the history of our society. And as children were seen as directly comparable to 'undeveloped races', their games and rhymes were seen as survivals of our own savage past.

Modern meaning-seekers have a much freer hand, and they are not shackled by any theory or need for historical accuracy. They never take into account that traditional forms exist in many versions and that the very hook they are using as a clue may be a recent introduction. Nor do they care about the documented age of the item, and simply assume that it has existed for hundreds or even thousands of years, and they always prefer romantic fiction over prosaic fact.

Some of these spurious origins have been around long enough to qualify as folklore in themselves, and they are still being created, with the Internet as the ideal breeding ground. This means that any respectable childlore researcher spends a great deal of unproductive time debunking myths about origin and secret meaning. It is, however, necessary. The legends are so often repeated and so widely believed that they dominate and warp the discourse and hamper genuine research by focusing everybody's attention in completely the wrong direction. Nevertheless, stories of plagues and slave auctions have romance and fascination on their side, and the boring old folklorist cannot offer anything much in their stead, because we simply do not know where any of it really originated.

There is no doubt that the *form* of the singing game goes back to the earliest documented times, and beyond. Dancing in a linked circle or in lines, with verses and chorus, with call and response, are all well attested in various ages and most parts of the world. But what is really at issue here is not the form of the game, but its content. To say that the form of a circle game goes back to pre-Christian times and therefore a particular game is that old is like saying that singing goes back to antiquity, so *Puff the Magic Dragon* must be 2,000 years old.

The Opies, in *The Singing Game*, opened up another fascinating avenue of research – looking for similar versions of British songs and games in other countries and cultures. Sometimes the parallels are so close that it looks as though a particular song or game might well have been imported and translated directly, though that still leaves the questions of which way, how and when. More often, the similarities and differences are more complex. There is clearly a need for further research.

OLDER SINGING GAMES

The Big Ship Sails

One of the great favourites in twentieth-century street and playground, *The Big Ship Sails* was sung all over the country and although not nearly so popular nowadays is still to be found on occasion. The basic action accompanying the song is very similar from place to place, as in the following from Sussex in the 1950s:

> The big ship sails through the Illy Ally oo
> The Illy Ally Oo, the Illy Ally Oo
> The big ship sails through the Illy Ally Oo
> On the last day of September
>
> The captain said it would never never do . . .
>
> The big ship sank to the bottom of the sea . . .

A line of children holding hands at 90 degrees to a wall. The last child starts to walk to the wall and passes between wall and under arm of first child; the whole chain follows; it effectively turns the first child round with crossed arms. The last child repeats by passing between and under arms of first child and second child, so the second child too turns 180 degrees and has crossed arms. This continues until the line has turned to face the other way all with crossed hands held. By the time the last verse is reached the crossing should be complete so that the whole chain squats down and bounces gently in a crouched position still holding crossed arms as 'the big ship sinks to the bottom of the sea'.

The first verse is essentially the same in nearly all versions, although the spelling of the 'Illy Ally' part varies considerably and the final line is sometimes 'on the 23rd of November' or 'December'. This verse is nearly always sung over and over until all the players are 'knotted up' and in many places the game simply finishes as they skip round in a circle, or they go through the whole process in reverse to unknot everybody. But in other versions, as in the Sussex one quoted above, there are other verses, with appropriate actions, which are sung at this stage in the game. A version from Northamptonshire continues:

> When all arms were crossed and linked, they sang
>
> > Dash, dash, dash, my blue sash (or 'Dip, dip, dip, my little ship')
> > Sailing on the water
> > Like a cup and saucer
> > Dash, dash, dash (or 'Dip, dip, dip')
>
> As they sang they lifted and dropped their linked arms, and on the last word, let go.

The action accompanying 'The Captain said . . .' verse is the gesture children invariably use when someone in authority is speaking: a vigorous shaking of the upraised index finger.

The 'Illy alley O' phrase has long fascinated commentators, and as the spelling varies considerably it is possible to read almost anything you like into it. But there is no indication that it was originally a real place, and the spelling is often simply the result of the collector's desperate attempt to approximate the accent of local children who do not have to worry about the finer points of orthography. In Scottish versions the first word is more usually 'Eely', and in the English versions published around the First World War, such as in Alice Gillington's *Old Hampshire Singing Games* (1909) and Norman Douglas's *London Street Games* (1916) it is 'Holly holly O'.

Despite the overall similarity of versions, there are occasional reports of very different local forms. The following, for example, was contributed to the *Lore of the Playground* website by Hilary Blencowe, as she remembered the game in Liverpool in the 1950s:

> Another one was 'The Big Ship Sails'. Girls and boys would stand opposite one another and raise and join hands to make a tunnel. The others would then go up and down the tunnel, under the hands, and everyone would chant:
>
> > The big ship sails through the alley alley o, the alley alley o,
> >   the alley alley o
> > The big ship sails through the alley, alley o on the last
> >   day of September
> > The big ships sails through the alley, alley o
> > Who'll be the master?

Then as someone was passing under the 'tunnel' two of the others who were joining hands would drop them to catch the person.

For all its widespread fame and popularity, *The Big Ship Sails* does not appear to be very old. The earliest known versions are reported by Brian Sutton-Smith in his *Games of New Zealand Children* (1972) as played in Nelson about 1870 and Christchurch in 1900, and the action and text for these are virtually identical to the later British versions. The earliest recorded in Britain are also from about 1900, and the game is regularly featured in books and collections from then on.

But the central feature of the game – a linked line going through an arch – is a great deal older, and it is likely that *The Big Ship Sails* is a reworking of an old game usually called *Thread the Needle*, which existed both as a children's game and as part of a number of calendar customs.

As described in Alice Gomme's *Traditional Games* (1898), the basic format of *Thread the Needle* was as follows:

The children stand in two long rows, each holding the hands of the opposite child, the two last forming an arch. They sing the lines, and while doing so the other children run under the raised arms. When all have passed under, the first two hold up their hands, and so on again and again, each pair in turn becoming the arch.

Alice Gomme gives more than a dozen versions of the accompanying words from around the country, the most complex being from London:

Thread my grandmother's needle!
Thread my grandmother's needle!
Thread my grandmother's needle!
  Open your gates as wide as high,
  And let King George and me go by.
  It is so dark I cannot see
To thread my grandmother's needle!
Who stole the money-box?

The contributor comments, 'The last line is called out in quite different tones from the rest of the rhyme. It is reported to have a most startling effect.'

In many localities *Thread the Needle* was also performed by adults on particular days, usually in spring – Shrove Tuesday, Easter, Whitsun, for example. Sometimes starting in a circle, but more often being simply a long line holding hands and snaking around the village, it gathered participants on the way and periodically turned back on itself to go through a proffered arch. Sometimes this was sufficient to itself, but on other occasions it was a prelude to another procedure, such as 'clipping the church'. This involved the villagers holding hands and trying to encircle the parish church (see p. 497).

Duke a-riding

My favourite game was 'There Came a Duke A-Riding'. The aim was for the 'Duke' to choose a wife. The players (usually the girls) would choose a 'Duke' (sometimes a boy) then the girls would stand in a line on one side of the play-ground. The 'Duke' would then skip towards the girls as if riding a horse and then the girls would skip towards the 'Duke' asking their questions.

DUKE: There came a duke a-riding, a-riding, a-riding
          There came a duke a-riding Y O U

GIRLS: What you riding here for, here for, here for?
          What you riding here for Y O U?

DUKE: I'm riding here to marry, marry, marry
          I'm riding here to marry Y O U.

LIVERPOOL, 1950S

This was an immensely popular singing game, reported all over the English-speaking world and with interesting continental analogues, and one of several 'courting' games.

> Here come three dukes a-riding
>   A-riding, a-riding
> Here come three dukes a-riding
>   With a hansom-tansom-tay.
>
> Pray what do you want with us, sirs? . . .
>
> We have come to marry, to marry . . .
>
> Will ever a one of us do, sirs? . . .
>
> You're all as stiff as pokers . . .
>
> We can bend as well as you, sirs . . .

FORFAR, C.1950

The commonest form is for boys and girls to form lines facing each other, holding hands. As each line sings, it advances and retires. The boys sing the first verse, the girls the second and so on.

More often than not it is dukes that come a-riding, but versions with kings, princes or Gypsies are also known, and sometimes the suitor is alone and sings, 'Here comes a duke a-riding'. The format varies little, but the actual verses are often different, and versions can be much longer than the Forfar example given above. In addition to the regular 'stiff as pokers', for example, there are sometimes further objections, such as 'too black and dirty', 'too poor and shabby', or simply 'your legs are too bandy', and often there is a defiant 'Good enough for you, sir!' in reply each time. After the general bandying of words, sometimes the suitors focus on a particular girl and she either joins them promptly, or, in many cases, shows defiance, or at least reluctance, and has to be pulled or pushed across. One particularly striking sequence is when the suitors ask for someone rather obliquely, 'We've come to marry Bacon Face', and the response is 'Who the 'eck is Bacon Face?'

The earliest example so far noted in Britain is a Lancashire version dating from the 1820s, as mentioned by Charlotte Burne in her *Shropshire Folk-Lore* (1883). The widespread distribution of the game in the nineteenth century is shown by the fact that Alice Gomme (1898) printed thirty different texts, from Britain alone, and numerous others were recorded in the twentieth century. There are also many very close analogues from the Continent, which the Opies identify and discuss at length in *The Singing Game* (1985). *Three Dukes* is another of those games for which the only hope for a better understanding would seem to be an in-depth international investigation.

Dusty Bluebells

This was one of the most popular singing games of the mid twentieth century, and recalled with particular affection by women remembering their childhoods in the 1960s and 1970s. The players form a circle, with raised hands to make arches. One girl dances in and out through the arches while everyone sings:

> In and out the dusty bluebells
> In and out the dusty bluebells
> In and out the dusty bluebells
> You shall be my partner.

Then she stops behind one of the others and taps her repeatedly on the shoulder, while everyone sings:

> Tap-a-rap-a-rap her on the shoulder
> Tap-a-rap-a-rap her on the shoulder
> Tap-a-rap-a-rap her on the shoulder
>   I'll be your partner.

The one whose shoulders have been tapped then joins on behind the first girl, holding her jumper or skirt, and they both dance in and out. The whole thing is repeated, the line grows and becomes unwieldy and the circle gets smaller. At the second verse each time, all the girls in the line belabour the shoulders of the one in front, sometimes gently, sometimes not.

The details of the words vary considerably – the bluebells are sometimes 'dusky', 'dusting', 'rushing', 'shady' and so on – but the overall pattern is remarkably stable, considering the number of versions that have been recorded.

Surprisingly, this does not seem to be a very old game, and no Victorian or Edwardian versions have come to light. *Running In and Out the Bluebells* is listed, but not described, by Norman Douglas in his *London Street Games* (1916), but the first definite sightings are in the 1920s and 1930s. The game was particularly popular in Scotland and Northern Ireland, and it is still to be found in the playground repertoire, but not nearly so widely as thirty years ago.

Dutch Girl

> I'm a little Dutch girl, Dutch girl, Dutch girl
> I'm a little Dutch girl, far across the sea
>
> I'm a little Dutch boy, Dutch boy, Dutch boy
> I'm a little Dutch boy, far across the sea
> I don't like you, like you, like you . . .
>
> Why don't you like me? . . .
>
> Because you stole my wedding ring . . .
>
> Here is your wedding ring . . .
>
> I still don't like you . . .

Why don't you like me? . . .

Because you stole my wedding dress . . .

Here is your wedding dress . . .

I still don't like you . . .

Why don't you like me? . . .

Because you stole my wedding necklace . . .

Here is your wedding necklace . . .

Now we're getting married . . .

A group of eight-year-olds at Andover C of E School in Hampshire sang this for me in the playground in 1983. They were ranged in two lines, each line taking alternate verses, and dancing forward and back as they sang. Long as it is (and the girls were quite out of breath at the end), versions from elsewhere follow the couple through life as they have babies, get older, die, go to heaven and become angels. There is also a certain amount of mimetic action: 'Here is . . .' is always accompanied with proffered hands; 'I hate you' with a stamp; babies are rocked, older backs bent and angels' wings are flapped.

The Opies report versions from various parts of the country from the 1950s onwards, and there have been occasional sightings in Canada and Australia. The earliest version to come to light so far is in Frank Rutherford's *All the Way to Pennywell*, where his text, from Birtley, Co. Durham, dates from the 1930s. There is no indication where it came from originally, although Alan Smith, in his collection of childlore published in *East London Papers* (1959), wrote that he suspected it to be 'a piece of dancing school sophistication'.

Fair Rosa

This little gem of the singing game tradition clearly tells the story of Sleeping Beauty, but it is interesting to note that no recorded versions seem to introduce that name. The heroine is variously 'Fair Rosie', 'Fair Rosa' or even 'Sweet Rosebud', but in the following version – collected by Julian Pilling in Nelson, Lancashire, in 1956 – she is a generic 'princess':

(1) The princess was a lovely child
Lovely child, lovely child

The princess was a lovely child
　Long, long ago.

(2) A wicked fairy cast a spell . . .

(3) The princess slept a hundred years . . .

(4) The palace trees grew tall and straight . . .

(5) A handsome prince came galloping by . . .

(6) He cut the trees down one by one . . .

(7) They all had a happy time . . .

One child in the middle is the princess; the rest hold hands, circle round, at a leisurely pace, and sing. (2) One child approaches the princess and mimes casting a spell with her hands; she 'sleeps' (3). (4) One child, or all the children, raises both arms and covers the princess with them. (5) One child rides around inside the circle. (6) She mimes cutting the trees with her sword. (7) The pace quickens and they all dance round.

　Although there are many minor differences between the documented versions, they all clearly derive from a poem, *Dornröschen war ein schönes Kind* ('Little Rose Thorn was a beautiful child'), published in Germany in the 1890s, which was probably written specifically for use in playschools there. This was translated into English and published several times, in Britain and America, from at least 1908 onwards, and became popular at parties. The song is therefore little more than 100 years old in Britain, and probably owes its survival to being taught to children by adults. But it certainly entered the tradition in its own right and was collected from children's singing a number of times across Britain and Ireland, and many times in North America. Some of its popularity can probably be explained by its haunting tune.

　The game, recorded in Belfast in 1971, can be seen in action on the *Dusty Bluebells* film, produced by David Hammond, and heard on the Flying Fox CD *Green Peas and Barley-O* (2000). But the song, at least, is guaranteed to live on in the minds of the next few generations of preschoolers, as it is included on the extremely popular DVD *Pop Go the Wiggles* (2008), by the Wiggles, which continues its long tradition of being taught by adults.

The Farmer's in His Den

This is another well-known singing game, played enthusiastically by nursery and preschool children all over the country, but probably rarely performed nowadays by anyone over reception-class age. As with many such games, though, it used to be an integral part of the playground repertoire, and was performed by much older children. A version played in Liverpool in the 1950s is representative:

> The farmer wants a wife, the farmer wants a wife
> Ee eye addio, the farmer wants a wife.
>
> The wife wants a child . . .
>
> The child wants a nurse . . .
>
> The nurse wants a dog . . .
>
> The dog wants a bone . . .
>
> We all pat the dog . . .

Everyone joined hands to make a circle and one person would be chosen to be the 'farmer'. The 'farmer' would stand in the middle of the circle while the rest went round chanting. At each verse another child is chosen to go into the middle. The person playing the dog is patted by everyone, and then becomes the farmer.

Considering its widespread popularity, the words and actions have changed little in over 100 years. That said, one or two variations have been recorded. One is that whereas the chosen figures often simply hang around in the middle until the 'patting' part, in some places they form a smaller circle and go round in the opposite direction to the outer one. Sometimes the game is extended to include a 'cat' who wants a 'mouse', who wants a 'cheese', though the principle remains the same. One aspect that has definitely changed over the years is the 'patting the dog', which is done gently in nursery schools under adult supervision, but was done much more robustly in the past when older children took part.

The only major textual variation is in the refrain line, which can be 'E I E I', 'Ee I addy O', 'Heigh-ho heigh-ho', 'I am the dairy O' or a number of other forms, as long as the rhythm is preserved.

Alice Gomme did not know of the game until after her first volume of *Traditional Games* was published in 1894, but she received one version in time for inclusion in the addenda in the second, four years later. This version was contributed by Mary Haddon from Auchencairn, Kirkcudbrightshire, and it was done in exactly the same way as the modern standard version, but had 'Oh my deary' as the refrain line, and had no reference to a bone. No earlier British version has been identified, but it was certainly widespread in Edwardian times, and all the major childlore collectors of the period, including Gavin Greig, Cecil Sharp and Alice Gillington, included versions, stretching from the Isle of Wight to Orkney, in their works.

However, there were numerous Continental versions (which the Opies' *The Singing Game* deals with extensively), and it seems clear that our game is a translation, probably from the German, which reached us in late Victorian times, via America. The only noticeable difference between the British and American versions is that Britons usually say that the farmer is in his 'den', whereas Americans say 'dell'.

Green Gravel

One of the most widely known singing games, collected dozens of times across Britain and Ireland in the nineteenth and twentieth centuries, *Green Gravel* has fascinated and dazzled commentators with its haunting tune and oblique references to young love and death:

> Green gravel, Green gravel
>   Your grass is so green
> And the fairest young damsel
>   That ever was seen
> I washed her in milk
>   And rolled her in silk
> And wrote down her name
>   With a glass pen and ink
> Dear Annie, your true love is dead
> I send you a letter to turn round your head.

This version was collected in Ireland in the 1920s, and represents the core of the song, which is remarkably stable across the country, considering how widely it was collected. Longer versions exist, but they show obvious signs of having been padded out by importation from other games.

In most places the children walk round in a circle, singing the words in unison, but at the ninth line one of them turns round to face the other way. They continue until all are facing outwards, and in some versions, if they wish to continue, they do it all again, each turning frontwards again.

Occasionally the chosen girl goes into the middle and mimes grief before rejoining the circle.

Despite its fascination for folklorists, no one has come up with any reasonable explanation of the imagery of the song. Why *green* gravel? Who are the maidens whose true loves have passed away? We do not know, but we sense a longer story. Unusually, though, there seem to be no Continental analogues to help us out. J. O. Halliwell included it in his *Nursery Rhymes of England* in 1842, and the Opies cite a version from Manchester in 1835, but in these it is already the short, apparently fragmentary story of the later versions.

Alice Gomme classifies it in *Traditional Games* (1894) as a 'funeral game', while the Opies include it in their chapter on 'Witch dances', because the children turn their backs to the centre of the circle, and this action was held by those early modern writers who were obsessed with witchcraft to be what witches did in their satanic dances. The unbelievably credulous witch-hunters certainly believed this as literal truth, but modern researchers must not fall into the trap of assuming that children's games with this feature are descended from witches' activities.

The plaintive *Green Gravel* of old was still going strong in the 1970s, and can be heard on the *Green Peas and Barley-O* CD recorded in Belfast in 1971, but may have disappeared from playgrounds by now. In the 1980s, though, there was a ring game that was almost a parody of the older form:

> Green gravel, Green gravel
> You are a naughty girl
> You told me you loved me
> But now it is not true
> So! Turn around you naughty girl
> And say no more to me [or 'And turn your back on me'].

The circle and the turning round to face outward were exactly the same as in the older version, but in this variant, as the girl turned, on the words 'naughty girl', one of the players smacked her bottom – none too gently, it has to be said.

Here We Go Round the Mulberry Bush

> Here we go round the mulberry bush
> The mulberry bush, the mulberry bush

> Here we go round the mulberry bush
> On a cold and frosty morning.
>
> This is the way we wash our hands . . .

There are various other verses to this song, mostly concerned with routine chores: 'This is the way we wash ourselves/dress ourselves/comb our hair/bake our bread/sweep the floor/go to school', and sometimes, 'This is way the ladies walk/the gentlemen walk', and so on. Traditionally, the children walk round in a circle, holding hands, while singing the chorus, and stand still to mime the verses. They then turn round on the spot before recommencing their circular movement.

Here We Go Round the Mulberry Bush is without doubt the best known of the 'mimed action' singing games, and is set to one of the most widely known traditional tunes in the English-speaking world, first published in 1760 as *Nancy Dawson*. The tune is also used for many other songs, including *Here We Come Gathering Nuts in May*. However, it only remains in the national consciousness because parents and nursery-school teachers are fond of it.

The song varies remarkably little from version to version, especially as performed in the twentieth century, but in the nineteenth century it was just as likely to be some other bush or tree as the mulberry, including ivy bush, ivory bush, bramble bush, gooseberry bush and holly bush. If nothing else, the sheer variety of plants mentioned in the past shows that it is dangerous to read too much significance into the mulberry bush element of the song.

There have been many theories of origin. Iona and Peter Opie, in their *The Singing Game* of 1985, drew attention to numerous dances across the world and throughout recorded history involving a linked ring around a tree or maypole, but unfortunately there is no reason to think that this game has anything beyond a generic connection with any of these. The earliest definite reference to the game dates only from the 1820s, although it may possibly be connected, at one remove, with a rhyme known in the eighteenth century, which started:

> The gooseberry grows on an angry tree
> About ye maids and about ye maids
> Others are merry as well as we
> Then about ye merry maids all.

A theory around in the 1970s, when the Opies were collecting, was that the song concerned the murderers of Thomas à Becket, who hung their swords on a mulberry tree, washed their hands of the blood and so on. This at least has the merit of being amusing in its unhistorical audacity, whereas the more recent notion that it concerns a mulberry tree in the exercise yard of Wakefield Prison, around which the poor prisoners marched, is just plain silly.

How Many Miles to Babylon?

This was a popular game certainly in the nineteenth century, collected all over Britain and Ireland and with a very long history, but it is now all but forgotten. A version published by J. O. Halliwell in 1842 provides the core text:

> How many miles is it to Babylon?
>   Threescore miles and ten
> Can I get there by candle-light?
>   Yes, and back again
> If your heels be nimble and light
>   You may get there by candle-light.

As is to be expected, the destination in the first line varies considerably, but it is remarkable how often the place starts with 'B' – Babylon, Bethlehem, Boston, Banbury, Barley Bridge, Barney Bridge, and so on.

There were several ways of playing the game. In one, the dialogue is simply a prelude to a chasing game:

> A line of children is formed, and the two standing opposite sing the questions, to which the line reply; then the two start running off in any direction they please, and the others try to catch them.   NORFOLK, 1890S

This was exactly how it was played in America, according to Eliza Leslie's *American Girl's Book* (1831), except that there the signal to run was the line, 'Take care the old witch don't catch you on the road!'

In other versions, the text usually includes a reference to a gate and the format is very similar to *Oranges and Lemons* and some versions of *London Bridge*:

> Then open the gates as wide as the sky
> And let King George and his men go by.
>
>   WARWICKSHIRE, 1890S

A version from Nairn, contributed to Alice Gomme's book by Walter

Gregor, proceeded in this way: two players take a secret name each, and stand facing each other, holding hands, to form a gate. The others form a line, one behind the other, holding the person in front by the waist. The leader of the line approaches the gate, and the dialogue takes place between them. The gatekeepers raise their arms to make an arch, and the line passes through. Without warning, they bring their arms down and capture one of the line, who is asked to choose one of the names, and who then stands behind the appropriate one. Once all players have been caught, the two sides have a tug of war.

The indefatigable researches of Iona and Peter Opie turned up a thirteenth-century Latin sermon in which:

> The preacher compared the behaviour of those Christians who at one moment make haste to Heaven and at other times relapse with the play of boys, and instances this very game: 'Quot leucas habeo ad Beverleyham?' The other says 'Eight'. The first asks if he can get there in daylight: 'Possum venire per lucem?' The other assures him he can, 'Ita potes', and begins running quickly, gets to where he wants, and then dances back to his original place, jeering at the other's slowness.

And as if this literary detective work were not brilliant enough, they also found a reference to the game being played at a school in Cumberland in the early seventeenth century.

The words continue to appear in books of nursery rhymes, but the game has long since disappeared from playgrounds.

London Bridge

This is another of the previously popular singing games which is still very widely known as a song, but hardly ever played as a game, except in preschool institutions. Indeed, *London Bridge is Falling* (or *Broken*) *Down* must be one of the most widely known rhymes in the English-speaking world.

> London Bridge is falling down
> Falling down, falling down
> London Bridge is falling down
> My fair lady.

This is the 'standard' version, and most people are also aware that it is followed by verses like 'Build it up with sticks and stones', even if they become increasingly vague about the words as the song progresses.

But in the historical record the physical game varies a great deal, and we do not know how it was originally done, or to what degree the recorded actions and words are intrinsically linked. In many cases, *London Bridge* is done in exactly the same way as the standard *Oranges and Lemons* (see p. 277), but without the tug of war that takes place in that song. Two children make an arch and the others parade through in single file; the arch is then lowered to catch an individual, who is assigned to a team by choosing 'sticks' or 'stones', or the equivalent pairs in other verses. In other versions the children caught in the arch are buffeted or swung to and fro to simulate the breaking of the bridge.

Five of the nine versions printed by Alice Gomme in 1894 include the notion of a prisoner who has stolen a gold watch and chain, or robbed a house, but this seems to be a late nineteenth-century addition, probably from another singing game, called *Hark the Robbers*. In these versions the child who is caught by the arch is designated the robber, and this child is often set aside and does not join in when the game starts again.

The first known printing of the full text is from the mid eighteenth century, in the influential *Tommy Thumb's Pretty Song Book* of 1744:

> London Bridge is broken down
> > Dance over my Lady Lee
> London Bridge is broken down
> > With a gay lady.
> Build it up with gravel and stone.
>
> Gravel and stone will wash away . . .
>
> Build it up with iron and steel . . .
>
> Iron and steel will bend and bow . . .
>
> Build it up with silver and gold . . .
>
> Silver and gold will be stolen away . . .
>
> Then we'll set a man to watch . . .

But there are indications that the song is much older. The *Gentleman's Magazine* of 1823, for example, includes a text that the contributor recalled from seventy years previously, sung by a woman who was born in the reign of Charles II (i.e. 1660–85) – not that this is definitive evidence that she learnt it that long ago.

Other early sources usually refer to a dance. The Opies, for example, discovered a reference in the comedy of *The London Chaunticleres* (1659), in which a female character says, 'When we kept the Whitson-Ale, where we daunc'd the building of London Bridge upon wool-packs and the hay upon a grasse-plot.' A dance called 'London Bridge' appears in early eighteenth-century dance manuals, but the tune bears no relation to that of the modern nursery rhyme, nor do the dance figures resemble the traditional singing game.

London Bridge is one of those nursery rhymes that has fascinated commentators for a long time, but we still do not have any solid information about its origin. Discussions of the development of the song are bedevilled by notions of human sacrifice being required for the successful construction of a bridge. There does seem to have been such a tradition in various parts of the world, but without further evidence of the existence of our rhyme before the seventeenth century it is hard to demonstrate any links between the text and such a practice. True, there are very close parallels on the Continent, but as we cannot be sure of their authenticity, date or earlier forms, no firm conclusions can be drawn.

Nuts in May

Here we come gathering nuts in May
Nuts in May, nuts in May
Here we come gathering nuts in May
May, May, May.

Who will you have for nuts in May? . . .

—, —, for nuts in May . . .

Very well, very well, so you may . . .

Who will you have to take her away? . . .

—, —, to take her away . . .

This text is from Belfast, as submitted to Alice Gomme's *Traditional Games* (1894) by W. H. Patterson. The only unusual feature of this version is the final line of each verse, which is more commonly something on the lines of, 'On a cold and frosty morning', or 'So early in the morning'.

In the game that traditionally accompanies the song, two lines of children take it in turns to skip towards each other, singing alternate verses.

The two people chosen in verses 3 and 6 try to pull each other over a line marked on the floor, and the loser joins the winner's team.

Alice Gomme printed nine versions, but listed many others too similar to give in full, and she commented:

> . . . this game is probably, unless we except 'Mulberry Bush', the most popular and the most widely played of any singing game. It might almost be called universal.

As the music is the same as that used in *Here We Go Round the Mulberry Bush*, the tune must have been truly ubiquitous. Later collecting confirmed Gomme's view, and the game continued in popularity until singing games declined in the later twentieth century. But although it was already widely known by 1880, *Nuts in May* cannot be shown to be very old, as the earliest description only dates from the 1860s.

A fair amount of scholarly ink has been expended in discussion of two mysteries concerning this song. Firstly, everyone knows that nuts are not available for gathering in May. The only plausible explanation here is that originally it was 'knots of May', a 'knot' in this case being a posy or bunch – and, indeed, some of the earlier versions do use those words. The second enigma is why verses of springtime flowers, more suited to love and courtship, are simply a prelude to a physical contest. Gomme managed to square this circle by proposing one of her favourite themes, 'marriage by capture', which she, and others of her generation, firmly believed had been a marked feature of previous societies. She argued that this was combined with the equally widespread customs of gathering spring flowers and celebrating love. In response, the Opies' more measured suggestion was that although there is scant evidence of genuine 'marriage by capture' being widely practised in the past, there were certainly numerous customs, in various countries, where brides' families were expected to put up a token show of resistance before surrendering her, and that something like this was possibly the game's original basis.

Plausible and sensible as this sounds, this line of argument has the usual problem: the lack of early references means all is speculation, and, in the case of *Nuts in May* in particular, we do not even have the usual plethora of foreign analogues to help us out.

Old Roger Is Dead

Old Rogers is dead and is laid in his grave
  Laid in his grave, laid in his grave
Old Rogers is dead and is laid in his grave
  He, hi! laid in his grave.

There grew an old apple tree over his head . . .

The apples grew ripe and they all fell off . . .

There came an old woman a-picking them up . . .

Old Rogers jumps up and he gives her a knock . . .

He makes the old woman go hipperty hop . . .

YORKSHIRE, C.1890S

In this song the girls sing the words as they stand or walk round in a circle, hand in hand while one of their number impersonates Roger by lying down in the centre to play dead. At the second verse another child stands over Roger, usually with arms outstretched in front to represent the branches of the tree. At verse 4, another child walks round pretending to pick up apples, and at verse 5 Roger jumps up and starts to belabour her. In most cases the 'old woman' becomes the new 'Old Roger' when the game starts again.

This was an extremely widely reported singing game, in North America as well as Britain. The commonest name for the main character is Old or Poor Roger or Rogers, but there are numerous variants, including Tommy, Johnnie, Cromwell and, especially in America, Grumble, Grimes, Pompey and Robin. Many of the words also vary, but considering its wide distribution, the story is remarkably stable across time and place.

The story, with its uncannily matter-of-fact handling of death and resurrection, and the hint of the supernatural, has long fascinated commentators, but apart from the fact that it was not uncommon to plant trees over graves, no one has come up with a reasonable theory that which explains the background to the story. The rhyme cannot be shown to be any older than the mid nineteenth century, and the Opies quote a version from Rhode Island from around 1850. The earliest sighting in Britain is *Cock Robin Is Dead and Lies in His Grave* from Derbyshire, published in the 1883 volume of the *Folk-Lore Journal*, but it was so widely reported, in Britain and America, in the 1880s and 1890s that it had clearly been around for a while.

A possible progenitor, however, was published in *Notes & Queries* in 1904, but referring to Cheshire in 1852:

Old Dobbin is dead
 Ay, ay
Dobbin is dead
He's laid in his bed
 Ay, ay
There let him lie
 Ay, ay
Keep watch for his eye
For if he gets up, he'll eat us all UP.

This was played in the street by little girls, who held hands and danced round the recumbent Dobbin, until he got up and chased them. The first one caught became the new Dobbin.

One Elephant

One elephant went out to play
 Upon a spider's web one day
They thought it such tremendous fun
 That they called for another elephant to come.

Two elephants . . .

Three elephants . . .

This rhyme was told to me by Lucy (aged eight) and Sarah (seven), two sisters from Andover, Hampshire, in 1982. They said, 'It's a Brownie game really', but that they also did it at school. The actions involve one child stomping round the outside of the circle pretending to be an elephant, and on the last words of each verse nudging another to join her.

Iona and Peter Opie confirm that the rhyme is usually found in an institutional setting, but also report versions from children's independent play. They date it from the 1930s, when it was probably introduced from France.

Orange Balls

The story of singing games is generally one of slow decline, but *Orange Balls* seems to be a relatively recent importation (or revival) and is still to be heard in playgrounds around the country. As sung by four eight-year-old girls walking round in a circle in East Finchley, London, in 2008, it goes:

> Orange balls, orange balls
> Here we go again
> The last one to sit down gets a boyfriend.

And then the last one to sit down has to go away and they have to not look, or close their ears, and the other people huddle up and discuss a boyfriend for them and then the person who is standing away has to come into the middle of the circle and everybody else would hold hands again.

> — has a boyfriend
> — has a boyfriend
> Simon likes —
> Simon likes —
> Stamp your feet if you hate him
> Hate him, hate him
> Stamp your feet if you hate him
> Hate, hate, hate
> Go under the bridge if you love him
> Love him, love him
> Under the bridge if you love him
> La la la.

A very similar version recorded in Andover, Hampshire, in 1982 has a jaunty 'hey hey' tacked on the end of 'Here we go again'. 'Stamp your feet' is pretty much universal in the 'hate him' lines, but instead of the London girls' bridge, it is more usual for the victim to be instructed to 'Clap your hands if you love him'. A version from Dublin in 1976, reported in the Opies' *The Singing Game* (1985), extends this sequence even further:

> Stamp your feet if you hate him . . .
> Roll your hands if you love him . . .
> Kneel up if you'll marry him . . .
> Stand up if you'll kiss him . . .

There is no shortage of rhymes and games where participants are assigned 'boyfriends', but this one has the added frisson of forcing the victim to admit openly to love or hate. The players sometimes choose pop singers or sports stars instead of identifiable boys.

Orange Balls seems to suddenly pop up in playgrounds about 1960, but it does have an interesting ancestry. An earlier song started with the lines:

> Orange boys, orange boys
> Let the bells ring
> Orange boys, orange boys
> God save the King.

SOUTHPORT, 1920

And years before that:

> Oliver, Oliver, follow the king
> Oliver, Oliver, last in the ring.

SHROPSHIRE, C.1883

This also involved ducking down and choosing a spouse. Further comparative research is needed on this game to pin its genealogy down satisfactorily.

Oranges and Lemons

> Oranges and lemons
>   Say the bells of St Clements
> You owe me five farthings
>   Say the bells of St Martins
> When will you pay me?
>   Say the bells of Old Bailey
> When I grow rich
>   Say the bells of Shoreditch
> When will that be?
>   Say the bells of Stepney
> I do not know
>   Says the great bell of Bow.

There was also *Oranges and Lemons* – rather like a country dance – two lines facing each other and holding hands with the opposite child. The top couple made an arch of their joined hands while the pairs split, danced up on the outside, met again at the top and went under the arch made by the top couple. At the end of all the *Oranges and Lemons* song (about the London church bells) the song continued, 'Here comes a candle to light you to bed. And here comes a chopper to chop off your head. Chip Chop, Chip Chop. The last man's head.' During this last part the top couple are bringing their joined hands in a circle down over the head of each pair passing underneath until the pair who are 'last man' are out.   *WOLVERHAMPTON, 1940S*

This description is slightly unusual in that it states that couples are trapped at the words 'The last man's head', whereas in most modern versions the children go through the arch singly, and are caught one at a time. In addition, the two making the arch have already decided, secretly, who is to be 'orange' and who 'lemon', and the player who is caught must choose one or the other fruit, stand behind the appropriate one, and when everyone is caught and assigned, a tug of war takes place.

Since at least the second half of the nineteenth century, *Oranges and Lemons* has been one of the most widely popular singing games in Britain. But in latter years it has had a strong 'official' existence – that is, popular at adult-organised children's parties – and it is now one of those rhyme games that survive mainly because they are taught by playgroup leaders, nursery-school teachers and parents, to preschool children. In these situations the 'chop off your head' feature, which was previously widespread, is often omitted or euphemised. Nevertheless, as so many children know the game so well, it still occasionally breaks out spontaneously in the playground, at least among the younger ones.

The history of the game is difficult to reconstruct with any confidence, and the endeavour is complicated by the fact that the text of the rhyme and the physical actions of the game were not necessarily linked in the past, and may well have different ancestries.

The words given above are a relatively standardised text, widely known today through popular publications, but as would be expected in a rhyme that has existed in the popular tradition for over 200 years, the historical record reveals dozens of different versions, many of which follow the basic pattern but differ greatly in detail.

The phrase 'Oranges and Lemons' was already known as the name of a dance published in the 1670 edition of John Playford's *English Dancing Master*, but the earliest known version of the words is to be found in *Tommy Thumb's Pretty Song Book* (1744). From then on, the rhyme appeared regularly in printed collections. There were also other songs based on local church bells, but it is probably because the London one was published so often that it became the most widely known and eventually eclipsed all others. Then again, of course, London has so many more churches to choose from.

It is highly unlikely that there is any intrinsic meaning in the phrases assigned to each name, or any geographical significance to the order in which they appear. If one looks through numerous versions collected or published over the last 200 years, it is abundantly clear that the song was constructed primarily by finding things to rhyme with the names of the churches, and the 'storyline' of debt and repayment developed later. A version published in the influential *Gammer Gurton's Garland* (1810) is a case in point:

> Gay go up and gay go down
>> To ring the bells of London Town
> Bull's eyes and targets
>> Say the bells of St Marg'ret's
> Brickbats and tiles
>> Say the bells of St Giles
> Halfpence and farthings
>> Say the bells of St Martin's
> Oranges and lemons
>> Say the bells of St Clement's
> Pancakes and fritters
>> Say the bells of St Peter's
> Two sticks and an apple
>> Say the bells at Whitechapel
> Old Father Baldpate
>> Say the slow bells at Aldgate
> You owe me ten shillings
>> Say the bells at St Helen's
> When will you pay me?
>> Say the bells at Old Bailey
> When I grow rich
>> Say the bells of Shoreditch
> Pray, when will that be?
>> Say the bells at Stepney
> I am sure I don't know
>> Says the great bell at Bow.

The words had been in circulation for a considerable time before there is any reference to an accompanying game. In 1823 Edward Moor included a reference in his dialect dictionary, *Suffolk Words and Phrases*, where he describes *Oranges and Lemons* as 'A juvenile pastime, playable by both boys and girls. I believe it is nearly the same as *Plumb-pudding and roast beef*, and under the latter name he equates it with the game *English and French*.

The first description of the game so far discovered is in Eliza Leslie's *American Girl's Book* (1831), where there is an arch, but no chopping or tug of war. The first mention of chopping off heads appears in the 1840s. Indeed, as the Opies perceptively point out, J. O. Halliwell, in the seminal *Nursery Rhymes of England* included the basic rhyme in his 1842 edition, added the 'Here comes a chopper' lines in 1844, and did not describe the game until the 1853 revision. This is far from proof, but is an indication that the connection between the bell rhyme and the head-chopping did not take place until the 1840s, at least 100 years after the rhyme was published.

But the mention of *Plum Pudding and Roast Beef* in Moor's description is particularly interesting. Choosing between 'Pudding' and 'Beef' was a widespread way of assigning teams in the nineteenth century, and it is clear from his words that it was this feature of choosing sides that most attracted his attention. 'English and French' is also a game of contesting sides.

Like many other nursery rhymes and singing games, *Oranges and Lemons* has been interpreted in all sorts of ways, usually on the basis of less than reliable evidence. One very common claim now is that the rhyme documents the route taken by condemned criminals, or more specifically, traitors, across London to their place of execution. This notion was first floated by Alice Gomme in 1898 and has recently been enthusiastically taken up by meaning-seekers. But, as usual, the theory extrapolates from supposed 'clues' within the text, and uses assumptions to support other assumptions, not least that the 'execution' lines were originally connected to the bell rhyme.

It is not even known which St Clement's is commemorated in the rhyme. St Clement Danes, in the Strand, boldly claims to be the one, and in 1924 a carillon was installed there, which still plays the well-known tune to passers-by every day, and a custom was inaugurated, in which oranges and lemons are given to the congregation every year in late March. The other St Clement's, in Eastcheap, does not get a look in.

Ring a-ring a-roses

Ring a-ring a-rosies
A pocket full of posies
A-tishoo, a-tishoo
We all fall down.

This, or something very similar, is taught to almost every preschool child in Britain, either at home or at nursery or playgroup, and is a great favourite. For that very reason it is shunned by older children as too babyish. Nevertheless, everyone knows it. The game itself is very limited, with players holding hands in a circle and walking round or standing and swinging their arms for the first three lines, and then suddenly ducking on the final word 'down'. The children try hard not to be the last one down, but there is no penalty or further development. Playgroup teachers have the dilemma of what to do next, and there have been various attempts to write a second verse. One, which has gained some general circulation, runs:

Cows in the meadow
Eating buttercups
One two three
And we all jump up.

The origin of the *Ring a-ring a-roses* rhyme has fascinated people for many years, but it is not easy to pin down the first recorded text in Britain. In 1875 James Fowler, of Wakefield, Yorkshire, contributed to *Notes & Queries* a number of local games which he had noted the year before. These texts also exist in a manuscript compiled by his daughter Wilelmine (born 1867), alongside one or two additional games, including two versions of *Ring a ring a-roses*. Wilelmine contributed these Yorkshire games to Alice Gomme for her *Traditional Games* volumes published in 1894. It is not clear whether *Ring o' roses* was collected by James in 1874, which would make them the earliest by about seven years, or by Wilelmine a few years later. According to the manuscript:

(Children dance in a circle and sing):

Ring a ring o' roses
A pocket full of posies
One for he and one for me

And one for little Moses
Husher! Husher! Cuckoo!

(At the words 'Husher! Husher!' the hands are raised up and down, and at 'Cuckoo', all the children sit suddenly on the ground. Another form of the words is):

Ring a ring o' roses
A pocket full o' posies
Upstairs and downstairs
In my lady's chamber
Husher! Husher! Cuckoo!

Whether this was the first sighting or not, it is clear that the game was already quite widely known in Britain by the 1880s as it was included in Kate Greenaway's *Mother Goose* (1881), Charlotte Burne's *Shropshire Folk-Lore* (1883) and other publications of the decade, and although the first two lines remained remarkably stable, the rest of the text varied considerably from version to version, which suggests that it had been around for some time.

The evidence from America is stronger, but still tantalising. William Newell, in his *Games and Songs of American Children* (1883), writes of the rhyme as 'universally familiar in America', and prints several variants. One, he claims, is from Massachusetts about 1790:

Ring a ring a rosie
A bottle full of posie
All the girls in our town
Ring for little Josie.

However, he does not indicate his source for this information or how reliable it is. Another version he gives is:

Round the ring of roses
Pots full of posies
The one who stoops last
She'll tell them who she loves best.

This is in line with some of the early British versions, where the children stoop, bow or curtsey rather than drop down, and suggests the idea that the rhyme was originally part of a sweetheart-choosing game.

Many commentators have noted how close our rhyme is to versions found on the Continent, notably in Germany, Switzerland, Italy and France, and indeed some of these texts are so close to ours that direct translation, in one direction or the other, is a real possibility, though more research is needed here. In general, the Continental rhymes are concerned with roses as symbols of love and courtship, and some imply a rose bush in the centre of the circle.

The notion that *Ring o' rosies* refers to, or dates back to, the plague, has to be addressed, because it is so widespread, and is accepted by many as gospel truth (see p. 255). Indeed, as the Opies wrote in *The Singing Game* (1985), 'we ourselves have had to listen so often to this interpretation we are reluctant to go out of the house.' The plague origin is complete nonsense, and was almost certainly invented, probably in the 1940s or 1950s, by somebody extrapolating from the word 'posy' in the rhyme, and then bending all other internal 'evidence' to fit. Neither sneezing nor red marks were symptoms of either the Great Plague of the 1660s or the Black Death of the mid fourteenth century; there is no indication of any such connection in the commentaries of contemporary writers; and there is, in any case, no evidence that the rhyme is old enough.

There is little chance that the plague explanation will shift from the general consciousness. Indeed, spurious plague-lore is very popular in a number of areas, and is proliferating rapidly. It has long been noticed by folklorists that any odd piece of unused land is said to have been a 'plague pit', and it is now extremely common for unlucky or haunted houses to be explained in the same way. Performers of the traditional folk song *The Foggy Dew* have even started to announce from the stage and on their websites that it is all about the Black Death. Further research into foreign-language versions may shed new light on the rhyme's history, and it will probably be found that *Ring a-ring a-roses* is about life and love, rather than death.

Roman Soldiers

Have you any bread and wine?
We are the Romans
Have you any bread and wine?
We are the Roman soldiers.

Yes we have some bread and wine
We are the Normans

> Yes we have some bread and wine
> We are the Norman soldiers.
>
> Will you give us some of yours? . . .
>
> No we won't give any of ours . . .
>
> Let us join and have a ring . . .

When performing this song, two lines of participants advance and retreat from each other, singing alternate verses. In the above version, noted in Northumberland in the 1920s, they all join hands in a circle and dance round at the end, but more usually there are further verses, such as:

> Are you ready for a fight? . . .
>
> Yes we're ready for a fight . . .

And then the two sides set upon each other.

This was another singing game that was collected widely in the later nineteenth century (Alice Gomme printed eighteen versions in 1898) and remained very popular for much of the twentieth. Older versions tend to be much longer; the one collected by Charlotte Burne in Shropshire, for example, extends to fourteen verses.

The basic format of a dialogue between two opposing sides is invariably present, but there is wide textual variation between versions, especially in respect of what they argue about, and this aspect is often so bizarre that the Opies commented on its 'spellbinding irrationality'. One side or other often appeals to higher authorities, and these include the magistrates, the new police, or even the 'big-bellied men'. Not too much should be read into the names of the protagonists, as these vary considerably: rovers and guardian soldiers; robbers and gallant soldiers; Romans and English; King George's, William's or James's men; and, after 1914, Germans and English. Quite often only one side is actually identified.

The earliest version is probably that printed by J. M. M'Bain in his *Arbroath Past and Present* (1887), which recalls life in the town fifty years previously:

> Have you any bread and wine
> Bread and wine, bread and wine
> Have you any bread and wine
> Cam a teerie, arrie ma torry.

Yes we have some bread and wine . . .

We shall have one glass of it . . .

One glass of it you shall not get . . .

We are King George's loyal men . . .

What care we for King George's men? . . .

Alice Gomme speculated that the origin of the game lies in some sort of traditional animosity between two groups, such as the long-running border conflicts between the English and Scots, or English and Welsh, or perhaps the habit of fighting between neighbouring parishes or villages.

It is certainly true that in the nineteenth century there was a widespread traditional animosity between neighbouring communities in various parts of the country, and this was often seen when neighbouring parish groups met while out 'beating the bounds', and at fairs that drew upon several rural communities, where fighting nearly always broke out. The sides in 'mass' football games, which still take place in a few places around the country, were also usually territorially defined. There is no evidence, though, that local rivalries inspired this particular activity, which may, when all is said and done, have always been simply a children's game.

It is interesting to note that Alice Gomme, who was never backward in suggesting historical meanings in games, did not propose what would be obvious to many modern meaning-seekers: the presence of 'bread and wine' in some versions and 'Romans' in others means that the song is about the age-old enmity between Protestants and Catholics. However, once again there is no evidence to support a notion based on such highly selective internal textual clues.

Sally Water

A very popular singing game, widely reported in the past across Britain and Ireland and also in the United States, and still found on occasion, *Sally Water* is in fact quite a slight little thing, usually comprising just one verse:

Little Sally Saucer,
Sitting in the water
Rise, Sally, rise
Wipe out your eyes

> Turn to the east and turn to the west
> And point to the one that you like best.

One person in the middle for Little Sally Saucer, and you skip round singing.

HAMPSHIRE, 1982

The heroine's name is nearly always Sally Water(s) or Walker, but in some versions she is called Sandy or another girl's name. Amy Stewart Fraser prints several Scottish versions in her collection *Dae Ye Min' Langsyne?* (1975), and makes the comment that in children's games of the past, 'Weeping for a sweetheart was a favourite theme':

> I'm a little Sandy Girl
>   Sitting on a stone
> Crying and weeping all day alone
>   Stand up, Sandy Girl
> Wipe your tears away
>   Choose the one you love the best
> And then run away.

If a boy wanted to play, the first line could be changed to 'Sandy Boy', or sometimes it was:

> Little Alexander sitting on the grass
> Weeping and wailing for a nice young lass.

SCOTLAND, NO DATE

Being so short, the Sally Water verse has been tacked on to other ring games, and one version, which has been played in the Brownies since at least the 1930s, is a 'Drop Handkerchief' type of game (see p. 43), in which Sally jumps up, touches one of the other players, and they race opposite ways round the circle, back to the vacant spot.

Alice Gomme prints no fewer than forty-eight versions in her *Traditional Games* of 1898, including one from Lincolnshire played 'seventy years ago', which would make it by far the earliest known example.

Sally, of course, often sits in water, but very many versions include other references to water, either directly or in phrases such as 'sprinkle in the pan'. Combining this insight with other internal 'evidence', such as Sally choosing her favourite, the meaning-seekers, led into the fray by Alice Gomme herself, have pronounced the rhyme's original as being a marriage ceremony coupled with water worship, and therefore a direct survival from the time of the 'pre-Celtic people of these islands'. The idea that a rhyme such as this, with a documented history of rather less than 200 years, is actually several thousand years old, need not detain us. But a different detail might provide a clue as to its origin. In a number of versions Sally is described as 'sitting in a saucer', and it may well be that the rhyme really commemorates the previously unknown pre-Christian invention of the tea set.

The Wind Blows High

(The children dance round in a ring, singing)

> The wind, the wind, the wind blows high
> The rain is falling from the sky
> — is sure to die
> Because there is such a rolling sky
> She is handsome, she is pretty
> She's the girl in this bright city
> She goes courting one two three
> Pray can you tell me who it can be?

(They all bend down to the ground, and the last that touches the ground must tell the name of her sweetheart. After she has whispered a boy's name, they all go round again, singing)

> — says he loves her
> All the boys are fighting for her
> Let the girls say what they will
> — loves her still.

ISLE OF WIGHT, C.1909

The Wind is known all over Britain and Ireland, usually sung to a distinctive and attractive tune, although nowadays it is used more for skipping than as a singing game. It was formerly particularly popular in Scotland and Ireland, where the versions were often longer and more complex. The following example is from Edinburgh in the 1960s, and has an effective change of tune and metre after the second verse:

> The wind, the wind, the wind blows high
> The snow comes falling from the sky

> Maisie Drummond says she'll die
>> For the want of the golden city.
>
> She is handsome, she is pretty
>> She is the girl of the golden city
> She is handsome one, two, three
>> Come and tell me who shall be.
>
> R is his first name
>> His first name, his first name
> R is his first name
>> E I O sir.
>
> S is his second name . . .
>
> Robert Sinclair is his name . . .
>
> Now's the time to hide your face . . .
>
> Now's the time to show your face . . .
>
> Now's the time to choose the one . . .

In the shorter versions little really happens, and the allocation of sweethearts seems its only purpose. But one major difference is whether the figure in the middle chooses her own sweetheart, or the players in the circle choose a name for him. Sometimes she gets to declare whether she likes or hates the chosen one, by nodding, stamping and so on, in a sequence probably borrowed from *Orange Balls* (see p. 276).

The earliest known version dates from about 1875, and a number of versions were collected in late Victorian times. Alice Gomme printed six in 1898. But the game seems to have gained in popularity as the twentieth century progressed, at least until the 1970s and 1980s.

RECENT SINGING GAMES

Cat's Got the Measles

A surprisingly tenacious image in popular playground imagery is the cat suffering from measles, and almost as common, the dog with influenza. First there is the rhyme, usually sung to the tune of *The Keel Row*, and probably known all over the country:

> Cat's got the measles
>> The measles, the measles
> Cat's got the measles
>> The measles got the cat.

HAMPSHIRE, 1980

Girls usually perform this by standing in a circle; and jumping up and down in time with the song, crossing and uncrossing their feet. On the last word, which abruptly ends the song, whoever has their feet crossed is out, or loses a point, or, in many cases, has to roll down one sock. The rhyme is repeated and if those who have suffered a penalty first time round end the song with their feet uncrossed they are allowed to roll their sock back up, but if they are again crossed, they have to roll down the other sock. The sequence continues with one shoe removed, then the other shoe, then one sock, then the other. A girl has to be spectacularly unlucky to get it wrong this many times, but as Megan, Mollie and Annie (aged eleven), from Godalming, commented, 'Some girls don't like doing that so we do "truth or dare". The words they used were slightly different:

> Cat's got the measles
>> Dog's got the flu
> Chicken's got the chickenpox
>> And out goes you.

Lucy (aged eight) and Sarah (seven) from Andover, in Hampshire, had a second verse:

> Send for the doctor
>> The doctor, the doctor
> Send for the doctor
>> The doctor's got the flu.

Perhaps inevitably, the same basic idea turns up as a counting-out rhyme (see p. 341):

> Ip dip do
>> The cat's got the flu
> The dog's got the chickenpox
>> Out goes you.

NORTH LONDON, 2009

Firecracker

A song with actions that was popular in British playgrounds in the late 1970s and early 1980s, and is still around, is clearly derived from an American cheer-leading chant:

> Firecracker firecracker boom boom boom
>   [*kick legs up, clap underneath*]
> Firecracker firecracker boom boom boom
>   [*wiggle, wiggle, wiggle*]
> Boys got the muscles, teachers got the brains
>   [*arms up, point to temples*]
> Girls got the sexy legs and we won the game
> Pepsi Cola, cola cola royal crown [*touch thighs, chest, head*]
> Turn on the radio, who do we hear
> Elvis Presley, star of the year
> Mother's toothache, father's [inaudible]
> Come on girls, let's show our muscles
> I'm gonna F-I-G-H-T [*kick up legs*]
> I'm gonna F-I-G-H-T
> I'm gonna fight fight fight until the morning light.

WILTSHIRE, 1978

Shirley Temple

Girls form a circle, with one in the middle, who does the actions:

> I'm Shirley Temple [*mime curls on side of head*]
> The girl with curly hair
> Got two dimples [*point to cheeks*]
> Wear my skirts up there [*raise skirt*]
> I'm not able to do the sexy cradle
> But I'm Shirley Temple
> The girl with curly hair
> Shirley, Shirley [*circle round with one in the middle*]
> We meet Shirley
> Hands up here [*hands up in the air*]
> Skirts up there [*raise skirts*]
> We meet Shirley.

WILTSHIRE, 1978

The Opies, in *The Singing Game* (1985), report that this game suddenly emerged in Scotland in the early 1960s and spread south to become a very popular playground routine by the 1970s. The 'Shirley, Shirley' lines are more usually, 'Salome, Salome/You should see Salome', and the 'sexy cradle' phrase was originally 'the Betty Grable'. Child-star Shirley Temple (born 1928) featured in numerous children's rhymes, and her name can still be heard occasionally, even though today's children know nothing of her.

Sunny Side Up

Kick the sunny side up up
　And the other side too too
See those girls in red white and blue
　See the boys say how do you do
So, kick the sunny side up up
　And the other side too too
See Cliff Richard singing a song
　See those soldiers marching along
So kick the sunny side up
　Right up, right up.

WILTSHIRE, 1978

From the early 1960s onwards, *Keep the Sunny Side Up* has been immensely popular in British playgrounds, with appropriate actions – chorus line kicks, marching, singing into microphones, waggling hips and so on – to accompany the song.

Keep your sunny side up
　Keep your sunny side up
See the soldiers marching along
　See Sabrina waggle her bum
Bend down and touch the floor
　Look like Diana Dors
Bend down and touch your knees
　And look like the Japanese
But keep your sunny side
　Wonderful sunny side
Keep your sunny side up.

LEEDS, 1960S

The original for this song and dance routine is the catchy dance-band number *Sunny Side Up* from the 1929 film *The Best Things in Life Are Free*, which has a good tune but most unpromising words:

> Keep your sunny side up, up
> > Hide the side that gets blue
> If you have nine sons in a row
> > Baseball teams make money, you know
> Keep your funny side up, up
> > Let your laughter come through, do
> Stand upon your legs, be like two fried eggs
> > Keep your sunny side up.

This was written by the well-known team of Ray Henderson, B. G. DeSylva and Lew Brown. According to the Opies' *The Singing Game* (1985), the song was already known in British playgrounds during the Second World War, but its later popularity was caused by its inclusion in a musical biopic of the song's writers, also entitled *The Best Things in Life Are Free*, which was released in 1956.

Tennessee Wig-Walk/Texas Girl

The Tennessee Wig-Walk was a novelty dance-song with a very catchy tune and somewhat ridiculous lyrics, written by Norman Gimbel and Larry Coleman, which got to number four in the UK charts in February 1954, sung by Bonnie Lou. The first verse ran:

> I'm a bow-legged chicken, I'm a knock-kneed hen
> > Never been so happy since I don't know when
> I walk with a wiggle and a giggle and a squawk
> > Doin' the Tennessee wig-walk.

And the chorus:

> Put your toes together, your knees apart
> > Bend your back, get ready to start
> Flap your elbows just for luck
> > And you wiggle and you waddle like a baby duck.

The movements are fairly obvious. It was just crying out for parody, and it soon entered the playground repertoire and the variant-making machine of the oral tradition. Many versions have been recorded and it can still be heard, to the original tune. A version from Glasgow printed in Maureen Sinclair's collection *Murder Murder Polis* (1986) remained remarkably faithful to the original, but as sung by an eight-year-old from Basingstoke, in 1982, it had drifted from Tennessee to Texas:

> I'm a bald-headed chicken and I got no sense
>> And been to heaven so I don't know when
> So she walks down the alleyway singing a song
>> Doing the Texas ping pang pong
> You're the king and I'm the queen
>> You're the one that stole my rings
> So she walks down the alleyway singing a song
>> Doing the Texas ping pang pong
> Indians come from far away
>> Cowboys come from USA
> So she walks down the alleyway singing a song
>> Doing the Texas ping pang pong.

And twenty years later the song has wandered even further away from the original, although it is still recognisable in parts:

> I'm a locked-up chicken
> I'm a locked-up hen
> Been locked up since the day I was ten
>> With a wiggle and a walk
>> And a turn right round
>> Doing the tension
>> Ping pang pong
> The girls are wearing mini-skirts
> The boys are wearing big T-shirts
>> With a wiggle and a walk
>> And a ping pang pong
> The girls are wearing red, white and blue
> The boys are saying we love you
>> With a wiggle and a walk
>> And a ping pang pong
> The girls are saying we love you
> The boys are saying we love you too

Doing the tension
Drop down dead.

YORKSHIRE, 2002

Within the same time frame, the song was also developing in a very different direction. Here are two versions of *Texas Girl* from Hampshire in the early 1980s:

I'm a Texas girl, I'm a Texas girl
  I can run, I can jump, I can swing a lasso
I can run, I can jump, I can swing a lasso
  Hands up, stick 'em up, fall down dead
Hands up, stick 'em up, fall down dead
  Hands up, stick 'em up, fall down dead
All from the land of Texas.

I'm a Texan girl, a Texan girl, I come from far
  I come from the land where the cowboys are
I can ride, I can shoot, I can throw a lasso
  If you don't believe me
Yahoo!

The words also form the core of a very interesting skipping rhyme, collected by Damian Webb in the North of England in the 1960s:

I'm a Texas girl
  I'm a Texas girl
I come from the land of – cowboys
  I can ride, I can shoot, I can do the hula-hoops
That's why they call me Bang Bang.

I'm an English girl
  I'm an English girl
I come from the land of – London
  I can dance, I can sing, I can do the ting-a-ling
That's why they call me [each says their name in turn].

There's a boy over there and he winks his eye
  He says that he loves me but he tells a lie
His hair don't curl and his shoes don't shine
  He ain't got the money so he can't be mine.

One day as I was walking
   I heard my boyfriend talking
To a little pretty girl with a strawberry curl
   And this is what he said:
[*Faster*] I'm going to marry her
   I'm going to marry her
I'm going to marry her
   Then drop dead.

Similar versions were also collected by Ewan McVicar in Scotland in the 1990s.

CHAPTER SEVENTEEN

Clapping Games

C lapping games existed over 100 years ago, but in the 1960s there was
an explosion of interest in the genre by girls (and occasionally boys)
all over the country, and this enthusiasm has continued and grown ever
since. Clapping is the real growth area of the late twentieth-century playground, and deserves a chapter of its own in any modern collection of
children's lore.

Enthusiasm has certainly not diminished among children of junior-
school age, and there has been a steady extension of both repertoire and
method over the past fifty years. Part of the reason why clapping games
have survived and flourished is that they are short and can be done almost
anywhere, anytime and quite spontaneously. Children also revel in them
because they are cooperative, fun, clever and patently modern. Although
they require concentration when a particular sequence is being learnt, expert
performers seem almost to operate on autopilot, and they often like to do
the actions as fast as they can. To the onlooker, the dexterity is quite bewildering. Nevertheless, when one analyses the movements, they are usually
quite few and simple: it is the speed and confidence that impresses.

The basic movements are: clap own hands, clap partner's right with
your right, or left with left, or both hands at the same time. Variations
include hitting backs of hands, interlacing your fingers and hitting partner's
hands palms first, or knuckles first, and – a particularly common movement nowadays – shifting the plane of movement so that the hands are
held horizontally while one hand claps down and the other claps up. The
sequence of horizontal – clap own hands – hit both partner's hands with
your hands, repeated over and over again, provides the basic three-part
beat that underlies many modern clapping games.

Another very different move is to hold hands together as if praying, but with fingers pointing at your partner, and then move the hands from side to side, bumping your partner's hands as you pass. Yet another is to hold right hands as if shaking hands, while the left hands clap each other above (high), below (low) or on the backs of the right hands. Those who are proficient at this can also move their right hand, and the result is an effective sinuous movement which looks as though each clapper is pulling down her partner's hand.

Further percussive effects can be achieved by tapping other parts of the body, such as shoulder, chest, elbows, hips and thighs, and as the games get more complex, other actions, gestures and body movements are added. As will be seen from this brief synopsis, it is a lot easier to demonstrate a clapping sequence than to describe it, and any baffled reader should ask a passing nine-year-old girl, who is sure to be adept in the art.

In the simpler rhymes (i.e. those where the clapping is relatively uninterrupted by other actions), the rhythm is relentless and quite hypnotic, but small changes can be very effective indeed, as in the still popular *Did You Ever Ever Ever*:

> Did you ever ever ever in your *long*-legged life
> See a *long*-legged sailor with a *long*-legged wife
> No I never ever ever in my *long*-legged life
> Saw a *long*-legged sailor with a *long*-legged wife.

In this rhyme, whenever the word *long* occurs the hands are thrown apart, and the regular sound of clapping is thus effectively punctuated. Succeeding verses introduce *short, tall, knock-kneed* and so on, with similar effect.

Several of the commonest rhymes share the same tune, and the words in others are often recited or chanted rather than sung. It is clear that the rhythm is what counts most, although there is not always a simple one-to-one rhythmic relationship between the words and the hands, and children are adept at variation.

In terms of content the texts vary widely and often make little literal sense, but it has been noted that whereas other rhyme traditions often include scatological references, the clapping games are more likely to include sexual references. These, however, are normally at the level of kissing boyfriends and mishaps with underwear. There seems to have been a gradual development in this sphere: the line 'Ooh aah I lost my bra, I think my 'lastic's gone too far' in *When Suzy Was a Baby* was probably regarded as sufficiently risqué in the 1960s, but it was not long before this became 'Ooh aah I lost my bra, I left my knickers in my boyfriend's car'. Adult listeners are often shocked when they hear this line, but on the whole it is pretty innocent stuff. In *My Boyfriend Gave Me an Apple*, for example, the girl's revenge for her date kissing another girl is usually nothing more than to stick bubblegum up his bum (see p. 307).

Three general principles can be identified in clapping games. The first is that the active repertoire of particular children's rhymes at any given time is relatively restricted, but as new songs have been introduced and the earlier ones not completely forgotten, the overall number in circulation has gradually increased over the last forty years.

The second is that, broadly speaking, the range of hand and body movements has been gradually extended, so that the performances have become more complex and flashy.

Indeed, in modern versions the rhythm of the song often changes halfway through, as the clapping gives way to other actions, or sections of other genres have been grafted on to a clapping sequence, which renders classification ever more difficult.

The third is that there is a definite progression within a child's development of the skills necessary to perform well. Children usually start with a simple rhyme and set of actions, as found in, for example, *A Sailor Went to Sea*, and they then gradually master the more complex rhythms over the next two or three years, before growing out of clapping by the time they reach the end of their junior-school years.

THE CORE REPERTOIRE

A number of rhymes that developed in the period from the 1960s to the 1980s grew immensely popular and were known in virtually every playground in the country. These became the core repertoire for succeeding generations, and although many of these can still be heard, others have lost some of their popularity and are being replaced by newer rhymes and procedures.

The rhyme most little girls start their clapping career on is *A Sailor Went to Sea* (often, in earlier years, *My Father Went to Sea*). The words are relatively simple:

> A sailor went to sea, sea, sea
> To see what he could see, see, see

But all that he could see, see, see
    Was the bottom of the deep blue sea, sea, sea.

As are the actions: clap own hands – slap each other's right hand – clap own hands – slap each other's left hand – clap own hands; then both slap each other's hands on 'Sea, sea, sea'. But this soon develops into variations with more verses:

A sailor went to eye, eye, eye [*touching eye*]
To see what he could eye, eye, eye . . .

A sailor went to love, love, love [*crossing arms across chest*]

A sailor went to you, you, you [*pointing to partner*]

A sailor went to I love you [*doing all three actions*]

And another very widely known version:

A sailor went to dis, dis, dis [*drawing circle on temple with finger*]

A sailor went to knee, knee, knee [*touching knee*]

A sailor went to land, land, land [*two open hands in front,
    palms down, jerked sideways across each other and back*]

A sailor went to Dis-ney-land [*doing all three actions*]

A further version has, in successive verses: *see* (pointing to eye), *chop* (chopping motion with right hand), *knee* (touching knee), with the final verse cumulating the actions as *see-chop-knee*, while another has *chest* (touching chest), *nut* (touching head), *tree* (arms up, moving outwards), ending with *chest-nut-tree*.

The other common beginners' rhyme was previously *Popeye the Sailorman*, which was ubiquitous in the 1970s and 1980s but seems to have rapidly lost favour in more recent years – in many schools children do not recognise it at all. In basic form, the verse is:

I'm Popeye the sailorman – toot toot!
I live in a caravan – toot toot!
And when I go swimming I kiss all the women
I'm Popeye the sailorman – toot! toot!

Early Clapping Rhymes

Clapping games are immensely popular in playgrounds all over Britain, but the modern liking for them seems only to date from the 1960s. Before then, they certainly existed, but they do not seem to have featured strongly in children's play, and few adults reported their existence when remembering the games of their childhood.

An exception here is the ubiquitous *Pat-a-cake, Pat-a-cake*, which was primarily done by adults with very small children. This was already in circulation by the 1690s and has remained a firm favourite, but it is unlikely that it was the ultimate ancestor of modern clapping styles. Other than this, the earliest description of clapping games as we now know them appeared in France in 1820s and it is not until the second half of the nineteenth century that we get any significant reference to them in Britain. Even then the evidence is patchy, and Alice Gomme makes no mention of clapping games in her *Traditional Games* (1894–8). Norman Douglas mentions only three, *One-two-three, Oranges, Oranges, Four a Penny* and *Twisters and Claps*, in *London Street Games* (1916). After the First World War our sources dry up almost completely. It is interesting to note that in the many volumes of the excellent *Within Living Memory* series, published in the 1990s by Countryside Books in association with the various County Federations of Women's Institutes, there are numerous memories of childhood games from the First World War to the 1940s that include items such as hoops, tops and marbles, and games such as hide-and-seek, tag and skipping are mentioned frequently – but there is barely a mention of clapping games.

That said, a few scattered rhymes dating from before the Second World War are recorded in various sources, although they tend to be the same small handful. The most popular seems to have been:

> My *mother said* that *I* should *not*
> *Play* with the *gipsies in* the *wood*
> *If* I *should*, then *she* might *say*
> *Naughty girl*, to *disobey*
> *Susan Brown went* to *town*
> *With* her *breeches hanging down*
> *When* she came *back*
> She *took* off her *hat*
> And *gave* it to *Miss* Ma*loney*.

BELFORD, NORTHUMBERLAND, C.1900

The italics are in the original, which states that 'the hands of the two players [are] to be clapped at the marked syllables. Another firm favourite with earlier clappers was *Pease Porridge Hot*:

> Two players faced one another, clapping one another's hands, now together, now singly, with hip-slapping between some claps, as all the time the steady chant went on

> Pease parritch hot
> Pease parritch cold
> Pease parritch in a pot
> Nine days old.
> Some like it hot
> Some like it cold
> Some like it in a pot
> Nine days old.
>
> CO. ANTRIM, C.1905

Frank Rutherford noted the following from a 57-year-old woman in Sunderland in 1965 – presumably from childhood:

> Sandy Doo, where were you
> All last night?
> Picking up cinders
> Breaking windows
> Feeding monkeys
> Riding donkeys
> Kicking up a row, row
> Bow-wow (*punch*). [The punch was acted, not spoken]

This has not been commonly reported in Britain, but it does have a long history. In Ian Turner's *Cinderella Dressed in Yella* (1978), for example, the following is recorded from Western Australia in about 1885:

> John, John, where have you been
> All this live-long day?
> Down the alley, courting Sally
> Picking up cinders, breaking windows
> Feeding monkeys, riding donkeys
> Chasing bull-dogs
> All this live-long day.

At the end of each line, you mime pulling a string while making the hooter sound. The words are much parodied and used as a general 'rude' rhyme. The clappers soon moved on to add punctuation:

> I'm Popeye the sailorman
> Full stop [*hands on shoulders then hands on hips*]
> I live in a caravan
> Full stop [*hands on shoulders then hands on hips*]
> I eat all the worms and spit out the germs
> I'm Popeye the sailorman
> Full stop [*hands on shoulders then hands on hips*]
> Comma comma [*thumbs over one shoulder then over other*]
> Dash dash [*head to one side then other side*]
> Turn around [*turn around*]
> Slap [*both hands on partner's*].
>
> HAMPSHIRE, 1980

Another easy rhyme, which has the advantage of a relatively leisurely pace:

> Number one at the baker's shop
> Who me?
> Yes you
> Couldn't be
> Then who?
> Number two at the baker's shop
> Who me? . . .
>
> EAST LONDON, 1978

The core of the following medium-difficulty rhymes, whose popularity reached epidemic proportions in the 1970s and 1980s, were two rather obscure pop songs of an earlier generation. As sung in the Vale of Glamorgan in the 1970s:

> Under the bramble bushes
> Down by the sea, boom boom boom
> True love for you, my darling
> True love for me
> And when we're married
> We'll raise a family

With a boy for you and a girl for me
And that's the way that it will be
Boom boom boom Es-so blue
And the same to you.

And as still sung by girls at Park Lodge School, Belfast, in 2010:

Under the bramble bushes
Under the sea
Boom boom boom
Johnny broke a bottle
And he blamed it on me
I told my mama
He hit me with a slipper
I told my dada
She hit me flipper
I told my teacher
And this is what she said
It was two plus two is eighty-four.
Shut your mouth and say no more.

These have a complicated history, as charted by the Opies in *The Singing Game* (1985). A comic song of 1895, *A Cannibal King*, and another of 1902, *Under the Bamboo Tree*, were later combined as a student song, *The Cannibal King Medley*. This included the following lines, which became the core of the clapping rhyme:

We'll build a bungalow big enough for two
And when we are married happy we will be
Under the bamboo, under the bamboo tree.

Another widely popular rhyme, less common nowadays but which can still be heard, is *See See My Playmate*. Despite a fair amount of variation, it still remains strangely true to its original:

Si si my baby
I cannot marry you
Your sister's got the flu
Chickenpox and measles too
Climb down the drainpipe

In through the kitchen door
We'll be for ever friends
   For ever more.

                                  KENT, 1970S/EARLY 1980S

Cissy my baby
   Come out and play with me
And bring your dollies three
   Climb up my apple tree
Slide down my rainbow
   Into my cellar door
And we'll be jolly friends
   For ever more, more, more

Cissy my baby
   I cannot play with you
My dolly's got the flu
   I don't know what to do
I've got no rainbow
   I've got no cellar door
But we'll be jolly friends
   For ever more, more, more.

                                       BELFAST, C.1980

Suzi my playmate
   I cannot marry you
My sister's got the flu
   She died at 82 [or 'She died at half past two']
Look down the drainpipe
   You'll see a little man
Look down the drainpipe
   You'll see a Pepsi can.

                                        COVENTRY, 1998

The original verses of *Playmates*, on which these were clearly based, were
written by Saxie Dowell in 1940:

Play-mate, come out and play with
   And bring your dollies three
Climb up my apple tree
   Look down my rain pipe

Slide down my kitchen door
   And we'll be jolly friends
For ever more.

   I'm sorry play-mate
I cannot play with you
   My dollies have the flu
Boo hoo hoo hoo hoo hoo
   Ain't got no rain pipe
Ain't got no kitchen door
   But we'll be jolly friends
For ever more.

Two clapping rhymes that were popular in the 1970s and 1980s and are still regularly heard today are *Chinese Restaurant* and *My Boyfriend Gave Me an Apple*. The first is interesting because it quickly developed into at least three distinct types, which were around at the same time. Indeed, some children knew versions of all three:

I went to a Chinese restaurant
   To buy a loaf of bread, bread, bread
They wrapped it up in a five-pound note
   And this is what they said, said, said
What is your name?
   My name is
Elvis Presley, girlfriend Lesley
   Sitting in the back seat, nudge nudge
Elvis died, Lesley cried
   Sitting in the back seat, nudge nudge
Les bought a coffin, tryin' not to squash him
   Sitting in the back seat, nudge nudge.

HAMPSHIRE, 1982

I went to a Chinese restaurant
   To buy a loaf of bread, bread, bread
He wrapped it up in a five-pound note
   And this is what he said, said, said
What is your name?
   My name is
Bend down and touch your knees [*touch knees*]
   Eyes like a Japanese [*pull corners of eyes*]

Hair like a golliwog [*hold out hair*]
  Boys go [*kiss kiss*] girls go wow! [*lift skirts*]
HAMPSHIRE, 1982

I went to a Chinese restaurant
  To buy a bag of chips
He wrapped it up in a five-pound note
  And this is what he said
My name is Elly Elly
  Shickely Shickely
Pom-pom-poodle
  Willy-willy whiskers
Chinese chop-sticks
  Indian chief says 'How'.
YORKSHIRE, 1982

And the second section of the rhyme continues to evolve:

I went to a Chinese restaurant
  To buy a loaf of bread, bread, bread
He wrapped it in a five-pound note
  And this is what he said, said, said
My name is Lucy Locket
  I'm a super star
I wear my curly-whirly knickers
  And my super bra
I've got my lips, my clips, my hips, my sexy legs
  Singing Ay-ay-ippy-ippy-ay yee-hah
Singing Ay-ay-ippy-ippy-ay yee-hah.
YORKSHIRE, 2002

The continued popularity of *My Boyfriend Gave Me an Apple* is probably due in part to the fact that it appears to tell a coherent story, in which the battle of the sexes can be played out in rhyme. In earlier versions the first eight lines constituted the whole rhyme, but nowadays the story is nearly always extended:

My boyfriend gave me an apple
  My boyfriend gave me a pear
My boyfriend gave me a kiss on the lips
  And threw me down the stairs

I gave him back his apple
  I gave him back his pear
I gave him back his kiss on the lips
  And threw him down the stairs
I threw him over China
  I threw him over France
I threw him over the football pitch
  And they saw his underpants
His underpants were yellow
  His underpants were green
His underpants were red and black
  And that was all I saw
He took me to a cinema
  To watch a sexy film
And when I wasn't looking
  He kissed another girl
I took him to the shop
  To buy some bubblegum
And when he wasn't looking,
  I stuffed it up his bum
I made him wash the dishes
  I made him mop the floor
I made him lick the baby's bum
  In 1994.

SURREY, 1990S

Instead of the cinema and bubblegum, another regular episode combines the cinema and dolly mixtures:

He took me to the pictures
  And bought me dolly mixtures
And every time the lights went out
  He stuffed them down my knickers.

HAMPSHIRE, 1983

The interesting thing about this rhyme is that its core had already done service for many decades as a skipping game. In the important collection of skipping rhymes put together by the Revd Moxon, published in the parish magazine of St Anne's, Soho, in 1907, the following gem makes an appearance:

A Miscellany of Clapping Rhymes
1960–90

The first two rhymes here were collected by Frank Rutherford in the mid 1960s, just as the clapping craze was taking off. *I'm a Pretty Little Dutch Girl* was the favourite of the day, and is clearly related to the *Boyfriend / Apple* rhymes and the 'Boys of the football match' theme quoted on p. 425. The next four rhymes were collected by Father Damien Webb, an enthusiastic folklorist from the early 1960s until his death in 1990 (some of his recordings have been issued by Saydisc and Folktrax). *Ali Ba Ba* is better known as a two-ball rhyme, *Nebuchadnezzar, the King of the Jews*, while *Abe, Abe* is based on the song *Abie My Boy*, written by H. Rule, T. McGee, L. Silberman and A. Grock in 1919. The final six rhymes come from various sources. Compare the first rhyme (*Zoom zoom zoom*) with *Number One at the Baker's Shop* (p. 302)

I am a little Dutch girl
As pretty as can be, be, be
And all the boys at the football match
Go crazy over me, me, me
My boy-friend's name is Harry
He comes from the land of Ko-ko-ko
He offered me an apple
He offered me a pear, pear, pear
To kiss him on the chair, chair, chair
I would not take the apple
I would not take the pear, pear, pear
To kiss him on the chair, chair, chair.
SUNDERLAND, 1965

Mrs Grady, she was a lady
She was a daughter who I adore
All day I court her
I mean the daughter
Every Monday, Tuesday, Wednesday,
Thursday, Friday
Saturday, Sunday afternoon at
half-past four.

I had the German measles
I had them very bad
They wrapped me in a blanket
And put me in a van
The van was very shaky

I nearly tumbled out
And when I reached the hospital
I heard the children shout
Mammy, daddy, I'll be home
From this place into our home
I've been here a year or two
Now I want to be with you
Here comes Doctor Banister
Sliding down the banister
Halfway down he ripped his pants
And now he's . . .
TRALEE, 1975

Ali Ba Ba Ba the king o' Jews, Jews, Jews
Bought his wife, wife, wife
A pair of shoes, shoes, shoes
When the shoes, shoes, shoes
Began to wear, wear, wear
Ali Ba Ba Ba began to swear, swear, swear
When the swear, swear, swear
Began to stop, stop, stop
Ali Ba Ba Ba bought a shop, shop, shop
When the shop, shop, shop
Began to sell, sell, sell
Ali Ba Ba Ba he bought a bell, bell, bell
When the bell, bell, bell
Began to ring, ring, ring
Ali Ba Ba Ba began to sing, sing, sing
When the sing, sing, sing

Began to stop, stop, stop
Ali Ba Ba Ba began to stop, stop, stop.
TRALEE, 1975

Abe, Abe, Abe my boy
Who are you wanting for now? Wooh!
Who are you wanting for now? Wooh!
Round at tea on Sunday, Monday
Never too late, never too soon
All my family are asking
Which day, what day
I don't know what to say
Abe, Abe, Abe my boy
Who are you wanting for now? Wooh!
Who are you wanting for now? You!
TRALEE, 1975

The spaceman said
Two legs together
Now and forever
Over the Irish Sea
My heart goes
Boom tattiarter
Like a tomato
Over the Irish sea
Chelsea, sexy
Maniac, tick tack.
HUDDERSFIELD, 1978

Zoom zoom zoom my heart went boom
Who stole the kitty from the boy next
door?
(1) Was it you?
(2) Who me?
(1) Yes you
(2) It couldn't have been
(1) Then who?
(2) Number two
(1) Who me? etc.
STOCKPORT, 1960S

In Bombay alli alli alli alli
Oh la Bombay ally away
Boom shig-a-lig-a lig-a boom
Boom shig-a-lig-a lig-a boom.
EDINBURGH, 1990

There was ten in the bed
And the little one said
Roll over, roll over
Then they all rolled over and one fell out
They hit the floor and screamed out loud
Please remember to tie a knot in your
pyjamas
Single beds are only made for
1 2 3 4 5 6 7 8 9 . . .
HAMPSHIRE, 1983

My boyfriend's name is Ella
He comes from Ellabella
He has a pimple on his nose
And cherries on his toes
And that's the way he goes.
SOUTH LONDON, 1960S

My boyfriend's name is Paddy
He comes from Switzerlandy
With a pimple on his nose
And three black toes
And this is how my story goes
One day as I was walking
I heard my boyfriend talking
To a pretty little girl
With a strawberry curl
And this is what I heard him say
I love you very dearly
But I love someone else sincerely
So jump in the lake
And swallow a snake
And come up with a belly-ache.
MIDDLESEX, EARLY 1960S

Eight o'clock bells are ringing
   Mother, may I go out?
My young man is waiting
   For to take me out
He will give me apples
   He will give me pears
He will give me sixpence
   For kissing me on the stairs
I don't want your apples
   I don't want your pears
I don't want your sixpence
   For kissing you on the stairs
Salt, mustard, vinegar, pepper.

Moxon commented that it was 'quite new' to him.

Two rhymes that were known in Britain before the great clapping boom of the 1960s were *My Mother Told Me* and *Three Six Nine*, but both were given a huge boost by inclusion in the hit record *The Clapping Song*, sung by Shirley Ellis in 1965. The texts were stabilised in this way, and they vary much less than most rhymes:

My mother told me, if I was goody
   That she would buy me a rubber dolly
My aunty told her I kissed a soldier
   Now she won't buy me a rubber dolly
Clap, clap, clap, clap.

LONDON, 1950S

Three six nine, the goose drank wine
   The monkey chewed tobacco on the old car line
The line broke, the monkey got choked
   And they all went to heaven in a little row boat
Clap clap, clap clap
Clap clap, clap clap
Clap clap.

HAMPSHIRE, MID 1960S

My Mother Told Me was already in use as a skipping rhyme in Edwardian times, and may perhaps be based on a music-hall song. *Three Six Nine* was known in America in the 1930s, but has much longer roots in the topsy-turvy language of fairy tales.

Another rhyme that is still going strong has, it must be said, a rather pedestrian rhythm:

> Miss Mary Mack, Mack, Mack
>   All dressed in black, black, black
> With silver buttons, buttons, buttons
>   All down her back, back, back
> She asked her mother, mother, mother
>   For fifty cents, cents, cents
> To see the elephant, elephant, elephant
>   Jump over the fence, fence, fence
> They jumped so high, high, high
>   Right up to the sky, sky, sky
> They never came back, back, back
>   Until Ju-lululululy.

LECHLADE, 2010

> Miss Mary Mack, Mack, Mack
>   All dressed in black, black, black
> With silver buttons, buttons, buttons
>   All down her back, back, back
> She cannot read, read, read
>   She cannot write, write, write
> But she can smoke, smoke, smoke
>   Her father's pipe, pipe, pipe
> She asked her mother, mother, mother
>   For fifty pence, pence, pence [some said 'cents']
> To see an elephant, elephant, elephant
>   Can climb her fence, fence, fence
> She climbed so high, high, high
>   She touched the sky, sky, sky
> And didn't come back, back, back
>   Till the fourth of July, July, July
> She went up stairs, stairs, stairs
>   And bumped her head, head, head
> Now she is dead, dead, dead.

SOUTH LONDON, 2010

This rhyme, or rather parts of it, also has a long history. In *Shropshire Folk-Lore* (1883) there is a rhyme that starts:

Betsy Blue all dressed in black
   Silver buttons down her back
Every button cost a crown
   Every lady turn around . . .

While in America in the 1860s it was Miss Mary Mack who had the silver buttons (see also 'Alligoshee', p. 9). But in its usual form, as presented here, the rhyme was almost certainly introduced from the USA, probably in the 1960s.

One more rhyme that has lasted well, and is still very popular, tells the story of Susie, through the various stages of her life:

When Susie was a baby, a baby Susie was
She went a-goo goo, a-goo goo goo.

When Susie was an infant, an infant Susie was
She went a-scribble scribble, scribble scribble scribble.

When Susie was a junior, a junior Susie was
She went a-miss, miss, I can't do this.

When Susie was a teenager, a teenager Susie was
She went a-Ooh Ah, I lost my bra,
I left my knickers in my boyfriend's car.

When Susie was a mummy, a mummy Susie was
She went a-rock rock, a-rock rock rock.

When Susie was an aunt, an aunt Susie was
She went a-sew sew, a-sew sew sew.

When Susie was a granny, – a granny Susie was
She went a-knit knit, a-knit knit knit.

When Susie was a-dying, – a-dying Susie was
She went a-aargh aargh, aargh aargh aargh.

When Susie was a skeleton, – a skeleton Susie was
She went a-rattle rattle, rattle rattle rattle.

When Susie was a ghost, – a ghost Susie was
She went a-ooooooh.

HAMPSHIRE, 1980

In other versions, Susie is variously a stripper, an angel, a devil and so on. There is also an effective cumulative version, in which the attributes for each age are listed at the end of each verse:

> When Susie was a baby
>   A baby, a baby
> When Susie was a baby
>   This is what she did
> Wah wah suck my thumb.
>
> When Susie was a child
>   A child, a child
> When Susie was a child
>   This is what she did
> Wah wah suck my thumb
>   Gimme a piece of bubblegum.
>
> When Susie was a teenager . . .
>   Gimme a piece of chocolate cake
>
> When Susie was a mother . . .
>   Ssh ssh the baby's sleeping
>
> When Susie was a grandmama . . .
>   Bang my head, dead. *South*

LONDON, 2010

The idea of a rhyme going through the stages of life pops up in many contexts in children's lore, and *When Susie Was a Baby* is probably derived from the much older singing game *When I Was a Lady* or *When I Was a Young Girl*, which was immensely popular in late Victorian times. Many of the clapping rhymes are also played abroad, but *Susie* seems to have travelled particularly well. Andy Arleo's international study of the game (2001) identifies versions in five different languages across the world.

THE RECENT REPERTOIRE

While it is true to say that many of the rhymes that made up the basic clapping repertoire from the 1960s to the 1980s came originally from America, either as earlier pop songs or already cast as clapping rhymes, the transatlantic influence was nevertheless relatively muted then, certainly when compared to nowadays. Of course, American children settling here, or British children spending time in the States, have always provided a channel for the import and export of games, as have cheerleading clubs and the like, not to mention American television series. However, the process has now been accelerated by direct Internet access. The latest rhyme can now be imported wholesale from anywhere in the world at the press of a button. Items can be replayed constantly, and words, tunes and actions can be copied directly, rather than filtered through the 'tradition' of the home country. In the case of clapping rhymes, in particular, it is interesting to note that most of the newer rhymes found in British playgrounds originated in Black American traditions. This is not the place to investigate the recent history of pop culture, but the prevalence of Black forms is almost certainly related to the pervasive influence of rap and hip-hop styles in popular youth culture in this country.

Some commentators deplore this direct electronic transmission, which they claim is a stultifying and ossifying force, creating a bland monochrome tradition on a worldwide scale. It is true that dominance from one country – in this case America – may well have a standardising effect across the globe. Another view, however, is that the Internet may potentially have the opposite effect. There is already a wealth of material posted there directly by children themselves, or by adults filming their children's performances, and it could be argued that the new medium will revitalise traditions by providing British children with infinitely greater opportunities to learn new games and rhymes, from children they will never meet. It could be argued that as the children of more countries and cultures get access to the medium, they will start posting their own traditions online, and the children of, say, Bengali immigrants in Britain will be able to keep up to date with developments in the family's homeland, and in their native language. As access increases, the result could well be *more* diversity, not less.

Nevertheless, it is important to keep a sense of proportion. While some girls are learning new rhymes or perfecting their clapping styles from YouTube, the majority of children are still learning their repertoire from friends and family, in the old-fashioned way. As I write this, my eldest granddaughter, aged six and a half, has just come home with her first clapping rhyme, which she learnt from her friend, who learnt it from her big sister.

A comparison of the clapping games of the 1970s and 1980s with those of the last two decades reveals a sea-change in repertoire and style. Perhaps that implies too sudden a change, and underplays the nature of folkloric transmission, but twenty or thirty years represents between five and eight generations in junior-school terms, which if translated into adult generations is equal to over 100 years.

A marked feature of the 'new' clapping is that whole sections of text now float from one rhyme to another, and overall texts are less stable than they used to be. This is not to argue that there was previously little variation between versions, far from it, but that the form of variation has changed. Perhaps it is because the newer rhymes have weaker narratives that they can be built in a modular fashion, with only the demands of rhythm to link them, and even here an effective change of rhythm is often a feature of performance. Paradoxically, the component sequences show remarkable internal stability; it is simply the way they are put together that appears to be new.

Furthermore, the newer rhymes seem to rely progressively less on the actual clapping, and increasingly on other actions. Indeed, there are already versions in which the girls do not even bother to clap but simply stand opposite each other, chant the words and do the actions.

Another feature of the new repertoire is again related to its closer links with pop culture. In America, and to a lesser extent in Britain, the rhymes turn up in a wide variety of forms, and are used, reused and adapted in the wider youth culture. The same rhymes and actions therefore turn up in various contexts, including, for example, adolescents' elaborate 'handshakes', and rap songs.

An excellent example is the following rhyme, known across the country, but printed here as collected in London in 2009:

> Eeny meeny decimeny
> > You are the one and only
> Educated, liberated, I like you
> > Sitting by the roller coaster
> Eating lots of candy
> > Greedy, greedy
> Wouldn't do your homework
> > Lazy, lazy
> Jumping out the window
> > Flipping crazy.

In a recent study, British childlore researcher Julia Bishop has documented dozens of versions in the USA, UK, Australia and New Zealand, and has shown that the first recorded mention of the rhyme, in America, dates from 1964, and the first in Britain from 1975. Significantly, the latter was noted from a child at the American School in London. More importantly, Dr Bishop has also identified a counting-out rhyme from which the clapping rhyme may have descended, and several pop songs, dating from 1946, 1957, 1963, 1998 and 1999, which feature elements from the rhyme.

Another rhyme, *Down Down Baby*, which is sometimes combined with *Eeny meeny decimeny*, has enjoyed a somewhat similar multimedia existence:

> This train goes down down baby
> Down by the roller coaster
> Sweet sweet cherry
> Mother won't let me go
> Sugar sugar Coco-pops
> Sugar sugar Aero
> Sugar sugar Coco-pops
> Sugar sugar Aero
> He makes chocolate biscuits
> He makes chocolate biscuits
> Ice cream with a cherry on top.

And you have to whack the other person's head on 'cherry on the top' to see who gets there first.   GODALMING, 2008

As documented in Kyra Gaunt's *The Games Black Girls Play* (1998) and Kathryn Marsh's *The Musical Playground* (2008), the song's words have roots in older rhyme traditions and were used in several pop songs. There was also an immensely influential version broadcast in a *Sesame Street* episode, and Tom Hanks used a version, which he had learnt from his son, who in turn had learnt it at summer camp, in his film *Big* (1988). In pre-digital days, such media exposure would have been highly influential, but would have been just one stage in the transmission process from person to person, community to community. Once this exposure had passed, its influence would gradually wane. But now these influential renditions can be played and replayed countless times. Other versions collected from British children include the following:

> Downtown baby
> Down by the roller coaster

Sweet sweet cherry, I like you
    Eeny meeny dessameeny
You are the one a-meeny
    Education, liberation, I like you
Apples on a stick, they make me sick
    They make my heart beat two-ninety-six
Boys, boys, having all the fun
    Here comes a lady with a big fat bum
She can wriggle, she can wraggle
    She can even do the splits
But I bet you ten bucks she can't do this
    Close your eyes and count to ten
If you mess up you're a big fat hen
    1, 2, 3, 4, 5, 6, 7, 8 9 10.

SURREY, 2008

My name is Ena Beena Boxer Beena
    Una Waller, Waller Weena
Inspiration, education
    I love you
Down down baby
    Down by the roller coaster
Sweet sweet baby
    No place to go
Wouldn't do the dishes
    Lazy, lazy
Stole a bit of candy
    Greedy greedy
Shared it with your boyfriend
    Sexy sexy.
My name is Ena Beena Boxer Beena
    Una Waller, Waller Weena
Inspiration, education
    I love you
Old Mother Hubbard
    Sick in bed
Called for the doctor and he said
    You'll be all right in a week or two
No more school for me or you.

COVENTRY, 1990S

A Miscellany of Modern Clapping Rhymes

Yankee Doodle went to town
[*clap / right / clap / left*]
A-riding on a po – ny
[*clap / clap / link own fingers, touch*
palms with each other twice]
Stuck a feather in his cap
[*clap / right / clap / left*]
And called it macar – oni [*right hand*
touches left elbow / left hand touches
right elbow / hands on hips / place left
hand on partner's right shoulder and
right hand on own left shoulder].

WEYBRIDGE, 2009/
WEST LONDON, 2009

Domino p-a-i-r
[the word 'pair' or 'pear' elongated]
Domino Sophia
[as in so-fi-ya]
Domino Sophia
Domino p—a—i—r.

CAMBRIDGESHIRE, 2009

In nineteen sixty-four, four, four
My granddad went to war, war, war
He brought me back a gun, gun, gun
And shot me up the bum, bum, bum.

YORKSHIRE, 2002

Super Sophie won a trophy
At St Mary's road race
In that road race she won first place
And now Sophie's a hero
La la la la la la la la la la la la la la
Now Sophie is a hero.

YORKSHIRE, 2002

Oliver, Oliver, Oliver Twist
I bet you a penny you can't do this
Number one, touch your tongue
Number two, touch your shoe
Number three, touch your knee
Number four, touch your floor
Number five, touch your sky
Number six, pick up sticks
Number seven, go to heaven
Number eight, sit on the gate
Number nine, swing on the line
Number ten, start again.

YORKSHIRE, 2002

I found a box of matches
Above the kitchen floor, floor, floor
And when I went to pick them up
They were dancing on the floor,
floor, floor
Singing Ay-ay-ippy-ippy-ay apple pie
[*twirling arm in arm*]
Singing Ay-ay-ippy-ippy-ay apple pie
[*clapping under leg*].

YORKSHIRE, 2002

Coca-Cola Coca-Cola
Alley alley pussy cat
Alley alley pussy cat
Boys got the muscles
Teachers can't count
Girls got the sexy legs
You'd better watch out
Hypnotise, candy lies
Turn around and faint.

COVENTRY, 2005

Ribena [*clap, clap, clap*]
Saffaseena(?) [*clap, clap, clap*]
Big boys [*clap, clap, clap*]
Crazy girls [*clap, clap, clap*]
Ribena [*clap, clap, clap*]
Saffaseena(?) [*clap, clap, clap*]
Big boys [*clap, clap, clap*]
Crazy girls [*clap, clap, clap*]
Statutes.

SOUTH LONDON, 2010

O Mary Anne, Mary Anne,
Mary Anne
Centory Anne, Mary Anne,
Mary Anne
Centory olay, olay O
Beat beat beat
Olay olay O
Beat beat beat.
Three, two, one.

BELFAST, 2010

Down down baby
Down down allay allaya
Sweet sweet baby
Sweet sweet allay allaya
Minnie minnie acker
Minnie minnie lay allaya
Minnie minnie acker
Minnie minnie lay allaya
Uckerbacka Uckerbacka
Uckerbacka stamp.

CAMBRIDGESHIRE, 2009

My mummy is a baker
Yummy yummy, fat tummy
My daddy is a dustbin-man,
poo-pooey poo-pooey
My sister is a show-off, curly wurly
curly wurly
My brother is a cowboy

Bang bang you're dead, fifty bullets in
your head
Turn around touch the ground
Singing ay yi yippy yippy yi (apple pie)
Singing ay yi yippy yippy yi (apple pie)
Singing ay yi yippy, my mother is
a hippy
Ay yi yippy yippy yi
yee-ha!

WEST LONDON, 2009

Pepsi Cola, Pepsi Cola
Irn bru, Irn bru
Boys got the muscles
Teachers got the brains
Girls got the sexy legs
So that's OK.

GATESHEAD, 2010

My name is Elvis Presley
Girls are sexy
Sitting in the back car
Drinking Pepsi
Borned a baby
Named it Pepsi
And that was the end of it.

LECHLADE, 2010

My mummy is a baker
Yummy yummy, fat tummy
My father is a dentist
Ga-gaa-ey, ga-gaa-ey
My sister is annoying
Curly wurly, curly wurly
My brother is a cowboy
Bang bang you're dead
Fifty bullets in your head
Turn around touch the ground
Bang bang you're dead.

LECHLADE, 2010

Down down baby
Down down the roller coaster
Sweet sweet baby
I'll never let you go
Gimme gimme cherry pop
Gimme gimme love
Gimme gimme cherry pop
Gimme gimme love
Doctor doctor
Grandma's sick
Doctor says
Let's put the rhythm in the head
Ding dong [*move head side to side*]
Let's put the rhythm in the head
Ding dong
Let's put the rhythm in the hands [*clap clap*]
Let's put the rhythm in the hands [*clap clap*]
Let's put the rhythm in the feet [*stamp stamp*]
Let's put the rhythm in the feet [*stamp stamp*]
Let's put the rhythm in the hot dog [*hands on
    hips, move hips sideways and back*]
Let's put the rhythm in the hot dog
Put 'em all together and what do you get
Ding dong [*clap clap, stamp stamp*]
Hot dog
Put it all backwards and what do you get
Dog hot [*stamp stamp, clap clap*]
Dong ding.

NORTH LONDON, 2009

It is interesting to note that the 'Let's put the rhythm' sequence was already being sung in London playgrounds in 1976, as reported in the Opies' *The Singing Game* (1985), in a rhyme which started, 'When Jimmy got drunk on a bottle o' gin'.

The following rhymes have all been noted in Britain within the last ten years, and exist alongside the older rhymes discussed above:

Miss Sue
   Miss Sue
Miss Sue from Alabama

She sat upon her rocker eating belacrocker
Watching the clock go tick tock, tick tock phenomenon
  Watching the clock go tick tock, tick tock phenomenon
A B C D E F G
  Wipe those coogies offa me
Moonshine, moonshine, moonshine
  Freeze!

EDINBURGH, 1990

Miss Moff [*clap clap clap*]
  Miss Moff [*clap clap clap*]
Miss Moff from California
  Sitting in a chair
Eating cockatair
  Watching the clock go
Tick, tock, tick tock shawalawala
  Tick, tock, tick tock shawalawala
A B C D E F G
  Wipe those cobwebs off my knee
Moonshine, moonshine, moonshine free
  Hello, goodbye, and that's the end of me.

GODALMING, 2008

Miss Mar [*clapping with partner: clap clap clap*]
Miss Mar [*clapping with partner: clap clap clap*]
From California
Sitting on a bench
Teaching French – bonjour!
Watching the clock go [*hands on hips, wiggle hips*]
Tick tock, tick tock [*two hands together, to right, left, right-left*]
Banana [*lean forward, roll arms*]
Tick tock, tick tock [*right arm, vertical, elbow bent, index finger
  up, to right, left, right-left*]
Banana [*lean forward, roll arms*]
A B C D E F G [*right hand up, left hand pats right elbow, repeat
  with left arm – seven times*]
Read those books of history [*hands as if opening and closing book*]
Wipe those cobwebs off your knee [*bend forward, hands moving
  across knees and back, twice*]
H I J K LMNOP [*elbow movements again*]

Moonshine, moonshine [*both arms extended, both*
    hands, fingers spread, swivel on wrists, four times]
Freeze!
Lalalala! [*mouth open, waggling tongue*]

CAMBRIDGESHIRE, 2010

Double double this this
Double double that that
Double this double that
Double double this that

You can use any connecting words that have one syllable, like:

Double double ice ice
Double double cream cream.

EAST FINCHLEY, 2008

The actions for *Double Double* are: on *double*, bang fists with partner; on
this, pat both palms with partner; on *that*, pat backs of hands with partner.
It is harder than it sounds when done at speed.
    Another popular rhyme goes as follows:

I know a little French girl
Called I-shoo-showella [*touch eye, shoe, wiggle, curtsey*]
All the boys in the football team
Know I-shoo-showella
How is your mother?
All right
Died in the fish shop
Last night
What did she die of?
Raw fish [*hold nose with one hand; other waves like a fish*]
What did she die like?
Like this! [*one falls into other's arms*]

ORKNEY, 2004

There was a little Chinese girl
Called Eye-Shoe-Shawana [*point to eye, then shoe,*
    then put fingertips together 'like a little roof']
All the boys in the football pitch
Loved Eye-Shoe-Shawana

How is your father, all right?
Died in the fish shop, last night
What did he die of?
Raw fish [*hold nose*]
How did he die?
Like this! [*feign swooning, back of hand to forehead*]

COVENTRY, 2008

One day I met an Irish girl
Called High Heel Tranner [*stand on tiptoe, touch heel,*
    show-off wiggle]
All the boys at the football pitch
Said High Heel Tranner
How's your mother?
All right
Died in the fish shop
Last night
What did she die of?
Rotten fish [*wavy hand movement*]
How did she die?
Like this [*fall back into partner's arms*].

LECHLADE, 2010

This rhyme has been around since at least the 1980s, when it began 'I am a little Dutch girl / Called Hi Susie Anna'. As recorded in Lechlade in 2010, it had also become:

My name is Anni Anni
Chickani chickani
Om pom poodle
Willy willy whiskers
Chinese chopsticks
Indian chiefs go woooh [*finger in mouth*]
Pow!

LECHLADE, 2010

Or, in a slightly different version:

My name is
Eli eli
Piccolo piccolo
Ump pum purley

Walla walla whiskey
Indian chief goes A-a-a-a [*hand on mouth*]
Pow.

ORKNEY, 2004

Another rhyme from Orkney of the same vintage goes as follows:

The girls in Spain
    Wash their knickers in champagne
And the boys in France
    Do the hoolie-hoolie dance
And the dance they do
    Is enough to tie a shoe
And the shoe they tie
    Is enough to tell a lie
And the lie they tell
    Is enough to ring a bell
And the bell they ring
    Goes ding-a-ling-a-ling [*tickle your partner*]

ORKNEY, 2004

One very common rhyme in the USA and in Britain is:

Apple sticky makes me icky
    Makes my heart beat two four sixty
Not because you're dirty
    Not because you're clean
Not because you're on our football team.

ESSEX, 2009

The wording of the first line is more usually 'Apple on a stick it makes me sick'. Girls in East Grinstead, Sussex, in 2010, had a version with a homely sounding first line, 'Apple crumble makes me rumble', which is more usually a line in a verse about farting.

At around the same time I heard the following impressive rhyme recited by a member of the school council at Ravenstone School in Balham, South London:

Wednesday, smells like coconuts
    Ooh ah, I want a piece of pie

Pie too sweet, I want a piece of meat
   Meat too tough, I want to ride a bus
Bus too full, I want to ride a bull
   Bull too black, I want my money back
Money back too green, I want a limousine
   Limousine too long, I want to write a song
Song too short, I want to read a book
   Book not read, I want to go to bed
Bed not made, I want some lemonade
   Lemonade's too sour, we got the power
To close our eyes and count to ten
   Whoever messes up has to do it again
1 2 3 4 5 6 7 8 9 10.

SOUTH LONDON, 2009

The others did not seem know it, and when I returned a few weeks later the girl who had recited it to me had moved away. It is well known in the USA, but not very common in Britain.

Any rhyme can make use of particular stylistic features, triggered by a key word. When the word 'freeze' (sometimes rendered as 'free') or 'statue' is added at the end of a rhyme, for example, whichever player is the last to freeze is out, or pays a penalty. The penalty is usually to do the rhyme again with only one hand, and when the movement calls for clapping with two hands you have to clap your body (usually the opposite shoulder). If you lose again you have to perform the following sequence with one eye shut, then both eyes shut, or kneeling down, or any other handicap which the players can devise.

Dum dum day
   Dum dum away away
See see kay see see away away
   Come on e-anker
Come on e-anker
   Icker backer, icker backer
Icker backer
   Freeze.

BELFAST, 2010

Lemonade [*three claps*]
Crunchy ice [*three claps*]
Beat it once [*three claps*]

Beat it twice [*three claps*]?
Lemonade, crunchy ice
Beat it once, beat it twice
Turn around, touch the ground,
FREEZE.

LONDON, 2009

Om dom day
   Om dom shawalla walla
See see say
   See see shawalla walla
Eenie meenie macker
   Eenie meenie ay
Ackerbom ackerbom acke bom
   Stash.

SOUTH LONDON, 2010

In the latter rhyme the clappers freeze on the word stash.

Other rhymes, especially ones with the final line 'I bet — can't do this', end with both players doing a jump which finishes with feet apart. The next time through, the feet are extended further, and so on. This usually continues until a player can extend no further, or falls over. When a rhyme ends in 'One, two, three' they make three jumps and that is usually enough to end the game. If not, they can do it again with three reducing jumps bringing the feet ever closer together.

Many children do this to a version of *Under the Apple Tree*:

Under the apple tree
My boyfriend said to me
Kiss me, hug me
Tell me that you love me
Wind up your body
One, two, three.

SOUTH LONDON, 2010

Under the apple tree
My boyfriend said to me
Kiss me [*touch lips*]
Hug me [*cross arms on chest*]
Tell me that you love me [*shake index finger at partner*]

ESSEX, 2009

A different rhyme used in the same way is:

> Milk man, milk man, do your duty
> Here comes Miss American beauty
> She can do the pom-poms [*twirl hands*]
> She can do the kicks [*kick legs*]
> But most of all
> She can do the splits
> One, two, three, four.

YORKSHIRE, 2002

> Milkman, milkman, do your duty
> Pick on Mrs Madarooty
> She can do the pom-pom
> She can do the splits
> Last of all a kiss on the lips
> One, two, three.
> [*Do it again with 'can't', and bring your feet back together*].

CAMBRIDGESHIRE, 2009

> Milkman, milkman, do your duty
> Visit Mrs Macaroni
> She can do the pom-pom – pom-pom
> She can do the twist – twi-ist
> But only can she not spell kiss
> K I S S.

DEVON, 2010

A few rhymes are based on a completely different style of hand movement: hands clasped as in handshake and the other clapped above on ('high') and below on ('low') or on them:

> High low jackalo, jackalo, jackalo
> High low jackalo, jackalo and high.

GODALMING, 2008

> My name is high low chickolo
> Chickolo chickolo
> High low chickolo
> Chickolo high.

EAST FINCHLEY, 2008

My name is
High low piccolo, piccolo, piccolo
High low piccolo, piccolo high.

WEYBRIDGE, 2009

ABC hit it
That's the way
     Uh-huh uh-huh
I like it
     Uh-huh uh-huh
That's the way
     Uh-huh uh-huh
I like it
     Uh-huh uh-huh
Scooby-dooby dooby do
     Hot chocolate
Scooby-dooby dooby do
     Hot chocolate.

EAST FINCHLEY, 2008

'That's the way . . . I like it' is from the 1975 pop song *That's the Way (I Like it)* by KC and the Sunshine Band, and appears in various guises:

Tic tac toe
     Give me a high
     Give me a low
     Give me a three in a row
Pull the chain and start again
A B C hit it
     That's the way, uh-huh uh-huh
     I like it, uh-huh, uh-huh
     That's the way, uh-huh uh-huh
     I like it, uh-huh, uh-huh
Pull the chain and start again.

BELFAST, 2010

This version introduces another rhyme distinguished by the memorable phrase 'Tic tac toe'. These words probably reveal the rhyme's recent American origin, as this is one of the standard American names for what is commonly called in Britain 'Noughts and Crosses'. However, 'Tick tack toe' was also one of the names for 'Noughts and crosses' on this side of the Atlantic in Victorian times, and so again usage in the USA can be seen to have preserved an earlier British form.

> Tic tac toe
>> Going high, going low
> Going three in a row
>> Tick tack lollipop
> Turn around
>> Touch the ground
> Bunny ears
>> Britney Spears
> Pull the chain
>> And start again.

NORTH LONDON, 2009

> Tic tac toe
>> Give me a high, give me a low
> Give me a three in a row
>> Bunny got shot by a UFO
> ['*Rock, Paper, Scissors*']
> Spider crawling up your back
>> Which finger did that
> I win, you lose
>> Now you get a big bruise.

LECHLADE, 2010

The complex game accompanying the example from Lechlade is found in very similar versions all over the country and needs a little explanation. On the fourth line (which is more usually 'Johnny . . .', but sometimes 'Granny . . .' or 'Polly . . .', etc.) the girls do 'Rock Paper Scissors' (see p. 342). Whoever loses that turns their back, and her partner draws a snake or pretends to be a spider crawling on her back, and then pokes with one or two fingers. The one whose back is turned has to guess which finger(s) did the poking and if she is correct she pounds on her partner's forearm, saying 'I win . . .'. If she is wrong, her partner bashes her arm in the same way. Sometimes there is a retort – 'I don't care, I don't care/Now I get to pull your hair' (compare Back Games, p. 105).

Returning to the 'That's the way . . .' and 'A B C . . .' motifs, the fluidity of the modern clapping repertoire is shown in the following two examples:

A B C, let's hit it
That's the way, uh-huh uh-huh
I like it, uh-huh uh-huh
That's the way, uh-huh uh-huh
I like it, uh-huh uh-huh
Brick wall [*one hand, palm forward, shoulder height,*
    joined by second hand a little lower]
Waterfall [*both hands mimic water falling*]
You think you know it all [*point to partner*]
But you don't [*shake index finger at partner*]
I do [*point to self*]
Whatever [*clap, big shrug, arms raised to side*]
Attitude! [*hands on hips, defiant look*].

LECHLADE, 2010

A B C hit it
Up together
Down together
Back to front
Head and toe
Wiggle your bum
And away we go
Flush the chain
Start again
A B C hit it
    That's the way, uh-huh uh-huh
    I like it, uh-huh uh-huh
    That's the way, uh-huh uh-huh
    I like it, uh-huh uh-huh
Boom boom
Peace peace
Kiss kiss.

[*Then hit it.*]

BELFAST, 2010

A fascinating example of continuity and change in the world of children is the clapping rhyme *Om Pom Pay*. Very widespread in the 1970s and 1980s, it is still heard from time to time today but seems to have lost most of its popularity. It was perhaps the first rhyme to feature the style of clapping that starts with both hands together side by side with a partner. The first time I encountered it was in Andover, Hampshire, in 1982:

> Om pom pay to a lay to a lassie
> Om pom pay to a lay
> > Yacker dandy
> Sugar candy
> > Yacker dandy
> Puff puff.

HAMPSHIRE, 1982

The last line varied rhythmically: sometimes it was two measured beats – *puff, puff*; sometimes a syncopated *puff-puff*; and sometimes a very definite *slam*! Other versions noted in the previous decade demonstrate something of the range of textual variation around at the time, although the kinship between different renditions is still obvious:

> In Pompeii alley askey
> In Pompeii far away
> > Alley askey so fairy
> > Alley askey
> Pompeii.

MANCHESTER, 1970S

> Om pom pay callallay callalasters
> Om pom pay callallay
> > Academus so famous
> > Academus
> Crack crack.

YORKSHIRE, 1976

> Em pom pee pomalee pomalassie
> Em pom pee comalee
> > Yackerdarmer so farler(?)
> > Yackerdarler
> Poof poof.

YORKSHIRE, 1978

Clearly, both performers and collectors found the spelling something of a challenge, and it is interesting to see that the person who remembered the version from Manchester renders the first line as 'Pompeii' rather than the meaningless 'Pom pay'. It is also interesting to note that many children who sang the song were convinced that it was a real foreign language.

The earliest version listed by the Opies in *The Singing Game* (1985) dates from 1965. In their usual brilliant fashion, they came up with the probable original: a song sung as a two-part round by members of the Holiday Fellowship, which was founded in 1913:

> Hi politi politaska, polita, polito
> Hi politi politaska, polita, polito
> O Nicodemus – O Sara numper
> O Nicodemusss, Sara – numper, umper, umper

Many organisations in the first half of the twentieth century like the Holiday Fellowship deliberately featured community singing in their activities and published their own songbooks (as it happens, I have not been able to trace this song in HF songbooks, but it is quite possible that members sang it anyway). It is likely that it was also sung in other organisations, as, at the time, there were many similar songs of an apparently nonsensical nature. It is also true that many of these organisations had strong internationalist agendas, and their songbooks were a channel through which songs from overseas entered Britain, sometimes in translation, but often in the original language. So it is feasible that the children who sang *Om Pom Pay* really were singing in a foreign tongue, even though a foreign original has not been traced.

The missing link between *Hi Politi Politaska* and *Om Pom Pay* may possibly be supplied by a sequence in the 1951 film of Edinburgh games *The Singing Street*. Here, the girls from Norton Park School are shown standing in a circle as one by one they go into the middle to dance solo.

> Oh alla tinker
>   To do the rhumba
> Oh alla tinker
>   Do the rhumba umber umber umber umber eh!
> I politi politeska
>   Politi polito
> I politi politeska
>   Politi polito
> Oh alla tinker
>   To do the rhumba

Oh alla tinker
Do the rhumba umber umber umber umber eh!

The tune changes for lines 4 to 8, and is close to the way *Om Pay Pay* is now sung, but the words are recognisably those of the Holiday Fellowship song. This seems to be the only recorded version of this particular game-song, and without it we would be hard put to understand the relationship between the original community song and the later clapping rhyme. The Edinburgh rhyme may well be the missing link.

The Pre-war Playground

Such were the extreme contrasts of wealth and poverty in Victorian and Edwardian England that it is very dangerous indeed to generalise too much about the experiences of children at play. For children from wealthier families, the Victorian era was probably the first in which 'childhood' as we understand it today, with its celebrations, toys and games, really existed. The children's writer E. Nesbit, for example, recalling her time at a small private school in Brighton in the 1860s, describes taking her toy pewter tea set to school, playing with dolls, and experiencing the various crazes that came and went – making dolls' beds out of matchboxes and selling them to others for marbles and gingerbread, and growing plants in herbaria. For children from poor families, on the other hand, childhood scarcely existed. The little watercress-seller encountered by the journalist Henry Mayhew in the 1850s was, at the age of eight, no longer a child. She had already been out selling in the streets for nearly a year, and before that had had to look after an aunt's baby.

The 1870 Elementary Education Act went a little way to bridge the social gap. It made education possible for all children aged five to thirteen years, and was followed ten years later by the introduction of compulsory education. The year after Queen Victoria's death a further Education Act set in motion the long march towards a truly integrated and national system of schooling, and in 1918 the school leaving age was raised to fourteen. The gulf between the rich and the poor, however, still remained.

Most schools of this period kept boys and girls strictly apart, a state of affairs that was to continue until after the Second World War. Writing of Govan in Glasgow in the 1930s, for example, George Rountree remembers:

In those days the playground was divided in two, the half nearest Nimmo Drive belonging exclusively to the boys . . . While most present day school playgrounds seem to have no rule of separation of the sexes, then it was a division strictly enforced by children themselves. There was no need for any supervisor to keep them apart, as no boy or girl would have been seen dead in the other playground, a strictly observed custom that remained throughout my schooldays.

Concerns about the moral and physical development of poor urban children went beyond seeking to provide them with basic education. The 'Children's Happy Evenings Association', founded in London in 1888, provided a place for poor children to go after school, and within a few years the influential 'Guild of Play' was founded by Grace Kimmins (née Hannam), a worker at the Bermondsey settlement. Kimmins's promotional literature explained that the Guild's main function was to 'counter the malign influence of the streets', and it evoked a spurious 'Merrie England' of the past where people had lived and played in harmony. Mrs Humphrey Ward's Vacation Schools, set up in 1902, and Evening Play Centres, two years later, had a similar ethos, and other schemes were set up in other cities. Then there was the Boy Scouts movement, founded in 1908, and the Girl Guides, set up in 1910.

All these schemes adopted a programme that included games, but the children were rarely left to organise themselves, being taught instead the games that the adults thought best for them. Indeed, many of the organisers were convinced that poor urban children did not know how to play.

Not that that was the case. By 1900 most of the staple repertoire of the playground and street was already in place. Hoops and tops, marbles and fivestones, skipping, chasing games such as tig, hide-and-seek and hopscotch were popular, and the singing games played on village greens by previous generations had made the transition to playground and street, and were still going strong in their new environment. Manufactured toys were beginning to find their way into the hands of children from wealthier backgrounds. Others were able to create toys and games out of a whole range of seemingly unlikely but very cheap or throwaway objects: cherry stones, scraps (see p. 236) and even broken bits of china (see p. 241).

New games started to make their way into the playground. Skipping, for example, which had been indulged in for a long time, began to acquire rhymes in the early part of the century. And sometimes a craze would suddenly sweep across swathes of the nation's children, just as it had done for E. Nesbit and continues to do today. In 1907 the craze was the diabolo. It was hardly a new invention, having been around for several centuries, but suddenly a major revival spread from France right across Europe. The diabolo was shaped like two cones joined at the point, which could be spun on a string fixed to two sticks, held in the player's hands. The diabolo could be thrown up and caught by those with skill, or passed from player to player, but memories of the game more often concentrated on the draw-backs rather than its fun. In Newcastle, Basil Peacock remembered:

> To be in the fashion I saved up my pocket money for four weeks to buy an outfit for fourpence. The amusement died almost as quickly as it arrived, and now only seems to be performed on stage by skilled music hall artistes who make diabolo a sort of juggling and ballet spectacle instead of a child's game.   NEWCASTLE, C.1907

And in London, at the same time, C. H. Rolph recalled:

> In the neighbourhoods where it could be afforded the flying diabolo top joined the tennis ball and the shuttlecock as another object always needing to be reclaimed from the garden next door.

One striking feature of play at this time – and indeed of play right up to and after the Second World War – was how much activity took place in the street. A lack of parks and municipal playgrounds was partly responsible for this – although the municipal playground movement was starting to take off, introducing an era of park keepers and swing ladies, recalled here by Doris Bailey in a description of Victoria Park, East London, in the 1920s:

> There were several lots of swings, each in a well-fenced enclosure and presided over by a swing lady. She had a little hut where she would brew tea, or bandage knees, or chat with her friends, while keeping a watchful eye on the children. She was most vigilant, and woe betide any rough who tried to push a small girl off a swing. One of our favourite games was tormenting the 'parkie'.

But a lack of public space was not the only factor. The comparative close-ness of pre-war urban communities meant that adults worried less about their children playing outside without adult supervision.

Many adults recalling pre-war childhood therefore remember games played in the street. Professor Richard Hoggart, talking about his child-hood in Leeds in the 1930s, wrote:

... the games of the street, with the lamp-post taking the place of the tree on the village green. Between five and fifteen, roughly, you play with your own sex. Games change as the year unfolds, following the products of the season (e.g. 'conkers') ... At one time everyone is playing 'taws', with his marbles ranked in prestige according to age and killing power; quite suddenly marbles go and everybody wants a threepenny shooter ... 'tig', hopscotch across the flags and a great number of games involving running round the lamp-posts or in and out of the closet areas, such as 'Cowboys and Indians', are still popular. Girls still like skipping-ropes, and almost peculiar to them is the game of dressing-up – trailing round the streets in grown-ups cast-off clothes and old lace, as 'a wedding' ...

Sometimes games brought together the whole community. Here, for example, is Ellen Morris (born in 1913) recalling her childhood on the Isle of Dogs:

Good Friday brought the skipping ... it began early in the day. Ropes were brought out from hidden places to be stretched and pulled to remove the kinks of storage. They reached from pavement to pavement across the roads. Every street would have several being turned slowly to become pliant and straight.

Almost everyone joined in. Those who could not skip took a turn at the end of the rope, sometimes sitting on chairs carried out from kitchens. Children adored the game, jumping and twisting as the ropes swung, showing how it should be done. Soon the streets would be full of people pushing each other into the skipping. 'Follow my leader', in one side of the rope and out the other. 'Over the waves', many a trip with that one too. Those too young to skip were caught up in strong arms and borne along, squealing with delight. Neighbours who may not have spoken for months found themselves moving together, quarrels forgotten for that day at least. Even the sick and bed-ridden tried to watch from the windows above the streets.

Ellen Morris's account also demonstrates how street activity was often linked with key fixtures of the calendar. Every November, children would beg a 'penny for the guy' (see p. 508) or indulge in the mischief-making that came in around Hallowe'en (see p. 498). At a more official level, in school, there was Empire Day, a day of patriotic songs, speeches, processions, flags and dressing-up, celebrating the existence of the Empire, and teaching children how lucky they were to be British (see p. 491).

Counting out, 1950

One potato, two potato, 2010

Lining up for school, *c.*1965

Time out, 2010

Rock, paper, scissors, 2010

Pinky promise, 2010

PART FIVE

Rules and Regulations

Black shoe, black shoe, change your black shoe, 2010

Rock, paper, scissors, c.2000

Eeny meeny miny mo, 1934

CHAPTER EIGHTEEN

Counting Out

One of the gems of children's tradition, which has fascinated adults for over a century, is the seemingly magical formula that children use to choose one of their number to be 'it'. Scholars have dubbed this process 'counting out', but the children themselves, if they have a name for it, use one of a range of local words, such as 'telling', 'counting', 'clipping', 'chapping', 'footin' and from the 1950s to the 1980s at least, the much-used 'dipping', taken from the rhymes which start 'Ip dip . . .' or 'Dip dip . . .'.

In fact, children do not just use counting-out rhymes to make a choice. They have various procedures that they can call on. The simplest is the race:

> We normally, like, race each other; we all have to start at one point and we have to finish, like, by the gate, and you have to run to it and whoever's last is 'it'.
>
> ESSEX, 2009

> Well, because there's quite a lot of us who play together and stuff, with my friends, we can't like go round in a circle going like that, so often we pick a place where we are playing it or tag, and we go, 'Last one to the —', and basically the last one there is 'it'.
>
> SOUTH LONDON, 2009

The same thing was happening in the 1950s:

> Just before break the word would go round that we'd be playing 'chain he' or something, and as soon as we got out we'd all race to the fence at the top of the playground, and the last one to get there was 'it'.
>
> SOUTH LONDON, 1950S

A little further back in time, a wider variety of options was available. Faced with a simple either/or choice, for example, where adults would think of tossing a coin, country children in particular would use anything to hand that had two identifiable sides:

> To decide who was 'het' we used to toss up for it but as we didn't have coins someone would select a small flat stone, spit on one side of it, and the call was 'wet or dry'. LANARKSHIRE, 1930S

A good way of choosing between two options – for example which captain would have first pick from the players – would involve a sort of walking duel:

> Occasionally boys would use this method of choice [i.e. a counting-out rhyme] – when playing with girls, for instance – but on the whole disdained it as 'soppy'. We used to 'Clip up'. For this, the first pair of boys would face each other from a yard or two apart and advance towards each other by placing one foot in front of another, heel to toe, alternating their 'goes'. At the end, the boy whose toecap 'clipped' over his opponent's had won. The loser would repeat the process with the next boy, and so on. The last loser was 'back' or 'it' or whatever the victim of the game was called.
> SOUTH-EAST LONDON, C.1915

Almost exactly the same process was recorded in Edward Moor's *Suffolk Words and Phrases* (1823), where it was also called 'clipping'. As each contender took a step they cried out either 'toe' or 'buckle', while a contributor to the *Lore of the Playground* questionnaire recalled that in East London in the 1960s the participants said 'bunny' and 'rabbit' alternately.

Another choosing method, which seems to be known in every playground in the country, is 'Rock, paper, scissors'. This can be played as an 'odd one out' game, but more often nowadays is employed by two players seeking to make some either/or decision, such as who will be 'it'. The players make gestures in competition with each other, and they have three choices: rock (clenched fist); paper (open hand, palm upwards); or scissors (index and forefinger extended in V-shape). In a neat circular rule, rock beats scissors, scissors beats paper, paper beats rock. Children are always introducing new categories (e.g. dynamite, volcanoes) half-jokingly, but they always revert to the basic three when they are being serious.

The important thing is to get the rhythm right, so that each player shows their hand at the same moment. In virtually all cases this is achieved by reciting a three-beat phrase, often with two emphatic downstrokes of the fist and then the chosen shape. Most children nowadays seem to chant simply, 'Rock, paper, scissors', but in the past there were more imaginative variants: 'Ick, ack, ock', 'Zig, zag, zog', 'Dib, dob, dab', and in my South London school, 'Ching, chang, choller'. One of Cathy Gould's informants, from Leicester in the 1980s, reported that they used to say, 'Ay, bab, boo', which the local children thought was Welsh for 'Rock, paper, scissors'.

A neat little touch, added by expert children, almost perfunctorily, is that if you both do 'rock' you bump fists, if 'paper' you slap each other's hand, and if 'scissors' you briefly insert your fingers into your opponent's.

The history of this procedure in Britain is not clear. It is not mentioned in Alice Gomme's *Traditional Games* (1894), nor, it seems, in any other Victorian game book. It is generally agreed that it was imported some time in the twentieth century from Asia, either directly or via the USA. There are certainly many versions in Asian countries, some exactly the same as the British one. The Japanese game of 'Jan-ken-pon' is mostly cited as the earliest version.

Another way of allotting players to teams that has a long pedigree is 'random' choice:

> Picking sides was managed by two leaders alternately choosing. Before them two boys with arms linked offered themselves, asking, 'Puddin' or Beef?', whereupon the leader, choosing 'Puddin'' or else 'Beef' was joined by the boy who answered to that name. Sometimes the choice offered was 'Sticks or Stones'; and sometimes some dirty alternative or other, when there would go up a bright-eyed and delighted laugh, and the boys who had the wit to suggest it were the more popular. But for this method of picking sides there was never any other name than 'Going in Puddin' or Beef'.
>
> FARNHAM, SURREY, 1860S

The basic problem with this method, of course, is that the two teams can end up hopelessly mismatched. Where the teams' strengths and abilities matter, it is common for the two captains to choose players alternately. To decide which captain gets first choice, or which team goes 'in' first, you can find a stick, or use the bat you are about to play with. Hold it vertically, and the first person grips it as near to the bottom end as possible, the second grips it just above the first hand (touching it), the first person puts a second hand next, and so on up the stick; the one whose hand cannot be placed fully when the top of the stick is reached is the loser.

A Miscellany of Early Counting-out Rhymes

One-ery, oo-ry, ick-ry, an
Bipsy, bopsy, Solomon san [or 'Little
Sir Jan']
Queery quaury
Virgin Mary
Nick, tick, tolomon tick
O U T out
Rotten, totten, dish-clout
Out jumps he.
DORSET, C.1818

Iroe diroe ducca medo
Where shall this poor Frenchman go?
To the east, to the west
To the upper crow's nest
Eggs butter cheese bread
Stick stock stone dead.
DEVON, C.1864

One-ery, two-ery, ziccary zeven
Hollow bone, crack a bone, ten or
eleven
Spin spon it must be done
Twiddledum, twaddledum,
twenty-one
O U T spells out
A nasty dirty dish-clout
Out, boys, out.
GAMES AND SPORTS FOR YOUNG
BOYS, 1859

Een-a, deen-a, dine-a, dust
Cat'll-a, ween-a, wine-a, wust
Spin spon, must be done
[Continues as previous rhyme].
GAMES AND SPORTS FOR YOUNG
BOYS, 1859

Hickety, pickety, pize-a-rickety
Pompalourum jig
Make a posset of good ale
And I will have a swig
O U T spells out
A hole in a shoe, and never a clout
Out, boys, out.
GAMES AND SPORTS FOR YOUNG
BOYS, 1859

[Boys] Meeny meeny miny mo
I ax ya whear maun this man go?
Sum gans eeast an' sum gans west
An' sum gans ower high crake nest.
EAST YORKSHIRE, 1880S

[Girls] Eeny meeny miny mo
Catalina si-ne so
Kay-o-way Kitty-ca-lan
Thou shalt be my soldier man
To ride my horse, to beat my drum
To tell me when my enemy come
O U T spells very fair
Rottom, bottom, dish clout
Out goes she.
EAST YORKSHIRE, 1880S

Icary Arry Ourey Ah
Bicary Bory Over Sah
Peer Peer Virgin were
Pit Pat out one.
CORNWALL, C.1880

Hickory Harry Oria Ah
Biddy Body Over Sah
Mere Mere Midger Mere
Pit Pat Out One.
CORNWALL, C.1880

Look upon the mantlepiece
There you see a ball of glass
Shining like a pocket-piece
O U T spells right out
Out goes he.
CORNWALL, C.1880

Polly in the garden
Counting out cinders
Cocked up her arse
And broke the church winders.
LEEDS, 1890S

A little old man and I fell out
How do you bring your matters
about?
I bring them about as well as I can
So get you out, you little old man.
NORFOLK, 1890S

Anery, twaery, tickery, seven
Aliby, crackiby, ten or eleven
Pin, pan, muskidan
Tweedlum, twodlum, twenty-one.
SCOTLAND, 1821

Me bindle, me bandle
Me soo, me goo, me gay
Me gandther, me sthradleum,
Dthradleum, dthrago, dthrathjean.
IRELAND, 1880S

One, two, three
I love coffee
And Billy loves tea
How good you be
One, two, three
I love coffee
And Billy loves tea.
ENGLAND, 1842

Winnery, ory, accory, han
Phillisy, phollisi, Nicholas, jam
Queby, quorby, Irish Mary
Sink, sank, sock.
ENGLAND, 1880S

Closer to the modern counting-out ritual was the following, reported from Wales about 1906:

> To decide who should be in, that is, the 'cuckoo', recourse was had to a very old and widely-spread counting-out device: each player put his finger on the inside of a cap while one counted, say, up to twenty, and the one on whose finger the twenty fell was the 'cuckoo'.

A similar system, also using fingers, was recorded in Belfast in 2010 (see p. 357). And a different variant on the counting procedure is also still current:

> 'Number 21': You say numbers, and the person who has to say '21' is on, and the maximum numbers you can say is three. In a circle; take it in turns to say numbers, you have to count to 21. Each person can say up to three numbers; so person 1 can say 'one, two, three'; next person can say 'four, five'; next person 'six', and so on; but whoever says 'twenty-one' is on, or out.   *ROCHESTER, 2010*

There are two basic types of the commonest counting-out procedure, in which the children stand in a line or circle, being pointed to in turn. The first could be called 'direct choice': a rhyme is chanted and whoever is indicated at the last word is chosen. The second method could be termed 'choice by elimination': the player on which the last word falls stands aside, and the rhyme is said again and again to eliminate the players one by one. The former is obviously more efficient, but children often opt for the elimination method, even if it means eating into valuable playing time, because they clearly relish the process itself.

It has often been pointed out that children regard the counting-out process as part of the game, or even as a game in itself, but its most important function is to satisfy one of the deepest psychological needs of childhood – that things must be *fair*. Nevertheless, there is in fact a great deal of scope for 'cheating' and manipulation during the process of counting out, and it is surprisingly easy to miss someone out when reciting and pointing at speed, and especially when pointing at people's feet. Consider, for example, the most widely known rhyme of all, *Eeny Meeny Miny Mo*. At normal speed there are four beats to each line and therefore sixteen people to be pointed at:

eeny / meeny / miny / mo
catch a / tiger / by his / toe

if he / hollers / let him / go
eeny / meeny / miny / mo (= 16)

But if you deliberately slow it down and change the rhythm, it is perfectly feasible, and some would say quite natural, to accentuate each syllable rather than each word:

ee / ny / mee / ny / mi / ny / mo
catch / a / ti / ger / by / his / toe
if / he / holl / ers / let / him / go
ee / ny / mee / ny / mi / ny / mo (= 28)

A careless or carefully manipulative counter can mix and match these approaches to his or her advantage. But there are sometimes built-in safe-guards. A regular way of prolonging the process, and randomising its result, is for the rhyme to ask a question:

Ippa dippa dation
My operation
How many people
At the station?

The one who is pointed at here replies with the number of their choice

Six.

The rhyme continues:

The one who comes to number six
Shall surely not be it
One, two, three, four, five, six.

Notice that in this version the count does not simply consist of the number given by the 'respondent', because this again could be calculated too easily, but is prefaced by two additional lines. Few children, or adults for that matter, would be mentally alert enough to instantly factor into the calculation the number of children, the fourteen extra syllables, and the number declared, to manipulate the result. Other randomising ques-tions, which have a similar effect, are 'What colour is it?' and 'When is your birthday?'

Again, procedures where the counter actually touches each player, as, for example, in *One Potato*, are intrinsically more difficult to manipulate than those where he or she simply points vaguely at people.

That said, two studies of 'strategy' in counting out, Goldstein (1971) in the USA and Arleo (1991) in France, demonstrated conclusively that not only was manipulation possible, but that the majority of children knew full well that some of their fellow players used such tactics. Missing out a person (especially themselves), interfering with the rhythm, adding a coda at the last minute, or simply choosing from their repertoire of different-length rhymes, were the most-used strategies. Arleo also offered anecdotal evidence that the same situation pertained in Denmark, Sweden and Norway.

Probably the most widely popular rhyme in England in the mid twentieth century was *One Potato*, which was certainly around in the 1940s and is possibly much older. It is still very well known but not normally the modern child's first choice for counting out. In this counting-out rhyme, players stand with their two fists held out vertically in front of them. The chooser goes round tapping his or her fist on each of the held-out fists, not forgetting their own, as each number is spoken:

> One potato, two potato, three potato, four
> Five potato, six potato, seven potato, more.

The fist on which 'more' falls is removed from the circle. The rhyme is repeated over and over again, until only one fist remains, who is 'it'. There are, of course, many variations. Some children, for example, say 'raw' as the last word, while in Andover in the 1980s they added 'One bad spud' on the end each time. The rhyme has been appropriated by a hand game (see p. 120), which may help to explain why it is still known.

The same pattern is found in one of the most widespread counting-out rhymes in playgrounds today:

> Coconut, coconut, coconut crack

The players, including the counter, start with both hands together, fingers intertwined. The first time 'crack' falls on a player, the two hands are separated into fists. The second time, one fist is removed. The third time the other fist is removed and the player is out. It is possible to elongate this by adding the rule that each fist is opened to a flat hand before being declared out. 'Coconut crack' is the most widely known version of the words, but the procedure allows for considerable variety: 'Lemonade,

lemonade, lemonade fizz', 'Banana, banana, banana split', 'Coca-Cola, Pepsi-Cola, Coca-Cola, split', and so on, are all employed, and some children delight in making up other suitable words; but the rhythm must stay the same.

Another extremely widespread simple rhyme nowadays is:

> Black shoe, black shoe, change your black shoe

As the counter says the words, he or she points to each player's feet. Participants stand with one foot forward, and the first time the count lands on them they swap feet, then the next time they are out.

Coconut Crack and *Black Shoe* are relative newcomers, but one rhyme that has stood the test of time is:

> Ibble obble black bobble
> Ibble obble out.

This has been in the active repertoire for at least fifty years.

These are examples of short and simple rhymes, even if the accompanying procedure is more complicated. But again children have choices here. Talking to the school council of Robert Arkenstall School in Haddenham, Cambridgeshire, in December 2009, I learnt that the children were aware of an impressive range of rhymes, which gave a surprising degree of choice, depending on a range of factors that included the number of players, the time available, the game chosen and the whim of the moment. Racing to a selected point was perhaps the quickest option, but the speediest alternative was to put feet in and count round, 'O U T spells out', then for the last two people do 'Rock, Paper, Scissors'. However, procedures can be mixed and matched:

If there's a lot of you, start with 'O U T spells out', and when there's only a few left you can do:

> Mickey Mouse in his house
> Pulling down his trousers
> Quick mum smack his bum
> That's the end of part one.

Or the last line could be:

> How many smacks does he get?

A Miscellany of Twentieth-century Counting-out Rhymes

The Lord made the mountain slippy
as glass
Down came the Devil sliding on his
arse
The elephant shit a monkey, the
monkey shit a flea
The flea shit a nanny-goat, out goes
he.
CO. DURHAM, C.1915

Egdom pegdom penny-a-legdom
Popped the lorum gee
Eggs, butter, cheese, bread
Stick, stock, stone dead
Out goes she.
TEWKESBURY, C.1917

Eena, deena, dina, do
Where shall these poor
Frenchmen go?
Some to the east, and
some to the west
And some to last year's
blackbirds nest.
CORNWALL, 1920S

As I was going down Icky Picky lane
I met some Icky Picky people
What colour were they dressed in?
Red
R E D spells red
So you are not it for making this up.
HULL, 1920S

Alla malla mink monk
Ting tong toozy
Oozy woozy wagtail
Ar var vat.
RAINHAM, KENT, 1930S

Ip dip dip my little ship
Sailing on the water like a cup and
saucer
You shall be IT.
SUSSEX, 1950S

Ickle ockle chocolate bokkle
Ickle ockle out.
NORTHAMPTONSHIRE, 1950S

Eeny meeny macka racka
Rair eye dommy nacka
Chicka packa lolly packa
Om pom push.
NOTTINGHAM, 1950S

Eeny meeny macaracca
Ere I dominacca
Chickapox, lollipop
Rom pom push.
LONDON, 1950S

Ip dip allaba da
Dutch cheese sentimar
Sentimar allaba da
Shah shah shah.
EAST LONDON, 1950S

There's a party on the hill,
will you come?
Bring your own cup and saucer
And your own cream bun
And the one who comes to number
three
Surely shall be he
1 2 3.
EAST LONDON, 1950S

One two three, mother caught a flea
She put it in the teapot and
made a cup of tea
The flea jumped out, mother
gave a shout
And in came Tommy with his shirt
hanging out.
EAST LONDON, 1950S

Ink pink, pen and ink
Who made that dirty stink?
Y O U.
YORKSHIRE, 1975

Eeny meeny macker acker
Rare ai dominacker
Chickabacka allipacker
Om pom push.
EAST LONDON, 1978

Ip dip sky blue
Who's it? Not you
Not because you're dirty
Not because you're clean
Cos my mum says you're the fairy
queen
So out you must go.
EAST LONDON, 1978

There's a party on the hillside, would
you like to come?
Bring your own cup and saucer and
your own currant bun
Choose your best chum
— will be there with a ribbon in her
hair
What colour will it be?
At the end of red we will surely tell you
Who is not on it
R E D.
HAMPSHIRE, 1982

Each peach pear plum
Choose your best chum.
HAMPSHIRE, 1982

Christmas is near
Christmas is here
How many lights on
the Christmas tree?
SOUTH LONDON, 1986

Hibble hobble chocolate bobble
Hibble hobble out
If you've got the chocolate bobble
You are OUT.
LANCASHIRE, 1980S

Ip dip dock shit
F—ing bastard
You are not it.
LONDON, 1980S

Ip dip do
The boys love you
Put you in the corner
And undress you
O U T spells out.
LONDON, 1980S

And it has to be higher than ten or lower than twenty, and they have like five seconds to think about it because if they had ages they could think [and count round].

Many of the verses that children recite consist of nonsense words strung together with more care for rhythm than meaning. Some, like *Mickey Mouse in His House*, make some sense, albeit in an often surreal way. Paradoxically, once a 'meaningless' word or phrase becomes widely used, it acquires its own meaning, which is why 'eeny meeny' is now in the *Oxford English Dictionary*.

Recurrent features and formulae may indicate how rhymes have developed from each other or may simply reveal that children's concerns are pretty universal. Feet, shoes and hands are often mentioned or implied, because they are an integral part of the procedure, and any word that rhymes with 'you', 'it' or 'out' stands a good chance of being incorporated somewhere down the line. There is also a lively sub-genre of 'rude ones', often lavatorial, but sometimes including swear-words, just for the fun of being naughty. These in themselves are traditional, although the children often think they have made them up themselves. The following has been around for over thirty years at least:

> Ip dip dog sh-t
> F—g bastard
> Silly git.

A SHORT HISTORY
OF COUNTING-OUT RHYMES

Numerous examples of counting-out rhymes can be found scattered among the general folklore literature and in other published sources of the past 130 years or so, but only a handful of compilations have concentrated on the genre. Henry Carrington Bolton's *The Counting-out Rhymes of Children* (1888) was the first, and includes over 460 English-language rhymes, although most were collected in North America and only about 95 from Britain and Ireland; Walter Gregor's *Counting Out Rhymes of Children* (1891) presents over 200 examples from Scotland; and Roger Abrahams and Lois Rankin's *Counting-out Rhymes: A Dictionary* (1980) gives 582 individual rhymes (plus numerous variants), although again American examples predominate.

A complicating factor for any collector is that because rhymes tend to be written down by adults, the spelling they adopt reflects not only their estimate of what the children mean, but an often exasperated approximation of how to spell it. There are, for example, at least four quite logical ways of spelling each word in the line 'Eeny meeny miny mo.' We often introduce meaning by our choice of spelling, and the problem is exacerbated by accent and dialect. We presume that children in one part of the country saying 'Wan-ery' is the same as others saying 'One-ery' because it is often followed by 'Two-ery', but it is rarely that simple.

We are fortunate nevertheless to have no shortage of textual material. Serious discussion, on the other hand, is much harder to come by. Bolton goes off into the flights of fancy on ancient origins that were fashionable at the time, though he does recognise that many counting-out rhymes have international parallels, but Abrahams and Rankin hardly address any historical or contextual issues. For a sustained discussion we must turn, as usual, to Iona and Peter Opie, whose *Children's Games in Street and Playground* (1969) includes an excellent section on the subject, with many examples. At that time they looked forward to the day when all the rhymes would be fed into a computer, their distribution mapped and their origins revealed. Forty years later we have still to grasp this particular nettle, and it looks increasingly unlikely that such an approach would tell us much, because the research ground has shifted considerably.

As with other genres of folklore, the field has been burdened with unsupported assumptions, which for many years have skewed our perspective and sent us looking for origins in completely the wrong direction. Put simply, the main problem is the assumption, which has grown stronger in recent years, that folk rhymes are necessarily very old, and that their origins should therefore be sought in ancient times. Unencumbered by any actual evidence, commentators are therefore free to invent origins almost at will, and it has become the norm to assert that the rhymes must be survivals of magical incantations or religious rituals. So, for example, *Eeny Meeny Miny Mo* has seriously been claimed as the way the Druids chose their victims for human sacrifice.

Along with *Eeny Meeny*, the rhymes beginning with 'Onery twoery' or 'Hickory dickory' are the ones that have attracted most attention, and it is commonplace to find them described as direct survivals from pre-Anglo-Saxon times; but the first two are not known before the nineteenth century, and even *Hickory Dickory Dock* has not been found before the 1740s. However, before the realms of bogus ancient history are left behind, it is necessary to notice the equally misunderstood 'shepherds' score'.

Folklorists and dialectologists have for some time been fascinated by reports from various parts of Britain of methods of counting that do not use modern English, but consist of words such as 'Yan, tan, tethera, pethera, pimp, sethera, letha, hovera, dovera, dick'. Most of these schemes only go up to twenty, and they are usually explained as old and traditional methods of sheep-counting, although there is rarely any first-hand evidence of their use for this purpose. Examples of these counting schemes have been reported from Yorkshire, Cumberland, Westmorland, Lancashire, Northumberland and Lincolnshire, and also parts of Scotland and Wales, and although there were regional differences, the overall similarity to Welsh quickly led to the notion that they were direct traditional survivals from ancient times. In England they were used as evidence that British (nowadays almost always referred to as 'Celtic') culture and customs continued, despite the upheaval of Anglo-Saxon and Danish settlement and the otherwise overwhelming weight of linguistic evidence to the contrary.

Unfortunately for this argument, there is no evidence to support the assumption that the 'shepherds' score' is of great age. The earliest mention of it in Britain is about 1745. In fact, in the opinion of many post-war experts, internal linguistic evidence, such as these numerals' affinity with modern rather than old Welsh, demonstrates that they were introduced into the areas in which they have been found a great deal later than the period of Anglo-Saxon settlement. Why or how this happened is still up for debate, but the idea of simple survival from an earlier population is no longer tenable.

It is important to get this into perspective, because the two very similar assumptions about counting-out rhymes and 'shepherds' scores' are regularly used to support each other in a circular argument. When writing of the ancient lineage of the 'shepherds' score', commentators almost always bring in the 'ancient' counting-out rhymes as evidence; and when discussing children's counting-out, the 'shepherds' score' is wheeled out to prove its long history. In fact, neither can be shown to be more than 300 years old.

Negative evidence is always problematic, but it would surely be expected that something so ubiquitous and deeply embedded in society's consciousness as child-based counting out would be echoed in the plays, poems and novels of the sixteenth to eighteenth centuries, however faintly. Plenty of other childish things, after all, are mentioned. In Shakespeare's *King Lear* (Act 4, scene 6), for example, the phrase 'handy dandy' appears: 'Hark, in thine ear; change places; and, handy-dandy, which is the justice, which is the thief?' This is a reference to the game of the same name in which a child chooses which hand an item is hidden in (see p. 122). Shakespeare and others also make regular mention of other children's games and activities. The fact that they make no reference to any recognisable counting-out rhymes must lead to the tentative conclusion that such rhymes did not exist, although it is just possible that they were simply not very widely known, or that we do not recognise them in the texts that have come down to us. If the latter is the case, then it is an indication that the tradition does not always preserve items over long periods of time.

But to return, with relief, to the firmer ground of real documented history, even the Opies could find nothing particularly old in the repertoire:

> No English counting-out rhyme, as such, is known to us earlier than the one the antiquary Francis Douce collected from his 'pretty little Sister Emily Corry' in 1795:

> > Doctor Foster was a good man
> > He whipped his scholars now and then
> > And when he had done he took a dance
> > Out of England into France
> > He had a brave beaver with a fine snout
> > Stand you there out.

They do, however, point out a possible earlier Continental reference in Randle Cotgrave's *A Dictionarie of the French and English Tongues* (1611):

> *Defendo*: A play with bits of bread (ranked one by another) which the player counts with certaine words, and the last his words end on, he takes, whether it be little, or great.

Iona and Peter Opie were each too careful a scholar to claim ancient origins where no evidence existed, but even they stated, a little wistfully perhaps, that 'it appears that the theory that these rhymes are centuries old is not to be lightly dismissed'.

One thing that puzzled the Opies in the 1960s was the relatively rapid change that children's rhymes seemed to undergo:

> No explanation is readily forthcoming why the most popular gibberish rhyme of the nineteenth century [*Onery, Twoery . . .*] (of which Bolton gives eighty versions) should be unknown to children today; while the gibberish that is now most common, 'Eenie meenie, macca, racca' was unknown in

A Miscellany of Modern Counting-out Rhymes

Black shoe, black shoe
Change your black shoe.
EAST FINCHLEY, 2008

Black shoe, black shoe
Change your dirty dirty black shoe
Not because you're dirty
Not because you're clean
Not because the King and Queen say so
You are not it.
COVENTRY, 2008

Coconut, coconut, coconut, split
[also:] Lemonade, lemonade,
lemonade fizz
[and:] Banana, banana, banana split.
CAMBRIDGESHIRE, 2009

Coca-Cola, Pepsi-Cola, Coca-Cola,
Split.
NORTH LONDON, 2009

Ip dip battleship, you are not it.
SHROPSHIRE, 2009

Ip dip sky blue
Who's it? Not you.
SCOTLAND, 2008

Ip dip do
Cat got the flu
Dog got the chickenpox
Out goes you.
CAMBRIDGESHIRE, 2009

Ip dip doo
Doggy did a poo
Went to the cinema at half-past two
When the film started
Everybody farted
Out goes you.
WEST LONDON, 2009

Ip dip sky blue
Granny sitting on the loo
Dropping bombs, singing songs
Out goes you.
EAST SUSSEX, 2008

Ip dip doo
The dog done a poo
The cat done another one
So out goes you.
EAST SUSSEX, 2008

Ibble obble black bobble
Ibble obble out
Turn your belly button
Inside out
If it wobbles let it go
Ibble obble black bobble
Ibble obble out.
CAMBRIDGESHIRE, 2009

Jimmy had a racing car
C A R
[*they pick a number*]
one, two, three . . .
ESSEX, 2009

Little Noddy in his car
C A R.

SOUTH LONDON, 2009

Racing car number nine
Losing petrol all the time
How many gallons did it lose?
One, two, three . . .

ORKNEY, 2004

Big Ben strikes ten, B − E − N.

KENT, 2009

Bubblegum, bubblegum, on a dish
How many pieces do you wish?

NORTH LONDON, 2008

Onniker bonniker see passoniker
Onniker bonniker nobs.

EAST SUSSEX, 2008

Onker bonker ally onker
Onker bonker split.

ROCHESTER, 2010

Up scout walk out.

SURREY, 2008

Put your pegs in box
Yes sir, no sir
Let me hear you cough sir
[*Cough cough*]
Very bad indeed sir
You have to leave the town sir.
[*Everybody puts both hands out, with
only middle and index finger
showing, slightly apart.*]

BELFAST, 2010

There's a party on the hill
Will you please please come?
[yes/no]
With your own cream cake
And your own cream bun?
[yes/no/can't afford it]
Who is your best friend?
[Hollie]
H O L L I E
You will see her up there
With her knickers in the air
Singing Ay-aye-ippee-ippee-aye
And you are not the one to be it.

ORKNEY, 2004

There's a soldier in the grass
With a bullet up his arse
Pick it out, pick it out
Like a good boy scout
Black cat counts to ten
1 2 3 4 5 6 7 8 9 10

COVENTRY, 2001

There was a little monkey
Ran across the country
Fell down a dark hole
Split his little arse-hole
What was the colour of his blood?
[Blue]
B L U E.

COVENTRY, 2001

Eechy, peachy
Peary, plum
Who has got the biggest bum?
[Cathy]
C A T H Y.

SOLIHULL, 2001

the nineteenth century . . . We know only that dips, even magical-sounding dips in which not a word is understandable, are not necessarily old, and need not originally have been for elimination.

Fifty years later, *Eenie Meenie Macca Racca* has gone the way of its Victorian predecessors, and is rarely heard.

Reaping the benefit of some further decades of systematic collecting of children's lore, we can now get a much clearer picture of how long particular items survive in the tradition, although, of course, it has to be borne in mind that children not only learn from other children, but also from their parents' and grandparents' repertoires. If children use these in their play, it is quite feasible for an item to pop up suddenly decades after its 'natural' life seems to be over. Some contemporary children I have spoken to will mention *One Potato* or *Eeny Meeny Macka Racka*, but then will go on to say that they do not generally use them in day-to-day play.

As a crude guide to how long particular rhymes last in tradition, here are eighteen 'dipping or counting-out rhymes' that Alan Smith gathered from a handful of East London schools in the 1950s and listed in *East London Papers* (1959):

(1)   One potato
(2)   Your shoes need cleaning
(3)   Dip dip dip, my little ship
(4)   Round and round the butter dish
(5)   Eeny meeny miny mo
(6)   1 2 3 mother caught a flea
(7)   Two little dicky birds
(8)   Pease pudding hot
(9)   There's a party on the hill
(10) I know a doctor, he knows me
(11) Piggy on the railway
(12) Ip dip allaba da
(13) Ibble bobble black bobble
(14) Old Mother Pink/Old Mother Mason
(15) Inky pinky ponky
(16) Ippy dippy dation
(17) As I was going down Inky Binky Lane
(18) I went into a Chinese shop

Number 18 comprises the first section of the widespread clapping rhyme *I Went to a Chinese Restaurant*, but then goes into *Eenie Meenie Macca Racca*.

At a glance it can be seen that few are now in active use. Number 13 is still common, Number 1 is well known but not used much for counting out, 5 is well known but hardly ever used, and 16, 9 and 3 are still met with on occasion. To all intents and purposes the rest have disappeared from London, and probably elsewhere. In fifty years, over two-thirds have apparently disappeared, while none of the current favourites (*Coconut Crack*, *Black Shoe*, etc.) appear on the old list at all.

It is perfectly possible that the speed of change in the playground has been much greater in recent times than in previous years, and we cannot therefore use the recent past as direct evidence for bygone eras. But it would seem at least a more fruitful exercise to try to learn how long items stay in the active repertoire, and how they are passed around and changed, than to make up spurious ancient origins.

CHAPTER NINETEEN

Truce Terms

One of the most interesting features of the research carried out by Iona and Peter Opie, and published in their *Lore and Language of Schoolchildren* in 1959, was the revelation that children up and down the country regulated their play with a local word, usually accompanied by a stipulated gesture, which would bring temporary respite during a game. 'Barley!' shouted children from Birmingham when they wanted to tie up a shoelace, 'Fainites!' cried a hard-pressed London child with the 'stitch', and in each case the person chasing them would respect their right to a few moments' breather to deal with whatever problem had arisen. The strength of this tradition was astonishing, and most children adhered strictly to the code as if it was the word of the law. The only exception was when a child was deemed to have misused the privilege by calling it too readily or too often.

A few folklorists and dialectologists had noticed and wondered about these words before, but nobody had investigated them to any great extent, nor had anyone attempted an overall collection. What the Opies found was that these 'truce terms', as they have come to be known, were markedly regional, and although several words might be known in particular areas, invariably one term was dominant in its own territory.

Fifty years later, children are still claiming temporary immunity with a word and gesture, but in many places the chosen word has changed beyond recognition, and the overall picture looks very different. With the benefit of further research in the intervening decades, we are in a position to re-examine the nature of the 'truce term' and to reassess both the history and development of its use. But it must be said that the situation turns out to be far more complex than it seems at first glance, and a neat and tidy picture cannot be expected to emerge.

There is no doubt that the Opies were broadly correct in their findings. Apart from one or two reservations, the regional pattern they identified has been confirmed by historical research into the period, and the pattern they identified seems to have held good through the 1960s and into the 1970s. Interviews with people born before about 1970 usually yield results that adhere to the 'Opie standard'. After that time, however, the picture starts to fragment. Nobody has done a national survey since the Opies' time, so it is not easy to map the changes, or even to understand them fully, but it is clear that the old pattern they identified has broken down, at least in part.

But first to the picture as revealed in 1959. It should be noted that in the 'oral tradition', which most children inhabit, they do not necessarily know how to spell the words they use every day, and it is always amusing when adults struggle to write down the words that tripped so easily off their tongues a few years before. The main seven words that the Opies identified as the dominant terms, and the territories over which they held sway, were as follows:

Barley: By far the biggest territory, including Eastern Scotland, the Borders, North-west England, the West Midlands, and all of Wales, except for an area in the South-east.

Keys: Western Scotland.

Skinch: Northumberland and Durham.

Kings or *kings and crosses*: The eastern half of England, from the Tees down to Bedfordshire, including most of East Anglia.

Fainites: London, the South-east, Essex, the West Country and parts of Wiltshire and Hampshire. Of all the terms, this is the one that varies most in spelling. The initial 'F' is often replaced by a 'V', and the second half often starts with 'L'. Thus 'fainlites', 'veinlights', 'vaynites', 'feignights' and so on.

Scribs: A relatively small area, including parts of Hampshire, West Sussex and Surrey. Variants include 'squibs' and 'cribs'.

Cree: On both sides of the Bristol Channel – South-east Wales and the area around Bristol.

Although these were the dominant terms, the Opies identified fifty-four words altogether; however, a number of these are probably variant spellings of each other.

The one qualification that needs to be made about the Opies' research concerns the truce term 'Pax'. This was undoubtedly the commonest word in private schools, and therefore also in school stories, and it was reported sporadically across the country, which prompted the Opies to label it 'group dialect not regional dialect'. But in subsequent research, many people who attended state schools in various parts of the country at that time have claimed 'Pax' as the usual word in their school. As one correspondent commented, 'We used this word in the 1950s in the fish dock area of Hull.' And in a survey undertaken in Croydon in 2004, twenty-three of the eighty-nine people asked about truce terms mentioned pax or paxes. Thirteen of these had attended state rather than private schools, and though most were from the South-east, several came from other parts of the country. Several contributors to the *Lore of the Playground* online questionnaire also reported 'Pax' as the truce term they used, and again no discernible regional pattern can be detected. It is probably the case, therefore, that 'pax' has been the 'second-choice' word in many schools, and was consequently under-reported in previous studies. Incidentally, in the Croydon study the most popular term among the fifty-nine who remembered a truce term was a version of 'Fainites' (recalled by twenty-nine people) – not surprising given the area most came from.

Since the Opies conducted their pioneering work, only three detailed studies of truce terms have been undertaken that I am aware of, and each of these covers a restricted area: Ian Beckwith and Bob Shirley's 'Truce Terms: a Lincolnshire Survey' (1975); Alasdair Roberts's 'Barleys, Key and Crosses' (1977) plus a section in his *Out to Play* (1980); and Kate and Steve Roud's 'Truce Terms in Croydon, Surrey, 1988' (1989).

In 1974 Beckwith and Shirley chose to investigate Lincolnshire because in the Opie report it was one of the areas where the territories of different words ('kings', 'crosses' and 'screams') overlapped. They reported that 'squits' was the most popular word, followed by 'kings', 'crosses', 'quits' (which was probably a variant of 'squits') and 'crog(g)s'. 'Screams' was hardly ever mentioned. They discovered that some of the words were concentrated in definable areas, but some, including 'crog(g)s' and 'quits', were found all over the place.

Alasdair Roberts's research, which focused on the Grampian region around Aberdeen in the late 1970s, also uncovered a complex picture. Five different words were found in significant numbers – 'barleys', 'crosses', 'pardies', 'keys' and 'chaps' – and although there was still a marked degree of regionalisation, it was more a complicated pattern of smaller territories than the broad regions suggested by the Opies. Roberts also reported a number of other terms, found in isolated areas, including 'thumbs', 'trucies', 'keppies', 'peacies', 'freezies', 'leeshies' and 'timies'.

My daughter and I undertook our Croydon survey, in which over half the borough's primary schools took part, in 1988. Back in 1959, Croydon had been firmly in the 'fainites' territory, and informal discussions with older local residents confirmed that this was the word they remembered. But in 1988 it came a relatively poor third in the list of preferred words. In terms of numbers of children reporting words, 'pax' came first (30 per cent), 'jecs' second (25 per cent) and 'fainites' third (20 per cent). The comments from the teachers were revealing in that they sometimes got the impression that 'fainites' was regarded as irredeemably old-fashioned, and some children said they knew it only from their parents or grandparents. 'Jecs' (or possibly 'jex') needs some explanation, as it does not appear in the Opies' findings at all. There is some evidence that it is short for 'injection', and probably comes from a particular game in which one can inoculate oneself against a 'virus'.

These three case studies demonstrate, at the micro level, that the pattern had changed considerably in twenty or thirty years. Some words had lost their dominant status, some had all but disappeared, others had been introduced, but in no area was there a clear-cut regional distribution.

The picture today is different again. While it is unwise to make sweeping generalisations, since not all parts of the country have been fully surveyed, it is clear that one new term, 'time out', has become very popular. It was not mentioned in the Opies' survey, and nor can I find it mentioned by any other British collector before the late 1990s, apart from Roberts's 'timies' in Aberdeen. The term is usually marked with a T-shape made with the hands, and in some schools you have to say 'time in' when you want to join back in, but in others this was thought unnecessary. The scale of the spread of 'time out' can be seen from the following list of places that have reported it in the last fifteen years – the places marked with an asterisk reported another truce term as well. Every school sampled in London in the last four years has reported it as the only word used.

London (six different areas)
*Rochester, Kent
Maresfield, Sussex
*East Grinstead, Sussex
Weybridge, Surrey
*Wivenhoe, Essex
*Ardleigh, Essex
Salisbury, Wiltshire
Bedfordshire

A Wealth of Truce Terms

In *The Lore and Language of Schoolchildren* (1959), Iona and Peter Opie mapped the distribution of truce terms the length and breadth of Great Britain. The list on the opposite page comprises all the terms they came across, as well as the ones that have come to my notice since. It should be remembered that the Opies' published list did not include terms that were rare or unique, and that later researchers would probably have grouped together some of their terms, for example 'arley' with 'barley'. Terms not included in the Opies' list are distinguished with an asterisk.

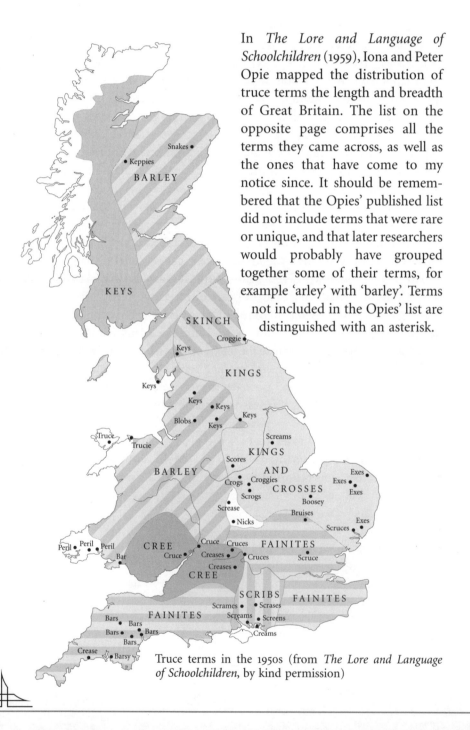

Truce terms in the 1950s (from *The Lore and Language of Schoolchildren*, by kind permission)

arley	keppies
ballow	Keys
bar	kings
barbee	*leeshies
barley	locks
barley-bees	*nicklas
barley-hay	nicks/nix
barley-o	*pardies
barley-play	parley(s)
barleys	*pause
barlow	pax
barrels	*peace/peacies
bars	*pears
bees	peas
blobs	peril
*block(s)	*pips
boosey	queens
*bugsies	quits
*chaps	scores
*checks	scrases
creams	screams
creases	screase
cree	screes
cribs	screws/screwsies/scruces
croggies/*crog(g)s	scribs/squibs
crosses	scrogs/scroggies
cross keys	skinch/skinge
cruce	snecks
den/denny	*squidsies
*dubs/dubbies	squits
eggshell	*thumbs
exes	*tibs
fains/fainites	*time out
finns	*timies
*finga-fongs	truce/trucie
*force field	twigs
free	twixes
*freezies	*uncle
*jecs/jex	vains/vainites

Lechlade, Gloucestershire
*Haddenham, Cambridgeshire
Aston on Clun, Shropshire
Coventry
Hackleton, Northamptonshire
Sheffield
Redcar, North Yorkshire
*Gateshead
Inverness

Other terms found in the same period are listed below. Places marked with an asterisk also claimed to say 'time out'.

Bugsies: Okehampton, Devon
Cross keys: Charlton Kings, Gloucestershire
Cross keys: *Rochester, Kent
Cross keys: *East Grinstead, Sussex
Crease: Coventry
Exes: Norfolk
Pause or paxies: Belfast
Pause or freeze: *Wivenhoe, Essex
Scribs: Godalming, Surrey
Scribs: *Haddenham, Cambridgeshire
Scribs: *Ardleigh, Essex
Skinches: *Gateshead
Truce: Waterford, Ireland
Twixes or truce: Chigwell, Essex
Uncle: Coventry

The evidence regarding the gestures that accompany truce terms is even more patchy than the words used, and it is again impossible to give a unified picture. Very broadly speaking, in the Opies' time, children in England and Wales crossed their fingers, while children in Scotland held up their thumbs. But there were isolated areas that did not follow this general pattern. In some parts of Lancashire and Yorkshire, the 'thumbs-up' fashion prevailed, and there were places where children did something completely different. At Lydney, for example, some held up a hand, palm forward, and at Bradford-on-Avon some held up three fingers.

After the Opies conducted their survey, the picture became even more complex. Alasdair Roberts reported in the late 1970s that more children around Aberdeen used crossed fingers than thumbs up. In the 1988 Croydon survey, 70 per cent of children crossed their fingers, but 6 per cent reported putting a thumb through the first two fingers, and 2 per cent crossed their arms across their chest. One girl in Andover, Hampshire (in 1978), said they crossed fingers on both hands, and then crossed their arms across their chests.

And then there are indications of gender difference. In the Croydon survey, in the schools where the boys put their thumb through their fingers, the girls usually crossed their fingers. The same pattern was reported in Gateshead in 2010 for the children who still said 'skinches' rather than 'time out', and the same again in Coventry in 2007 for children saying 'crease'. Clearly there is much more research to be done. It is probably still true to say that crossed fingers is the most used truce-term gesture. But if the spread of 'time out' continues, with its obvious T-shape, then most of these other gestures will fade away.

Gender differences might explain another anomaly in the documentary record. In the area in which 'kings' prevailed, on the eastern side of England, there were occasional reports of people saying 'queens', and it is possible that this was a result of girls and boys using gender-specific terms.

TRUCE WORD ORIGINS

Derivations are clear for a few of the terms used, and many suggestions have been made for some of the others, not always convincingly. Some, of course, come from standard English words that mean a brief respite: truce/trucie, pax/paxies, peace, peas, freezies and pause (which may have come in with the video/DVD generation). Some words appear to have been taken from specific games, 'blocks', for example, 'jecs' (which may be short for 'injections'), 'den/denny' and so on. Some seem to be a reflection of the gesture used – 'thumbs', for instance. 'Crosses' probably fits the same pattern, as do 'cruces', 'scruces', 'exes' and even 'cross keys'. If 'cross keys, is derived from crossed fingers, then 'keys' can perhaps be explained in the same way. That said, it is true to say that we have no idea where many truce terms came from.

Incidentally, in children's language, not only does '-ie' get added to the end of any word, but consonants are often hardened. Thus, 'elastics' becomes 'laggies', and 'first' becomes 'fogs' or 'foggy'. So 'croggies' and 'crogs' may well derive from 'crosses'.

Barley

Barley has fascinated antiquarians and dialectologists since the nineteenth century:

> *Barley*, a Yorkshire word, to indicate a cessation of play for a time; a boy's truce. One writer thinks it is a coalition of the words 'By your leave'; another says it is 'Parley'; and Sir Walter Scott explains it as a contraction of 'Byrlady, for our lady' (the Virgin Mary). There is a game in Scotland called Barley-Brake, and Allan Ramsay writes, 'While he cried "Barley-fummil", meaning while he wished for a stoppage to the game . . .'   YORKSHIRE, 1891

'Barley' is the earliest recorded word used explicitly as a truce term: John Jamieson records it in his *Etymological Dictionary of the Scottish Language* (1808) as, '*Barley*: A term used in the games of children, when a truce is demanded.' But there are earlier examples, when it may have meant either a 'surrender' or a 'truce', as in Tobias Smollett's *The Reprisal* (1757): 'Never fash your noddle about me; conscience! I'se no be the first to cry Barley' (Act 2, scene 3). And the word appears in a similar context in the four-teenth-century poem *Sir Gawain and the Green Knight*. And then there was 'Barlafummill', a term of surrender in a wrestling match, first docu-mented in *Christ's Kirk on the Green* of about 1550.

Despite the ingenious etymologies of the nineteenth century, the most likely derivation is the most obvious one, that, like the word 'parley', it comes from the French *parlez*.

The historical picture is clouded, however, by the fact that 'barley' was also regularly recorded in the nineteenth century as a claiming word, equiv-alent to the more widespread 'bags, or 'bagsy' (see p. 376).

Cribs/Squibs/Scribs

There is no shortage of the meanings of these words in the *Oxford English Dictionary* and the *English Dialect Dictionary*, but none of them seems to have any connection with games or truces, so the etymology of these words remains obscure.

Fainites

Fainites/vainites/veins and so on appear to be derived from *fain*, a word commonly used in the medieval period to mean 'to decline' or 'back out of' something and probably ultimately from the French *défendre*, in the sense of 'to forbid'. It apparently survived in English dialect forms, connoting a negative, or forbidding something, as in these three examples:

> *Fen*: a preventative exclamation, imperatively used to negative or prevent any undesirable action. A boy at marbles, his taw slipping, cries 'slips over again!' to authorise another attempt; which his adversary averts by sooner, or more quickly, exclaiming 'Fen slips over again'. SUFFOLK, 1820S

> *Fainites* or *Fainlites* obviously had relation to that other expression we used to excuse ourselves from a bothersome or dangerous task – *Fains I* – 'Not me, chaps'. SOUTH-EAST LONDON, C.1915

> When Touch succeeds in touching another, he cries, *Feign double-touch!*, which signifies that the player so touched must not touch the player who touched him, until he has chased somebody else.
> GAMES AND SPORTS FOR YOUNG BOYS, 1859

But 'fainites' as a truce term (in any of its spellings) is not recorded until 1870, although it was then said to be already in common use by London schoolboys. On the present evidence, it seems that the use of the word forbidding an action in a game is the immediate root of the truce term, although how the former survived 500 years or so without being recorded remains a mystery.

Kings/Queens

'Kings' is first mentioned as a truce term in Thomas Sternberg's *Dialect of Northamptonshire* (1851), where it is explained as 'An exclamation in use among boys to give notice of a cessation of game'. But in some areas during the nineteenth century the truce term was more commonly a phrase – 'king's-cruise' in Lincolnshire, and 'king's-speech and barley bay' in Northumberland, for example. Countless children's games also contain the word 'king' somewhere, in the name, the dialogue or as one of the characters. The *English Dialect Dictionary* has a representative sample in its entry for 'king'.

Nicks/Nix

The predominant truce term in Warwick, according to the Opies, 'nix' was a widespread slang word from at least the 1780s as a general negative term, and from at least the 1860s as a schoolboy word for 'look out someone's coming'. G. F. Northall, in his *Warwickshire Word-Book* (1896), claims unconvincingly that as a truce term it must derive from St Nicholas, whom, being the patron saint of children, schoolboys would call to when in need of assistance.

Screens/Screams/Creams

'Screens' is included in J. E. Brogden's *Provincial Words and Expressions Current in Lincolnshire* (1866), and it is possible that it is related to one of the meanings of the word listed in the *Oxford English Dictionary* as 'To shield or protect from hostility or impending danger'. This may be clutching at straws, though. The attempt to equate 'screams' and 'creams' with 'screens' is equally conjectural.

CHAPTER TWENTY

Rituals

PROMISES, OATHS AND LIES

All across the country, modern children routinely link little fingers to seal a promise, which they call making a 'pinky promise', or, if more serious, a 'pinky swear' (although children in Belfast say 'piggy promise'). Sometimes they say these words while performing the action, but there does not seem to be any other verbal component to the procedure. The 'pinky promise' appears to be a relatively recent invention, as it is not mentioned in previous childlore literature, although it may well be a survival of older finger traditions.

'Pinky', incidentally, has been the word for a little finger for centuries. It is recorded in exactly that sense in John Jamieson's *Etymological Dictionary of the Scottish Language* (1808), and since 1594 as a word for anything small. 'Pink' is also the word for a little finger in Dutch.

The other very widespread method of making a promise nowadays is to say, 'Cross my heart and hope to die', sometimes also making an X across the chest with the finger. But few children are satisfied with this, and nearly every child interviewed in the last three years has chanted:

> Cross my heart and hope to die
> Stick a needle in my eye

as the strongest way of attesting their truthfulness. This is much older than the 'pinky promise'.

Children interviewed about such things sometimes mentioned holding up their hands when promising or swearing something. I found this a little confusing, as I had assumed that the hands-up gesture was more commonly used to indicate surrender. But a girl from St Mary's in Ardleigh, in Essex, cleared up my confusion by explaining that you hold both hands up in front of you, palms forward, fingers spread, to show that you do not have your fingers secretly crossed, which would of course negate the promise. She further commented that some people cross their legs and, even more deviously, 'some people can cross their tongues'.

Aware of these underhand tricks, Maddie, Rhea and Dahlia from Ealing said that you always say, 'Pinkie promise – no crosses count', or, as some Coventry children told collector Cathy Gould:

> Swear down
> On me Gran's ashes
> Only hands included.

Crossed fingers is a widespread feature in British folklore, and it has a variety of meanings, depending on the circumstances. Sometimes it is protective, guarding against ill-wishing or even witchcraft, or against the power of the person who is 'it' in the game of tag, while at other times the gesture is to ensure good luck, as in 'I'll cross my fingers for you'. But sometimes the fingers are crossed to negate the power of the spoken word, as when the gesture cancels a promise or secretly contradicts a statement made in apparent good faith.

There has never been full agreement about whether duplicate crossings enhance or negate the effect. So, for example, a few people have always maintained that crossing the fingers on the second hand cancels out the power of the single hand, but most believe that using both hands doubles the effectiveness. Hence, also, the idea that crossing the legs is similarly effective, and in some circumstances when crossing the fingers is not possible – for example when sitting an exam or playing cards – crossing the legs is a good substitute.

In the past, children took their oaths and promises a lot more seriously, and they could choose from a range of colourful expressions, most of which have since disappeared from children's vocabulary.

When children at school make oaths or promises to each other the deponent wets his finger and shows it to the other children in order that they may see that it is wet. As soon as the finger is dry the deponent draws it across his throat like a knife and says:

Is it wet? Is it dry?
I'll cut my throat before I die
Here's the knife to cut it with
And here's the dish to catch the blood.

DERBYSHIRE, 1890S

And in Yorkshire, about 1906:

Oath taking amongst our local children is definitely fixed, a ceremonial of contract and promise. (1) Wet the forefinger, dry it again, and cross the throat. (2) Link the little fingers of the right hand.

This 'wet and dry' procedure was very widely known, and probably still survives in some playgrounds. The precedents for the linked fingers are obscure, but may have contributed to the modern popularity of the 'pinky promise'. The Opies mention, in their *Lore and Language of Schoolchildren* (1959), for example, that girls in Swansea linked little fingers and said, 'Pull the dying oath', and a mid nineteenth-century report reads:

In the Midland counties when I was young it was very common for boys, who wished to bind each other to an engagement, to link the little fingers of their right hands and say

Ring finger, blue bell
Tell a lie, go to hell,

after which, if either failed to perform, the little finger, as a matter of course, would be sure to divulge.

There are other scattered references to fingers and hands being concerned with truthfulness and trust:

When I was a boy, I remember often pinching and being pinched. Boys pinched the little finger of girls, and vice versa, to see whether they could keep a secret or not. If anyone screamed out under the operation, it was a sign the person pinched could not keep a secret, and vice versa. Of course boys pinched harder than girls, and so the latter were deemed unworthy of confidence. I believe the like operation was performed by lovers to try each other's constancy. *MID NINETEENTH CENTURY*

Two relatively obscure passages from Shakespeare's plays might be relevant here. In *Henry IV, Part I* (Act 2, scene 4), Lady Percy says:

> In faith I'll break thy little finger, Harry
> An if thou wilt not tell me all things true.

In *The Winter's Tale* (Act 1, scene 2) Leontes says of his wife and his best friend, 'But to be paddling palms and pinching fingers'. Florence McDowell adds another dimension, in her account from Co. Antrim in about 1905:

> A test of truthfulness could be easily administered. If a child's word was in doubt, his inquisitor was entitled to take his hand, palm upward, and tickle it very gently with a finger, all the while reciting
>
> > Tickle-y, tickle-y, on the han'
> > If you are a funny wee man
> > If you laugh or if you smile
> > You'll never be a lady's child
>
> Any hint of a smile meant instant punishment for a liar, or, of course, for a truthful child who was ticklish.

Another interesting aspect of the 'wet and dry' declaration is the use of spittle. Like crossing the fingers, spitting serves many different purposes in British folklore, including protection from evil influence, for luck, and to underline the truth or seriousness of a declaration or action. A writer from Devon contributed this observation to *Notes & Queries* in 1911:

> In this parish there is a traditional custom amongst the boys of 'spitting their death' to confirm a promise. This is done by crossing the forefingers, looking earnestly at them while repeating the promise, and then spitting upon the ground. A boy who breaks this solemn asseveration is regarded as unworthy of any confidence.

And this is clearly related to a custom noted by John Brand in the 1777 edition of his *Popular Antiquities*:

> The boys in the north of England have a custom amongst themselves of spitting their faith or, as they call it in the northern dialect, 'their saul' (i.e.

soul), when required to make asseverations in matters which they think of consequence.

In past years, children making an oath or a solemn promise often resorted to swearing on God's name, the Bible or their mother's life. This approach seems to be much less widespread nowadays, although the mention of 'Gran's ashes' in the Coventry example above shows that the idea has not completely disappeared.

When it comes to accusing someone of not telling the truth, every child I have spoken to recently immediately volunteered:

> Liar, liar, pants on fire!

There is often a second line, which exists in a number of versions:

> Liar, liar, pants on fire
> Halfway up the electric wire.
>
> *LECHLADE, 2010*

> Liar, liar, pants on fire
> Hair sticking up like a ten-foot wire.
>
> *GATESHEAD, 2010*

> Liar, liar, your bum's on fire
> Your nose is bigger than Blackpool Tower.
>
> *LANCASHIRE, 1980S*

This verse has been around for at least fifty years, as the following collected in California in 1954 shows:

> You liar, you liar
>   Your pants are on fire
> Your nose is as long
>   As a telephone wire.

Nowadays, the clever retort is along the lines of:

> I don't care, I don't care
> I'll just get another pair.

This is all very different from how it was in the nineteenth century. The taunting call in 1842 was:

Liar, liar lickspit
Turn about the candlestick
What's good for liar?
Brimstone and fire.

And in Lancashire in 1914, the less brutally reproachful:

You've told a lie
Beneath the sky
You'll be sorry by and by
And then when you come to die
You'll wish you'd never told a lie.

CLAIMING AND AVOIDING

One of the most remarkable examples of the rule of custom in the playground is the respect that most children have for the law of precedence. In most situations the one who speaks first gains the desired item or avoids an undesirable role, and the most powerful word in this context is 'bags'. In its many guises, including 'bagsy', 'bags I', and often sounding more like 'bugsie' or 'bogsie', the utterance of this word is respected the length and breadth of Britain.

'Bagsy' is undoubtedly the dominant word for claiming or avoiding, but there are also others in children's vocabulary. Occasionally, for example, one might hear people say that they have put their 'dibs' on something. In some circumstances, however, something with a subtly different nuance is called for, such as 'poison'. Cherry and Ella, two eleven-year-olds from Camden in North London, recorded in 2009, explained the difference:

When we're playing 'Champ' [which involves waiting in line for your turn], say you needed to go to the toilet or you wanted to go and speak to someone else who was asking after you, and you wanted your place in the line to stay, you said, 'Poison', and then you'd go to the toilet or get a drink, and then you'd come back and your friend, if they were nice, they'd let you come back.

But it is always best to take into account the literalness of playground ritual:

Sometimes you might say, 'Poison after so-and-so', instead of saying, 'Poison second in line', because I probably could have been in fourth square by that time . . . 'Bagsy' is more like before you've got something, 'poison' is when you've got it and you want to keep it. It's quite complicated . . . Then there's 'Turn around, touch the ground, bagsy not something', and the last person to say it would have to do it.

Indeed, 'Turn around, touch the ground' turns out to be widely known and practised, and it is often extended to 'Turn around, touch the ground, touch wood, it's mine'. But many children comment that it takes too long and by the time you have done it someone else has simply 'bagsied' it. Yet another word that seems to have arisen in recent decades is 'shotgun', used in exactly the same way as 'bagsie', as in 'shotgun that cake' or 'shotgun first place'.

To confuse things further, the Year 6 children from St Mary's in Ardleigh, Essex, explained that the girls say 'bagsy' or 'shotgun', or even occasionally 'bagsy shotgun' to make really sure. But the boys often say 'dibs' or even 'shotgun dibs'.

The earliest evidence for 'bags' that the compilers of the *Oxford English Dictionary* have so far located dates from 1866, but the supporting quotation indicates that it was already in general usage at the time – '"Bags I first drink," says Bob, according to the polite practice of schoolboys.' It is probably derived directly from an older use of the verb 'to bag', meaning to seize, catch or take possession of.

'Dibs' was also a name for fivestones or jacks (see p. 157), going back to at least the 1730s, but in the sense of claiming something, it seems to be American slang from the early 1930s.

One thing that confused nineteenth-century writers on 'truce terms' (see p. 360) was that the word 'barley' was used both for gaining respite in a game and for claiming, particularly in northern counties of England:

Barley: To claim. The word is used in a curious sense, almost always by children in play. The expressions, 'He barleyed that seat', 'Aa barleyed the shul', mean that at sight of the articles one has been first to cry out, 'Barley me that seat, or that shovel.' The first to do so has a right to the use of the article named, and it is a point of honour among lads to acknowledge and give place to the one so doing. NORTHUMBERLAND, C.1890

A range of other words were used in the nineteenth and twentieth centuries, including 'ballow', 'chaps', 'cogs', and 'pike', but none of them seems to have achieved anywhere near the level of general acceptance that 'bags' did.

'SAME WORDS' RITUAL

Little fingers were a very important part of a special charm. If you and your friend happened to say the same word at the same time, you immediately linked your wee fingers together without uttering a single word until you had both silently wished. When each of you had said the name of a poet, you might safely disengage your fingers. Shakespeare and Wordsworth were very much favoured poets, perhaps because they often appeared in the Readers of the day.　　　　　　　　　　　*CO. ANTRIM, C.1905*

When the Opies were compiling their *Lore and Language of Schoolchildren* in the 1950s, they found that accidental simultaneous utterance was marked by little rituals all over the country, but that these took a wide variety of forms from place to place.

The commonest elements were the linking of little fingers, a temporary silence, the idea that if the ritual was carried out correctly both participants would get a wish, and the naming of a poet. Sometimes only the first to name a poet would, it was believed, be favoured, and in some places there was the delightful detail that Shakespeare and Burns should not be named, because they would 'spear' or 'burn' the wish and thus nullify it.

In Glasgow, they link pinkies and press thumbs together, reassuring each other:

Pinkety, pinkety, thumb to thumb
Wish a wish and it's sure to come
If yours comes true
Mine will come true
Pinkety, pinkety, thumb to thumb.

Not all believed that the procedure would lead to the granting of a wish. Some believed it would ensure that the participants would receive a letter. More often than not the future event would be favourable or exciting, but for some it was something to be feared:

Saying the same thing was bad luck, so you had to say, 'Crosses' and cross your fingers at the same time to ward it off.　　　*NOTTINGHAM, 1950s*

All this has changed dramatically in recent decades, though. In modern playgrounds there is no talk of wishes or poets, but instead it is a question of 'jinx'.

> When two people said the same thing at the same time you had to be quick
> to yell, 'Jinx', otherwise you had to stay silent until someone said your full
> name. The penalty for speaking was a punch or a pinch.
>
> *NORTH YORKSHIRE, 1990S*

The change seems to have occurred in the 1970s, and the new style appears now to be known all over Britain. The main feature, which stays pretty constant, is the idea that the person who has been 'jinxed' must remain silent until their name is said out loud, but the number of times the name must be spoken varies considerably from one to ten, even within the same school. Some also say that it is only the 'jinkster' who can release the victim; others, more practically, that anyone can do it by saying the name. They relate amusing anecdotes about how they have had to try, in dumb show, to get a friend to say their name. There are also extensions:

> If you said, 'Jinx private jinx', it was only you who could say their name for
> them to be able to talk. If you said, 'Jinx personal padlock', supposedly the
> person could not talk for the rest of the day.   *BEDFORDSHIRE, 1990S*

> Jinx personal padlock, throw away the key.
>
> *WEST LONDON, 2009*

> Jinx padlock, touch wood, eat the key.
>
> *SOUTH LONDON, 2009*

The Opies' research into this subject in the 1950s also revealed the astonishing similarities they found at the international level. Not only does the United States have corresponding rituals to ours, but children (and not a few adults) all across Western Europe were doing and saying remarkably similar things.

FIRST THE WORST

> First the worst
> Second the best
> Third the one with the hairy chest.
> [But if it's a girl we usually say 'treasure chest'].

One of the innumerable bits and pieces of rhyme that float around in a child's repertoire is this little gem, which is probably known, in some form or other, by almost every junior-school child in the country, and is therefore remembered into many adult lives. It is readily available for quotation whenever someone else is first in a queue, or achieves something you do not, or is boasting and needs to be taken down a peg or two. It is an excellent example of the way in which children's traditional lore subverts and parodies, and while it is usually said in taunting fun, it can be used with real venom, depending on the situation and the relationship between the protagonists.

The first two lines are almost always the same, but then things get more interesting and creative, and the third line is variously: 'the one with the treasure chest/hairy chest/fancy dress/ballet dress, and so on. The rhyme can be extended at both ends, and my personal favourite, from Maddie, Rhea and Dahlia (all aged ten), of Ealing, West London, runs:

> Minus the highness
>   Zero the hero
> First the worst
>   Second the best
> Third the one with the hairy chest
>   Fourth the one with the golden gun
> Fifth the one with the Chinese bum.

When they told me this in November 2009, there was some discussion as to what constituted a 'Chinese bum', but we reached no conclusions. Two generations of the rhyme follow from Sheffield: Natasha (aged five) learnt the first version in 2005; her father came across the second in the mid 1970s:

> Zero the hero
>   First the worst
> Second the best
>   Third the hairy princess
> Fourth the golden eagle.

> First the worst
>   Second the best
> Third the hairy princess
>   Fourth the dwarf.

Another format, with a different second line, seems to be much less common but might be older, as in this example, which was in use in Leeds in the 1980s:

> First the worst
>> Second the same
> All the rest are down the drain.

The rhyme has its own history, stretching back to at least the later nineteenth century and probably further. Charlotte Burne included the following 'fragments of a children's racing game' in her *Shropshire Folk-Lore* (1883):

> First, for the golden purse
>> Second, for the same
> Fourth, for the sugar loaf
>> Seven, for the key of heaven
> Last, for the bag of brass.

G. F. Northall, in his *English Folk-Rhymes* (1892), states that in Warwickshire and Staffordshire it was the following (very close to our Leeds example):

> First the best, second the same
> Last the worst in all the game.

These are clearly ancestors of our modern rhyme, but the most obvious difference is that they have the exact opposite meaning. The Victorian versions follow the 'official' line that coming first is the best, while the modern style shows a refreshing irony and irreverence.

An older rhyme has a similar feeling to 'First the worst' and, if not its direct ancestor, is perhaps a second cousin. In England in 1842 it went as follows:

> One's none
>> Two's some
> Three's a many
>> Four's a penny
> Five is a little hundred . . .

The Scottish version is far more complex:

Ane's nane
  Twa's some
Three's a pickle
  Four's a curn [= small quantity]
Five's a horse-lade
  Six'll gar his back bow
Seven'll vex his breath
  Aught'll bear him to the grund
And nine'll be his death.

The kinship with our modern rhyme is revealed in the editor's explanation that the words are satirical, 'Said when anxious to get more of some delicacy, such as comfits, which a companion may chance to have'.

CHAPTER TWENTY-ONE

Teasing and Making Up

TAUNTS

Children have always had a good line in taunts, and answers, but it seems that many traditional rhymes and phrases that were ubiquitous only a few decades ago have largely disappeared from British playgrounds, and it is not clear what is replacing them. *Liar, Liar* is still around (see p. 375), but others, such as *Telltale tit* and *Cowardy cowardy custard*, have apparently lost their hold on the childish imagination.

When asked what they call a 'telltale', nearly every child interviewed in the last two years has replied 'snitch', 'sneak', 'grass', 'snake' or other epithet drawn from general adult parlance. Even when I prompted them with 'telltale tit' there was rarely any flicker of recognition, except in the cases where they said something on the lines of, 'My gran says that.'

But well into the 1970s and 1980s it was quite common to hear a chanted taunt aimed at anyone suspected of telling tales, as in these two examples from the 1970s collected by Cathy Gould in Coventry:

> Tell tale tit
>   Your mother can't knit
> She can't even walk
>   With a walking stick.

> Tell tale tit
>   Your tongue will be split
> And all the little doggies
>   Will get a little bit.

These two verses perpetuate the two commonest images that have been found, probably simply because 'knit' and 'slit' or 'split' rhyme with 'tit'. The 'knit' verse occurs throughout the twentieth century, but the motif of the dogs having their bit of the tongue goes back to at least 1744, when it was included in *Tommy Thumb's Pretty Song Book*.

Such taunts do not exactly reach the heights of poetry or even invention. Earlier generations, by contrast, had a wider range to choose from:

> Johnny Brown is a telly-pie-tit
> > Sits on the church wall
> Eating an apple and kepping a ball
> > His tongue shall be slit
> And all the little dogs shall have a bit.
>
> > > *NORTH SHIELDS, 1895*

> Telly-pie-tit
> > Sat upon a wall
> Eating raw cabbages
> > And letting bits fall.
>
> > > *CUMBERLAND, 1950S*

And from Co. Wicklow in 1977:

> Tell tale tattler
> Buy a penny rattler.

> Tell tale, tell tale
> > Stick to the cow's tail
> When the cow begins to kick
> > — cries for sugar stick.

A similar situation pertains to the traditional treatment of cowards. When asked about what they call a coward, nearly every child I have spoken to recently has said 'chicken' (and makes a clucking noise), or occasionally they say 'yellow', but nobody volunteers the phrase 'cowardy cowardy custard', which only thirty years ago was still very common in playgrounds around the country. In 1977, for example, Siobhán Lynch of Co. Wicklow contributed the following couplet to the Irish Folklore Commission:

> Cowardy cowardy custard
> Stick your head in mustard.

The second line varies, but nearly always ends in 'mustard', for obvious reasons. The phrase was already well known in mid Victorian times, as this entry in Anne Baker's *Glossary of Northamptonshire Words and Phrases* (1854) makes clear:

> Cowardy! Cowardy! Custard! Repeated by children playing at the game of 'One Catch All', when they advance towards the one who is selected to catch them, and dare, or provoke her to capture them.

Alice Gomme confirms this usage in her *Traditional Games* (1898), from her own girlhood in the 1850s and 1860s.

As a child, I assumed the basis of the phrase was the connection between cowardice and being 'yellow', but this cannot be the correct derivation, because the phrase long pre-dates the use of that colour to denote cowardice. Nor does the idea, occasionally voiced, that custard 'shakes' as if in fear ring true as a genuine derivation. Anne Baker made the suggestion that it was originally 'cowardy costard' and that 'costard' was a derisive term for the 'head'. But again this is not convincing, mainly because the word 'costard' seems to have been no longer popular when the phrase 'cowardy custard', became well known.

The two earliest references that I can find to 'cowardy custard' are in the titles of two nineteenth-century pantomimes: an anonymous production performed at the Adelphi Theatre, London, in December 1836, entitled *Cowardy Cowardy Custard, or Harlequin Jim Crow and the Magic Mustard Pot*, and another by Richard Thorne, *Cowardy Cowardy Custard Ate His Father's Mustard, or Harlequin the Demon Vice and the Fairy Queen Virtue*, which was produced in December 1851. Interestingly, both contain the word 'mustard', but whether they were capitalising on an existing phrase, or the catchphrase actually originated with these productions, cannot be ascertained without further research.

Another widespread rhyme, which was available for any occasion when derision was needed, but in my experience was usually employed in fun, and often directed towards the teachers, was sung to the tune of *The Ash Grove*:

> —, you're a funny 'un
> Got a face like a pickled onion
> A nose like a squashed tomato
> And legs like matchsticks.

> SOUTH LONDON, 1950S

The inclusion of a version from Leeds in Rowland Kellett's *Heritage of the Streets* (1966) shows that this particular rhyme was certainly current in the 1920s.

Crybabies have always tended to get short shrift:

> Cry baby cry
>> Put your fingers in your eye
> Go home and tell your mother
>> It wasn't I.

> Cry baby cry
>> Put your fingers in your eye
> Hang him on the lamp-post
>> And leave him there to dry.

BELFAST, C.1980

The endlessly curious can also suffer:

> Ask no questions and you'll be told no lies
> Shut your mouth and you'll catch no flies.

YORKSHIRE, 1978

The immortal *Made You Look . . .* is still used when a child has tricked another into looking at nothing:

> Made you look
>> Made you stare
> Made the barber cut your hair
>> Cut it long, cut it short
> Cut it with a knife and fork.

This was how it was said in Birmingham in the 1970s, and it is exactly how I remember it from the 1950s, but there were other versions, with less-than-subtle variations:

> I made you look, I made you stare
>> I made you cut the barber's hair
> The barber's hair was full of lice
>> I made you cut it over twice.

SUFFOLK, C.1918

> Made you look, you dirty duck
> Stuck your head in cow muck.
>
> *LANCASHIRE, 1980S*

The following shows that the same principle held in Forfarshire in the 1850s:

> I gar'd ye luik
> I gar'd ye cruik
> I gar'd ye thraw yer neck aboot.

And it is good to see that the same poetic muse still stalks the twenty-first-century playground:

> Made you look, made you look
> Turned you into turtle soup.
>
> *INVERNESS, 2008*

> Made you look, made you stare
> Made you lose your underwear.
>
> *SHROPSHIRE, 2009*

These can also be said when someone is staring at you, as can the older variant, recorded in Leeds in the 1920s:

> Stare stare you big fat bear
> When you grow up you'll have no hair.

When my daughter Kathy was at school in Andover, Hampshire, in the early 1980s, she used to get indignant that the boys on her lunch table would regularly ruin her day by suddenly declaring:

> Silence in the courtyard
> Silence in the street
> The big fat monkey's just about to speak!

It was no use telling her to ignore it. She hated being called 'the big fat monkey', and desperately tried to avoid it by remaining silent. Elsewhere in the country there were similar declarations. In Coventry in the 1970s, for example, it was:

Silence in the graveyard
Silence in the court
The biggest fool in all the world
Is just about to talk.

It is interesting to see that this particular rhyme is still very much alive and well. When I was recently alking to the children on the school council of Ravenstone School, Balham, South London, one Year 6 boy volunteered:

Silence in the jury
Silence in the court
The big fat monkey's just about to talk.

We normally do that like when the teacher goes out to talk to another teacher and we all get noisy, and someone just shouts it out, and someone will say [something] and then they're the big fat monkey.

The wording may have changed, but the basic framework and meaning has been around for well over 100 years. The Opies found a number of versions in the 1950s, including:

Silence in the pig market or the pigs won't sell.

Silence in the frying pan, the sausage is going to speak.

Silence in the court, the monkey wants to talk; speak up, monkey, speak.

Silence in the pig market, the fat pig wants to speak.

A flurry of correspondence in *Notes & Queries* demonstrated that the pig-market imagery was common in the 1880s and 1890s, at schools and in large families. One regular form was 'Silence in the pig market of Anjou!', although why that particular place was singled out, nobody seemed to know. More straightforward was the version noted by G. F. Northall in the Worcestershire and Warwickshire area:

Silence in the pig-market
And let the old sow have a grunt.

And finally, here are a few prose items to round off this selection of barbed rhymes and comments:

Nottingham [in the 1950s] had its own particular word used universally for ridicule and disdain: 'Awer' (possibly 'oo-er'). The first syllable was short, and the second was drawn out and had a rise and fall. It meant an automatic cast-out, unless the victim immediately stopped doing or wearing whatever it was that caused the call. 'Awer' was often used by girls, but it was dangerous to use against boys because it invited a thump.

If anyone was naughty we'd 'tell on them': we'd hold two fingers to our lips, the other hand stretched out in front of us, with two fingers up (and together) with fist clenched, and say 'umm, I'm telling of you'. It struck fear into the heart of the kid it was directed at, but made the director feel quite powerful.

GLOUCESTERSHIRE, 1980S

The whole 'your mum is so fat that when she wore a yellow jumper people yelled taxi' really took off in Year 6. There were lots of other 'your mum' ones as well. *SOUTH LONDON, C.2002*

RIPOSTES

Children are not defenceless against verbal abuse. They have a range of answers for instant deployment, and the following can be used in offence or defence, as appropriate:

Twinkle, twinkle, little star
What you say is what you are
No returns back.

HAMPSHIRE, 1982

Twinkle, twinkle, little star
    What you say is what you are
With bedknobs and broomsticks
    No back answers.

YORKSHIRE, 1982

The same to you with knobs on
Cabbages with clogs on
And you with dirty knickers on.

LEEDS, 1920S

I know you are but what am I?

YORKSHIRE, 1980S

If I could have your picture
  It would be very nice
I'd hang it on the attic wall
  To scare away the mice.

YORKSHIRE, 1982

I'm telling
  You're smelling
You jumped in a pond
  And you kissed James Bond.

COVENTRY, 2007

Generally speaking, there is a riposte for just about every occasion. If you are told to 'shut up', for example, you might respond:

I wasn't shut up, I was brought up
And a monkey like you should be locked up.

CO. WICKLOW, 1977

If someone says, aggressively, 'What are you laughing at?' you could say:

I'm laughing at you
Your face is so blue
And your nose is like a kangaroo.

CO. WICKLOW, 1977

The suggestion that your physical appearance is not everything it might be could be countered with:

Are you looking in a mirror?

YORKSHIRE, 1980s

Some children prefer the more direct approach:

See my finger, see my thumb
See my fist – and here it come.

SUFFOLK, C.1918

Others favour a more disdainful response. The only danger is that you might be told:

Don't care was made to care
Don't care was hung
Don't care was put in the pot
And boiled until he was done.

ESSEX, TWENTIETH CENTURY

Don't care, won't care
Won't care was hung
Don't care was put in the pot
Till he was done.

WILTSHIRE, 1960S

Children also tend to be dubious about the efficacy of:

Sticks and stones may break my bones
But words will never hurt me.

Every child I have spoken to comments that they never say this in the playground because it does not work, and it is only their parents and teachers who think it worth repeating. One sharp ten-year-old at Okehampton Primary School quipped, 'Chuck a dictionary at them – words'll hurt then.' Older versions were often longer, but, one suspects, no more effective than the modern ones:

Sticks and stones may break my bones
But names will never hurt me
And when I'm dead an' in my grave
You'll suffer what you callt me!

CO. ANTRIM, C.1905

MAKING UP

I remember a ritual from South London in the 1950s, performed more by girls than boys, when there had been any disagreement or rift between friends. The two concerned would link the little fingers of their right hands and say, in unison, 'Make up, make up, never never break up', or 'Make up, make up, never do it again, if you do you'll get the cane', shaking their hands up and down in time with the rhythm of the words.

Numerous informants have confirmed that this little rhyme and ritual was known all over the country, from at least the 1950s, with only small variation. Sometimes the participants shook hands rather than linked fingers:

> Make friends, make friends
> Never never break friends
> If you do you'll catch the flu
> And that will be the end of you.
>
> *BUCKINGHAMSHIRE, 1980S*

We crossed arms and held hands, facing each other and swung our hands up and down in time to the rhyme. We also used the opposite, i.e. 'Break friends, break friends' as a taunt when we fell out.   *COVENTRY, 1970S*

But this is another of those traditional rhymes that seem to be fading away. Many children I have interviewed recently have not heard of it at all, and of those who have, most learnt it from their parents (often forced to when they fell out with a brother or sister) and do not use it much in the playground. Judging by the present situation, I do not think it will last much longer.

The Multicultural
Playground

The fact that childlore spreads so readily around the world shows that children do indeed, like snails, carry their culture with them. The permissions game 'Mother, May I?', which has been popular in Britain for decades, was also being played in 1950s Indiana. The skipping rhyme *Teddy Bear, Teddy Bear, Touch the Ground*, heard now everywhere from London to Belfast, was also recorded in Canberra in 1961 and has a German version which I was amazed to see being demonstrated in Tokyo in 1999. It is not surprising therefore that British children whose families originate from outside the UK may well not only witness and participate in the games and songs that others play and sing but bring their own rich heritage into the country with them. They do not necessarily, however, bring those games and songs into the playground.

Generally speaking it seems to be the case that where children from a particular ethnic background are in the minority in the playground, they are wary about sharing their traditions more widely. Kathy Marsh, for example, observed in 2008 of one West Yorkshire school:

Several girls had come in from schools in other villages or towns and were diffident about revealing games that deviated from the standard forms played in the school. A number of girls of Pakistani descent demonstrated Pakistani games such as Zig Zag Zoo and string games taught by family members. They told us that they played these at home but not usually at school.

It also seems to be the case that such children may well happily integrate into all sorts of classroom activities, but will tend to stick with members of their own group when they go outside to play. When they do participate in games with others, they tend to play the ones known by the majority, not the ones they know at home.

What is fascinating, though, is how much the situation changes once an ethnic minority is actually in the majority in a particular school. Now games and songs appear that may be subtly or completely different from those found elsewhere. And, in some cases, they actually preserve forms that died out in Britain some years ago but that continue to thrive elsewhere – rather in the way that 'Trick or Treat', which we tend to regard as an American import, probably has its origins in the traditions of Irish and Scottish settlers in the USA a century or so ago.

An example of this is a sticks game described by two Bangladeshi boys in West Yorkshire in 1993. They called it 'Eeteedanda' and described it as follows:

> Miss, you have a short stick and a long stick and, miss, you make a hole in the ground and you put the short stick in it. Then, miss, you hit the short stick with the long stick so it goes up up up in the air. Then you hit the short stick far far. As far as you can. Then, miss, you see how far the stick has gone. You put the long stick on the ground and measure.

The temptation is to assume that this is a Bangladeshi game. Certainly, it is not familiar to most other Yorkshire children today. Yet, in fact, what these two boys were describing is the classic game of 'Tip Cat', or 'Pig and Stick' or 'Billet and Stick' as it was known in Yorkshire. It is now no longer played by indigenous children, though their grandfathers sometimes make the pig and stick out of broom handles, to show their grandchildren how they played as boys. The game seems to have died out in Keighley, where the Bangladeshi boys lived, sometime in the 1940s.

Hopscotch is another good example of a game where children from a non-English background have preserved older traditions. Hopscotch squares are often to be found in playgrounds because, one suspects, teachers like the idea of a children's game that involves numbers. When watching children at play in Yorkshire schools, though, I noticed that the indigenous children didn't quite understand how the numbers work. They knew about hopping up and down the pattern, but when it came to throwing a stone to determine the sequence, they let it land in any square, and hopped around it accordingly. One group had realised that the numbers were there for a reason, and had incorporated the numbers into their game by scoring points. If the stone landed in, say, the 3 square, and you managed to retrieve the stone successfully, you counted three as your score. This made the game not just a test of whole-body coordination and number recognition, but one of addition as well.

Among children of Pakistani or Bangladeshi origin, on the other hand, I noticed that the game was played largely as the Opies described it fifty years ago. The stone was thrown or kicked in sequence starting at the first square and proceeding up the number ladder, with the stone being picked up on the return journey. Towards the end of the game, when the whole sequence had been completed successfully, squares could be claimed and decorated by one player. This made the progression up and down the grid much more difficult since the squares which had been claimed could not be used by other players.

Fivestones is another game that it is much rarer among the indigenous white population than it used to be, but adults in Yorkshire's Pakistani community are adept at it. One lady, Shanaz, said that she had played the game every day until the age of seventeen because 'there was nothing else to do'. Primary-school-age children are less practised but nevertheless find the game interesting enough for there to be small groups of girls crouching in circles with five pebbles, much as they must have done thousands of years ago in Egypt, Greece and Rome.

The girls choose five stones of roughly the same size. They are thrown in the air and one of the five is caught on the back of the hand. This stone is then thrown in the air while the player attempts to pick up the other stones one by one. If successful she will then go on to pick up the stones in twos, then three and one, then all four. There are then several further moves demonstrated by the mother of one girl but not by the children. Shanaz asked her daughter to choose one of the stones, then made a bridge with the fingers of her left hand and knocked each stone through the arch as she threw the chosen stone into the air. Then she made a curved barrier with her hand into which the stones had to be knocked, again without the chosen stone being touched.

In an attempt to provide variety in playground activities one local school had introduced jacks, brightly coloured pronged objects that can be thrown up like the pebbles, and were accompanied by a small bouncy ball. Being made of plastic they are very light. The children rejected these because the ball was too bouncy and introduced an extra complication to an already elaborate and difficult game. They put the highly coloured jacks to one side and played with pebbles.

Another game, called 'Seven Stones', could be found among the indigenous population in Denholme, Bradford, back in the 1930s, at which time it was also recorded in the East End of London and as far away as Ethiopia. In the course of his work for the Centre for Creativity in Education and Cultural Heritage in Jerusalem, Simon Lichman has found that while the Arab children participating in the scheme know the game, the Jewish children do not. It is currently very popular indeed in West Yorkshire among children of Pakistani and Bangladeshi origin and is played in the street by both girls and boys. They call it 'Pitoo'.

In 'Pitoo' there are two sides, one of which, side A, must build a tower of seven stones. The other team, side B, has a ball and bowls at the tower in order to knock it down. If they succeed their team runs and tries to tag as many of the other team as possible while side A tries to rebuild the tower. When the tower is rebuilt, the tagging must stop. Anyone tagged retreats to the sidelines and watches.

COUNTING-OUT RHYMES

When it comes to games with words, children not surprisingly mix and match languages. In Yorkshire, for example, children from Punjabi families have an extensive repertoire of games in Punjabi and English, and sometimes a mixture of the two. Back in 1993 the following three Punjabi counting-out rhymes were collected in two Keighley schools with large Punjabi speaking populations:

> Eessi peesi nack pareessi
> Garae wun galae peessi.
>
> Kerava keravoom bay bo
>   Asee na baer poor a so
> So koloda dital mo
>   Sa pel sa koda.
>
> Insinse sin sikha slanie
> Ga tika hazoor ki
> Beti lambhie latiy.

Versions of English rhymes the children knew and which were shared by the indigenous community were:

Mickey Mouse built a house
What colour was it?

Inky pinky ponky
   Daddy bought a donkey
The donkey died.
   Daddy cried
Inky pinky ponky.

Eeny meeny mackera acka
   Dare die dominacka
Sticka bocka lollipop
   Om pom push.

There's a party on the hill
Will you come?
Bring your own cup and saucer and a bun.
Who is your very best friend?
   Safia
Safia will be there with a ribbon in her hair
   What colour will it be?

Racing car, number nine
Losing petrol all the time
How many gallons did it lose?

Ip dip do
   The cat's got flu
Mother's got the chicken pox
   So out goes you.

Ickle ockle
Chocolate buckle
Ickle ockle out.

Ip dip dog sh-t
F-cking b-st-rd
Dirty g-t.

Or, as one ethnic English child recited in a rather more self-censored way:

Ip dip dog um
Um um, dirty um.

Intriguingly, a small group of English rhymes known to Punjabi speakers were not known to the indigenous population that surrounded them. Where did the children learn these rhymes? The most plausible explanation seems to lie in the holiday visits they were making to extended family in such places as Leicester or Bury, or in visits from other family members to West Yorkshire.

One of the rhymes, though modelled on an English rhyme, has a distinct flavour of Bollywood about it:

> Ip dip do
> The girl kiss you
> When she die, she say
> 'I love you'.

Another rhyme which appears to mix Punjabi and English goes as follows:

> Abba babba blue babba
> Pissing in the sea
> If you want another babba, please choose me.

The children were convinced this was a Punjabi rhyme because the word 'peess' means 'fart' in Punjabi. However, it seems more likely that it is a variation of *Ickle Ockle*, recorded by the Opies in the 1960s. One version from Spennymoor went as follows:

> Ickle ockle blue bottle
> Fishes in the sea
> If you want a pretty maid, please choose me.

And another, from Hampstead:

> Ibble ubble black bubble
> Ibble ubble out.

The Punjabi version uses the Hampstead 'b' rather than the Spennymoor 'k' sound, but otherwise follows the longer Spennymoor rhyme.

Various other rhymes have taken a hold, too. One recorded in the 1990s in West Yorkshire goes as follows:

> One two three
> You go free.

Several years later in 2003 in Bradford this had become:

> One two three
> Michael Jackson goes free.

Another well-known rhyme, which crops up in a variety of forms and is one of the rhymes collected by the Camden World Song Project, as well as in West Yorkshire in 1993 and 2003, is:

> Ippy dippy dation
> Mother had an operation
> What colour was her blood?

The Opies published a slightly different version in 1969, presumably collected from the indigenous population:

> Dic-a-dic-adation.
> My operation.
> How many stitches did I have?

Another rhyme, current in the 1990s and 2003, is:

> Egg, sugar, butter, tea
> Fairy liquid, bumble bee
> What would you rather be?

There appear to be no modern examples of this in any recent collection. However, in a mammoth collection of counting-out rhymes from around the world, compiled in 1888 by Henry Carrington Bolton, the following appears, recorded in Connecticut:

> Eggs, butter, cheese, bread.
> Stick, stock, stone dead.

Finally a version of *Eeny Meeny Miny Mo*. Over a ten-year period from 1993 to 2003, the indigenous population in West Yorkshire chanted:

> Eeny meeny miny mo
>> Put the baby on the po
> When it's done, wipe its bum
>> With a piece of chewing gum.

The version used by children of Pakistani ethnicity in 2003 was:

> Eeny meeny miny mo
>> Put the baby on the floor
> When it cries, smack it twice
>> Eeny meeny miny mo.

CLAPPING RHYMES

Clapping rhymes show a similar pattern to counting-out rhymes, though, whereas counting-out rhymes are used by both boys and girls, clapping rhymes tend to be performed almost exclusively by girls. Over the years clapping has become very elaborate, with a great many body and hand movements incorporated as well as the standard clapping against the hands of a partner.

First a rhyme that was popular in the 1990s among Pakistani girls in Keighley, West Yorkshire, but not among their ethnic English peers:

> Zig zag zoo
> Khabi ooper ['Sometimes on top']
> Khabi neechay ['Sometimes underneath']
> Khabi sithay ['Sometimes facing']
> Khabi photay ['Sometimes the opposite way'].

The game was played by two girls facing one another. Each player holds the left hand in a vertical position at right angles to the body with the back of the hand against the back of the partner's. The right hands are then clapped above the left hands, then below. Then both right and left hands are clapped against the partner's, palm to palm, followed by the back of the hands clapped together.

The first line is similar to a counting-out rhyme recorded by the Opies in Manchester in the 1960s: 'Zig zag zooligar,/Zim zam bum'. The game itself was recorded both in Australia in the 1980s and among native English children in Keighley in 1976, with minor differences:

One two three together
Up together
Down together
Back, front, knee.

By the first decade of the twenty-first century, the Punjabi version had changed slightly:

Zig zag zoo
Khabi ooper ['Sometimes on top']
Khabi neechay ['Sometimes underneath']
Khabi oonchey ['Sometimes high']
Khabi taley ['Sometimes low']
Khabi mukkey. ['Sometimes punches']

In this version the game ended with both girls trying to punch one another. When asked, children said they had learnt the game either from various family members or on visits to Pakistan. This might seem a bit puzzling, given that native British children were playing the game in the 1970s. It is not uncommon, however, to find games seeping from one culture to another, and children have a tendency to view a slight variation of a well-known game as a completely new game in its own right.

A favourite clapping rhyme at another school in Bradford in 2003 was *Charm Charm Charm.*

Charm charm charm ['Dark dark dark']
Nana abo sotai hai ['Mum's dad is sleeping']
Mitti goli catta hai ['Eating a sweet tablet']
Nam ['Name'] [*clap clap clap*]
Io mitti ['You are sweet'] [*clap clap clap*]
Io ben ki shadi ['Your sister's wedding'] [*clap clap clap*]
Kachai cheval ['Uncooked/green rice'] [*clap clap clap*]
I say stop.

The verse is repeated until one of the girls decides to stop and catches the other one out. This game was played in Rawalpindi forty years ago, according to a lunchtime supervisor, though the first line was different ('Tum tum tum', meaning 'You you you') and there was no English in the older version.

As with counting-out rhymes, some clapping rhymes are entirely in

English. *That's the Way, uh-huh, uh-huh, I Like It*, for example, seems to be pretty ubiquitous in the twenty-first century. Among Punjabi-speaking children in Yorkshire, other popular ones include *I Know a Chinese Girl, Chinese Girls are Very Funny, A Sailor Went to Sea* and the following, rather complicated, one:

> I'm a pretty little Dutch girl
> As pretty as can be
> And all the boys in the football team
> Go crazy over me
> And this is how my story goes
> My boyfriend gave me an apple
> My boyfriend gave me a pear
> My boyfriend gave me twenty-five cents
> I gave him back his apple
> I gave him back his pear
> I gave him back his twenty-five cents
> And I throwed him down the stair.

Because most children's rhymes are quite short, if they want to give a longer performance they have a tendency to link together rhymes from different sources, using a linking line such as 'And this is what he said' or, in this case, 'And this is how my story goes', which can be found in a completely different rhyme recorded by the Opies back in the 1980s. The section starting 'My boyfriend gave me an apple' is frequently found on its own, without the twenty-five cents but with 'a kick up the bum'. It was first collected by Norman Douglas in London in 1916, and has since cropped up in countries as far apart as Australia and the USA (see also p. 306).

Another clapping game that has been recorded in various countries involves children sitting in a circle with their hands spread at either side of them. The clap is passed round the circle from one girl clapping her right hand on to the right hand of her neighbour. In some versions it is an elimination game. At the end of the rhyme the last player must try to snatch her hand away so she is not eliminated. If she does not do so and inadvertently accepts the clap, she is out.

The rhyme the indigenous children of West Yorkshire used in the 1990s to accompany the game was as follows:

> Who stole the cookie from the cookie jar?
> Debbie stole the cookie from the cookie jar

What me? [*clap clap clap*] Couldn't be! [*clap clap clap*]
So who stole the cookie from the cookie jar?

The use of 'cookie' here suggests that the rhyme might have originated in the USA or Canada and had been learnt by some of the children at Brownies.

By the first decade of the twenty-first century the game was popular worldwide. It has been collected in the North and South of England, in Norway, the USA and Australia. It was played by both children of Pakistani descent and the indigenous white children in one school in Keighley, West Yorkshire. The indigenous children used the rhyme *Down in the Jungle Where Nobody Goes*, while girls of Pakistani descent used to two different rhymes:

> Down by the river goes hanky panky
> > Where the two fat frogs go back to banky
> With a hip hop solo pop
> > And this is where it stops.

> Sella ella oola quack quack quack
> Say yes chigga challi chap chap
> Say one two three four five.

The melody of the first rhyme may originate in *Three Little Fishies*, a popular song from 1939 composed by Saxie Dowell and Lucy Bender Sokole, which became a hit when it was performed by Kay Kyser and his band. The second rhyme, for its part, has proved very popular in the USA and Canada.

SINGING GAMES

Children from ethnic backgrounds generally know the standard singing games taught in English in nursery schools such as *The Farmer's in His Den*, *Here We Go Round the Mulberry Bush*, *The Hokey Cokey*, *Ring a-ring a-roses* and *In and Out the Dusty Bluebells*. The only Bangla game I was able to collect, though I am sure there will be many more, was:

> Aix a hale barma batee
> Roll de heetoo

> Kazakdi korbaneeta
> 　Oota sollee moohatolla
> Plassa peep loondaloo.

The gist of the rhyme is 'Why are you crying? Wake up and wash your face. Choose your partner.' The child who sang this said it was a singing game her mother had taught her. No one else knew it and the suspicion was that the child herself had only learnt it the night before. She organised a group of children into a ring with one child sitting in the centre and they chanted as they skipped round.

What is fascinating about the song is that it bears a striking resemblance to *Sally Water*, a song recorded in forty-eight versions by Alice Gomme in the 1890s, one of which goes:

> Here sits poor Sally on the ground
> 　Sighing and sobbing for her young man.
> Arise, Sally, rise and wipe your weeping eyes,
> 　And turn to the east and turn to the west
> And show the little boys that you love best.

The game was later recorded in 1936, in *Traditional Singing Games for Brownies* (see also p. 285). The question is, of course, how a Bangladeshi child should come to know it some sixty years later. One possibility is that it accompanied Christian missionaries to the Raj who then passed it on to the indigenous population. Another possibility is that precisely the opposite happened. It might have started out as a Bengali song and game played and chanted by native nurses to their European charges and then brought back to Britain. After all, that quintessentially British game 'Snakes and Ladders' started out as a Hindu game that was played in India for many centuries and was meant to encourage such virtues as generosity, faith and humility, and to discourage such evils as vanity and theft.

One rhyme that can be confidently said to have started its life in Europe is *Kuna Mtu Shambani*, a Swahili song from Kenya collected by the Camden World Song Project. No prizes for guessing the original!

> Kuna mtu shambani ['There is a man in the garden']
> Kuna mtu shambani ['There is a man in the garden']
> Iya iya kuna mtu shambani ['Iya iya there is a man in the garden']
> Mtu ataka mke ['The man wants a wife']

Mtu ataka motto ['The wife wants a baby']
Mtoto ataka yaya ['The child wants a childminder']
Yaya ataka mbwa ['The childminder wants a dog']
Mbwa ataka mfupa ['The dog wants a bone']
Tumpapase mbwa ['Let's all pat the dog'].

Even the tune is the same as the English version.

A further example from the Camden project is a clapping rhyme from Trinidad learnt by a girl called Coral from her mother:

Mosquito one, mosquito two
   Mosquito jump in the old man's shoe.
The old man cried, the old man cried.
   The old man cried like a little child.
Ten pound ten the Dominica hen
   The monkey jump up and jump up again.
My mother said, I must not
   Play with the bad boys in the wood.
If I did, she would say
   What a naughty boy I am to disobey.
Where have you been all this time?
   Down in the alley kissing Sally
Riding donkey, shooting monkey
   If I had known
I would have rung the bell
   And blow the shell
And knock that old man down the well.

The beginning of this rhyme seems to be purely West Indian, but the middle section can be traced back to Victorian Britain and was recorded in West Yorkshire in 1999 as the very latest in clapping rhymes:

My mother said that I never should
   Play with the gypsies in the wood
If I did, she would say
   Naughty girl to disobey
Your hair shall curl, your eyes shall shine
   You gypsy girl, you shall be mine
Because she said that if I did
   She'd smack my bottom with the teapot lid.

Apart from lines 5 and 6 an almost identical rhyme used for clapping was recorded in Walmersley, Lancashire, in 1875 (see also p. 300). Lines 5 and 6 have crept in from who knows where – a ballad, perhaps. There are references in the second half of the Trinidadian verse to another rhyme, recorded by Frank Rutherford, an enthusiastic collector of children's folklore in the North-east of England in the 1960s:

> Sandy doo where were you
>   All last night?
> Down in the alley courting Sally
>   Picking up cinders, breaking windows
> Feeding monkeys, riding donkeys
>   Kicking up a row row bow wow.

Rutherford collected this in 1965 from a 57-year-old woman in Sunderland. As so often in children's rhymes, all sorts of words and phrases have been brought together here simply because they sound good and support the rhythm of the game.

Not all popular children's rhymes can claim quite such lengthy pedigrees. Pop songs and, for many children of Asian origin, Bollywood also exert an influence. In 2002, for example, Kathy Marsh recorded a group of Punjabi-speaking girls who were using *Bole Chudyan* from the movie *Khabi Kushi Kabhi Gham* as a clapping game in which they copied not just the music but some of the choreographic details as well. This was followed seamlessly by a song by Madonna, one by Gareth Gates, who had just reached number one 1 in the charts with his version of *Unchained Melody*, and contributions from pop bands S Club 7 and Steps, Atomic Kitten and the American singer Britney Spears.

The following year, girls at a different school were found to be using material culled from S Club Juniors and Liberty X. They, too, were familiar with tunes and dances from Bollywood movies and could move with ease between the two traditions, some of them being able to imitate with great accuracy both kinds of source material. They found all these via the Internet, videos and Sky Digital. They watched *Top of the Pops* and bought CDs of the material they liked, both Indian and Western. One girl commented that what she particularly liked about the Indian dancing was the hand movements.

Meanwhile, one boy gave a tuneful rendition of *Greensleeves*, though without the words – another example of a song handed down through the generations, perhaps. In fact, it turned out that he had heard it played by his local ice-cream van.

ACTING GAMES

Make-believe games based on television and computer games are common. But two games collected in Keighley in 1993 and again in 1994 from a small group of girls show that other influences are sometimes at work. The girls called them 'Grandma' games, and an adult recalled that she had played one of them when she was a girl in Rawalpindi twenty years before. They consisted of a character – grandma – and a group of children. After quite a protracted dialogue at the end of which the children are very cheeky, they are chased by the grandma and beaten if she can catch them. They could perhaps equally well be classified as chasing games with a dialogue, except that when watching them it appeared that the dialogue and acting of the parts, particularly that of the grandma, seemed to take precedence over the chasing.

The plot of the first, as told by the children, was:

> The little children ask to the grandma, 'Can we go to town?' And grandma says, 'No, you can't go to the town.' Then the little children say again to grandma. Grandma says, 'Go.' And then grandma says, 'Come back', and the children don't come back. And she says that 'I will give you gold earrings' and they say that I'm not going to come back and the grandma says, 'I give you a gold crown', and they say, 'All right, we'll come then.' Then they come. Grandma says, 'Where have you been?' And they say, 'We've been to uncle's house, right?' And grandma says, 'What did you have to eat?' And they say, 'We ate a lot of things.' Grandma says, 'What did you bring for me?' And they say, 'Nothing.' Then grandma chases the children.

This has parallels with a nineteenth-century English game called 'Old Mother Grey', which was still being played when the Opies were collecting games in the 1960s. They describe a set dialogue in which the children plead to go out to play and eventually are allowed to. When they return they say they have been to see the Queen. The dialogue then goes:

> What did she give you?
> A loaf of bread as big as your head,
>   a piece of cheese as big as our knees,
>   a lump of jelly as big as our belly
>   and a teeny weeny sixpence.
> Where's my share?

> Up in the air.
> How shall I get it?
> Stand on a chair.
> What if I fall?
> We don't care.

At this point the grandma chases the children and whoever is caught becomes the next grandmother.

The second game played by the Punjabi children was in much the same vein. Grandma searches in the dust and is questioned by the children:

> What are you looking for?
> I'm looking for a needle.
> Why do you want a needle?
> To sew my husband's coat.
> Where is your husband?
> He's gone to town to buy some pears.
> Can we have some?
> No. Go and eat sh-t.
> Eat it yourself.

The grandma now chases the children as she did in the previous game.

There are parallels in the dialogue with the question-and-answer formula to be found in 'Hen and Chickens', another game much described by Alice Gomme in 1894. In this game there is a mother hen who guards her chicks from 'the Outsider'. The dialogue between the two characters is:

> What are you scratching for?
> Pins and needles.
> What do you want pins and needles for?
> To mend my poke.
> What do you want to mend your poke for?
> To put some sand in.
> What do you want sand for?
> To sharpen knives with.
> What do you want your knives for?
> To cut off the little chickens' heads.

Obviously there are differences in the dialogue towards the end, but the beginning is quite strikingly similar and, as with several of the games described, it may be that there has been 'seepage' between the two cultures at some time in the past.

Such games and rhymes as these run just below the surface of playground play in Britain, and tend to be largely unnoticed and unappreciated by others. Yet the communities who cherish them and pass them on to the next generation are keeping alive games which have been played for hundreds of years and which were often once enjoyed but then lost by the host population. It is a rich and fascinating cultural seam.

Mavis Curtis

Playing in the park, 2010

Children of all ages gather in the street, c.1920

Girls chatting, 2000s

Chasing game, 2010

Playground scene, 1990s

Stockport street, 1966

PART SIX

Just
for Fun

Playing with a hoop, 2010

On the swings, 2010

Playing at shops, 1904

CHAPTER TWENTY-TWO

Nonsense Rhymes and Parodies

Even before they can speak, children seem to like songs and rhymes and their appreciation of such material continues throughout their primary years and beyond. In a very real sense, verbal lore is as important to children's development as are physical and imaginative games, as it is through rhymes and riddles, jokes and repartee, that children learn the rhythms and possibilities of their language. It may seem to be stretching the point to imply that a parody of *Happy Birthday* is a major piece of poetic achievement, but it is precisely these apparently trivial everyday utterances on which children sharpen their linguistic skills and mental faculties. Many folklorists and linguists are well aware of the developmental importance of such ditties, as Joanne Green and John Widdowson of Sheffield University's National Centre for English Cultural Tradition comment in the introduction to their work on *Traditional English Language Genres* (2003):

> The penchant which children have for linguistic play is commonly expressed through rhyme. This early informal learning experience not only aids the acquisition of a wide range of linguistic skills, but also introduces children to the rudiments of literature, through familiarisation with rhyme, rhythm, figures of speech, and other rhetorical devices, not to mention the innate fascination of wordplay itself, and the characteristic humour of many rhymes which children find so enjoyable.

At any time there are dozens of rhymes in active circulation, with old and new rubbing shoulders. New rhymes are coined, often borrowed or parodied from pop songs or other mass media material, while old ones are being constantly repeated, recycled and updated. Only a small selection can be given here, but there is plenty more where these came from.

NONSENSE RHYMES

Ching Chang Chinaman

'Chinamen' and 'Chinese' crop up often in children's rhymes, usually when there are nonsense words, which children often believe are a real foreign language. But *Ching Chang* (or *Ching Ching*, or *Ching Chong*) *Chinaman* seems to have a life of his own, and is an interesting case study in the continuity and variation of children's rhymes, showing how a line or phrase can take children's fancy and then pop up in various guises in many places, over many years.

Iona and Peter Opie printed this ball-bouncing rhyme in their *Lore and Language of Schoolchildren* (1959), as collected in Scotland and Northern England in 1952–3:

> Little Shirley Temple
>   She bought a penny doll
> She washed it, she dried it
>   Then she let it fall
> She called for the doctor
>   The doctor couldn't come
> Along came the ambulance
>   Rum, tum, tum.

They also recorded an alternative ending:

> She phoned for the doctor
>   The doctor couldn't come
> Because he had a pimple
>   On his bum, bum, bum.

They included this is in their section on 'topical rhymes' as an example of the incidence of film stars of a previous era, but they made the comment that 'in the south the hero of this rhyme is Ching Ching Chinaman'. Their observation was confirmed by the following, which was sung in South London in the 1940s:

Ching Chang Chinaman
Bought a penny doll
Washed it, dried it
Then it caught a cold
Sent for the doctor
Doctor couldn't come
Cos he had a pimple
On his rum-tum-tum.

In more recent times our Chinaman has changed quite a bit:

Ching chong chinaman
Went to milk a cow
Ching chong chinaman
Didn't know how
Ching chong chinaman
Pulled the wrong bit
Ching chong chinaman
Got a bucket of sh-t.

COVENTRY, 1990S

Almost exactly the same wording was recorded in Yorkshire and Nottinghamshire in the 1970s. It is difficult to say whether this later version is a parody of the earlier rhyme, or simply the reuse of the phrase 'Ching Chong Chinaman'.

Interestingly, versions of both the *Bought a Penny Doll* and *Went to Milk a Cow* variants are included in Ian Turner's *Cinderella Dressed in Yella* (1978), a collection of Australian rhymes, sung in the 1930s and the 1960s, along with a completely different version with the same first line. And then there is a counting-out rhyme collected in Portland, Oregon, in the 1880s:

Ching Chong Chineeman
How do you sell your fish?
Ching Chong Chineeman
Six bits a dish
Ching Chong Chineeman
Oh! that is too dear
Ching Chong Chineeman
Clear right out of here.

'Ching Chong Chinaman' has appeared in many other guises, on both sides of the Atlantic, sometimes merging into racial stereotypes of Chinese laundries and so on, and he still appears in the playground repertoire.

Topsy-turvy Rhymes

'Tangletalk' or topsy-turvy imagery has been a popular characteristic of children's rhymes for many years and has also featured strongly in adult folk traditions, and in the routines of some professional comedians. Essentially, it involves putting contradictory or paradoxical ideas or words next to each other, and there is a small repertoire of topsy-turvy verses that have been passed on down the years. Almost inevitably, every new generation thinks they have made them up.

Each verse can stand on its own, although a child who knows more than one can join them into a little nonsense song:

> One fine day in the middle of the night
> 　Two dead men got up to fight
> Back to back they faced each other
> 　Drew their swords and shot each other.
>
> The elephant is a pretty bird
> 　It flits from bough to bough
> It lays its eggs in a rhubarb tree
> 　And whistles like a cow.
>
> 'Twas in the month of Liverpool
> 　On the city of July
> The rain was snowing heavily
> 　And the streets were very dry.

NEWCASTLE, 1960S

The first verse here is particularly well known and has been around for 100 years or so. It is still heard in playgrounds around the country.

> One fine day in the middle of the night
> 　Two dead men got up for a fight
> A blind man was there to see fair play
> 　A deaf and dumb man to shout hurray
> A scabie-eyed donkey came scampering by

Kicked the blind man in the eye
Knocked him through a nine-inch wall
Into a dry ditch and drowned them all.

LEEDS, 1920S

One fine day in the middle of the night
Two dead men got up to fight
They drew their swords to shoot each other
And drew their guns to stab each other.

One fine day in the middle of the night
Two dead dogs got up to fight
Back to back they faced each other
Drew their swords to shoot each other.

I went to the playhouse tomorrow
And got a front seat at the back
A woman gave me a banana
I ate it and gave it her back.

I took a photograph of Carol
Although it looks so nice
I put it in the toilet
To scare away the mice.

YORKSHIRE, 1980

I went to the pictures tomorrow
I got a front seat at the back
A lady gave me a nana
I ate it and gave it straight back
I walked down a straight, crooked alley
I saw a dead donkey alive
I got out my penknife and shot it
It got up and kicked me in the eye.

COVENTRY, 2005

The verse 'I went to the playhouse' is also more than a century old, and was current in Co. Antrim about 1905, as recorded in Florence McDowell's book of memories, *Roses and Rainbows*. Another rhyme from her time lasted at least fifty years in the playground, and probably more:

Ladies and jellyspoons
  I stand upon a speech
To make a platform
  The train didn't arrive, so
I took a cab and walked it
  I come before you
To stand behind you
  And tell you something I know nothing about.

CO. ANTRIM, C.1905

Another popular rhyme goes:

One night as I was dreaming
  The snow was raining fast
A barefoot boy with clogs on
  Came zooming past
He turned a straight, crooked corner
  He saw a dead donkey die
Pulled out a knife and shot it
  And saw it was deaf in one eye.

COVENTRY, 1990S

And here are two less common ones:

One bright September morning
  In the middle of July
The sun lay thick upon the ground
  And the snow shone in the sky
The flowers were singing gaily
  The birds were full of bloom
I went upstairs to the cellar
  To clean a downstairs room
I saw ten thousand miles away
  A house just out of sight
It stood alone between two more
  And it was black-washed white.

LEEDS, 1920S

I went to letter a post
  I saw a bark and it dogged at me
I went down a stone

And picked up a street
And nearly necked me nock out.

LEEDS, 1920S

PARODIES

Happy Birthday to You

Dispute surrounds the writing of *Happy Birthday to You*, arguably the best-known song in the English language. Although it was copyrighted in 1935 in the USA as the composition of Preston Ware Orem and R. R. Forman, it has been claimed that it was actually written in the 1890s. Children, of course, do not care, and have parodied it mercilessly since at least the 1950s. There are numerous versions, but they follow relatively restricted lines.

In the 1960s, this was a favourite:

> Happy birthday to you
>   Squashed tomatoes and stew
> Bread and butter in the gutter
>   Happy birthday to you.

This is still heard, but sounds quite dated compared to the most common one nowadays, which rhymes 'zoo' with 'you':

> Happy birthday to you
>   You live in a zoo
> You look like a monkey
>   And you smell like one too.

GATESHEAD, 2010

Another widespread series of variants rhyme 'loo' with 'you':

> Happy birthday to you
>   Stick your head down the loo
> If you taste it don't waste it
>   Happy birthday to you.

OKEHAMPTON, 2010

These two parodies are so common that it was a relief to find a completely different one at a Balham school:

Happy birthday to me
   I'm a hundred and three
I still go to nursery
   With a nappy on me.

SOUTH LONDON, 2010

Roses Are Red

Written in countless valentine cards and autograph books over the years, or simply said by schoolchildren whenever the fit takes them, *Roses Are Red* rhymes are ubiquitous. One of the interesting things about traditional language is the way that simple verbal formulae can carry a great deal of meaning, not just as a cliché but as a marker, identifying the context and meaning of what is to follow. There are many traditional formulae like this in the English language – 'Once upon a time . . .' and 'Knock knock . . .' are good examples – but 'Roses are red . . .' is slightly different because it works at more than one level. Everyone immediately recognises it as a stock lover's or friend's poetic tribute, but because everyone also knows that the genre is mercilessly parodied, the listener's interest is heightened and humorous dramatic tension thereby created.

Roses are red
   Violets are blue
Sugar is sweet
   And so are you.

This is probably the one most people would regard as the standard form, and is not too far from the earliest known version, published in *Gammer Gurton's Garland* (1784):

The rose is red
   The violet's blue
The honey's sweet
   And so are you
Thou art my love and I am thine
   I drew thee to my valentine
The lot was cast and then I drew
   And fortune said it should be you.

But the negative parodies are not usually known for their subtlety:

> Roses are red
> > Violets are blue
> Some people are ugly
> > But not like you.
>
> *CROYDON, 1989*

> Roses are red
> > Cabbages are green
> My face is funny
> > But yours is a scream
>
> *SOUTH LONDON, 1950S*

> Roses are red
> > Violets are blue
> A face like yours
> > Belongs in a zoo.
>
> *SOUTH LONDON, 1950S*

> Roses are red
> > Violets are blue
> There's something weird about me
> > Have you noticed it too?
>
> *CROYDON, 1989*

For other aspects of Valentine's Day, see p. 474.

Jingle Bells

One of the most parodied songs in recent years has been *Jingle Bells*, and nearly every child I have spoken to during that time has known at least one version and sometimes two or three. Nevertheless, most versions follow a relatively narrow band, and the first line, 'Jingle bells, Batman smells,' is almost ubiquitous.

> Jingle bells, Batman smells
> > Robin flew away
> Landed on a football pitch
> > And didn't know how to play.
>
> *LECHLADE, 2010*

A Miscellany of Nonsense Rhymes

Mickey Mouse is dead
He died last night in bed
She cut his throat with a ten-pound note
And this is what he said
Red, white and blue
My mummy's lost her shoe
My daddy is a hunter
And you're a kangaroo.
HAMPSHIRE, 1982

Donald Duck
Did some muck
On the kitchen floor
Mrs Duck mopped it up
And Donald did some more.
COVENTRY, 1990S

Not last night but the night before
Three big tom cats came
knocking at my door
One with a fiddle, one with a drum
And one with a pancake stuck to his bum.
YORKSHIRE, 1975

Mrs Wright had a fright
In the middle of the night
She saw a ghost eating toast
Halfway up a lamp-post.
YORKSHIRE, 1980

What's the time?
Half past nine
Hang your knickers on the line
When the copper comes along
Hurry up and put them on.
HAMPSHIRE, 1983

What's the time?
Half past nine
Hang your knickers on the line
When they're dry take them in
Put them in the biscuit tin
Take a biscuit, take a cake
Eat your knickers by mistake.
ORKNEY, 2004

A wonderful bird is the pelican
Holds more in its beak than its belly can
It holds enough in its beak
To last it a week
And I don't know how the hell he can.
NOTTINGHAMSHIRE, 1970S

It's raining, it's pouring
The old man is snoring
He went to bed and bumped his head
And couldn't get up in the morning.
COVENTRY, 1970S

What's your name?
Mary Jane
Where do you live?
Down the lane
What's your street?
Pot of meat
What's your number?
Lollipop
What's your car?
Jaguar.
YORKSHIRE, 2002

Girls' faults are many
Boys have only two
Everything they say
And everything they do.
YORKSHIRE, 1984

Mr Brown went to town
Singing high and lowly
He let fart behind a cart
And paralysed the pony
The fart went rolling down the street
Knocked a copper off his feet
There was a man with a bottle of gin
He opened his mouth and the fart went in
The fart came out the other end
Round the corner and back again.
HAMPSHIRE, 1950S

Down in the jungle pretending to sleep
I saw three elephants there at my feet

One had a trumpet, one had a drum
And one had a lollipop stuck to his bum.
SUSSEX, 1966

England for ever
Chuck them in the river
Pull them out
Make them shout
Scotland for ever.
EDINBURGH, 1990

Guess what?
Teapot
Guess who?
Down the loo.
GATESHEAD, 2010

I see London
I see France
I see —'s underpants.
GATESHEAD, 2010

Easy peasy lemon squeezy
Apple pie and custard
Don't forget the mustard.
GATESHEAD, 2010

Three little angels all dressed in white
Tried to get to heaven on
the end of a kite
But the kite string broke and
down they fell
Instead of going to heaven,
they all went to –
Two little angels . . .
One little angel . . .

Three little Girl Guides
dressed in blue
Tried to get to heaven on the
end of a loo
But the loo seat broke and
down they fell
Instead of going to heaven,
they all went to –
Two little Girl Guides . . .
One little Girl Guide . . .

Three little devils dressed in red
Tried to get to heaven on the
end of a bed

But the bedpost broke and
down they fell
Instead of going to heaven
they all went to –
Two little devils . . .
One little devil . . .
Don't be mistaken, don't be misled
Instead of going to heaven
they all went to bed.
YORKSHIRE, 1980

There was a boy
Der ner ner ner ner, der ner
ner ner ner
And a girl – der ner . . .
They went for a drive
They saw a lake
They fancied a swim
They jumped in
They swam far
They swam fast
Daddy shark
Mommy shark
Brother shark
Sister shark
Baby shark
Boy swam fast
Girl swam faster
They took a leg
The other leg
They took an arm
The other arm
They took the head
The water was red
They were DEAD!

[The obvious actions were miming
driving and front crawl; the sharks
were illustrated by making the shape
of snapping jaws with your hands in
various sizes to show how big each
shark was – so baby shark only had
thumb and forefinger for jaws,
mummy shark used the hand from
the wrist, while daddy shark had your
whole arms from the elbow. The
daddy shark's line was sung in a gruff
voice, the mummy shark in a soft
voice, and the baby shark's in a
squeak].
NORTH YORKSHIRE, 1990S

Jingle bells, Batman smells
  Robin flew away
Uncle Billy lost his willy
  On the motorway, hey!

DEVON, 2010

Some children sing the following verse with the third line as 'Auntie Ruby lost her boobie'.

Jingle bells, Batman smells
  Robin flew away
He lost his pants in the middle of France
  And found them in Marbay. Hey!

GATESHEAD, 2010

Jingle bells, Batman smells
  Robin flew away
The Batmobile lost its wheel
  And the penguin got away.

COVENTRY, C.1972

Jingle bells, Batman smells
  Robin flew away
He did a fart behind the cart
  And blew up the USA.

ROCHESTER, 2010

Jingle bells, Batman smells
  Robin flew away
Lisa lost her lollipop
  And got a Milky Way.

HAMPSHIRE, 1982

Jingles like these have been around since at least the 1960s. Frank Rutherford gives one, very similar to the modern versions, in his *All the Way to Pennywell* (1971) collection from Co. Durham:

Jingle bells, Batman smells
  Robin's flew away

> The Batmobile's lost a wheel
> And landed in the hay.

He also comments, 'A more critical, mildly obscene, version was sung, perhaps by older children', but unfortunately gives no clue to its text.

The first verse of the song seems less amenable to parody, but has not escaped entirely:

> Dashing through the snow
>   On a rotten piece of cheese
> Jumping over rocks
>   Crashing into trees
> The snow is turning red
>   I think I might be dead
> I'm sitting in a hospital
>   With a knife stuck in [or bandage on] my head
>   Hey!

CAMBRIDGESHIRE, 2009

Batman and Robin verses also exist in forms designed for reciting rather than singing:

> Batman and Robin in a batmobile
>   Robin did a fart and paralysed the wheel
> The wheel couldn't take it, the car fell apart
>   All because of Robin's supersonic fart [*fart noise*]

CAMBRIDGESHIRE, 2009

The first *Jingle Bells* parody I mentioned includes a reference to a football pitch, and this allows children to move seamlessly from Batman and Robin to the lines beginning 'Fatty passed to Skinny' from another perennial favourite, *My Old Man's a Dustman*:

> My old man's a dustman
>   He wears a dustman's hat
> He found a penny ticket
>   To go to the football match.
>
> Fatty passed to Skinny
>   Skinny passed it back

Then Fatty took a rotten shot
  And knocked the goalie flat

Where was the goalie
  When the ball was in the net?
Halfway up the goal post
  With a dummy round his neck.

They put him on a stretcher
  They put him in a bed
They rubbed his belly with raspberry jelly
  And this is what he said:
COR BLIMEY!

COVENTRY, 1970S

Christmas carols

Parodies of Christmas carols abound, and it is interesting to see that a verse based on *We Three Kings* that I remember from fifty years ago is still current and almost unchanged:

We three kings from Orientar
  One in a taxi, one in a car
One on a scooter blowing his hooter
  Playing electric guitar.

CAMBRIDGESHIRE, 2009

The last line we sang was 'Smoking a big cigar', and other, slightly different versions, have been recorded, too. Like contemporary children, we too thought that 'Orientar' was a real place.

And then there is the ubiquitous parody of *While Shepherds Watched*, which is also still around. The original words were written by Nahum Tate, an Irish Protestant clergyman, in about 1700, but there can hardly be a person in the land who does not know that the shepherds were really washing their socks, rather than watching their flocks. The rhyme keeps up with the times by the product placement that has crept in – with various brands of soap and detergent being immortalised in verse:

While shepherds washed their socks by night
  All seated round the tub

The angel of the Lord came down
  And taught them how to scrub.

SOUTH LONDON, 1950S

While shepherds washed their socks by night
  All seated round the tub
A bar of Sunlight Soap came down
  And they began to scrub.

HAMPSHIRE, 1960S

While shepherds washed their socks by night
  In Omo bright and blue
The angel of the Lord came down
  And said, 'Use Daz, it's new!'

NEWCASTLE, 1967

While shepherds washed their socks by night
  In Persil sixty-nine
An angel of the Lord came down
  And said, 'Those socks are mine.'

NEWCASTLE, 1960S

Pop songs

Any pop song is fair game for the parodist, although because the parody
often outlives the original song in the popular consciousness, eventually
only the expert can spot the latter:

Ta-ra-ra bum-de-ay
  My knickers flew away
They came back yesterday
  They'd been on holiday.

COVENTRY, 1960S

Daisy, Daisy
  The coppers are after you
If they catch you
  You're in for a year or two
They'll tie you up with wire
  Behind a black maria

So ring your bell
    And pedal like hell
On your bicycle made for two.

COVENTRY, 1970S

We all piss in a blue and white pot
    A blue and white pot ... [Tune = *Yellow Submarine*]

YORKSHIRE, 1978

I'm walking in the air
    I've lost my underwear
I went to Mothercare
    And got another pair
So there!

WOLVERHAMPTON, 1990

Nursery rhymes are not exempt either:

Georgie Porgie, pudden and pie
    Kissed the girls and made them cry
When the boys came out to play
    He kissed them too, he's queer that way.

YORKSHIRE, 1980

Twinkle, twinkle, chocolate bar
    My mum drives a rusty car
Turn the handle, pull the choke
    Off we go in a puff of smoke
Twinkle, twinkle, little star
    My mum drives a rusty car.

SOUTH LONDON, 2010

CHAPTER TWENTY-THREE

Rude and Horrible Rhymes

Bodily functions and anything faintly 'naughty' have always fascinated children, and over the years there have been hundreds of risqué rhymes. Only a representative sample can be included here. What is noticeable is how often the same sort of ideas and patterns crop up from generation to generation.

TEASER RHYMES

Children seem invariably captivated and delighted by verses that proceed as though an improper word is about to rear its ugly head but then avoid it and use an innocuous word instead. Perhaps because most children do not know that many rude words, the repertoire is quite small, and the rhymes have changed remarkably little in the last fifty or sixty years.

>Some say he died of a fever
>>Some say he died of a fit
>But we all know what he died of
>>He died of the smell of the sh–
>–ine your buttons with Brasso
>>One and three ha'pence a tin
>Buy it or swipe it from Woolies
>>But I doubt if they've got any in.
>Some say he's buried in a coffin
>>Some say he's buried in a box

But we all know what he's buried in
　　He's buried in a pile of sh—
—ine your buttons . . .

HAMPSHIRE, 1950S

As I was walking by St Paul's
　　A woman grabbed me by my elbow
She said, 'You look a man of pluck
　　So come inside and have a ham sandwich
It may cost a penny, it may cost a bob
　　But that depends on the size of your appetite.'

YORKSHIRE, 1978

Mary had a little lamb
　　She thought it rather silly
She threw it up into the air
　　And caught it by its
Willy was a watchdog
　　Who was kicked up the
Ask no questions, tell no lies
　　Have you ever seen a policeman
Doing up his
　　Flies are a nuisance
Fleas are worse
　　And this is the end of my little verse.

YORKSHIRE, 1980

Miss Susie had a steamboat
　　The steamboat had a bell
Miss Susie went to heaven
　　The steamboat went to
Hello operator fetch me number nine
　　If you disconnect me, I'll kick you from
Behind the fridgerator
　　There was a piece of glass
Miss Susie fell upon it
　　And hurt her little
Ask me no more questions
　　Tell me no more lies

Miss Susie's in her kitchen
   Baking her mud pies.

WEST LONDON, 2009

Rule Britannia, two monkeys up a stick
   One fell down and paralysed his
Dicky was a watchdog lying in the grass
   Along came a bumble-bee and stung him up his
Ask no questions, tell no lies
   Have you ever seen a Chinaman doing up his
Flies are a nuisance, bugs are worse
   And that is the end of my Chinese verse.

VERY GENERAL

These lines often appear in their own right, but sometimes they are stuck on the end of the *My Old Man's a Dustman* rhyme quoted above. And in another incarnation of the *Dustman* rhyme, the following lines appear, which can also stand on their own.

My wife she had a baby
   She called him Sonny Jim
She put him in the toilet
   To see if he could swim
She got so excited, she pulled him by his
   Cocks and muscles if you don't like
Then stick it up his
   Ask no questions tell no lies
I saw a copper zipping up his
   Flies are a nuisance
Bees are worse
   This is the end of my silly verse.

YORKSHIRE, 1982

The next example of the genre was popular on school coach trips in Gateshead in the late 1960s:

Samson was a warrior
   His mother was as well
Samson went to heaven
   And his mother went to

Helensburgh Castle
　　Is built upon a rock
If you want to go there
　　You'll have to show your
Cockles and Mussels
　　Are very good for colds
If you do not like them
　　You can shove them up your
Hold on, ladies
　　The train is going fast
And if you do not hold on
　　You will fall upon your
Ask no questions
　　Tell no lies
Samson was a warrior
　　Because he ate mince pies.

The following only works if you slur the ends of the lines a bit:

Have you ever had it up?
　　Have you ever had it up?
Have you ever had a tuppenny cornet?
　　Have you ever had it in?
Have you ever had it in?
　　Have you ever had a tin of corned beef?

HAMPSHIRE, 1960S

RUDE AND HORRIBLE

Worm Rhymes

Children seem to be perennially fascinated with worms, and they have a number of rhymes on the subject. Here are three versions of a very widely known rhyme:

Nobody likes me
　　Everybody hates me
I'm going to eat some worms

Long thin slimy ones
Itsy bitsy, titsy bitsy worms.
  First you bite their heads off
Then you suck the guts out
  Ooh how they wiggle and squirm
Big fat juicy ones . . .

HAMPSHIRE, 1950S

Nobody loves me
  Everybody hates me
I'm going out in the garden to eat worms
  Long thin juicy ones
Small fat slimy ones
  Some that go down easy
And some that stick
  Nobody loves me
Everybody hates me
  I'm going out in the garden to be sick.

HAMPSHIRE, 1960S

Nobody likes me
  Everybody hates me
So I'm just going to eat worms
  Big fat juicy ones, little thin squirmy ones
That's what worms are like
  Bite off their head
Suck out their juice
  Throw away the skin
Nobody likes me
  Everybody hates me
So I'm just going to eat worms.

YORKSHIRE, 1980

The same rhyme has been recorded in Canada and the USA.
  The worm theme has been dealt with in other ways as well:

Have you ever thought as the years go by
  That one of these days you're going to die
They put you in a wooden box
  And cover you over with smelly socks

The worms crawl in, the worms crawl out
　　They crawl in thin, and crawl out stout
They bring their friends, and their friends too
　　And oh what a mess they make of you.

HAMPSHIRE, 1950S

Little worm upon the ground
　　Little worm so fat and round
There it lays upon its belly
　　So I squash it with my welly.

YORKSHIRE, 1980

Scatological rhymes and others

It is well known that, much to the embarrassment of their parents and teachers, children delight in rhymes and songs about forbidden or gross subjects. Some of them are clever or amusing in their own right, others are not, but the children seem to make little distinction. They are clearly learning about boundaries of behaviour, and how much these can be pushed or stretched, and they are also often simply enjoying being 'naughty'. Children learn at different stages in their development when to recite these rhymes and when not, but most of them do learn that valuable social lesson sooner rather than later.

The first few I am including here are about taboo subjects, but in adult terms are more 'horrible' than 'rude', although children do not always make this separation. As detailed in the Introduction, I have decided to omit the outright offensive 'gross' material. Even so, look away now if you are easily offended.

If you see a bunny
　　With a runny nose
Don't think it's funny
　　'Coz it's SNOT!

COVENTRY, 1970S

Climbing up a lamp post
　　With a bottle of milk
Want to go toilet
　　Whoops, too late!

COVENTRY, 1960S

Tarzan in the jungle,
  Had a belly ache,
Went to the toilet,
  Ptthhrrp [*short raspberry*] too late.

COVENTRY, 1970S

Old King Cole was a merry old soul
  And a merry old soul was he
He called for a light in the middle of the night
  To go to the WC
The WC was occupied
  So he stuck his bum out the window side
Queen Victoria passing by
  Caught a sausage in her eye
She looked east and she looked west
  Caught a sausage down her vest
She looked up to the window pane
  And caught a shower of golden rain.

NEWCASTLE, 1960S

Milk, milk, lemonade
  Round the corner
Chocolate's made.

NEWCASTLE, 1960S

Eyes, nose, mouth, chin
  Running down to Uncle Jim
VJ makes lemonade
  Round the corner
Chocolate's made.

SOUTH LONDON, 1971

What do you do if you can't find a loo
  In an English country garden
Pull down your pants and fertilize the plants
  In an English country garden
Pull off a leaf and wipe your underneath
  In an English country garden.

YORKSHIRE, 1980

Mummy I'm unhappy
  There's something in my nappy

It's long and brown
  I can't sit down
Cos if I do I'll squash it
  And then you'll have to wash it
Oh what is it
  A lump of shit
It's sliding down my leggy
  Just like a boiled eggy
Now it's in my shoe
  It is a lump of poo.
[Tune = *The Conga*]

HAMPSHIRE, 1982

In 1966
  The queen pulled down her knicks
She licked her bum and said yum yum
  This is better than Weetabix.

HAMPSHIRE, 1983/COVENTRY, 2005

Yum yum bubblegum
  Stick it up your mother's bum
When it's brown pull it down
  Yum yum bubblegum.

HAMPSHIRE, 1983

All these deal with basic bodily functions. Some range a little more widely around the human anatomy:

Ee by gum
Can your belly touch your bum?
Can your tits hang low?
Can you tie them in a bow?
Can your balls hang flat?
Can you tie them in a plait?
Ee by gum, say yes to that!

COVENTRY, 1990S

And inevitably some take an earthy view of sex:

Jack and Jill [or 'Mum and Dad'] went up the hill
  To fetch a pail of water

God knows what they did up there
    But now they've got a daughter.

YORKSHIRE, 1980

In Jamaica, under the tree
They sell condoms for 99p
    Big ones, small ones
    Take your pick
It all depends on the size of your dick!

COVENTRY, 2005

I be a farmer
    Me name be Bob
I'm widely renowned
    For the size of me knob
It's too big for women
    It just makes them weep
But it's just the right size
    For me cows and me sheep!

COVENTRY, 2005

Food, too, is a particular favourite:

Cody cody custard, green snot pie
    All mixed up with a dead dog's eye
Caterpillar sandwich mixed up thick
    Wash it all down with a cup of sick.

YORKSHIRE, 1980

Yellow belly custard
    Green snot pie
All mixed together
    With a dead dog's eye
Get a bit of brown bread
    Slap it on thick
And wash it all down
    With a cold cup of sick.

COVENTRY, C.1970

CHAPTER TWENTY-FOUR

Down with School

ANTI-SCHOOL SONGS

The modern British schoolchild seems sadly ill-equipped to greet the end of term in an appropriate manner – certainly when compared to previous generations. Anyone over thirty-five is likely to know *One More Day of School, We Break Up, We Break Down* or *No More English, no More French* . . ., but very few of the children I have interviewed recently recognised these songs, and the ones who did had usually learnt them from their parents. The nearest I could find was when a boy in Gateshead told me how they all played *School's Out for Summer* on their iPods as they left on the last day of term. When I quoted some of the end-of-term songs of my youth to some present-day children they looked blankly at me and said, 'But we *enjoy* school . . .' Perhaps that is the problem. All is not lost, however, for the forces of subversion. Ewan McVicar's definitive collection of Scots children's rhymes, *Doh Ray Me, When Ah Wis Wee* (2007), shows that many of the following rhymes, and others, were still current in the late 1990s, and most likely still are. And even in England, some anti-teacher ditties continue to circulate.

One anti-school rhyme I clearly remember from the 1950s was very widely known:

> One more day of school
> One more day of sorrow
> One more day of this old dump
> And we'll be home tomorrow.

It was sung to the tune of *One Man went to Mow*, and we usually started a day or two early. 'Two more days of school . . .' worked fine; 'We'll be home the day after tomorrow' did not scan very well, but it did not worry us unduly.

Another popular rhyme from the 1950s went as follows:

> We break up, we break down
>> We don't care if the school burns down
> There'll be no more English, no more French
>> No more sitting on the old school bench.

This was sung to the tune of *Nick Nack Paddy Whack*, and also existed in an extended version:

> We break up, we break down
>> We don't care if the school falls down
> No more English, no more French
>> No more sitting on the old school bench
> If the teacher interferes, dynamite and box her ears
> If that does not shut her up, dynamite'll blow her up
>> Teacher, teacher, we declare, we can see your underwear
>> Is it black or is it white, oh my god it's pink and white.

HAMPSHIRE, 1983

Or the shorter one:

> No more school
> No more stick
> No more dirty arithmetic.

NORTHAMPTONSHIRE, 1950S

> No more teachers
> No more books
> No more teacher's dirty looks.

SOUTH LONDON, 1950S

And, from a private school in Cambridgeshire:

> No more Latin, no more French
>> No more sitting on a hard school bench

No more beatles in my tea
　　Making goggling eyes at me
No more spiders in the bath
　　Trying hard to make me laugh
Kick the tables, kick the chairs
　　Kick the teachers down the stairs.

CAMBRIDGESHIRE, 1960S

Then there was the ubiquitous *Build a Bonfire*, sung to the tune of *Clementine*:

Build a bonfire, build a bonfire
　　Put the teachers on the top
Put the prefects in the middle
　　And burn the blimmin' lot.

LONDON, 1950S

Come to —, come to —
　　It's a place of misery
There's a sign-post at the corner
　　Saying 'Welcome unto thee'
Build a bonfire, build a bonfire
　　Put the teachers on the top
Put the prefects in the middle
　　And burn the ruddy lot.

BATH, 1970S

And the admirably direct:

Hip hip hooray
　　No school today
We can go and play
　　Hey!

NORFOLK, 1990S

And the resigned:

God who made the bees
　　Bees who made the honey

We do all the mucky work
Teachers get the money.

YORKSHIRE, 1982

When it came to mocking teachers, the following verse was popular from at least the 1950s and can still be heard. It goes to the tune of *John Brown's Body*:

Glory glory hallelujah
  Teacher hit me with a ruler
The ruler broke in half
  And the class began to laugh
On the last day of September.

ESSEX, 1970S/EARLY 1980S

One of the oldest teacher rhymes, which can be adapted to suit any name, was already in circulation in 1795 (and was also used as a skipping rhyme, see p. 184):

Billy Timms is a very good man
He tries to larn us all he can
Radin', 'ritin' and 'rithmetic
But he don't forget to give us the stick
When he does he makes us dance
  Out of England into France
  Out of France into Spain
  Over the hills and back again.

WORCESTERSHIRE C.1910

And one of the most recent, which is widely known in Britain and America, is the following parody of the Christmas hymn *Joy to the World*, originally by Isaac Watts (1719) but recorded by all and sundry in recent years:

Joy to the world, the teacher's dead
We barbecued her head
And where was the body?
We flushed it down the potty
  And round and round it goes

And round and round it goes
And round and round
And down it goes.

SOUTH LONDON, C.2002

Modern school dinners probably do not deserve the opprobrium heaped on them in traditional rhyme, but old habits die hard. The most commonly found is sung to the tune of *Frère Jacques*, and has been in circulation since at least the 1950s:

School dinners, school dinners
  Concrete chips, concrete chips
Soggy semolina, soggy semolina
  I feel sick, toilet quick
It's too late, I've done it on the plate.

HAMPSHIRE, 1982

School dinners, school dinners
  Irish stew, Irish strew
Sloppy semolina, sloppy semolina
  No thank you, no thank you.

YORKSHIRE, 1982

And from about the same period:

They say here at —
  The food is very fine
A pea rolled off the table
  And killed a friend of mine
Ooooh boarding life
  Jeepers I wanna go
But they won't let me go
  Jeepers I wanna go home.

BATH, 1970S

Other rhymes about school dinners have not stood the test of time as well as the above, presumably because the songs they parodied have also disappeared. This, for example, parodies the first verse of *Out of Town*, a minor hit in the UK for Max Bygraves in 1956:

Say what you will
School dinners make you ill
Davy Crockett died of shepherd's pie.

SUSSEX, 1960s

And to the tune of *Sixteen Tons*:

If you stay to school dinners
    Better throw them aside
A lot of kids didn't
    A lot of kids died
The meat is made of iron
    The spuds are made of steel
If they don't get you
    The afters will.

YORKSHIRE, 1978

Some children insist on reciting certain rhymes at school dinner-time, which we will not quote here in case they put the reader off their food. But a couple of versions can be found in the 'Scatalogical rhymes and others' section in the previous chapter (p. 437), starting with *Cody Cody Custard*.

The Post-war Playground

The period since the Second World War has seen such huge changes in children's lives that it is often difficult for those who have not lived through them to comprehend just how different things were only a few decades ago. In terms of play, it is not simply that modern children are inundated with toys, pre-packaged entertainment and electronic gadgetry, but that there has been a sea-change in the way childhood is viewed and, in particular, a sharp reduction in the environments available for self-organised play.

The period starts with the huge upheaval of the war itself, which clearly had a major effect on children's lives. Hundreds of thousands of urban children were evacuated to predominantly rural areas, and for many there was a marked culture clash highlighting the vast differences not only between city and country but also between the classes in British society. Sometimes the local children and the evacuees integrated well, although it often took a while, but occasionally their interaction was little short of all-out war.

As factories moved over to more vital areas of production and imports were suspended, there were severe shortages of new toys, and therefore a rise in home-made efforts and the vigorous recycling of second-hand toys. Children were given new things to do as they were roped in on campaigns to help the war effort, such as collecting scrap metal, waste paper, and even acorns to feed the pigs. New war-related hobbies, such as collecting army cap badges and pieces of shrapnel, became widespread, and any self-respecting boy could tell the difference between a Spitfire and a Hurricane. In many urban areas, exciting new playgrounds appeared, in the shape of bomb-sites and derelict buildings galore.

As the austerity and rationing of the immediate post-war years receded, Britain entered a period of relative affluence, which gave many children access to toys and entertainment that had previously been out of their reach. Cinema, radio and comics, which had achieved mass popularity in the 1930s, maintained and strengthened their grip, and the first glimmerings of the new 'youth culture' appeared, with rock and roll and skiffle. These soon filtered into the children's repertoire, and pop singers' names began to replace film stars in playground rhymes. The 1956 Davy Crockett craze, which came on the back of a Disney film, was probably the first American-style orchestrated commercial campaign aimed at children. Soon every child wanted a coon-skin hat. By the 1960s full employment and a rapidly rising standard of living were reflected in new fashions for children's clothes and increasingly aggressive commercial campaigns aimed at children as consumers. In the Swinging Sixties, television and pop music became the major media influences on the playground.

The late 1950s and early 1960s also marked the heyday of 'Saturday morning pictures', when it seemed as if every child in the land was packed into their local cinema cheering and booing their way through a weekly fare of cartoons, newsreels, interminable serials featuring cowboys and Indians, Robin Hood, Flash Gordon and many others. There was community singing, and occasional live action such as demonstrations of yo-yo tricks or even a visit from a celebrity like Robbie the Robot from *Forbidden Planet* (1956). Many cinemas had clubs – the ABC Minors, Granadiers Club, Empire Rangers and so on – complete with a badge and a special song, and they would read out your name from the stage if it was your birthday.

The middle of the post-war period also saw major changes in the games played, although it is difficult to put firm dates on these developments because they took place at different times across the country. By the dawn of the 1970s, hoops and tops had completely disappeared from childhood play, although there was a major craze for hula hoops in the early 1960s. By the 1980s, cigarette cards had all but disappeared, and even two-balls had begun to fade away. Traditional singing games had been in decline for some time, and continued their descent from the playground to the nursery and preschool environment.

On the other hand, a new craze for clapping games occurred in the early 1960s and has lasted to the present day, while frisbees arrived in the mid 1970s. The increase in child-centred mass media also provided innumerable models for songs and dances in the playground, and hugely stimulated imaginative play – a state of affairs that still prevails today.

Commercial interests have made sure that there are plenty of things for children, or at least those who can afford them, to collect and swap, from Pokémon cards to My Little Pony, which adults often despise, but children love.

Other changes in society, and more particularly changes in schools and teaching, also had their effect on the playground. In 1967 the hugely influential Plowden Report (*Children and Their Primary Schools*) ushered in an era of 'child-centred' education, stressing the uniqueness of each child, learning by discovery and so on, and doing away with traditional 'learning by rote' systems. In the same period, significant numbers of immigrant children came into the educational system. Concerns about racism, sexism and bullying began to tell in the way that playground activity was organised and regulated.

The 1970s onwards saw the biggest change in children's play environments since the rapid urbanisation of the nineteenth century took place, as the long-standing occupation of the street by children went into rapid decline. The inexorable increase in road traffic was the most obvious factor in this change. Not only were streets more dangerous because of passing traffic, but even in the back streets, parked cars dominated the playing space, and the owners of those cars were not keen on hordes of children playing around and over them. But other contributing factors were at work, such as the spread of large-scale slum-clearance schemes, which broke up many existing working-class communities, and the unfortunate fact that neither the tower blocks nor the housing estates built to replace them turned out to be conducive to outside play.

But it is arguable that playing in the street was doomed anyway. As the twentieth century advanced there was a gradual upward shift in the class attitudes of British society, which came with rising prosperity and the spread of education. Street-play was already restricted mainly to the working classes, and was one of the markers of class identity that upwardly mobile parents were keen to shake off. This, in turn, went hand in hand with an increase in the general concern for 'health and safety', and a specific concern about the dangers posed by strangers and outsiders.

What was lost for children in these changes – particularly for those under eleven – was the opportunity for *unsupervised* play, and the idea that children should be simply left alone most of the time to amuse themselves all but disappeared. As many smaller rural schools began to close, and increasing numbers of children were driven to school by car, the casual games that accompanied walking to school were also lost – though, in some cases, they were replaced by games played on school buses. Parents, teachers and other adults became more and more involved, or, as some would argue, interfered more, in children's free time.

In the playground in recent years there have been widespread moves to 'civilise' children's behaviour, with written codes of conduct stressing thought for others, discouraging bullying and rough and potentially dangerous play. Not that this is necessarily a completely new phenomenon: I remember acorns being banned at my school in 1955 because someone got hit in the eye, and 'British Bulldog' was already forbidden.

Some deplore the more regulated playground of recent years. Others deplore the cultural dominance of television and computer games. Both groups fear that 'children are forgetting how to play', just as they did in the 1890s. Now, as then, there is no evidence that there is much to panic about.

Penny for the guy, 1896

Avoiding the cracks, 2010

Penny for the guy, 1956

Empire Day, 1930s

Trick or treating, c.2009

Buying fireworks, 1949

Whit walk, Lancashire, 1930s

May Day, 1900s

Ring-pull fortune-telling, 2010

CHAPTER TWENTY-FIVE

Superstitions and Customs

SUPERSTITIONS AND LEGENDS

Discussions of 'superstition' in society are fraught with difficulty, as there are no firm definitions and everyone has a different perspective. On the broadest level, many people are convinced that 'we' are more superstitious than ever, while others, including myself, argue that people nowadays play at being superstitious and that we are, as a society, infinitely more rational and secular than ever before.

In some ways, childhood is the perfect breeding ground for superstition. Children have not yet sorted out what is real and what is not, they have only a tentative grasp of cause and effect, and they can slip from 'magical thinking' to 'rationality' in a moment. The stories that adults tell them, of tooth fairies and Father Christmas, Wombles and super-heroes, are designed to stimulate the wonder and imagination necessary for an active mind, but at some point in its development, each child needs to understand the difference between fiction and fact.

When interviewing children, I routinely ask about 'lucky' and 'unlucky' things. I am nearly always told nowadays about common adult superstitions such as walking under ladders, Friday 13th, umbrellas indoors, broken mirrors, horseshoes and black cats. Rarely do children today mention anything that formerly would have been considered a 'child's superstition', except, perhaps, 'stepping on the cracks'. Only two or three generations ago, many superstitions were almost exclusive to childhood, but these seem to have largely disappeared, or at least to have drastically weakened their hold over the minds of the young.

It is easy to jump to the conclusion that children nowadays are more street-savvy, better informed, precociously grown-up and so on, and therefore less superstitious. There is an element of truth here, but what seems to be happening in the children's sphere is a mirror of what has been happening to adult superstitions for some time. Although many people still claim to be superstitious, the number of superstitions in the active repertoire has narrowed sharply in recent years, and whereas a 'superstitious person' fifty years ago would have had a couple of dozen that they followed avidly, today that figure has shrunk to perhaps a quarter of that number. And even the self-confessed superstitious person does not really expect to live by their beliefs. They would be most offended if they were refused a job because they were the wrong star sign, or their staff did not turn up for work because they saw a magpie outside their door.

Detailed below is a selection of the superstitious beliefs common to British children over the past 100 years, including those still to be found in certain families or playgrounds. It is impossible to be dogmatic about whether or not particular beliefs survive, because evidence tends to be patchy. Superstitions can lie dormant in people's minds and easily skip a generation if grandparents pass on their beliefs to their grandchildren. But two obvious developments in society in general have had a direct influence on children's beliefs, although it is unclear (at least to me) what the long-term effect is likely to be.

The first is that professional sporting heroes now talk openly about their superstitious practices, which the media gleefully report in detail. Indeed, it is now an essential accessory for the 'real' sports star to have a few pet superstitions, and children, boys especially, feel that they must join in. The underlying superstitious principle is that where people have jobs which rely to a large extent on 'luck' they often try to gain control over uncertain outcomes by preventative or protective actions. The most popular notion nowadays is that if something works once, it will work again, so the temptation is to follow exactly the same patterns each time – the journey to the match, the 'lucky' socks, putting your right boot on first, touching the doorpost on the way out and so on. The charitable response is that this is simply a bit of fun, does no harm and may even be helpful if it contributes to a positive frame of mind. The less under-standing perspective is that it is obsessive behaviour which if left unchecked can become psychologically damaging, and it teaches our children that an understanding of scientific cause and effect is not necessary in life.

The other development is that children's popular culture is now awash with images of the supernatural, to a degree never seen before. Wizards, witches, vampires and other fictional supernatural beings are all around us, in addition to super-heroes, who share many of the attributes of traditional supernatural beings.

It may be that the daily exposure to the fictional world of magic has, in effect, taken the magic out of it for children by desensitising them, so that most of them are well aware that magic really is fiction. But it seems almost de rigueur for adolescents to flirt with the occult, and to dabble in ouija boards, tarot cards and the like, and their 'belief' often appears much stronger than children's, perhaps because it has a countercultural element.

This has probably always been the case, and most of them grow out of it, but again the difference nowadays is the sheer ubiquity of material. Fifty years ago you had to find a specialist shop to buy a set of tarot cards; now you can buy them in almost any corner shop; and there seems to be an endless diet of vampire and werewolf television programmes on offer. But then a while ago the same seemed to be true of martial arts, and that seems to have left little trace behind.

Many children's superstitions can only be dated for sure to the 1950s because that is when Iona and Peter Opie began collecting material for their books – no one had bothered with such trifling matters before. The Opies were the first to point out that many people – adults as well as children – took note of the serial number on their bus ticket. The basic belief was that if it added up to twenty-one it was lucky, and some would actually keep it as a lucky token. A girl could give such a token to a boy, and if he kept it, or kept half and gave her back the other half, he was definitely interested in her. Others decided that if it added up to thirteen it was an unlucky omen for the day, while some constructed more complicated meanings from the numerals. Although the basic twenty-one superstition is still mentioned today, it is unlikely to be so prevalent as it was in the past.

One of the commonest motifs of superstition for any age is that certain things are unlucky to *see* or meet. These things vary considerably, from the fairly obvious ambulance or funeral, to the rather more obscure single magpie:

> When I was a girl, if an ambulance passed us when we were out playing in the street, we would cross our fingers and hold our breath until it had passed. We believed that if we didn't do that we would catch TB or polio or something. *LINCOLN, 1940S*

Many of us in post-war years followed the ritual that if you saw a funeral or ambulance you held your collar until you saw a four-legged animal, and then you were safe. The idea of holding the collar may have derived from the previous generation holding their hats to their chests as a funeral passed by as a mark of respect. Children made little distinction between hearses and ambulances: they both might have dead people in them. And it was not just the sight of a funeral that was dreaded:

> We trotted most of the way [from school] and had to hold our breath, when we passed the undertakers, because Georgie told us that if you breathed in the undertaker's smell, you'd catch your death. The undertaker made coffins in the yard behind his premises, and the acrid smell that wafted up the alley from the yard was from elm sawdust, but to us that alley was the jaws of hell.   *LONDON, 1920S*

Childlore collector Cathy Gould was told in Coventry in 1998, 'Always cross your fingers when passing a graveyard.'

Many children share the adult superstition about seeing magpies and know at least the first couple of lines of the rhyme:

> One for sorrow
> Two for joy
> Three for a girl
> Four for a boy
> Five for silver
> Six for gold
> Seven for a secret never to be told.

The belief about magpies is first mentioned in the 1780s. The rhyme used to exist in many different versions, but this standardised text has probably wiped out most local wordings. Children who know that the magpie is unlucky usually know that to counteract the bad luck you simply say hello and are polite to the bird in question.

A surprisingly widespread children's superstition, current since at least the 1950s, focuses on Royal Mail vans, although there has apparently been no consensus about whether it is lucky or unlucky to see one. Some people have thought you can get a wish, especially if you can touch the crown painted on the side; others have thought it distinctly unlucky, especially if you see the back of the van. A letter published in the *Mirror* (31 October 1974), from a woman in Suffolk, stated:

A saying we had as youngsters after seeing a Royal Mail van was, 'Royal Mail, touch the ground, the first boy you speak to you love.' We would then spend ages avoiding the boys we did not like!

The ritualised touching of something specific in this case seems to have developed a little later. Cathy Gould was told by Danielle Sharp, who was born in Coventry 1983, that if you saw a mail van you should chant (and do):

> Touch green,
> Never to be seen,
> Touch black,
> Don't look back.

Surprisingly, this belief still seems to be current. 'Stephen from Cumbernauld', for example, contributed the comment 'Whenever I see a Royal Mail van I touch something red' to a BBC *Newsround* chatroom (6 January 2003).

One of the most widespread, and most puzzling, of childhood superstitions is the notion that it is unlucky to step on the cracks of the pavement, along with the related idea that to walk on 'three drains' is particularly ominous. When I was a boy in the 1950s, we played a game on the way to and from school called 'Broken Biscuits'. The rule was that you must not step on the lines between the paving stones, and could only step on a stone that was complete. If it was cracked, or cut into by a manhole cover or drain, you had to jump over or go round it. But I am sure we had no notion of good or bad luck in this regard, and I remember being surprised, a few years later, when someone said that stepping on the cracks was 'unlucky'.

Nevertheless, research has shown that the inadvisability of stepping on the cracks dates back at least to 1890 and perhaps to the 1860s, although it presumably cannot pre-date the introduction of paving stones. The penalty for treading on a crack has varied so much that it is difficult to reach any conclusions about the original notion. One of the major themes is marriage, and in more racist times in the mid twentieth century it was often said that you would 'marry a black man' or 'have a black baby'. An alternative, made famous by A. A. Milne's 'Lines and Squares' in *When We Were Very Young* (1924), was that the bears will get you, though others have said that it will be snakes. Another theme was broken dishes – you will break your mother's best china, or the devil's dishes, and so on. Mothers feature fairly often in these predicted consequences, but the prevalent notion nowadays, that it will 'break your mother's back', is the American version, imported relatively recently.

The related superstition that it is unlucky to step on any place where three drains or manhole covers are laid out in a row is also puzzling. Iona Opie and Moira Tatem's *Dictionary of Superstitions* (1989) does not mention it, and I had not come across it until I was doing research for my own *Dictionary* in 1998. But several people remembered it from their own childhoods, and it has become, if anything, more widely known in recent years. Nothing more specific than 'bad luck' is usually predicted for those who are unwise enough to ignore the 'three-drains' warning.

Another children's superstition concerns *Araucaria araucana* or the monkey puzzle tree, a tree that has presumably delighted and mystified people in equal measure since its introduction from Chile in the 1790s. Stories circulated about its connection with the devil, which varied from 'the tree is lucky because the devil cannot hide in it' to the exact opposite idea that 'it is only the devil who can hide there'. Nevertheless, the dominant belief for children fifty years ago, and still occasionally heard today, is that it is unlucky to speak as you pass it by. No reason is ever given, but it is possible that the idea grew from vague notions of the devil hiding there.

One superstition that has definitely disappeared is the 'luck' of finding certain brands empty cigarette packet. Children in the 1950s would deliberately step on a packet of Black Cat or Navy Cut cigarettes, and say:

> Black cat, black cat, bring me luck
> If you don't I'll tear you up

Or:

> Sailor, sailor, bring me luck
> Find a shilling in the muck.

These two can be explained by the prominent picture on the packet, as both black cats and sailors featured in other common superstitions, but children also did it with other brands as well, such as Woodbines.

In the days of corporal punishment at school, children had several notions about how to ameliorate the pain of being caned, and they were convinced that if you managed to stretch a human hair across the palm of your hand, the cane would split in two. This idea lasted from at least the 1870s to the post-Second-World-War period. Rubbing your palm with a raw onion was also said to make the punishment less painful.

Children often keep unusual things that they find – shells, strangely shaped or coloured pebbles and so on – often regarding them as 'lucky charms'. In this, they are definitely following in the footsteps of many ancestors, who behaved similarly when they came across things by chance. Horseshoes, for example, had to be found by accident if they were to be efficacious, and any other piece of metal was also believed to bring luck in the same way. Since at least the seventeenth century in Britain, and earlier in other parts of Europe, a stone with a natural hole in it was particularly prized:

> In the gravel formations around Poole, perforated pebbles are not uncommon, and the occurrence of one of these was considered 'lucky'; such a stone being denominated a 'lucky stone'. But in order to realise to the full the felicitous results of such a find, it was important to go through the following ceremony. The stone was picked up, spat upon, and then thrown backward over the head of the fortunate finder, who accompanied the action with the following rhyme:
>
> > Lucky stone! Lucky stone! Go over my head
> > And bring me some good luck before I go to bed.
>
> *DORSET, C.1818*

A lively sub-genre of folklore exists in the intersection between belief and legend. They are not quite superstitions, because they have no element of luck, premonition and so on, but they are nonetheless founded on erroneous beliefs. Many parents, for example, have resorted to a turn of phrase to discourage their children from making faces or doing other grotesque things, by saying, 'If you're not careful, the wind will change and you will be stuck like that for ever.' Where the phrase came from is not clear, but it has been around for over 100 years, and countless children have believed it to be literally true, as evidenced by Alison Uttley's memory of Derbyshire in the 1880s:

> She actually saw the little girl who was squinting when the wind changed, and her eyes got stuck, a strange cross-eyed infant.

And the same author also drew attention to another widespread notion:

> She was told of a little boy who drank water from a trough at the side of the road, and swallowed a frog. It grew and grew in his inside, till he swelled like a balloon, and the frog hopped out of his mouth.

Ladybird Rhymes and Beliefs

Everyone seems to love the ladybird; wherever they are found in the world they tend to be regarded as lucky and are protected from harm, and many European countries have rhymes similar to that which British children still recite when one lands on them:

> Ladybird, ladybird
> Fly away home
> Your house is on fire
> And your children are gone.

This is the commonest version nowadays, but in earlier times the text varied much more widely, and the insect also went under a plethora of local names, including lady-cow, cushy-cow lady, marygold, lady beetle, lady bug, lady-clock, and even God Almighty's cow. One Scottish version of the rhyme, noted in the early nineteenth century, ran:

> Lady, Lady Landers
> Lady, Lady Landers
> Take up your coats about your head
> And fly away to Flanders.
> *SCOTLAND*

Creatures regarded as lucky are usually also protected by the notion that to kill or harm them is unlucky:

> A marygold was as sacred in our eyes as a robin.
> No injury should be done to it on any account.
> *HEREFORDSHIRE, 1930S*

This was indeed high praise, as robins were everywhere protected by the notion that they were 'God Almighty's' bird, and saved from harm or harassment because of it. In addition to the general good luck of a ladybird landing on your hand, the insect was also used in a minor form of divination, which focused on the direction in which it 'flew away':

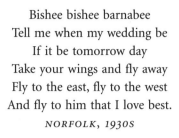

Bishee bishee barnabee
Tell me when my wedding be
If it be tomorrow day
Take your wings and fly away
Fly to the east, fly to the west
And fly to him that I love best.

NORFOLK, 1930S

Alternatively, the number of spots it has on its back was noted:

The better or deeper the red of the ladybird, the better the luck. Also the more spots the better. Seven spots especially – we always looked for these.

CAMBRIDGESHIRE, 1938

In Sussex at the same period, they said you would get as many happy months as there were spots.

It is no surprise that the ladybird is generally liked – its attractive colour and appearance account for that, and in the insect world it has few competitors in that department – but there is a great mystery as to what, if anything, lies behind the widespread 'house on fire' rhymes. Unusually, there seem to be no traditional stories that seek to explain it, although there are, of course, several spurious explanations in circulation put forward by commentators looking for ancient origins. The two commonest are that the mention of fire must be a relic of ancient sun worship, or that there is hidden religious symbolism behind the fact that the 'lady' in its name must be a reference to the Virgin Mary. There is indeed evidence that some of the ladybird's names are references to Mary, but this is hardly uncommon in dialect names for birds, flowers and other natural phenomena, and is no indication of genuine religious symbolism or great age.

The earliest known version in Britain, which is very similar to the modern standard wording given above, only dates from 1744, and none of the many versions noted across Europe, as far as I can tell, is older than the nineteenth century. Some of the latter are so close that direct and recent translation is most likely.

Stories of creatures who invade the human body, and grow there, are extremely common in British tradition and have been firmly believed over the years by adults as well as children. The belief often manifests itself in a 'contemporary legend' told as a true story and localised to give it credibility, and the roster of animal invaders is large – earwigs entering the brain through the ears, spiders living in beehive hairdos or laying their eggs under the skin, and countless frogs, newts and snakes living in people's stomachs. How they got there varies considerably. It can be that the person drank unclean water, slept out in the open or, very popular these days, got infected when abroad or when handling imported goods. Many science fiction and horror stories depend on similar ideas for their effect.

A major health worry of the 1950s was tetanus, which we children knew as 'lockjaw' because of the muscle spasms it could cause. We were convinced that if you cut yourself in the skin where the thumb and index finger join, even just a little bit, you would get lockjaw and die. We told each other stories about a child in the nearby school who was sitting in class with his friends watching in horror as his face became distorted and he died in agony.

One of the commonest legends of childhood varies with each community but is usually concerned with a particular object or place; often a scary thing like a tomb, but occasionally something relatively innocuous, like a well or small building. The legend is that if you run round it X times and tap on it, or look through the crack, or listen, or say something three times, you will see or hear the dead, the ghost, the devil and so on:

> One of the scary games we played at Chasetown was running round a certain flat tombstone seven times and then spitting on it – the dead were then supposed to talk to us. Fortunately, they never did.
>
> *STAFFORDSHIRE, 1940S*

> My mother had told me that if I wanted to see the Devil, I was, on the eve of All Hallows, to run three times in an anti-clockwise direction around the well then peep through the holes in the wall of the well and I would see Old Nick. It was also bad luck to say 'The Devil'. I tried it once but I didn't see anything.
>
> *LINCOLN, 1940S*

TELLING FORTUNES

A huge sub-category of superstitious belief and practice in the past was concerned with divining or influencing future love prospects, and young women especially had a surprising range of procedures they could adopt when they felt the need. These procedures ranged from the simply romantic, such as placing a piece of wedding cake under pillow to dream of their future love, to complex quasi-witchcraft spells designed to force a reluctant lover to change his allegiance, or fall in love them. The general name for these matters is 'love divination'. Most of these superstitious procedures were carried out by adolescents and young women, but as seen in the sections on singing games and skipping, as soon as girls started playing games they were involved in beginner's level divination and were concerned, however innocently, with courtship and questions of love and marriage.

However disparate they may seem, most adult superstitions rely on one of a limited number of underlying principles, and the beliefs only make sense when those principles are identified. One of the commonest is the notion of *beginnings*. Whatever you are doing, whatever your situation, whatever you want to happen, the beginning is the time for key influence. The beginning of the year is obviously the most important here, but also the beginning of a journey, a life, a marriage, or, of particular importance in love divination, symbolic beginnings, such as when you see the first new moon of the cycle, when you hear the first cuckoo and so on. In love divination there were also other symbolic times, including Valentine's Day, Hallowe'en, Christmas Eve and St Agnes Eve (20/21 January); St Agnes was the patron saint of young girls. Procedures carried out at these times were particularly potent.

Everybody knows that you can ask a flower, particularly a daisy, a question as you pluck its petals. Nowadays the petals are usually asked to reveal whether 'He loves me' or not, but in the nineteenth century there were more choices – 'much, little, devotedly, not at all', for example – or the questions were on the lines of the *Tinker, Tailor* rhyme.

> The bigger girls often used the fern to find out whether the boy they liked loved them – 'yes', 'no' – until the final leaf gave the answer. Sometimes they varied the procedure, using the alphabet instead of the affirmative and negative; the last leaf giving the initial of the boy who loved them. With adequate manipulation, the right letter could finally be got.
>
> *CARMARTHENSHIRE, C.1905*

'Plucking daisies' is associated with love divination as far back as Thomas Killigrew's play *Thomaso* (1663), but it is not clear whether he meant the petal-counting or not. The earliest definite reference to the latter is as late as 1831.

Another simple traditional divinatory procedure was tossing or bouncing a ball:

> It was played at by one girl, who sent the ball against a tree, and drove it back again as often as she could, saying the following rhymes, in order to divine her matrimonial fortune:
>
>> Keppy ball, keppy ball, coban tree
>> Come down the long loanin' and tell to me
>> The form and the features, the speech and degree
>> Of the man that is my true love to be.
>>
>> Keppy ball, keppy ball, coban tree
>> Come down the long loanin' and tell to me
>> How many years old I am to be.
>>
>> One a maiden, two a wife
>> Three a maiden, four a wife, etc.
>
> NORTHUMBERLAND, 1860S

Exactly the same procedure was adopted by girls who made balls out of cowslip blossoms, called 'teesty-tossty', or something similar, throwing them up and catching them, and by others while bouncing a shuttlecock on their battledore (see p. 146).

Tinker, Tailor, easily the best-known traditional rhyme for simple divination, has been recited by children and young people while counting cherry stones or petals on flowers, or bouncing a shuttlecock, for 200 years or so. It was clearly very widely practised in the nineteenth century, the earliest definite reference being provided by Edward Moor in his *Suffolk Words and Phrases* (1823). Moor's description is worth quoting in full, for the context as well as the words of the rhyme itself:

> We have a curious old *sortes fibularae*, if such a phrase may be tolerated, by which the destiny of school-boys is fore-shadowed. On a first appearance with a new coat or waistcoat, a comrade predicts your fate by your buttons, thus: sowja, sailor, tinker, tailor, gentleman, apothecary, plow-boy, thief – beginning at top and touching a button, like dropping a bead, at each epithet. That which applies to the lower button is your promised or

threatened avocation in life. Another reading gives this course – tinker, tailor, sowja, sailor, rich man, poor man, plow-boy, poticarry, thief.

Young ladies gather similar results as to the station and character of their future husbands; by taking hold, in lack of buttons, of a bead of their own or school-fellow's necklace, touching and passing one onward to the end. The tallying of the last bead with the word, denotes that which 'makes or mars them quite'.

The rhyme was obviously already well established, and if Moor was writing about his own boyhood, this would put it back to the 1770s at least. It is interesting to note that there were already two versions of the text, and that they were very close to how we know it today. There are tantalising hints of antecedents, such as the line in William Congreve's *Love for Love* (1695), which lists 'A soldier and a sailor, a tinker and a taylor', but as yet there is no firm evidence of the rhyme's existence much before Moor's time.

Twentieth-century children used the words in various ways, including as a part of a skipping rhyme:

> Red currants, black currants, gooseberry tart
> Tell me the name of my sweetheart
> A B C etc.
> Tinker, tailor, soldier, sailor
> Rich-man, poor-man, beggar-man, thief;
> Silk, satin, muslin, cotton, rag;
> Coach, carriage, wheelbarrow, muck-cart;
> Church, chapel, cathedral;
> Little house, big house, pig sty, barn.

HUNTINGDONSHIRE, 1947

Every line from 'Tinker' onwards was repeated until the skipper made a mistake, and predicted, respectively, the husband's profession or status, the wedding dress, the wedding carriage, the wedding venue and the couple's future home.

Modern girls still have a wide range of ways to divine their future love life, and their repertoire includes some from the past and some seemingly brand new. Younger ones still chant 'A B C D' when skipping, or the equivalents of *Tinker, Tailor*, but their older sisters have a vast range of procedures, which, typically, rely on complex calculations with letters and numbers to arrive at answers. These are often perpetuated, or started, by girls' magazines.

But they also have some simple ones, for example using a ring pull on a drinks can to function in the same way as a flower petal.

The following selections are taken mainly from three collections, made, respectively, by Cathy Gould in Coventry in the 1970s and in 2007; Kate and Steve Roud in Croydon, South London in the 1980s; and Heather Laird in Glasgow in 2005. They are generally taken from interviews with twelve- to fourteen-year-olds. As will be seen, the procedures again include certain recurrent features. Some are simple yes/no procedures on the lines of the traditional 'He loves me, He loves me not' principle, but whereas the younger ones are content with simply revealing the first letter of the love's name, the older girls are keen to test their future prospects with named boys. In nearly every case, the test is carried out by a series of calculations involving numbers and letters of the names of the people involved. Others involve simply listing things in categories – names, places, colours – with a randomising element, usually a number, which selects the old favourites of honeymoon destinations, colours of wedding dresses and so on.

Apple stems

Twist the stem of an apple back and forth while reciting the alphabet. When the stem breaks off the first initial is revealed. Then the stalk is stabbed into the apple's flesh, again while reciting the alphabet, and when the skin breaks the second initial is shown.   COVENTRY, 1998

Bus tickets

Add up all the numbers that appear on your bus ticket. If the number is above 26 add the digits together until a number below 26 is the total. This number then relates to the alphabet and gives you the initial of your future love.

COVENTRY, 1970S

Chewing gum wrappers

Wrigley's chewing gum wrapper has symbols to encourage purchasers to dispose of their chewing gum responsibly, i.e. a mouth – a hand and wrapper – a rubbish bin. Tear into three, with one symbol on each piece, and three people pick a piece each. Mouth = a snog; Hand = you will get picked up by a boyfriend; Bin = you will be dumped.   GLASGOW, 2005

Hand game 1

A draws round B's hand. A asks B for the names of two boys she wants to marry, and writes them on the little finger of the drawing, and adds another name under them. A then asks for two colours, for the wedding dress, writes them on the next finger, and adds one herself. Then two places for honeymoon, two wedding ring stones, and two places to live, respectively, adding her own choice each time. Then two numbers to represent children, adding one herself, in the palm of the hand. A then asks B's ideal age for marriage and uses this number to count round, starting from the bottom number of children, then bottom to top on little finger, and so on across the hand. Either the first reached in each category is 'true' or they are gradually eliminated, and the last in each category is selected. A will usually choose something ludicrous to add in each category, such as an ugly teacher, North Pole, 100 children or a black wedding dress. *CROYDON, 1988*

Hand game 2

A says to B, 'How many letters in the name of the man of your dreams?'; B says, 'Five'; A draws five lines on the back of B's hand; A says, 'Sun or moon?'; B says, 'Sun'; A draws a sun with rays under the five lines (or a moon shape); A says, 'Now close your eyes and make a wish about him.' While B does so, A draws a love-heart around the lines and sun. B must now do this procedure to six other people to make the wish come true. As Kate wrote at the time: 'There are 125 girls in our year, so that means 250 hands, and with everyone rushing around trying to complete their six we soon ran out of hands. I believe that in the beginning you were only allowed to have this done once, on just one hand, but as we ran out of hands, both hands and palms were used.' *CROYDON, 1988*

'Love, Hate, Marry, Adore'

Write two full names one below the other. Any letters which appear in both names are cancelled out. Take each name individually using remaining letters, count Love, Hate, etc. *GLASGOW, 2005*

Love percentages

You write down your full name and someone else's full name and in the middle write LOVES, and then you see how many L's, O's, etc. there are in both names. If a letter does not appear, use 0. Write down the five digits, eg 11003. Add first & second, second & third, etc. = 2103. Repeat = 313. Repeat = 44%.   *LEICESTER, 1980S/GLASGOW, 2005*

Matches

Once we were smokers, e.g. about 14 years of age, we twisted a match against the sandpaper on the matchbox, pressing hard. This randomly caused 'crack' sounds. Each sound stood for a successive letter of the alphabet. Finally the match would ignite and that letter would be the initial of your future love.   *COVENTRY, 1970S*

'Noughts and crosses'

Draw a noughts and crosses grid. Working clockwise from top left, write H in the first corner, and P R S in the other corners (these stand for Happy, Poor, Rich, Sad). Choose five numbers between one and ten (for numbers of children) and write them all in the top-row middle space. In the middle row: five colours for wedding dress in left space; five boys' names in right space. Bottom row: five places to live in middle space. Add together the numbers in top-row middle, and write the total in the middle space. Use this number in your counting round. Ignore the corner spaces for now. Working clockwise, start with the first number in top-row middle, count each number, then each name in middle-row right, and so on, round the grid. When the count finishes on a number or word, cross it out, and continue round, but do not cross out or count the last item in each box. Once you have one item left in each category, use the same number to alternate between H and S, and again between P and R, to find out if you will be happy or sad, rich or poor.   *CROYDON, 1988*

Ring pulls

A ring pull on a soft drinks can is bent backwards and forwards while the child recites the alphabet. When it finally breaks off the letter reached indicates future (or present) love interest. *COVENTRY, 1998/GLASGOW, 2005*

Six boys' names

A table 6 x 6 is drawn: Six boys, six places, six boy body parts, six girl body parts, six actions and six numbers are added into the boxes. Again important to have a good mixture of romantic, mundane, gross, rude, etc. Then the victim chooses a number between 1 and 7. Let's say 3 is chosen. Each third item is crossed out and this is repeated until only one of each category is left. This is what the girls wants to do. Example – Donny Osmond, in the park, his ear and your mouth, kissing 24 times. Again we thought this was hilarious!

COVENTRY, 1970S

Square game

Draw a square. 1) Write the year you were born along the top edge. 2) Write the names of four boys you fancy, one under the other, to the left of the square. 3) Write P M R B under the lower edge (= Poor, Rich, Millionaire, Beggar). 4) Write four places, one under the other, to the right of the square. These are honeymoon destinations or places to live. 5) Think of a number between one and ten and write it in the middle so you do not forget it. 6) Starting with the first boy's name, count round the square, anti-clockwise, counting each name, letter or numeral, until the number you thought of. Cross out the name or letter on which that number falls. 7) Carry on counting round and crossing out. 8) Do not cross out, or count, the last word, letter or numeral on each side. 9) When you only have one item left on each side, it will tell you who you are to marry, whether you will be poor, etc., your honeymoon or place of residence, and how many children you will have.

CROYDON, 1988

Ten boys' names

(1) 10 boys names are chosen – these include choices from the player herself, i.e. film stars, boys she genuinely fancies, etc. However, onlookers must also choose some, for example horrid or embarrassing boys, teachers, etc. (2) The writer lists these names randomly and secretly against the numbers 1–10. (3) Then 10 actions are called out by onlookers in question form, e.g. 'Who would you marry?' To each question the victim (for want of a better word – people say they enjoyed it) has to answer with a number that refers to one of the boys' names but she can't see to whom she is referring each time. Much hilarity follows. Questions can range from 'Who would you go for a romantic meal with?' to 'Who would you "69" with'? (4) When all 10 have been answered the list is read to the victim as questions, e.g. 'Would you marry Mel Gibson?' Each 'yes' is counted up and the boy linked to the final number is the boy the victim is destined to be with. A very funny game.

COVENTRY, 1970S

True Love percentage

To calculate how much people love each other. Write down their names,
e.g.: Kate Roud 4 Russell Evans. Write down 'True Love':

T	L
R	O
U	V
E	E

Count how many times the letters 'T', 'R', 'U', etc. occur in the two names,
and enter them beside the appropriate letter, and add the columns:

T = 1	L = 2
R = 2	O = 1
U = 1	V = 1
E = 3	E = 3
———	———
7	7
———	———

The answer is therefore 77%.   CROYDON, 1988

CHAPTER TWENTY-SIX

The Children's Year

The calendar by which we live our daily lives has changed dramatically over the past 100 years or so, and we have lost a great many special days, along with the particular customs and festive food that went with them. At the same time the main festivals of the modern child's life – Christmas and Hallowe'en, especially – have grown out of all recognition.

The history of days and customs is rarely simple. Local variations, gradual changes of emphasis plus the occasional deliberate reshaping of old traditions, and the creation of new ones, are rarely documented, and the cultural historian is left with many more questions than answers. The problems start with the history of the calendar itself, which is far more complex than most people realise, even without going back to the early days of how it was first devised.

In Britain the bedrock of the way our time is organised is the Christian calendar. The Christian church was by far the prevailing cultural and social force in British society for many centuries, and the way it ordered the year set a pattern that still largely determines the way our year proceeds. The major religious festivals – Shrove, Easter, Whitsun, Christmas – dominated people's lives, and there were many minor festivals and saints' days in between, each with their highly prescribed character and rules. Local events such as fairs, and legal matters such as rent-paying, were all geared to saints' days.

In addition, the physical year, which determines our seasons, and shapes the agricultural year, with its cycles of sowing and harvesting, of lambing and shearing, of picking hops, apples, and so on, also plays a major role.

Laid on top of these is the secular year, decreed by sovereigns and political events. Guy Fawkes Night and Royal Oak Day are festivals created to mark historical events; New Year's Day is the start of the secular, not ecclesiastical, year; the August bank holiday was created in 1871 and was the first official non-religious holiday; and so on.

All of these, and other minor calendars, had a major effect on the way our ancestors' lives were ordered, and the way they perceived time. But the study of folklore is based on the belief that people will always create 'unofficial' ways of perceiving and doing 'official' things, so while these major forces may set the pattern, people then make things their own. We were ordered by King and Parliament to celebrate their miraculous survival when the Gunpowder Plot was foiled, but this does not mean that patriotic thoughts are uppermost in our minds when we set off a rocket in the back garden on 5 November. Nor do most of us care about forty days of fasting when we eat pancakes on Shrove Tuesday. Children, in particular, are highly adept at redefining things to suit their own needs, and all the festivals and events discussed below have been shaped or claimed in some way by them.

One general point needs to be made about calendar customs, because there is widespread misinformation on the subject: none of the calendar customs included here can be shown, or even reasonably thought, to date back to pagan times.

1 JANUARY: NEW YEAR'S DAY

New Year's Day in most parts of Britain formerly involved children calling on friends and relatives to 'wish them a happy New Year' and hoping for something in return. This soliciting of New Year gifts, or *Calenig*, was particularly strong in Wales. D. Parry-Jones, writing of his childhood about 1905, gives many details of the custom, which involved groups of children going door to door, and points out the importance of personal knowledge and contact within traditional communities:

> As soon as it was light enough for them to see their way, off the children would go, each family group keeping to itself, for the arrangement had worthwhile advantages – a motley crowd would be treated as a crowd. A family group, on the other hand, would have more personal treatment. Immediately the short traditional formula had been shouted at the door: *Blwyddyn newydd dda I' chwi a phawh sydd yn y ty* (a happy New Year to you and all that are in the house) – or the customary rhyme recited, some member of the family would be sent to the door to find out who they were. If they were reported to be Ann's children, something extra would have to

be given, for the sake of Ann and old times. She may at one time have been maid there.

There was a special toffee, made of butter, flour and treacle, made for the occasion, and another special item was a decorated apple or orange called *rhodd calenig*. The same author also comments that the custom of New Year visiting was still kept up by many Welsh children in the mid 1960s.

Writing about Guernsey in 1975, Marie de Garis commented:

> The habit of children going around soliciting gifts on *le jour dé l'an* only died out in the west of the island after the Second World War. Elsewhere, it had been abandoned a long time before. The children always carried baskets in which to put any commodities given and a bag made of striped ticking, in which to place coins handed out.

Another Welsh New Year custom, still active in the mid 1960s, involved children going round with 'New Year Water', freshly drawn from well or spring, with which they sprinkled the hands and faces of people they met, provided, of course, that the privilege was paid for. This is presumably allied to the belief, found in various parts of Britain, that the first water drawn in the New Year was lucky and, like May Dew, particularly good for the complexion. It was called the Flower of the Well.

First-footing is one of the most well known of Scottish calendar customs, but in the past there were similar beliefs all over Britain and Ireland, including England. The idea that the first events of the year must be lucky is one of the fundamental principles underlying superstitious belief, and is more or less universal. What changes from place to place, and over time, is what attributes are considered lucky or unlucky. The idea that the first-footer should be dark-haired is a relatively recent intro-duction. Once nobody would have accepted anyone who was, say, disabled or ill-favoured. The one thing that almost all first-footing traditions agree on is that the person must be male – to have a female first-footer would be disastrous.

> Much excitement and interest attached to the appearance and character of the first visitor to cross the threshold after the advent of the New Year as upon him the happiness and prosperity of the households was supposed to depend for the ensuing twelve months. Maidens of the house gener-ally arranged beforehand that some favoured and 'well-fawiet' youth of

their acquaintance should be their first visitor. Several physical types were deemed unlucky, for example, those who were flat-soled 'first-foot' or one whose character was conspicuously sanctimonious.

SCOTTISH REVIEW, 1905

Boys were often 'hired' to visit certain houses to 'first-foot' them, especially where there was no male in the household.

FEBRUARY, MARCH: SHROVE TUESDAY

Unless you live in one of those places where a special Shrove Tuesday custom still takes place, or come from a strict, old-fashioned Christian family, Shrove Tuesday is unlikely to mean much more than pancakes for tea, but in the past it was one of the busiest festival days of the year.

It owes its origin to the ecclesiastical year: the celebration of Christ's crucifixion on Good Friday was preceded by Lent – forty days of fasting and penance, during which there were strict rules about what could be done and what could be eaten. Shrove Tuesday, or Fastern's Eve as it was called in Scotland, was the last day before Lent, so it became a day of fun and feasting, before the lean period began. Foods that were forbidden during Lent had to be consumed, and since Shrove Tuesday occurred in early spring, boisterous outdoor activities such as football, throwing at cocks, and cock-fighting were extremely popular, especially with young people. Because Easter is a movable feast, Shrove Tuesday can fall on any date between 3 February and 10 March.

This religious history explains the background to the day, but the picture is complicated by the fact that because Protestant Churches placed a lot less emphasis on Lent than the Roman Catholic Church did, it withered away as a religious festival faster in countries such as England than it did in, for example, Ireland. Nevertheless, remarkably similar descriptions of the activities of the day occur in sources from all over Britain and Ireland. The traditional customs and sports had taken root and continued long after Lent had ceased to be important.

In England and Scotland especially, the day was particularly important to apprentices, who were an identifiable and often volatile group in urban society for centuries, and also to schoolchildren. Both groups believed that they should have a half-holiday on the day, and they often took direct action to achieve it. Throughout the nineteenth and early twentieth centuries, for example, schoolchildren on the Isle of Man would lock their teacher out of the school and chant:

> Holly, holly, holly pancake day
> If you don't give us holly we'll all run away.

'Holly' is, of course, short for 'holiday'.

One of the earliest mentions of football in Britain demonstrates its connection both with young people and with Shrovetide. William Fitz Stephen, writing about London in around 1180, observed:

> After dinner all the youth of the city goes out into the fields to a much-frequented game of ball. The scholars of each school have their own ball and almost all the workers of each trade have theirs also in their hands. Elder men and fathers and rich citizens come on horse-back to watch the contents of their juniors, and after their fashion are young again.

This is not modern football, but a much rougher game, more akin to rugby but without many rules, and as many as wanted joined in on each side. Mass games like these were played in the streets of towns, and in rural fields, up and down the country till well into the nineteenth century, and still survive in a few places, such as Alnwick in Northumberland and Atherstone in Warwickshire.

For some unknown reason, cockerels were closely associated with Shrove Tuesday, and there was a widespread traditional game in which a bird was tethered to the spot by one leg and people paid to throw heavy sticks at it. Whoever killed it kept the bird.

But another close connection was with cock-fighting, in which specially bred fighting birds were pitted against each other. As odd as it may seem to modern sensibilities, for centuries cock-fights were particularly associated with schools, and at many schools the pupils were required to pay the schoolmaster a fee (the so-called 'cock-penny') so that he would supply game-cocks for the fights on Shrove Tuesday.

For smaller children, the high spot of the day was 'going shroving', which meant going from house to house singing a ditty and hoping for food, drink or money. The 'respectable' end of the custom is usually remembered fondly, as here by Margaret Lale:

> When I was quite a small child all the school children were let out early at dinnertime on Shrove Tuesday to go shroving. First to 'Veniscombe' where

the Misses Hargrove lived, then to the Shop, where Mr John Wheeler the
baker lived, on to the Pointer Inn and finally to the Vicarage. We sang a
little ditty which went

> Shroven, shroven, here we come a-shroven
> A piece of bread, a piece of cheese, a piece of your fat bacon
> The roads are very dirty, my boots are very clean
> I've got a little pocket to put a penny in.

We were rewarded with money (coppers) and boiled sweets which were
thrown and we scrambled for them when we had to watch out we didn't
get our fingers trodden on.   NEWCHURCH, ISLE OF WIGHT, C.1920

But in some places the requests were backed up by threats, and it was
traditional for the shrovers to carry stones or pieces of broken crockery.
Anyone who refused to give, or who the gang did not like for some reason,
got their front door pelted.

As with all these 'rough' customs, the children (and many adults)
genuinely believed that such behaviour was allowed on the day on the
grounds that it was 'immemorial custom' and the law could not stop them.

Other traditions included playing the singing game of *Thread the Needle*
(see p. 259), and, in Scarborough in Yorkshire, public skipping (see p. 177)

Today, just about the only aspect of Shrove Tuesday that children are
aware of is the tossing and eating of pancakes. The traditional connection between Shrove Tuesday and pancakes goes back to the time when
foodstuffs needed to be used up before Lent. A custom takes place at
Westminster School in London, for example, in which boys scramble for
a piece of a specially made pancake, which is thrown into their midst by
the school cook. This has been the annual custom since at least the 1750s.
Pancake races came along rather later: they were invented just before or
after the Second World War, at Olney in Buckinghamshire.

14 FEBRUARY: VALENTINE'S DAY

The festival of St Valentine looms so large in the modern festival year, at
least in the media, that it is difficult to appreciate that its present mani-
festation is little more than fifty years old. A great deal of inaccurate
information about Valentine's Day was peddled by both Victorian
antiquarians and twentieth-century romantics, and a spurious early
history was invented. They were desperate to give the festival ancient

pagan roots, and sought to show it as a direct survival of the Roman festival Lupercalia, which occurs on roughly the same date, and to portray St Valentine as a fertility figure. In reality, not only did the Lupercalia bear no relation to the later festival, but there is nothing in the legends of any of the possible St Valentines to link him with love, courtship and the like. The simple fact is that this saint's day just happened to fall on 14 February, which was regarded in medieval times as the first day of spring. Geoffrey Chaucer, John Gower and other writers between 1370 and 1400 certainly believed this, and they introduced the notion that this was the day the birds chose their mates.

Tellingly, these writers did not make any mention of human love; John Lydgate's poem of 1440, *A Valentine to Her that Excelleth All*, however, did. From that time on, regular references to valentine customs can be found, including the giving of gifts to loved ones, the choosing of valentines by lot, and other notions such as the belief that the first eligible person you see on Valentine's Day will be your lover. The choosing of a valentine by placing names in a hat was a widespread party game, and diarists such as Samuel Pepys give us lively accounts of how mock-seriously it was all taken in the seventeenth century.

By the early nineteenth century commercially produced cards were available, and the day took on something of the aura it has today, but by the end of the century it was dying out, in large part because of the fashion for spoof anti-valentine cards and cruel joke presents. *The Graphic* (17 February 1894) commented:

> St Valentine's day, which fell on a Wednesday this year, attracts very little attention in England, but across the Atlantic the Saint is still honoured.

The festival never quite died out in Britain, but it was not until after the Second World War that it began to revive, under the influence of the USA, and the commercial card manufacturers.

For most of its history the day has been generally an adult affair, although there was often a romantic conceit of including children's names in the family fun of choosing valentines by lot. But children were far more interested in what they could get out of the day. Several places made special traditional cakes, and there was a lively house-visiting custom, known all over the country, but particularly well reported in East Anglia, by which children would go from door to door around their neighbourhood, singing a song or reciting a rhyme, and expecting, as in all such visiting customs, food, drink or money in return.

Parson Woodforde, who lived in Weston Longeville, Norfolk, is one of the first people to mention the custom, and he recorded in his diary almost every year from 1777 to 1802 that he gave a penny to every village child who called at his house on the day and said, 'Good morrow, Valentine.'

Children did not entirely ignore the 'love' aspect of the day, and older girls, especially, knew that the Eve was one of the key nights in the year for divination.

George Swinford, writing about his childhood in Filkins, on the Oxfordshire–Gloucestershire border in the 1890s, remembered the girls of the village taking direct action:

> I remember girls forming a ring and surrounding a boy if they could. Then they would say this verse:
>
> > Good morning, Valentine
> > I'll be yours if you'll be mine
> > If no apples you can find
> > Please to give us a bacon chine.
>
> Then the girls would close in and try to kiss him.

These rhyming and visiting customs had not entirely died out when the Opies were doing their research in the 1950s, but those children were probably the last generation to keep the old custom of the day alive.

MARCH/APRIL: MOTHERING SUNDAY/MOTHER'S DAY

Mothering Sunday is the fourth Sunday in Lent, or Mid-Lent Sunday, which means that it can fall anywhere between 1 March and 4 April, depending on where Easter falls in the year. In its original form, Mothering Sunday was not really about children, but about young working people. When first mentioned, in the mid seventeenth century, it was the traditional day that young people working away from home, in service, as apprentices or as live-in farm-workers, would try to get home to visit their families. The first reference is in the diary of Richard Symonds for 1644:

Every Sunday is a great day at Worcester, when all the children and grandchildren meet at the head chief of the family and have a feast. They call it
Mothering-day.

And soon afterwards, Robert Herrick included these lines in his poem
Hesperides (1648):

> I'll to thee a simnell bring
> Gainst thou go'st a mothering.

There are many later references to the day and this custom, but it seems
that the day was never universally observed, because for every two or three
references that mention it there is one that makes it clear that it was
unknown, or only partially understood. By the early twentieth century it
is clear that it was on its way to being abandoned.

But then in 1916 a Mr J. A. Whitehead inaugurated a movement to found
a 'Mother's Day', and on 2 August 1917 *The Times* reported that the Queen
had given it her support. The day was held in early August, and the same
newspaper gave it coverage each year until about 1920. In 1928 *The Times*
reported on a meeting at which Mrs Stanley Baldwin proposed to inau-
gurate a 'Mother's Day'. This, however, seems to have failed to get off the
ground. Meanwhile, in Philadelphia in 1907, a schoolteacher named Miss
Anna Jarvis proposed an annual 'Mother's Day'. This was agreed by Congress
in 1913, and it was designated to take place on the second Sunday in May.

The situation in Britain changed rapidly after the Second World War.
Presumably because of the presence of American troops, the British public
suddenly decided they wanted a Mother's Day after all, but being tradi-
tionalists opted for the old movable Mothering Sunday date instead of a
fixed one on the US pattern. The new Mother's Day took hold quite quickly,
primarily because both the church and commercial interests saw it as a
grand opportunity, and under their twin guidance it has grown in importance ever since. From the 1950s onwards, local churches began special
services, with features such as giving out little posies for children to give
to their mothers, while schools and nurseries up and down the land encouraged children to make Mother's Day cards. All of this is official practice
and out of the control of the children themselves, but what happens within
individual families is of more interest.

One recurrent theme is that the mother gets breakfast in bed and other
members of the family take on the chores she would normally carry out,
although as it is a Sunday their contribution is often more token than

truly effective. Adults are also encouraged to remember their mothers on the day, by sending cards, flowers or chocolates in advance, or at least by phoning for a chat.

17 MARCH: ST PATRICK'S DAY

It is no surprise that it is generally the Irish, or those of Irish descent, who take note of St Patrick's Day, and their celebrations are as to be expected on a day that is both a national and a religious holiday. There do not seem to have been any customs specifically carried out by children on the day, although, as Kevin Danaher describes in detail in *The Year in Ireland* (1972), children and others wore emblems. In the nineteenth and early twentieth centuries, the most favoured item was a St Patrick's Cross, usually home-made. Girls' crosses were formed by placing two pieces of stiff cardboard across each other, wrapped in silk or ribbon of various colours, with a green rosette in the centre. The boys' crosses were more complex. One type was described in 1895 as:

> A small sheet of white paper, about three inches square, on which is inscribed a circle which is divided by elliptical lines or radii, and the spaces thus formed are filled in with different hues, thus forming a circle of many coloured compartments.

Both boys and girls proudly wore these on their breasts or shoulders, but St Patrick's Crosses gradually died out as the twentieth century progressed. Today Irish children still wear badges, but these are usually a harp, sham-rock, or green ribbon or rosette.

Where Catholic and Protestant lived side by side, St Patrick's Day could be one of those days when local tensions surfaced, even in the children's sphere. In the booklet entitled *Skin Street Scallywags* (1991), Gordon Mills recalled his childhood in Edinburgh in the 1920s. As a newcomer to the city, he was one day accosted in the street by two boys who demanded of him, 'Scotch or Irish?' 'Scotch,' he replied, and was immediately assailed by the boys with strange weapons of balled-up paper on a long string. He ran off, made himself a weapon of the same design and joined in the fights throughout the day, although he soon discovered that some boys had stones inside the paper. He had no idea what was going on.

In a booklet of stories from the St Ann's Reminiscence Group (1990),

Norman Forsyth explains it all: St Patrick's Day was the one day of the year when it mattered whether you were Protestant or Catholic:

> We kids, for the rest of the year, were one big happy family, bound together no doubt by the poverty of our times. But come the 17th March, we boys were expected to stand up and be counted and join ranks of either Scotch or Irish. This meant we confronted each other to do 'battle' and inflict as much fear and humiliation as we could. Sometimes if you were on your own, and confronted by three or four lads and were not known to each other – when asked if you were 'Scotch or Irish?' you hurriedly made a guess, and woe betide if you made the wrong one – you got 'clattered'.

MARCH/APRIL: GOOD FRIDAY GARDENS

An otherwise unremarked children's custom was reported in *The Times* in April 1944:

> The day before Good Friday I saw three young children in the now railing-less enclosure of Brook Green, apparently stripping small branches from the shrubs and green shoots. What I saw on the bare earth were three small gardens, about 18in. square. Neatly scored out in lines, each was planted with 12 tiny shoots of privet and protected by branches.

This was clearly not simply a one-off affair, as another reader contributed his own memory of the subject, in Camberwell, more than forty years previously:

> It was the regular custom on the day before Good Friday for the children to make such little gardens, which they called 'grottoes', on the pavement. They used to tear handfuls of grass out of the front gardens, with which they set out a little square, inside which they put small stones, gravel, etc. Some were quite elaborately laid out with twigs of privet and empty cockle shells. Then the children stood alongside and asked passers-by for 'a penny for the grotter'.

One of the reasons this custom is under-reported is that it gets over-shadowed by the much better known custom of building shell grottoes on the pavement in July and August (see p. 496). The construction of these Easter gardens is clearly different, although the picture is further complicated by the fact that the last summer grottoes reported in Mitcham in the 1960s were flat affairs of mud flowers and twigs, not unlike 'gardens'.

In the absence of other examples, it is impossible to say anything further of these gardens, but another somewhat mysterious custom, called 'Tommy on the Tub's Grave', may be of relevance:

> Last evening (23 May 1894) I was much interested, in passing through Bloomsbury Square, by some children coming up to me with hand extended, and saying, 'Please to remember Tommy on the tub's grave.' I found that they had got, set out on the pavement a little arrangement like a cemetery, made principally of sand. It was enclosed with sand walls, and there were various hieroglyphics arranged in sand inside, and having flowers (cowslips, I think) laid on them. In the centre was a large bunch of flowers on a bigger heap, and this was pointed out to me as the 'tub's grave'.

Children in the area claimed it was an annual event, and another contributor stated that he had often seen them in the Lincoln's Inn area. Again, there is no more information about this custom, nor any idea who 'Tommy on the tub' might have been.

MARCH/APRIL: EASTER

Considering the importance of Easter in the religious sphere, there is a distinct paucity of traditional customs attached to the period, especially in the southern half of England, where the season is hardly mentioned in folklore books at all, except in terms of superstitions to do with Good Friday. But in the counties of Lancashire, Cheshire, Yorkshire, Cumbria, Northumberland and Co. Durham, and in Scotland, Northern Ireland and the Isle of Man, there was a much wider variety of customs, usually involving eggs, at least nominally.

Eggs were collected, decorated, thrown, rolled and eaten in abundance, and any of these customs were likely to be called pace- or peace-egging, after *Pasch*, the Latin word for Easter. The word pace-egg was already in use by 1579, but there is no record of any egg-decorating or house-visiting customs until 1778.

The commonest form of the custom took place within the family, as it was traditional for children to be given hard-boiled eggs, either already coloured or which they then helped to decorate, often using dyes made from plants and other methods handed on from generation to generation. These eggs were usually played with before being eaten, and the most popular game was egg-rolling, in which the eggs were literally rolled down-hill, or bowled at each other, to see whose egg lasted the longest before being cracked or broken.

> Jarping hard-boiled pace eggs (sometimes the painted ones, but often we didn't want to sacrifice our laboriously decorated works of art) on Easter Monday; it was like conkers – you jarped one end of your pace egg against the end of someone else's and the winner was the egg that hadn't cracked, or still had one end intact. My dad cheated one year using a realistic-looking ceramic egg. *GATESHEAD, 1960S*

Most of the egg-rolling customs were low-key family or local affairs, but in some places they developed into major events:

> On Easter Monday the singular custom of rolling oranges and dyed eggs down the slopes of Avenham Park, Preston, Lancashire, was adhered to by all the youngsters of the neighbourhood. The grounds, comprising upwards of twenty-two acres, were covered by a dense multitude of people who come annually from places in the vicinity to witness or take part in this unique festivity. When the eggs and oranges are eaten, dancing and all kind of games are kept up until darkness compels a cessation of the festivity. *LANCASHIRE, 1880*

Egg-rolling and jarping still take place in many families.

Pace-egging was also the name of a type of mummers' play found exclusively in the Lancashire, Yorkshire and Cumbria region, but performed at Easter rather than over the more usual Christmas period. The vast majority of mumming plays elsewhere were performed by adults, or at least by youths, but in the pace-egg areas there was a strong tradition of children's teams. Pace-egg plays also included characters not usually found elsewhere, such as Lord Nelson, Jovial Jack Tar, Toss Pot, Bessie Brown Bags and Molly Masket, but these often simply appear in the introductory song and take little part in the core action of the play, in which two combatants fight, one is wounded or killed, but is then revived by a doctor.

In Cumbria the teams were usually called the 'Jolly Boys', and correspondence in the *Cumberland and Westmorland Herald* on 8 March 1952 included a number of ex-participants' memories, giving details of how they made their costumes, blackened their faces with burnt cork and went from house to house performing their play:

A typical scene for this paschal drama was the kitchen of a farm house with the family gathered round the fireside for the night. Suddenly the door sneck would be lifted. There followed the sound of the oncoming pace-eggers . . . rendering the opening verse of the pace-egging song which was completed as they marched round the supper table:

> Here come two or three jolly boys, all in one mind
> We've come a pace-egging, I hope you'll prove kind
> I hope you'll prove kind with your eggs and strong beer
> And we'll come no more near you until the next year.

A curious custom recorded in Kendal in 1875, which does not seem to have a parallel elsewhere, was submitted to *Notes & Queries*:

The little boys and girls in this town have a curious custom they go through on the eve of Good Friday . . . Some half a dozen or so boys and girls, usually companions, obtain an old tin can, tie a string to it, and one of the lads starts off at a good run, trailing the can after him, whilst his companions follow, striking the can with stocks, at the same time singing the following peculiar refrain:

> Trot hearin, trot horn
> Good Friday to morn,

which they repeat until the poor old tin can has not a jingle left in it.

MARCH/APRIL: SPANISH WATER

A children's custom that was surprisingly popular in Derbyshire and elsewhere in the English Midlands involved making a drink on a particular day:

Elecampane on Easter Monday: During a recent visit to the little village of Castleton, Derbyshire, I noticed every child without exception had a bottle of this mixture – the younger ones having one tied around their necks – all sucking away at this curious compound of Spanish juice [liquorice] sugar and water, with great assiduity. I was informed by a very old man that this custom had always obtained at Castleton on Easter Monday as long as he could remember.

1870

The day and the custom went by various names – Spanish Sunday, Sugar-cupping Day, Sugar-and-water Day, Rinsing Day, Shakking Monday – and took place on a variety of special days, including Ascension Day and Palm Sunday, but most often Easter Sunday or Easter Monday.

The ritual of making the drink was deemed important, and often involved a trip to a particular well or spring that had a reputation for good water. Sometimes the children believed they had to do something special, such as walking three times round the well, or they visited at an earlier time and dropped new pins into the water, to ensure a plentiful supply on the day.

Folklorist Christina Hole included a note on the custom in her *Dictionary of British Folk Customs* (1976), which shows the local popularity of the tradition, although it is not clear which village she is referring to:

An informant from Stonesfield (Oxon) said that when she was a child, about 1905, she went to the Lady Well at Wilcote to fill her Palm Sunday bottle, and found about a hundred children gathered there.

An alternative to liquorice was peppermint:

Easter Monday is called 'Shakking Monday'. At Bradwell, children fill glass bottles with spring water and put therein pieces of peppermint cakes of various colours, but usually pink. These peppermint cakes are quite different from ordinary peppermint lozenges; they are big things, two or three inches wide and are square or oblong in shape. The children break them up, put broken pieces into the bottles, shake the mixture and drink it; the sweetened water lasts for several days.

There is no indication that this was a particularly old custom, and it does not seem to have been noticed before the second half of the nineteenth century.

1 APRIL: APRIL FOOL

April Fool's Day seems to have been celebrated in a similar way in every part of Britain and Ireland. It was previously called 'All Fools' Day', in direct parody of the existing church festivals of All Souls' Day and All Saints' Day, but it also has many local names.

The origins of the day are unknown. The earliest known reference is in the manuscript *Remaines of Gentilisme and Judaisme*, compiled by antiquarian John Aubrey about 1686. Commenting on the mention of the Roman Festival of Fools in Ovid's *Fasti*, Aubrey states, 'Fooles holy day – we observe it on ye first of April', and then adds a note, 'and so it is kept in Germany everywhere'. But the absence of any mention in earlier plays, poems and diaries is suspicious, and it seems likely that it was introduced to Britain from Germany or France not long before Aubrey noted its existence.

As with several other children's customs, the rule was, and is, that the fooling had to stop at twelve noon, and anyone who tried it beyond that time could be mocked:

> April Noddy's past and gone
>   You're a fool for thinking on
> Up a ladder, down a tree
>   You're a bigger fool than me.
>
> LANCASHIRE, 1930S

There were several names for the person fooled – 'Noddy', for example. A recurrent theme in earlier days was that they were a 'cuckoo', or 'gowk' in Scotland, where the day was often called Huntigowk Day.

The tricks played on people on the day have been many and various, and children seem to get great pleasure out of even the simplest ones. Telling someone that their shoelace is undone is as old as shoelaces – previously people were told their buckles were undone. But the classic trick of the day, carried out mostly by adults on children or young people, was to send the victim to ask for something, and for the person then being asked (who was in on the joke) to send the victim to the next person and so on.

The demise of April Fool's Day in the children's calendar has been predicted many times over the last fifty years or more, but it still hangs on. That said, its future now seems to lie with the media, especially newspapers, who delight in publishing spoof stories on the day.

APRIL: THE OXFORD AND CAMBRIDGE BOAT RACE

The Oxford and Cambridge Boat Race can hardly be called a children's calendar custom, but the odd thing is that until fairly recently children up and down the country, most of whom would never have any connection with any university, let alone Oxbridge, chose their sides and vehemently defended the honour of their team:

Between the wars, Boat Race Day was a great occasion and everyone wore favours. You could buy them in all the shops in Eastbourne, and elsewhere – crossed oars with a light or dark blue bow, pale blue or dark blue fluffy monkeys, or rosettes you made yourself. We all had our favourite teams.

It seemed that everyone in the land knew that Cambridge was light blue and Oxford dark blue. Some knew even more, as revealed by a letter in the *Sunday Express* on 9 April 1972:

Casting my mind back to pre-war days, I vividly remembered that for weeks before the big day schoolboys would take sides and make supporters of the opposing boat's crew their arch-enemies (until the race was over). We knew the name of the cox and all his crew, and sported our dark or light blue rosettes with pride ... My twin daughters don't even know what the Boat Race is.

The race was founded in 1829, and the teams adopted their present colours in 1836.

1 MAY: MAY DAY GARLANDS

One of the most picturesque of children's customs is the May garlanding tradition that was widely practised across much of England throughout the nineteenth century and into the twentieth. In its simplest form, children made garlands of spring flowers and went round their neighbourhood showing everyone their handiwork and hoping for a contribution in return. As with all these visiting customs, a song or rhyme, sometimes a dance, and sometimes characters, in costume, completed the picture.

Within the broad category of May garlands there were many differences – in the construction of the garland, the 'shape' of the custom, the behaviour of the children and so on. May Day was one of the main festivals 'taken in hand' by reformers during the Victorian and Edwardian period, cleaned up, and remodelled to fit into a new notion of 'Merrie England'. One direct result of this interference was the separation of what folklorists have termed 'independent' and 'organised' garlanding traditions. In the 'independent' style, children made their own garlands (albeit usually with assistance from parents) and went round on their own. With 'organised' traditions the whole affair was taken over by worthies of the local church or school. One large garland was made and carried around, the other children attended in procession, and there was usually a tea or other organised event at the end. The organisers frequently took the opportunity to introduce new songs and to formalise the interaction between the 'characters' in the party.

It is not surprising that these community leaders wanted to take control of the custom. As with most customs, many of the children who kept it up were 'working class', their behaviour relatively 'rough and ready', and their efforts did not meet the standards expected by their social betters. And when the custom was in full swing, it could be a real nuisance to householders:

> Hitherto the advent of May Day has been anything but a happy one with the principal inhabitants here, owing to the custom of innumerable children in straggling groups keeping up an incessant knocking at one's door for the usual dole. OXFORDSHIRE, 1882

'Organisation' did not happen everywhere and took place at different times in different locations, so the result was very patchy. Some places were not affected; in others it lapsed after a short while, leaving the custom to disappear, return to its old ways or, as sometimes happened, become a hybrid. In the latter case there might be one main garland, but organised largely by the children themselves. Some independent garlanding continued in many places right up to the Second World War, as in the following letter from the Rectory, Westcott Barton, Oxfordshire, in 1931, published in *The Times*:

> Last year, and again this year groups of little girls have visited me on May Day, bringing with them garlands of wild and cottage garden flowers either in the form of hoops or sprays arranged in a very comely fashion, which is probably also traditional. The little girls chant a little song, the same essentially, but with variations:

> > Maypole, maypole, trip, trip, trot
> > See what a maypole I have got
> > Gentlemen and ladies, I wish you all good day
> > I come to show my garland
> > Because it is May Day
> > Because it is May Day
> > I've come to show my garland
> > Because it is May Day.

I have a little garden
I dig it well, I rake it well
I weed it well, and throw the weeds away
Oh I have a garden of my own
And on the summer day
I rake it well, I dig it well
And throw the weeds away.

The little girls told me that their mothers had taught them the song, and their grandmothers had instructed their mothers.

A very different impression is given by a description from Brighton, Sussex, in 1910:

Children, in bands of five, were to be met in almost every street, bedecked not only with brightly coloured paper garlands, but with paper flowers liberally attached to every part of their outer garments. Halting at intervals, and four solemnly walking round and round their companion stationary in the centre, they sang a curious compound of old melodies and new, passing abruptly from a sweet air dealing with that which is 'underneath the trees' or 'underneath the ground' to

John Brown's body's on a sour apple tree
As we go marching round,

and then to what sounded very much like a rhymed invocation. The version seemed common to all the quaintly dressed little bands.

Garlands varied considerably in size and shape. The larger ones were usually constructed on a bell-shaped wickerwork frame, but others were constructed of two hoops at right angles to each other. Both types were usually carried on a pole between two people, but there were also smaller hand-held ones, and some that were little more than decorated sticks. Some of the larger ones had a doll suspended in the middle.

Many of them had a 'May Queen' with attendants. In Flora Thompson's famous description in *Lark Rise* (1939), her remembrances of her Northamptonshire village in the 1880s, the entourage consisted of: 'Boy with flag', 'Girl with money box', 'The garland carried by two bearers', 'King and Queen', 'Two maids of honour', 'Lord and Lady', 'Two maids of honour', 'Footman and footman's lady', 'Rank and file walking in twos', 'Girl known as "Mother"', and 'Boy called "Ragman"'.

May garland customs are known to have existed from the 1790s onwards, but they did not take place all over the country. In England they were found across the South, South-east and Midlands, and the southern coast of the West Country, but there seem to have been none in the northern counties, and few in East Anglia. Wales and Ireland certainly had many traditions that centred on bringing flowers and greenery into the village, setting up boughs and decorating buildings, but no children's garlanding as such. In Ireland the dominant custom was the setting up of the May Bush, but, according to Kevin Danaher's *The Year in Ireland* (1972), this sometimes involved something on the lines of the English garland tradition:

> In more recent times the May bush has been almost entirely a matter for the children, who might request adult help where the task was too great for their strength or skill . . . and who, in places, went in a group around the village or the townland carrying the bush and asking for contributions of material to decorate it, or sweets and other goodies, or money with which to buy these.

And in Northern Ireland the May Queen had all the features of the one at Lark Rise except for a large garland. Florence McDowell's delightful description from Antrim in 1905 is included in her *Roses and Rainbows* (1972). Their Queen, dressed in a lace curtain and transported in a 'go-chair camouflaged with a patchwork quilt', was crowned with Mayflowers (kingcups) and carried a large bouquet. Her entourage had also done their best to look the part, and carried ash plants, hawthorn blossoms and Mayflowers.

Garlands were the most widespread of the children's May Day customs in England, but there were other variations on the house-visiting theme. The doll in the middle of the garland has already been mentioned, and in some areas this became the main feature:

> I cannot claim that we danced round the Maypole in those days, but we certainly looked forward each year to the 'May Boxes', brought round on May morning by groups of little girls. Large wooden or cardboard boxes were filled with spring flowers, and in the centre lay a doll dressed as the May Queen.   *LEICESTERSHIRE, 1920S*

1 MAY: MAYPOLES

The adult custom of setting up a maypole is well known and well documented, but there was also a spin-off tradition, undertaken by children, of carrying a portable maypole around the village or neighbourhood. In this sense it was very similar to the May garlands (see above), but with the maypole taking the central role. In Burnley in 1922:

> One of the party acts as May Queen and sits on a stool, holding the pole, while the others dance round her. As far as I can make out, what they sing is something like this:
>
>> Round and round the maypole
>> Merrily we go
>> Hippy, chippy, cherry
>> Singing as we go
>> All the happy past days
>> Round the village green
>> Courting in the sunshine
>> Hurrah, hurrah, for our May Queen.

> Another song they sing goes something like this:
>
>> I'm the Queen, the merry merry Queen
>> We've come to show our flowers
>> Hail, oh hail! the merry merry Queen
>> We've come to show our flowers
>> Hail, oh hail, to our beautiful Queen.

Robert Roberts described the girls' maypole custom at Salford before the First World War, in his *Ragged Schooling* (1976):

> Nearly every street of any length had its own gay totem, the event being organised almost invariably by the daughters of labourers, artisan's children being forbidden by parents to go 'begging'.

A similar picture is painted by a journalist on the *Evening Standard* (1 May 1928), who saw, on a patch of waste ground in Bermondsey, London:

> A dozen small children were moving solemnly in a circle, each grasping in a grubby hand a piece of string about four foot long, the other end of

which was tied to the top of a broomstick, the latter embedded a few inches in the earth. The broomstick was crowned with a piece of faded ribbon.

1 MAY: MAY DAY BEARS

A May Day custom that seems to have been unique to the Burnley area of Lancashire was for boys to dress up as dancing bears and to go from house to house doing their performance and asking for money. One boy would get a sack, cut holes for eyes and mouth, and put it over his head and shoulders to become the bear. He would be led on a string by his leader, who also carried a pole. As the leader chanted words like 'Addy om bombay' or 'Aye-dee aye, dee om pom pey', and gestured with the pole, the bear danced and did acrobatic tricks.

The whole thing was in imitation of real dancing bears, even down to the nonsense recited by the leader, which was an approximation of what the real bear-leaders used to say. Dancing bears were a fairly regular sight in villages around Britain, even as late as the 1920s, usually brought over from Eastern Europe.

It is often stated that the boys started the bear custom to give themselves something in imitation of the girls' visiting maypole custom. This is quite possible, as the May Day bear is only documented from about the First World War to the 1940s.

1 MAY: MAY GOSLINGS

According to a contributor to the *Gentleman's Magazine* (1791):

> A May gosling on the 1st of May is made with as much eagerness in the north of England, as an April noddy (noodle), or fool, on the first of April.

There seems to be no logical reason why the North of England needs a second 'Fool's Day', but the Opies (in *The Lore and Language of Schoolchildren* (1959)) found the May gosling tradition still current in the 1950s in Cumbria, north Yorkshire and elsewhere, and subsequent research has found it also existed in Lincolnshire, which is where the *Gentleman's Magazine* correspondent was writing from. There seems to be no difference between the tricks played in April and May, and it is unlikely that the latter is now remembered anywhere.

13 MAY: MAY GARLANDS, ABBOTSBURY

At Abbotsbury in Dorset they have one of the last surviving May garland customs in the country, which takes place on 13 May every year. That date may seem unusual, but it is probably simply that the day is 'old May Day', caused by the change of the calendar in 1752, when eleven days were skipped to bring the country in line with the internationally accepted Gregorian calendar. The garland is a large bell-shaped framework completely covered in flowers and carried on a pole by two people. It is taken from door to door round the whole village and shown to the inhabitants, who usually donate to the collection in appreciation.

The earliest documentary evidence for the custom occurs in John Hutchins's *History of Dorset* (1867), which shows that on 'Garland Day' each of the local fishing families made a garland of flowers and paraded them round the village in the morning. There was also a church service, and in the afternoon there was merrymaking on the beach and some of the garlands were thrown into the sea from the fishing boats. As the twentieth century progressed, the local fishing industry declined, and other families became involved in the garland custom. The school also became a major force in keeping the custom alive, and children were given the afternoon off to parade the garlands. After the Second World War, other social changes threatened to wipe out the garlanding. A decline in the number of children in the village meant that the local school was closed in 1981, and the custom became one of adults making the garlands during the day, and children taking them round in the evening after school.

Many of the other villages in the area had May garland customs, but Abbotsbury is unique in continuing the tradition.

24 MAY: EMPIRE DAY

One of the high points of the school year in the first half of the twentieth century was Empire Day, which, being official, was organised for the children rather than by them. Nevertheless, many children enjoyed the colour and spectacle of the celebrations, and when they reached adulthood looked back on the day with great fondness:

> I was eight years old when I was chosen to be Britannia. I wore a white tunic and a golden helmet, and carried a trident and a Union Jack shield.

I had to say 'I am Mother Britannia, my birthday is today, boys and girls remember the 24th May.'   *YORKSHIRE, 1930S*

A day to celebrate the achievements of the British Empire was first organised in Canada in 1899, but following the death of Queen Victoria in 1901, an official Empire-wide day of celebration was suggested. It was inaugurated in 1903, on 24 May, the late Queen's birthday, and was at first called Victoria Day.

The annual event soon blossomed into a major set piece of patriotic fervour, aimed largely at educating the children about the glories of the Empire and Britain's wonderful achievements.

It was a day of pageantry, patriotic songs, marching and flag-waving, of red-white-and-blue bunting and hair bows. One regular feature was that each country was represented:

> Various classmates represented the countries of the Empire and as they paraded before us they spoke a short rhyme describing the country they in particular represented, listed its products and industries, and as they did so held up the items, such as sugar, cocoa tea, coffee, etc.
>
> *WORCESTERSHIRE, 1930S*

After the Second World War, with many of the countries in the Empire agitating for independence, Empire Day was felt to be out of step with the mood of the times. It was officially replaced in 1958 by Commonwealth Day (12 June, Elizabeth II's official birthday), which never captured the public's attention in the same way.

MAY/JUNE: WHITSUN

Whit Sunday is the seventh Sunday after Easter and was previously one of the most popular days of the year in both the religious and secular spheres. Whit Monday was an official bank holiday from 1871 to 1971, but has now been supplanted by the May Day and Spring bank holidays. Falling in early summer, it was a favourite time for fêtes and other village gatherings, and many customs such as morris dancing and well-dressing took place on the day.

For children in many areas, particularly in the towns of Lancashire, Whitsun was the time of the Whit walks. These were organised by the local churches and involved grand processions of children, dressed in white, marching behind colourful banners to the music of a brass band. On the whole, children loved being involved, and it was a great honour to be asked to carry the banner or to hold one of the many ribbons that draped from it; weeks of preparation and rehearsal went into getting everything just right.

The walks stemmed from the late eighteenth-century Sunday School movement, and the first Anglican walk in Manchester was held in 1801. They grew in size and importance as the century progressed, and by mid century were an established part of the urban scene.

Interestingly, different denominations walked on different days, and it was a long time before there was sufficient tolerance to allow them to share the same day. Indeed, there was a great deal of rivalry between some denominations, and there is no doubt that the Catholic Church put much more effort into the day than the others. In his study 'The Catholic Whit-Walk in Manchester and Salford, 1890–1939', Steve Fielding explains the downside of this need for perfection. Quoting people's memories of the 1920s and 1930s, he comments that children whose parents could not afford new white clothes, or the rosettes and other paraphernalia required to 'put on a good show', were ashamed and excluded. The pressure was not so great on Anglican children, because the established church had less to prove and could take a more relaxed view.

The glory days of Whit walks were already over by the Second World War, and they gradually dwindled away as church attendance declined. There are enthusiastic revivals, and some still take place, but usually on Spring bank holiday.

29 MAY: ROYAL OAK DAY

Royal Oak Day is another of the previously important days of celebration in the year, and has now disappeared almost completely. It was officially inaugurated to celebrate the Restoration of the monarchy in 1660, and set on 29 May because that was not only Charles II's birthday but also the day he rode back into London after his long exile. It was therefore an 'official' day, characterised by patriotic fervour, bell-ringing, bonfires, and an official Prayer of Thanksgiving, which was only removed from the day's church service in 1859.

The oak leaf, which rapidly became the recognised symbol of Charles and the restored monarchy, referred to the story of Charles hiding in an oak tree after the Battle of Worcester in 1651, a legend refashioned as a miraculous survival rather than proof of his ignominious defeat. Houses, shops and churches were decorated with oak boughs and for a while Royal Oak Day stole some of May Day's glory.

It was everybody's patriotic duty to wear a sprig of oak on the day, and children took it upon themselves to punish any of their number who did not comply with tradition. As one writer in the *Leiestershire & Rutland Magazine* of September 1949 remembered:

> Walking to school in the early summer of 1924, I was horrified to see several parties of boys armed with bunches of stinging nettles. It was Oak Apple Day and for once I had forgotten to wear a sprig of oak leaves. So I had to take my punishment and was well stung on the legs for my disloyalty.

And in Bradford, about 1912:

> We always remembered 29 May as Oak Apple Day, and we would not have dared to go to school without a sprig of oak, preferably with the apple on, pinned to our clothes. We also took a few nettles with us, and anyone who had not got a sprig of oak was well and truly nettled. We chanted this rhyme:

> The twenty-ninth of May
> Is Oak Apple Day
> If you don't give us a holiday
> We'll all run away.

As with many other children's customs, it was generally agreed that you could only attack people before midday.

The oak-leaf customs lasted well into the 1950s and 1960s, mostly in midland and northern counties of England, but rapidly faded after that time. A few places with a special connection to Charles II, including the Royal Hospital at Chelsea, still celebrate the day, but for the general population it is now completely forgotten.

The day went by various local names, including Oak Apple Day, Shick-shack Day, Shig-shag Day, Yak-bob Day, Bobby-ack Day and Nettling Day.

JUNE: DERBY DAY

Major sporting events attract crowds, crowds attract food vendors, fairground rides, sideshows, stallholders and others who cater for people's leisure time, and the occasion often becomes a major feature of the year for local children. The Derby Stakes at Epsom, one of the most famous horse races in the country, was first run in 1779, and quickly established itself as a major day out for Londoners of all kinds. As Blanchard Jerrold wrote in his *London: A Pilgrimage* (1872), illustrated by Gustave Doré, 'On the Downs London is in the highest spirits, and all classes are intermingled for a few hours on the happiest of terms.' Hundreds of families who lived within walking distance made a point of visiting the Downs for the day every year.

But children who lived on the routes out of town created their own calendar custom by bunking off school and lining the streets to admire the coaches and carriages carrying the race-goers. A resident of Wandsworth, South London, in the 1920s, recalled:

> On Derby Day, full of daring, my brother and I would go 'down the lane' and watch the carts and carriages on their way to the Derby on Epsom Downs, especially the 'costers' with their feather boas and gaudy hats. The children, mostly shoeless, would dart out into the road and yell out, 'Throw out your mouldy coppers', and the good-hearted crowd would throw out their loose change. There was a scramble, and sometimes a fight to pick up the coins.

5 AUGUST: RUSH-BEARING

Another of the adult-organised customs that strongly feature children is rush-bearing. Its ultimate origin lies in the time when churches (and most homes) were strewn with rushes as a floor covering, and these had to be changed periodically. Bringing the new rushes to the church became a popular occasion with local parishioners. In many cases it was a relatively low-key affair, mainly involving the women of the parish, but in other places, particularly in Lancashire, it developed into a major festival, with the rushes piled high on a cart and decorated with flowers and ribbons, escorted by a procession of villagers, morris dancers, a band and so on.

Somewhere between these two extremes there developed a more sedate custom that featured children carrying token rushes and other symbols in the procession. Five places in the Lake District continue this tradition each year. Grasmere is perhaps the best known, thanks to the William Wordsworth connection, where the custom takes place on the Saturday nearest 5 August, St Oswald's Day. Here, the rush-maidens – six girls wearing green dresses and yellow flowers in their hair – carry between them a sheet on which flowers and rushes are placed, and in their other hand a few tall rushes. Others in the procession carry symbolic shapes, such as crosses, harps and crowns, made of rushes and flowers on wooden frames.

Other places that have, or had until recently, similar traditions include Warcop (29 June), Ambleside (first Saturday in July), Urswick (29 September) and Great Musgrave (first Saturday in July).

AUGUST: GROTTOES

Formerly, at any time from late July to early September, the streets of London and several other places would be encumbered by 'grottoes' made of shells. Their child creators would stop passers-by and ask them for money:

> Please to remember the grotto
> My father has run off to sea
> My mother's gone to fetch 'im back
> So please give a farthin' to me.

The grotto was usually a bee-hive shaped construction, about two foot tall, with an open doorway in the middle at ground level. It was originally built of oyster shells, when these were plentiful, but later the children used any material to hand, such as clinker from the local gasworks, or stones. They decorated the grotto with anything they could find, such as bits of pottery, glass, pictures, beads, ribbons and flowers, and they often made a little garden in front and around it. A most important feature was a candle, to be placed in the aperture.

Dozens of recorded descriptions make it clear that the custom was common all over London, from at least the 1820s to the 1930s, and it was also reported from various other places, including Essex, Norfolk, Hampshire, Sussex and Swansea, during the same time. It survived the Second World War in only a few places, and the last known grottoes were seen in the 1960s in Mitcham, Surrey, now in Greater London. The main reason it survived here was that the local fair happened to fall on 12 August and was always associated with oyster-eating.

The earliest known reference is in *Time's Telescope* (1823), but the writer speaks of it as an established custom, and it was certainly well known enough in 1833, when *The Times* reported two incidents that happened to take place at grottoes. The first was the unfortunate case of a six-year-old girl in Finchley who was carrying a lighted candle to put into her grotto when her clothes caught fire. The second concerned two boys in Blackheath, who had built their grotto and had placed two old pictures, which had been knocking about at home, on each side to decorate it. A passing dealer offered them sixpence for the pictures, which they declined, and they were eventually sold for £1,400. In neither case does the writer express any surprise at the grotto-building, or feel the need to explain what they were to his readers. Indeed, the first piece referred to 'those mimic grottoes which at this season they delight in constructing'.

The proper time for 'Grotto Day' was unclear, and could be any time in late summer or early autumn. This is probably because the custom was tied to the opening of the oyster season, which would have varied from year to year, according to the state of the oyster crop. Right from the first published reference, it was assumed that the custom had some connection with St James of Compostela, whose feast day is 25 July and whose symbol is a scallop shell, but this is most unlikely. That saint's fame died out centuries before the grottoes appeared, and it is more likely that the children's custom was either a celebration of the start of the oyster season, or simply took advantage of the ready availability of shells.

Romantic 'grottoes' were very popular in adult society in the first decades of the nineteenth century. Parks and pleasure gardens often had them, and fashionable people's fêtes and parties often featured a poetic grotto, specially built for the occasion. Adverts for houses for sale in the news-papers between 1800 and 1820 often mention a grotto in the garden, and there was at least one pub in London at the time called 'The Grotto'. It is conceivable that children picked up on this fashion and spotted a commer-cial use for the millions of oyster shells available at that time of year. But this is speculation.

There is another complication to this story of grottoes. Although the majority of descriptions clearly refer to the three-dimensional construc-tions, there was another tradition of making flat 'gardens' on the pavements, usually around Good Friday. These were also called 'grottoes', and indeed the last known grottoes displayed in Mitcham took this form. See p. 479 for more information.

19 SEPTEMBER: CHURCH CLIPPING

On the Sunday closest to 19 September the people of Painswick, in Gloucestershire, gather for their annual 'church clipping' ceremony. 'Clipping' is Old English for embracing, and they carry out the ceremony by encircling the church. The local children play an essential part – without them there probably would not be enough adults to complete the circuit. A contributor to the Women's Institute's book *Gloucestershire Within Living Memory* (1996) remembered taking part in the 1930s:

> When I was a little girl we had just the same procession and hymns we do today. The children wore flowers, usually in a garland round the girls' hair, and a buttonhole for the boys. I can remember the Sunday School teacher poking hair pins into my head to keep the flowers in place. The band played the hymns and round the churchyard went in procession led by our splendid cross, then the choir, then the clergy, the sidesmen and children. Once assembled all round the outside of the church we had the Clipping Hymn, 'Daily, daily sing the praises', and all moved forward and back, embracing the church, rather in the style of the *Hokey Cokey*.

It is usually claimed that the ceremony goes back many hundreds of years, and some people even claim a pagan origin, but this is nonsense for a patently Christian ceremony which is clearly relatively modern. The current tradition at Painswick only goes back to Victorian times, although it is usually claimed that it was revived then, rather than started. But there is no record of any church clipping anywhere before the late eighteenth century.

Painswick is the most famous clipping ceremony, but other churches have similar customs, and even more are known to have had them in the past. Shrovetide and Easter were popular times for the custom, but at Painswick the date is that of the church's patronal festival, the feast day of Saint Mary the Blessed Virgin – 8 September – plus the eleven days 'lost' in the calendar reconstruction in 1752.

OCTOBER: PUNKIE NIGHT

At Hinton St George, Somerset, they have an annual custom in late October called 'Punkie Night'. The punkies are hollowed-out turnips or mangold-wurzels, with faces or other designs cut into them so that a lighted candle placed inside shines through. This is exactly what used to happen in areas that celebrated Hallowe'en before the influx of the American carved pumpkins, and it is often assumed that the Somerset custom is a survival of the older Hallowe'en tradition.

The custom at Hinton St George (and other nearby villages) was probably a simple house-visiting custom, but it was reorganised in the mid twentieth century to feature a children's procession, fancy-dress party and the crowning of a Punkie King and Queen. The history of the celebration has not been researched, or at least not yet published, but at present it cannot be shown to be any older than the twentieth century. The local rhyme that goes with the custom is:

> It's punkie night tonight
> It's punkie night tonight
> Give us a candle, give us a light [or 'Adam and Eve could never believe']
> It's punkie night tonight.

30 OCTOBER: MISCHIEF NIGHT

The night before Hallowe'en is one of those nights that in certain areas is called 'Mischief Night', when local children and young people indulge in an orgy of antisocial behaviour and vandalism. The history of 'Mischief Nights' is explored under 5 November, but 30 October – the eve of Hallowe'en – has proved a very strong pull in places like Liverpool:

> Mischief Night Crackdown: More than 1000 police officers will take to Merseyside's streets to tackle crime and anti-social behaviour on Mischief Night. Extra officers have been brought in to reassure older people who are frightened and intimidated in the run-up to Hallowe'en. Police today thanked shopkeepers who have agreed not to sell flour and eggs to youths after incidents in previous years when gangs ran riot across Merseyside.
>
> LIVERPOOL, 2008

Local police regard the whole autumn period, with Mischief Night, Hallowe'en and Bonfire night following in quick succession, as being particularly trying. That said, reports in recent years have actually shown an annual decrease in the numbers of incidents reported.

The day after 30 October, Hallowe'en, has been the standard night for mischief and pranks in Scotland, and the list of traditional misdeeds associated with the time and included in Mrs Macleod Banks's *British Calendar Customs: Scotland III* (1941) is almost identical to the tricks played elsewhere in Britain: blocking up and bombardment of doors, attacking the doors of houses with turnips, blowing smoke through keyholes, stopping chimneys, window tapping, pretending to smash windows, knocking on doors with kail runts and so on. Inevitably, the pranks vary slightly between urban and rural settings, according to the items children can lay their hands on:

> Parties of youths would congregate at night, steal into their neighbour's yards, and, pulling up their best cabbages, proceed to batter their doors and windows with them. If an individual happened to be disliked in the place, he was sure to suffer dreadfully on these occasions. His doors would be broken, and frequently not a cabbage left standing in his garden.
>
> JOHN O'GROATS, 1911

31 OCTOBER: HALLOWE'EN

Hallowe'en is one of three traditional festivals – Christmas and Valentine's Day being the others – that has mushroomed in terms of popularity, media coverage and public awareness. The commercial potential of Christmas and Valentine's Day was actually first spotted in Victorian times; however, the sharp rise in the popularity of Hallowe'en is relatively recent and, like Valentine's Day, Hallowe'en has been strongly influenced over the past three decades or so by customs on the other side of the Atlantic.

Many people instinctively feel that the modern festival is simply an American import. They are largely correct, but it can be argued that trick or treating is loosely based on traditional 'guising', when children disguised themselves and went from house to house begging food and money, and that carved pumpkins are similar to the old turnip heads they carried. Even the dressing up as witches, ghosts and aliens by teenagers and twenty-somethings, which is such a godsend to costume-hire shops, has some roots in the Hallowe'en fancy-dress parties that once took place. However, it is the scale and media emphasis which is completely new, and perhaps even unnerving.

Inevitably, Hallowe'en's history has been reinvented to fit what happens now, and the usual spurious notions of ancient history are accepted both by those who enjoy it and by those who oppose it on religious grounds. In fact, far from being a pagan 'day of the dead', Hallowe'en is a wholly Christian invention. It was deliberately started in medieval times as two adjacent festivals: All Saints or All-Hallows (1 November), inaugurated in the eighth century, and All Souls (2 November), added about AD 1000. The former was the designated day to commemorate saints and martyrs, and the latter to remember the departed Christian faithful. This short period therefore became a focus of concern for the dead, and nothing that has happened since has been outside the normal Christian worldview. For much of Britain the festival was weakened by the Reformation and its rejection of the notion of purgatory, where human souls were kept hanging about waiting for onward shipment to either heaven or hell, and therefore amenable to prayers and rituals from the living.

For most people in England, until the post-war growth of the festival, Hallowe'en had dwindled to almost nothing, and many simply regarded it as a Scottish festival, primarily because of Burns's famous poem on the subject. In Scotland and Northern Ireland, however, the date continued to be enthusiastically celebrated with bonfires, house-visiting customs such as 'guising' and 'love divination'. It is more than likely that Scottish and Irish emigrants took their customs with them to the USA, that they were modified over time there, and then re-imported to the UK in recent years.

As usual, the Opies offer an excellent snapshot of the state of play in the mid twentieth century. When collecting childlore in the 1950s, they discovered:

> Britain has the appearance of a land inhabited by two nations with completely different backgrounds. The frontier between these two peoples appears to run from somewhere around the mouth of the Humber southwest to Knighton, and then southwards along the Welsh border, counting Monmouthshire in with Wales, and then – although this line is less certain – south again through Dorset.

They pointed out that English children to the north and west of this line had more in common with Ireland and America than with other parts of England.

The old Hallowe'en in the northern and western areas included a number of traditional activities, including children who went from house to house as 'guisers', singing a song and hoping to collect money, apples, nuts and so on. Traditional disguises on these occasions included blackened faces, jackets worn inside out and cross-gender dressing, and in some places the householders were expected to guess who the guisers were. At Hallowe'en gatherings, the still well-known games of apple-bobbing and ducking were popular, along with others on similar lines, such as having to nibble treacle-covered scones hanging from a string, or picking up an apple or nut placed on a mound of flour with one's mouth. One tradition that our modern health-and-safety concerns would not allow us to offer to children involved a horizontal stick suspended on a string from the ceiling, with an apple fixed to one end and a lighted candle at the other.

Fires were also a major feature of the season, as Jeanne Cooper Foster wrote of Ulster about 1950:

> Bonfires are still one of the features of Hallowe'en celebrations, in the towns as well as in the country, and letting off squibs and rockets appears to be an ineradicable practice among children, who are usually aided and abetted by their elders.

And it was also the accepted Mischief Night in some areas (see p. 499), again as described by Jeanne Foster:

> A peculiar aspect of the Hallowe'en celebrations is that it is recognised as a time of revelry for the young men. Nowadays the revelry is, fortunately, of a milder order than in bygone days. During the hours of darkness bands of young men parade about the countryside playing pranks and carrying off property which they deposit in inaccessible places. Most country people are careful not to leave implements around on this night, and doors are bolted. Few care to be alone on isolated country roads lest they should become the victims of the revellers.

In *Scenes and Legends of the North of Scotland* (1835), Hugh Miller comments that Burns's poem of 1786 concentrates almost exclusively on the divinatory procedures that took place on the night, and ignores other widespread aspects of the festival. He sets the record straight by writing about the mischief and mayhem:

> The Scottish Halloween, as held in the solitary farmhouse and described by Burns, differed considerably from the Halloween of our villages and smaller towns. In the farmhouse it was a night of prediction only; in our towns and villages there were added a multitude of wild mischievous games, which were tolerated at no other season . . . After nightfall, the young fellows of the town formed themselves into parties of ten or a dozen, and breaking into the gardens of the greater inhabitants, stole the best and heaviest of their cabbages. Converting these into bludgeons, by stripping off the lower leaves, they next scoured the streets and lanes, thumping at every door as they passed.

Miller continues, 'Woe to the inadvertent female whom they encountered!' She was dragged into the cart, manhandled and forced to remain while it was raced around the streets. He then writes about the games, such as apple-bobbing.

'Trick or treating' hit Britain in the late 1970s, and nowadays it is quite common for children to go out in small groups and in costume, although because of safety fears they are often accompanied by their parents or responsible older siblings. Householders prepare stocks of sweets – often specially made or packaged, with a ghoulish theme – and it is commonly accepted that if you wish the trick or treaters to call, you place a lighted pumpkin outside your house. Although the children who come round sometimes have a rhyme, they more often simply say, 'Trick or treat!', and there is no real threat of retribution against those who are not forthcoming.

2 NOVEMBER: ALL SOULS

The festival of All Souls, discussed more fully under Hallowe'en, was inaugurated by the Church some time around AD 1000, but it was not till the codification of the doctrine of purgatory that the day took on a wider significance. It became the duty of all Christians, on this day in particular, to help souls trapped in purgatory, by their prayers and ritual actions such as ringing bells and lighting purifying fires. It was a popular time for charity doles, on the grounds that good deeds in this life could help those in the hereafter, and these often took the form of giving out specially made cakes, usually referred to as 'soul-cakes'.

It was also the day for 'souling', one of the many customs in which children went from door to door singing a song and hoping for money or food in return. In England, children's souling always seems to have been confined to Cheshire, Staffordshire and Lancashire, but it was also popular in Wales. Many contributors to antiquarian journals such as *Notes & Queries* and *Bye-gones* in the 1880s and 1890s reported that the custom was still popular with children, but, like most house-visiting customs, it certainly went into decline from that point and by the 1930s was very rare indeed.

All these visiting customs had a very similar outline, but the songs and rhymes were usually more distinctive than the actions that were carried out. Many soulers sang one simple verse, but there were also longer versions, such as the one submitted to *The Times* on 13 December 1935 by Archdeacon Howson, as remembered from the 1880s on the borders of Cheshire, Shropshire and Staffordshire:

A soul, a soul
  An apple or two
If you have not an apple
  A pear will do
I pray you good lady, a soul cake
  Go down to your cellar
Your cellar goes deep
  By walking and talking
You'll get a good name
  My clothes are very dirty
My shoes are very thin
  I've got a little pocket
To put a penny in
  One for Peter, and two for Paul
Three for the one who made us all
  Up with the kettle
And down with the pan
  Give us an answer
  And we'll be gay.

Given the time of year, it is not surprising that apples and pears featured in the goodies expected by the singers, but years after the practice of giving special cakes had died out, the children often called all their booty 'soul-cakes'.

A wider variety of All Souls visiting customs were recorded in Wales, carried out by adults, but the children also went on their rounds on the day in the same way as their English counterparts. The custom there had various names, including *hel bwyd cennad y meirw* (collecting the food of the messenger of the dead), *hel solod* (collecting souls or soul-cakes), *bara-a-chawsa* (bread and cheesing), and also sowling, dole-bread and doling day. Some of them simply stood at the door and said what translates as 'Please may I have a little food for the messenger of the dead?', while others recited a rhyme somewhat similar to that given above. But there was more variation in the imagery of the verses in Welsh, one of which translates as:

Bread and cheese
  Bread and cheese
If I get some I'll jump
  If I don't, I won't.   *1891*

And in Denbighshire in the 1890s:

> *Dega, dega,* come to the door
> And give to the messenger of the dead.

But if nothing was forthcoming:

> *Deca, deca,* under the door,
> And the wife's head in smithereens.

Although the house-visiting type of souling custom is often assumed to be of great age, and the tunes used for the rhymes are often described as archaic, there is no evidence of their existence before the turn of the nineteenth century. The characteristic custom before that time was, as already indicated, the making and distribution of special cakes, often specifically to family and friends, as well as to the poor, and this was practised over a much wider geographical area.

See also other children's visiting customs: Clementing and Catterning (p. 512) and pace-egging (p. 480).

4 NOVEMBER: MISCHIEF NIGHT

In a few places in England, mostly in Yorkshire, local children and young people still celebrate Mischief Night (or 'Miggy Night') on the day before 5 November. All kinds of 'mischief' are perpetrated, sometimes shading into petty or real vandalism, and it has long been the idea that those involved have a right to behave badly on this day, and the police cannot stop them.

Mischief Night: At the Huddersfield Guildhall on Tuesday [May 1857], four youths were summoned for upsetting a straw-stack, belonging to Mr William Wilkinson, of Salendine Nook. The boys pleaded guilty legally, with the historical excuse of mischief night, and they had since the 'malek', as they termed it, paid a man for putting the stack up again. On hearing this, the Magistrates discharged the case on the payment of expenses.

Even apart from the idea of a time in which the law is powerless, which is not as unusual as we might think, there are two strange things about Mischief Night: firstly, the restricted area in which it took place, even in the past when it was more widely practised; and secondly, the fact that for much of its 200 years of documented history, it actually took place on a different night entirely – 30 April.

Records of the custom show that it took place in a relatively narrow geographical area, across northern England, taking in Lancashire, Yorkshire, Derbyshire, and northern parts only of Cheshire, Nottinghamshire and Lincolnshire. But the earliest definite reference to come to light so far is completely outside this area and refers to the Scilly Isles. George Woodley wrote in 1822:

> In the Island of St Mary, Scilly Isles, early in the morning of May-day, or, rather, during the previous night, numbers of youths and girls go into the country and unhinge gates, injure fences, and otherwise damage property and annoy the inhabitants.

One reference that might be earlier appears in a series of articles called 'Rambles by the Ribble' in the *Preston Guardian* (19 March 1864), in which the author recorded meeting a old inhabitant of Clitheroe who described the custom in his youth there, presumably about 1810.

All the earlier sources refer to 30 April as Mischief Night, and it is not clear why or even when the alteration took place. The change in date seems to have started happening around the turn of the twentieth century, but apparently took some years to spread across the region, and it may be the only example of a custom being moved to a totally different time of year. A search of the local newspapers should be able to help map the change, as articles on the damage caused on the night were a regular feature in the period. But the main result of the move is obvious, as it brought it into the ambit of Guy Fawkes Night, which was not only a time when wild behaviour was already commonplace, but also when fireworks were available and minds focused on gathering material for bonfires.

There is a definite pattern in descriptions of what went on during Mischief Night. The nineteenth-century sources almost always mention gates and signs being removed or swapped around, carts wheeled away and left in odd places, and any farm or household utensils similarly spirited away. It was often explicitly stated that if you were fool enough to leave anything portable lying around outside on that evening, you deserved to have it taken away. Another traditional feature seems to have been to collect all these items into a central place.

As the twentieth century progressed, the focus was much more on direct 'assaults' on property – tying people's door knockers together, putting treacle on doorknobs, blocking chimneys and so on – although there was still a strong tradition of removing anything combustible. Indeed, the mischief nighters had to guard their own bonfires, which were ready for the next day's celebrations, against premature firing by rival gangs.

Latter-day reports also show a strong tradition that students took to Mischief Night in a big way and used it as an excuse for various stunts. A sad piece in *The Times* on 5 November 1963, for example, reported on a road accident in which three students were killed. They were on their way, with friends, to set fire to a bonfire built by students of a rival college just outside Lincoln.

Police in Sheffield and other parts of Yorkshire still have problems with vandalism and general bad behaviour on Mischief Night. One of the main features nowadays is throwing flower and eggs at people and vehicles. To confuse things further, in some parts, Mischief Night is on the night before Hallowe'en; see (p. 499).

Children living in areas without a Mischief Night tradition were not totally starved of opportunities for traditional misbehaviour. Guy Fawkes Night itself provided plenty of scope, and many Shrovetide customs also gave traditional sanction to antisocial activities (see p. 472). Nor was the idea of the law being powerless confined to this time. Indeed, the local mythology surrounding many customs included the notion that 'tradition' over-rode the usual legal niceties, and there were also particular hours or days that were thought to be 'lawless' (see Roud (2006)).

5 NOVEMBER: GUY FAWKES NIGHT

Now that 5 November is a time of set-piece displays or back-garden firework parties strictly controlled by adults, that part of the celebration once organised by children has largely been taken out of their hands.

Until the late nineteenth century, celebrations of the Fifth were very public affairs, especially in urban areas. Bonfires took place in the streets or on waste ground, huge, none-too-sober crowds gathered and fireworks were let off indiscriminately, blazing tar barrels were rolled, and until the 1830s the crowd even discharged firearms as part of the fun.

Mass celebrations like these began to be suppressed in the 1870s, often in the teeth of violent opposition from those who enjoyed them, and it was in reaction to this mass mode of celebration that the middle classes, and increasingly the respectable working classes as well, took to holding their bonfire nights in private in their own gardens. This became the predominant form of celebration for much of the twentieth century.

But working-class children continued to inhabit the streets, at least in the lead-up to the Fifth every year, and their concerns were focused on acquiring enough combustible material to make a good bonfire, the necessary ingredients for a good guy, and enough money to buy fireworks. The latter two goals were connected, of course, in the 'penny for the guy' custom, and it is this aspect of the tradition that is worth saying a little more about.

It is not clear whether the same procedures were common in the eighteenth century, but certainly by the 1820s, children were making guys, carrying them around and asking for money from passers-by. Many cartoonists of the period depicted a scene with a guy seated on a chair, mounted on two poles, being paraded around the streets, and there are occasional newspaper reports of something that went wrong – for example, when there was a pitched battle between Catholic and Protestant boys for the possession of a guy: the anti-Catholic nature of the festival was never far below the surface.

By the twentieth century the static 'penny for the guy' was the norm, and was widely seen in the run-up to the big day. Almost inevitably, opinion was divided about the tradition. There were those who simply saw it as a harmless childish tradition. But then there were those who said that it constituted outright begging, that the children were rude, insistent, aggressive, disrespectful; that they did not even try to make decent guys; that they were manipulated by adults who sent them out to earn money which was then spent on drink; and that it taught them that they could get something for nothing. There was a strong class element to this criticism. The children who carried out the custom were virtually all working class. Their opponents were not and they tended to adopt the view – familiar today, too – that things were getting worse.

The battle was, to a large extent, carried out in the press – national and local – and at times it almost reached the proportions of a full-blown moral panic. Paradoxically, the voices that were particularly vocal against the custom sound very similar to those who nowadays are so vociferous against 'health and safety' and who maintain that our children should be allowed the freedom to play.

As in all moral panics, the righteous indignation, on both sides, was fuelled as much by rumour, legend and prejudice as by factual information, but there is no doubt that both camps had a certain amount of justice on their side. Their viewpoints, however, were simply irreconcilable.

Guy Fawkes night is rapidly degenerating into an excuse for hooliganism and organized begging. Last year a man apologetically gave a small boy a penny. It was all he had, he explained. There were no thanks, and the donor caught sight of another man lurking round a dark corner. He watched him, and saw the child hand over his takings.

TIT-BITS, 6 NOVEMBER 1954

This can be contrasted with the incident in Rose Gamble's *Chelsea Child* (1979), in which she and her siblings made a guy and worked hard in the streets to earn 7d, which their brute of a father promptly took off them, and Rose's sister got a smack across the face because it was not more. On a rather lighter note:

> Just before Guy Fawkes night, an Ealing woman was asked for a contribution by two little girls. 'But where's your guy?' she enquired. It was raining at the time. 'At home,' retorted one of the girls scornfully. 'You don't think we'd bring him out in this weather, do you?'
>
> TIT-BITS, 6 NOVEMBER 1954

A recurrent motif in stories both for and against 'penny for the guy' operations is the group who dress up one of themselves as the guy instead of making an effigy. 'They didn't even bother to make a guy,' say one side; 'Oh, what a clever little wheeze,' says the other. Tom McCarthy described doing just this during his boyhood in Islington, North London, in the 1930s, though in this case there was a tragic outcome:

> When we were dressing up as a guy we blacked our faces and put on tatty, dark clothes and topped the whole outfit off with the largest old hat we could get. Sometimes the effect was very good and we fooled many people if we sat still long enough, especially in the dark. Sometimes the effect was altogether too realistic, and on this occasion the result was tragedy. One local group dressed one of their mates as a guy and pushed him round the shops in Stroud Green Road in a battered old pram to collect money. He was sitting very still in the pram when they passed a butcher's shop, the butcher was standing outside the shop talking to a friend as they walked past and they asked him for a penny for the guy. The bloke was holding one of his very sharp knives, and thinking the lad was a bundle of rags, ran him through with the knife, killing him outright.

This has all the hallmarks of an urban legend, and one can just imagine the story flashing round the neighbourhood in the hushed and excited tones children reserve for this kind of fascinatingly horrible tale.

The 'penny for the guy' custom was not the only aspect of Guy Fawkes

Night to come in for criticism. The general behaviour of the children at this time of year was often roundly condemned, though again not always without justification. As part of their research for their *Lore and Language of Schoolchildren* (1959), Iona and Peter Opie asked teachers to get their pupils to write compositions about 'special days in the year'. Many of these make fascinating reading fifty years later, because they represent the relatively unfiltered voices of children of the period. Those who advocate a return to the freedom of pre-health-and-safety days should read some of the accounts. A fourteen-year-old boy from Forfar, whose name we will withhold, in case any of his victims are still around, wrote in 1954:

> On Guy Fawkes Day there are lots of fireworks in the shops and everybody makes a rush to get them. When night comes they go outside to set them off. The bangers make more noise if they are set off in an enclosed space and rain-pipes and drains are ideal for this. With small bangers you can light them and drop them behind some unsuspecting person. Sometimes you put them on the doorstep of a house then ring the bell and hide. When the occupant of the house opens the door he cannot see anybody and the banger goes off beneath his feet. Sometimes it goes off before the door is opened but usually it goes off as the door is opened. With rockets we usually see who can get the biggest one and which goes farthest. If there are any animals in the fields we set them off near those and they run away. If there are a lot we surround them and set them off all at once. The animals do not know which way to run. At November the fifth every year boys gather round bonfires and set off fireworks. There were two sides picked, each person having bangers and matches. One side would attack and one side defend a bonfire. Each side if they saw an enemy they would throw a lighted banger at them. This would continue until one side set the bonfire on fire.

Many children of that era will remember such antics, and worse.

But not all celebrations were like this. A more affectionate view of Guy Fawkes Night is given by Jacqueline Simpson, writing about her native town of Worthing, Sussex, from the 1930s onwards:

> I loved the free-and-easy cheerful crowds around Splash Point and the Pavilion with their own bangers and sparklers – and above all, the Jumping Jacks (now banned, I believe) which flashed and banged at one's feet . . . [In 1958] the Town Council had forbidden people to light their family bonfires on the beach. This was a much-loved custom. I remember how, in the 1930s, all along the beach there were dozens of little fires, three or four between each break-

water, lovingly built up several days in advance. During the War, the beach was, of course, blocked off with barbed wire, but after 1945 we were free to use it again and Guy Fawkes fires very much part of that freedom.

Various songs and rhymes were associated with the custom, but by the post-war period they were largely forgotten, or had dwindled down to the ubiquitous single verse starting 'Remember, remember, the fifth of November'. A contributor to the *Times Literary Supplement* (7 December 1951) sent in the following, remembered from between sixty and seventy years previously:

> Please to remember the fifth of November
>> The Gunpowder treason and Plot
> I have no reason why gunpowder treason
>> Should ever be forgot
> Guy Fawkes Guy
>> Stick him in the eye
> Hang him on a lamp-post
>> And there let him die
> A ha'penny loaf to feed the Pope
>> And a penn'orth of cheese to choke him
> A pint of beer to rinse it down
>> And a tuppenny faggot to burn him
> Holler boy! holler boys!
>> Let your voice ring
> Holler boys! holler boys!
>> God save the Queen!
> Hip! hip! hooray!

'Cob coalin' was the Lancashire term for collecting material for the fire, and the collectors had a song that they sang at people's doors:

> We've come a-cob-o'-coalin' at bonfire time
>> Your coal and your money we hope to enjoy
> Fol-a-day, fol-a-day, fol-a-diddle-i-do-day
>> Down in our cellar there's an owd umberella
> There's nowt in our cornish [mantelpiece] but an owd pepper pot
>> Pepper pot, pepper pot, mornin' till neet
> If you give us nowt, we'll steal nowt
>> But bid you good neet.

OLDHAM, C.1930

And another from the children's compositions in the Opie Collection:

When I go guisin' on Guy Fawkes night dressed up, I repeat as verse after having sang as we are about to leave:

> Rise up auld wives and shake your feather
> We've no come here as tinks or beggars
> We're only wee bairnies oot tae play
> So see aw're pennies and let's away.

23 NOVEMBER: ST CLEMENT'S DAY

In the area around Warwickshire and Staffordshire there was a children's house-visiting custom called 'clementing', that involved begging for apples, money and so on. The rhyme the children recited was published in *Notes and Queries* in 1863, as current about fifty years previously:

> Clemeny, clemeny, God be wi' you
> Christmas comes but once a ye-ar
> When it comes, it will soon be gone
> Give me an apple and I'll be gone.

This was very similar to another custom called 'catterning', which took place on St Catherine's Day (25 November), and the two were often combined. Both were also very similar to 'souling' (2 November). Most of the references to clementing come from the nineteenth century, but it was mentioned in print in 1686, and before that in 1540 (see 25 November, below).

25 NOVEMBER: ST CATHERINE'S DAY

One of several house-visiting customs that took place on special days in November, in the Midlands, was called 'catterning', because it took place on St Catherine's Day (25 November). It was very similar to 'clementing', on St Clement's Day, two days before, and indeed it was often reported as 'cattern and clementing' and done on either or both days.

The following was the verse used in a Worcestershire version in the 1880s.

It is longer than the usual house-visiting rhyme, but includes all the usual elements, plus the last five lines, which are specific to the local area:

> Catherine and Clement come year by year
> Some of your apples and some of your beer
> Some for Peter, some for Paul
> Some for the merry boys under your wall
> Peter was a good old man
> For his sake then give us some
> None of the worst, but some of the best
> And pray God send your souls to rest
> Butler! Butler! fill the bowl
> Dash it up against the wall
> Up the ladder and down with the can
> Give us a red apple and we'll be gone
> A plum, a plum
> A cherry, a cherry
> A good cup of perry
> Will make us all merry
> We go a-Cattin, a-Cattin go we
> From Hitton to Titton as soon as you shall see
> From Mitton to Pitton, Hartleybury all three
> Round by old Kiddy and good Hillintree
> Then down to old Arley, Astley, and Shaweley go nimbly
> And finish we up at Holty, Hallow and Grimley.

The majority of references to both catterning and clementing are from the counties of Worcestershire, Staffordshire, Shropshire and Warwickshire, but they were clearly much more widespread in the past. W. D. Parish, for example, includes both in his *Dictionary of the Sussex Dialect* (1875) and claims a long history for the custom:

> In spite of a proclamation made at London, July 22 1540, that 'neither children should be decked ne go about on St Nicholas, St Catherine, St Clement, the Holy Innocents, and such-like days', the children in Sussex still keep up the custom of catterning and clemening.

Other customs also took place at this season, including festivities to do with the lace-making trade, and the day was clearly more important in the traditional calendar than it is usually given credit for. A letter to *The*

Times on 5 December 1935, from Aylesbury, Buckinghamshire, for example, reads:

> Older parishioners here tell of a merrymaking known as Kattern, which used to take place on St Katherine's Day. Friends and families met for games and a meal; special oval seed-cakes were eaten, washed down by ale, and the chief game was bob-apple.

See also 'clementing' (p. 512) and 'souling' (p. 503).

DECEMBER: CHRISTMAS: OLD TUP

There were formerly a number of customs around the country in which men or youths dressed up as animals, usually in the form of a hobby horse, but occasionally other species. These could be quite raucous, hard-drinking affairs.

Sometimes, however, the local tradition included children's teams, and an example of this is the 'Owd Tup' or 'Old Tup' play, which was found in the nineteenth and twentieth centuries in the area around Sheffield, straddling the Yorkshire–Derbyshire–Nottinghamshire border. The play is based on the very widely known traditional song *The Derby Ram*, which is about a prodigious ram with horns that reached to the moon, and feet that covered an acre of ground. Beyond dressing up as the ram, the only potential for action, however, is the verse:

> The butcher that killed this ram, sir
> Was up to his neck in blood
> And the boy who held the basin
> Was washed away in the flood.

The killing of the ram was the core of the performance, and has definite echoes of the standard mumming play, which also included a stabbing. It is no surprise, therefore, that the two were sometimes incorporated into one performance. An example of the latter was published in the journal *Lore and Language* (July 1969), as it used to be performed in Sheffield in Edwardian times. It was usually done on the evening of Christmas Day and on New Year's Day:

> They went from door to door, always knocking and asking permission to perform first. They acted outside by the light of the house lamps, each

stepping forward in turn to say his part. The play was passed on orally by the boys of the village. They started performing at the age of nine or ten and continued for three or four years.

The Tup was constructed in the same way as most traditional animal characters: its head was made from a large mallet with a hole bored in it to take a broom handle, which was held by a boy leaning forward, with a sack over him. The other characters in this version were Me and Our Old Lass, Butcher, Doctor, Beelzeebub, Little Devil Doubt; all had blackened faces, and they always made a collection after each performance.

28 DECEMBER: HOLY INNOCENTS' DAY

In the Christian calendar, Holy Innocents, or Childermas, is the day set aside to commemorate the slaughter of the innocent children by Herod, in his attempt to kill the baby Jesus (Matthew 2:16). It was therefore a day of repentance, despite coming within the ambit of the Twelve Days of Christmas, and in popular tradition it was regarded as one of the unluckiest, 'cross' days of the year. Indeed, in some parts, the day of the week on which Holy Innocents fell was regarded as a 'cross' day for the following year.

There are no recorded children's customs on the day, but, paradoxically, children benefited from its gloomy nature. Up to the nineteenth century, one of the features of Holy Innocents was that children were not chastised on the day, but indulged more than usual.

SCRAMBLING CUSTOMS

'Scrambling customs' are a category of traditional customs that are organised by adults, but that children join in with enthusiastically. Typically, something is thrown to a crowd of waiting children and they scramble around to get it.

Scrambling often took place on an ad hoc basis, such as when a newly married couple left the church, or the local squire visited the village fête, but there were also special occasions that included the feature, and some of these were annual events. Mayor-making celebrations and other civic events often included it, as did many charity doles, when food was thrown to the crowd rather than being distributed in a more orderly fashion.

A contributor to *West Yorkshire Within Living Memory* (1996) described the scene at Meltham Mills, between Meltham and Netherton, about 1930:

> At twelve o'clock precisely the mill owner and his manager came out into the mill yard armed with a bag of pennies, which they proceeded to toss in handfuls into the crowd of children waiting there. We were allowed to leave school early that morning, at eleven-thirty, and by running all the way we would get there in time.

But the one time he joined in he returned empty-handed because the bigger boys, wearing clogs, got all the pennies.

Scrambling customs still take place around the country, either annually or periodically. Extant examples include: Harwich (Essex), bun-throwing, part of the mayoral celebrations on the third Thursday in May; Abingdon (Oxfordshire), bun-throwing, where the custom has been in practice since at least 1809, special occasions only; Rye (Sussex), coin-throwing, as part of the mayor-making, 23 May; Durham, coin-throwing as part of mayor-making, mid May; Hungerford (Berkshire), oranges thrown as part of their Hocktide celebrations; St Briavels (Gloucestershire), bread and cheese dole, Whit Sunday; Hallton (Leicestershire), 'hare pie' thrown as part of their bottle-kicking game, Easter Monday.

Bibliography

Abrahams, Roger D., *Jump-Rope Rhymes: A Dictionary* (Austin: University of Texas Press, 1969).

Abrahams, Roger D., and Rankin, Lois, *Counting-out Rhymes: A Dictionary* (Austin: University of Texas Press, 1980).

Addy, Sidney Oldall, *A Glossary of Words used in the Neighbourhood of Sheffield* (London: English Dialect Society, 1888).

Arleo, Andy, 'The International Diffusion of the Jump-Rope Game "Elastics"', *Australian Children's Folklore Newsletter* 19 (Dec 1990) 5–9; 20/21 (Sep 1991) 16–21.

—, 'Strategy in Counting-Out Saint-Nazaire, France', *Children's Folklore Review* 14:1 (Fall 1991) 25–9.

—, 'The Saga of Susie: The Dynamics of an International Handclapping Game', in Bishop & Curtis (2001) 115–32.

Atkinson, Robert, *Belfast Street Games* (Belfast?: No Publisher, 1977).

Aubrey, John, *Remaines of Gentilisme and Judaisme*, in John Buchanan-Brown (ed.), *Three Prose Works* (Carbondale: Southern Illinois University Press, 1972).

Avery, Valerie, *London Morning* (London: Pergamon, 1967).

Baker, Anne Elizabeth, *Glossary of Northamptonshire Words and Phrases* (London: John Russell Smith, 1854).

Balfour, M. C., *County Folk-Lore: Northumberland* (London: Nutt, 1904).

Banks, M. Macleod, *British Calendar Customs: Scotland* (London: William Glaisher, 1937–41).

—, *British Calendar Customs: Orkney and Shetland* (London: William Glaisher, 1946).

Bason, Fred, 'Street Games in Southwark', in John Hadfield, *The Saturday Book*, No. 31 (London: Hutchinson, 1971).

Baumann, Paul, *Collecting Antique Marbles*, 2nd edn. (Radnor, PA: Wallace-Homestead, 1991).

Beckwith, Ian, and Shirley, Bob, 'Truce Terms: A Lincolnshire Survey', *Local Historian* 11:8 (Nov 1975) 441–4.

Berkeley, Mildred, and Jenkins, Caroline E., *A Worcestershire Book* (Worcester: Worcestershire Federation of Women's Institutes, 1932).

Bishop, Julia, *Eeny Meeny Dessameeny: Continuity and Change in the 'Backstory' of a Children's Playground Rhyme* (unpublished paper delivered at the 'Children's

Playground Games & Songs in the New Media Age Interim Conference', London, Feb 2010).

Bishop, Julia, and Curtis, Mavis, *Play Today in the Primary School Playground* (Buckingham: Open University Press, 2001).

Black, G. F., *County Folk-Lore: Orkney and Shetland Islands* (London: Nutt, 1903).

Blair, Anna, *Tea at Miss Cranston's: A Century of Glasgow Memories* (Edinburgh: Birlinn, 1985).

Blakeborough, Richard, *Wit, Character, Folklore and Customs of the North Riding of Yorkshire* (London: Henry Frowde, 1898).

Bosanquet, Rosalie E., *In the Troublesome Times* (Newcastle: Northumberland Press, 1929).

Boy's Own Book, 24th edn. (London: Longman, Brown, 1846).

Boyes, Georgina, 'Children's Clapping Rhymes from Newfoundland and Sheffield', *Folk Song Research* 3:3 (Dec 1984) 33–42.

Brady, Eilis, *All in! All in!: A Selection of Dublin Children's Traditional Street-Games with Rhymes and Music* (Dublin: Comhairle Bhéaloideas Éireann, 1984)

Brain, Jennifer, *Children's Games* (London: Bethnal Green Museum of Childhood, 1984).

Brand, John, *Observations on the Popular Antiquities of Great Britain* (London: Bohn, 1849; 1st edn. published 1777).

Brewster, Paul G., *Games and Sports in Shakespeare* (Helsinki: FF Communications No. 177, 1959).

Britten, James, and Holland, Robert, *A Dictionary of English Plant-Names* (London: English Dialect Society, 1886).

Brockett, John Trotter, *A Glossary of North-Country Words* (Newcastle: Emerson Charnley, 1829).

Brockie, William, *Legends and Superstitions of the County of Durham* (Sunderland: B. Williams, 1886).

Buckinghamshire Federation of Women's Institutes, *Buckinghamshire Within Living Memory* (Newbury: Countryside Books, 1993).

Bullock, Jim, *Bowers Row: Recollections of a Mining Village* (East Ardsley: E. P., 1976).

Burne, Charlotte, *Shropshire Folk-Lore* (London: Trubner, 1883).

Burrows, Ray, *Beckery Burrows: Somerset in the Thirties* (London: Research Pub., 1978).

Cameron, Archie, *Bare Feet and Tackety Boots* (Barr, Ayrshire: Luath Press, 1988).

Care, Noel, *A Rye Childhood in the 1920s* (Hastings: Hastings & Rother Family History Society, c.1987).

Cassell's Book of Sports and Pastimes, new and revised edn. (London: Cassell, 1907).

Chambers, Robert, *The Popular Rhymes of Scotland* (Edinburgh: William Hunter, 1826).

—, *Popular Rhymes of Scotland*, new edn. (Edinburgh: W&R Chambers, 1870).

Chesterton, Thomas, *Organised Playground Games*, revised edn. (London: Educational Supply Association, 1908).

Clancy Children, *So Early in the Morning: Irish Children's Songs, Rhymes and Games* (Tradition CD TCD 1053, 1997).

Coles, E. G. M., 'Huntingdonshire Children at Play', *Hunts County Magazine* 1:4 (Spring 1947) 151–2.

Cooper, Ernest R., *Mardles from Suffolk* (London: Heath Cranton, 1932).

Cox, J. Charles, *Memorials of Old Derbyshire* (London: Bemrose, 1907).

Craig, Patricia, *The Oxford Book of Schooldays* (Oxford: Oxford University Press, 1994).

Cram, David, Forgeng, Jeffrey L., and Johnston, Dorothy, *Francis Willughby's Book of Games: A Seventeenth Century Treatise on Sports, Games and Pastimes* (Aldershot: Ashgate, 2003).

Crombie, J. W., 'History of the Game of Hop-Scotch', *Journal of the Royal Anthropological Institution* 16 (1886) 403–8.

Cumbria Federation of Women's Institutes, *Cumbria Within Living Memory* (Newbury: Countryside Books, 1994).

Curtis, Mavis, 'A Sailor Went to Sea: Theme and Variations', *Folk Music Journal* 8:4 (2004) 421–37.

Danaher, Kevin, *The Year in Ireland: Irish Calendar Customs* (Cork: Mercier, 1972).

Darlington, Thomas, *The Folk-Speech of South Cheshire* (London: Trubner, 1887).

De Garis, Marie, *Folklore of Guernsey* (Channel Islands: The Author, 1975).

Douglas, Norman, *London Street Games* (London: St Catherine Press, 1916).

Dublin University Magazine, 'An Irish Hedge-School, by a Constant Visitor', *Dublin University Magazine* 60 (1862) 600–616.

Dyer, Joanne, 'Elastics', *Australian Children's Folklore Newsletter* 1:2 (Apr 1982) 7–8.

Dyer, Samuel, *Dialect of the West Riding of Yorkshire* (Brighouse: John Hartley, 1891).

Dyer, T. F. Thistleton, *Folk Lore of Shakespeare* (London: Griffith & Farran, 1883).

—, *The Folk-Lore of Plants* (London: Chatto & Windus, 1889).

English Dialect Dictionary (London: Henry Frowde, 1898–1905).

English Folk Dance & Song Society, *Have You Ever Seen . . . a Penguin Come to Tea?* (London: EFDSS, 2008).

Ferguson, Robert, *The Dialect of Cumberland* (London: Williams & Norgate, 1873).

Fielding, Steve, 'The Catholic Whit-Walk in Manchester and Salford 1890–1939', *Manchester Region History Review* 1:1 (1987) 3–10.

Flying Fox Films, *Green Peas and Barley-O: Children's Street Songs and Rhymes from Belfast* (Belfast: Flying Fox Films CD, c.2000).

Foster, Jeanne Cooper, *Ulster Folklore* (Belfast: H. H. Carter, 1951).

Fraser, Amy Stewart, *Dae Ye Min' Langsyne* (London: Routledge & Kegan Paul, 1975).

Games and Sports for Young Boys (London: Routledge Warne, 1859).

Gaskell, Alfred, *Those Were the Days* (Swinton: Swinton & Pendlebury Public Libraries, 1963).

Gaunt, Kyra D., *The Games Black Girls Play: Learning the Ropes from Double-Dutch to Hip-Hop* (New York: New York University Press, 2006).

Gilcraft's Book of Games: A Collection of Games Suitable for Scout Troops (London: C. Arthur Pearson, 1928).

Gill, W. Walter, *Manx Dialect: Words and Phrases* (London: Arrowsmith, 1934).

Gillington, Alice E., *Old Hampshire Singing Games and Trilling the Rope Rhymes* (London: Curwen, 1909).

—, *Old Isle of Wight Singing Games* (London, Curwen, 1909).

—, *Old Surrey Singing Games and Skipping-Rope Rhymes* (London: Curwen, 1909).

—, *Old Dorset Singing Games: With a Few from Wilts. and New Forest* (London, Curwen, 1913).

Gloucestershire Federation of Women's Institutes, *Gloucestershire Within Living Memory* (Newbury: Countryside Books, 1996).

Goldstein, K., 'Strategy in Counting-Out: An Ethnographic Folklore Field Study', in E. Avedon, and B. Sutton-Smith, *The Study of Games* (New York: John Wiley, 1971) 167–78.

Gomme, Alice Bertha, *The Traditional Games of England, Scotland and Ireland*, 2 vols. (London: David Nutt, 1894 and 1898).

Gosse, P. H., 'A Country Day-School Seventy Years Ago', *Longman's Magazine* 13 (1888–9) 512–24.

Gould, D. W., *The Top: Universal Toy, Enduring Pastime* (New York: Clarkson N. Potter, 1973).

Green, Joanne, and Widdowson, J. D. A., *Traditional English Language Genres: Continuity and Change, 1950–2000*, 2 vols. (Sheffield: NATCECT, 2003).

Gregor, Walter, *Notes on the Folk-Lore of the North-East of Scotland* (London: Elliot Stock, 1881).

—, *Counting Out Rhymes of Children* (London: David Nutt, 1891).

Grey, Edwin, *Cottage Life in a Hertfordshire Village* (Harpenden: Harpenden & District Local History Society, 1977).

Grimes, Dorothy A., *Like Dew Before the Sun: Life and Language in Northamptonshire* (Wellingborough: W. D. Wharton, 1996).

Gurdon, Eveline Camilla, *County Folk-Lore: Suffolk* (London: Nutt, 1893).

Gutch, Mrs, *County Folk-Lore: North Riding of Yorkshire and the Ainsty* (London: Nutt, 1901).

Gutch, Mrs, and Peacock, Mabel, *County Folk-Lore: Lincolnshire* (London: Nutt, 1908).

Hackwood, Frederick William, *Staffordshire Customs, Superstitions and Folklore* (Lichfield: Mercury Press, 1924).

Halliwell, James Orchard, *The Nursery Rhymes of England* (London: Percy Society, 1842) plus later editions.

Harris, Mollie, *A Kind of Magic* (London: Chatto & Windus, 1969).

Haworth, Don, *Figures in a Bygone Landscape: A Lancashire Childhood* (London: Methuen, 1986).

Henderson, William, *Notes on the Folk Lore of the Northern Counties of England and the Borders* (London: Longmans, 1866).

Herefordshire Federation of Women's Institutes, *Herefordshire Within Living Memory* (Newbury: Countryside Books, 1993).

Heslop, Richard Oliver, *Northumberland Words: A Glossary of Words Used in the County of Northumberland and on the Tyneside* (London: English Dialect Society, 1892).

Hinkson, Katharine (Tynan), *Victorian Singing Games* (London: Folklore Society, 1991); reprints articles from the *Monthly Packet*, 1896–7.

Hole, Christina, *A Dictionary of Folk Customs* (London: Paladin, 1978).

Hubbard, Jane, 'Children's Traditional Games from Birdsedge: Clapping Songs and Their Notation', *Folk Music Journal* 4:3 (1982) 246–64.

Humphries, Steve, Mack, Joanna, and Perks, Robert, *A Century of Childhood* (London: Sidgwick & Jackson, 1988).

Hunter, Joseph, *The Hallamshire Glossary* (London: William Pickering, 1829).

Husenbeth, F. C., *The History of Sedgley Park School, Staffordshire* (London: Richardson, 1856).

Hutton, Ronald, *The Stations of the Sun: A History of the Ritual Year in Britain* (Oxford: Oxford University Press, 1996).

Inglis, James, *Oor Ain Folk*, 4th edn. (Edinburgh: David Douglas, 1909).

Jamieson, John, *An Etymological Dictionary of the Scottish Language* (Edinburgh: Edinburgh University Press, 1808).

Joughin, J. J., 'Folk-Lore Notes: Peel Street Games', *Mannin* (Nov 1916) 486–8; (May 1917) 530–33.

Kellett, Rowland, *Heritage of the Streets: A Collection of Children's Songs, Games and Jingles* (unpublished typescript in Vaughan Williams Memorial Library, 1966).

Kenneally, Christy, *Maura's Boy: A Cork Childhood* (Cork: Mercier, 1996).

Kent Federation of Women's Institutes, *East Kent Within Living Memory* (Newbury: Countryside Books, 1995).

King, Madge, and King, Robert, *Street Games of North Shields Children*, 2nd series (Tynemouth: Priory Press, 1930).

Kirkup, James, *The Only Child: An Autobiography of Infancy* (London: Collins, 1957).

Knight, Sid, *Cotswold Lad* (London: Phoenix House, 1960).

Lancashire Federation of Women's Institutes, *Lancashire Lore* (Preston: Lancashire Federation of Women's Institutes, 1971).

Lancashire Federation of Women's Institutes, *Lancashire Within Living Memory* (Newbury: Countryside Books, 1997).

Lawson, John, and Silver, Harold, *A Social History of Education in England* (London: Methuen, 1973).

Leather, Ella M., *The Folk-Lore of Herefordshire* (Hereford: Jakeman & Carver, 1912).

Lee, W. R., 'Pastimes of Youth', *Papers of the Manchester Literary Club* 61 (1936) 144–53.

Lessels, David H., 'Bools, Babs and Cockie-Dunty', *Scots Magazine* (Feb 1990) 542–6.

Leyden, Maurice, *Boys and Girls Come Out to Play: A Collection of Irish Singing Games* (Belfast: Appletree, 1993).

Little Penny Pocket Book (London: John Newbery, 1767; facsimile reprint, London: Oxford University Press, 1966).

Long, W. H., *A Dictionary of the Isle of Wight Dialect* (London: Reeves & Turner, 1886).

Low, Frances H., 'The Street Games of Children', *Strand Magazine* 2 (1891) 513–20.

Lynch, Geraldine, 'The Lore of a Wicklow Schoolgirl', *Bealoideas* 45 (1977) 46–62.

Mackenzie, A. W., *Games for Scouts*, 3rd enlarged edn. (Glasgow: Brown, Son & Ferguson, 1928; reprinted 1948).

Maclagan, Robert Craig, *The Games and Diversions of Argyleshire* (London: David Nutt, 1901).

MacTaggart, John, *The Scottish Gallovidian Encyclopedia* (London: The Author, 1824).

Madders, Jane, and Horseman, Grace, *Growing Up in the Twenties* (Bovey Tracy: Cottage Publishing, 1993).

Marsh, Kathryn, *The Musical Playground: Global Tradition and Change in Children's Songs and Games* (Oxford: Oxford University Press, 2008).

Marshall, John J., *Popular Rhymes and Sayings of Ireland* (Dungannon: Tyrone Printing Co., 1924).

—, *Popular Rhymes and Sayings of Ireland*, 2nd edn. (Dungannon: Tyrone Printing Co., 1931).

Mary Erskine School, Edinburgh, *Children's Street Games Project* (unpublished MS in Edinburgh Room, Edinburgh Central Library, 1990).

May, Phil, *Gutter-Snipes: 50 Original Sketches in Pen and Ink* (London: Leadenhall Press, 1896).

Mayhew, Henry, *London Labour and the London Poor* (London: Griffin, Bohn, 1861–2).

M'Bain, J. M., *Arbroath Past and Present* (Arbroath: Brodie & Salmon, 1887).

McCarthy, Tom, *Boysie* (Braunton: Merlin, 1986).

McDowell, Florence Mary, *Roses and Rainbows* (Belfast: Blackstaff, 1972).

McGlinchey, Charles, *The Last of the Name* (Belfast: Blackstaff, 1986).

M'Nair, Robert, 'Childish Sports and Games', in Senex, *Glasgow Past and Present* II (Glasgow: David Robertson, 1884).

Miller, Hugh, *Scenes and Legends of the North of Scotland* (Edinburgh: Black, 1835).

Mills, Gordon, and Hardie, Alastair, *Skin Street Scallywags and Town and Country* (Edinburgh: Stylus, 1991).

Moor, Edward, *Suffolk Words and Phrases* (London: R. Hunter, 1823).

Moore, A. W., *The Folk-Lore of the Isle of Man* (London: Nutt, 1891).

—, *A Vocabulary of the Anglo-Manx Dialect* (Oxford: Humphrey Milford, 1924).

Moore, John, *Portrait of Elmbury* (London: Collins, 1946).

Moxon, T. Allen, 'Games of Soho', *St. Anne's Soho Monthly Paper* (Jun, Jul & Aug 1907) 152–6, 180–84, 222–5.

Newbery, Maggie, *Reminiscences of a Bradford Mill Girl* (Bradford: Bradford Libraries, 1980).

Newchurch Women's Institute, *Newchurch Remembered* (Newchurch: Newchurch Women's Institute, 1988).

Nicholson, John, *Folk Lore of East Yorkshire* (London: Simpkin Marshall, 1890).

Nicolson, James R., *Shetland Folklore* (London: Robert Hale, 1981).

North Yorkshire Federation of Women's Institutes, *North Yorkshire Within Living Memory* (Newbury: Countryside Books, 1995).

Northall, G. F., *English Folk-Rhymes* (London: Kegan Paul, Trench, Trubner, 1892).

—, *Folk-Phrases of Four Counties* (London: English Dialect Society, 1894).

—, *A Warwickshire Word-Book* (London: Henry Frowde, 1896).

A Nosegay for the Trouble of Culling, or Sports of Childhood (London: William Darton, 1813).

O'Flynn, Criostoir, *There is an Isle: A Limerick Boyhood* (Cork: Mercier, 1998).

Ogden, James, 'Marbles and Conkers', *Lore & Language* 2:9 (1978) 70–72.

Ogilvie, Mary I., *A Scottish Childhood* (Oxford: George Ronald, 1952).

Opie, Iona, *The People in the Playground* (Oxford: Oxford University Press, 1993).

Opie, Iona, and Opie, Peter, *I Saw Esau: Traditional Rhymes of Youth* (London: Williams & Norgate, 1947.)

—, *Oxford Dictionary of Nursery Rhymes* (Oxford: Oxford University Press, 1951).

—, *Lore and Language of Schoolchildren* (Oxford: Oxford University Press, 1959).

—, *Children's Games in Street and Playground* (Oxford: Oxford University Press, 1969).

—, *The Singing Game* (Oxford: Oxford University Press, 1985).

—, *I Saw Esau: The Schoolchild's Pocket Book*, new edn. (London: Walker Books, 1992).

—, *Children's Games with Things* (Oxford: Oxford University Press, 1997).

Opie, Iona, and Tatem, Moira, *A Dictionary of Superstitions* (Oxford: Oxford University Press, 1989).

Owen, Trefor F., *Welsh Folk Customs* (Cardiff: National Museum of Wales, 1968; 4th ed., Dyfed: Gomer, 1987).

Palmer, Roy, *The Folklore of Leicestershire and Rutland* (Wymondham: Sycamore Press, 1985).

Parish, W. D., *A Dictionary of the Sussex Dialect* (Lewes: Farncombe, 1875).

Parry-Jones, D., *Welsh Children's Games and Pastimes* (Denbigh: Gee & Sons, 1964).

Paton, C. I., *Manx Calendar Customs* (London: Folk-Lore Society, 1942).

Paul, Albert, *Poverty-Hardship but Happiness: Those Were the Days 1903–1917*, 3rd edn. (Brighton: Queenspark Books, 1981).

Peacock, Basil, *A Newcastle Boyhood, 1898–1914* (Sutton: Sutton Libraries, 1986).

Penny, C. W., 'Caps: A West Country Game', *Somerset Notes & Queries* 5 (1896–7) 193–4 (and 283).

Porter, Enid, *Cambridgeshire Customs and Folklore* (London: Routledge & Kegan Paul, 1969).

Pugh, Edwin, 'Some London Street Amusements', in George R. Sims, *Living London*, Vol. III (London: Cassell, 1906) 266–71.

Rayner, Daisy, *Our Knickers Were Interesting: A Norfolk Village Childhood* (Dereham: Susan Palmer, 1989).

Ritchie, James T., *The Singing Street* (Edinburgh: Oliver & Boyd, 1964).

—, *Golden City* (Edinburgh: Oliver & Boyd, 1965).

Roberts, Alasdair, 'Barleys, Keys and Crosses', *Scots Magazine* (Dec 1977) 268–72.

—, *Out to Play: The Middle Years of Childhood* (Aberdeen: Aberdeen University Press, 1980).

Roberts, Robert, *A Ragged Schooling: Growing Up in the Classic Slum* (Manchester: Manchester University Press, 1976).

Robinson, F. K., *A Glossary of the Words Used in the Neighbourhood of Whitby* (London: Trubner, 1876).

Rodgers, Jean C., *Lang Strang* (Forfar: Forfar Press, c.1950).

Rolph, C. H., *London Particulars* (Oxford: Oxford University Press, 1980).

Roud, Steve, 'Random Notes from an Andover Playground', *Downs Miscellany* 2:1 (1984) 21–32.

—, 'Random Notes from an Andover Playground Pt.2: Elastics', *Downs Miscellany* 3:1 (1985) 10–15.

—, *The Penguin Guide to the Superstitions of Britain and Ireland* (London: Penguin, 2003).

—, *The English Year* (London: Penguin, 2006).

Rountree, George, *A Govan Childhood: The Thirties* (Edinburgh: John Donald, 1993).

Rutherford, Frank, *All the Way to Pennywell: Children's Rhymes of the North East* (Durham: University of Durham Institute of Education, 1971).

St Ann's Reminiscence Group, *More Tales of the Old Town* (Edinburgh: Community Printshop, 1990)

Salisbury, Jesse, *A Glossary of Words and Phrases used in S.E. Worcestershire* (London: J. Salisbury, 1893).

Sangster, Eve, *Children of the Angel: Growing Up in Hertford 1910–1935* (Hertford: Hertford Oral History, 1998).

School Boys' Diversions, 2nd edn. (London: Dean & Munday, c.1820).

Sinclair, Maureen, *Murder Murder Polis* (Edinburgh: Ramsey Head, 1986).

Sluckin, Andy, *Growing Up in the Playground: The Social Development of Children* (London: Routledge & Kegan Paul, 1981).

Smith, A. W., 'An Introduction to East London Folklore', *East London Papers* 2:2 (1959) 63–78.

Smith, R. A., *Blue Bell Hill Games* (Harmondsworth: Kestrel Books, 1982).

Somerset Federation of Women's Institutes, *Somerset Within Living Memory* (Newbury: Countryside Books, 1992).

Staffordshire Federation of Women's Institutes, *Staffordshire Within Living Memory* (Newbury: Countryside Books, 1992).

Sternberg, Thomas, *The Dialect and Folk-Lore of Northamptonshire* (London: John Russell Smith, 1851).

Strutt, Joseph, *Sports and Pastimes of the People of England* (London: Tegg, 1833; first published 1801, and in many editions since).

Sturt, George, *A Small Boy in the Sixties* (Cambridge: Cambridge University Press, 1927).

Surrey Federation of Women's Institutes, *Surrey Within Living Memory* (Newbury: Countryside Books, 1996).

Sutton, Maureen, *We Didn't Know Aught* (Stamford: Paul Watkins, 1992).

Sutton-Smith, Brian, *The Folkgames of Children* (Austin: University of Texas Press, 1972); includes *The Games of New Zealand Children*.

Swinford, George, *The Jubilee Boy: The Life and Recollections of George Swinford of Filkins* (Filkins: Filkins Press, 1987).

Tapp, Wilfrid B., *When I Wor a Lad* (Bradford: Bradford Libraries, 1992).

Tate, George, *History of the Borough, Castle and Barony of Alnwick* (Alnwick: H. H. Blair, 1866–9).

Thompson, Flora, *Lark Rise to Candleford* (Oxford: Oxford University Press, 1945); previously published as 3 vol.: *Lark Rise* (1939), *Over to Candleford* (1941), *Candleford Green* (1943).

Tobin, Barbara, *Eenie-Meenie-Des-O-Leenie: The Folklore of the Children of Alps Road Elementary School* (unpublished paper, 1983).

Townsend, Hilary, *Blackmore Vale Childhood* (Oxford: Isis, 2007).

Tredinnick, L. C., 'The Game of Five Stones', *Old Cornwall* 2:7 (1931–6) 38–40.

Turnbull, E., 'Schoolboy Games of 60 Years Ago', *Journal of the Lakeland Dialect Society* 7 (1945) 6–8.

Turner, Ian, Factor, June, and Lowenstein, Wendy, *Cinderella Dressed in Yella*, 2nd edn. (Richmond: Heinemann Educational Australia, 1978).

Turner, W. F., 'I Remember Rabbiting, Popguns and Boxing in the Barn', *East Anglian Magazine* 13 (1953–4) 647–51.

Udal, J. S., 'Dorsetshire Children's Games', *Folk-Lore Journal* 7 (1889) 202–64.

—, *Dorsetshire Folklore* (Hertford: Stephen Austin, 1912).

Uttley, Alison, *The Country Child* (London: Faber, 1931).

—, *Country Things* (London: Faber, 1946).

Vickery, Roy, *A Dictionary of Plant-Lore* (Oxford: Oxford University Press, 1995).

Wales, Tony, *Long Summer Days: Games and Pastimes of Sussex Children* (Horsham: Field & Furrow Books, 1983).

—, *A Treasury of Sussex Folklore* (Seaford: S. B. Publications, 2000).

—, *A Sussex Childhood* (Seaford: S. B. Publications, 2001).

Walker, Harold W., *Games Forgotten (or Nearly So)* (Waltham Abbey: Sewardstone Investments, 1989).

Ward, Zoe, *Curtsy to the Lady: A Horringer Childhood* (Lavenham: Terence Dalton, 1985).

Warwickshire Federation of Women's Institutes, *Warwickshire Within Living Memory* (Newbury: Countryside Books, 1993).

Williams, Alfred, *A Wiltshire Village* (London: Duckworth, 1912).

Willughby, Francis, *see* Cram, David et al.

Wolveridge, Jim, *Ain't it Grand (or This was Stepney)* (Newham: Stepney Books, 1976).

Woodley, George, *A View of the Present State of the Scilly Isles* (London: Rivington, 1822).

Wright, A. R., and Lones, T. E., *British Calendar Customs: England* (London: William Glaisher, 1936–40).

Wright, Elizabeth Mary, *Rustic Speech and Folk-Lore* (London: Humphrey Milford, 1913).

Yeatman, E. F. E., and Hall, Maud R., *On the Green: Village Games* (London: Wells Gardner, Darton, 1894).

Young, George, *A History of Whitby* (Whitby: Clark & Medd, 1817).

References

Where rhymes or games are identified with a 'Roud Number', e.g. (Roud 1368), this refers to the numbering system used in my Folk Song Index, which can be used to locate other versions in books, unpublished collections and recordings. The Index is available on the website of the Vaughan Williams Memorial Library, http://library.efdss.org/cgi-bin/home.cgi.

'SR collection' designates material collected by Steve Roud, 1970 to the present day.

Page 3–4 'Four Corners': SR collection, Simon Furey (b.1945), Nottingham, 2008

4 'Corner Wall': Steve Gardham collection, Barbara Pawson, Beverley, Yorkshire, 1975

4 'The Tree Game': SR collection, Ravenstone School Council, Balham, South London, 2010

5 'I'm the king of the castle . . .': SR Collection, Natasha (11), Aston on Clun, Shropshire, 2009

5 'King of the Castle': Forrest (1858) 233–4

5 'Chwarae Cadw'r Castell, neu'r Twmpyn': Parry-Jones (1964) 122

5, 8 'Willie Willie Wassle . . .': *Notes & Queries* 4S:2 (1868) 554

6 'Granny's Fridge': SR collection, Park Lodge School Council, Belfast, 2010

6 'Red Lips': SR collection, Park Lodge School Council, Belfast, 2010

6 'Granny in the Graveyard': SR collection, Park Lodge School Council, Belfast, 2010

6–7 'Fly Away Peter': SR collection, Sîan Cleaver (1960s), South Wales, 2009

7 'Roadkill': SR collection, year 6 schoolchildren (11/12), Ardleigh, Essex, 2009

7 'Human Dominoes': SR collection, Maddie, Rhea & Dahlia (all 10), Ealing, West London, 2009

7 'Solomon Had a Great Dog': *Folk-Lore Journal* 5 (1887) 50

8 'If a defender . . .': Forrest (1858) 233–4

8 'I was in the junior school . . .': Gamble (1979) 143

9 'An enterprising parent . . .': Somerset Fed WIs, *Somerset Within Living Memory* (1992) 123

9 'The children form pairs . . .': Gomme I (1894) 7–8

10 'Upon Latchford Heath . . .': Lowe (2004)

10–11 'The game I liked best . . .': *Boy's Own Paper* (5 Nov 1887) 87

12 'The formula for joining . . .': Gamble (1979) 137–8

13 'Long before playtime . . .': Paul (1957) 37

13 'There was no need . . .': Avery (1964) 70

13 'Allee 'ome . . .': Avery (1964) 70

13 'All-ee, All-ee in . . .': Cathy Gould collection, own recollection (1970s), Coventry

16 'One boy touches . . .': *Francis Willughby's Book of Games* (1660s) fol.222

19–20 List of tig variants: Mary Erskine School, Edinburgh, Children's Street Games Project, 1990

21 'Touch off ground': SR collection, Caroline Brewser (b.1967), Vale of Glamorgan, Wales, 2007

22 'Nobody fancied . . .': Blair (1985) 83

24 'Feet-off-ground': Paul (1957) 47

24 'During Off-ground Tig . . .': Cathy Gould collection, Richard Lamb, (b.c.1969), Solihull, 2004

24 'Egarty Budge': Steve Gardham collection, Ian Kilpatrick, Beverley, Yorkshire, 1982

25 'Bob 3 Times . . .': Steve Gardham collection, schoolchild, Beverley, Yorkshire, c.1975

25 'Feet-off-ground': *Notes & Queries* 11S:1 (1910) 483

25 'This was followed . . .': Avery (1967) 68–9

25 'Lame Tig': Nicholson (1890) 145

25 'English touch': Opie (1969) 75

25 'Bum it': SR collection, Maddie, Rhea & Dahlia (all 10), Ealing, West London, 2009

26 'Nothing in after life . . .': Paul (1957) 43–4

26 'Spiral': SR collection, Jolian Searles (b.1977), Tiptree, Essex, 2007

26 'The Blob': SR collection, Helena (9), Charlton Kings, Gloucestershire, 2008

27 'If they let go hands . . .': Opie (1969) 95

27 'Stag-a-rag-a-roaring . . .': Burne (1883) 523

27 'Widdy widdy way . . .': Heslop (1892) 788

28 'Well, it's called . . .': SR collection, Claire (10) & Emma (7) Taylor, Andover, Hampshire, 1979

29 '. . . generally instigated . . .': SR collection, Rachel Nussey (born 1976), Middlesbrough, Yorks., 2007

32 'Lurgies': SR collection, Ravenstone School Council, Balham, South London, 2010

32 'There's one group . . .': SR collection, Maddie, Rhea & Dahlia (all 10), Ealing, West London, 2009

33 'Sticky Toffee': SR collection, Rebecca, Ella, Helena & Luckshie (all 8), East Finchley, North London, 2008

33 'Cross Touch': *Games and Sports for Young Boys* (1859) 1

33 'Cross tig': Husenbeth (1856) 107

34 'Last-Bat-Poison': Heslop (1892) 107

34 'But be it remembered . . .': Blakeborough (1898) 257–8

34 'Tiggy-Touchwood . . .': Addy (1888) 260

35 'Or scamper. . .': Anderson (1805) 32

35 'This fast-moving game . . .': Opie (1969) 95

37–8 'Bulldog': SR collection, Maddie, Rhea & Dahlia (all 10), Ealing, West London, 2009

38 'A more violent version . . .': SR collection, David Pye (b.1972), Bingham, Nottinghamshire, 2009

38 'We play Bulldog . . .': SR collection, Kate (11) & Joanna (12), Weybridge, Surrey, 2009

38 'In "Subject Bulldog" . . .': Steve Gardham collection, Michael Brumpton (13), Beverley, Yorkshire, c.1996

39–40 'Two teams of players . . .': Cathy Gould collection, girls, Coventry, 2004

40 'Bulldog and Red Rover . . .': SR collection, Catherine McKiernan (b.1976), Leeds, 2007

40 'Coockoo . . .': Steve Gardham collection, Avis Butterfield (b.c.1908), York, 1996

41 'Everybody on one side . . .' SR collection, own memory, Streatham, South London, 1950s

41 'Octopus': SR collection, Park Lodge School Council, Belfast, 2010

42 'One [game] . . .': Herefordshire Fed WIs, *Herefordshire Within Living Memory* (1993) 128

42 'While I was still . . .': Sturt (1927) 235

44 'In this game . . .': SR collection, Lynda Rose (b.1956), Birmingham, 2009; (Roud 13188)

45 'A peculiar custom . . .': *Westminster Gazette* (10 Aug 1899)

45 'After "Postman's Knock" . . .': Thompson (1945) 438

46 'The lads and lasses . . .': *Little Penny Pocket Book* (1767)

46 'When this game is played . . .': Strutt (1833) Bk 4, Ch. 4

47 'In this last . . .': *Folk-Lore Journal* 7 (1889) 211–12

48 'Down in the jungle . . .': SR collection, Maddie, Rhea & Dahlia (all 10), Ealing, West London, 2009

49 'Doctor, Doctor we're in a twist . . .': Cathy Gould collection, girls (1990s), Coventry, 2004

49 'Doctor Doctor': SR collection, Megan, Mollie & Annie (all 11), Godalming, Surrey, 2008

49–50 'The players should toss up . . .': *Games and Sports for Young Boys* (1859) 18

50 '. . . pull or buffet . . .': Gomme I (1894) 145–6

50 'From in the middle . . .': Leslie (1831) 19

50 'Where is the key . . .': Burne (1883) 519–20

52 'At my little boy's . . .': SR collection, L. Davis (b.1958), Haywards Heath, Sussex, 2008

54 'Boys had to be . . .': Haworth (1986) 169–70

54 'Normally girls did not . . .': Haworth (1986) 166, 169–70

54–5 'The playground . . .': Townsend (2007) 27

55 'Although most of us . . .' Care (*c*.1987) 37

55 'It may be noted . . .': Gaskell (1964) 3

55 'The marked . . .': Low (1891) 51–4

55 'In nothing is the change . . .': *Notes & Queries* 4S:2 (1868) 98

59–60 Hopscotch patterns: Opie (1997) 95–109; Gomme I (1894) 190, 223; Gomme II (1894) 182, 307, 451; Ritchie (1965) 96–110

60 'On the first one . . .': SR collection, Claire (10) & Emma (7) Taylor, Andover, Hampshire, 1979

60–61 'You drew squares . . .': SR collection, Jennifer Henson (b.1950), Stroud Green, North London, 2007

62 'Throw your stone . . .': SR collection, Caroline Oates (b.1955), Gateshead, 2009

64 'Hopscotch, for example . . .': Rolph (1980) 36

64–5 'Girls' games . . .': Pugh (1906) 271

66 '"Bays" was . . .': Tait (1953) 19

66–7 'London': Low (1891) 515–16

67 'To play a pebble . . .': Cathy Gould collection, Sue Sanders, Halifax, Yorkshire, 1960s/1970s

68 'He was very desirous . . .': Tennant (1885) 605

68–9 'Next came handstands . . .': 'Keeping up with the Joneses', *The Times* (16 Apr 1956)

69 'Rain, snow . . .': SR collection, East Street School playground, Andover, Hampshire, 1982

69 'You all do handstands . . .': SR collection, Robert Arkenstall School Council, Haddenham, Cambridgeshire, 2009

69–70 'At several Dunedin schools . . .': Sutton-Smith (1972) 74

70 'Head, head . . .': Cathy Gould collection, Coventry, 2008

70 'Salt and pepper . . .': Cathy Gould collection, girls (11), Coventry, 2008

70 'We would play . . .': SR collection, Catherine Burke (b.1989), Waterford, Ireland, 2007

70 'Twisting . . .': Bason (1971) 109

71 'They are still enjoying . . .': Opie (1993) 147

71 'London Bridge is broken . . .': Northall (1892) 353

72 'The "monkey battle" . . .': *Notes & Queries* 4S:2 (1868) 554

72–3 'In my younger days . . .': *Notes & Queries* 9S:2 (1898) 497

73 'It was always "pig-a-back" . . .': *Notes & Queries* 9S:2 (1898) 497

73 'There was another game . . .': Parry-Jones (1964) 108

73 'You could write . . .': Douglas (1916) 24

75 'It was the sort . . .': Charles Dickens, *The Pickwick Papers* (1836–7) Ch. 28

75 'A very rustic sort . . .': MacTaggart (1824) 320

76 'The first as he jumps . . .': *Folk-Lore Journal* 5 (1887) 60

76 'Leap Frog was another . . .': Bullock (1976) 73

76 'One boy stoops down . . .': Douglas (1916) 30

76–7 'Hi Jimmie Knacker': SR collection, John Earl, South-east London, 2009

77 'The melee . . .': Walker (1989) 13

78 'There was usually found . . .': Parry-Jones (1964) 75

78 'Challey wag . . .': A. H. Pye, unpublished letter to *The Times* (Jan 1951)

78 'One, two, three . . .': Donald Wolfit, unpublished letter to *The Times* (Jan 1951)

78–9 'The game was played . . .': F. C. Clarke, letter to *The Times* (Jan 1951)

79 '. . . was no namby-pamby . . .': Knight (1960) 37–8

79 'Whilst I was serving . . .': C. Farthing, letter to *The Times* (Feb 1951)

79 'When I was a schoolgirl . . .': M. V. Batey, letter to *The Times* (Jan 1951)

83 'Draw a large ring . . .': Peter Millington collection, A. Coleman (b.*c*.1903), Selston, Nottinghamshire, 1973

83–4 'Another exciting . . .': Walker (1989) 13–14

84 'Spy Ann': MacTaggart (1824) 435

84 'But-Thorrin': Moore (1924) 25

84 'If the finder failed . . .': Buckinghamshire Fed WIs, *Buckinghamshire Within Living Memory* (1993) 111

85 'A child's cry . . .': Baker I (1854) 164, 336

85 'Hoopie': Long (1886) 29

85 'Among the . . .': Gaskell (1964) 3

85 'Hide and seek': Bullock (1976) 74–5

86 'There's "Forty Forty Touch" . . .': SR collection, Megan, Mollie & Annie (all 11), Godalming, Surrey, 2008

86 'The person who was it . . .': SR collection, Caroline Brewser (b.1967), Vale of Glamorgan, Wales, 2007

87 'Before the game starts . . .': Cathy Gould collection, boy (9), Coventry, 2007

87 'There's an itter . . .': SR collection, Maddie, Rhea & Dahlia (all 10), Ealing, West London, 2009

87–8 'Dickie Dickie Shine-a-Light': Cathy Gould collection, father's recollection

88 'Hare and Hounds': Joughin (1916) 486

88 'Sound your holler . . .': Northall (1892) 357

88 'Uppa uppa holye . . .': *Folk-Lore Journal* 5 (1887) 61

88 'The best time of all . . .': Surrey Fed WIs, *Surrey Within Living Memory* (1996) 123

88 '[Laura] never really . . .': Thompson (1945) 36

90 'We play it like . . .': SR collection, schoolchildren (10/11), Okehampton Primary School, Okehampton, Devon, 2010

91 '"On" facing wall. . .': Gareth Whitaker collection, Denholme, Yorkshire, 2002

91 'London': SR collection, G. J. Anderson (male, b.1936), Glasgow, 2010

91 'Chocolate Fudge': Mary Erskine School, Edinburgh, Children's Street Games Project, 1990

92 'It starts off . . .': SR collection, Megan, Mollie & Annie (all 11), Godalming, Surrey, 2008

92 'Everyone will stand . . .': SR collection, Georgia (13), Inverness, 2008

93 'Please, Your Majesty . . .': SR collection, Megan, Mollie & Annie (all 11), Godalming, Surrey, 2008

93 'In this game . . .': SR collection, Chantel Cousins (b.1979), London, 2008

93 'Other versions . . .': Cathy Gould collection

93 'In Glasgow . . .': Tamsin Watt, *Playground Games in Grandtully Primary School* (student project MD 1998.13, School of Scottish Studies, Edinburgh, 1998)

94 'There would be an "it" . . .': SR collection, Sharon Forrester (b.1968), Edinburgh, 2007 (wording modified)

94 'Red Square . . .': Mary Erskine School, Edinburgh, Children's Street Games Project, 1990

94 'The first person . . .': SR collection, Megan, Mollie & Annie (all 11), Godalming, Surrey, 2008

95 'Jack, Jack . . .': SR collection, Sîan Cleaver (1960s), South Wales, 2009

95 'Crocodile, crocodile . . .': SR collection, Lucy (8) & Sarah (7) Bawden, Andover, Hampshire, 1982

95 'Please Mr Crocodile . . .': SR collection, Megan, Mollie & Annie (all 11), Godalming, Surrey, 2008

96–7 'Basically, someone's on . . .': SR collection, Megan, Mollie & Annie (all 11), Godalming, Surrey, 2008

97 'Peter Pan said to Paul . . .': Ritchie (1964) 89–90

97 'Television game': SR collection, Claire (10) & Emma (7) Taylor, Andover, Hampshire, 1979

97–8 'TV Game': SR collection, Kate Roud (12), Croydon, South London, 1987

98 'Pop Groups': Steve Gardham collection, Barbara Pawson, Beverley, Yorkshire, 1975

98–9 'Whatever the name . . .': Parry-Jones (1964) 106–7

99 'Please We've Come . . .': Douglas (1916) 40

99 'Honeypots': (Roud 19197)

100 'Buy my fine . . .' Gomme I (1894) 220

100 'Take her and bake her . . .': Gomme I (1894) 220

100 'Honey pots, honey pots . . .': Gomme I (1894) 220

100 'Hinnie-Pigs': MacTaggart (1824) 270

100 'Sometimes we has . . .': Mayhew, *London Labour and the London Poor* I (1861) 152

100 'The game lasted . . .': Douglas (1916) 39

100–1 'Concentration . . .' [1]: SR collection, Rebecca, Ella, Helena & Luckshie (all 8), East Finchley, North London, 2008

101 'Concentration . . .' [2]: Mary Erskine School, Edinburgh, Children's Street Games Project, 1990

101, 104 'A major game . . .': SR collection, Jane Chadwick (b.1961), Berkshire, 2007

102 'There was always an element . . .': Devon Fed WIs, *Devon Within Living Memory* (1993) 110

103 'The local lads . . .': Cumbria Fed WIs, *Cumbria Within Living Memory* (1994) 108

103 'With chewing-gum . . .': Rolph (1980) 125–6

104 'It's got to be . . .': SR collection, Harry (8), Harry (9), George (10) & Justin (9), Maresfield, Sussex, 2008

104 'When the commander . . .': *Round About the Coal Fire* (1740)

104 'Suppose you and I . . .': Opie (1969) 266

105 'Buck Buck': (Roud 16f287)

105 'Another boys' game . . .': Nicholson (1890) 149

105 'If the one stooping . . .': Williams (1912) 247–8

106 'If the guess was wrong . . .': Gomme I (1894) 47

106 'Inkum, jinkum . . .' Gomme I (1894) 46

106 'Trimalchio . . .': Opie (1969) 294–7

107 'Handie Back . . .': *Francis Willughby's Book of Games* (1660s) f.221

108 'They go on to suggest . . .': Opie (1969) 294

108 'Strokey back . . .': Opie (1969) 292–3

108 'I draw a snake . . .': SR collection, Jim Duerdin (b.1957), Newcastle, 1977

109 'Tick tack toe . . .': SR collection, Ravenstone School Council, Balham, South London, 2009

110 'Little finger . . .': SR collection, Robert Arkenstall School Council, Haddenham, Cambridgeshire, 2009

110 'You win . . .': SR collection, Robert Arkenstall School Council, Haddenham, Cambridgeshire, 2009

110 'Spiders crawling . . .': SR collection, Cherry & Ella (both 11), Camden, North London, 2009

110 'Dot dot . . .': Katharine Beavan, *Children's Playground Rhymes* (project MD2004.02, School of Scottish Studies, Edinburgh, 2004)

111 'Line line . . .': SR collection, schoolchildren (10/11), Okehampton Primary School, Okehampton, Devon, 2010

111 '10 nails in your back . . .': Australian Children's Folklore Newsletter (Nov 1984) 4

113 'Marco Polo . . .': SR collection, Maddie, Rhea & Dahlia (all 10), Ealing, West London, 2009

113–14 'All stand in a circle . . .': SR collection, Adam (13), Irma (8), Bethany (11) & Adele (11), Gateshead, 2010

114 'Statues': Madders & Horseman (1993) 196

114–15 'There are . . .': Douglas (1916) 41

115 'You have someone sat . . .': SR collection, schoolchildren (10/11), Okehampton Primary School, Okehampton, Devon, 2010

115 Buff dialogue: Gomme I (1894) 48–50

116 'When sitting round . . .': Nicholson (1890) 148

116 'Jack's Alive': Addy (1888) 118

116–17 'Robbin-a-Ree': MacTaggart (1824) 410

117 'In this game . . .': Moore (1924) 51

117 'Children wave . . .': Burne (1883) 530

117–18 'Robin Alive': *Francis Willughby's Book of Games* (1660s) f.230 (spelling and punctuation modernised)

118 'Players in a circle . . .': *Gilcraft's Book of Games* (1928) 46

119 'A well-known game . . .': Gomme I (1894) 98

119–20 'Neivies': Gill (1934) 20; Rodger (c.1950) 8

120 'A singular rustic amusement . . .': MacTaggart (1824) 173

120 'What have you there . . .': Leslie (1831) 18–19

121 'Here's one hammer . . .': Northall (1892) 418

121 'Handy dandy . . .': *Notes & Queries* 6S:7 (1883) 235; (Roud 19429)

121 'Handy Andy . . .': *Notes & Queries* 6S:7 (1883) 235; (Roud 19429)

121 'Handy spandy . . .': *Notes & Queries* 6S:7 (1883) 235; (Roud 19429)

122 'Nievie, nievie nack . . .': *Notes & Queries* 6S:7 (1883) 235; (Roud 19144)

122 'Nievie nievie nick-nack . . .': *Transactions of the Rymour Club* 3 (1928) 137; (Roud 19144)

122–3 'It was a favourite . . .': Marshall (1924) 33

123 'This is the king . . .': MacTaggart (1824) 257–8

123 'A quieter indoor game . . .': Nicholson (1890) 145–6

123 'Bwch mewn llwyn . . .': Parry-Jones (1964) 142–3

123–4 'Dyma'r hawl . . .': Parry-Jones (1964) 142–3

124 'Pi – pa – po – pin . . .': Parry-Jones (1964) 142–3

124 'Hey the button . . .': Rodger (c.1950) 8

124 'Four, three, two, one . . .': SR collection, Robert Arkenstall School Council, Haddenham, Cambridgeshire, 2009

124 'Five, six, seven, eight . . .': Gareth Whitaker collection, Denholme Primary School, Yorkshire, 2002

124–5 'Two boys stand . . .': SR collection, own recollection (1950s), South London

125 '[This game] transferred . . .': Rolph (1980) 34

125 'You and your friend . . .': McDowell (1972) 152

125 'One particular two-person . . .': SR collection, Nigel Wilcockson (b.1961), Cambridge, 2009

126 'If the slappee . . .': Cathy Gould collection, Graeme Daniels (b.1962), Coventry, c.2004

126 'Two players hold . . .': Cathy Gould collection, boys (year 8), Coventry, 2004

126–7 'Along come the crabs . . .': SR collection, Cherry & Ella (both 11), Camden, North London, 2009

127 'Write "THIS" . . .': SR collection, Kate (11) & Joanna (12), Weybridge, Surrey, 2009

127 'This [show "THIS"] . . .': Cathy Gould collection, Lucy Sharp (11), Coventry, 2000

128 'Write "THIS" on fingers . . .': SR collection, Sam (11) & Caitlin (7), Rochester, Kent, 2010

130 'The wet sleeve . . .': Cathy Gould collection, Graeme Daniels (b.1962), Coventry, 2010

130 'Chicken scratching': Cathy Gould collection, Craig Robins (1970s), Coventry, 2010

130 'In Warwickshire . . .': Northall (1892) 354

130 'Pile on': SR collection, Liam Robinson (b.1976), Grimsby, 2010

131 'A game popular . . .': Church (1955) 144–5

131 'Another playground favourite . . .': SR collection, Steve Gardham (b.1947), Hull, 2010

131 'A perennial favourite . . .': SR collection, Paul Sartin (1975–1982), Cricklewood, North-west London, 2010

132 'When a "Cobbing match" . . .': Henderson (1866) 18

132 'Should a boy . . .': Nicholson (1890) 146–7

132–3 'A particularly nasty . . .': SR collection, Paul Davenport (b.1950), Hull, 2010

133 'I was evacuated . . .': SR collection, John Earl (b.1928), South London, 2010

133 'Tabbing': SR collection, Tom Randall (b.1944), Mansfield, Nottinghamshire, 2010

133 'Cauliflower ear': Cathy Gould collection, boys (year 9), Coventry, 2010

133 'Wet willies': Cathy Gould collection, boys (year 11), Coventry, 2010

134 'A boy met me . . .': Craig (1994) 101

134 'The punishment . . .': Moor (1823) 53

134–5 'Returning to birthdays . . .': Cathy Gould collection, Graeme Daniels, Judith Roberts and Karla Gould (b.1962/3), Coventry; Cathy Gould collection, Richard Lamb (b.c.1969), Solihull, 2004

135–6 'A very popular game . . .': Steve Gardham Collection (1980s/1990s), Beverley, Yorkshire, 2010

136 'Adam and Eve . . .': SR collection, own recollection (1950s), Streatham, South London, 2010

136 'The basic rhyme . . .': Notes & Queries 10S:4 (1905) 77

136 'Punch and Judy . . .': SR collection, Steve Gardham (b.1947), Hull, 2010

136 'Smell my cheese': Steve Roud collection, Liam Robinson (b.1976), Grimsby, 2010

137 'What does the Queen Mary . . .': SR collection, Malcolm Smith (b.1949), Isle of Wight, 2010

141 'Lolly Sticks': SR collection, own memory, (1950s), Streatham, South London

141 'Sunderland children . . .': SR collection, Alex Branthwaite (b.1939), Sunderland, 2009

141–2 'Cat's Cradle': Caroline Furness Jayne's String Figures (1906) was one of the first serious attempts to plot the worldwide distribution of the game

142–3 'Ducks and Drakes': Moor (1823) 115–16

143 'Torri Cwt y Gath . . .': Parry-Jones (1964) 53

143–4 'Ali Bwl Dab . . .': Parry-Jones (1964) 109

144–5 'In "Duck" . . .': Low (1891) 516

146 'As for "Knifey" . . .': Lessels (1990) 543

146–7 'Battledore and shuttlecock . . .': Uttley (1946) 64–6

147 'Shuttlecock, shuttlecock . . .': Notes & Queries 3S:3 (1863) 87

147 'This year, next year . . .': Gomme II (1898) 194

148–9 'One day . . .': Uttley (1946) 66–7

149 'Hoops were one . . .': Parry-Jones (1964) 51

150 'Girls kept their hoops . . .': Tapp (1992) 98–9

150 'A good hoop-stick . . .': Sturt (1927) 151

150 'A hoop was the best . . .': Uttley (1946) 66–7

151 'A well-spun top . . .': Uttley (1946) 55–7

151 'For boys tops . . .': Haworth (1986) 169–70

151 'But then, the little peg-tops . . .': Sturt (1927) 150

152 'Boys always had . . .': Care (c.1987) 34–5

152 'Another way in which . . .': Care (c.1987) 34–5

152–3 'Chip'ems': Gamble (1979) 138

153 'The spinning tops were . . .': Rolph (1980) 31

154 'Top': *Francis Willughby's Book of Games* (1660s) f.222

158–9 'Knuckle bones in 1881': *Boy's Own Paper* (28 May 1881) 557

159 'Order of Knucklebones . . .': *Boy's Own Paper* (2 Jul 1881) 648

162–3 'Skipping was a favourite . . .': Uttley (1946) 62–3

163 'Young skippers . . .': Ritchie (1965) 112

164 'We used plastic hoops . . .': SR collection, Sally Cole (b.1978), St Leonard's-on-Sea, Sussex, 2007

164 'In pairs you stand . . .': SR collection, Megan, Mollie & Annie (all 11), Godalming, Surrey, 2008

165 'One of the girls . . .': Brady (1984) 70

165 'Keep the kettle boiling . . .': SR collection, Valerie Groves & Kerry Newman (b.c.1960), Mitcham, Surrey, 1974

165 'Down in the meadow . . .': SR collection, Tracy Slipp (b.1969), Ludgershall, Wiltshire, 1978

165 'Over and Under the moon': Warwickshire Fed WIs, *Warwickshire Within Living Memory* (1993) 119–20

166 'Over the sun . . .': SR collection, Joanne Wallwork (b.1965), Manchester, 2007

166 'Back to back . . .': SR collection, Maddie, Rhea & Dahlia (all 10), Ealing, West London, 2009; SR collection, Megan, Mollie & Annie (all 11), Godalming, Surrey, 2008

166–7 'High, low, swing . . .': SR collection, Caroline Brewser (b.1967), Vale of Glamorgan, Wales, 2007

167 'In Hampshire . . .': SR collection, Kathy Roud (8), Andover, Hampshire, 1983

167 'F. C. Husenbeth . . .': Husenbeth (1856) 105–6

167 'Ali Baba . . .': Ritchie (1965) 118

167 'What we called French skipping . . .': *The Listener* (25 Nov 1954) 917–18

167 'In Redcar . . .': SR collection, Sophie (b.1988), Redcar, North Yorkshire, 2008

168–9 Skipping rhymes in 1898: Gomme II (1898) 200–4

169 'All the boys . . .': Moxon (1907) 156

170 'Bluebells, cockleshells . . .' [1]: SR collection, Natasha (8), Sheffield, 2008

170 'Bluebells, cockleshells . . .' [2]: SR collection, Tracey Slipp (9), Ludgershall, Wiltshire, 1978

170 'Bluebells, cockleshells . . .' [3]: Cathy Gould collection, Sue Sanders (1960s/1970s) Halifax, Yorkshire

170 'Bluebells, cockleshells . . .' [4]: Cathy Gould collection, Danielle Sharp (b.1983), Coventry, 2007

170 'Eaper Weaper . . .': Douglas (1916) 53

171 'Swish swosh . . .': Opie (1997) 179

172 'Well, whoever went . . .': Steven Clarke, Queen's University student project, Maureen Hutcheson (b.1916), Belfast, 1995/6

173 'Skipping with a rope . . .': Husenbeth (1856) 105–6

173 'By the holy . . .': Babcock (1886) 332

173 'Curiously enough . . .': *Girl's Own Paper* (12 Mar 1892) 372–3

174 'The second class . . .': Gomme II (1898) 201–2

174 'I'm a little bumper car . . .': SR collection, Laetitia (11), London, 2009

175 'Bumper car, bumper car . . .' [1]: SR collection, Alison Agnew (7/8), Andover, Hampshire, 1980

175 'Bumper car, bumper car . . .' [2]: SR collection, Kathy Roud (8), Andover, Hampshire, c.1983

175 'Then you count down . . .': SR collection, Megan, Mollie & Annie (all 11), Godalming, Surrey, 2008

175 'Teddy bear . . .' [1]: SR collection, Laetitia (11), London, 2009

176 'Teddy bear . . .' [2]: SR collection, Park Lodge School Council, Belfast, 2010

176 'All in together, girls . . .' [1]: SR collection, Natasha (8), Sheffield, 2008

176 'All in together, girls . . .' [2]: M. Lynn, Mrs Anne Lynn (62), Omagh, Co. Tyrone, 1992 (student project, University of Belfast)

177 'When it was time . . .': Gamble (1979) 105

177 'I like coffee . . .' [1]: SR collection, Megan, Mollie & Annie (all 11), Godalming, Surrey, 2008

177 'I like coffee . . .' [2]: SR collection, Sharon Forrester (b.1968), Edinburgh, 2007

178 'Cowboy Joe . . .': SR collection, Valerie Groves & Kerry Newman (b.c.1960), Mitcham, Surrey, 1974

178 'Cinderella, dressed in yellow . . .': SR collection, Tina & Lisa Roud, Leytonstone, East London, 1978

178 'Cinderella, dressed in yella . . .' [1]: SR collection, Jessica (b.1989), Norfolk, 2007

178 'Cinderella, dressed in yella . . .' [2]: SR collection, Kate (11) & Joanna (12), Weybridge, Surrey, 2009

178–9 'Rosy apple . . .': SR collection, Park Lodge School Council, Belfast, 2010

179 'Not last night . . .': SR collection, Natalie Harbury (8), Andover, Hampshire, 1982

179 'I'm a little girl-guide . . .' [1]: SR collection, Tracy Slipp (9), Ludgershall, Wiltshire, 1978

179–80 'I'm a little Brownie . . .': Harcus Moodie, *A Study of a Family's Recollections of Primary School Playground Games* (student project MD 2007.03, School of Scottish Studies, Edinburgh, 2007)

180 'I'm a little girl guide . . .' [2]: SR collection, South London, 1970

180 'Jelly on a plate . . .' [1]: Leyden (1993) 129

180–1 'Jelly on a plate . . .' [2]: Rodger (c.1950) 21

181 'On the corner . . .': SR collection, Margaret Wilton (b.c.1952), Andover, Hampshire, 1975

181 'On a mountain . . .' [1]: SR collection, Valerie Groves & Kerry Newman (b.c.1960), Mitcham, Surrey, 1974

181–2 'On a mountain . . .' [2]: SR collection, Nicola Meads (b.1965), Andover, Hampshire, 1975

182 'The wind . . .': SR collection, Geraldine (b.c.1947), Lancashire, 1975

182–3 'Sometimes we got two . . .': SR collection, year 6 schoolchildren (11/12), Ardleigh, Essex, 2009

183 'One of my favourite games . . .': SR collection, Georgia (13), Inverness, 2008

183 'We also played colours . . .': SR collection, Phil Morant (1950s), Bedfont, Middlesex, 2009

183 'Colour Wand': Cathy Gould collection, girls (1990s), Coventry, 2004

184 'Teddy on the railway . . .': SR collection, Joyce Kerr (b.c.1929), Dundee, 2009

184 'Ipsy gypsy Caroline . . .': SR collection, Bob Webb (1940s), Bradford on Avon, Wiltshire, 2009

184 'My pink pinafore . . .': Coles (1947) 151

184 'Little Fatty Doctor . . .': SR collection, Andrea (1950s), Leeds, 2009

184 'House for sale . . .': SR collection, Pat Gillies (b.1953), Cardiff, 2007

184 'Schwah schwah . . .': SR collection, Nikki Collins (b.1957), Southampton, Hampshire, c.1984

184 'All the girls in our town . . .': SR collection, female, South London, 1970

184–5 'Mr Speed . . .': SR collection, female (b.c.1947), Lancashire, 1975

185 'Mrs D . . .': SR collection, Diana Roud (b.1946), Mitcham, Surrey, 1970

185 'Mrs M . . .': SR collection, Margaret Wilton (b.c.1952) Andover, Hampshire, 1975

185 'Down to Mississippi . . .': SR collection, Valerie Groves & Kerry Newman (b.c.1960), Mitcham, Surrey, 1974

185 'Ice cream . . .': SR collection, Valerie Groves & Kerry Newman (b.c.1960), Mitcham, Surrey, 1974

185 'Vote, vote, vote . . .': SR collection, Anne White (b.1953), Streatham, South London, 1970

185 'Policeman, Policeman . . .': SR collection, female (b.1953), Streatham, South London, c.1970

185 'Drip, drop, drops . . .': SR collection, Anne White (b.1953), Streatham, South London, c.1970

185 'London County Council . . .': SR collection, Jayne Eggert (b.1953), Norbury, South London, 1970

185 'Saucy Mary Ann . . .': SR collection, female (b.1953), Streatham, South London, c.1970

186 'In "Polly Tell Me the Time" . . .': Douglas (1916) 49

186 'As a child . . .': *Notes & Queries* 172 (1937) 262

187 'At Worship Street.': *The Times* (8 Apr 1874)

188 'We did it in year 3 . . .': SR collection, Megan, Mollie & Annie (all 11), Godalming, Surrey, 2008

188 'In 1989 . . .': Arleo (1989; 1991)

189 'The craze came back . . .': Roud (1985) 10

189 'England, Ireland . . .' [1]: Roud (1985) 11

189 'England, Ireland . . .' [2]: SR collection, Cherry & Ella (both 11), Camden, North London, 2009

189 'England, Ireland . . .' [3]: SR collection, Georgia (13), Inverness, 2008

190 'England, Ireland . . .' [4]: SR collection, Megan, Mollie & Annie (all 11), Godalming, Surrey, 2008

190 'Banana, banana . . .': SR collection, Wendy (8), Joanna (9) & Sonai (10), Croydon, Surrey, 1985

190 'Jingle jangle . . .': SR collection, Tina & Lisa Roud, Leytonstone, East London, 1978

190 'Jack be nimble . . .': SR collection, Wendy (8), Joanna (9) & Sonai (10), Croydon, Surrey, 1985

190 'Romans, Saxons . . .': Steve Gardham collection, Amanda Allenby, Beverley, Yorkshire, 1982

191–7 Ball-bouncing: Opie (1997) 128–59; Rutherford (1971) 77–87; Ritchie (1965) 80–95; McVicar (2007) 40–8; Brady (1984) 53–68

191 'One, two, three a'leary . . .': SR collection, Sylvia Elkins (1950s/1960s), Willesden/Kingsbury, North London, 2009

191 'One, two, three O'Leary . . .': SR collection, Joy Gallagher (b.1956), Abbots Ann, Hampshire, 1977

192 'One two three alairy . . .': Kellett (1966) 56

192 'For certain games . . .': Gamble (1979) 139–40

193 'Our playground . . .': North Yorkshire Fed WIs, *North Yorkshire Within Living Memory* (1995) 95

193 'We would start . . .': Warkwickshire Fed WIs, *Warwickshire Within Living Memory* (1993) 118

193–4 'We had *plainsies* . . .'; 'Drink a pint . . .'; 'Big Ben . . .': SR collection, Caroline Brewser (b.1967), Vale of Glamorgan, 2007

194–5 '*Plainsies* . . .': SR collection, Chantel Cousins (b.1979), London, 2008

195 'Every time you miss . . .': SR collection, Jo Robinson (b.1971), Leigh on Sea, Essex, 2008

195–6 'Juggling two balls . . .': SR collection, Caroline Oates (b.1955), Gateshead, 2009

197 'One girl takes a ball . . .': Gomme II (1898) 64–5, 405–6

197–8 'Want a cigarette . . .': SR collection, Nicola Mead (b.1965), Andover, 1975

198 'Johnny get up . . .': SR collection, Jim Duerdin (b.1957), Newcastle, 1977

198 'Nebuchadnezzar, King of the Jews . . .': SR collection, Anne Rogers (b.1942), Paddock Wood, Kent, 2007

199 'Matthew, Mark, Luke and John . . .' [1]: SR collection, Joy Gallagher (b.1956), Abbots Ann, Hampshire, 1977

199 'Matthew, Mark, Luke and John . . .' [2]: Opie (1951) 303–5

199 'When I was one . . .' [1]: SR collection, Nicola Mead (b.1965), Andover, Hampshire, 1975

200 'When I was one . . .' [2]: SR collection, Geraldine (b.c.1947), Lancashire, 1975

200 'When I was one . . .' [3]: SR collection, Anne White (b.1953), Streatham, South London, 1970

202 'I went into the garden . . .': Rodger (c.1950) 25

202 'Alice in Wonderland . . .': SR collection, Nicola Thomson, Norbury, South London, 1978

202 'Upsy Walls ice cream . . .': SR collection, Amanda Martin (b.1975), Preston, Lancashire, 2007

202 'Poor Mrs Fluffyball . . .': SR collection, Rachel Nussey (b.1976), Middlesbrough, Yorkshire, 2007

202 'Mrs Minny had a pinny . . .': SR collection, Jessie Richards (b.1959), Clapham, South London, 1971

202 'Gipsy Ipsy lived in a tent . . .': SR collection, Diana Roud (b.1946), Mitcham, Surrey, 1970

202 'Over the garden wall . . .': SR collection, Monica Southwell (b.1953), Streatham, South London, 1971

202 'Each peach pear plum . . .': SR collection, Monica Southwell (b.1953), Streatham, South London, 1971

202 'Oliver, Oliver . . .': SR collection, Christine, Cheryl & Karen (b.c.1960), Mitcham, Surrey, 1971

203 'P K penny a packet . . .': SR collection, Jessie (12), Pollards Hill, South London, 1971

203 'Brownie number one . . .': SR collection, Nicola Mead (b.1965), Andover, Hampshire, 1975

203 'Peter Pan said to Paul . . .': SR collection, girl (b.1955), South London, 1970

203 'Under, over . . .': SR collection, Joy Gallagher (b.1956), Abbots Ann, Hampshire, 1977

203 'Plainsies, Clapsies': Lynch (1977) 51

203 '1, 2, 3 . . .': SR collection, Linda Shoben (b.1950), Caernarvon, 2007

203 'Eight girls' names . . .': SR collection, Jim Duerdin (b.1957), Newcastle, 1977

203 'I went over . . .': SR collection, Jenny (b.c.1948), Andover, Hampshire, 1977

203 'Plainsy, clapsy . . .': SR collection, Monica Southwell (b.1953), Streatham, South London, 1971

204 'Ball in a stocking . . .': SR collection, Joanne Wallwork (b.1965), Manchester, 2007

204 'The ball was what . . .': Cumbria Fed WIs, *Cumbria Within Living Memory* (1994) 110–11

204 'Queenie, Queenie': (Roud 19361)

204–5 'Queenie, Queenie . . .' [1]: SR collection, Hazel Fortune (b.1950), London, 2007

205 'Alla balla boosha . . .': SR collection, Simon Furey (b.1945), Nottingham, 2008

205 'Queenie, Queenie . . .' [2]: SR collection, Lucy (8) & Sarah (7) Bawden, Andover, Hampshire, 1982

205 'In Southwark . . .': Bason (1971) 105–6

205 'Lady Queen Anne . . .': Leslie (1831) 2

205 'In 1898 . . .': Gomme II (1898) 90–102

206 'It was only played . . .': Bason (1971) 106–7

206 'The girls stand in a line . . .': Rodger (c.1950) 30

206–7 'Bad Eggs': SR collection, own recollection (1950s/1960s), South London

207 'You throw the ball up . . .': SR collection, Megan, Mollie & Annie (all 11), Godalming, Surrey, 2008

208–9 'Caps': C. W. Penny (1896–7) 193–4

210 'A ball was thrown . . .': Ronne Randall collection, Lynne Chapman (b.c.1955), Nottingham, 2003

210 'Kerby': Steve Gardham collection, schoolchild, Beverley, Yorkshire, 1980

210–11 'Slam': Steve Gardham collection, Michael Brumpton (13), Beverley, Yorkshire, c.1996

211 'Children line up . . .': Cathy Gould collection, girls, Coventry, 2004

211 'Dodge Ball': SR collection, Maddie, Rhea & Dahlia (all 10), Ealing, West London, 2009

211–12 '4 Square': Steve Gardham collection, A. Smith, Beverley, Yorkshire, c.1975

212 'In a circle . . .': SR collection, Adam (13), Irma (8), Bethany (11) & Adele (11), Gateshead, 2010

212 'You all stood . . .': SR collection, G. J. Anderson (male, b.1936), Glasgow, 2010

213 'Two boys stand . . .': Douglas (1916) 5

213 'There's a circle . . .': SR collection, Maddie, Rhea & Dahlia (all 10), Ealing, West London, 2009

215 'The playing of marbles . . .': Bishop & Curtis (2001) 46

215–16 '*Different types of marble . . .*': Wright (1913) 309

216 '*Dobbing . . .*': Baker (1854) 188

216–17 'Let me tell you . . .': Forrest (1858) 80

217 'Cullies . . .': SR collection, Jonnie Robinson (b.1964), Sutton Coldfield, West Midlands, 2007

217 'Queenies . . .': SR collection, Amanda (b.1972), Ramsgate, Kent, 2008

217 'Skettis . . .': SR collection, Jo Robinson (b.1971), Leigh on Sea, Essex, 2008

217 'Marbles that were opaque . . .': SR collection, Chris (male, b.1968), Bristol, 2007

217–18 'Ring taw': Nicholson (1890) 145–6

218 'It was along the gutters . . .': Kent Fed WIs, *East Kent Within Living Memory* (1995) 121

218 'Now guttery . . .': Mills & Hardie (1991) 6

218–19 '[Of all the marble games] . . .': Rolph (1980) 32

219 'Cob-castle': Willughby (2003) 188

219 'Another game . . .': Gloucestershire Fed WIs, *Gloucestershire Within Living Memory* (1996) 95

219 'The object being . . .': Lee (1936) 147

220 '[Another] favourite game . . .' Lee (1936) 147

220 'But there was a certain . . .': *Nottingham Journal* (22 Apr 1952)

220 'We used to find . . .': SR collection, Sylvia Elkins (1950s/1960s), Willesden/Kingsbury, North London, 2009

221 'A quieter indoor game . . .': Nicholson (1890) 145–6

221 'Of course, you never . . .': Lessels (1990) 542–3

221 'You have stuck . . .': Forrest (1858) 79–80

222 'This is no small ordeal . . .': Lee (1936) 147

222 'Boys *and* girls played the game . . .': Harris (1969) 101–2

223 'There are many different . . .': *Games and Sports for Young Boys* (1859) 43

224 'Were the newest . . .': *Notes & Queries* 9S:3 (1899) 65

225–6 'One very odd amusement . . .': *The Life and Correspondence of Robert Southey* I (1849) 55–6

226–7 'Conquerors': Sturt (1927) 158–9

227 'Oblionker': *Notes & Queries* 5S:10 (1878) 177

228 'In the course . . .': *Notes & Queries* 5S:12 (1879) 28

228 'I can assure you . . .': Margaret Acland, *The Times* (29 Sep 1952)

228–9 'The date of their advent . . .': Uttley (1946) 54

230 'Obli, Obli . . .': *Notes & Queries* 5S:10 (1878) 378

230 'Cobley Co . . .': Parry-Jones (1964) 108

230 'Hick, hack . . .': *The Times* (26 Sep 1952)

230 'Fuggy smack . . .': Ogden (1978) 71

230 'Conkers are not lightly . . .': *The Times* (26 Sep 1952)

230–31 'The rules of combat . . .': *Pall Mall Gazette* (6 Oct 1898)

233 'Cigarette cards were our passion . . .': Paul (1957) 48–9

233 'Almost everything . . .': Paul (1957) 48–9

233 'We got most . . .': Gamble (1979) 138

235 'In the playground . . .': Rolph (1980) 33

235 'Exchanging "scraps" . . .': Lancashire Fed WIs, *Lancashire Within Living Memory* (1997) 108

236 'You took the scraps . . .': SR collection, Jane McOwan (b.1951), Glasgow, 2007

236 'Boys buy . . .': Mayhew I (1861–2) 85

237 'Paip': Jamieson, *An Etymological Dictionary of the Scottish Language* (1808)

237 'The simplest one . . .': *Scots Magazine* (Jul 1991) 370–3

237 'I recall, too . . .': Church (1955) 121

238 'Us boys used to go . . .': Paul (1981) 31

238 'A screw would be placed . . .': Walker (1989) 8

238 'Cherry time was lovely . . .': Lakeman (1982) 56

238 'We used to sit for hours . . .': North Kensington Amenity Trust, *They were Happy Days* (1982–3) 6

239 'Every night . . .': *Scots Magazine* (Jul 1991) 370–3

239 'Buttons': Grey (1977) 141

240 'The girls played buttons . . .': Paul (1981) 32

240–41 'Buttons': Low (1891) 51–4

241 'Passing the button': Bullock (1976) 75

242 'Guy': Moore (1924) 76

242 'When we were kids . . .': Folkways LP *The Elliots of Birtley* (FG 3565, 1962)

242 'I remember well . . .': Gomme II (1898) 41–2

243 'A pinnet a piece . . .': Addy (1888) 325

243 'Then there were grottoes . . .': North Kensington Amenity Trust, *They were Happy Days* (1982–3) 6

243 'One of the respectable . . .': Rolph (1980) 32

244 '. . . from the hazel hedge . . .': Parry-Jones (1964) 45–7

245 'At the age of four . . .': North Yorkshire Fed WIs, *North Yorkshire Within Living Memory* (1995) 106

245–6 'Until my brother . . .': Shakespeare (1990) 86

246 'I was like everyone else . . .': Ward (1988) 87

247 'Rock the cradle. . .': Moore (1924)

252 'Then, beneath the long . . .': Thompson (1939) 142–52

257 *The Big Ship Sails*: (Roud 4827)

257 'The big ship sails through . . .': SR collection, Heather Rendall (b.1946), Sussex, 2007

258 'When all arms . . .': Grimes (1996) 194

258–9 'Another one was . . .': SR collection, Hilary Blencowe (1950s), Liverpool, 2009

259 'The children stand . . .': Gomme II (1898) 228–32

259 'Thread my grandmother's needle . . .': Gomme II (1898) 228–32

260 *Duke a-Riding*: (Roud 730)

260 'My favourite game was . . .': SR collection, Hilary Blencowe (1950s), Liverpool, 2009

260 'Here come three dukes . . .': Rodger (c.1950) 32

261–2 *Dusty Bluebells*: (Roud 13206)

262–3 *Dutch Girl*: (Roud 13205)

263 *Fair Rosa*: (Roud 7889)

263–4 'The princess was . . .': *English Dance & Song* 21:6 (Jul/Aug 1957)

264–5 *The Farmer's in His Den*: (Roud 6306)

265 'The farmer wants a wife . . .': SR collection, Hilary Blencowe (1950s), Liverpool, 2009

266 *Green Gravel*: (Roud 1368)

266 'Green gravel . . .' [1]: Marshall (1924) 30

267 'Green gravel . . .' [2]: SR collection, East Street School playground, Andover, Hampshire, 1983

267–8 *Here We Go Round the Mulberry Bush*: (Roud 7882)

268 'The gooseberry grows . . .': James Hook, *Christmas Box* (1798), quoted in Opie (1985) 289

269 *How Many Miles to Babylon?*: (Roud 8148)

269 'How many miles is it . . .': Halliwell (1842) 157

269 'A line of children . . .': Gomme I (1894) 236

269 'Then open the gates . . .': Gomme I (1894) 234

270 'The preacher compared . . .': Opie (1985) 45

270 *London Bridge*: (Roud 502)

271 'Five of the nine versions . . .': Gomme I (1894) 333-50

272 *Nuts in May*: (Roud 6308)

273 '. . . this game is probably . . .': Gomme I (1894) 424-33

274 *Old Roger Is Dead*: (Roud 797)

274 'Old Rogers is dead . . .': Gomme II (1898) 17

275 'Old Dobbin is dead . . .': *Notes & Queries* 10S:2 (1904) 348-9

275 *One Elephant*: (Roud 22569)

275 'Iona and Peter Opie confirm . . .': Opie (1985) 367-9

275–7 *Orange Balls*: (Roud 22561)

276 'Orange balls . . .': SR collection, Rebecca, Ella, Helena & Luckshie (all 8), East Finchley, North London, 2008

276 'Stamp your feet . . .': Opie (1985) 235

277 'Orange boys . . .': Anne Gilchrist MSS, Vaughan Williams Memorial Library, London (AGG/1/18/38)

277 'Oliver, Oliver . . .': Burne (1883) 508

277–80 *Oranges and Lemons*: (Roud 13190)

277–8 'There was also . . .': SR collection, Margo Crispin (b.1936), Wolverhampton, 2009

279 'Gay go up . . .': *Gammer Gurton's Garland* (1810) 28-9

281 *Ring a-ring a-roses*: (Roud 7925)

281 'In 1875 James Fowler . . .': *Notes & Queries* 5S:3 (1875) 481-3

281–2 'Ring a ring o' roses . . .': Neale (1975) 156-7

282 'Ring a ring a rosie . . .': Newell (1903) 127-8

283 '. . . we ourselves . . .': Opie (1985) 221

283–5 *Roman Soldiers*: (Roud 8255)

283–4 'Have you any bread and wine . . .' [1]: Bosanquet (1929) 131

284–5 'Have you any bread and wine . . .' [2]: M'Bain (1887) 342-3

285–7 *Sally Water*: (Roud 4509)

285–6 'Little Sally Saucer . . .': SR collection, Lucy (8) & Sarah (7) Bawden, Andover, Hampshire 1982

286 'I'm a little Sandy boy . . .'; 'Little Alexander . . .': Fraser (1975) 109

286 'Alice Gomme prints . . .': Gomme II (1898) 149-79

287 '. . . pre-Celtic people . . .': Gomme II (1898) 179

287–8 *The Wind Blows High*: (Roud 2649)

287 'The wind, the wind . . .' [1]: Gillington (1909) 1-2

287–8 'The wind, the wind . . .' [2]: Ritchie (1965) 169-70

288–9 *Cat's got the Measles*: (Roud 19597)

289 'Cat's got the measles . . .' [1]: SR collection, Williams family (10–14), Andover, Hampshire, 1980

289 'Cat's got the measles . . .' [2]: SR collection, Megan, Mollie & Annie (all 11), Godalming, Surrey, 2008

289 'Send for the doctor . . .': SR collection, Lucy (8) & Sarah (7) Bawden, Andover, Hampshire, 1982

289 'Ip dip do . . .': SR collection, Cherry & Ella (both 11), Camden, North London, 2009

290 *Firecracker*: (Roud 19983)

290 'Firecracker firecracker . . .': SR collection, Tracey Slipp (9), Ludgershall, Wiltshire, 1978

290–91 *Shirley Temple*: (Roud 16291)

290 'I'm Shirley Temple . . .': SR collection, Tracy Slipp, Ludgershall, Wiltshire 1978

291–2 *Sunny Side Up*: (Roud 18992)

291 'Kick the sunny side up up . . .': SR collection, Tracey Slipp (9), Ludgershall, Wiltshire, 1978

291 'Keep your sunny side up . . .': Kellett (1966) 53-4

292–5 *Tennessee Wig-Walk*: (Roud 19008)

293 'I'm a bald-headed chicken . . .': SR collection, Wendy Hill (8), Basingstoke, Hampshire, 1982

293–4 'I'm a locked-up chicken . . .': Gareth Whittaker collection, Denholme, Yorkshire, 2002

294 'I'm a Texas girl . . .' [1]: SR collection, Wendy Hill (8), Basingstoke, Hampshire, 1982

294 'I'm a Texan girl . . .': SR collection, East Street School playground, Andover, Hampshire, 1983

294–5 'I'm a Texas girl . . .' [2]: Folktrax recording FTX 196; recorded by Damian Webb in the North of England, 1960s

296–333 Although clapping rhymes have featured strongly in the playground for nearly fifty years, there have been few studies in Britain which concentrate on the genre, and folklorists were a little slow in taking notice. Frank Rutherford was probably the first to devote a special section to clapping in his collection from the North-east published in 1971, and this was followed by studies by Jane Hubbard (1982) and Georgina Boyes (1984), who reported on their fieldwork in different parts of Yorkshire, and some of my own collecting in Hampshire and London was printed in 1984. R. A. Smith included a section in his book of rhymes from Blue Bell School in Nottingham (1982); Eilis Brady devotes two pages of her Dublin collection (1984) to it. But as usual it is Iona and Peter Opie who present the biggest sample from across the country in *The Singing Game* (1985). In recent years there has been a noticeable revival of interest in the genre. Ewan McVicar devotes some pages in his book of Scottish rhymes (2007); Mavis Curtis (2004) concentrates on the tunes (again from fieldwork in Yorkshire); and Green & Widdowson (2003) provide a detailed analysis of the language of several clapping texts. Andy Arleo demonstrates how British rhymes fit into the international scene with his study of *When Susie Was a Baby* (2001).

299 'I'm Popeye the sailorman . . .': SR collection, Alison Agnew (7/8), Andover, Hampshire, 1980

300 'My *mother* said . . .': Balfour (1904) 120

301 'Pease parritch hot . . .': McDowell (1972) 152

301 'Sandy Doo . . .': Rutherford (1971) 77

301 'John, John . . .': Turner et al (1978) 36

302 'Number one at the baker's shop . . .': SR collection, Tina & Lisa Roud, Leytonstone, East London, 1978

302–3 'Under the bramble bushes . . .' [1]: SR collection, Caroline Brewser (b.1967), Vale of Glamorgan, 2007

303 'Under the bramble bushes . . .' [2]: SR collection, Park Lodge School Council, Belfast, 2010

303–4 'Si si my baby . . .': SR collection, Amanda (b.1972), Ramsgate, Kent, 2008

304 'Cissy my baby . . .': Quigley (1993) 8

304 'Suzi my playmate . . .': Cathy Gould collection, Danielle Sharp (15), Coventry, 1998

305 'I went to a Chinese restaurant . . .' [1]: SR collection, East Street School playground, Andover, Hampshire, 1982

305–6 'I went to a Chinese restaurant . . .' [2]: SR collection, East Street School playground, Andover, Hampshire, 1982

306 'I went to a Chinese restaurant . . .' [3]: Steve Gardham collection, Julia Blake, Beverley, Yorkshire, 1982

306 'I went to a Chinese restaurant . . .' [4]: Gareth Whittaker collection, Denholme, Yorkshire, 2002

306–7 'My boyfriend gave me an apple . . .': SR collection, Lucy Kelley (b.1987), Belmont, Surrey, 2007

307 'He took me to the pictures . . .': SR collection, Kathy Roud & friends (all 8), Andover, Hampshire, 1983

308 'I am a little Dutch girl . . .': Rutherford (1971) 74

308 'Mrs Grady . . .': Rutherford (1971) 76

308 'I had the German measles . . .': Damian Webb Collection, Saydisc CD-SDL 338

308–9 'Ali Ba Ba Ba . . .': Damian Webb Collection, Saydisc CD-SDL 338

309 'Abe, Abe, Abe my boy . . .': Damian Webb Collection, Saydisc CD-SDL 338

309 'The spaceman said . . .': Damian Webb Collection, Saydisc CD-SDL 338

309 'Zoom zoom zoom . . .': SR collection, Clare Higginson (b.1963), Stockport, 2008

309 'In Bombay . . .': Mary Erskine School, Edinburgh, Children's Street Games Project, 1990

309 'There was ten in the bed . . .': SR collection, East Street School playground, Andover, Hampshire, 1983

309 'My boyfriend's name is Ella . . .': SR collection, Jessie Richards, (b.1959), Clapham, South London, 1971

309 'My boyfriend's name is Paddy . . .': SR collection, Laura Hyde (b.*c*.1953), Stanmore, Middlesex, 1970

310 'Eight o'clock bells . . .': Moxon (1907) 153

310 'My mother told me . . .': SR collection, Lynn Davis (b.1949), Herne Hill, South London, 2007

310 'Three six nine . . .': SR collection, Lesley Dawe (b.1956), Hook, Hampshire, 2007

311 'Miss Mary Mack . . .' [1]: SR collection, Rebecca (9, from Lechlade) & Maddie (10, from Salisbury), Lechlade, Gloucester, 2010

311 'Miss Mary Mack . . .' [2]: SR collection, Ravenstone School Council, Balham, South London, 2010

312 'When Susie was a baby . . .' [1]: SR collection, Williams family (10–14), Andover, Hampshire, 1980

313 'When Susie was a baby . . .' [2]: SR collection, Ravenstone School Council, Balham, South London, 2010

315 'Eeny meeny decimeny . . .': SR collection, Laetitia (11), London, 2009

316 'This train goes . . .': SR collection, Megan, Mollie & Annie (all 11), Godalming, Surrey, 2008

316–17 'Downtown baby . . .': SR collection, Megan, Mollie & Annie (all 11), Godalming, Surrey, 2008

317 'My name is Ena Beena . . .': Cathy Gould collection, Danielle Sharp (15), Coventry, 1998

318 'Yankee Doodle . . .': SR collection, Kate (11) & Joanna (12), Weybridge, Surrey, 2009; SR collection, Maddie, Rhea & Dahlia (all 10), Ealing, West London, 2009

318 'Domino p-a-i-r . . .': SR collection, Robert Arkenstall School Council, Haddenham, Cambridgeshire, 2009

318 'In nineteen sixty-four . . .': Gareth Whittaker collection, Denholme, Yorkshire, 2002

318 'Super Sophie . . .': Gareth Whittaker collection, Denholme, Yorkshire, 2002

318 'Oliver, Oliver . . .': Gareth Whittaker collection, Denholme, Yorkshire, 2002

318 'I found a box . . .': Gareth Whittaker collection, Denholme, Yorkshire, 2002

318 'Coca-Cola . . .': Cathy Gould collection, girls (5), Coventry, 2005

319 'Ribena . . .': SR collection, Ravenstone School Council, Balham, South London, 2010

319 'O Mary Anne . . .': SR collection, Park Lodge School, Belfast, 2010

319 'Down down baby . . .': SR collection, Robert Arkenstall School Council, Haddenham, Cambridgeshire, 2009

319 'My mummy is a baker . . .' [1]: SR collection, Maddie, Rhea & Dahlia (all 10), Ealing, West London, 2009

319 'Pepsi Cola . . .': SR collection, Adam (13), Irma (8), Bethany (11), Adele (11), Gateshead, 2010

319 'My name is Elvis Presley . . .': SR collection, Sophie (7), Lechlade, Gloucestershire, 2010

319 'My mummy is a baker . . .' [2]: SR collection, Sophie (7), Lechlade, Gloucestershire, 2010

320 'Down down baby . . .': SR collection, Cherry & Ella (both 11), Camden, North London, 2009

320–21 'Miss Sue . . .': Mary Erskine School, Edinburgh, Children's Street Games Project, 1990

321 'Miss Moff . . .': SR collection, Megan, Megan, Mollie & Annie (all 11), Godalming, Surrey, 2008

321–2 'Miss Mar . . .': SR collection, Jacqueline Faulkner (6), Haddenham, Cambridgeshire, 2010

322 'Double double this . . .': SR collection, Rebecca, Ella, Helena & Luckshie (all 8), East Finchley, North London, 2008

322 'I know a little French girl . . .': Katharine Beavan, *Children's Playground Rhymes* (Project MD2004.02, School of Scottish Studies, Edinburgh, 2004). Introduced by girl who had moved there from England

322–3 'There was a little Chinese girl . . .': Cathy Gould collection, girls (11), Coventry, 2008

323 'One day I met an Irish girl . . .': SR collection, Rebecca (9, from Lechlade) & Maddie (10, from Salisbury), Lechlade, Gloucester, 2010

323 'I am a little Dutch girl . . .': Opie (1985) 480

323 'My name is Anni Anni . . .': SR collection, Rebecca (9, from Lechlade) & Maddie (10, from Salisbury), Lechlade, Gloucester, 2010

323–4 'My name is Eli eli . . .': Katharine Beavan, *Children's Playground Rhymes* (Project MD2004.02, School of Scottish Studies, Edinburgh, 2004)

324 'The girls in Spain . . .': Katharine Beavan, *Children's Playground Rhymes* (Project MD2004.02, School of Scottish Studies, Edinburgh, 2004)

324 'Apple sticky . . .': SR collection, year 6 schoolchildren (11/12), Ardleigh, Essex, 2009

324–5 'Wednesday, smells like coconuts . . .': SR collection, Ravenstone School Council, Balham, South London, 2009

325 'Dum dum day . . .': SR collection, Park Lodge School Council, Belfast, 2010

325–6 'Lemonade . . .': Chris Richards and Rebekah Willett collection, Christopher Hatton Primary School, London, 2009

326 'Om dom day . . .': SR collection, Ravenstone School Council, Balham, South London, 2010

326 'Under the apple tree . . .' [1]: SR collection, Ravenstone School Council, Balham, South London, 2010

326 'Under the apple tree . . .' [2]: SR collection, year 6 schoolchildren (11/12), Ardleigh, Essex, 2009

327 'Milk man, milk man . . .' [1]: Gareth Whittaker collection, Denholme, Yorkshire, 2002

327 'Milkman, milkman . . .' [2]: SR collection, Robert Arkenstall School Council, Haddenham, Cambridgeshire, 2009

327 'Milkman, milkman . . .' [3]: SR collection, schoolchildren (10/11), Okehampton Primary School, Okehampton, Devon, 2010

327 'High low jackalo . . .': SR collection, Megan, Mollie & Annie (all 11), Godalming, Surrey, 2008

327 'My name is . . .' [1]: SR collection, Rebecca, Ella, Helena & Luckshie (all 8), East Finchley, North London, 2008

328 'My name is . . .' [2]: SR collection, Kate (11) & Joanna (12), Weybridge, Surrey, 2009

328 'ABC hit it . . .': SR collection, Rebecca, Ella, Helena & Luckshie (all 8), East Finchley, North London, 2008

328 'Tic tac toe . . .' [1]: SR collection, Park Lodge School Council, Belfast, 2010

329 'Tic tac toe . . .' [2]: SR collection, Cherry & Ella (both 11), Camden, North London, 2009

329 'Tic tac toe . . .' [3]: SR collection, Rebecca (9, from Lechlade) & Maddie (10, from Salisbury), Lechlade, Gloucester, 2010

330 'A B C let's hit it . . .': SR collection, Rebecca (9, from Lechlade) & Maddie (10, from Salisbury), Lechlade, Gloucester, 2010

330 'A B C hit It . . .': SR collection, Park Lodge School Council, Belfast, 2010

331 'Om pom pay . . .' [1]: SR collection, East Street School playground, Andover, Hampshire, 1982

331 'In Pompeii . . .': SR collection, Joanne Wallwork (b.1965), Manchester, 2007

331 'Om pom pay . . .' [2]: Damian Webb Collection, Garforth, Yorkshire, 1976

331 'Em pom pee . . .': Damian Webb Collection, Huddersfield, Yorkshire, 1978

332 'Hi politi politaska . . .': Opie (1985) 428, 464

332 'Oh alla tinker. . .': Opie (1985) 428

334 'The children's writer . . .': Nesbit (1966) Ch. 1

335 'In those days . . .': Rountree (1993) 177

336 'To be in the fashion . . .': Peacock (1986) 107

336 'In the neighbourhoods . . .': Rolph (1980) 61–2

336 'There were several . . .': Humphries, Mack & Perks (1988) 73

336 '. . . the games of the street . . .': Hoggart (1957) 66–7

337 'Good Friday brought . . .': Morris (1982)

341 'We normally, like . . .': SR collection, year 6 schoolchildren (10/11), Ardleigh, Essex, 2009

341 'Well, because there's . . .': SR collection, Ravenstone School Council, Balham, South London, 2009

341 'Just before break . . .': SR collection, Peter Roud (b.1947), Streatham, South London, 2009

342 'To decide who . . .': SR collection, George Smith (b.c.1928), Newmains, Lanarkshire, 2009

342 'Occasionally boys . . .': Paul (1957) 40–41

343 'Picking sides . . .': Sturt (1927) 235

344 'One-ery, oo-ry . . .': Gosse (1888–9) 518

344 'Iroe diroe . . .': *Notes & Queries* 3S:5 (1864) 395

344 'On-ery, two-ery . . .': *Games and Sports for Young Boys* (1859) 68

344 'Een-a, deen-a . . .'; 'Hickety . . .': *Games and Sports for Young Boys* (1859) 68

344 'Meeny meeny . . .': Nicholson (1890) 153–4

344 'Eeny meeny . . .': Nicholson (1890) 153–4

345 'Icary Arry . . .': *Old Cornwall* 1:5 (1927) 41

345 'Hickory Harry . . .': *Old Cornwall* 1:5 (1927) 41

345 'Look upon the mantelpiece . . .': *Old Cornwall* 1:5 (1927) 41

345 'Polly in the garden . . .': Kellett (1966) 48–9

345 'A little old man . . .': A. G. Fulcher collection, Norfolk, *c.*1897; (Roud 19793)

345 'Anery, twaery . . .': *Blackwood's Magazine* (Aug 1821)

345 'Me bindle . . .': Bolton (1888) 123

345 'One, two, three . . .': Halliwell (1842) 86

345 'Winnery, ory . . .': Bolton (1888) 94

346 'To decide who should . . .': Parry-Jones (1964) 107

346 'Number 21': SR collection, Sam (11) & Caitlin (7), Rochester, Kent, 2010

349, 352 'If there's a lot . . .': SR collection, Robert Arkenstall School Council, Haddenham, Cambridgeshire, 2009

350 'The Lord made . . .': Rutherford (1971) 53

350 'Egdom pegdom . . .': Moore (1946) 28

350 'Eena, deena . . .': *Old Cornwall* 1:8 (1928) 39

350 'As I was going down . . .': Rutherford (1971) 50

350 'Alla malla . . .': East Kent Fed WIs, *East Kent Within Living Memory* (1993) 107–8

350 'Ip dip dip . . .': SR collection, Heather Rendall (b.1946), Sussex, 2007

350 'Ickle ockle . . .': SR collection, Ruby Tait (b.1946), Corby, Northamptonshire, 2007

350 'Eeny meeny macka racka . . .': SR collection, Simon Furey (b.1945), Nottingham, 2008

350 'Eeny meeny macaracca . . .': SR collection, Ann Ennis (b.1950), London, 2007

350 'Ip dip allaba da . . .': Smith (1959) 71

351 'There's a party . . .': Smith (1959) 71

351 'One two three . . .': Smith (1959) 70

351 'Ink pink, pen . . .': Steve Gardham collection, schoolchild, Beverley, Yorkshire, 1975

351 'Eeny meeny macker acker . . .': SR collection, Tina & Lisa Roud, Leytonstone, East London, 1978

351 'Ip dip sky blue . . .': SR collection, Tina & Lisa Roud, Leytonstone, East London, 1978

351 'There's a party on the hillside . . .': SR collection, Kathy Roud (7), Andover, Hampshire, 1982

351 'Each peach pear plum . . .': SR collection, East Street School playground, Andover, Hampshire, 1982

351 'Christmas is near . . .': SR collection, Kathy Roud (11), Norbury, South London, 1986

351 'Hibble hobble . . .': SR collection, Amanda Martin (b.1975), Preston, Lancashire, 2007

351 'Ip dip dock shit . . .': SR collection, Chantel Cousins (b.1979), London, 2008

351 'Ip dip do . . .': SR collection, Ruth Maurice (b.1982), Rotherhithe, London, 2007

355 'No English counting-out . . .': Opie (1969) 39

355 'Doctor Foster . . .': Bodley, Douce Adds. R 227

355, 358 'No explanation . . .': Opie (1969) 53

356 'Black shoe . . .' [1]: SR collection, Rebecca, Ella, Helena & Luckshie (all 8), East Finchley, 2008

356 'Black shoe . . .' [2]: Cathy Gould collection, Coventry, 2008

356 'Coconut, coconut . . .': SR collection, Robert Arkenstall School Council, Haddenham, Cambridgeshire, 2009

356 'Coca-Cola . . .': SR collection, Cherry & Ella (both 11), Camden, North London, 2009

356 'Ip dip battleship . . .': SR Collection, Natasha (11), Aston on Clun, Shropshire, 2009

356 'Ip dip sky blue . . .': SR collection, Harris (11), Inverness, 2008

356 'Ip dip do . . .': SR collection, Robert Arkenstall School Council, Haddenham, Cambridgeshire, 2009

356 'Ip dip doo . . .' [1]: SR collection, Maddie, Rhea & Dahlia (all 10), Ealing, West London, 2009

356 'Ip dip sky blue . . .': SR collection, Harry (8), Harry (9), George (10) & Justin (9), Maresfield, Sussex, 2008

356 'Ip dip doo . . .' [2]: SR collection, Harry (8), Harry (9), George (10) & Justin (9), Maresfield, Sussex, 2008

356 'Ibble obble . . .': SR collection, Robert Arkenstall School Council, Haddenham, Cambridgeshire, 2009

356 'Jimmy had a racing car . . .': SR collection, year 6 schoolchildren (11/12), Ardleigh, Essex, 2009

357 'Little Noddy . . .': SR collection, Ravenstone School Council, Balham, South London, 2009

357 'Racing car number nine . . .': Katharine Beavan, *Children's Playground Rhymes* (Project MD2004.02, School of Scottish Studies, Edinburgh, 2004)

357 'Big Ben strikes ten . . .': SR collection, Sam (8), Rochester, Kent, 2009

357 'Bubblegum . . .': SR collection, Rebecca, Ella, Helena & Luckshie (all 8), East Finchley, North London, 2008

357 'Onniker bonniker . . .': SR collection, Harry (8), Harry (9), George (10) & Justin (9), Maresfield, Sussex, 2008

357 'Onker bonker . . .': SR collection, Sam (11) & Caitlin (7), Rochester, Kent, 2010

357 'Up scout . . .': SR collection, Megan, Mollie & Annie (all 11), Godalming, Surrey, 2008

357 'Put your pegs in box . . .': SR collection, Park Lodge School Council, Belfast, 2010

357 'There's a party on the hill . . .': Katharine Beavan, *Children's Playground Rhymes* (Project MD2004.02, School of Scottish Studies, Edinburgh, 2004)

357 'There's a soldier in the grass . . .': Cathy Gould collection, boys (11), Coventry, 2001

357 'There was a little monkey . . .': Cathy Gould collection, boy (8), Coventry, 2001

357 'Eechy, peachy . . .': Cathy Gould collection, girls (9–11), Solihull, 2001

358 List of eighteen rhymes: Smith (1959) 69–73

361 List of seven main words: Opie (1959) 141–53

368 '*Barley*, a Yorkshire word . . .': Dyer (1891) 47–8

369 '*Fen*: a preventative . . .': Moor (1823) 125

369 '*Fainites* or *Fainlites* . . .': Paul (1957) 46–7

369 'When Touch succeeds . . .': *Games and Sports for Young Boys* (1859) 1

372 'Pinkie promise . . .': SR collection, Maddie, Rhea and Dahlia (10) Ealing, West London, 2009

372–3 'When children at school . . .': Addy (1895) 127

373 'Oath taking . . .': *Yorkshire Notes & Queries* 3 (1906) 233

373 'In the Midland counties . . .': *Notes & Queries* 4S:11 (1873) 22

373 'When I was a boy . . .': *Notes & Queries* 5S:6 (1876) 108, 214, 337–8

374 'A test of truthfulness . . .': McDowell (1972) 151

374 'In this parish . . .': *Notes & Queries* 11S:3 (1911) 217

374–5 'The boys in the north . . .': Brand III (1849) 261; *see* the dictionaries of superstitions by Roud (2003) and Opie and Tatem (1989) for more on the folklore of spitting

375 'Liar, liar, pants on fire . . .' [1]: SR collection, Rebecca (9, from Lechlade) & Maddie (10, from Salisbury), Lechlade, Gloucester, 2010

375 'Liar, liar, pants on fire . . .' [2]: SR collection, Adam (13), Irma (8), Bethany (11), Adele (11), Gateshead, 2010

375 'Liar, liar, your bum's on fire . . .': SR collection, Amanda Martin (b.1975), Preston, Lancashire, 2007

375 'You liar, you liar . . .': *Western Folklore* 13 (1954) 191

376 'Liar, liar lickspit . . .': Halliwell (1842) 135

376 'You've told a lie . . .': Gaskell (1964) 9

376 'When we're playing . . .': SR collection, Cherry and Ella (11), Camden, North London, 2009

377 'Sometimes you might say . . .': SR collection, Cherry & Ella (both 11), Camden, North London, 2009

377 '*Barley*. To claim . . .': Heslop (1892) 36

378 'Little fingers . . .': McDowell (1972) 152–3

378 'In Glasgow . . .': Opie (1959) 311

378 'Saying the same thing . . .': SR collection, Simon Furey (b.1945), Nottingham, 2008

379 'When two people . . .': SR collection, Sophie (b.1988), Redcar, North Yorkshire, 2008

379 'If you said . . .': SR collection, Heather Saunders (b.1992), Gravenhurst, Bedfordshire, 2008

379 'Jinx, personal padlock . . .': SR collection, Maddie, Rhea & Dahlia (all 10), Ealing, West London, 2009

379 'Jinx padlock, touch wood . . .': SR collection, Ravenstone School Council, Balham, South London, 2009

379 'First the worst . . .' [1]: SR collection, very general, 2008–10

380 'Minus the highness . . .': SR collection, Maddie, Rhea & Dahlia (all 10), Ealing, West London, 2009

380 'Zero the hero . . .': SR collection, Natasha Wiltshire, 2005–6, Sheffield, 2009

380 'First the worst . . .' [2]: SR collection, Robin Wiltshire (1974–8), Sheffield, 2009

381 'First the worst . . .' [3]: SR collection, Catherine McKienan (b.1976), Leeds, 2007

381 'First, for the golden purse . . .': Burne (1883) 572

381 'First the best . . .': Northall (1892) 359

381 'One's none . . .': Halliwell (1842) 133; (Roud 20589)

382 'Ane's nane . . .': Chambers (1870) 147; (Roud 20589)

383 'Tell tale tit . . .' [1]: Cathy Gould collection, Karla Gould & Graeme Daniels, Coventry

383 'Tell tale tit . . .' [2]: Cathy Gould collection, Judith Roberts, Coventry

384 'Johnny Brown . . .': King (1930) 10

384 'Telly-pie-tit . . .': Opie (1959) 190

384 'Tell tale tattler . . .': Lynch (1977) 56–7

384 'Cowardy cowardy custard . . .' [1]: Lynch (1977) 56–7

385 'Cowardy! Cowardy! Custard! . . .' [2]: Baker I (1854) 149

385 '—, you're a funny 'un . . .': SR collection, own recollection (1950s), Streatham, South London

386 'Cry baby cry . . .': Quigley (1993) 10

386 'Ask no questions . . .': Steve Gardham collection, schoolchild, Beverley, Yorkshire, 1978

386 'Made you look . . .': Cathy Gould collection, Richard Lamb, (b.c.1969), Solihull, 2004; (Roud 20455)

386 'I made you look . . .': Ward (1985) 121

387 'Made you look, you dirty duck . . .': SR collection, Amanda Martin (b.1975), Preston, Lancashire, 2007

387 'I gar'd ye luik . . .': Inglis (1909) 103

387 'Made you look, made you look . . .': SR collection, Georgia (13), Inverness, 2008

387 'Made you look, made you stare . . .': SR collection, Natasha (11), Aston on Clun, Shropshire, 2009

387 'Stare stare you big fat bear . . .': Kellett (1966) 49

387 'Silence in the courtyard . . .': SR collection, Kathy Roud, Andover, Hampshire, 1980s

388 'Silence in the graveyard . . .': Cathy Gould collection, own recollection (1970s), Coventry

388 'Silence in the jury . . .': SR collection, Ravenstone School Council, Balham, South London, 2010

388 'Silence in the pig market . . .' [1]: Opie (1959) 194–5

388 'A flurry . . .': Notes & Queries 174 (1938) 155, 193, 233

388 'Silence in the pig-market . . .' [2]: Northall (1894) 22

389 'Nottingham . . .': SR collection, Simon Furey (b.1945), Nottingham, 2008

389 'If anyone was naughty . . .': SR collection, Catherine Jones (b.1981), Stroud, Gloucestershire, 2007

389 'The whole . . .': SR collection, Maddy (b.1992), Sydenham, 2008

389 'Twinkle, twinkle, little star . . .' [1]: SR collection, East Street School playground, Andover, Hampshire, 1982

389 'Twinkle, twinkle, little star . . .' [2]: Steve Gardham collection, Kevin Hughes, Beverley, Yorkshire, 1982

389 'The same to you with knobs on . . .': Kellett (1966) 49

389 'I know you are . . .': SR collection, Rachel Nussey (b.1976), Middlesbrough, Yorkshire, 2007

390 'If I could have your picture . . .': Steve Gardham collection, Susan Cunningham, Beverley, Yorkshire, 1982

390 'I'm telling . . .': Cathy Gould collection, May Gould (12), Coventry, 2009

390 'I wasn't shut up . . .': Lynch (1977) 56–7

390 'I'm laughing at you . . .': Lynch (1977) 56–7

390 'Are you looking . . .': SR collection, Rachel Nussey (b.1976), Middlesbrough, Yorkshire, 2007

390 'See my finger . . .': Ward (1985) 122

391 'Don't care was made to care . . .': SR collection, Nigel Wilcockson's grandmother (b.1890s), Leigh on Sea, Essex, 2010

391 'Don't care, won't care . . .': SR collection, Sara Cording (b.1961), Redlynch, Wiltshire, 2007

391 'Sticks and stones . . .': McDowell (1972) 151

392 'Make friends . . .': SR collection, Toni (female, b.1975), Hanslope, Buckinghamshire, 2008

392 'We crossed arms . . .': Cathy Gould collection, Kathy & Karla Gould, Coventry

393-409 Material in this chapter dated 2003 was collected in a project funded by the Joseph Rowntree Foundation which looked at how disabled children are integrated, or not, into the playground culture. The project was headed by Helen Woolley, Senior Lecturer and a director of the Centre for the Study of Childhood and Youth at the University of Sheffield. The report, entitled *Inclusion of Disabled Children in Primary School Playgrounds*, was published by the National Children's Bureau in 2005.

393 'Several girls . . .': Marsh (2008) 94

394 'Miss, you have a . . .': Mavis Curtis collection, Keighley, 1993

394-5 'Hopscotch . . .': Mavis Curtis collection, Keighley, 1993 & 1999

395-6 'Fivestones . . .': Mavis Curtis collection, Keighley, 1993 & 1995

396 'Pitoo': Mavis Curtis collection, Keighley, 1996; Mavis Curtis collection, Bradford, 2003

396 'Eessi peesi . . .': Mavis Curtis collection, Keighley, 1993

397 'Inky pinky ponky . . .': Mavis Curtis collection, Keighley, 1993

397 'Ip dip dog um . . .': Mavis Curtis collection, Keighley, 1993

398 'Abba babba . . .': Mavis Curtis collection, Keighley, 1993

399 'One two three . . .' [1]: Mavis Curtis collection, Keighley, 1993

399 'One two three . . .' [2]: Mavis Curtis collection, Bradord, 2003

399 'Ippy dippy dation . . .': Mavis Curtis collection, Keighley, 1999

399 'Dic-a-tic-adation . . .': Opie (1969) 58

399 'Egg, sugar . . .': Bolton (1888) 111

399 'Egg, sugar, butter, tea . . .': Mavis Curtis collection, Keighley, 1993; Mavis Curtis collection, Bradford, 2003

400 'Eeny meeny miny mo . . .': Mavis Curtis collection, Keighley 1993, 2002; Mavis Curtis collection, Bradford, 2003

400 'Zig zag zoo . . .': Mavis Curtis collection, Keighley 2002; Mavis Curtis collection, Bradford, 2003

401 'Charm charm charm . . .': Mavis Curtis collection, Bradford, 2003

402 'I'm a pretty little Dutch girl . . .': Mavis Curtis collection, Bradford, 2003

402-3 'Who stole the cookie . . .': Mavis Curtis collection, Keighley 1999

403 'Down by the river . . .': Mavis Curtis collection, Keighley, 2002

403 'Sella ella oola . . .': collected by Kathryn Marsh, Keighley, 2002

403-4 'Aix a hale . . .': Mavis Curtis collection, Keighley, 1993

404 'Here sits poor Sally . . .': Gomme II (1898) 165

405 'My mother said . . .': Mavis Curtis collection, Keighley, 1999

406 '. . . an almost identical rhyme . . .': Opie (1985) 441

406 'Sandy doo . . .': Rutherford (1971) 77

406 *Greensleeves*: Mavis Curtis collection, Bradford, 2003

407 'The little children ask . . .': Mavis Curtis collection, Keighley, 1993

407-8 'Old Mother Grey': Opie (1969) 307

408 'What are you looking for . . .': Mavis Curtis collection, Keighley, 1993

408 'What are you scratching for . . .': Gomme I (1894) 202

413 'The penchant which children . . .': Green & Widdowson (2003) 12

414 'Little Shirley Temple . . .': Opie (1959) 113

414 'She phoned for the doctor . . .': Opie (1959) 113

415 'Ching Chang Chinaman . . .': SR collection, Jacky Roud (b.1940), Streatham, South London, 1970

415 'Ching chong chinaman . . .': Cathy Gould collection, Lucy Sharp (1990s), Coventry

415 'Ching Chong Chineeman . . .': Bolton (1888) 116

416 'One fine day . . .' [1]: SR collection, Jim Duerdin (b.1957), Newcastle, 1977

416-17 'One fine day . . .' [2]: Kellett (1966) 45-6

417 'One fine day . . .' [3]: Steve Gardham collection, Julian Kaye, Beverley, Yorkshire, c.1980

417 'I went to the pictures . . .': Cathy Gould collection, Coventry, 2007

418 'Ladies and jellyspoons . . .': McDowell (1972) 153

418 'One night as I was dreaming . . .': Cathy Gould collection, Lucy Sharp (1990s), Coventry; Kellett (1966) 45

418 'One bright September . . .': Kellett (1966) 45

418-19 'I went to letter a post . . .': Kellett (1966) 45

419 'Happy birthday to you . . .' [1]: SR collection, own recollection (1960s), South London

419 'Happy birthday to you . . .' [2]: SR collection, Adam (13), Irma (8), Bethany (11) & Adele (11), Gateshead, 2010

419 'Happy birthday to you . . .' [3]: SR collection, schoolchildren (10/11), Okehampton Primary School, Okehampton, Devon, 2010

420 'Happy birthday to me . . .': SR collection, Ravenstone School Council, Balham, South London, 2010

420 'Roses are red . . .' [1]: SR collection, own recollection (1950s), Streatham, South London

421 'Roses are red . . .' [2]: SR collection, Gail Coley (b.c.1975), Croydon, 1989

421 'Roses are red . . .' [3]: SR collection, own recollection (1950s), Streatham, South London

421 'Roses are red . . .' [4]: SR collection, own recollection (1950s), Streatham, South London

421 'Roses are red . . .' [5]: SR collection, Sarah Proberts (b.c.1975), Croydon, 1989

421 'Jingle bells . . .' [1]: SR collection, Sophie (7), Lechlade, Gloucester, 2010

422 'Mickey Mouse is dead . . .': SR collection, East Street School playground, Andover, Hampshire, 1982

422 'Donald Duck . . .': Cathy Gould collection, Lucy Sharp (12/13), Coventry, 2001

422 'Not last night . . .': Steve Gardham collection, schoolchild, Beverley, Yorkshire, c.1975

422 'Mrs Wright had a fright . . .': Steve Gardham collection, Pamela Middleton, Beverley, Yorkshire, 1980

422 'What's the time . . .' [1]: SR collection, Kathy Roud & Natalie Harbury (both 8), Andover, Hampshire, 1983

422 'What's the time . . .' [2]: Katharine Beavan, *Children's Playground Rhymes* (project MD2004.02, School of Scottish Studies, Edinburgh, 2004)

422 'A wonderful bird is the pelican': SR collection, Nottinghamshire (1970s)

422 'It's raining, it's pouring . . .': Cathy Gould collection, own recollection, Coventry

422 'What's your name . . .': Gareth Whittaker collection, Denholme, Yorkshire, 2002

422 'Girls' faults are many . . .': Steve Gardham collection, Lesley Donkin, Cottingham, Yorkshire, 1984

422 'Mr Brown went to town . . .': SR collection, Margaret Wilton (b.c.1952), Andover, Hampshire, 1975

422-3 'Down in the jungle . . .': Kellett (1966) 46

423 'England for ever . . .': Mary Erskine School, Edinburgh, Children's Street Games Project, 1990

423 'Guess what . . .': SR collection, Adam (13), Irma (8), Bethany (11) & Adele (11), Gateshead, 2010

423 'I see London . . .': SR collection, Adam (13), Irma (8), Bethany (11) & Adele (11), Gateshead, 2010

423 'Easy peasy . . .': SR collection, Adam (13), Irma (8), Bethany (11) & Adele (11), Gateshead, 2010

423 'Three little angels . . .': Steve Gardham collection, Wendy Oxley, Beverley, Yorkshire, 1980

423 'There was a boy. . .': SR collection, Sophie (b. 1988), Redcar, Yorkshire, 2008

424 'Jingle bells . . .' [2]: SR collection, schoolchildren (10/11), Okehampton Primary School, Okehampton, Devon, 2010

424 'Jingle bells . . .' [3]: SR collection, Adam (13), Irma (8), Bethany (11) & Adele (11), Gateshead, 2010

424 'Jingle bells . . .' [4]: Cathy Gould collection, Graeme Daniels (school 1968–1973), Coventry, 2000

424 'Jingle bells . . .' [5]: SR collection, Sam (11) & Caitlin (7), Rochester, Kent, 2010

424 'Jingle bells . . .' [6]: SR collection, Donna Cooper (7), Andover, Hampshire, 1982

424-5 'Jingle bells . . .' [7]: Rutherford (1971) 116

425 'Dashing through the snow . . .': SR collection, Robert Arkenstall School Council, Haddenham, Cambridgeshire, 2009

425 'Batman and Robin . . .': SR collection, Robert Arkenstall School Council, Haddenham, Cambridgeshire, 2009

425-6 'My old man's a dustman . . .': Cathy Gould collection, Graeme Daniels (b.1962), Coventry

426 'We three kings from Orientar . . .': SR collection, Robert Arkenstall School Council, Haddenham, Cambridgeshire, 2009

426–7 'While shepherds washed . . .' [1]: SR collection, own recollection (1950s), Streatham, South London

427 'While shepherds washed . . .' [2]: SR collection, Joy Gallagher (b.1956), Abbots Ann, Hampshire, 1977

427 'While shepherds washed . . .' [3]: Rutherford (1971) 127

427 'While shepherds washed . . .' [4]: SR collection, Jim Duerdin (b.1957) Newcastle, 1977

427 'Ta-ra-ra bum-de-ay . . .': Cathy Gould collection, various people (1960s), Coventry

427–8 'Daisy, Daisy . . .': Cathy Gould collection, Graeme Daniels (b.1962), Coventry

428 'We all piss in a blue and white pot . . .': Steve Gardham collection, James Ellis, Beverley, Yorkshire, 1978

428 'I'm walking in the air . . .': SR collection, Gemma (5), Wolverhampton, 1990

428 'Georgie Porgie . . .': Steve Gardham collection, schoolchildren, Beverley, Yorkshire, 1980

428 'Twinkle, twinkle, chocolate bar . . .': SR collection, Ravenstone School Council, Balham, South London, 2010

429–30 'Some say he died of a fever . . .': SR collection, Margaret Wilton (b.c.1952), Andover, Hampshire, 1975

430 'As I was walking . . .': Steve Gardham collection, schoolchild, Beverley, Yorkshire, 1978

430 'Mary had a little lamb . . .': Steve Gardham collection, Louise Hugill, Beverley, Yorkshire, 1980

430–31 'Miss Susie had a steamboat . . .': SR collection, Maddie, Rhea & Dahlia (all 10), Ealing, West London, 2009

431 'My wife she had a baby . . .': Steve Gardham collection, Christopher Rodger, Beverley, Yorkshire, 1982

431–2 'Samson was a warrior . . .': SR collection, Caroline Oates (b.1955), Gateshead, 2009

432 'Have you ever had it up . . .': SR collection, Joy Gallagher (b.1956), Abbots Ann, Hampshire, 1977

432–3 'Nobody likes me . . .' [1]: SR collection, Margaret Wilton (b.c.1952), Andover, Hampshire, 1975

433 'Nobody loves me . . .': SR collection, Joy Gallagher (b.1956), Abbots Ann, Hampshire, 1977

433 'Nobody likes me . . .' [2]: Steve Gardham collection, Martin Brigham, Beverley, Yorkshire, 1980

433–4 'Have you ever thought . . .': SR collection, Margaret Wilton (b.c.1952), Andover, Hampshire, 1975

434 'Little worm upon the ground . . .': Steve Gardham collection, schoolchild, Beverley, Yorkshire, 1980

434 'If you see a bunny . . .': Cathy Gould collection, Graeme Daniels (b.1962), Coventry

434 'Climbing up a lamp post . . .': Cathy Gould collection, own recollection (1970s), Coventry

435 'Tarzan in the jungle . . .': Cathy Gould collection, Graeme Daniels (b.1962), Coventry

435 'Old King Cole . . .': SR collection, Jim Duerdin (b.1957), Newcastle, 1977

435 'Milk, milk, lemonade . . .': SR collection, Jim Duerdin (b.1957), Newcastle, 1977

435 'Eyes, nose, mouth, chin . . .': SR collection, girls (12) Pollards Hill, South London, 1971

435 'What do you do . . .': Steve Gardham collection, schoolchild, Beverley, Yorkshire, 1980

435–6 'Mummy I'm unhappy . . .': SR collection, East Street School playground, Andover, Hampshire, 1982

436 'In 1966 . . .': SR collection, East Street School playground (female), Andover, Hampshire, 1983; Cathy Gould collection, Coventry, 2005

436 'Yum yum bubblegum . . .': SR collection, Kathy Roud & Natalie Harbury (both 8), Andover, Hampshire, 1983

436 'Ee by gum . . .': Cathy Gould collection, Lucy Sharp (1990s), Coventry, 2007; similar collected from Graeme Daniels (1970s), Coventry

436–7 'Jack and Jill . . .': Steve Gardham collection, schoolchildren, Beverley, Yorkshire, 1980 (many versions)

437 'In Jamaica, under the tree . . .': Cathy Gould collection, girls (year 9), Coventry, 2005

437 'I be a farmer . . .': Cathy Gould collection, boys (year 10), Coventry, 2005

437 'Cody cody custard . . .': Steve Gardham collection, Martin Brigham, Beverley, Yorkshire, 1980

437 'Yellow belly custard . . .': Cathy Gould collection, Graeme Daniels (b.1962), Coventry

438 'One more day of school . . .': SR collection, own recollection (1950s), Streatham, South London

439 'We break up, we break down . . .' [1]: SR collection, own recollection (1950s), Streatham, South London

439 'We break up, we break down . . .' [2]: SR collection, East Street School playground, Andover, Hampshire, 1983

439 'No more school . . .': SR collection, Ruby Tait (b.1946), Corby, Northamptonshire, 2007

439 'No more teachers . . .': SR collection, Lynn Davis (b.1949), Herne Hill, London, 2007

439–40 'No more Latin, no more French . . .': SR collection, Nigel Wilcockson (b.1961), Cambridge, 2009

440 'Build a bonfire . . .': SR collection, Jennifer Henson (b.1950), Stroud Green, London, 2007

440 'Come to . . .': SR collection, Caroline Sykes (b.1963), Bath, c.1980

440 'Hip hip hooray . . .': SR collection, Jessica (b.1989), Norfolk, 2007

440–41 'God who made the bees . . .': Steve Gardham collection, schoolchild, Beverley, Yorkshire, 1982

441 'Glory glory hallelujah . . .': SR collection, Lisa Rowles (b.1972), Ilford, Essex, 2007

441 'Billy Timms is a very good man . . .': Knight (1960) 76; (Roud 19288)

441–2 'Joy to the world, the teacher's dead . . .': SR collection, Maddy (b.1992), Sydenham, 2008

442 'School dinners . . .' [1]: SR collection, East Street School playground, Andover, Hampshire, 1982

442 'School dinners . . .' [2]: Steve Gardham collection, Heather Cooper, Beverley, Yorkshire, 1982

442 'They say here at . . .': SR collection, Caroline Sykes (b.1963), Bath, c.1980

443 'Say what you will . . .': SR collection, L. Davis (female, b.1958), Haywards Heath, Sussex, 2008

443 'If you stay to school dinners . . .': Steve Gardham collection, schoolchild, Beverley, Yorkshire, 1978

453 'When I was a girl . . .': Sutton (1992) 136

454 'We trotted . . .': Gamble (1979) 143

455 'A saying we had . . .': Opie & Tatem (1989) 237

455 'Touch green . . .': Cathy Gould collection, Danielle Sharp (b.1983), Coventry, 2007

456 'Black cat . . .': Opie (1959) 222

456 'Sailor, sailor . . .': Opie (1959) 222

457 'In the gravel . . .': Gosse (1888–9) 519

457 'She actually saw . . .': Uttley (1931) 49

457 'She was told . . .': Uttley (1931) 49

458 'Ladybird, ladybird . . .': (Roud 16215)

458 'Lady, Lady Landers . . .': Chambers (1870) 201

458 'A marygold was . . .': *Folk-Lore* 49 (1938) 32

459 'Bishee bishee barnabee . . .': *Folk-Lore* 49 (1938) 32–3

459 'The better or deeper . . .': *Folk-Lore* 49 (1938) 197

459 'In Sussex . . .': *Folk-Lore* 49 (1938) 35

460 'One of the scary games . . .': Staffordshire Fed WIs, *Staffordshire Within Living Memory* (1992) 130

460 'My mother had told me . . .': Sutton (1992) 125

461 'The bigger girls . . .': Parry-Jones (1964) 63

462 'It was played at . . .': Tate (1866) 436

462 *Tinker, Tailor.* (Roud 802)

462–3 'We have a curious . . .': Moor (1823) 377–8

463 'Red currants . . .': Coles (1947) 151

464 'Apple stems': Cathy Gould collection, girls (13), Coventry, 1998; Cathy Gould collection, girls, Coventry, 2007

464 'Bus tickets': Cathy Gould collection, own recollection (1970s), Coventry, 2007

464 'Chewing gum wrappers': Heather Laird, *He Loves Me, He Loves Me Not: the Divinatory Activity of Children in the Barlanark Area of Glasgow* (MA dissertation, School of Scottish Studies MH 2005.03, University of Glasgow, 2005)

465 'Hand game 1': SR collection, Kate Roud (12/13), Croydon, 1988

465 'Hand game 2': SR collection, Kate Roud (13), Croydon, 1989

465 'Love, Marry, Hate, Adore': Heather Laird, *He Loves Me, He Loves Me Not: the Divinatory Activity of Children in the Barlanark Area of Glasgow* (MA dissertation, School of Scottish Studies MH 2005.03, University of Glasgow, 2005)

465–6 'Love percentages': Cathy Gould collection, Zoe Hampson (1980s), Leicester, 2007; Heather Laird, *He Loves Me, He Loves Me Not: the Divinatory Activity of Children in the Barlanark Area of Glasgow* (MA dissertation, School of Scottish Studies MH 2005.03, University of Glasgow, 2005)

466 'Matches': Cathy Gould collection, own recollection (1970s), Coventry, 2007

466 'Noughts and crosses': SR collection, Kate Roud (13), Croydon, 1989

466 'Ring pulls': Cathy Gould collection, girls (13) Coventry, 1998; Heather Laird, *He Loves Me, He Loves Me Not: the Divinatory Activity of Children in the Barlanark Area of Glasgow* (MA dissertation, School of Scottish Studies MH 2005.03, University of Glasgow, 2005)

466–7 'Six Boys Names': Cathy Gould collection, own recollection (1970s), Coventry, 2007

467 'Square game': SR collection, Kate Roud (12/13), Croydon, 1988

467 'Ten boys' names': Cathy Gould collection, own memory (1970s), Coventry

468 'True Love percentage': SR collection, Kate Roud (age 12/13), Croydon, 1988

469–516 For anyone interested in the history of our calendar customs in general, there is an extensive literature, but as a starting point see the following (listed in the Bibliography): *England*: Roud (2006); Wright & Lones (1936–40). *Scotland*: Banks (1937–41 & 1946). *Isle of Man*: Paton (1942); Moore (1891). *Wales*: Owen (1968). *Ireland*: Danaher (1972). *General*: Hutton (1996).

470–71 'As soon as it was light . . .': Parry-Jones (1964) 222

471 'The habit of children . . .': De Garis (1975) 69

471–2 'Much excitement . . .': *Scottish Review* (21 Dec 1905)

473 'Holly, holly . . .': Paton (1942) 18

473 'After dinner . . .': Fitz Stephen (1990) 56–7

473–4 'When I was quite . . .': Newchurch W.I. (1988) 74

476 'I remember girls . . .': Swinford (1987) 22

477 'Every Sunday . . .': Symonds (1644/1909) 27

477 'I'll to thee . . .': Herrick (1648) 'A Ceremonie in Gloucester'

478 'A small sheet . . .': *Journal of the Cork Historical Society* (1895) 553–5

478 'Gordon Mills recalled . . .': St Ann's Reminiscence Group, 1990

479 'The day before Good Friday . . .': *The Times* (13 Apr 1944)

479 'It was the regular custom . . .': *The Times* (20 Apr 1944)

480 'Last evening . . .': *Folk-Lore* 5 (1894) 290–2

481 'Jarping hard-boiled eggs . . .': SR collection, Caroline Oates (b.1955), Gateshead, 2009

481 'On Easter Monday . . .': *Notes & Queries* 6S:1 (1880) 337

482 'The little boys and girls . . .': *Notes & Queries* 5S:3 (1875) 247

482 'Elecampane . . .': *Notes & Queries* 4S:5 (1870) 595

483 'An informant . . .': Hole (1978) 290

483 'Easter Monday is called . . .': Cox (1907) 363

484 'April Noddy's . . .': Lancs Fed WIs, *Lancashire Lore* (1971) 13

485 'Between the wars . . .': East Sussex Fed WIs, *East Sussex Within Living Memory* (1995) 244

486 'Hitherto the advent . . .': *Banbury Guardian* (4 May 1882) 8

486–7 'Last year . . .': *The Times* (1 May 1931)

487 'Children, in bands of five . . .': *Notes & Queries* 11S:1 (1910) 383

488 'In more recent times . . .': Danaher (1972) 91

488 'I cannot claim . . .': *Leicestershire & Rutland Magazine* (Sep 1949) 207

489 'One of the party . . .': *Burnley News* (6 May 1922) 9

489 'Nearly every street . . .': Roberts (1976) 62–4

489–90 'A dozen small children . . .': *Evening Standard* (1 May 1928)

490 'A May gosling . . .': *Gentleman's Magazine* (1791) 327

491–2 'I was eight years old . . .': East Yorkshire Fed WIs, *East Yorkshire Within Living Memory* (1998) 206

492 'Various classmates . . .': Worcestershire Fed WIs, *Worcestershire Within Living Memory* (1995) 242

494 'Walking to school . . .': *Leicestershire & Rutland Mag* (Sep 1949) 207

494 'We always remembered . . .': Newbery (1980) 20

495 'On Derby Day . . .': Surrey Fed WIs, *Surrey Within Living Memory* (1992) 259

497 'Those mimic grottoes . . .': *The Times* (30 Aug 1833/11 Oct 1833)

498 'When I was a little girl . . .': Gloucestershire Fed WIs, *Gloucestershire Within Living Memory* (1996) 217–18

499 'Mischief Night Crackdown . . .': *Liverpool Echo* (28 Oct 2008)

500 'Parties of youths . . .': Banks III (1941) 162

501 'Britain has the appearance . . .': Opie (1959) 268

502 'Bonfires are still . . .': Foster (1951) 26

502 'A peculiar aspect . . .': Foster (1951) 27

502 'The Scottish Halloween . . .': Miller (1835) 61–2

504 'A soul, a soul . . .': *The Times* (13 Dec 1935) 10

504–5 'Bread and cheese . . .': *Bye-gones* (25 Mar 1891); quoted in Owen (1987) 139

505 '*Dega, dega,* come to the door . . .': *Bye-gones* (25 Jul 1891); quoted in Owen (1987) 139

505 'Mischief Night . . .': *Leeds Mercury* (14 May 1857)

506 'In the Island . . .': Woodley (1822) 231–2

509 'When we were dressing up . . .': McCarthy (1986) 102

510 'On Guy Fawkes Day . . .': Opie Archives, Calendar Customs, Folklore Society

510–11 'I loved the free-and-easy . . .': *Worthing TV Review* (16–29 Nov 1991) 11

511 'Please to remember. . .': *Times Literary Supplement* (7 Dec 1961) 785

511 'We've come a-cob-o'-coalin' . . .': Opie Archives, calendar customs, Folklore Society

512 'When I go guisin' . . .': Opie collection, child (13), Forfar, 1954

512 'Clemeny Clemeny . . .': *Notes & Queries* 3S:4 (1863) 492

513 'Catherine and Clement . . .': Wright & Lones III (1942) 180–1

513 'In spite of . . .': Parish (1875) 22

514 'Older parishioners . . .': letter to *The Times* (5 Dec 1935) 17

514–15 'They went from door to door . . .': *Lore and Language* 1:1 (Jul 1969) 6–8

516 'At twelve o'clock precisely . . .': West Yorkshire Fed WIs, *West Yorkshire Within Living Memory* (1996)

Index